D0788586

THE HISTORY OF THE BAPTIST
MISSIONARY SOCIETY

THE HISTORY OF THE BAPTIST MISSIONARY SOCIETY 1792-1992

by

Brian Stanley

T&T CLARK
EDINBURGH

T&T CLARK
59 GEORGE STREET
EDINBURGH EH2 2LQ
SCOTLAND

Copyright © T&T Clark, 1992

All rights reserved. No part of this publication may be reproduced, stored in a
retrieval system, or transmitted, in any form by any means,
electronic, mechanical, photocopying recording or otherwise,
without the prior permission of T&T Clark.

First Published 1992

ISBN 0 567 09614 9

British Library Cataloguing-in-Publication Data
A catalogue record for this book is
available from the British Library

Typeset by Trinity Typesetting, Edinburgh
Printed and bound in Great Britain by Biddles Ltd, Surrey

*To all missionaries of
the Baptist Missionary Society,
past and present.*

Contents

Foreword

By the Most Reverend and Right Honourable Dr George Carey,
Archbishop of Canterbury

It is an honour to have been asked to write the Foreword to this book, not least because on its very first page it speaks of 'the Anglican monopoly of power' and the marginalisation of those – including Baptists – who dissented from it in the late eighteenth century. For an Anglican Archbishop to be invited to contribute to the official bicentenary history of the Baptist Missionary Society is an indication, therefore, not only of how much the ecclesiastical world has changed since those days, but of the generosity of the BMS today. (I don't suppose the fact that one of the principal founders of the Society was called Carey had anything to do with it . . .)

No-one reading through Dr Brian Stanley's text can fail to be struck by the remarkable way in which so many of the issues surrounding the formation to the BMS and its work since are still very much alive today. In 1792, for example, there were those who raised theological scruples about the propriety of the motivation for direct evangelism. The scruples then were mainly based on certain forms of Calvinism: our own age has different theological hesitations but the effect can be just the same, a paralysis of the Church, preventing it speaking of Christ and inviting commitment to Him.

Those who clamour for speedy results today would do well to ponder the patience and faithfulness of William Carey and his companions in India who laboured for seven years before seeing a single convert. In Africa too growth was initially slow and discouraging whereas today that continent is predominantly Christian and possesses a vibrancy and boldness which puts Europeans to shame. Equally thought-provoking is the high loss of life sustained by the Mission: ten people in a single twelve-month period in the early years in India; six doctors in China between 1913 and 1923. We are tempted to speak of 'waste'; they talked of 'sacrifice'. We are challenged by the vision, urgency and undergirding with prayer which so characterised the missionaries and their supporters back home. Can we match their fervour and constancy?

Particularly striking is the way in which the early missionaries, though faithful to their primary task of saving souls, soon found themselves having to address issues of social injustice, as, for example, in the slave plantations of the West Indies.

Commitment to making Christ known is inseparable from a commitment to remove injustice and oppression; though the latter must never replace the former.

There is much else that could be highlighted: church planting, attitudes to other faiths, indigenous leadership, post-colonial issues, the charismatic movement – they are all here. For me part of the interest of the book lies in the way familiar subjects are approached from unfamiliar angles. It is instructive for an Anglican to read of the Church in China or the formation of the Church of North India from a Baptist perspective.

This book, then, has a relevance not just to Baptists or to historians of Christian mission, especially at this juncture when evangelism is an explicit priority for so many of our Churches. Let me extract from it one further note of encouragement. William Carey in his well-known dictum, challenges us to 'attempt great things for God'. Many of us, however, feel that 'great things' are beyond our reach. Let us take heart then that the Baptist Missionary Society which has lasted for two hundred years and brought thousands of souls to Christ began in complete domesticity: 'in the back parlour of Mrs Beeby Wallis's home in Kettering'. Who knows where our own small, local efforts may not lead under the might hand of God?

GEORGE CANTUAR

Acknowledgments

A book of this size and character must always be the product of the hard work and enthusiastic co-operation of many people other than the author. To acknowledge all the debts which I have incurred in the process of its production is perhaps impossible, but I shall endeavour to mention all whose contributions have been particularly significant.

Much of the research and writing was accomplished during the academic year 1989-90, when I was granted leave from my post at Spurgeon's College to work on the book full-time. I owe thanks to the Principal and Council of Spurgeon's College for granting me leave of absence. The year was financed through generous grants from the Twenty-Seven Foundation, the Particular Baptist Fund, the Whitley Trustees, the Whitefield Institute, and the Hinchley Charitable Trust. Congenial facilities for this year of study were provided by Regent's Park College, Oxford, where the superb research resources of the Angus Library, now enriched by the deposit in 1989 of the archives of the Baptist Missionary Society, were made freely available to me. I owe a particular debt to the enthusiastic co-operation and efficiency of the librarian, Sue Mills, and the BMS archivist, Elizabeth Doull.

The list of those on whose wisdom and experience I have drawn in various ways is a long one. I apologise to them all that I can only mention their names, rather than the nature of their contribution: Len Addicott, Basil Amey, Margot Bafende, Eric Blakebrough, Barbara Boal, Professor A. E. Bottoms, Kathleen Brain, Peter Brewer, Raymond Brown, Mali Browne, Stanley and Dorothy Bushill, Stuart Christine, Kathleen Chesterton, John Clark, Roy and Margaret Deller, David Doonan, Fred Drake, John Dyer, Arthur and Kathleen Elder, Avelino Ferreira, David Grainger, Jim Grenfell, Geoffrey Grose, Bruce and Joyce Henry, Gareth Hutchinson, David Jelleyman, Joy Knapman, George and Betsy Lee, Samuel Lokangu, Angus MacNeill, Ernest Madge, the late Peter Manicom, David Martin, Bishop D. K. Mohanty, Koli Mandole Molima, the late Leslie Moore, Stanley Mudd, Geoffrey Nuttall, John Nicholson, Wai Nlemvo, Ruth Page, David Pountain, Malcolm Purdy, Derek Rumbol, Keith Skirrow, A. H. Spillett, Fred Stainthorpe, Roger Standing, Jim Sutton, Stanley Thomas, Leslie Wenger, Morris West, David Wilson, Derek Winter, Pat Woolhouse.

Two overseas trips to Zaire in 1987 and India/Bangladesh in 1988 were made a pleasure as well as extremely profitable through the generous hospitality and efficient arrangements of many BMS missionaries and Zairean, Indian and Bangladeshi church leaders. There is unfortunately no space to mention their names here.

The chapters of the book were read in draft by a working group set up by the Society. Its members - Donald Monkcom, Reg Harvey, Maureen Sleeman, Brian Tucker and Barrie White - have all contributed to the improvement of the book through their careful and informed criticisms. I must also thank my friend David Bebbington, who read the whole manuscript in draft, and whose acute comments and creative suggestions have been of immense value. The index has been compiled with painstaking care and professionalism by Miss Rosemary Taylor, MA, MPhil, ALA, formerly of the Institute of Historical Research, University of London. I am deeply grateful to her.

My colleagues at Spurgeon's College and, more recently, at Trinity College, Bristol, have given good-natured encouragement when my energies began to flag. My wife, Rosemary, and two children, Jonathan and Rebecca, have sacrificed a great deal of family time over several years to allow Daddy to get on with his 'big book'. Their patient forbearance has contributed to this history in ways that cannot be quantified.

My publishers, T&T Clark, have performed miraculous feats in producing the book so rapidly. To all involved, and especially to Geoffrey Green, Elizabeth Nicol, and Callum Fisken, I am most grateful.

Finally, I must express my gratitude to the Baptist Missionary Society itself for having the vision and courage to perceive that a substantial official history of the Society ought to be produced for its bicentenary. Its General Secretary, Reg Harvey, has steered the project through to a successful completion amidst many competing pressures. I hope the missionaries and supporters of the Society will feel that the finished product is worthy of the vision which led to its commissioning. The constraints imposed by the 1992 deadline for publication have dictated that research has not always been as exhaustive as I should have liked. Hard decisions have had to be made regarding the emphasis and overall balance of the history. In particular, it was decided to weight the book towards the twentieth century, partly to rectify the striking inbalance in the existing secondary literature, and partly to facilitate concentration on those issues which have greatest relevance for Christian mission today. Inevitably, there are many individuals who have made major contributions to the life of the Society over the last two centuries whose names do not appear in the text. For that reason, and by way of apology to those whose role has had to be minimized or omitted altogether, I gladly dedicate this history to all those who have served Christ as missionaries of the Baptist Missionary Society.

Brian Stanley
Trinity College, Bristol
June 1992

Lists of Maps

List of Illustrations

List of Abbreviations

ABFMS	American Baptist Foreign Mission Society
ABMU	American Baptist Missionary Union
BBU	Bengal Baptist Union
BBS	Bangladesh Baptist Sangha
BCC	British Council of Churches
BM	*Baptist Magazine*
BMS	Baptist Missionary Society
BQ	*Baptist Quarterly*
BT	*Baptist Times*
BU	Baptist Union
BUNI	Baptist Union of North India
BUP	Baptist Union of Pakistan
BWA	Baptist World Alliance
BZM	Baptist Zenana Mission
CBBF	Communauté Baptiste du Bas-Fleuve
CBCNI	Council of Baptist Churches in Northern India
CBFZ	Communauté Baptiste du Fleuve Zaire
CBHC	Communauté Baptiste du Haut-Congo
CBMF	Communauté Baptiste du Moyen-Fleuve
CBMS	Conference of British Missionary Societies
CCP	Chinese Communist Party
CCT	Church of Christ in Thailand
CEBADER	Centro Batista de Desenvolvimento Rural, Potinga
CECO	Centre Evangélique de Co-opération, Kimpese
CES	Chinese Evangelization Society
CEZ	Communauté Evangélique de Zaire
CLS	Christian Literature Society
CMS	Church Missionary Society
CNI	Church of North India
CR	Central Register of Documents, BMS headquarters, Didcot
DNB	*Dictionary of National Biography*
ECZ	Eglise du Christ au Zaire
EPI	L'Ecole de Pasteurs et d'Instituteurs, Kimpese

FMLN	Farabundo Marti de Liberacion Nacional
FNLA	Frente National de Libertação de Angola
FOMECO	Fonds Médical de Co-opération
GBMS	General Baptist Missionary Society
HCB	Huileries du Congo Belge
IEBA	Igreja Evangélica Baptista em Angola
IMC	International Missionary Council
IME	Institut Médical Evangélique, Kimpese
ISTY	Institut Supérieur Théologique de Yakusu
JBU	Jamaica Baptist Union
JBMS	Jamaican Baptist Missionary Society
KETI	Kimpese Evangelical Training Institution
LIM	Livingstone Inland Mission
LMS	London Missionary Society
MH	*Missionary Herald*
MMA	Medical Mission Auxiliary
MPR	Mouvement Populaire de la Révolution
MPLA	Movimento Popular de Libertação de Angola
NCC	National Christian Council (of India)
NMC	National Missionary Council (of India)
PA	*Periodical Accounts relative to the Baptist Missionary Society*
SCM	Student Christian Movement
SCU	Shandong Christian University
SDK	Society for the Diffusion of Christian and General Knowledge among the Chinese
SLBS	Sri Lanka Baptist Sangamaya
SMF	Svenska Missions Förbundet
SPCK	Society for Promoting Christian Knowledge
SPG	Society for the Propagation of the Gospel in Foreign Parts
SVMU	Student Volunteer Missionary Union
TBMF	Thailand Baptist Missionary Fellowship
TSPM	Three-Self Patriotic Movement
UCCCC	Utkal Christian Central Church Council
UMN	United Mission to Nepal
UPA	União das Populações de Angola
UPNA	União das Populações do Norte de Angola
UTCWI	United Theological College of the West Indies
WCC	World Council of Churches
WJ	William Ward's journal
WMA	Women's Missionary Association
YMCA	Young Men's Christian Association

I

The Origins and Early Domestic History of the Society

I: The New Horizons of Late-Eighteenth-Century English Dissent

On 7 November 1793 the Danish East Indiaman the *Kron Princessa Maria* dropped anchor in the mouth of the Hooghli river south of Calcutta. On board were two Englishmen. One, John Thomas, had already spent some years in Bengal as a surgeon employed by the East India Company. The other, William Carey, was accompanied by his wife, Dorothy, her sister, and four young children. Carey was a thirty-two year old Baptist pastor and former shoe-maker who had never before left his native land. Both Thomas and Carey had now come to India convinced that divine providence was calling them to proclaim the message of the redeeming love of Christ to the Hindus. They were the first two missionaries of the Baptist Missionary Society, and the first English nonconformists to travel to India with the sole aim of evangelizing the national population. When, on 10 November, Thomas began to preach in Bengali to a curious audience in a bazar on the banks of the Hooghli river, a new chapter had opened, not just in Christian history, but also in the history of the relations between the Western and non-Western world. These early missionaries of the BMS were among the first expressions of a renewed endeavour by Western Christians to refashion the rest of the globe in a Christian image - a movement which was to have profound implications for the history of the non-European world over the next two centuries.

Thomas and Carey were not the first foreign missionaries to be sent out by the Protestant churches of Europe. From the Church of England, clergy supported by the Society for the Propagation of the Gospel in Foreign Parts (founded in 1701) had ministered throughout the eighteenth century, not merely to the settlers in the North American colonies, but in some measure

1

also to the indigenous Indian population. Moravian missionaries had been sent to Greenland, the West Indies, and the Cape of Good Hope. John Wesley's lieutenant, Thomas Coke, had issued his *Plan of the Society for the Establishment of Missions among the Heathens* as early as 1783, and from 1786 had missionaries working in the West Indies.[1] In India itself, the Danish settlement of Tranquebar had been the scene of Protestant missionary activity since 1706, mainly by Lutheran pietists from Halle, although from 1728 the mission had been the responsibility of the Anglican Church, through the Society for Promoting Christian Knowledge (founded in 1699). The SPCK had confined its work to the south, but in 1789 sent one missionary, Abraham Clarke, to Calcutta. However, Clarke soon abandoned his missionary work, and accepted a post as an East India Company chaplain.[2] Despite these precedents, the formation of the Baptist Missionary Society in 1792 marks a turning-point in the history of Christian missionary endeavour. The BMS set the pattern for the voluntary society model of missionary agency which became so widespread in the nineteenth century. Its foundation was one of the first indications in Britain of the new self-confidence and breadth of vision which the Evangelical revivals of the eighteenth century had nurtured in both British and American Protestantism, qualities which, in the nineteenth and twentieth centuries, became an integral part of national culture and self-understanding on both sides of the Atlantic.

As dissenters from the established Church of England, Thomas and Carey came from a community which had been on the defensive for most of the eighteenth century. The Toleration Act of 1689 had given dissenters freedom of worship, but their religious liberty remained fragile and their civil liberties few. As orthodox dissenters who believed in the Trinity, Particular (Calvinistic) Baptists such as Thomas and Carey had additional theological reasons for adopting a defensive mentality. The central truths of the Christian revelation had been repeatedly attacked from without by deists and sceptics, and undermined from within by a creeping rationalism, which impelled some dissenters towards Unitarianism. It is no wonder that some (though by no means all) Particular Baptists had responded by raising the drawbridge of their Calvinism higher and still higher.[3] In these circles,

---

1.   J. Vickers, *Thomas Coke: Apostle of Methodism* (London, 1969), 132-54.

2.   On Clarke see S. Piggin, *Making Evangelical Missionaries 1789-1858: The Social Background, Motives and Training of British Protestant Missionaries to India* (Sutton Courtenay Press, 1984), 20, 254.

3.   R. Brown, *The English Baptists of the Eighteenth Century* (London, 1986), 72, 84-5.

Baptist ministers became pastors of the chosen few rather than preachers to the many. Evangelism was not so much forgotten as ruled out of court as an attempt to usurp God's prerogative of salvation. If mission at home had become theologically suspect to some English dissenters, mission overseas remained unthinkable to all except the most visionary. Until the closing years of the eighteenth century, India was to Britain little more than a trading post. British influence in the East was as yet slender in comparison with the commercial might of the Dutch, though that was now past its peak. European industrial innovation had not yet progressed far enough to tip the scales of world power away from the grandiose empires of Asia towards the new economic expansionism of the West. To British eyes, the world beyond the troubled European continent remained largely unknown and threatening. In short, at the time of the French Revolution in 1789, British Baptists appeared to be an inward-looking sect in an insular nation in an unstable continent - hardly the most likely candidates for originating a movement which was to transform world history.

The insularity of eighteenth-century Dissent was, nonetheless, far from absolute, even before the advent of the Evangelical Revival. Among the Independents, Isaac Watts and Philip Doddridge are notable examples of dissenting leaders who took a keen interest in the early missionary ventures of the Halle pietists or the Moravians.[4] Among Particular Baptists also, a warmer, more evangelical stream of Calvinism can be discerned even in the first half of the eighteenth century, flowing chiefly from the source of the Bristol Baptist Academy. The Academy was put on a more systematic basis in 1770 through the formation of the Bristol Education Society, whose objects were said to be, firstly, the training of candidates for the ministry, and secondly, 'the encouragement of missionaries to preach the gospel wherever providence opens a door for it'.[5] Although this second objective was not immediately realized, Bristol-trained ministers provided a counter-weight to the more rigid Calvinism which predominated in Particular Baptist churches in London and East Anglia. Later these ministers helped to create the new mood of expansion which began to capture Baptist imagination in the 1780s and 1790s. Yet the influence of the Bristol Academy was insufficient to break the hold of theological passivity on Particular Baptists as a whole. An injection

4.   E. A. Payne, 'Doddridge and the Missionary Enterprise', in G. F. Nuttall (ed.), *Philip Doddridge 1702-51* (London, 1951), 79-101; G. F. Nuttall, 'Continental Pietism and the Evangelical Movement in Britain', in J. van den Berg and J. P. van Dooren (eds.), *Pietismus und Réveil* (Leiden, 1978), 207-36.

5.   C. Evans, *The Kingdom of God* (Bristol, 1775), 24, cited in Brown, *The English Baptists*, 115.

of spiritual dynamism from an entirely different quarter was needed. That infusion of new life came from across the Atlantic.

On 23 April 1784 John Ryland, the young co-pastor of College Lane Baptist Church, Northampton, received a parcel of books from Dr John Erskine of Edinburgh.[6] Among them was a pamphlet written by the New England theologian, Jonathan Edwards, *An Humble Attempt to Promote Explicit Agreement and Visible Union of God's People in Extraordinary Prayer.*[7] Edwards believed that the 'Great Awakening' in New England in the 1730s and 1740s was a sign that the last days of history were about to begin - an era which would be marked above all by the spread of the gospel throughout the globe. The specific burden of his *Humble Attempt* was, however, that the latter-day expansion of the Church would not come without 'extraordinary and united prayer'. God in his sovereignty was laying before the Church the prospect of unprecedented blessing, yet the appropriation of that blessing hinged on the believing prayers of his people. The pamphlet had a profound impact on Ryland and his friends, John Sutcliff of Olney and Andrew Fuller of Kettering. Edwards' finely-struck balance between divine sovereignty and human responsibility was immensely appealing to the developing moderate Calvinism of these young pastors. Of the three, only Sutcliff was a product of the Bristol Academy; Ryland had learnt his theology on the job as apprentice to his father, J. C. Ryland (who was Bristol-trained) at College Lane; Fuller was largely self-taught.

When the ministers and delegates of the Northamptonshire Association of Baptist churches gathered for their meetings in Nottingham on 2 and 3 June 1784, what they heard was dominated by the message of Edwards' *Humble Attempt.* Andrew Fuller preached on 'The Nature and Importance of Walking by Faith', a sermon which was later printed with the addition of some notes, significantly entitled 'Persuasives to General Union in Extraordinary Prayer for the Revival and Extent of Real Religion'.[8] At the business session the next day John Sutcliff moved successfully that the

6.　　The date is given by Ryland in his *The Work of Faith, the Labour of Love, and the Patience of Hope Illustrated; in the Life and Death of the Reverend Andrew Fuller ...* (London, 1816), 153n. The following account of the prayer call of 1784 is based on E. A. Payne, *The Prayer Call of 1784* (London, 1941).

7.　　Printed in *The Works of Jonathan Edwards, A M,* ed. E. Hickman (2 vols.; London, 1834), ii, 278-312.

8.　　The sermon is printed in A. G. Fuller, *The Complete Works of the Revd Andrew Fuller, with a Memoir of his Life* (London, 1841), 538-46. For the notes see Payne, *The Prayer Call of 1784,* 2, and T. S. H. Elwyn, *The Northamptonshire Baptist Association* (London, 1964), 17.

churches should agree to meet on the first Monday of every month for united prayer for the revival of religion at home and 'the spread of the Gospel to the most distant parts of the habitable globe'. This call to prayer was duly issued to the twenty or so churches in the Association (which stretched well beyond the borders of Northamptonshire itself), and by the following year the pattern of monthly prayer meetings was well established. Before long the prayer movement had spread further afield, to the churches of Warwickshire, Yorkshire, and the Western Association centred on Bristol. By 1789 the popularity of the prayer call was such that Sutcliff decided to issue an English edition of the *Humble Attempt*.

In the later months of 1784 Andrew Fuller was at work preparing a manuscript of his own for publication. *The Gospel Worthy of all Acceptation* was originally written in 1781 without any intention of publication, but Fuller eventually acceded to the persuasion of his friends, and the work was finally published in 1785.[9] It was a rebuttal of the central tenet of the current hyper-Calvinist creed - namely, that unconverted sinners were under no moral obligation to repent and believe the gospel, since they were rendered incapable of doing so by total depravity, and could not justly be held accountable for failing to do what they were unable to do. Fuller's argument depended chiefly on two earlier works: Abraham Taylor's tract, *The Modern Question* (1742), and Jonathan Edwards' major philosophical treatise, *An Inquiry into the Modern Prevailing Notions Respecting that Freedom of the Will which is Supposed to be Essential to Moral Agency* (1754).[10] Once again Edwards' theology was crucial for Fuller, convincing him that the inability of people to believe without the aid of the Holy Spirit (which was not at issue) was the consequence, not of a natural state over which they had no control, but of a culpable act of the will. Fuller's work was concerned with the moral obligation of those who had had an opportunity to respond to the gospel, rather than with the plight of the 'heathen' who had never heard it.[11] Yet his book was of prime importance in preparing the ground for Baptist missionary endeavour, precisely because it enabled Particular Baptists to restore concepts of moral obligation and human responsibility to the very

9. Ryland, *Life and Death of Andrew Fuller*, 204-7; Fuller, *Complete Works of Andrew Fuller*, 150.

10. G. F. Nuttall, 'Northamptonshire and the Modern Question: A Turning-Point in Eighteenth-Century Dissent', *Journal of Theological Studies* 16 (1965), 101-23; E. F. Clipsham, 'Andrew Fuller and Fullerism: A Study in Evangelical Calvinism', *BQ* 20 (1963-4), 110-113; Fuller, *Complete Works of Andrew Fuller*, 151; Ryland, *Life and Death of Andrew Fuller*, 58.

11. Fuller, *Complete Works of Andrew Fuller*, 175.

centre of their theology of salvation. Fuller had established that divine sovereignty did not eliminate the responsibility of the unconverted to believe in Christ. What was now needed was someone to make explicit the logical corollary of that position - that it was equally the responsibility of the converted to bring the gospel to the world.

II: The Young William Carey

That inference was first drawn publicly by a Baptist at the Northampton-shire Association ministers' meeting, most probably in September 1785. The chairman, J. C. Ryland, had demanded that the two most junior ministers present should each propose a question for discussion. The suggestion offered by the first - J. W. Morris of Clipstone - was deemed unacceptable. The other junior minister had only recently taken up his first pastorate at Moulton, and was not yet even ordained. His name was William Carey. He pleaded excuses, but Ryland was adamant - a topic must be submitted. Eventually the young pastor offered his question: 'Whether the command given to the apostles to "teach all nations", was not obligatory on all succeeding ministers to the end of the world, seeing that the accompanying promise was of equal extent'. To Ryland and doubtless to others present this was a novel interpretation of the Great Commission of Matthew 28. Protestants had always insisted that the office of apostle had been given for the first century only, and was it not to the apostles that the Great Commission had been given? Ryland accordingly dismissed Carey's question as unworthy of serious consideration:

> certainly nothing could be done before another Pentecost, when an effusion of miraculous gifts, including the gift of tongues, would give effect to the Commission of Christ as at first ... he was a most miserable enthusiast for asking such a question.

Our knowledge of this celebrated episode is solely dependent on one first-hand source, J. W. Morris's life of Fuller, published in 1816.[12] Indeed, John Ryland junior denied that his father could have voiced such senti-ments, and insisted that the topic was not even raised for discussion.[13]

---

12.   J. W. Morris, *Memoirs of the Life and Writings of the Revd Andrew Fuller* (London, 1816), 96-7. Morris dates the episode 'before the end of 1786', but John Ryland points out that his father had left Northampton before the ministers' meeting in 1786, which took place in Oakham.

13.   Ryland, *Life and Death of Andrew Fuller*, 175.

Furthermore, Morris's recollection of the incident was subsequently questioned by Carey himself.[14] Nevertheless, the substantial authenticity of Morris's account seems probable, not least because Carey in his *Enquiry* specifically contests the claim that a restoration of the miraculous gifts of the apostolic age was necessary before the Great Commission could again be discharged by the Church.[15] The twenty-four year old Carey was, according to Morris, 'greatly abashed and mortified' by his public rebuke, and Fuller did his best to console him.[16] Yet Carey's youthful naivety had brought into the open a question which he was to keep on the agenda of discussion within the Association until it received an answer seven years later.

There is no evidence that the young Carey had read Fuller's *The Gospel Worthy of all Acceptation* by September 1785. He had, however, read Robert Hall senior's sermon on stumbling blocks to Christian progress, *Help to Zion's Travellers* (1781), and derived great spiritual profit from it.[17] He had also regularly made the twenty-mile journey to Arnesby to hear Hall preach. It was no accident that the teaching and example of Robert Hall brought William Carey to espouse the same active and keenly moral strain of Calvinism as Hall had already encouraged in his protégé, Andrew Fuller.[18]

In 1785 Carey was still a newcomer to the Baptist family. Born in 1761, he had been brought up as an Anglican in the Northamptonshire village of Paulerspury. As a teenager he had begun to attend a dissenting prayer-meeting in the village of Hackleton, where he worked as an apprentice shoe-maker. In his attendance at Sunday worship he remained a faithful Anglican until February 1779, when a fast-day sermon, preached by Thomas Chater, the Independent minister at Olney, convinced him that he must 'bear the reproach of Christ among the dissenters'.[19] From 1779 to 1783 Carey was

14.   At an earlier date Carey had recalled the incident, and on this basis Eustace Carey accepts its authenticity; see E. Carey, *Memoir of William Carey, D.D.* (London, 1836), 53-4. More recent biographies tend to report Ryland's words as 'Young man, sit down. When God pleases to convert the heathen, He will do it without your aid or mine'. This version first appears in J. Belcher, *William Carey: A Biography* (Philadelphia, 1853), 19, and there must be some doubt about its authenticity.

15.   W. Carey, *An Enquiry into the Obligations of Christians, to Use Means for the Conversion of the Heathens* (facsimile edn., London, 1961), xiv, 11.

16.   Morris, *Memoirs of Andrew Fuller*, 97.

17.   Carey, *Memoir of William Carey*, 16-17.

18.   Ibid., 46-7, but see also 67-8. For Hall's influence on Fuller see Ryland, *Life and Death of Andrew Fuller*, 56, 58, 68, 153.

19.   Carey, *Memoir of William Carey*, 12-13.

by denominational affiliation an Independent, but his views on infant baptism gradually changed. On 5 October 1783 he was baptized by John Ryland junior at Northampton. Soon afterwards, John Sutcliff recommended Carey to the small congregation at Earls Barton, whither Carey now travelled to preach on Sundays, while continuing his trade as a shoe-maker, and studying Latin, Greek and Hebrew under Sutcliff's supervision during the week. Sutcliff's benevolent patronage was also responsible for Carey's move in March 1785 to his first residential pastorate at Moulton, which qualified him to attend the ministers' meeting for the first time at Northampton in September.

At Moulton Carey received a stipend of £11 per annum, topped up by a grant of £5 from the Particular Baptist Fund in London.[20] This meagre income was insufficient to support his growing family, and had to be supplemented by school-mastering. As a school-master Carey was far from successful. The village school declined to such an extent that before long he was back at the shoe-maker's bench. In other respects, however, the period at Moulton was a fruitful one. Residence at Moulton brought Carey closer to Andrew Fuller in Kettering and John Ryland in Northampton, forging ties of friendship which were later to prove invaluable.[21] Moreover, it was during the Moulton pastorate that Carey's distinctive and exceptionally informed global vision took shape. Before he left Moulton (and probably as early as 1784-5) he had read the published accounts of Captain James Cook's voyages to Australasia and the South Seas - 'the first thing that engaged my mind to think of missions'.[22] Teaching geography to his village pupils gave Carey further opportunity to ponder the immensity of the new world opening up to European eyes in the Pacific. By 1788 he was convinced that something must be done about the vast portion of humanity which had never heard the name of Christ. Indeed, he had already done something himself. In either 1787 or 1788, while visiting Birmingham to raise funds for the Moulton chapel building, Carey called on Thomas Potts, a wealthy member of the Cannon Street Baptist Church, who had developed an interest in missions as a result of contact as a youth in North

---

20. Ryland, *Life and Death of Andrew Fuller*, 239; J. C. Marshman, *The Life and Times of Carey, Marshman, and Ward* (2 vols.; London, 1859), i, 7.

21. Marshman, *Life and Times of Carey*, i, 8-9.

22. Carey, *Memoir of William Carey*, 18; M. Drewery, *William Carey: Shoemaker and Missionary* (London, 1978), 27. The accounts of Cook's second and third voyages were not published until 1784, and it was presumably these that Carey read, rather than the account of Cook's first voyage, published in 1773.

America with mission work among the Indians. Carey told Potts of his burden that 'something should be done for the heathen', indicated that he would be willing to go himself to Tahiti, and confessed that he had 'written a piece on the state of the heathen world', which, if published, might awaken public interest in the subject. Potts then urged him to publish, and promised £10 towards the cost of publication.[23]

On his return from Birmingham, Carey met Ryland, Fuller and Sutcliff in Ryland's study in Northampton, and at first urged one of them to publish on the subject. They were sympathetic, but raised objections 'on the ground of so much needing to be done at home, etc'. Carey then revealed that he had told Potts of his determination 'to do all in his power to set on foot a Baptist mission', and that Potts had offered financial support if Carey would publish. Carey did not, however, reveal that he already had something in writing, but modestly told the others that he had reluctantly promised Potts that he would write a pamphlet if no one of greater competence for the task could be found. At this, the three senior ministers united in urging Carey to go ahead and put his thoughts on paper, and undertook to provide constructive criticism of his manuscript. Thus encouraged, Carey resumed work on his existing material, first at Moulton, and then, from May 1789, in Leicester, following his acceptance of a call to the pastorate of the Harvey Lane church. The editorial team of Ryland, Fuller, and Sutcliff found that Carey's submitted text needed 'very little correction', and by April 1791 the first stage of revision was complete.[24]

III: The Genesis of a Missionary Society, 1791-1792

The Easter 1791 meeting of the Northamptonshire Baptist ministers was held at Clipstone. The two sermons preached before the gathering both had a missionary aspect. John Sutcliff's sermon on 1 Kings 19:10 urged the necessity of the Church being, like Elijah, 'very jealous' for the glory of the Lord of hosts. This characteristically Puritan sentiment was matched by an

---

23. F. A. Cox, *History of the Baptist Missionary Society, from 1792 to 1842* (2 vols.; London, 1842), i, 7-8. Cox's account derives from Samuel Medley of Chatham, who was present on this occasion, and corrects the version given by Ryland, *Life and Death of Andrew Fuller*, 238-9, which implies that Carey had written nothing before seeing Potts. Most sources date this episode in 1788; W. Finnemore, *The Story of a Hundred Years 1823-1923: Being the Centenary Booklet of the Birmingham Auxiliary of the Baptist Missionary Society* (Oxford, n.d.), 9, gives the date as 1787.

24. This paragraph is based on Ryland, *Life and Death of Andrew Fuller*, 238-9, supplemented by Cox.

humanitarian emphasis typical of the age of the Enlightenment: jealousy for the honour of God implied sharing his character of universal benevolence. Christ's answer to the question 'Who is my neighbour?' made clear that benevolence could not be confined to the man next door, but must extend to any member of the human race:

> Let him be an ignorant Negro, dwelling in the unexplored regions of Africa; or an untutored Savage, wandering in the inhospitable forests of America; he is your fellow creature; he is your neighbour; he is your brother. He has a Soul, - a Soul that will exist for ever.[25]

Sutcliff was followed by Andrew Fuller, whose sermon on Haggai 1:2 warned of the danger of delay in doing the work of God. The convenient plea that 'the time is not come' for building the Lord's house went a long way to explain why 'so few and so feeble efforts have been made for the propagation of the gospel in the world'. No longer could it be claimed that there were 'no opportunities for societies, or individuals, in Christian nations, to convey the gospel to the heathens'.[26]

Carey needed no further exhortation. Immediately after dinner that evening he proposed that something should be done, there and then, towards the formation of 'a society for propagating the gospel among the heathen'. The reactions of his fellow ministers to this proposal will never be known in any detail. According to Carey's nephew, Eustace, those present were sympathetic in principle but sceptical about the feasibility of what was proposed.[27] J. C. Marshman, writing decades after the event, and even more concerned to portray Carey as a lone warrior for truth fighting against the complacency of his ministerial colleagues, depicted the reactions of the others in a still more unfavourable light. Marshman followed Eustace Carey in interpreting the outcome of the meeting - a request that Carey should further revise his manuscript and proceed to publication - as an attempt to fob Carey off and play for time.[28] This seems manifestly improbable in view of the sermons they had just heard (and preached), and also of the fact that Fuller, Ryland and Sutcliff supposed that Carey had begun to write on the

---

25. *Jealousy for the Lord of Hosts: and, the Pernicious Influence of Delay in Religious Concerns: Two Discourses Delivered at a Meeting of Ministers at Clipstone ... The Former by John Sutcliff of Olney ...* (London, 1791), 7.

26. Fuller, *Complete Works of Andrew Fuller,* 551.

27. Carey, *Memoir of William Carey,* 74.

28. Marshman, *Life and Times of Carey,* i, 14.

topic only as a result of their persuasion. Eye-witness accounts of the meeting paint a more plausible picture. John Ryland had to abandon the discussion at an early point for a preaching engagement in Northampton, but stayed long enough to observe that everyone with whom he spoke was convicted of 'the evil of negligence and procrastination'.[29] Fuller's official account for later public consumption records that the discussion was characterized by 'a good degree of serious and earnest concern to exert ourselves for the propagation of the kingdom of our Lord'.[30] Most illuminating of all is J. W. Morris's comment that 'a society would then have been formed, but for the well-known deliberative prudence of Mr Sutcliffe'.[31] It seems that the leading figures in the Northamptonshire Association no longer needed convincing of the theological case for missionary endeavour; what Carey still had to persuade at least some of them of was that an immediate initiative on their part was both 'prudent' and realistic.

Carey's desire to see some form of missionary society established was shared by at least one other Baptist minister outside his own Association. At some point between the end of 1789 and May 1791 Carey paid a second visit to Birmingham to see Samuel Pearce, fresh from his studies at the Bristol Academy, and newly settled in the pastorate at Cannon Street. He found in Pearce a kindred spirit who could trace his concern for the fate of the 'heathen' back to within a week of his conversion in 1782. Since coming to Birmingham, Pearce's missionary zeal had been fanned into a flame by a sermon preached in one of the city's Wesleyan chapels by Thomas Coke. Carey's resolve must have been strengthened by hearing Pearce describe the work of Coke's missionaries in the West Indies, and he was further encouraged by promises of support from Pearce's friends, among them, no doubt, Thomas Potts.[32]

In May 1791 Pearce preached the evening sermon at Carey's ordination and formal induction to the pastorate at Harvey Lane, Leicester - Carey's lengthy period of ministerial probation was at last over. At Pearce's request Carey concluded the proceedings by reading to the assembled company the greater part of his revised manuscript, entitled *An Enquiry into the Obligations of Christians to use Means for the Conversion of the Heathens*.[33] During

29. Ryland, *Life and Death of Andrew Fuller*, 241.

30. J. Rippon (ed.), *The Baptist Annual Register*, i (1790-3), 375.

31. Morris, *Memoirs of Andrew Fuller*, 99.

32. Fuller, *Complete Works of Andrew Fuller*, 766; Carey, *Memoir of William Carey*, 74.

33. Fuller, *Complete Works of Andrew Fuller*, 766.

the following winter Carey took his completed text to a Leicester printer and bookseller. On 12 May 1792 the pamphlet was published at a price of 1s. 6d.

The most significant words in the title of the *Enquiry* were 'Obligations' and 'Means'. The first and most important section of the pamphlet returned to the theme of Carey's question of September 1785 by establishing that the global commission given to the apostles was still binding on the Church. Carey described the consequences of the widespread denial of this obligation in language which corresponded closely to a passage in Fuller's April 1791 sermon on the dangerous tendency of delay.[34] The question of obligation and the question of means were inextricably connected, for where 'a command exists nothing can be necessary to render it binding but a removal of those obstacles which render obedience impossible, and these are removed already'.[35] The Church's failure to take the gospel to the world was thus comparable to the inability of natural man to believe in Christ, as expounded by Fuller in *The Gospel Worthy of all Acceptation:* both should be attributed, not to natural circumstances beyond human control, but to a culpable refusal on the part of the human will.

In the second section of the *Enquiry* Carey presented an historical review of missionary endeavour from apostolic times to the most recent efforts of the Moravians and Methodists. Its purpose was to prove that 'the success of the gospel has been very considerable in many places already', and thus to counter the claim of some hyper-Calvinists that no missionary success could be anticipated until the slaying of the two witnesses of Revelation 11, and the fulfilment of other prophecies of the end-time.[36] Once again Carey was developing themes initially explored by Fuller: 'This people say, "the time is not come"' was as much the text for the *Enquiry* as for Fuller's Clipstone sermon.

The lengthy third section of the pamphlet, with its remarkable statistical survey of world geography and population, was less vital to the logic of the argument. It served merely to emphasize the immense numbers of the human race - conservatively estimated by Carey at 731 million - and the 'vast proportion' of them who remained in heathen darkness, destitute of

---

34. Compare Carey, *Enquiry*, 8, and Fuller, *Complete Works of Andrew Fuller*, 551. It is possible that Fuller had borrowed from Carey's text, rather than vice versa.

35. Carey, *Enquiry*, 11.

36. Ibid., 12; see W. R. Ward, 'The Baptists and the Transformation of the Church, 1780-1830', *BQ* 25 (1973), 167-70.

all knowledge of the gospel.[37] In the following section Carey returned to the theme of 'means' at greater length. In attempting to show 'the Practicability of something being done, more than what is done, for the Conversion of the Heathen',[38] he was addressing himself less to hyper-Calvinist opponents than to the very Northamptonshire friends who had proved sympathetic but hesitant about the feasibility of actually engaging in overseas missionary work. Here Carey was speaking with his own voice, in no sense Fuller's mouth-piece, but rather a goad in his side.

The fifth and final section of the *Enquiry* hinged in classic moderate Calvinist fashion on the necessary connection between prayer and responsible Christian action. Carey followed Edwards' *Humble Attempt* in teaching on the basis of Zechariah 12 and 13 that 'an universal conjunction in fervent prayer' would be the prelude to that 'glorious outpouring' of the Spirit on the missionary labours of the Church which would characterize the last days. Furthermore, he believed that 'some tokens for good' could already be discerned, as God's initial response to the prayer movement instituted in 1784. Carey then came to the crux of the whole pamphlet: 'We must not be contented however with praying, *without exerting ourselves in the use of means* for the obtaining of those things we pray for.' Divine sovereignty demanded human means; prayer required action; obligation called for obedience.[39]

Within three weeks of the publication of the *Enquiry* Carey seized his opportunity to bring to fruition the proposals for forming a missionary society which occupied the final pages of his pamphlet. On Wednesday, 30 May 1792 he was due to preach before the annual meeting of the Northamptonshire Association at Nottingham.[40] Carey chose as his text Isaiah 54: 2-3: 'Enlarge the place of thy tent, and let them stretch forth the curtains of thine habitations: spare not, lengthen thy cords, and strengthen thy stakes ...'. In the plight of exiled Judah, apparently forgotten by God her husband, Carey saw a picture of the barren and desolate Church of his own day, and in the promise of a new and wider destiny for Judah lay the prospect of countless new children in the Christian family to be drawn from all the

---

37. Carey, *Enquiry*, 62-3.

38. Ibid., 67.

39. Ibid., 77-87.

40. The correct date of the sermon is given in the minutes of the Northamptonshire Association, printed in Rippon (ed.), *The Baptist Annual Register*, i (1790-3), 418-19. *PA* i, 2-3, gives the incorrect date of 31 May, an error which has been followed by many of Carey's biographers.

earth. Once again, however, Carey insisted that God's promise was also his command. God was about to do great things by extending the kingdom of Jesus throughout the globe, and for that very reason Christians were bound to attempt great things in spreading the gospel overseas: 'Expect great things. Attempt great things.'[41]

John Ryland found Carey's exposition of 'the criminality of our supineness in the cause of God' so forcible that he would not have been surprised 'if all the people had lifted up their voice and wept'.[42] Yet when it came to the business meeting the following morning nobody was willing to make a proposition. Carey, writes J. C. Marshman, seized Fuller by the hand in desperation, inquiring whether 'they were again going away without doing anything?'[43] Carey's appeal evidently moved Fuller, who then took the initiative from which others had held back. The following resolution was recorded in the minutes: 'Resolved, that a plan be prepared against the next Ministers' meeting at Kettering, for forming a Baptist society for propagating the Gospel among the Heathen.'[44]

So it was on 2 October 1792 that 'the Particular-Baptist Society for propagating the Gospel among the heathen' was formed in the back parlour of Mrs Beeby Wallis's home in Kettering. Although there was no reference in the title to the Northamptonshire Association, the Society was in every respect a child of the Association, and the assumption of its founding members was clearly that the Society's support would derive largely from the Association in the foreseeable future. All except two of the thirteen persons whose presence at the inaugural meeting is recorded in the minutes came from churches currently or subsequently in membership with the Association.[45] The two exceptions were William Staughton, a student from

41. The text of the sermon has not been preserved. That the original form of Carey's motto was 'Expect Great Things; Attempt Great Things' rather than 'Expect Great Things from God; Attempt Great Things for God' has been argued by E. A. Payne, 'John Dyer's Memoir of Carey', *BQ* 22 (1967-8), 326-7, and A. C. Smith, 'The Spirit and the Letter of Carey's Catalytic Watchword', *BQ* 33 (1989-90), 226-37.

42. Ryland, *Life and Death of Andrew Fuller*, 242.

43. Marshman, *Life and Times of Carey*, i, 15.

44. Rippon (ed.), *The Baptist Annual Register*, i (1790-3), 375, 419.

45. The thirteen were John Ryland (Northampton), Reynold Hogg (Thrapston), John Sutcliff (Olney), Andrew Fuller (Kettering), Abraham Greenwood (Oakham), Edward Sharman (Moulton), Samuel Pearce (Birmingham), Joseph Timms (deacon at Kettering), William Heighton (Roade), William Staughton (Bristol Baptist Academy), Joshua Burton (Foxton), Thomas Blundel (Arnesby), John Eayre (Braybrooke). The congregations at Thrapston (not yet formally constituted as a church) and Braybrooke did not join the Association till later.

Bristol Academy who happened to be in the county preaching with a view to succeed John Ryland at Northampton; and Samuel Pearce, Staughton's pastor, who had preached at the ministers' meeting that afternoon, and had set his heart on being present as soon as he had heard of the plan to form a society.[46] Staughton, and very probably Pearce as well, were regarded as welcome guests rather than full participants.[47] There is in fact no record of attendance as such in the minutes; the thirteen names recorded are the names of those who pledged annual subscriptions. As has frequently been observed, Carey's name does not appear on the list, although he was appointed a member of the five-man Committee. However, we have the testimony of Andrew Fuller, who was appointed as secretary of the Society, that Carey was present; it seems probable that even the lowest level of subscription pledged by those present (half a guinea) was beyond Carey's limited means.[48] In fact Carey attended only two more Committee meetings before his departure for India in June 1793.

IV: Laying the Foundations of Public Support

Perhaps the most crucial issue facing a missionary society formed by a group of impecunious Northamptonshire ministers was how to construct a sufficiently broad base of domestic support to finance overseas operations. The first step towards resolving this problem was taken by Samuel Pearce, when he presented the second meeting of the Society on 1 November 1792 with two surprises. The first of these was the princely sum of £70 raised from the Cannon Street congregation - a gift which, in Ryland's words, 'put new spirits into us all'.[49] The second was the news that Pearce's church had on their own initiative formed a 'distinct society' to receive funds for the mission and 'co-operate by every other means in their power with the primary society'.[50] The Northampton meeting not only placed its seal of approval on Pearce's action, but expressed the hope that 'similar corresponding united Societies' would be formed elsewhere, and promptly made

46. R. Hayden, 'Kettering 1792 and Philadelphia 1814', *BQ* 21 (1965-6), 3-20, 64-72; E. A. Payne, *The First Generation* (London, 1936), 55-9; Fuller, *Complete Works of Andrew Fuller,* 766.

47. S. P. Carey, *Samuel Pearce, MA: the Baptist Brainerd* (London, n.d.), 136-7.

48. BMS Committee Minutes, 2 Oct. 1792, pp. 2-3; Carey, *Memoir of William Carey,* 75.

49. Ryland, *Life and Death of Andrew Fuller,* 242.

50. *PA* i, 5.

Pearce a member of the Committee.[51] At the third meeting of the Society two weeks later it was agreed that any 'corresponding society' should have the right to send two delegates (or one delegate with two votes) to any meeting of the primary society.[52] The term 'corresponding society' was short-lived, being replaced in 1793 by 'assistant society', no doubt because the former term was becoming the conventional nomenclature for the newly founded reform societies, which were currently championing the dangerous causes of constitutional reform and the 'Rights of Man', as expounded by Tom Paine's book, published in 1791. This act of political prudence was ultimately of less significance than the commitment which the infant mission had now made to the principle of nationwide organization. How the achievement of this general objective could be reconciled with the continuing direction of the Society by Northamptonshire hands was to prove a more taxing problem than Fuller or his associates then realized.

The need to establish an adequate base of financial support in the churches would become acute as soon as the BMS had candidates to send out and a destination in view. Samuel Pearce's preference for the first field of service was the Pellew Islands, a tiny group situated to the east of the Philippines.[53] The rejection of this unlikely venue in favour of Bengal was due largely to fortuitous circumstances. At the third meeting of the BMS on 13 November 1792 a letter was read from Carey (who was unable to attend both this and the previous meeting), proposing that the Society should take under its patronage a friend of Sutcliff's, John Thomas, who had recently returned from Bengal and intended to return to India with a companion to work as an evangelist amongst the Hindu population. The Committee deputed Fuller to make appropriate enquiries regarding Thomas. Abraham Booth, pastor of the Prescot Street church in London, who had known Thomas long enough to be cautious, supplied a guarded but not unfriendly reference. Fuller proceeded to interview Thomas, and was impressed by the evangelistic warmth of his Calvinism. Thomas was then invited to meet the Committee at Kettering on 9 January 1793. Characteristically he arrived late, only to find himself all but accepted. No sooner had he satisfied the Committee with his answers to their remaining questions than Carey volunteered himself as Thomas's companion. Fuller's minutes of the

51. *PA* i, 5-6.

52. *PA* i, 6.

53. Carey, *Samuel Pearce*, 139-40.

meeting record that the members present could do no other than accept Carey's offer, since they had 'long considered him as a person peculiarly formed and fitted for so arduous an undertaking; and had formed themselves into a Society with a view to carry into execution what he had proposed'.[54]

In the latter part of January 1793 Andrew Fuller wrote upwards of fifteen letters to Baptist ministers in different parts of the country, enclosing a printed account of the Society's origins and pleading for the financial support of their congregations.[55] His repeated theme was that, whereas for eight or nine years the churches had been praying for the spread of the gospel among the 'heathen', 'we now think we ought to do something more than pray'.[56] One of those to whom he wrote was Dr Samuel Stennett, minister at Little Wild Street in London, and one of the most influential Baptists of his day. It was Stennett who took the chair at a meeting of eight London ministers and twenty-three laymen convened at the Devonshire Square church to consider the propriety of forming a London auxiliary to the BMS.[57] However, Stennett told the meeting that the mission would 'come to nothing' for want of any support save what was contributed 'for once in a fit of zeal', and consequently advised the London ministers to 'stand aloof and not commit themselves'.[58] As a result, the great majority of London Baptist ministers did precisely that. The one London minister who gave strong support to the BMS from the beginning, Abraham Booth, was prevented by illness from attending the Devonshire Square meeting. His two principal deacons - William Fox and Joseph Gutteridge - were, however, present, and imbibed (or were confirmed in) a deep suspicion of the Society's management which was to have serious consequences in years to come.[59]

54. BMS Committee Minutes, 13 Nov. 1792, pp. 10-13; 9 Jan. 1793, pp. 14-18; *BM* 8 (1816), 452.

55. Bound volume of original letters of Fawcett, Fuller, Morris, Ryland, 1773-1813, Fuller to Sutcliff, 5 Feb. 1793.

56. [J. Fawcett, junior], *An Account of the Life, Ministry, and Writings of the late Rev. John Fawcett, DD* (London, 1818), 294; see also M. H. Wilkin, *Joseph Kinghorn of Norwich* (Norwich, 1855), 216-17.

57. G. Laws, *Andrew Fuller: Pastor, Theologian, Ropeholder* (London, 1942), 66.

58. *BM* 8 (1816), 453; H/1/1, Fuller to Ward, 5 Mar. 1813.

59. Laws, *Andrew Fuller*, 66; Fox and Gutteridge may be meant by Cox's reference in *History of the BMS*, i, 21, to 'two of the principal people in a leading church' who 'spoke decidedly against the formation of such a society'.

The failure of the BMS to attract much support from London Baptists may have had less to do with theology than with social prejudice and metropolitan disdain for rustic provincial initiatives. Equally marked, though ultimately less serious, was the Society's inability to make much headway in the counties of Norfolk and Suffolk. Here the opposition was specifically theological. The High Calvinist churches of the Norfolk and Suffolk Association suspected Fullerite theology as a half-way-house to Arminianism, a suspicion which eventually bore fruit in the formation of a new Strict Baptist Association in 1828-9.[60]

Happily London and East Anglia were not representative of the country as a whole. Baptists in Yorkshire and Lancashire had derived fresh evangelistic zeal from the impact on the north of England of George Whitefield, William Grimshaw, and other leaders of the Evangelical Revival. Yorkshire in particular proved fruitful ground for Fuller, thanks in large measure to John Fawcett of Hebden Bridge, whose Wainsgate Academy had nurtured both John Sutcliff and William Ward. One of the earliest assistant societies affiliated to the BMS was formed at Halifax in March 1793; Fawcett, its secretary, became a member of the BMS Committee.[61] Another early and active assistant society was established in Hampshire and Wiltshire in July 1793.[62] Its prime movers were John Saffery of Salisbury and William Steadman of Broughton. Although its primary function was naturally to collect funds for the overseas work of the BMS, the Hampshire and Wiltshire assistant society was distinguished by its eager promotion of the cause of home mission through itinerant or village preaching. In September 1795 the BMS Committee agreed to seek the approval of its subscribers for devoting some of the Society's funds to village preaching in Britain. The response was favourable, and as a result Saffery and Steadman were dispatched to Cornwall in June 1796 on an evangelistic tour financed by the Society.[63] This was the first of sevє al such home mission tours which the BMS or its auxiliaries sponsored until as late as 1815-16. The same evangelical enthusiasm which fired the foreign missionary movement also inspired an urgent concern for the 'heathen' at home, expressed through the

---

60. *BM* 8 (1816), 454; H/1/1, Fuller to Ward, 27 Oct. 1804; E. A. Payne, *The Baptist Union: A Short History* (London, 1959), 41, 56.

61. BMS Committee Minutes, 20 Mar. 1793, pp. 20-22.

62. H/4, Minute Book of Hants. and Wilts. Auxiliary to the BMS, 1793-1818.

63. BMS Committee Minutes, 16 Sept. 1795, p. 55; notes for June 1796, pp. 66-7; *PA* i, 117-18, 153-6, 262-71.

promotion of itinerant preaching; the two movements were not in competition but fed off each other.[64]

William Steadman's removal from his Broughton pastorate to Devonport in 1798 was a natural sequel to his evangelistic campaigns in Devon and Cornwall in 1796-7, but it threatened to weaken the foothold which the BMS had established in Hampshire and Wiltshire. John Saffery feared that he would now be left 'almost alone' to keep alive missionary exertions in the neighbourhood.[65] Further west, Bristol itself had been dependable ever since John Ryland's assumption of the presidency of Bristol Academy in 1793, a step which Fuller regarded as of great strategic significance for the spread of correct views of divine truth.[66] It could not be assumed that the existing influence of the Academy would automatically secure the whole-hearted support of churches throughout the Western Association for the BMS. J. W. Morris, pastor at Clipstone, remarked perceptively in 1800 that 'a *Western* Calvinist is a very different kind of animal from a Northampton-shire one'.[67] The precise nature of the difference is elusive, but it is clear that an existing tradition of moderate Calvinism was not in itself sufficient to create active Baptist enthusiasm for the BMS.

Ryland's personal influence in the Bristol area was matched by that of Samuel Pearce in Birmingham. In October 1795 the Birmingham assistant society was, 'for the sake of convenience', fully incorporated into the parent society, and its chief officers became members of the BMS Committee.[68] Among them were Thomas King, who now succeeded Reynold Hogg as treasurer, and Thomas Potts, benefactor of the *Enquiry*. Even though Pearce was lost to the Society in 1799 by his death at the early age of thirty-three, his deacons, King and Potts, survived till 1831 to champion the missionary cause so dear to their pastor's heart.[69]

Although the endeavours of men such as Fawcett, Saffery, Ryland, and Pearce were crucial in promoting the BMS cause in different parts of the country, the lion's share of such work fell on the shoulders of Andrew Fuller throughout the period of his secretaryship. To the regret and almost certain

---

64. D. W. Lovegrove, *Established Church, Sectarian People: Itinerancy and the Transformation of English Dissent, 1780-1830* (Cambridge, 1988), 25.

65. Ibid., 32-3.

66. Angus Library, transcript of Fuller to Ryland, 3 Dec. 1793.

67. Bound volume of original letters of Fawcett, Fuller, Morris, Ryland, 1773-1813, Morris to Sutcliff, 19 Nov. 1800.

68. BMS Committee Minutes, 16 Sept. 1795, p. 56.

69. Finnemore, *The Story of a Hundred Years,* 21-2.

detriment of his church, he was away from Kettering for up to three months of the year travelling vast distances for the Society. As late as 1814, when already a sick man, Fuller travelled in one month a total of 600 miles, preaching on twenty-eight occasions, and collecting for the mission 'about a pound a mile'.[70] Nowhere were Fuller's travels more profitable than in Scotland, which he visited five times, in 1799, 1802, 1805, 1808 and 1813.[71] At first sight Scotland was most unpromising territory for the BMS, since the Baptist churches were of the 'Scotch' variety, adhering to the Sandemanian principles of Archibald McLean, who taught that faith was not a moral act of the will but merely a simple process of intellectual assent. However, Fuller, despite sharp theological differences with McLean, was happy to solicit Scotch Baptist support for the BMS. More productive still were the churches founded around the turn of the century through the evangelistic ministry of the brothers Robert and James Alexander Haldane. Some of these churches adopted Baptist principles, especially after the Haldanes themselves became Baptists in 1808, and forged close links with Fuller and English Particular Baptists.[72] By his later years Fuller was probably better known, and certainly better loved, in Scotland and the North of England than in London. After 1807 one of the Haldanes' disciples, Christopher Anderson of Edinburgh, became, not just the Society's leading advocate in Scotland, but increasingly the man to whom Fuller looked as his most likely successor.

V: The BMS, Evangelical Ecumenism, and Politics

William Carey had expressed the hope in his *Enquiry* that the missionary obligation would be accepted by 'every one who loves our Lord Jesus Christ in sincerity', but had recognized that 'in the present divided state of Christendom, it would be more likely for good to be done by each denomination engaging separately in the work, than if they were to embark in it conjointly'.[73] This concession to ecclesiastical reality was faithfully echoed in the founding minutes of the BMS: 'As in the present divided state of Christendom it seems that each denomination by exerting itself seperately

---

70. H/1/1, Fuller to Ward, 5 Sept. 1814.

71. Ryland, *Life and Death of Andrew Fuller*, 249-50, 261-338.

72. D. W. Bebbington (ed.), *The Baptists in Scotland: A History* (Glasgow, 1988), 19-24, 30-4.

73. Carey, *Enquiry*, 84.

[*sic*] is most likely to accomplish the great ends of a mission, it is agreed that this Society be called *The Particular-Baptist Society, for propagating the gospel amongst the heathen.*'[74]

The BMS was thus founded in a spirit of ecumenical idealism tempered by a liberal dose of denominational realism. From the beginning Fuller and his colleagues not merely welcomed support from non-Baptists, but actively sought it. By May 1794 Fuller's collecting book could boast contributions from leading London Independents, as well as such distinguished Anglican names as William Wilberforce, Henry Thornton of Clapham, Thomas Scott, and John Newton.[75] However, in September 1795 the missionary enthusiasm of Independents and Anglican Evangelicals gained an alternative outlet. What later became known as the London Missionary Society (LMS) originated in a small interdenominational group, which first met in London in the spring of 1794 to discuss Melvill Horne's appeal in his *Letters on Missions* for the formation of a truly ecumenical evangelical missionary agency.[76]

Initial Baptist responses to 'the Missionary Society', as the new society styled itself, were generally favourable. Until about 1810 the LMS was careful not to poach on BMS territory by collecting from Baptist congregations.[77] Nevertheless, the BMS rapidly lost most of the paedobaptist support which it had enjoyed up to 1795. By September 1802 Ryland was voicing the fear that 'we shall miss some money thro' the notion some people entertain that THE Society supports *all* the Missions'.[78] Writing the definite article in the new society's pretentious title in capitals was also a favourite device of Fuller's, and relations between the two societies became markedly more strained once the LMS began collecting from Baptist churches after 1810.[79]

Although the missionary awakening encouraged a 'pan-evangelical' spirit of interdenominational co-operation in the cause of domestic and

---

74. BMS Committee Minutes, 2 Oct. 1792, pp. 1-2.

75. [J. Wilson], *Memoir of ... Thomas Wilson, Esq.* (2nd edn.; London, 1849), 126n.-127n.

76. M. Horne, *Letters on Missions: Addressed to the Protestant Ministers of the British Churches* (Bristol, 1794), 21-2; see R. H. Martin, *Evangelicals United: Ecumenical Stirrings in Pre-Victorian Britain, 1795-1830* (Metuchen, N.J., and London, 1983), 40-8.

77. Martin, *Evangelicals United,* 48-9, 63.

78. Bound volume of original letters of Fawcett, Fuller, Morris, Ryland, 1773-1813, Ryland to Sutcliff, 23 Sept. 1802.

79. Marshman, *Life and Times of Carey,* i, 395; Martin, *Evangelicals United,* 62-3.

foreign mission, there were clear limits to the scope of ecumenical enthusiasm, at least as far as Andrew Fuller was concerned. Fuller was glad to associate publicly with the Anglican Evangelicals who founded the Church Missionary Society (CMS) in 1799, and proudly reproduced for the benefit of his wayward missionary John Fountain an eulogy on Carey from the pen of John Newton, in which Newton exclaimed: 'he is more to me than Bishop or Archbishop; he is an apostle'.[80] Yet Fuller retained a profound conviction of the harmful consequences of religious establishment, and in 1806 felt bound to warn the Serampore Trio (Carey, Joshua Marshman, and William Ward) that their friendship with the East India Company's Evangelical chaplains Claudius Buchanan and David Brown might draw them off from the simplicity of Christ into a 'worldly, *political* religion'.[81] For Fuller national establishments of religion were but a compounding of the first and fundamental error of paedobaptism: 'the one introduces the unconverted posterity of believers, the other of all the inhabitants of a country, considering none but jews and deists as unbelievers'.[82] Fuller's belief that infant baptism led inexorably to a fatal mingling of the Church and the world lay at the root of his unflinching opposition to the growing popularity of open communion among Baptists in both England and India. The adoption of open communion at Serampore in 1805 on William Ward's initiative was deplored repeatedly by Fuller in terms which reveal the boundaries of his commitment to evangelical unity. When Ward added the name of John Wesley to a list of paedobaptist worthies whose right of admission to the Lord's table could hardly be denied, Fuller replied with a blunt statement that even if 'Mr W had been a Baptist I could not have joined him at the L[ord's] S[upper] ... how a person who opposed the doctrine of salvation by grace as he did, and who held with sinless perfection in this life, could know either himself or the Saviour I do not understand'.[83] While the Serampore missionaries derived from their strengthening Anglican contacts a new breadth of Christian sympathy, the BMS secretary remained a typically eighteenth-century Particular Baptist in his staunch attachment to Baptist and Calvinistic principles. Carey's famous proposal

---

80. H/2/3, Fuller to Fountain, 7 Sept. 1797. The point of citing Carey's example to Fountain was that Carey had dropped his former enthusiasm for politics 'for things of greater consequence'.

81. H/1/2, Fuller to Marshman, 8 Nov. 1806.

82. H/1/1, Fuller to Ward, 21 Sept. 1800.

83. H/1/1, Fuller to Ward, 16 July 1809. On this episode see E. D. Potts, 'A Note on the Serampore Trio', *BQ* 20 (1963-4), 115-17.

in 1806 of 'a general association of all denominations of Christians', to meet every ten years or so at the Cape of Good Hope, was politely dismissed by Fuller as 'one of bro' Carey's pleasing dreams'. Fuller could see no purpose or prospect of unity in such a meeting, and justified his scepticism by pointing to the 'endless strifes' which, he said, were already marring the interdenominational spirit of the LMS.[84]

Whilst BMS relationships with paedobaptist dissenters and Anglicans were to some extent circumscribed by Fuller's theological convictions, the realities of contemporary ecclesiastical politics were in practice a more substantial determinative force. At a time when evangelical dissenters were widely suspected, not without reason, of political disloyalty and republican sympathies, Fuller was concerned to distance the BMS from any appearance of political radicalism.[85] His own political views were in any case decidedly conservative. Fuller wrote to Carey in 1799 that he had observed that 'those Ministers who have been the most violent partizans [sic] for democratic liberty ... are commonly not only cold hearted in religion, but the most imperious in their own churches'; the leaders of the French Revolution were mostly, in his view, 'unprincipled infidels' bent on supreme power and the extirpation of Christianity itself; there was little to choose between monarchical and democratic government, and no hope of peace except through the spread of the gospel.[86]

BMS missionaries who gave voice to overtly democratic sentiments on the field soon felt the weight of Fuller's reproof. Jacob Grigg, one of two Bristol-trained missionaries sent to establish a mission in Sierra Leone in 1795, was the first such offender. When in October 1796 John Ryland received a letter from Zachary Macaulay, the Evangelical governor of the colony, complaining that Grigg had 'conducted himself with great impropriety', Fuller was quick to recognize that there was 'great danger of the

---

84. H/1/1, Fuller to Ward, 2 Dec. 1806. Carey's proposal was made in a letter to Fuller dated 15 May 1806 (original in possession of St Mary's Baptist Church, Norwich), cited in E. D. Potts, *British Baptist Missionaries in India 1793-1837* (Cambridge, 1967), 53.

85. D. W. Lovegrove, 'English Evangelical Dissent and the European Conflict', in W. J. Sheils (ed.), *The Church and War* (Studies in Church History, 20; Oxford, 1983), 263-76. For William Ward's background in radical journalism and politics see A. C. Smith, 'William Ward, Radical Reform, and Missions in the 1790s', *American Baptist Quarterly* 10 (1991), 218-44.

86. H/1/3, Fuller to Carey, 18 Apr. 1799; see P. S. E. Carson, 'Soldiers of Christ: Evangelicals and India, 1784-1833', Ph.D. thesis (London, 1988), 79-80.

African Mission being utterly destroyed thro' Grigg's Imprudence'.[87] Grigg's offence had been to interfere in the political affairs of the colony by, for example, objecting to the imposition of taxation without elected representation. Although the BMS Committee acted promptly to censure his conduct, the damage had been done. Macaulay, assured of the full support of the Committee, expelled Grigg in 1797 and the Sierra Leone mission came to an untimely end.[88]

The consequences of Grigg's behaviour in Africa made Fuller doubly nervous in September 1797 when John Fountain, newly arrived in India, showed signs of confirming the Committee's suspicions that he had too great an 'edge for politicks'.[89] Despite repeated admonitions from home, Fountain continued to make pro-republican statements which imperilled the survival of the India mission and challenged Fuller's deepest convictions about the scriptural duty of civil obedience.[90] The receipt of Fountain's journal for 1798 caused the BMS Committee in April 1800 to pass a series of resolutions deploring its general spirit and 'many obnoxious passages in particular', and undertaking to recall Fountain at once if the next mailing from India displayed no improvement.[91] Fuller subsequently informed William Ward that, whilst he had left the Committee to form their own judgment on the journal, he would, if no adverse comment had been passed, have resigned his office, 'persuaded as I am that God will never bless us while any amongst us can so fly in the face of the whole tenor of the S[cripture]s'.[92] Although there appears to have been some subsequent moderation in the tone of Fountain's utterances, he remained a source of constant anxiety to Fuller up to his death in 1801.

Andrew Fuller's sensitivity to the fact that the India mission hung by the slenderest of political threads was amply vindicated in 1807-8. A mutiny

---

87. BMS Committee Minutes, 22 Sept. 1796, pp. 73-4; Bound volume of original letters of Andrew Fuller to John Sutcliff, 1790-1814, letter of 3 Oct. 1796.

88. On the Grigg case see S. Jakobsson, *Am I not a Man and a Brother? British Missions and the Abolition of the Slave Trade and Slavery in West Africa and the West Indies 1786-1838* (Uppsala, 1972), 84-100; B. Amey, 'Baptist Missionary Society Radicals', *BQ* 26 (1975-6), 368-9. The other Sierra Leone missionary, James Rodway, had already been invalided home in 1796.

89. H/2/3, Fuller to Fountain, 7 Sept. 1797; see Amey, 'Baptist Missionary Society Radicals', 370-1.

90. Bound volume of original letters of Andrew Fuller to John Sutcliff, 1790-1814, letters of 18 Feb. and 26 Apr. 1799; H/1/3, Fuller to Carey, 18 Apr. 1799.

91. BMS Committee Minutes, 17 Apr. 1800, pp. 4-5.

92. H/1/1, Fuller to Ward, 13 June 1800.

amongst the East India Company's sepoy troops at Vellore in 1806 was widely attributed to fears induced by missionary activity, and plans were made to introduce a motion in the Court of Proprietors demanding the expulsion of all missionaries from Company territory.[93] Initially the BMS Committee authorized a statement defending its missionaries against the charges being levelled against them, which Fuller proposed to distribute to the Proprietors, Directors, and members of the Board of Control before the meeting on 17 June 1807 at which the anti-missionary motion was expected.[94] However, Charles Grant, the Evangelical deputy chairman of the Company, persuaded Fuller to postpone circulation of the BMS statement, and leave the matter in the sympathetic hands of himself, Edward Parry the chairman of the Company, and Lord Teignmouth, president of the British and Foreign Bible Society and formerly governor-general in India. This low-key diplomatic strategy paid off. The anti-missionary motion on 17 June 1807 was safely neutralized by the benevolent intervention of Parry as chairman.[95] Even though the publication by the Serampore missionaries of an ill-judged pamphlet attacking Muslim belief prompted a renewed political onslaught on the BMS India mission in January 1808, Fuller was sufficiently confident of friends at court to have few fears.[96] A new motion for the recall of the missionaries was put to the Court of Directors at the end of the month, but was defeated by thirteen votes to seven after a two-hour speech by Charles Grant.[97]

Andrew Fuller's political discretion played a part in ensuring that the East India Company continued to turn a blind and generally benevolent eye towards the activities within its territory of Baptist and other missionaries who had never applied for the requisite Company licence. Unofficial but uneasy approval of the missionary presence in Bengal remained the rule

93. Carson, 'Soldiers of Christ', 117-24; S. K. Mitra, 'The Vellore Mutiny of 1806 and the Question of Christian Mission to India', *Indian Church History Review* 8 (1974), 75-82.

94. *PA* iii, 374. The BMS Committee minutes for 1805-15 are unfortunately not extant. The statement is printed in J. Ivimey, *A History of the English Baptists* (4 vols.; London, 1811-30), iv, 94-107.

95. Carson, 'Soldiers of Christ', 134-8; bound volume of original letters of Fuller to Sutcliff, 1790-1814, letters of 11 and 20 June 1807; H/1/1, Fuller to Ward, 9/29 July 1807.

96. H/1/1, Fuller to Ward, 11 Jan. 1808. For the 'Persian pamphlet' see Carson, 'Soldiers of Christ', 159-77; Potts, *British Baptist Missionaries*, 183-91.

97. Carson, 'Soldiers of Christ', 144-50.

until 1811, when Company attitudes began to harden again, in tandem with the attempts of Lord Sidmouth to restrict the freedom of nonconformist itinerant preaching at home. In view of the worsening prospects for the toleration of missionary work in India, the BMS joined enthusiastically with the LMS and the CMS in petitioning parliament in 1813 for the insertion of a 'pious clause' in the East India Company charter which would, for the first time, give missionaries an assured legal status in the Company's territories. Although the public leadership of the campaign was assumed by William Wilberforce, the decisive pressure was applied by the 895 petitions, signed by half a million people, which were presented to the House of Commons between April and June 1813, 281 of them from Baptist congregations.[98] However, the outcome was something of a hollow victory for nonconformists. The new charter set up an Anglican establishment of a bishop and three archdeacons to be financed from Company revenues. Although it stated that 'sufficient facilities' ought to be afforded to persons going to India in order to disseminate 'useful knowledge' and 'religious and moral improvement', such persons still had to apply to the Company for a licence.[99] Co-operation between evangelicals of different denominations had secured toleration for missionary activity in India, but on terms which few Baptists could applaud.

VI: Union Essential to Prosperity: The BMS and the Origins of the Baptist Union

Andrew Fuller feared that the coming of an ecclesiastical establishment to India would strengthen the hand of those who were jealous for the honour which the considerable translating achievements of the Serampore missionaries had earned for the BMS. 'When we began in 1792', he reflected in a letter to William Ward written in March 1813, 'there was little or no respectability amongst us ... not so much as a squire to sit in the chair at our meetings, nor an orator to address him with speeches.'[100] What the Serampore translations had done, continued Fuller, was to attract the attention of 'respectable men', who were impatient to wear such an impressive feather in their own caps. He saw evidence of a general

---

98.   Ibid., 218, 240, 412.

99.   Ibid., 246-8.

100. H/1/1, Fuller to Ward, 5 Mar. 1813, cited in Marshman, *Life and Times of Carey*, ii, 78.

conspiracy by 'respectable men', both within and beyond the Baptist denomination, to impose their will and ways on a society which remained unashamed of its humble origins. Fuller may perhaps have been over-suspicious by nature, but his perceptions cannot be lightly dismissed. Behind his analysis lay real issues of power, style, and management which became increasingly contentious as his secretaryship drew towards its end.

The narrow base of management of the BMS had become a cause of anxiety to the Serampore missionaries, particularly to Carey and Joshua Marshman, as early as 1805. Marshman wrote at length to John Ryland voicing his concern for the future of the mission should Ryland, Fuller, Sutcliff and Morris follow Samuel Pearce to the grave. The LMS, Marshman pointed out, had so many in their management that if three or four were taken away, they would hardly be missed. If the BMS were to give a greater say within its Committee to ministers from outside the Northamptonshire Association, its desperate weakness in London and some other parts of the country might be remedied. Marshman also suggested that the Society could with profit follow the example of the LMS by holding annual meetings to rouse the missionary zeal of the public.[101] Marshman's comments were passed on to Sutcliff, and presumably also to Fuller, but neither of his recommendations was implemented. Fuller's suspicions that the London ministers were fatally compromised by hyper-Calvinist 'antinomianism' were, if anything, more intense in 1804-5 than they had been in 1792.[102] Wariness of London theology was supplemented by a distaste for London culture: the annual London meetings of the LMS exhibited qualities of ostentation and display which Fuller and his colleagues found uncongenial. The idea of holding an annual public meeting in London for the BMS was given serious consideration in 1808, but the objections raised in some quarters were so strong that the proposal was dropped.[103]

In the eyes of many provincial Baptists, to go down the road of public meetings, presided over by wealthy notables and full of 'speechifying', would be a dangerous concession to worldliness. When John Ryland informed Robert Hall junior in 1815 that plans were afoot to organize a city-wide BMS auxiliary in Bristol which would hold 'public days' with all their associated paraphernalia, Hall was quick to voice his concern that the

101. Bound volume of original letters of Fawcett, Fuller, Morris, Ryland, 1773-1813, Ryland to Sutcliff, 21 Sept. 1805, citing Marshman to Ryland [1805].

102. H/1/1, Fuller to Ward, 27 Oct. 1804, and 14 Jan. 1805.

103. Ryland, *Life and Death of Andrew Fuller*, 324-5.

BMS, so long marked by 'unobtrusive modesty', should now be attempting to 'vie with the London society in the noise and ostentation of its proceedings'. Large public meetings with a panoply of speakers drawn from all over the country would, warned Hall, prove more expensive than productive to the Society, and injurious to Christlike humility.[104] Auxiliary 'pomp and pride' were 'a species of necromancy' in that they sought to consult with the unregenerate - the spiritually dead - about the best methods of propagating the religion of Christ.[105] Far better, insisted Hall, would be a systematic effort to ensure that every Baptist minister made an annual collection from his own congregation. He was defending the traditional nonconformist conviction that all Christian work must be firmly based in the gathered congregation of Christ's people. That principle was now being challenged by the impact of the new world of evangelical philanthropy, a world in which those who held the purse-strings would increasingly hold the power.

In the June 1811 edition of the *Baptist Magazine* appeared an article entitled 'Union Essential to Prosperity'. Its author was Joseph Ivimey, pastor of the Eagle Street church in London. Its argument was controversial. The present age, Ivimey pointed out, was an age of Christian union, which the new Bible, tract and missionary societies had done much to promote. The annual London meetings of these institutions had quickened zeal and brought to each society 'a gradual accumulation of talents, of property, and of exertions ... by which the deficiencies made by death and otherwise, have been repaired'. The BMS had already done much to unite the Baptist denomination, yet it must be questioned whether every suitable means had been adopted to ensure Baptist unanimity in the missionary cause. The main obstacle to more widespread support was the lack of any 'general bond of union' between Particular Baptist churches. Ivimey went on to propose an annual assembly of ministers, messengers of churches, and association representatives, to be held either in London or in the provinces. Its primary purpose would be to raise support for the BMS. Why, pleaded Ivimey, should Baptists lag so far behind others in plans to promote the union, peace, and prosperity of the Church? 'Some of our friends', he admitted, 'object to bustle and parade', and point to the model of the '*quiet* and

104. Selly Oak Colleges Library, MS Letters of Robert Hall to John Ryland, 1791-1824, Hall to Ryland, 10 April [1815]. This letter is printed in part (but inaccurately and wrongly dated) in *The Works of Robert Hall, AM*, ed. O. Gregory (6 vols.; London, 1832), v, 502-5.

105. Selly Oak Colleges Library, Hall to Ryland, 1 May 1815.

persevering zeal' of the Moravians - yet even they had septennial synods and 'numerous plans to keep them a compact body'. Although veiled in places, Ivimey's message was plain to the initiated. It was a plea for the BMS to abandon its provincial distaste for 'bustle and parade'. Ivimey's plan for a 'Baptist union' was first and foremost a plan for the prosperity of the BMS.[106]

Andrew Fuller's initial reaction to Ivimey's proposal was predictably 'very cold': 'you will only show the poverty of the denomination by such a meeting.'[107] However, by January 1812 Fuller viewed the idea more favourably, and was suggesting arrangements for a mid-week service concluding with missionary 'intelligence' and a collection, which would enable ministers to attend without abandoning their own congregations on a Sunday.[108] In June Ivimey's plans came to fruition in precisely the shape which Fuller had suggested. The BMS held its first London public meeting at the Dutch Church, Austin Friars, on Wednesday 24 June. What was termed a 'meeting' was in fact a morning and an evening service, each comprising a sermon followed by a report from Fuller on the present state of the mission, and a collection for BMS funds. It was a meeting without the evils of bustle and parade; there were no rich laymen in the chair and no resolutions. At a meeting held the following day in John Rippon's vestry at Carter Lane, Southwark, it was agreed to form a 'general union' of Particular Baptist churches. The inaugural meetings of the union were held in London in June 1813. The Baptist Missionary Society had given birth to the first Baptist Union.[109]

VII: Contending for the Ark: The Succession to Andrew Fuller

Shortly before the London meetings of June 1812 Fuller received an anonymous letter from 'a Baptist Friend'.[110] He recognized the hand as that of Joseph Gutteridge, deacon of the Prescot Street church, treasurer of the new Baptist Academy at Stepney, and vice-chairman of the Protestant Dissenting Deputies.[111] The tone of the letter was friendly, commending

106. *BM* 3 (1811), 234-7; see also 326-30.

107. Ivimey, *History of the English Baptists*, iv, 124.

108. H. Anderson, *The Life and Letters of Christopher Anderson* (Edinburgh, 1854), 198.

109. *BM* 4 (1812), 351-9; see also Payne, *The Baptist Union*, 15-21.

110. Gutteridge correspondence, 1812-31, [Gutteridge] to Fuller, [-] May 1812, Fuller to Gutteridge, 13 June 1812.

111. E. Steane, *Memoir of the Life of Joseph Gutteridge, Esq.* (London, 1850), 110-18.

those who presently directed the Society for their quiet but well-directed efforts, but expressing anxiety for the future of the mission, if they were to be removed from the scene. Gutteridge's solution was to propose the formation of a corresponding committee in London (and possibly of another in Edinburgh), to act under the direction of the present leadership, but ready - by clear implication - to assume control as soon as death or infirmity incapacitated Fuller and his colleagues. Gutteridge also suggested more tentatively that the time had come to allow paedobaptists some say in the management of the Society. This latter proposal could safely be ignored. What could not be avoided was the fact that Gutteridge had repeated more pointedly the concerns raised in Ivimey's article of 1811. He was warning Fuller that the BMS could not continue for much longer to be run by the Northamptonshire circle which had brought the Society into existence.

Fuller took Gutteridge's letter seriously and sounded out the advice of trusted friends. Some favoured the plan of several committees in London, Bristol, Edinburgh, and elsewhere on the grounds that if the Society passed into the hands of a sole committee in London, 'it goes into a vortex of vanity'. More congenial to Fuller was the contrary opinion, which urged a single, indivisible committee with 'a few brethren from London among them, but ... the seat of the Society ... where it is, in your own Association'.[112] This advice emanated from Christopher Anderson, former pupil of John Sutcliff at Olney and John Ryland at Bristol Academy, and now pastor of Richmond Court Baptist Chapel in Edinburgh. Ever since 1807 Fuller had had his eye on Anderson as a potential successor to both the Kettering pastorate and the BMS secretaryship.[113] On 4 May 1812 he had written to Anderson inviting him to become co-pastor at Kettering with a view to succeeding Fuller in the mission.[114] Anderson declined the offer in the light of his current Scottish commitments, although holding out some hope that in two or three years he might be available. Fuller was disappointed, but remained determined that whoever might succeed him should maintain the brotherly and informal spirit which he had cultivated in correspondence with missionaries on the field: 'We have not imagined ourselves to be legislators,' Fuller wrote to Ward in 1812, 'but brethren, acting with you in the same object'.[115]

112. H/1/1, Fuller to Ward, 15 July/9 Aug. 1812.

113. H/1/1, Fuller to Ward, 10 Dec. 1807; Anderson, *Life of Christopher Anderson*, 183.

114. Anderson, *Life of Christopher Anderson*, 200-2.

115. H/1/1, Fuller to Ward, 15 July/9 Aug. 1812.

Despite his resolve to perpetuate a spirit of partnership between the Committee and the missionaries of the BMS, Fuller was aware that changes would have to be made if the Society were to outlive its founding fathers. At a general meeting of the Society held in Kettering on 29 September 1812 agreement was reached to double the size of the Committee by the addition of nineteen names, among them Christopher Anderson.[116] It was also laid down for the first time that there should be an annual meeting of the Society, to take place at the ministers' meeting of the Northamptonshire Association, which was held alternately in Kettering and Northampton in late September or early October of each year. The tenor of the changes was, nevertheless, conservative. A resolution was passed approving the proceedings of the Committee and recommending perseverance 'in the same unostentatious and prudent course in which things have hitherto been conducted'. Those added to the Committee were mainly middle-aged provincial ministers who would make good advocates of the Society but could not ordinarily be expected to attend the Committee meetings in Northamptonshire. Only three of the new members (William Newman, Francis Cox, and Joseph Ivimey) came from London, making a total London representation of no more than four out of thirty-seven.[117] The intention, as Fuller confessed openly in a letter to the Society's India missionaries published in the *Periodical Accounts*, was to keep 'the seat of the Society' in the Northamptonshire Association, 'where we trust it will be conducted in the same quiet and harmonious way which it has hitherto been'.[118]

These constitutional changes can have afforded scant satisfaction to Gutteridge and the advocates of reform. By the annual meeting in October 1814 Sutcliff was dead and Fuller was failing. The meeting urged every Baptist minister to do all in his power for the Society, since 'those who have hitherto been most active in collecting for the Mission are becoming less capable of exertion'.[119] By the spring of 1815 Fuller knew he was dying. He wrote both to Ryland and to William Burls, the Society's London agent, reiterating his wish that his successor should be Christopher Anderson. This step was regretted even by some who shared many of Fuller's views on the conduct of the Society. Robert Hall wrote to Ryland on 1 May, deeming

---

116. *PA* iv, 456-7. The existing eighteen members are listed in *PA* iv, 292.

117. The only existing London member was the layman, William Burls.

118. *PA* iv, 458; see Marshman, *Life and Times of Carey*, ii, 79-80.

119. *PA* v, 407.

it 'a great pity' that Fuller had interfered, and voicing his opinion of Anderson as 'totally unfit for the office proposed'. Hall thought Anderson a poor writer of English, deficient in sound judgment, narrow in Christian sympathy, and suspected that his views of church government had been infected by the principles of the Scotch Baptists on the plurality of elders. Above all he was sure that Anderson would never secure the confidence of the younger ministers who would soon be the leading agents in the Society.[120] In the light of this letter, Ryland wrote to Anderson, explaining that, whilst he and some others had thought of Anderson as a fit successor to Fuller, 'we are not yet sure whether others would think with us'. He asked Anderson whether, if a united invitation from the Committee did prove possible, he would consider it, and whether he could be comfortable in the pastorate of a church such as Olney or Kettering, without wanting 'any material change of discipline'.[121] Anderson replied that he would consider a united invitation from the whole Committee, that his duties as secretary would leave him little time for questions of church order, and that in any case Fuller's experience inclined him to think that the secretaryship ought no longer to be combined with a pastoral charge.[122] Ryland also replied to Hall, asking him whom he judged to be the best person to succeed Fuller. Hall responded on 9 May, having heard the previous night of Fuller's death on 7 May. If it were thought necessary to 'retain the Mission within the bounds of the Northamptonshire Association', he ventured to suggest the name of his own nephew, John Keen Hall, Fuller's assistant at Kettering. If no such limitation were thought expedient, he urged Ryland himself to consider the post.[123]

The BMS Committee met on 17 May and invited Ryland to discharge the duties of secretary until the annual meeting in October.[124] On 22 May Ryland wrote to Anderson warning him that 'great skill and caution' would be needed to prevent discord within the Society.[125] Anderson also received letters from Kettering urging him to accept both the secretaryship and the

---

120. Selly Oak Colleges Library, Hall to Ryland, 1 May 1815. The suspicion that Anderson was sympathetic to Scotch Baptist views on church government seems to have been unfounded.

121. Anderson, *Life of Christopher Anderson*, 236-7.

122. Ibid., 237-9.

123. Selly Oak Colleges Library, Hall to Ryland, 9 May 1815.

124. *PA* v, 526.

125. Anderson, *Life of Christopher Anderson*, 241-2.

Kettering pastorate, but conceding that the invitation from the church would not be unanimous. Anderson, anxious to avoid any rivalry with J. K. Hall - whom many in the Kettering congregation regarded as the heir-apparent - made no reply. His silence was misconstrued by Hall's supporters as meaning the very opposite of what he intended. According to Anderson's nephew and biographer, this misunderstanding of his motives was largely responsible for Robert Hall's opposition to his candidacy for the secretary-ship, but it is clear that Hall's convictions of Anderson's unsuitability were more deeply rooted.[126] More convincing is Hugh Anderson's statement that what disqualified his uncle from the secretaryship was 'the well-founded conviction that he would carry out Mr Fuller's policy'.[127] Anderson soon deduced from the letters of Ryland and others that the matter had become a party question. Glad to yield to J. K. Hall so far as the Kettering pastorate was concerned, he now withdrew from the heat of the wider battle over the secretaryship, and awaited the outcome of the October meeting in North-ampton.

On Tuesday evening, 10 October 1815, the BMS Committee met privately in the College Lane vestry from 8 till 11 o'clock. There was 'much conversation' about the business to be decided on the morrow, and Ryland was 'greatly wearied'. The consensus appears to have been that Ryland should continue as secretary, but with the assistance of a colleague still to be agreed. Ryland went to bed 'sorely frightened' that he would be left with 'an intolerable load'. The Committee met again for prayer from 6.30 to 8 next morning to seek divine guidance. The crucial business meeting at 4 in the afternoon was attended by many subscribers in addition to Committee members. William Burls read an official letter from Fuller expressing his wish that Anderson should succeed him. A motion was then put that Anderson should become joint-secretary with Ryland. A debate ensued, less violent than Ryland had feared, but strong enough to necessitate the withdrawal of the motion. Ryland then fell back on a name which had come to him during the night, and proposed James Hinton of Oxford as joint-secretary. This was passed unanimously. Ryland's compromise had defused the crisis. Further resolutions instructed the Committee to prepare such revisions to the rules of the Society as were judged necessary, and provided for future annual meetings to be held 'at such places in various parts of the kingdom' as should be decided at the previous annual meeting. Resolutions were also passed thanking Burls and Anderson for their services to the

126. Ibid., 235-6.
127. Ibid., 244.

Society, and expressing the hope that these would continue. Harmony had, for the moment, been preserved, but at the price of ignoring Fuller's declared wishes.[128]

A. C. Underwood expressed the opinion in his *A History of the English Baptists* that, if Anderson had succeeded Fuller in the secretaryship, the unhappy schism which developed between the Serampore missionaries and the Society after 1817 would never have taken place.[129] Underwood was almost certainly correct, but it must also be said that the prospects of Anderson being able to unite all sections of the domestic constituency under his leadership were slim. Anderson remained in Edinburgh, and as minister of Charlotte Chapel became the Serampore missionaries' most trusted advocate during the controversy.[130] He believed that even Fuller's former supporters on the BMS Committee had forgotten Fuller's insistence that 'we do not consider ourselves as legislators for our brethren; but merely as co-workers with them'; the result, as Fuller had predicted in 1813, was 'a declaration of independence'.[131] The sharpest thorn in the side of Carey, Marshman, and Ward after 1819 was none other than Joseph Gutteridge. Gutteridge was at the head of a London deputation which waited on the Committee in March 1819, urging them to implement the changes in management which had for so long been resisted. At the annual meeting in October Gutteridge and his supporters gained their objectives.[132] Gutteridge joined the Committee, and a London office was opened at Fen Court. It was staffed by John Dyer, who had been assistant secretary of the Society since 1817, and was appointed its full-time salaried secretary at the 1818 annual meeting. London had, in William Ward's words, 'gained the prize'.[133] John Ryland's well-known prophecy that he 'trembled for the ark of the mission, when it should be transported to London and fall into the hands of mere

---

128. This account is based on Anderson, *Life of Christopher Anderson*, 244-5; BMS Committee Minutes, 10-11 Oct. 1815, pp. 3-8; *PA* v, 679-83; Cox, *History of the BMS*, i, 270 -1; Marshman, *Life and Times of Carey*, ii, 136.

129. A. C. Underwood, *A History of the English Baptists* (London, 1947), 195.

130. A. C. Smith, 'The Edinburgh Connection: Between the Serampore Mission and Western Missiology', *Missiology* 18 (1990), 185-209.

131. Anderson, *Life of Christopher Anderson*, 279; H/1/1, Fuller to Ward, 5 Mar. 1813.

132. BMS Committee Minutes, 30-31 Mar. 1819, p. 70; 6 Oct. 1819, pp. 85-6; Steane, *Memoir of Joseph Gutteridge*, 118-20.

133. Marshman, *Life and Times of Carey*, ii, 203, 209. Dyer had succeeded Hinton as joint-secretary in 1817.

counting-house men' was about to be put to the test.[134] The BMS had at last been cut free from the apron-strings of the Northamptonshire Association which had nursed it, and was now established at the heart of evangelical philanthropy and respectable society. It could now expect a corresponding increase in efficiency and prosperity. Whether these benefits had been purchased at an unacceptable price in terms of the relationship between the Committee and its missionaries was a question which only events in India could answer.

134. Marshman, *Life and Times of Carey*, ii, 190.

II

India, 1793-1837

I: Convictions: The Sovereignty of God

John Thomas and William Carey landed in Bengal on 10 November 1793 convinced, in Carey's words, that 'the work is God's - it has been favoured by God - we shall surmount all difficulties, and the glory will redound to God again'.[1] This conviction was shared by all the early BMS missionaries to India. Nurtured in the Calvinistic tradition of the Particular Baptists, they believed that the work on which they were engaged was God's before it was man's - hence its ultimate success was guaranteed. That work they defined as winning the souls of men and women for God, and thus building the kingdom of Christ in India. For such a work, they held it to be 'absolutely necessary that we set an infinite value upon immortal souls; that we often endeavour to affect our minds with the dreadful loss sustained by an unconverted soul launched into eternity'. Their belief that the 'heathen' must be presumed to be eternally lost was matched by an unshakable confidence that they could be redeemed and transformed: 'He who raised the sottish and brutalized Britons to sit in heavenly places in Christ Jesus, can raise these slaves of superstition, purify their hearts by faith, and make them worshippers of the one God in spirit and in truth'.[2] What God had done in Britain in the Dark Ages, he was now about to do in India.

For Carey and his colleagues, these convictions were unshakable. They needed to be to survive. The tenacity with which the Hindus adhered to the caste system was a revelation to the missionaries. On 4 December 1793 Carey wrote to his sisters that caste was 'one of the strongest bonds that ever the devil used to bind the souls of men; and dreadfully effective it is indeed'.[3]

1. *PA* i, 65.

2. 'Form of Agreement', 7 Oct. 1805, in *PA* iii, 199.

3. E. Carey, *Memoir of William Carey*, 124; see D. B. Forrester, *Caste and Christianity: Attitudes and Policies on Caste of Anglo-Saxon Protestant Missions in India* (London, 1980), 23-8.

By 19 April 1794 he was confiding to his journal that his hope of the conversion of the heathen, so very strong when he left England, would 'utterly die away' among so many obstacles, unless it were upheld by God.[4] Confronted by a religious system far more obdurate than he had anticipated, Carey's continual resort was to the 'promise, power, and faithfulness of God' who could as 'easily convert a superstitious Bramin [*sic*] as an Englishman'.[5] The immediate reactions of William Ward, who arrived in Bengal in October 1799 with Joshua Marshman, Daniel Brunsdon, William Grant and their families, were very similar. It was easy, reflected Ward, to believe in the millennium when listening to Samuel Pearce preaching on the subject and surrounded by Christians; but in India 'all the rapid conversions we have heard of, except in apostolic times, would scarcely thin the ranks of idolators'. Yet Ward refused to despair, placing his confidence in the 'almighty breath of God', whose word brings his will to reality.[6] Nonetheless, Ward could not avoid the fact that the caste system of India loaded the dice against conversion to Christ in a way that was not true in England: 'If religion walked in her golden slippers, as in England, the professors of the Gospel would soon become more numerous'.[7]

The nagging tension between confidence in the promises of God and dismay at the obduracy of Hindu resistance to the gospel was alleviated but not dispelled by the missionaries' first conversion, which came in December 1800, fully seven years after Carey landed in India. The decisions of Krishna Pal and his friend Gokul to renounce caste and profess conversion led Ward to exclaim jubilantly in his diary that 'thus the door of faith is opened to the Hindoos - Who shall shut it?'. The unstable John Thomas was 'almost mad with joy', but three days later Thomas was literally 'quite mad', a pathetic figure tied down on his bed and mouthing profanities.[8] Krishna Pal's baptism on 28 December was the beginning of a steady trickle of conversions at Serampore, but the lives of the converts were so marked by backslidings and bickerings that the missionaries' spirits at times became almost more depressed than they were before.[9]

4. *PA* i, 175.

5. Carey to Fuller, 19 June 1796, in *PA* i, 303.

6. William Ward's journal (hereafter WJ), 21 Mar. 1800. Ward refers to Pearce's sermon on Psalm 90:16-17 preached at the Kettering ministers' meeting in Oct. 1798; see Fuller, *Complete Works of Andrew Fuller*, 778.

7. WJ, 12 Aug. 1802.

8. WJ, 22 and 25 Dec. 1800.

9. WJ, 19, 21 May and 20 Oct. 1802; S. P. Carey, *William Carey*, 236-7.

The deaths of missionary colleagues and members of their families placed
further strain on the missionaries' faith. William Grant's death in October
1799 caused Ward to question the purpose of God in leading Grant on a
15,000- mile errand to convert the Hindus and then cutting him off on the
threshold of his work.[10] Within a period of twelve months in 1811-12, the
mission lost ten persons by death, including Ward's daughter Mary, Joshua
Marshman's infant son William, and the three children of John Chamberlain, who had joined the mission in 1803. To these grievous human losses
was added the crowning blow of the Serampore fire of 11 March 1812,
which destroyed some of Carey's most precious manuscripts and a large
collection of type founts and paper. It was entirely characteristic of Carey
that his report to Andrew Fuller of this 'providence' passed rapidly from the
losses suffered to a list of eight 'merciful circumstances' surrounding the
fire, for which Carey wished to give thanks; the eighth was the fact that all
the missionaries had been preserved from discouragement. To Carey the
disaster of the fire was simply another reminder of the infinitely wise
providence of God, and hence also of his promises regarding the extension
of his kingdom.[11] Missionaries whose minds were thus captivated by the
sovereignty of God possessed an extraordinary ability to transform
discouragements into renewed incentives to faithfulness.

The survival of the Bengal mission in its first two decades required an
extraordinarily high degree of personal motivation on the part of its leaders.
Their Calvinistic convictions regarding the sovereignty of God and the
lostness of the 'heathen', although uncongenial to some modern palates,
were the primary source of that motivation. They also help to explain the
remarkably modest self-evaluation displayed by Carey in particular. For a
man who was primarily responsible for the translation of the entire Bible
into six languages and of parts of it into a further twenty-nine, to describe
himself, as Carey did in 1817, as a 'loiterer', may appear as absurdly false
modesty.[12] But for Carey divine grace was an overpowering reality which
threw all his achievements into miniature. On reviewing his life on his
seventieth birthday, Carey found 'much, very much, for which I ought to
be humbled in the dust', and his 'negligence in the Lord's work' to be great.[13]
People who thus insisted on their ultimate insignificance in the light of the

10.   WJ, 31 Oct. 1799.

11.   IN/13, Carey to Fuller, 25 Mar. 1812; see also Carey to Fuller, 30-31 July 1812.

12.   Angus Library, Carey to Jabez Carey, 3 Feb. 1817.

13.   Angus Library, Carey to Jabez Carey, 17 Aug. 1831.

grandeur of the divine purpose possessed a unique capacity to withstand the immense pressures which were applied to the Indian mission in its early history.

The Life of the Missionary Community

William Carey was a remarkable individual, but he was no individualist. His vision for the evangelization of India consisted, not in the heroic efforts of isolated individuals, but in the corporate witness of ordered Christian communities. The mission community which came into existence at the Danish settlement of Serampore in January 1800 was originally conceived as the model for missionary organization throughout the BMS India mission, although Carey, Marshman and Ward soon recognized that their principles were too distinctive to command the support of many who followed them to India. These principles derived from the example of the Moravian missions which so interested the young Carey, and ultimately from the pioneering Moravian community founded by Count Zinzendorf at Herrnhut in 1722.[14] The Moravian influence is already apparent in the pages of the *Enquiry*, in which Carey outlined his conception of the missionary community as an economically self-supporting colony of married couples.[15]

Once in Bengal, it was not long before Carey was writing to Fuller, urging the Society to send out sufficient reinforcements to constitute a Moravian-style colony of seven or eight families, supporting itself by agriculture, and living according to a common rule, administered by elected stewards.[16] It would be essential for missionary wives 'to be as hearty in the work as their husbands', in order that their families could become 'nurseries for the Mission'. All would live together 'in a number of little straw houses forming a line or square', and all property would be held in common. Carey hoped that converted Indians would join the community, and be treated on the same basis as European missionaries. Such communitarian practice would, he believed, yield four advantages. It would facilitate economical

---

14. S. P. Carey, *William Carey,* 90, 185-7. The Moravian influence on Carey is investigated, but not satisfactorily, in A. H. Oussoren, *William Carey Especially his Missionary Principles* (Leiden, 1945), 219-69.

15. Carey, *Enquiry,* 73-4; see A. G. Spangenberg, *An Account of the Manner in which the Protestant Church of the Unitas Fratrum ... Carry on their Missions among the Heathen* (English transl., London, 1788), 58, 96.

16. IN/13, Carey to Fuller, 16 Nov. 1796.

living, encourage the training up of more missionaries from the children of missionaries and converts, provide a standing witness to the excellence of the gospel, and ensure harmony within the missionary community by the clear allocation of tasks.

Carey's vision for Christian community living was never fulfilled in every detail, but it was a consistent and profound influence on the policy of the Indian mission. His involvement from 1794 to 1799 in indigo planting at Mudnabati, which caused more than a few raised eyebrows in England, was both a recognition of economic necessity and a principled attempt to secure a self-supporting basis to the mission: 'after a bare allowance for my family', Carey assured the anxious BMS Committee, 'my whole income, and some months much more, goes for the purposes of the gospel, in supporting pundits and school-teachers and the like. The love of money has not prompted me to this indigo-business'.[17] The same objective was from the beginning pursued by the enlarged missionary community at Serampore; the intention of making the mission as soon as possible independent of funds from the home Committee derived from a conviction that 'without this the gospel could never be permanently planted in India'.[18] Hence the Serampore missionaries resolved (apparently as early as January 1800) 'to have all things in common, and that no one should pursue business for his own exclusive advantage': all the proceeds of trade, schools, government employment, printing and translations, were to be devoted to the common purse for the sake of the gospel.[19] This determination was to be tragically misinterpreted in years to come.

The set of rules for community life which the mission 'family' at Serampore, as it termed itself, adopted within weeks of its inception in January 1800, reveal that the power of the Moravian example was not confined to principles of financial management. Roles within the family were clearly allotted, and the week followed a regular pattern, with Saturday evenings being devoted to 'the adjusting of differences, and the pledging ourselves to love each other', and Thursday evenings to 'experience meetings', in which missionaries and, latterly, converts gave testimonies of their experience of divine grace.[20] As Carey desired, the missionary sisters (and

17. S. P. Carey, *William Carey*, 164; see IN/13, Carey to Fuller, 17 June 1796; *PA* i, 233.

18. Serampore missionaries to BMS Sub-Committee, 4 Sept. 1817, printed in J. Ivimey, *Letters on the Serampore Controversy, Addressed to the Rev. Christopher Anderson* (London, 1831), 118.

19. The 'Form of Agreement' insists that the resolution on the subject of private trade was formed 'when we first united at Serampore'; *PA* iii, 211.

20. WJ, 18 Jan. 1800, 15, 22 Jan., 5 Feb. 1801.

William Carey, Founder of the BMS and Missionary in Bengal, 1793-1834.　*Andrew Fuller, Secretary of the BMS, 1792-1815.*

William Ward, Missionary in Bengal, 1799-1823.　*Joshua Marshman, Missionary in Bengal, 1799-1837.*

supremely Hannah Marshman) played an essential part in the household management of the family; according to William Ward, a sister might have to make tea for twenty to thirty people in one evening.[21] In one significant respect, the mission departed from Moravian precedent. Moravian mission communities were accustomed to appoint a permanent 'housefather' to direct the affairs of the settlement; but at Serampore such direction was rotated on a monthly basis.[22]

Traditional nonconformist convictions of the liberty and equality of all believers blended with the corporate emphases of the Moravian tradition to produce a community which initially exhibited a remarkable degree of harmony. 'We are, through divine mercy', Carey reported to Fuller in 1806, 'all well, and living in the utmost harmony'.[23] Carey was overjoyed at the quality of the new recruits sent out in 1799. Ward, he declared to be 'the very man we wanted'; Marshman, 'a prodigy of diligence and prudence'.[24] The relationship between the three men was close and enduring, but not devoid of tension. Marshman was a zealot, utterly absorbed in his work, 'excessively tenacious of any idea which strikes him as right or important'; his regard for the feelings of others was, Carey admitted, 'very little, when the cause of God is in question'.[25] Inevitably, there were collisions between Marshman and the more placid Carey, but they were never sufficiently serious to disrupt the underlying unity of purpose between the Trio.[26]

In August 1811 Carey again reported to Fuller that 'we, viz. Bro' M., Ward, and myself live in the utmost harmony'.[27] The limitation now applied to his statement was significant. A bond of union ideally suited to three kindred spirits did not fit so comfortably once the family became larger and more diverse. In October 1805 Ward produced a written statement of missionary objectives, which included a re-affirmation of the principle that all private income was to be devoted to the common fund.[28]

21. WJ, 14 July 1802.

22. S. P. Carey, *William Carey*, 186.

23. IN/13, Carey to Fuller, 14 Mar. 1806.

24. IN/13, Carey to Fuller, 5 Feb. 1800, and 27 Feb. 1804.

25. Carey to Fuller, 2 Aug. 1811; cited in Potts, *British Baptist Missionaries*, 21.

26. W. Carey, *Thoughts upon the Discussions which Have Arisen from the Separation between the Baptist Missionary Society and the Serampore Missionaries* (Liverpool, 1830), 5.

27. IN/13, Carey to Fuller, 2 Aug. 1811.

28. *PA* iii, 198-211. Ward's authorship is asserted by Marshman, *Life and Times of Carey*, i, 229.

This 'Form of Agreement' was signed by John Chamberlain, Richard Mardon, John Biss, William Moore, Joshua Rowe and Felix Carey, in addition to the Trio. Carey subsequently recalled that within a year the Agreement was found impracticable and 'consigned to oblivion'.[29] He meant, presumably, that the financial provisions of the Agreement soon proved incapable of application beyond the Trio themselves. Chamberlain in particular resented the claim of the Trio to have the right to superintend the finances of the Katwa out-station which he had opened. By 1807 the Trio had reached the conclusion that all missionaries not resident at Serampore ought to be directly dependent on BMS funds rather than on Serampore, although Fuller in England continued to regard them as subject to the Trio's authority.[30] Irritation at the Trio's continuing pre-eminence combined with dislike of Joshua Marshman's inflexible personality to create among the younger missionaries the sense of unease which Carey reported to Fuller in August 1811. Amongst the next generation of missionaries, who arrived in Bengal from 1814 onwards, this dissatisfaction was to become more acute and infinitely more troublesome.

Encounter with Hinduism

Carey and his colleagues believed that Hinduism was not merely devoid of salvific value but an idolatrous system which was an affront to God's sovereign rule of his world. In common with all other missionaries of their day, they regarded other religious systems as satanic edifices to be brought low in the name of the all-conquering Christ. Their initial impressions of Hinduism were of a religion of fear and darkness which held its devotees in a regime of terror and cruelty. They judged the Hindus to be almost entirely lacking in ordinary human morality: 'Avarice and servility are so joined in, I think, every individual, that cheating, juggling, and lying, are esteemed as no sins with them'.[31]

The missionaries quickly identified the Brahmins - the priestly caste - as the controlling influences in popular Hinduism, and hence as their chief religious opponents. William Ward, observing in his journal that many attributed quasi-divine status to the Brahmins, exclaimed for the benefit of

29. J. Marshman (ed.), *Letters from the Rev. Dr Carey* (3rd edn., London, 1828), 56.

30. Potts, *British Baptist Missionaries*, 23-4.

31. IN/13, Carey to Fuller, 30 Jan. 1795. Compare the published version in *PA* i, 129: Fuller has altered Carey's text to read 'united in almost every individual'.

his readers in Britain 'Oh! Pray that Brahmanism may come down! It is here the great black devil indeed'.[32] Open-air preaching sessions frequently ended in bitter doctrinal disputes with local Brahmins, although after a while the Brahmins seem to have lost heart for the fight and kept out of the missionaries' way. 'It would entertain you', Carey wrote to Fuller in 1802, 'to see the Brahmans wheel off to the other side of the way when we are disputing in the streets; and it would grieve you to hear the torrents of abuse, and obscenity with which the vile sort frequently assault us'.[33] Carey was quite prepared to concede in public debate that both the Hindu shastras and the Qur'ān contained 'many good observations and rules'; but he would go on to point out that they were silent on the crucial question of how a God of justice could save sinners, and to compare their sacred books to a loaf of bread in which a considerable quantity of good flour was mixed with some 'very malignant poison', making the whole so poisonous as to be fatal.[34] There was no reluctance to engage in open confrontation with Hindu apologists, or to run down the character of the Hindu deities in public.[35] Inevitably the first converts at Serampore followed their missionary mentors in this respect, with a zeal which even the missionaries could find excessive. They were grieved in August 1801 when Krishna Pal flew into a violent passion against a Brahmin; 'his hatred to Brahmanism', commented Ward, 'almost exceeds ours'.[36]

The missionaries' negative response to Hinduism was coloured above all by the prevalence of religious practices which struck them as disgusting and inhumane. The practice of *sati* - the burning of widows on their husbands' funeral pyres - was the most horrific of all. In theory an act of voluntary devotion (though later shown to be without any shastric authority), *sati* in Bengal had become an obligation enforced by the Brahmins and the woman's relatives. Ward reported in 1802 that estimates of the number of widow murders performed each year in Bengal varied between 25,000 and 30,000.[37] The estimates may have been exaggerated, but a survey conducted by Carey in 1803 at the request of the government revealed a total of 438 *satis* within a thirty-mile radius of Calcutta.[38] The missionaries conducted

32. WJ, 31 Aug. 1800.

33. IN/13, Carey to Fuller, 21 Jan. 1802.

34. *PA* i, 199.

35. WJ, 14 Sept. 1800.

36. WJ, 18 Aug. 1801.

37. WJ, 5 Jan. 1802.

38. Potts, *British Baptist Missionaries*, 146.

a protracted publicity campaign to alert public opinion in Britain to the enormity of the problem and dissuade the East India Company from its refusal to interfere. Eventually their efforts bore fruit: in 1829 Governor-General Bentinck declared *sati* illegal throughout Bengal; the governments of Madras and Bombay followed a year later.[39]

Other inhumane practices which aroused the moral indignation of the missionaries included the exposure of infants or sick and dying relatives on the banks of the Ganges.[40] To the missionaries these were further examples of virtual murder masquerading as religious devotion: infants abandoned to the Ganges were offered in fulfilment of vows that one of a pair of twins would be offered to the sacred river. The practice of hook-swinging at Hindu festivals, when devotees were suspended by hooks attached to the flesh of their backs, was more innocent, but seemed to constitute further evidence to Christian minds that there was an inescapable connection between Hindu 'idolatry' and cruelty. Graphic confirmation of this conclusion was offered by the mass pilgrimages to the temple in honour of Jagannath situated only a mile and a half from Serampore; the image of the god was dragged along on a heavy carriage, and pilgrims were sometimes crushed beneath its wheels by the press of the crowds, or even threw themselves to their deaths. 'Come ye admiring philosophers of enlightened Europe', wrote William Ward on seeing the festival for the first time, 'and join the Hindoos in drawing Juggernaut's carriage, or in laying yourselves under its wheels to be crushed to death.'[41] Soon to become still more notorious among missionary supporters in Britain was Jagannath's main temple at Puri in Orissa, which was visited, on Carey's estimation, by over a million pilgrims a year.[42] After 1805 this temple was actually maintained by the East India Company government by means of a tax levied on the pilgrims. Such government support for Hindu 'idolatry' became a *cause célèbre* of evangelical agitation in Britain, especially after the General Baptist Missionary Society began work in Orissa in 1821. One of the first two General Baptist missionaries, James Peggs, became after his return to

---

39. For a full account see Potts, *British Baptist Missionaries*, 144-57.

40. Potts, *British Baptist Missionaries*, 140-4.

41. WJ, 21 June 1803; cf. *Address of the Committee of the General Baptist Missionary Society* (Derby, 1816), 12. The current English word 'juggernaut' is, of course, derived from this source.

42. *Address of the Committee of the GBMS*, 7.

Britain in 1826 a tireless propagandist on behalf of 'India's Cries to British Humanity' and against the Jagannath grant in particular.[43]

There can thus be little doubt that the missionary apologetic of the early Baptist missionaries was of an uncompromising and even confrontational character. However, their observation of Hinduism was neither unintelligent nor undiscriminating. Carey informed John Sutcliff in 1798 that Hindu modes of worship and customs varied from district to district, and observed that such regional variation helped to explain the discrepancies in the published accounts of Hinduism. In the same letter he noted that hook-swinging was not commanded by any of the shastras.[44] As their knowledge of Hindu sacred literature increased, the missionaries became more sensitive to the gulf which frequently separated local religious practice from the Hinduism of the written authorities. They were also willing to concede that on a purely literary or cultural level the Hindu classics compared very favourably with their Western counterparts. Thus Carey rated the *Mahabharata* 'much upon a par' with Homer's *Iliad* from a literary standpoint, yet insisted that, since it was 'the ground of Faith to Millions', it must ultimately be held 'in the utmost abhorrence'.[45]

There is, moreover, some evidence that the Serampore missionaries subsequently moderated their attacks on Hinduism and saw the wisdom of a more positive evangelistic approach which concentrated on preaching the distinctive Christian message of redemption. The 1805 'Form of Agreement' explicitly warned against attacking Hindu prejudices 'by exhibiting with acrimony the sins of their gods; neither should we upon any account do violence to their images, nor interrupt their worship: the real conquests of the gospel are those of love'.[46] Nevertheless, the change was one of strategy only, not of theology. In an article published in 1823 the Trio acknowledged that to insult a man's religion was not the mode best calculated to win his confidence, yet insisted that as men of integrity they were still bound to inform Indians of the essential vanity of their religion.[47]

---

43. J. Peggs, *India's Cries to British Humanity* (2nd edn., London, 1830); K. Ingham, *Reformers in India 1793-1833* (Cambridge, 1956), 39-40.

44. IN/13, Carey to Sutcliff, 5 Apr. 1798; see also WJ, 11 Apr. 1800.

45. Carey to Fuller, 23 Apr. 1796, cited in M. A. Laird, *Missionaries and Education in Bengal 1793-1837* (Oxford, 1972), 56.

46. *PA* iii, 200.

47. *The Friend of India* ix (Dec. 1823), 16, cited in Potts, *British Baptist Missionaries,* 37-8. *The Friend of India* first appeared as a monthly periodical in 1818. As a quarterly from 1820 to 1825, edited by Joshua and J. C. Marshman, *The Friend of India* was an important means of articulating the missionary programme for social reform.

William Ward's massive study of Hinduism, *A View of the History, Literature and Religion of the Hindoos*, was in places very respectful of the achievements of Hindu civilization, but Ward would not have disputed his biographer's statement that the purpose of the work was to correct mistaken notions of the 'simple, mild and virtuous nature' of Hinduism, and establish that 'like every other *dark part of the earth*, India also was *full of the habitations of cruelty*'.[48] Although the Serampore pioneers were more prepared than many later missionaries to see good qualities in Hindu culture, their essential conviction remained that Hinduism was a religion of darkness waiting for the light of the Christian gospel to dawn.

II: Strategy: The Planting of a National Church

The fourth section of Carey's *Enquiry* had set out to prove 'the practicability of something being done, more than what is done, for the Conversion of the Heathen'. It was concerned in particular to show that it was not unreasonable to expect European Christians to preach the gospel with success even amongst the 'barbarous heathen'. Carey placed relatively little emphasis in his pamphlet on the role of national converts in winning their own countrymen for Christ, although even at this stage he could perceive that 'it might be of importance' for missionaries to encourage the development of evangelistic gifts in national Christians, since these would have the advantage of knowing the language and indigenous customs.[49] The realities of missionary life in India soon convinced Carey and his colleagues that the role of Europeans in the evangelization of India would in fact be an indirect one.

Carey's own thinking about church-planting strategy drew its initial inspiration from British examples. He was impressed by those churches of the eighteenth-century Evangelical Revival which had made the encouragement of preaching and evangelistic gifts a priority - the success of Welsh nonconformity and of Wesleyan Methodism was, he believed, testimony to the wisdom of this policy. Conversely, the mission churches of South India appeared to him to be in danger of neglect, because their Danish and German missionaries had declined to use anyone in the ministry who had not received a formal college training. Carey informed Fuller in 1801 that

---

48. S. Stennett, *Memoirs of the Life of the Rev. William Ward* (London, 1825), 255; cited in Potts, *British Baptist Missionaries*, 93; see also Laird, *Missionaries and Education*, 56. Ward's work first appeared in 1806.

49. Carey, *Enquiry*, 67-76.

the Serampore missionaries hoped to profit from such reflections by making 'all the use we can of the gifts God may give us in the Church'.[50]

However, what was decisive in persuading the missionaries that the potential for the evangelization of India lay in Indian hands was their discovery of the linguistic and cultural barriers which stood in the way of their communicating successfully with the population. It was these obstacles which led William Ward in November 1802 to confess he was

> ready to doubt whether Europeans will ever be extensively useful in converting souls by preaching, in this country. God can do all things. Paul could become a Jew to win Jews, and as a Gentile to win Gentiles; but, however needful, we cannot become Hindoos to win them, nor Mussulmans to win Mussulmans.[51]

Ward had in fact penetrated close to the heart of what twentieth-century missiologists would term the problem of cross-cultural communication. Although the first BMS missionaries were ignorant of the modern concept of a culture as an integrated system of social values, they did at least perceive that it was no brief of the missionary to change those practices which could be regarded as 'the innocent usages of mankind', and that there was a limit to the capacity of any Englishman to distance himself from 'those parts of English manners' which were naturally offensive to an Indian audience.[52] Ward went on to report that the missionaries had therefore decided to despatch their convert Petumber Singh to commence his own evangelistic ministry, and hoped that Krishna Pal would similarly soon be ready to engage in itinerant evangelism. Although Serampore's first experiments with Indian evangelists were not devoid of disappointments, by October 1805 the missionaries had reached a conclusion which was radical indeed:

> It is only by means of native preachers that we can hope for the universal spread of the gospel through this immense continent. Europeans are too few, and their subsistence costs too much, for us ever to hope that they can possibly be the instruments of the universal diffusion of the word amongst so many millions of souls ... If the practice of confining the ministry of the word to a single individual in

---

50. IN/13, Carey to Fuller, 13 July/4 Aug. 1801.

51. WJ, '13' [in fact 15] Nov. 1802.

52. See the 'Form of Agreement' in *PA* iii, 200, 208.

a church be once established amongst us, we despair of the gospel's ever making much progress in India by our means.[53]

From this bold conclusion derived three strategic priorities.

It followed, firstly, that the translation of the Scriptures into the major languages of India was of the utmost importance. An indigenous evangelistic ministry presupposed the availability of the Bible in a tongue which was native both to the evangelist and his hearers. 'The translation of the Scriptures becomes more and more important in my mind', Carey informed Sutcliff in March 1809:

> I think (between you and me) that we may hope to see such a number of persons raised up in the Church at Calcutta who will be fitted to preach the word to the natives with more acceptance than Europeans ever will as to supersede the necessity of sending Europeans out.[54]

In the short term, however, more missionaries were essential, not least because it would be some years before national Christians were sufficiently educated to supervise translation work themselves. In fact, most of the spade-work on the Serampore translations was from the beginning done by Indian pandits; the role of Carey and Marshman was to edit their drafts and check them against the Hebrew or Greek original. The Serampore translations have been criticized, and with some justice, as being hasty and unidiomatic to the point of incomprehensibility. But the criticisms were generally made by later missionaries and linguists whose own efforts depended on the pioneering work which Serampore had already achieved.[55] For all their imperfections, and giving due credit to the substantial contributions of the pandits who assisted him, Carey's six complete and twenty-nine partial translations of the Bible remain perhaps the most remarkable individual achievement in the history of Bible translation.[56] In addition to his biblical translations, Carey was wholly or partly responsible

---

53. Ibid., 205-6.

54. IN/13, Carey to Sutcliff, 8 Mar. 1809. At this stage Carey had particularly in mind converted Portuguese Indians, but his argument was all the more applicable to Indian nationals.

55. For a critical assessment see Potts, *British Baptist Missionaries*, 83-9.

56. The whole Bible was translated into Bengali, Oriya, Hindi, Marathi, Sanskrit, and Assamese; for the incomplete translations see the table in S. P. Carey, *William Carey*, 415.

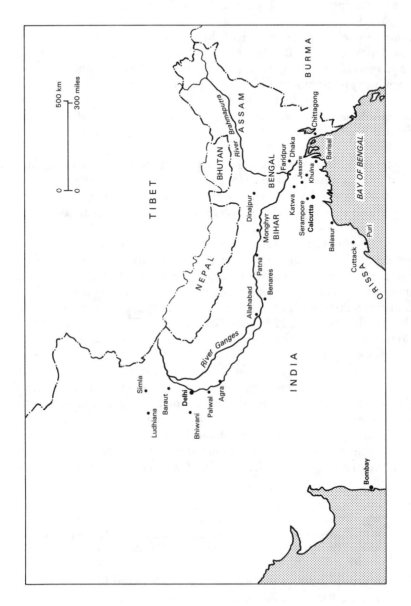

Map 1: Northern India in the Nineteenth Century

for the publication of grammars in seven Indian languages and the compilation of dictionaries in Bengali, Sanskrit and Marathi. These would have been signal achievements for a scholar with formal linguistic training; for someone whose formal education had finished at the age of twelve, they must be judged extraordinary.

A second deduction from the conclusion that national Christians were to be the primary agent of India's evangelization was that education must be accorded a high priority. In common with almost all evangelicals of their day, the Serampore missionaries possessed an unshakable belief that the dissemination of useful knowledge must in itself promote the ultimate advance of the gospel. Carey reckoned schools to be 'one of the most effectual means of spreading the light of the Gospel', and even ranked the system of non-denominational elementary education devised by Joseph Lancaster as one of the three 'powerful engines', alongside missionary and Bible societies, which God was now using to spread blessings over the face of the world.[57] Lancaster's system was the model followed by Joshua Marshman after 1811 in establishing a network of native schools around Serampore, which by 1818 could boast a total of some 10,000 pupils in 92 schools.[58] Before becoming a missionary, Marshman had been a teacher in Bristol at the school supported by Broadmead Baptist Church, and it was he who became the chief architect of the educational policy of the mission. The Trio did not expect elementary schools to produce immediate and direct conversions; rather they believed that educating the heathen in their childhood would enable them 'to see things just as they are when their understandings are matured'.[59] The mission's extensive educational programme was neither a substitute for evangelism nor an act of pure social benevolence: it was a long-term investment in the benefits of an anticipated 'Christian Enlightenment' which would gradually irradiate the darkness of heathenism.[60]

There was, however, a more direct sense in which the Serampore missionaries intended education to further the growth of an indigenous church. Serampore College was established in 1818 with the primary

---

57. Angus Library, Carey to Jabez Carey, 15 Apr. 1814, 12 Jan. 1815. Lancaster's system, based on the use of abler pupils as monitors to teach the others, was employed in the schools of the British and Foreign Schools Society (1814), favoured by nonconformists.

58. Laird, *Missionaries and Education*, 64-5; Potts, *British Baptist Missionaries*, 119.

59. *PA* v, 659.

60. Laird, *Missionaries and Education*, 86-7.

purpose of training Christian Indians to be missionaries to their own people. It was to be first and foremost a missionary institution. For that very reason, the curriculum was to be more than just theology - it was to include both Western science and the study of Oriental languages, supremely of Sanskrit, which the Trio held to be the key to understanding Hindu culture and learning Indian languages. Teaching was to be in Bengali, with the study of English being reserved for the more advanced students.[61] More controversially, the College admitted Hindu and Muslim as well as Christian students. In the eyes of many of the younger missionaries and their supporters on the BMS Committee this fact seemed to deny the missionary character of the College. The Trio, on the contrary, regarded such breadth of educational experience as essential if future missionaries were to 'obtain that knowledge of the character, the feelings, and the prejudices of the heathen among whom they were designed to labour'.[62]

The vision which lay behind the foundation of Serampore College - of a missionary force staffed primarily by Indian nationals - remained no more than a long-term goal.[63] Nonetheless, the confidence in native agency which Serampore showed from an early date had a third and immediate implication: the role of the European missionary had to be given a narrower and more specific definition than was assumed in the pages of the *Enquiry*. He had to be neither the pastor nor the evangelist of a local church, but a blend of apostle and bishop, planting new churches in virgin territory and exercising superintendence over the doctrine and discipline of established churches with national pastors.[64] This missionary philosophy (which bears some similarity to the later and better-known theory adumbrated by Henry Venn of the CMS)[65] undergirded the geographical expansion of the India mission, which began with the sending of John Chamberlain to Katwa in 1804.

A Pattern for Missionary Expansion

Carey intended that the Katwa station should be the first of a network of mission stations, located about 100 miles distant from each other, and

61. Ibid., 142.

62. Marshman, *Life and Times of Carey*, ii, 463.

63. *Letters from the Rev. Dr Carey*, 54.

64. For Ward's exposition of this theme see *PA* iii, 206-7; WJ, 19 Oct. 1805.

65. For Venn's theory see C. P. Williams, *The Ideal of the Self-Governing Church: A Study in Victorian Missionary Strategy* (Leiden, 1990).

linked to Serampore by ties of both spiritual and financial dependence. Each missionary would be given a capital sum to invest in trade which, Carey hoped, would soon make the outstation self-sufficient and indeed a contributor to the common fund at Serampore.[66] As has been seen, the financial aspects of this scheme soon proved ill-advised: within a year Chamberlain was asking to be released from any business connection with Serampore, and the Trio had to abandon the attempt to make the outstations financially dependent upon the parent station.[67] However, the essential concept of a network of stations radiating outwards from Serampore proved viable. By August 1805 Carey had framed plans for a further seven stations in addition to those already established at Katwa, Dinajpur and Jessore: the proposed locations ranged from Agra or Delhi in the north-west to Chittagong in the east. Each of the contemplated stations would itself have ten satellite outstations manned by native evangelists.[68] To bring this vision to reality required three things: additional missionary recruits, increased funding from Britain, and the necessary sanction of the East India Company government for the undertaking of missionary work on British territory.[69]

New missionary personnel were provided: eight recruits were added to the India mission between 1810 and 1818. But their numbers were inadequate and their cost disproportionate: Carey estimated in 1812 that even a capable missionary cost the Society at least £600 before he began to be effective on the field; by 1827 he had revised the figure to £1,000.[70] Missionary extension on the scale Carey envisaged was possible only through the employment of other human resources. Thus, by the time of Carey's death in 1834, the nineteen stations then connected with Serampore were staffed by fifty workers, of whom no more than six had been sent out from Britain.[71]

A potentially more serious limitation on the realization of Carey's strategy was the fact that all Europeans intending to reside in British territory in India were supposed to apply to the East India Company for a

66. IN/13, Carey to Fuller, 27 Feb. 1804; Cox, *History of the BMS,* i, 118-19.

67. WJ, 22 and 30 Mar., 11 Apr. 1805; W. Yates, *Memoirs of Mr John Chamberlain* (London, 1826), 153; see above, p. 43, n. 30.

68. IN/13, Carey to Sutcliff, 22 Aug. 1805.

69. IN/13, Carey to Fuller, 10 Dec. 1805.

70. IN/13, Carey to [?], 15 Jan. 1812; *Letters from the Rev. Dr Carey,* 53.

71. Potts, *British Baptist Missionaries,* 33.

licence to do so. Serampore was Danish territory (apart from two periods of British control from May 1801 to July 1802 and from 1808 to 1815), and hence exempt from this requirement. But even to establish a church in Calcutta seemed to the Trio too risky an undertaking until David Brown, a Company chaplain and a leading Evangelical Anglican, assured Carey in 1802 that there was nothing to fear from government.[72] From then on, the missionaries began to look for a permanent meeting place in Calcutta, although the first church building at Lall Bazar was not erected until 1806. For a time, the Company seemed happy to wink at the illegal presence of missionaries on its territory, but the Vellore mutiny of June 1806 produced an immediate change of climate. The governor-general, Sir George Barlow, imposed severe restrictions on itinerant preaching, and ordered William Robinson and James Chater, newly arrived from Britain, to leave the country. Although the growing threat to the continuance of missionary activity in Company territory was eventually averted by the representations of sympathetic persons of influence in Britain, the presence of missionaries in British Bengal remained precarious until after the revision of the East India Company charter in 1813.[73]

Although the deportation order of 1806 was soon suspended, it was clear that Robinson and Chater were best out of reach of Calcutta. Robinson, sent initially to Katwa, was then refused permission to remain anywhere in Bengal, and was accordingly dispatched in 1808 to commence a mission among the hill tribes of Bhutan. Chater, together with Richard Mardon, was commissioned to investigate the possibility of a mission in Burma.[74] Neither of these ventures proved conspicuously successful. Robinson abandoned the Bhutan mission in 1811. Chater left Burma in 1812, although the BMS mission there survived long enough under the rather eccentric care of Carey's eldest son Felix to be inherited by Adoniram Judson and the American Baptists. Nevertheless, this rather tortuous chain of events had consequences of permanent significance. Robinson sailed in 1813 for the East Indies, where he worked first in Java, and then from 1821 in the Sumatra mission, established three years previously by William Ward's nephew, Nathaniel. The Sumatra mission survived until the 1840s, eventually in the sole hands of Nathaniel Ward. The Society's work in Java

72. WJ, 24 Dec. 1802; E. S. Wenger, *The Story of the Lall Bazar Baptist Church Calcutta* (Calcutta, 1908), 26.

73. Potts, *British Baptist Missionaries*, 177-9; Carson, 'Soldiers of Christ', 122-4, 180-7, 197-8.

74. IN/13, Carey to Sutcliff, 11 Feb. 1807.

was continued until 1847, latterly by the solo efforts of a German, Gottlob Brückner. In both islands the results in terms of church-planting were meagre, although Brückner's translation of the New Testament into Javanese laid the foundation for subsequent translation work by Dutch missionaries.[75] As for Chater, he moved on to Colombo in 1812 to found the Society's Ceylon (Sri Lanka) mission. Chater found the Sinhalese population unresponsive: he reported in 1815 that he had yet to find fifty Sinhalese in Colombo 'who have so much regard for religion as to wish to hear a sermon'. By January 1816 he was admitting his inability to collect even ten Sinhalese together to hear him preach.[76] Nonetheless, the mission survived under Chater's care to nurture an indigenous church which can trace its origins indirectly to the reluctance of the British government to permit any expansion of missionary activity in Bengal.

Frictions with government had temporarily slowed the pace of missionary expansion within British India, but ironically had facilitated the extension of BMS activity to new fields within South and South-East Asia. Carey's strategic vision was never confined to British India, but encompassed Bhutan, Burma, Ceylon, and the East Indies, whilst Afghanistan, Nepal, Tibet, Assam, and Indo-China remained on the list of unfulfilled aspirations.[77] Carey informed Fuller in October 1809 that his preference was for all future recruits to be posted, not to Bengal, but to one of the surrounding countries, as selected by the Serampore missionaries. Such pioneering work had the advantage of removing new recruits from the fatal attractions of European society in Calcutta, which, complained Carey, had in a number of cases encouraged a spirit of self-indulgence to the detriment of missionary zeal.[78]

Integral to the programme of missionary expansion initiated by Serampore was the work of the General Baptist Missionary Society in Orissa. The Society was formed at the annual Association meeting of the General

75. On the BMS East Indies missions see E. A. Payne, *South-East from Serampore* (London, 1945). In 1814 Carey sent his third son, Jabez, to Amboyna in the Moluccas, where he remained until the closure of the mission soon after the islands returned to Dutch control in 1817. William Robinson returned to India in 1825 to conduct successful ministries at Lall Bazar, Calcutta (1825-38) and Dhaka (1839-53).

76. *PA* vi, 56, 221-2.

77. IN/13, Carey to Fuller, 4 Oct. 1809; Carey to Dyer, 15 July 1819, printed in *Letters from the Rev. Dr Carey*, 6-17.

78. IN/13, Carey to Fuller, 25 Oct. 1809.

Baptist New Connexion at Boston on 26 June 1816.[79] Its prime mover and first secretary was John Gregory Pike, a minister in Derby. In the autumn of 1812 Pike had roused General Baptists to contribute to making good the losses incurred by the Serampore fire, and the contacts thus established with Andrew Fuller laid the foundations for a General Baptist mission. In its early years the Society struggled to find a suitable field, considering first Madagascar, and then Assam or the Punjab. Its selection of a field so close to Bengal was due ultimately to the influence of William Ward. George Wilkins, a founding Committee member of the Society, and printer of its *Quarterly Papers,* had been a fellow apprentice printer with Ward. During his brief visit to England in 1821 Ward preached at the ordination of the Society's first missionary, William Bampton, and two weeks later Bampton and James Peggs sailed for India with Ward. The Society instructed them to seek the advice of the Serampore missionaries regarding a suitable sphere of labour, and that advice was unanimous in urging them to commence work in Orissa. It had the advantages of being under British rule, having the entire Bible already translated into Oriya (by Carey), while the Jagannath temple at Puri gave the province obvious strategic significance as 'the head-quarters of Hindoo idolatry'.[80] A BMS preacher, the Armenian John Peters (or Peter) had already worked in Orissa at Balasur, but had returned to Calcutta in 1817. The Orissa mission of the General Baptists was to develop into one of the most fruitful Baptist fields in India.

The Orissa mission made an important contribution to the progressive realization of Carey's vision for missionary expansion within the Indian sub-continent. By 1837 other centres of Baptist work included Calcutta, Katwa and Suri in West Bengal; Jessore, Dinajpur, Dhaka, and Chittagong in modern Bangladesh; Monghyr in Bihar; and Allahabad, Agra, and Delhi in north-west India.[81] Unfortunately, no adequate records exist of the size of the churches established at the various centres, although it seems likely that in most cases the numbers of members were to be reckoned in tens rather than hundreds. Baptismal records were kept at Serampore itself: a total of 1,407 persons were baptized between 1800 and 1821.[82] These early

79.   For the origins and early history of the GBMS see J. B. and J. C. Pike (eds.) *A Memoir and Remains of the Late Rev. John Gregory Pike* (London, 1855). The General Baptist New Connexion was formed in 1770 to unite those General (Arminian) Baptist churches founded or renewed as a result of the influence of the Evangelical Revival.

80.   Ibid., 163; *General Baptist Repository and Missionary Observer,* 1822, p. 308.

81.   Cox, *History of the BMS,* i, 297-429; Ingham, *Reformers in India,* 134-6.

82.   Potts, *British Baptist Missionaries,* 47.

converts were not preponderantly outcastes or of low caste; indeed, a disproportionate number appear to have been Brahmins.[83] Most modern historians would take the view that what has to be explained is not why there were not more converts, but why there were any at all, given the cohesion of Hindu culture and what would now be judged the unsophisticated nature of the Baptists' missionary approach. The missionaries themselves believed that God had done it all. The relative paucity of converts in the early decades was in harmony with their own conviction that the only effective force for the evangelization of India would be well-trained indigenous evangelists. The problem in the years to come would be how such competent leaders could be both recruited from, and supported by, a Christian community which was numerically and spiritually weak, and economically dependent on missionary patronage.

III: Controversy

The history of the BMS India mission between the death of Fuller in 1815 and the death of Joshua Marshman in 1837 was marred by protracted and bitter controversy. The dispute between the Serampore missionaries and the home Committee was complex in its origins and frankly tedious in its course. However, unlike most other aspects of the early history of the Serampore mission, which have been thoroughly analyzed in recent writing, the controversy has been largely neglected by historians. To perpetuate this neglect would be to belittle the convictions of the protagonists and to miss the broader issues of policy which lay beneath the surface of the argument.

The roots of the controversy were embedded in the status of the Serampore mission as a largely self-supporting entity - a status which was founded on fundamental principle, and not merely on economic necessity.[84] Over the years of Fuller's secretaryship, the Trio built up a complex of buildings at Serampore, purchased with their own money, supplemented by loans from the Society. The premises were held on behalf of the Society, but the legal status of the trust deeds was unsatisfactory. To the home Committee - especially the younger element who had found aspects of Fuller's regime unbusinesslike and irksome - it seemed imperative after Fuller's death that the mission property at Serampore should speedily be

83. Ibid., 44-5.

84. See above, pp. 39-40 , n. 15-19.

placed on a basis which would secure its proprietorship to the Society. Thus among the 'proposals for consideration' minuted by the Committee at its meeting on 23 January 1816 was the item: 'Whether, for securing the large property of the Society in India additional trustees ought not to be forthwith appointed?'[85]

At the same time in India, the Trio also were considering what steps ought to be taken to safeguard the distinctive principles of the Serampore mission after their own deaths. William Ward put on paper some of his own thoughts on the subject, and sent them, in the name of the Trio, to John Ryland, William Burls and Joseph Ivimey. Ward proposed, *inter alia*, that new members of the 'Serampore Mission Family Station' should be elected by the existing members, but with the Society holding a right of veto, and that all mission property should be held by the 'family' in trust for the Society.[86] Ward's document, although a private and personal communication which Carey and Marshman may not have even seen, was read at the meeting of the BMS Committee held in Birmingham from 15 to 17 October 1816.[87] The Committee, seizing on a statement made by Ward in an accompanying letter, authorized Ryland and Hinton to call a special meeting of the Committee as soon as they had received 'the corrected plan which the brethren in India have promised to send respecting the affair of the trust deed of the property at Serampore'.[88] In fact, no such collective promise had been made, and no corrected plan was ever received.

The October meeting of the Committee also appointed a sub-committee to meet twice a year in an executive capacity. The sub-committee met first in Oxford on 31 December. It was concerned chiefly with some of the problems which had arisen between the Trio and the younger missionaries, but also addressed the question of the Serampore premises. William Burls presented a legal opinion recommending that the premises be vested in trustees, part in India and part in Britain, and the meeting proceeded to nominate eight persons to serve as trustees in Britain.[89]

85. BMS Committee Minutes, 23 Jan. 1816, p. 16.

86. Ward's communication is printed in Ivimey, *Letters on the Serampore Controversy*, 105-7.

87. For Carey and Marshman's insistence that Ward's communication was never officially sanctioned by them see *Letters from the Rev. Dr. Carey*, 47-8.

88. BMS Committee Minutes, 15-17 Oct. 1816, p. 23. Ward's covering letter had indicated that he would discuss the matter with Carey and Marshman, after which a revised plan would be sent to the Committee.

89. BMS Committee Minutes, 31 Dec. 1816, p. 29.

The resolutions of the sub-committee were sent out to Serampore, and produced consternation in the minds of the Trio. The first communication they had received from the home Committee since Fuller's death seemed to be questioning their integrity. They took alarm at a phrase which implied that the national workers whom the Trio supported out of their own funds were ultimately responsible to the Society, for it suggested that the Committee considered the funds themselves as belonging to them. They were even more perturbed at the proposal to vest the mission premises in a majority of trustees resident in England, which seemed to them to constitute a demand that the Trio surrender control of property purchased with their own funds. Serampore's reply was in the form of a printed letter, penned by Marshman in his most combative mood, and sent to every member of the Committee.[90] To the letter was appended an 'Explanatory Declaration', drafted by a Serampore lawyer, which asserted that the premises were held in trust by Carey, Marshman and Ward, and such additional trustees as they should subsequently appoint, and declared that 'no other person or persons in England or in India belonging to the ... Baptist Missionary Society ... shall have the least right or title to the property or the administration of the said premises'.[91]

Neither Marshman's letter nor the Explanatory Declaration was happily worded. But a private letter from Carey to Ryland left the Society's new secretary in no doubt that the sense of grievance was acute. Matters had been made worse by the arrival in Serampore of Samuel Pearce's son, William, armed with instructions from London that he was to serve at Serampore as assistant to Ward in the printing office. All previous new missionaries had been located by the Trio: the family union at Serampore was a covenant community which could be entered only by invitation. The combined impression created by Pearce's arrival and the Oxford resolutions was of a Committee hungry for a power hitherto denied them. 'We are your brethren, not your servants', Carey reminded Ryland: 'I beseech you not therefore to attempt to exercise a power over us to which we shall never submit'.[92]

The breakdown of trust between the Trio and the home Committee was paralleled by a breakdown of relationships between the Trio and the

90. Carey, Marshman and Ward to BMS Sub-Committee, 4 Sept. 1817, in Ivimey, *Letters on the Serampore Controversy*, 107-33. For Marshman's authorship see Marshman, *Life and Times of Carey*, ii, 143-4.

91. Ivimey, *Letters on the Serampore Controversy*, 133-5.

92. IN/13, Carey to Ryland, 1 Oct. 1817.

younger missionaries at Calcutta, William Yates, Eustace Carey, John Lawson and James Penney. William Carey traced the beginnings of the estrangement to an attempt by Yates and Penney to convert the Lall Bazar church to open communion principles[93] Yates himself attributed the argument to his exclusion from the privileges of the Serampore confraternity. The publication of the Trio's letter to the sub-committee was for him the last straw. Yates withdrew from his translation work at Serampore, and joined his younger colleagues in a new missionary union at Calcutta, founded on the principle of complete submission to the authority of the home Committee.[94] From 1817 onwards, the 'younger brethren' in Calcutta became the spokesmen for the Committee's view that all mission property belonged by right to the Society. The chief object of their suspicion (and, according to Carey, their envy) was Joshua Marshman, who soon became branded, both in India and at home, as the villain of the piece - scheming, ambitious for himself and his family, and suspected of amassing his own private fortune.[95] Carey in his turn suspected Yates, Pearce, and his nephew, Eustace, as 'plants' commissioned by the new party on the BMS Committee to bring the recalcitrant Trio to heel.[96] The dispute between the Trio and the younger brethren was not of the essence of the controversy, but it served to fuel the flames of the fundamental argument between Serampore and the home Committee.[97]

The Trio's letter and Explanatory Declaration arrived in England in May 1818, and were considered by a shocked BMS Committee over several days in June. There was considerable debate over the exact meaning of the documents. Some concluded quite simply that the Trio had denied the Society any claim to the Serampore property; others that they had merely denied the right of the BMS to appoint trustees or interfere in the management of the premises. But the Committee members united in despatching a reply to the Trio, disclaiming the 'spirit of domination' which had been attributed to them, yet insisting that all the mission property in

93.   IN/13, Carey to Ryland, 1 Oct. 1817 and 11 Apr. 1818.

94.   J. Hoby, *Memoir of William Yates, D.D., of Calcutta* (London, 1847), 99-108.

95.   IN/13, Carey to Ryland, 11 Apr. 1818. Carey was prepared in private to admit that Marshman was ambitious and prone to 'a certain kind of crooked policy', but stoutly defended him from any charge of misappropriation of funds.

96.   IN/13, Carey to Dyer, 15 July 1819; Ivimey, *Letters on the Serampore Controversy*, 18-19.

97.   See Ryland's comment cited in Mrs E. Carey, *Eustace Carey: A Missionary in India* (London, 1857), 301-2.

India belonged to the Society. The letter implied that the Trio, by asserting that the premises were theirs to dispose of as they pleased, were now breaking their vows made in the 1805 Form of Agreement.[98] The Committee further agreed to send the assistant secretary, John Dyer, to India in an attempt to defuse the crisis.[99]

John Dyer never went to India. At its next meeting in August the Committee resolved that circumstances subsequent to the June meeting made his visit unnecessary.[100] Apparently the Committee had in the main been persuaded that the Trio had not meant to deny the Society's proprietorship of the mission premises.[101] Subsequent letters from Serampore confirmed that this was indeed the case: 'Assure yourself', Carey wrote to William Burls, 'that no such thought as that of alienating the property at Serampore from the Mission Society ever entered our minds.'[102] The August 1818 meeting of the Committee reached a unanimous definition of the status of the Serampore property, which proved almost entirely acceptable to the Trio when communicated to them.[103] The signs were that the controversy was nearing its end.

On 9 January 1819 John Dyer, newly in the saddle as the first full-time secretary of the Society, wrote privately to Carey, putting to him certain questions regarding the controversy. He asked whether Carey had 'seriously and calmly' weighed the 'natural and necessary consequence' of the Trio's printed letter of September 1817.[104] Carey replied that he had, and reiterated that there had been no intention of removing the ultimate right to the property from the BMS.[105] More pointedly, Dyer asked whether there were no grounds for the charges of extravagance and ostentation laid against Marshman by the younger brethren. In reply Carey dealt with each of the criticisms levelled at Marshman, but Dyer's letter created deep resentment, and began to undo the good done by the resolutions of the previous August. The damage was compounded by two letters from John

---

98. Ivimey, *Letters on the Serampore Controversy*, 136-41.

99. BMS Committee Minutes, 23 June 1818, pp. 54-5.

100. Ibid, pp. 60-1.

101. Marshman, *Life and Times of Carey*, ii, 177; *Letters from the Rev. Dr. Carey*, 49n.-50n.

102. IN/13, Carey to Burls, 19 Aug. 1818, postscript dated 3 Sept.

103. Ivimey, *Letters on the Serampore Controversy*, 24-8; Marshman, *Life and Times of Carey*, ii, 178.

104. Dyer to Carey, 9 Jan. 1819 [this letter appears not to be extant in the BMS archives, but is cited in Carey's reply].

105. Carey to Dyer, 15 July 1819, in *Letters from the Rev. Dr. Carey*, 6-17.

Ryland repeating the same charges against Marshman, one addressed to Carey, and one written to Marshman himself. Carey found these letters, coming as they did from an old friend, hurtful in the extreme, and wrote a pained reply on behalf of them both.[106]

William Ward had left Serampore in December 1818 to travel home to England. The principal objects of his visit were to restore his ailing health and raise funds for the new College at Serampore, but it was also understood that he would take the opportunity of discussion with the home Committee. However, Ward found himself received with 'great shyness and reserve' on his arrival in England in June 1819. Over twelve months elapsed before he was invited to meet the Committee.[107] In the interim the London businessman Joseph Gutteridge joined the Committee and rapidly became its dominant influence.[108] At a meeting in December 1819 the Committee passed a further series of resolutions on the controversy. On the whole these maintained the conciliatory spirit of the August 1818 meeting. The Committee stated its view that the various Serampore premises should be consolidated into a single trust, and that additional trustees approved by the Committee should be appointed, some of whom should be resident in Britain. This suggestion was in fact now acceptable to Serampore, but one unguarded sentence had disastrous effects when communicated to India: the Committee warned that 'were they to consent to the alienation of the property from the Society, they would violate the confidence reposed in them by the public'.[109] This amounted to a repetition of the old allegation that the Trio were out to deprive the BMS of their proprietary rights. Once again Carey and Marshman felt that their good faith had been impugned.

The apparent rapprochement of 1818 was now evaporating under the impact of renewed misunderstanding and unfounded accusations. The fault was not all on one side. Serampore made matters worse by issuing a set of Articles of Union in January 1820, which sought to provide for the continuation of the union after the deaths of its present members. To the Committee the Articles appeared to be 'a declaration of independence'.[110] Ward was invited to meet the Committee in August 1820 to discuss the

106. Carey to Ryland, 28 Sept. 1819, in ibid., 17-19.

107. Marshman, *Life and Times of Carey*, ii, 209; Stennett, *Memoirs of Ward*, 198.

108. On Gutteridge see above, ch. I, pp. 29-30, and E. Steane, *Memoir of the Life of Joseph Gutteridge, Esq.* (London, 1850).

109. BMS Committee Minutes, 31 Dec. 1819, pp. 22-3.

110. Cox, *History of the BMS*, i, 282.

issues raised by the document, and came away convinced that there was no possibility of compromise.[111] In point of fact, the Committee was eager for peace, not least because the controversy was by now proving damaging to the public reputation of the Society. A special meeting of the Committee on 25 April 1821 authorized the sending of a letter to Serampore, which indicated the Society's continuing dissatisfaction with the status of the mission premises, but attempted to explain in what sense the Committee was prepared to concede independence to Serampore.[112] Ward met the Committee again on 16 May, and after lengthy discussion appeared satisfied by the Committee's explanation of its letter. Carey's reaction to the 25 April letter was less positive, yet he still held out hopes of a reconciliation, and was prepared to admit that 'there has been much wrong on both sides'.[113] Relations in India between the Serampore and Calcutta missionaries had indeed been more cordial following a meeting in July 1820 which produced a measure of harmony.[114]

A restoration of peace between Serampore and the BMS once again seemed possible. But a tragic misunderstanding intervened to thwart this prospect. The Serampore missionaries were now willing to appoint additional trustees, and reconstruct the deeds of the properties in the sense desired by the Society. But legal advice indicated that the BMS, not being a chartered body, could not hold lands in India. That being so, Serampore let the matter rest, and waited for the Society to make a firm proposal regarding a new trust. The Committee, however, expected Serampore to take the initiative, and the question remained thus suspended on the mutual expectation of action until 1825.[115]

The long-standing dispute over the Serampore property had reached an impasse, but it was not the immediate cause of the separation in 1827 of the Serampore mission and its subsidiary stations from the BMS. What finally precipitated the schism was the role of Serampore College. From its foundation in 1818 the College had been criticized by the Calcutta brethren and their domestic supporters for the breadth of its curriculum and its

111. Marshman, *Life and Times of Carey*, ii, 209-12; cf. BMS Committee Minutes, 1819-23, pp. 68-70.

112. BMS Committee Minutes, 25 Apr. 1821, pp. 113-15.

113. IN/13, Carey to Burls, 5 Oct. 1821.

114. Angus Library, Carey to Jabez Carey, 15 Aug. 1820; Marshman, *Life and Times of Carey*, ii, 225-6.

115. Ivimey, *Letters on the Serampore Controversy*, 143; *Letters from the Rev. Dr Carey*, 39, 49-50.

readiness to admit non-Christian students. The College also proved to be inordinately expensive, absorbing an ever-increasing proportion of the independent funds of the Serampore Union. Faced with the prospect of inadequate resources to maintain the subsidiary stations, Serampore applied to the BMS for aid, and a sum of £1,000 was promptly voted in March 1824. It was not enough. Severe flooding had hit Serampore in October 1823, and repair works proved costly. Carey and his colleagues therefore applied to the Society for a further £1,000 in January 1825. Again the money was granted, but this time with considerable reluctance. The letter notifying Serampore of the second grant was penned by Gutteridge himself.[116] It chided the missionaries for failing to submit any account of the expenditure of the first £1,000 (as they had been asked to do) and went on to complain that the Committee was still waiting for Serampore to take the necessary steps to secure the mission property. On receiving this letter, Carey was incensed, and had a mind instantly to 'break off all connection with the Society'. Carey and J. C. Marshman (Joshua's son, who had replaced Ward in the Serampore Union after Ward's death in 1823) replied on behalf of Serampore, confessing that the Committee's letter had 'inflicted a wound which it is scarcely in the power of time to heal'.[117]

By this time Joshua Marshman was en route for Europe. His mission was to obtain a charter of incorporation for the College from the King of Denmark, and to secure more financial aid from the BMS. His first meeting with the Committee on 3 August 1826 was satisfactory, but when letters arrived from India bringing news of the letter from the Committee that had so incensed Carey, and also of a commercial crisis in Calcutta which made the financial plight of Serampore still more desperate, the whole complexion of the negotiations was changed. Marshman increased his demands for financial assistance, and the tone of the Committee became less friendly in response.[118]

Matters came to a head at a special meeting of the Committee on 15-17 March 1827.[119] A letter from Carey and J. C. Marshman to the Society was read, in which they informed the Committee that lack of funds compelled them to hand over four of Serampore's stations to the BMS. Dyer then made a proposal that the Society should take over all the Serampore stations, and

---

116. Marshman, *Life and Times of Carey*, ii, 290-1, 303-4, 307-9, 345.

117. *Letters from the Rev. Dr Carey*, 36-40.

118. Marshman, *Life and Times of Carey*, ii, 318-20, 327-30.

119. The fullest account (obviously sympathetic to Marshman) is in ibid., ii, 337-46. For a pro-BMS view see Cox, *History of the BMS*, i, 292-6, and BMS Committee Minutes, 15-17 Mar. 1827, pp. 296-306.

that the whole should be managed by a committee comprising all BMS missionaries in India, under Carey's presidency. When Marshman rejected this proposal as a recipe for strife, Gutteridge and Dyer suggested that the management of the stations should be left in the sole hands of Carey and Marshman for as long as they both were living. To Marshman this was equally unacceptable, for it promised the Society a free hand within the foreseeable future. Marshman held out for control of the stations by the council of Serampore College, which he and Carey had come to regard as the only possible successor to the old 'family union': if the College were to be the source of India's Baptist missionaries, it seemed to them only logical that it should also have the management of India's Baptist missions.[120] This the Committee could not concede, for Carey and Marshman were the only two of the five members of the council to be BMS missionaries. The Society understandably refused to put its funds at the disposal of a body which it deemed 'irresponsible' - in the sense that it owed no corporate responsibility to the BMS.[121] On this rock the negotiations foundered. On 23 March 1827 the Committee publicly announced that the BMS and the Serampore missions were henceforward to be considered as two entirely independent bodies.

From 1827 to 1837 Serampore and its missions were supported independently of the BMS by a committee of which Christopher Anderson was the first secretary. The reunion negotiated in 1837 excluded Serampore College, and provided for the direct superintendence of the Serampore station itself to remain in Marshman's hands during his lifetime. Marshman in fact died before the news of the settlement reached India. The College continued as an autonomous body until taken over by the BMS in 1855. The parting of the ways between Serampore and the BMS was sadly not the end of the controversy. In Britain the pamphlet war between the two sides rumbled on into the 1830s, while in India relations between Serampore and the Calcutta missionaries remained frosty right until Carey's death in June 1834. 'Nothing has filled my last years with so much distress', reflected Carey in 1830, 'as the division in the mission first brought about by the junior Brethren and still maintained with an implacable hostility'.[122]

It is hard to resist the conclusion that Carey's distress could have been avoided, in view of the fact that agreement on the immediate issues in contention seemed so close on more than one occasion. It is equally

120. *Letters from the Rev. Dr. Carey*, 52-6.

121. *BMS Annual Report*, 1826-7, p. 16.

122. Angus Library, Carey to Jabez Carey, 16 Jan. 1830.

plausible to attribute the schism to ordinary human failings of communication and personality, and to suggest that it could never have occurred in
the era of the air mail letter and the telephone. Yet any assessment of the
controversy which looks no deeper than this remains ultimately unconvinc-
ing. For at its roots were two mutually incompatible conceptions of what
a missionary society is.

Carey, Marshman, and Ward regarded the home Society as essentially an
agency for the recruitment of missionaries and for the raising of the funds
required to send them to the field. Under Fuller's regime the Committee
did little more than this. It followed that the mission was not a body located
entirely or even primarily in Britain, but an entity whose heart was on the
field.[123] By making themselves rapidly independent of domestic funding,
the Trio had committed Serampore to a degree of independence of
domestic control. They regarded their own funds, 'earned with the sweat of
our brows', as being in no sense at the disposal of the home Committee,
although certainly devoted to the work of the mission. For Carey the nub
of the issue was not the Serampore property, but the Society's claim to
dominion over the membership and funds of the private 'family union'
formed by the Serampore missionaries as a covenant of shared life, work,
and personal finances. From their perspective, it seemed that the Committee was claiming control over that which they had devoted to God alone.[124]

On the other side of the controversy was an equally deep conviction,
represented by the Calcutta brethren in India, and typified in England by
Gutteridge's businessman's approach to the affairs of the Society, that a
missionary was a servant and employee of the society which sent him out.
A missionary society was a body of expatriate workers, who were responsible
to the home Committee that sent them to the field, and ultimately to the
subscribers who provided the funds. Sadly this conviction seems to have had
as its corollary a tendency to undervalue the work of the national workers
on whom the Trio placed such reliance: insistence on the dependence of
missionaries tended to go hand in hand with an even greater insistence on
the dependence of the national church.[125] The immediate future of the

123. Ivimey, *Letters on the Serampore Controversy*, 128.

124. IN/13, Carey to Ryland, 14 June 1821, printed in *Letters from the Rev. Dr. Carey*, 21-
   3. The original of this letter (which includes Carey's famous complaint that John
   Dyer's letters were 'like those of a Secretary of State') was discovered when the BMS
   vacated its Gloucester Place premises in 1989, and has now been lodged in the archives
   at Regent's Park College.

125. IN/13, Carey to Ryland, 1 Oct. 1817; Marshman, *Life and Times of Carey*, ii, 212-13;
   Potts, *British Baptist Missionaries*, 32-4.

missionary movement lay with those who emphasized Committee control, but the argument in favour of independence was to reappear later in the nineteenth century, and is indeed still on the agenda of missiological debate at the end of the twentieth century.

III

The West Indies, 1813-1892

I: The Baptist Tradition in the West Indies

The West Indies mission occupies a unique place in the nineteenth-century history of the Society. Alone among the early BMS fields, the West Indies were not wholly unevangelized territory: BMS missionaries came, not primarily as evangelists of the 'heathen', but as pastors and teachers of an existing Christian negro community. In no other Baptist field during the nineteenth century was church growth so spectacular, and nowhere else was progress towards the autonomy of the indigenous church so rapid, nor so firmly insisted on by the Society. Perhaps most notable of all, Baptist missionaries in the West Indies exercized a more decisive influence on the course of secular history than they did in any other part of the world. As a result, British Baptist missionaries in Jamaica were the subject of public debate and criticism in Britain to a degree that finds no parallel in the Society's history.

The Baptist churches of the Caribbean owe their origin to the transplantation to the West Indies of the Baptist revivalism which became an increasingly marked feature of the religious life of much of the slave population in the southern United States in the late eighteenth century. In some cases (such as in Trinidad), the transplantation was effected by the migration of Christian negro communities from America; in others (as in Jamaica) a greater share of the responsibility for implanting the Baptist tradition lies with individual negro preachers. The religion which Christian communities and preachers brought with them to the Caribbean was enthusiastic and experiential. It was a faith more of the Spirit than of the Word - a Christianity of the poor and non-literate. The uninhibited emotionalism of the 'camp-meetings' of the American revivalist tradition held much the same attraction for the slave communities of both the southern States and the Caribbean. Revivalism enabled them to express the joy of new Christian experience in old cultural forms: slaves filled with the Holy Spirit worshipped in ways that their African forefathers possessed by the spirits of African traditional religion would have found not entirely unfamiliar.[1]

The missionaries whom the BMS sent to the Caribbean, and the indigenous Baptists whom they encountered there, both possessed an evangelical faith whose roots lay in the transatlantic religious awakenings of the 1730s and 1740s. Nevertheless, the differences between the two evangelical traditions were substantial. Missionaries with a profound respect for godly learning found the ignorance of the indigenous Baptists shocking. The mainstream of evangelical religion, which accorded reason a high ranking in the scale of Christian virtues, now came into contact with one tributary of evangelicalism that had no fear of 'enthusiasm' and its physical manifestations.[2] Ministers who had derived from their theological training an elevated conception of the pastoral office were confronted with approaches to church leadership that valued charismatic gift more highly than formal status. Given such divergences of cultural and theological background, the periodic difficulties which beset the Society's West Indian missions are hardly surprising.

In Jamaica the pioneer of Baptist work was George Liele (or Lisle), an emancipated slave born in Virginia. He came to the island in 1783 as one of a body of 4-5,000 slaves who, with their masters, had left America as a result of the War of Independence. Liele had exercized a preaching ministry in Georgia, and now began to do the same in Kingston and elsewhere. In December 1791 he wrote to John Rippon, the influential pastor of the Carter Lane church in London, reporting that he had gathered a church in Kingston of nearly 350 members, most of them slaves, and appealing to English Baptists for assistance in completing the building of a chapel to house the congregation. Liele claimed that the total Baptist community on the island now numbered about 1,500 - which may indicate that some of the immigrants of 1783 came from a Baptist background in America. Rippon published Liele's letter in his *Annual Register*.[3] Thus, even before

1.   P. D. Brewer, 'The Baptist Churches of South Trinidad and their Missionaries 1815-1892', M.Th. thesis (Glasgow, 1988), ch. 1.

2.   For the indebtedness of Evangelicalism to the Enlightenment see D. W. Bebbington, *Evangelicalism in Modern Britain: A History from the 1730s to the 1980s* (London, 1989), ch. 2.

3.   J. Rippon, *The Baptist Annual Register*, i (1790-3), 332-7; see also 338-9, 343-4, 541-3. On Liele see E. A. Payne, 'Baptist Work in Jamaica Before the Arrival of the Missionaries', *BQ* 7 (1934-5), 20-6; E. A. Holmes, 'George Liele: Negro Slavery's

the formation of the BMS, Jamaican Baptists were brought to the attention of Particular Baptists in England.

One of the 1783 immigrants baptized by Liele was Moses Baker, a mulatto from New York. Baker formed his own church on the Adelphi estate in the north-west of the island, where he worked as a religious teacher for a Quaker planter, Isaac Winn. In 1806 the Jamaican House of Assembly passed a law prohibiting Christian teaching on the plantations. The mounting opposition of the planters to Christian work amongst the slaves prompted Baker to begin a regular correspondence with John Ryland, drawing his attention to the religious needs of the slave population.[4] In response, the Society in December 1813 appointed John Rowe, one of Ryland's students at Bristol Baptist Academy, to go to Jamaica to assist the now ageing Baker.[5] The partnership between British and Jamaican Baptists had begun.

II: Slavery and the Gospel: 1814-1838

John Rowe landed at Montego Bay on 23 February 1814. He found Moses Baker's slave congregation in serious disarray. The law against Christian preaching to the slaves had prevented Baker from teaching his flock for eight years; there had been no baptisms for over three years, and no celebration of the Lord's Supper for ten. Nevertheless, it is estimated that total Baptist membership on the island was about 8,000.[6] A Moravian missionary praised Baker in 1818 as a 'blessed and active servant' of God, and testified that some of the other negro Baptist preachers were clever and gifted men.[7] More often, however, the missionary verdict on the negro Baptist leaders was less favourable. An appeal to British Baptists for contributions towards the erection of a new chapel in Kingston described the leaders of the black Baptists as 'exceedingly ignorant and superstitious ... very unqualified for the service', and claimed that this explained their failure to gain the approval of the authorities.[8] On these grounds John Rowe devoted his brief mission-

Prophet of Deliverance', *BQ* 20 (1963-4), 340-51, 361; C. Gayle, *George Liele: Pioneer Missionary to Jamaica* (Kingston, n.d. [1982]).

4. *Evangelical Magazine* (1803), 365-71; (1804), 469-72; E. A. Payne, *Freedom in Jamaica* (London, n.d. [1933]), 18-19; Gayle, *George Liele*, 29.

5. *PA* v, 289-91.

6. Ibid., 502-5; *BM* 7 (1815), 168; Gayle, *George Liele*, 20, 33.

7. *BM* 11 (1819), 96.

8. *BM* 10 (1818), 438.

ary career to running a day and Sunday school in Falmouth. For Rowe, hope of a purer Christianity in the future lay in teaching slave children reading and the first principles of Christianity, with the full sanction of the planters.[9] According to his obituary, Rowe had, by his death in 1816, won the respect and approval of the chief magistrate of the district and other neighbouring slave-owners.[10] He had also paved the way for other missionaries whose contribution to Baptist church life in Jamaica was more substantial and enduring. James Coultart, sent out to Kingston in 1817, saw one thousand new members added to the church within five years.[11]

John Rowe had fulfilled to the letter the BMS Committee's parting instructions to avoid interference in political matters and 'endeavour by a respectful demeanor to recommend yourself and the gospel to the white inhabitants of the Island'.[12] Lee Compere, sent out to join Rowe in 1815, was not so scrupulous in his obedience. In 1816 Compere acceded to a pressing invitation from the black Baptists of Kingston to come and teach them the way of God more perfectly, but within a year his connection with the BMS had been severed, apparently on account of his refusal to keep silent on the issue of slavery.[13] Compere had imperilled the initially tolerant attitude which Rowe's 'prudence' had secured from at least some of the slave-owners. Nonetheless, until 1823 the planters appear to have turned a continuing blind eye to the rapid expansion of the BMS mission, some perhaps regarding the missionaries as a restraining influence on those of their slaves who were Baptists.

From 1823 the climate for evangelical missionary work throughout the British West Indian colonies became less favourable. On 15 May 1823, Thomas Fowell Buxton, heir-apparent to William Wilberforce as leader of the anti-slavery lobby in Britain, introduced a motion in the House of Commons, affirming that slavery 'ought to be gradually abolished throughout the British colonies with as much expedition as may be found consistent with a due regard to the well-being of the parties concerned'.[14]

Although Buxton's motion was unsuccessful, the launching of his 'gradualist' campaign for the abolition of slavery had an immediate impact,

9. *PA* v, 677-8.

10. *BM* 10 (1818), 47.

11. Cox, *History of the BMS,* ii, 39.

12. *PA* v, 293.

13. *BM* 9 (1817), 74, 470; see B. Amey, 'Baptist Missionary Society Radicals', *BQ* 26 (1975-6), 371-2.

14. *Parliamentary Debates* 9 (1823), 274-5.

both on opinion in Britain and on West Indian politics. In July the *Baptist Magazine* published an article claiming that it was 'high time for the British nation to awake from its slumber', and for Christians in particular to petition both Houses of Parliament to take 'such measures for the gradual abolition of slavery as in their wisdom they shall deem expedient and just'.[15] The response of the British colonial government to Buxton's campaign was to attempt to make the face of slavery more acceptable by encouraging Christian instruction among the slaves. The slave-owners, thrown on to the defensive, now perceived nonconformist missions as an ally of the abolitionist cause and a direct threat to planter interests. Among the slaves themselves, rumours began to circulate that in Britain moves for their freedom were afoot. In August the slaves of Demerara, in what is now Guyana, rose in revolt, believing that the governor and planters were withholding their freedom. John Smith, a missionary of the LMS, was arrested, tried and falsely convicted for allegedly inciting the slaves to rebellion.[16]

The Baptist missionaries in Jamaica soon felt the chill wind of the planters' heightened antagonism. J. M. Phillippo, newly arrived in Spanish Town at the close of 1823, found his application to the magistrates for a licence to preach turned down on the grounds that he was (allegedly) an emissary of the Anti-Slavery Society, and that John Smith had been the cause of the recent insurrection at Demerara. Phillippo's second application was similarly rejected, and it was not until January 1825 that his credentials, certified, as the magistrates demanded, by the Lord Mayor of London himself, were finally accepted.[17]

Unsuccessful in their efforts to exclude dissenting missionaries from the island, the Jamaican planters turned instead to legislative sanctions. In December 1826 the House of Assembly passed a Consolidated Slave Law intended to render missionary activity impossible. Slaves found guilty of preaching or teaching without their owners' permission were to be subject to severe penalties; dissenting meeting-houses were not permitted to open between sunset and sunrise; and religious teachers who took money from the slaves were to be fined.[18] To the jubilation of the missionaries and the

15. *BM* 15 (1823), 278, 283.

16. For the effects of the 'gradualist' campaign see M. Turner, *Slaves and Missionaries: The Disintegration of Jamaican Slave Society, 1787-1834* (Urbana, 1982), 102-26.

17. E. B. Underhill, *Life of James Mursell Phillippo* (London, 1881), 34-5, 38-42; WI/1, MS autobiography of Phillippo, 79b-89.

18. *BM* 19 (1827), 244.

consternation of the House of Assembly, the Consolidated Act was disallowed by the Colonial Secretary. In response, protest meetings were held throughout the island in November 1827 which passed resolutions defending the Act as essential for the protection of the slave population from 'the spurious tenets of the sectarians'. The nine BMS missionaries on the island replied to the resolutions passed at the Kingston protest meeting with a published statement, proclaiming that they had 'studiously kept aloof from all interference with every party in politics', and that Christianity taught its adherents to promote the welfare of the government under which they lived. The statement continued by claiming that the restrictions of the Slave Law were not calculated to promote the welfare of the colony, and were contrary to the 'equitable and peaceable doctrines of Christianity'.[19] As late as December 1827, therefore, the Society's Jamaican missionaries were, without exception, prepared to endorse publicly the insistence of the BMS Committee that it was no part of the missionary's role to engage in politics; all agreed that, even in a slave society, Christianity taught peaceful submission to lawful authority.[20]

The House of Assembly, intent on sustaining the pressure on the colonial government, had appointed a committee to investigate the activities of 'all Sectarians and Dissenters' in Jamaica. Between December 1827 and December 1828 this 'Sectarian Committee' examined twenty-five persons, including five BMS missionaries. The Committee's report concluded, predictably, that the principal object of the dissenting missionaries was to extort money from their congregations, and that, in order to further this object, they inculcated 'the doctrines of equality and the rights of man', and taught sedition from the pulpit.[21] The *Missionary Herald* was severely critical of the accuracy of the report, and J. M. Phillippo subsequently dismissed it as a 'disreputable, base and untruthful document'.[22] That Baptist and Methodist missionaries taught the *spiritual* equality of all men was true enough, but neither group had yet deduced from this principle any inference that Christians could no longer tolerate the structures of a slave society.

19.   *BM* 20 (1828), 95. See also MS autobiography of Phillippo, p. 109-facing p. 110.

20.   For the committee's instructions to William Knibb on his departure for Jamaica in 1824, see J. H. Hinton, *Memoir of William Knibb* (London, 1847), 149-50.

21.   For the Sectarian Committee and its report see S. Jakobsson, *Am I Not a Man and a Brother?* (Uppsala, 1972), 407-16.

22.   *BM* 21 (1829), 132; MS autobiography of Phillippo, 121.

The report of the Sectarian Committee stiffened the resolve of the slave-owners to see the Consolidated Slave Law come into force. A revised version of the Law was passed by the House of Assembly in 1829, and received the assent of the new Governor, Lord Belmore. Once again, however, the Colonial Office withheld its assent, with the result that the persecuting clauses were eventually dropped from the Act. The legal status of missionary activity thus remained confused throughout 1829 and 1830, but the reality confronting the nonconformist missions was one of increasingly irksome restrictions on their freedom of action.

The planters' resort to legal sanctions against the missions was a reflection of the extraordinary growth which the Baptist churches in particular were now experiencing. William Knibb, writing to his mother in September 1828 after his first three years of missionary service in Kingston, reported that, despite most determined opposition from the authorities, thousands were flocking to hear the word.[23] In April 1829 Joseph Burton, stationed at Port Maria, informed John Dyer that the prosperity of the Jamaican churches was greater than he had ever imagined while in Britain: 'With you the blessings of the Gospel descend like dew; but with us they are heavy showers of rain'.[24] The meeting of the Jamaica Baptist Association held that month reported an aggregate church membership in twelve churches of 7,001, an increase of 2,017 over the twenty-one months since the last meeting.[25] Growth had been most spectacular in the west of the island: by 1830 Thomas Burchell's church at Montego Bay, formed in 1824 with a membership of twelve, had 1,216 members, and a further 3,348 enquirers.[26] Confronted with such a spiritual harvest, missionaries began to speculate that the period of the universal triumph of the Saviour's kingdom might not be far distant.[27]

In April 1830 William Knibb, now in charge of a new mission station at Savanna-la-Mar, informed John Dyer that one of his deacons, the slave Sam Swiney, had been arrested, tried and sentenced for 'illegal preaching'. In fact Swiney had participated in a prayer meeting held in Knibb's home while Knibb was unwell. Swiney's case received widespread publicity both

23. WI/3, W. Knibb to his mother, 9 Sept. 1828.

24. *BM* 21 (1829), 487-8.

25. *BM* 21 (1829), 397; 22 (1830), 132. The figures exclude the church at Spanish Town, which made no returns. The Association had been formed at Kingston in 1827.

26. W. F. Burchell, *Memoir of Thomas Burchell* (London, 1849), 55; *BM* 28 (1826), 541-2; 22 (1830), 262.

27. WI/3, Knibb to his mother, 9 Sept. 1828; *BM* 22 (1830), 362.

in Jamaica and in Britain. In Jamaica Knibb published a letter in *The Struggler* newspaper which severely criticized the magistrates responsible. In Britain Dyer sent an extract of Knibb's letter to the Colonial Secretary, who then instructed Governor Belmore to investigate the case. Belmore sought to vindicate the magistrates, but further pressure from the Colonial Office resulted in their dismissal.[28]

Swiney's case, together with a similar case involving Henry Williams, a Methodist class-leader, added to the growing body of evidence that the Jamaican magistracy was prepared to resort to almost any means to slow the influx of the slaves to the nonconformist churches. As a result, abolitionist, and specifically nonconformist, opinion in Britain moved in the course of 1830 and 1831 from its former 'gradualist' view to the conclusion that slave-holding was a crime in the sight of God, and that immediate abolition was, therefore, the only option.[29] The news that the anti-slavery movement in Britain was now pressing for immediate abolition soon reached Jamaica. During the second half of 1831, rumours abounded among both planters and slaves that the British parliament had granted, or was about to grant, the slaves their freedom. By December, some slaves had concluded that their freedom was being delayed only by the intervention of the planters. One of Burchell's deacons at Montego Bay, Sam Sharpe, was also recognized as a 'daddy' or leader among groups of Baptists unaffiliated to the BMS - who were increasingly denominated 'native Baptists'.[30] Sharpe began to plan a campaign of passive resistance whereby the slaves would refuse to return to work after the Christmas holiday until the planters granted them their freedom. Some of his native Baptist associates made preparations, not just for 'strike' action, but for armed revolt. Burchell, meanwhile, was on his way back from a period in England. It was widely expected that he would return in triumph, bearing proof of the slaves' emancipation with him.[31]

28.   On the Swiney case see Turner, *Slaves and Missionaries*, 139-40; Jakobsson, *Am I Not a Man and Brother?*, 433-8.

29.   Turner, *Slaves and Missionaries*, 141-4; J. Walvin, 'The rise of British popular sentiment for abolition, 1787-1832', in C. Bolt and S. Drescher (eds), *Anti-Slavery, Religion and Reform* (Folkestone, 1980), 155-6.

30.   The native Baptists were not always a clearly identifiable separate group, but often a tendency existing around and beyond the fringe of those churches which had become affiliated to the BMS mission. See Turner, *Slaves and Missionaries*, 17-18, 57-8, 152-3.

31.   On the insurrection see Turner, *Slaves and Missionaries*, 148-73; M. Reckord, 'The Jamaican Slave Rebellion of 1831', *Past and Present* 39 (1968), 108-25.

The BMS missionaries on the island remained in total ignorance of Sharpe's plot until December 26, when the Presbyterian missionary, George Blyth, warned William Knibb that the slaves in the parish of St James were on the brink of rebellion. Knibb spent that evening and the following day urging the Baptists of Montego Bay and Salter's Hill to report for work as normal the next day, and to desist from violence.[32] But on the night of the 27th, a sugar works on Kensington estate was set on fire, and Knibb's worst fears were realized. The insurrection itself - which soon became known as 'the Baptist war' - was speedily and brutally suppressed. Martial law was imposed. Knibb and three other BMS missionaries, W. Whitehorne, T. F. Abbott, and Francis Gardner, were arrested, ostensibly because they had initially declined to serve in the militia to help put down the rebellion. In reality they were suspected of inciting the slaves to rebellion.[33] Burchell too was arrested as soon as his ship anchored in Montego Bay on 7 January 1832.

By the end of March the charges against the Baptist missionaries had all been dropped through lack of evidence. Burchell was compelled for his own safety to flee to the United States. 312 slaves (including Sharpe) were, however, convicted and executed. Furthermore, during February white mobs, orchestrated in each parish by a body called the Colonial Church Union, had destroyed fourteen Baptist and six Methodist chapels, including Burchell's spacious building at Montego Bay, erected following a special appeal by the BMS in 1826.[34] By persecuting the missions so openly, the slave-owners unwittingly ensured the imminent demise of the slave system. J. H. Hinton, biographer of William Knibb, was careful to emphasize that up to this point even those Baptist missionaries, such as Knibb, who had for long held slavery in private moral abhorrence, had obeyed the Committee's instructions to say nothing against the system and do all they could to conciliate the planters. However, now that the planters had declared open war on evangelical Christianity, the BMS missionaries 'declared hostility against slavery itself, and resolved to identify themselves with those who had long been seeking its abolition'.[35] Hinton's analysis corresponds with that given in February 1832 by J. M. Phillippo, then recovering his health in England. Phillippo saw the colonial backlash following the insurrection as a classic instance of God's propensity to allow human evil to overreach itself

---

32. Hinton, *Memoir of Knibb*, 117-18.

33. Ibid., 122; *BM* 24 (1832), 174.

34. *BM* 25 (1833), 317-19; Jakobsson, *Am I Not a Man and a Brother?*, 471.

35. Hinton, *Memoir of Knibb*, 136-7.

and so effect its own downfall. The doom of slavery was fixed, and its death warrant signed by its own defenders. 'This is the time', continued Phillippo, 'for the nation to arouse itself and without delay to demand the total and final extinction of Slavery throughout the dominions of the Patriot King'.[36]

It would not be long before Phillippo's prophecy was fulfilled. True, the BMS Committee had not yet reached the same radical conclusion as Knibb, Phillippo and others of their Jamaican missionaries. The Committee's concerns were wholly with the infringement of the civil and religious liberties of dissenters that had taken place in Jamaica. The Committee made representations to this effect to the Protestant Dissenting Deputies, who appointed a deputation to the Government.[37] The same concerns predominated at a special BMS public meeting at Finsbury Chapel on 25 May: it appears that nothing was said on the subject of slavery itself.[38] The Jamaican missionaries were, indeed, anxious to see their wrongs redressed and their shattered work rebuilt. Knibb was dispatched to England at the end of April to solicit the Committee's aid on these very matters; to agitate for immediate abolition was no part of his commission, although evidently very much in his mind.[39]

Knibb and his family arrived in England in early June. At an open meeting of the Committee on the 19th, Knibb gave a lengthy account of the insurrection and its aftermath. John Dyer, fearing that Knibb's public utterances would arouse political controversy, urged the necessity of 'prudence, and a temperate policy'. Knibb's celebrated response was to assert that he was prepared to take his family by the hand, and 'walk barefoot through the kingdom' (in other words, to resign from the Society), rather than keep silence before British Christians about the sufferings of their Jamaican brethren. Hinton records that this declaration 'quelled all active opposition'. There is no evidence that Knibb said anything explicit about campaigning for abolition: it is reasonable to suppose merely that he won the Committee's approval for pulling no punches in his public depiction of the outrages inflicted on Jamaican Baptists.[40]

36. MS autobiography of Phillippo, 143b. These remarks were made in a letter dated by Phillippo 7 Feb. 1833, but by that date it would have been unnecessary to call for the exercise of public opinion to secure the downfall of slavery; the letter reads as if written in February 1832.

37. BMS Committee Minutes, 21 Apr. 1832, p. 109; 24 May 1832, p. 113.

38. *BM* 24 (1832), 272, 274.

39. Hinton, *Memoir of Knibb*, 137-9.

40. Ibid., 142-3; BMS Committee Minutes, 19 June 1832, p. 119. That Knibb spoke explicitly about abolition is assumed by Payne, *Freedom in Jamaica*, 38-9.

On the morning of 21 June, Knibb and Phillippo made their way together to the Mission House to be ready for the annual public meeting at Spa Fields Chapel at 11.00 a.m. Outside Fen Court, they met Dyer about to leave for the meeting. Dyer spoke to Knibb in a lowered voice and a tone which Phillippo judged to be 'admonitory'. He then turned to Phillippo, and warned him 'not to anticipate Brother Knibb about the insurrection, or you will destroy the interest of the meeting'. At the meeting Phillippo, who spoke before Knibb, accordingly confined himself to a general appeal for renewed effort to sustain the Jamaican mission; it was quite unfair of Hinton to put an unfavourable construction on his failure to speak out on slavery.[41] It thus fell to Knibb to expound the thesis that Phillippo equally accepted: that the questions of colonial slavery and freedom for missionary activity were now inseparably connected. Knibb claimed that hitherto it had been right for missionaries to keep silence on political affairs, but now that freedom to preach the gospel was at issue, it could be right no longer: 'He could assure the meeting that slaves would never be allowed to worship God till slavery had been abolished'. At this point, Dyer tugged at Knibb's coat-tails to urge him to desist, but to no avail. Knibb again declared his readiness to sacrifice his connection with the Society, and concluded with an impassioned appeal to Christians to unite with politicians and philanthropists to secure the immediate emancipation of the slaves.[42] Amidst an atmosphere of 'amazingly intense' excitement, several of the speakers who followed aligned themselves with Knibb.[43]

In view of Knibb's warm reception by the meeting, there was no going back for the Society. The Committee's conversion was, nonetheless, gradual. At its meeting on 25 June, the Committee agreed to consult with T.F. Buxton and representatives of other missionary societies about arranging a public meeting in Exeter Hall, but the object in view was still defined in terms of securing religious liberty in Jamaica.[44] In August the *Missionary Herald* raised the subject of abolition for the first time: the article was sanguine that better times were approaching 'both for the slaves and their masters', but warned that emancipation was a question surrounded by greater practical difficulties than many were aware of, and that some time

41. MS autobiography of Phillippo, 146-7; Hinton, *Memoir of Knibb,* 144.

42. Cox, *History of the BMS,* ii, 193-5; Hinton, *Memoir of Knibb,* 145-8.

43. R. E. Cooper, 'The diary of William Newman - II', *BQ* 18 (1959-60), 278; *BM* 24 (1832), 326-8.

44. BMS Committee Minutes, 25 June 1832, p. 125.

Thomas Burchell, Missionary in Jamaica, 1823-46.

James Phillippo, Missionary in Jamaica, 1823-79.

William Knibb, Missionary in Jamaica, 1825-45

E.B. Underhill, Secretary of the BMS, 1849-76.

would probably be necessary before it could be safely accomplished.[45] The *Herald's* conservatism was soon overtaken. At the interdenominational meeting at Exeter Hall on 15 August, convened to adopt such measures as were necessary to safeguard religious liberty in Jamaica, a resolution calling on the legislature and Government to implement the 'complete and immediate extinction of slavery throughout the British dominions' was moved by John Dyer himself.[46] In the closing months of 1832 Knibb, Burchell (who arrived in England from the States in September) and, to a lesser extent, Phillippo, toured England and Scotland, mobilising humanitarian opinion in favour of immediate abolition.[47] In the general election campaign of December 1832, nonconformist ministers urged their congregations to vote only for candidates willing to pledge their support for emancipation. A bloc of up to 200 such candidates was returned, laying the foundation for the passing of the Emancipation Act in August 1833. Christian opinion had been decisive in effecting major political change.[48]

On 1 August 1834 slaves throughout the British West Indies received their freedom. In Jamaica jubilant crowds flocked into the chapels for the celebratory services. Jubilation was premature. The Emancipation Act had decreed that slaves were bound to work as apprentices for their former masters, in the case of domestics and tradesmen until 1838, and in the case of plantation workers until 1840. Special magistrates were appointed by the Colonial Office to oversee the operation of the apprenticeship system. James Phillippo, the first of the three leading Baptist missionaries to return to Jamaica after the passing of the Emancipation Act, was also the first to criticize apprenticeship. Within a month of emancipation, Phillippo had written to the governor of Jamaica, Lord Sligo, and to others in England, citing instances of the special magistrates brutally flogging former slaves, and warning of the dangers of a new insurrection if apprenticeship were not speedily abolished. Phillippo soon received an admonitory letter from Dyer, pointing out that his view of apprenticeship did not seem to be shared by any of his missionary brethren.[49] Dyer's claim was not true for long. On 18 December 1834 Thomas Burchell, while acknowledging that the

45. *BM* 24 (1832), 370-2.

46. Ibid., 419.

47. Hinton, *Memoir of Knibb*, 151-2; Burchell, *Memoir of Burchell*, 255; Underhill, *Life of Phillippo*, 103-4. Phillippo's more limited activity was due to ill health.

48. R. Anstey, 'The pattern of British abolitionism in the eighteenth and nineteenth centuries', in Bolt and Drescher (eds.), *Anti-Slavery, Religion and Reform*, 27-8.

49. MS autobiography of Phillippo, 172-3; Underhill, *Life of Phillippo*, 125.

apprenticeship system was working efficiently, reported similar cases of gross maltreatment of apprentices.[50] By late February 1835, Knibb had added his voice to the criticism of the special magistrates.[51]

By 1837 the missionaries of the BMS had earned a reputation on the island as the most vocal and consistent critics of the apprenticeship system. Missionaries of other societies, notably the Wesleyan Methodists, included some stalwart defenders of apprenticeship.[52] In Britain the leading opponent of apprenticeship was the Birmingham Quaker, Joseph Sturge. In 1837 Sturge and three companions visited six West Indian islands to investigate the workings of the system. In Jamaica Sturge consorted freely with the BMS missionaries. At the annual meetings of the Jamaica Baptist Association in March, the missionaries presented Sturge with an address condemning apprenticeship as a 'mockery of freedom', and urging him to use his influence to effect the total abandonment of the system in 1838.[53] On his return to Britain, Sturge did precisely that, orchestrating a radical campaign, based largely in the provinces, for an immediate end to apprenticeship. The pressure generated in Britain was sufficient to compel the various West Indian legislatures to end apprenticeship by statute. On 1 August 1838 all apprentices throughout the British West Indies were declared free. On the night of 31 July, in Knibb's chapel at Falmouth, as the clock struck the last stroke of midnight, Knibb exclaimed before the packed congregation, 'The monster is dead: the negro is free'.[54] The monument which stands to this day in the William Knibb Memorial Baptist Church commemorates the abolition of slavery as having taken place, not on 1 August 1834, but on 1 August 1838.[55]

The former apprentices now became wage labourers in a free market economy. The planters attempted to draw up a pay scale designed to depress wages to levels far below those paid under apprenticeship. Knibb, Burchell and other BMS missionaries assumed the role of mediators in the labour disputes which accordingly developed between workers and overseers on the plantations. Although the missionaries strongly opposed the pittance of

50.   Burchell, *Memoir of Burchell*, 294-6.

51.   Hinton, *Memoir of Knibb*, 228.

52.   Jakobsson, *Am I Not a Man and a Brother?*, 565-7.

53.   J. Sturge and T. Harvey, *The West Indies in 1837* (London, 1838), 249-51.

54.   Hinton, *Memoir of Knibb*, 256-7.

55.   Ibid., 305. For an extended commentary on this fact see A. Tyrrell, 'The "Moral Radical Party" and the Anglo-Jamaican campaign for the abolition of the Negro apprenticeship system', *English Historical Review* 392 (1984), 481-502.

sixpence sterling a day offered by the planters, they also discouraged the workers from holding out for unrealistic wage demands. Most frequently their intervention was made at the request of sympathetic estate managers. Their role was a conciliatory one, designed to promote social harmony and at all costs avert a backlash from the planters.[56] However, few of the estate-owners appreciated the missionaries' attempts to preserve social cohesion; it was at this time that Knibb earned his reputation in planter demonology as a 'pope', a 'Mahomet', an 'agitator', 'the Dan O'Connell of Jamaica'.[57]

From November 1838 the planters began to charge the estate workers high rents for the cottages and provision grounds which previously they had occupied free of charge. Missionaries had other ideas. Baptist 'free' villages or townships were intended to encourage the growth of a Christian peasantry who could be quite independent of the economic power of the planters. J. H. Hinton, who was not averse to a little inflation of Knibb's achievements in comparison with those of Phillippo or Burchell, claimed that the credit for originating the free village concept belonged to Knibb.[58] In fact, as early as 1835, Phillippo had anticipated the need for freehold land on which to settle former apprentices, and had purchased an area in the mountains above Spanish Town, partly with this object in view. The first freeholder bought his plot in July 1838. By the end of 1840, Phillippo's free township at 'Sligoville' comprised over 100 families, and he had founded five similar free townships elsewhere.[59] Knibb had followed suit by buying land in November 1838 in southern Trelawny, where he planted the free village of 'Birmingham', named in honour of Sturge.[60] Whoever originated the idea, it rapidly became integral to the vision, shared by all the BMS missionaries, of a new Christian social order in Jamaica, founded on a free peasantry able to support their own religious life.[61] No-one in 1838 could foresee the obstacles which were to prevent that vision from becoming reality.

56.   S. Wilmot, 'The Peacemakers: Baptist missionaries and ex-slaves in Western Jamaica, 1838/40', *The Jamaican Historical Review* 13 (1982), 42-8.

57.   Hinton, *Memoir of Knibb*, 317; Payne, *Freedom in Jamaica*, 58; Tyrrell, 'The Moral Radical Party', 501-2. Daniel O'Connell was the popular champion of Home Rule in Ireland.

58.   Hinton, *Memoir of Knibb*, 299.

59.   Underhill, *Life of Phillippo*, 183-8.

60.   Hinton, *Memoir of Knibb*, 299-300. Phillippo's second township, Sturgetown, was also named in honour of Sturge.

61.   Tyrrell, 'The Moral Radical Party', 483, 487-8.

III: The Problems of Independence: The Jamaica Mission, 1839-1860

The Baptist churches of Jamaica grew even more rapidly after 1834 than they had done in the final years of slavery. Aggregate membership in the BMS churches grew from 10,838 in 1831 to 13,818 in 1835, and 27,706 in 1840.[62] Enquirers were almost as numerous as members. Furthermore, the expanding Baptist membership seemed to have espoused the principles of Christian stewardship with an avidity which warmed the hearts of the BMS Committee. In 1844 the total receipts of the churches amounted to £13,000; some churches had an annual income of over £1,000, whilst most averaged between £300 and £400.[63]

Such statistics impressed the BMS Committee, and confirmed members in their long-standing aversion to spending money on the West Indian mission. As early as 1826, Thomas Burchell had been so exasperated by the Society's unwillingness to commit funds to Jamaica that he had actually proposed to the Committee that they should abandon the mission to others.[64] The rapid expansion of the Jamaica mission during the 1830s played havoc with the Committee's parsimonious intentions: in 1841, a year when the Society's finances were in a critical condition, expenditure on Jamaica amounted to £9,016 out of a total expenditure of £25,165. A sub-committee set up in May 1841 to suggest means of retrenchment recommended that Jamaican expenditure be reduced to £5,000 per annum. In October the possibility of total financial independence for the Jamaica mission was first raised in the BMS Committee. A letter detailing plans for substantial reductions in expenditure was sent to the annual meeting of the Jamaica Baptist Association at Kingston in January 1842.[65] Among the strong churches which comprised the Western Union, there was a ready response to the Committee's letter. On Thomas Burchell's initiative the meeting went even further than London had requested, resolving that, from 1 August 1842, the Association should become fully independent of the

62. West Indies and Africa Sub-Committee Reports, Report of the Deputation to Jamaica, 1859-60, p. 4. No membership returns are available for 1832, 1833, or 1834.

63. Notes of Deputation to Jamaica, 1846-9, 19-20; G. A. Catherall, 'Thomas Burchell, gentle rebel', *BQ* 21 (1965-6), 358.

64. Burchell, *Memoir of Burchell*, 106; cf. BMS Committee Minutes, 17 Aug. 1826, pp. 246-8. Burchell's ultimatum prompted the Committee into authorizing the special appeal for the new chapel at Montego Bay.

65. *BMS Annual Report*, 1840-1, p. 81; BMS Committee Minutes, 1 July 1841, pp. 205-6; 5-7 Oct. 1841, pp. 249-56; 11 Nov. 1841, pp. 12-13. See below, ch. VII p. 213.

parent society.[66] Although the resolution was unanimous, some of the other missionaries, generally those who had large debts outstanding on their chapels, had their reservations.[67] Phillippo in particular felt the step was premature and 'likely to be a death-blow to the mission'. He supported the resolution only on condition that loans could be obtained from the BMS. As an old man in 1876, Phillippo looked back on the 1842 decision and pronounced his solemn verdict that 'our mission began to decline from this day onwards to the present time'.[68]

The decision reached at Kingston meant that no more BMS missionaries would be sent to Jamaican pastorates after August 1842. Those who had advocated this independence had done so in full confidence that the Jamaican churches were ready for self-support and self-extension; as Baptist churches they already possessed self-government, at least in theory. Burchell and Knibb intended, not merely that the money saved on the Jamaica field would enable the BMS to seize new missionary opportunities elsewhere in the West Indies and in Africa, but also that independence would stimulate the Jamaican Baptists to engage in mission elsewhere on their own account. The formation of the Jamaican Baptist Missionary Society (JBMS) was thus a natural first-fruit of the 1842 decision.[69] The Jamaica missionaries had first proposed the idea of a West African mission staffed by Jamaican nationals in January 1839, and in June 1840 the BMS resolved to accede to the requests of their Jamaica brethren and commence a mission in West Africa.[70] During that year, six young men began studying under Joshua Tinson, pastor of Hanover Street Chapel, Kingston, with a view to going to Africa. The same Association meeting in January 1842 which opted for financial independence also resolved to establish a permanent theological institution at Calabar, near Rio Bueno. Premises were purchased with proceeds from the BMS Jubilee Fund, and the Calabar Institution opened, under Tinson's presidency, in October 1843. By that date, the original conception of a training college for the African mission was already being eclipsed by the more pressing need to train men for the Jamaican pastorate, now that recruitment of missionaries from Britain had ceased. In the event,

66. Burchell, *Memoir of Burchell*, 363.

67. Underhill, *Life of Phillippo*, 203; WI/5, W. Dendy to J. Angus, 29 Aug. 1843.

68. Underhill, *Life of Phillippo*, 201.

69. H. O. Russell, 'A question of indigenous mission: the Jamaican Baptist Missionary Society', *BQ* 25 (1973-4), 86-93.

70. Cox, *History of the BMS*, ii, 352-3; see below, ch. IV, pp. 106-7.

only one Calabar student in the first twenty years of the Institution joined the African mission.[71]

J. M. Phillippo's observation that the prosperity of the Jamaica mission began to decline from about 1842 was accurate enough, but it was hardly fair to lay the blame wholly on the decision reached at Kingston. The problems which increasingly afflicted the Jamaica field after the abolition of apprenticeship were in part the problems of church growth whose scale exceeded its qualitative depth and in part a reflection of the decline in the Jamaican economy.

From the early 1830s the BMS mission in Jamaica was the object of repeated public criticism - not merely, as had always been the case, from the planter interest - but now, more painfully, from the representatives of other evangelical societies. The critics included George Blyth and H. M. Waddell of the Scottish Missionary Society, W. G. Barrett of the LMS, and Richard Panton, an Anglican clergyman who was corresponding secretary for the CMS. The common theme running through their allegations was that the phenomenal growth of the Baptist churches had been achieved at the expense of spiritual discipline and purity. Criticism focused on the Baptist use of the 'ticket and leader' system.[72]

From an early date in the history of the Jamaica mission, BMS missionaries had organized their congregations on the Methodist pattern of classes, supervised by class leaders. Admission to the classes was regulated by the issue of tickets, which were renewed quarterly to members at communion, but withheld in cases of moral failure. A second category of ticket was issued to enquirers seeking baptism and church membership.[73] Ultimately this pattern was derived from the Methodist societies on the island, but its essential features, at least, were borrowed in the first instance from the existing Baptist congregations. In the black Baptist churches the class leaders (or 'daddies') were often the headmen of the old slave-gangs who worked the estates, elected by their class members more in recognition of their status within slave society than for any spiritual qualities. The critics alleged that the BMS missionaries had frequently taken over the black

71. For the origins of Calabar College see Underhill, *Life of Phillippo*, 199, 204-6; idem, *The West Indies: Their Social and Religious Condition* (London, 1862), 292-4; Payne, *Freedom in Jamaica*, 105-6. The one student who went to Africa was Francis Pinnock.

72. P. T. Rooke, 'Evangelical missionary rivalry in the British West Indies', *BQ* 29 (1981-2), 341-55; H/9, 'Memorandum of a communication made by the Revd Richard Panton...' and 'Replies to the charges of the Rev. Richard Panton'.

73. *BM* 12 (1820), 438-9; *BM* 15 (1823), 402; Cox, *History of the BMS*, ii, 69-76.

Baptist leadership structures intact when black Baptist congregations affiliated themselves to the BMS. The ticket and leader system, they argued, had become a Trojan horse, introducing into the BMS congregations the 'African' superstition and immorality which characterized the church life of the 'native Baptists'. Baptist members, it was said, were buried clutching their class tickets, as if they were passports to heaven. No such criticism was levelled against the Methodist class system, because the Methodists had not normally appointed slaves as class leaders, and had no indigenous Christian tradition resistant to missionary control.[74]

The usual defence adopted by the BMS missionaries was to concede that their churches were not perfect, but to defend the ticket and leader system as the most efficient method of maintaining spiritual discipline and pastoral care in such vast congregations. Instances of superstitious regard for tickets were very few, and class leaders did not exercize the power which was alleged.[75] Baptists suspected that the allegations were motivated by envy of their disproportionate success, a charge which one modern historian has largely substantiated.[76] The controversies may have injured the reputation of the BMS churches, but they did not impair their growth. They also revealed the ignorance prevailing in the BMS Committee regarding the native Baptists. Edward Steane, one of a small group deputed to hear Panton's allegations in 1838, remarked in the course of the meeting that the importation of the native Baptists from America 'must have been so many years ago that they must have all pretty well died off'. In fact, as Panton was quick to point out, they remained strong in the east of the island, notably in Kingston.[77] In the west, their adherents had largely been absorbed into the BMS churches, but remained as a penumbra around the fringe of chapel membership.[78] There, as in other parts of the West Indian mission, the currents of negro revivalism continued to run beneath the placid surface of British evangelical orthodoxy. To that extent, the critics were right.

74. H/9, 'Memorandum of a communication', pp. 4-10, 59; W. G. Barrett, *Baptist Mission in Jamaica: An Exposition of the System Pursued by the Baptist Missionaries in Jamaica* (London, 1842), 8; W. J. Gardner, *A History of Jamaica* (new edn.; London, 1909), 359-60. Jakobsson, *Am I Not a Man and a Brother?*, 433, says that the Methodists began to appoint slaves as class leaders in 1829.

75. H/9, 'Replies to the charges of the Rev. Richard Panton', *passim*.

76. Ibid., 38-9; Rooke, 'Evangelical missionary rivalry', 347-9.

77. H/9, 'Memorandum of a communication', 48-9; cf. Underhill, *The West Indies*, 191.

78. Turner, *Slaves and Missionaries*, 58, 152-3; see also Joshua Tinson in H/9, 'Replies to the Charges of the Rev. Richard Panton', p. 18.

Persistent criticism could be rebutted or ignored. More damaging to the life of the Jamaican churches was the impact of the deterioration of the island economy. After 1842 the financial problems of the field escalated rapidly. In 1845 the BMS Committee, in response to urgent representations from the Jamaican ministers for assistance in tackling the crippling burden of chapel debt, authorized a special appeal for £6,000. The grant was made on the understanding that it represented 'a full and final discharge' of all claims by the Jamaican ministers on the Society, except for the payment of the salary of the theological tutor at Calabar.[79] Nevertheless, some influential voices in Jamaica, including Phillippo, continued to argue that the BMS should resume financial responsibility for the Jamaica mission. Knibb and Burchell, the doughtiest advocates of autonomy, were now dead.

The renewed pressure from Jamaica for a review of the financial relationship with the Society resulted in the BMS secretary, Joseph Angus, and a respected Liverpool minister, C. M. Birrell, being sent to the island in November 1846. Their deputation report was, however, adamant in maintaining the Committee's existing view that Jamaica 'is no longer a field for the bounty or efforts of our Society'. The deputation reported that the island was much better supplied with Baptist ministry than was Britain, and its churches too well off to merit any claim on BMS funds. The Jamaican people, concluded Angus and Birrell, were 'among the most prosperous peasantry in the world'. This conclusion was reached despite evidence that the receipts of the churches had declined from £13,000 to £10,000 over the previous three years.[80] Worse was to come. In 1846 the British parliament began the reduction of the duties which had protected imported Jamaican sugar from foreign competitors. In 1847 a commercial crisis in Britain led to the failure of several West Indian merchant houses and the Planters' Bank in Kingston. The price of sugar on the London market fell by a third.[81] The declining fortunes of Jamaica's staple export commodity hit wage levels hard. By 1849 the average annual contribution to church funds per Baptist member was only seven shillings and fourpence, compared with nearly

---

79. *BMS Annual Report*, 1844-5, xii-xiii; Underhill, *Life of Phillippo*, 246. The BMS was also prepared, in cases of the illness or death of those sent out as missionaries before May 1840, to consider paying the return passage expenses of the pastor, or his widow and children.

80. Notes of Deputation to Jamaica, 1846-9 ([*sic*] in fact 1846-7), 18-20.

81. P. D. Curtin, *Two Jamaicas: The Role of Ideas in a Tropical Colony 1830-1865* (Cambridge, Mass., 1955), 151-2.

twelve shillings before 1844.[82] Economic depression was followed by demographic disaster. In 1850-1 a cholera epidemic removed between 25,000 and 30,000 of the Jamaican working classes; a smallpox epidemic came in its wake.[83]

Jamaica's problems were not fully understood at the Mission House. Even E. B. Underhill, secretary since 1849 and confidant of D. J. East, principal of Calabar College, seemed to imagine that the effects of economic depression were providentially limited to the planters - the former oppressors - while the one-time oppressed were evolving into a prosperous free peasantry.[84] Although he had Jamaica's interests at heart, Underhill saw no continuing role for the BMS in Jamaica beyond assisting the churches in the training of a native pastorate and Christian school-teachers. To this end he pressed the BMS Committee to sponsor promising students at Calabar College, and encouraged East to add a Normal School department in 1854.[85] However, in 1859-60 Underhill, accompanied by J. T. Brown of Northampton, visited Jamaica in the course of a deputation tour of the West Indies. To sympathetic interest was now added a measure of accurate understanding. For the first time (and for the next fifteen years) the West Indies mission had the benefit of a BMS secretary who, whilst remaining firmly committed to the ideal of autonomy for the Jamaican churches, was prepared to defend the interests of the West Indies both in the Committee and beyond it.

Underhill and Brown's visit was a response to a request from Jamaica in April 1857 that a deputation be sent to investigate the churches and their difficulties, in the hope that measures would be adopted which would save the mission from 'further declension, and restore it to its former efficiency'.[86] At the heart of the churches' difficulties lay the problem of an insufficient number of pastors. Underhill and Brown found that only thirty-six pastors were available to serve seventy-seven churches. Every pastor had at least two churches under his care. The pastor was to be found in a particular pulpit only on alternate Sundays, and many church members came to worship only on 'minister's Sunday'. Pastoral care had suffered,

82.   Underhill, *The West Indies*, 329.

83.   Curtin, *Two Jamaicas*, 160.

84.   Correspondence of D. J. East and E. B. Underhill, 1852-95; Underhill to East, 6 Nov. 1852 and 16 Nov. 1853.

85.   Ibid., Underhill to East, 14 Aug. 1852, 13 and 29 Apr. 1854.

86.   W. Indies and Africa Sub-Committee Reports, Letter of Instructions to Underhill and Brown, 13 July 1859.

especially where members migrated annually into the mountains in search of work or land. Perhaps the most significant of all the deputation's observations on this point was the comment that, as a result, 'the deacons and leaders have thrown upon them a larger responsibility, and an influence may be acquired over the people which may be harmful to the churches' welfare and the pastor's peace'. This, of course, had been the burden of the accusations laid against the mission in the 1830s, but strenuously denied by both the missionaries and the home Committee. An official BMS deputation was now conceding the existence in the Jamaican churches of 'evils of no inconsiderable magnitude', and attributing these defects in large measure to the influence exercised by untrained class leaders. Although Underhill and Brown did not say so explicitly, the spectre of the native Baptists was continuing to haunt the BMS Jamaica mission.[87]

Underhill and Brown made two major recommendations. They urged, firstly, that the Society should offer financial incentives to attract European pastors to Jamaica (such as paying their passage money), and should even be prepared to subsidize a few selected stipends for a short period. In the second place, the deputation report addressed itself to the problem of the paucity of Jamaican candidates for the ministry, noting that in fifteen years Calabar College had produced only fourteen serving Jamaican pastors. Underhill and Brown diagnosed the problem as the low level of education of the people, and as a solution recommended that the length of the pastoral course be increased from four to six years.

The deputation had accurately diagnosed the sickness, but had prescribed strangely inappropriate medicine. Measures to increase the numbers of European pastors were short-sighted, in view of the fact (which the deputation recognized) that Europeans tended to hold more than one pastorate in order to make up their income to a level capable of sustaining a European standard of living. Not surprisingly, the suggestion that the BMS should permit some temporary infringement of the maxims of self-support was not taken up in London.[88] Increasing the length of the Calabar pastoral course for the few who qualified for it was hardly likely to expedite the entry of Jamaicans into the ministry - rather the reverse. The possibility that the solution lay rather in a programme of lower-level Christian education aimed at the deacons and class-leaders seems never to have been considered.

87. Ibid., Report of the Deputation to Jamaica, 21 Sept. 1860 [printed, with slight amendment, in *BM* 52 (1860), 787-97].

88. W. Indies and Africa Sub-Committee Reports, Report of the Sub-Committee on the Jamaican Deputation Report, 16 Jan. 1861.

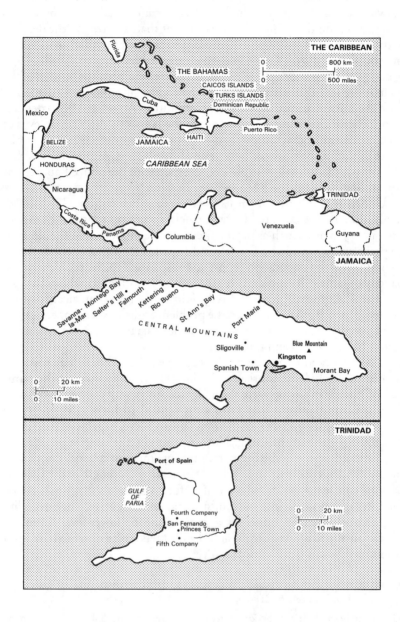

Map 2: The West Indies

IV: The Other West Indian Missions, 1822-1860

In addition to his visit to Jamaica in the company of J. T. Brown, E. B. Underhill visited the BMS missions in the Bahamas, Haiti and Trinidad. The granting of financial independence to Jamaica in 1842 had been intended, in part, to release resources for other areas of the West Indies. In the short term, this objective was pursued, but the Society lacked the corporate will to give the other West Indian stations a realistic chance of success. In comparison with the Jamaica mission, they received little publicity and few missionary recruits. Church growth was patchy. If the strong churches of Jamaica found the maintenance of financial autonomy difficult, the prospects for the establishment of a self-supporting church elsewhere in the West Indies were slim indeed.

From 1822 to 1850 the BMS maintained a small mission in British Honduras. The mission was established as a result of the trading activity in Honduras of G. F. Angas of Newcastle, a wealthy benefactor of the Society. The first missionary, James Bourne, a student of William Steadman's at Bradford Academy, was sent out at Angas's expense.[89] A second missionary, John Fleming, was sent to join Bourne in 1824, but died almost immediately on arrival.[90] Bourne laboured alone at Belize until 1835, when he was transferred to the Bahamas mission. He was replaced by Alexander Henderson, a man of strict communion principles. Two missionaries were despatched to join him in 1841, but one died en route.[91] Henderson's strict communion views began to create tensions with the BMS, and his connection with the Society was terminated in 1846. In 1850 the BMS withdrew from Honduras altogether. The Baptist church at Belize eventually became the responsibility of the JBMS.[92]

The Honduras mission was alone among the West Indian fields in being a pioneer evangelistic situation: there is no evidence of any previously existing Baptist community. Elsewhere the Society faced, to a greater or lesser degree, the same problem as it encountered in Jamaica: how to marry British standards of church practice and discipline to an indigenous Baptist tradition. The most flourishing and important of these secondary West Indian fields was the Bahamas mission.

89. Cox, *History of the BMS*, ii, 42-3; *BM* 14 (1822), 82; BMS Committee Minutes, 27 Dec. 1821, pp. 169-70.

90. *BM* 16 (1824), 226, 498-9, 544-5.

91. Cox, *History of the BMS*, ii, 348-9.

92. J. B. Myers (ed.), *The Centenary Volume of the Baptist Missionary Society 1792-1892* (London, 1892), 213.

The Bahamian churches originated in the migration to the islands at the close of the American War of Independence of loyalist proprietors, some of whose slaves were Baptists.[93] Contact with British Baptists was established as early as 1815, but the first BMS missionary, Joseph Burton, did not arrive till January 1833, having worked previously in Jamaica. Burton found twenty churches in existence, but afflicted by an illiterate leadership and prevalent 'superstition'. At Nassau the departures from scriptural order were deemed so serious that Burton and his fellow missionary, Kilner Pearson, decided to disband the existing churches and re-form them, admitting to membership only those whom they judged would be received 'by other Baptist churches in any other part of the world'.[94] At least one group, no doubt threatened by this process, seceded to form their own native congregation.[95] Others declined to affiliate to the mission. A pattern was thus created in the Bahamas of mission and native churches existing in close proximity to each other.

Underhill in 1860 was impressed that nearly one half of the population of the eighteen islands of the Bahamas group which had churches in connection with the BMS was 'distinctively Baptist'. Even allowing for the substantial minority who were native Baptists, membership of the BMS churches was thus higher in proportion to total population even than in Jamaica. However, Underhill was less impressed with the continuing low standard of literacy of the church leaders, and the form of pastoral supervision adopted by the churches in the northern district of islands. Each island had appointed a pastor, jointly supported by the churches of that island, who circulated among the churches providing teaching of a higher standard than the resident church leaders could supply. Underhill felt the arrangement was un-Baptist and discouraging to the voluntaryist spirit: the pastor's visits were resented by the church leaders, and his support granted unwillingly by the people. Nonetheless, he recommended that the churches were now sufficiently strong for their dependence on BMS support to be limited to the provision of two missionary salaries.[96] The home Committee in fact went further still, ruling that the Nassau church, with a membership of over 800, should assume responsibility for the

---

93. On Bahamian Baptist history see M. C. Symonette and A. Canzoneri, *Baptists in the Bahamas: An Historical Review* (El Paso, 1977); also P. Brewer, 'British Baptist missionaries and Baptist work in the Bahamas', *BQ* 32 (1987-8), 295-301.

94. *BM* 26 (1834), 359.

95. Symonette and Canzoneri, *Baptists in the Bahamas,* 12-13.

96. *BM* 52 (1860), 807-11.

support of its own missionary pastor, leaving the salary of one missionary to serve the central and southern districts as the principal remaining charge on BMS funds.[97]

The BMS mission on Haiti, an offshoot of the Bahamas work, was, by contrast, feeble in the extreme. Here Protestantism struggled in an oppressive atmosphere of Catholicism laced with voodoo belief and practice. In 1841, as part of the BMS Committee's encouragement of forward movement in the West Indies beyond Jamaica, the BMS extended the Bahamas mission by stationing one missionary, W. Littlewood, in the Turks and Caicos Islands.[98] From his base on Turks Island, Littlewood made a visit towards the end of 1842 to Puerto Plata on the north coast of the Spanish-speaking eastern part of Haiti (San Domingo). Here he found a small Baptist community of former American slaves, some of whom met for worship in the home of Samuel Vincent, an ordained negro preacher. Littlewood formed them into a church of fourteen members, and asked the Society to send a missionary.[99] The war of independence of 1844, which led to the establishment of the Dominican Republic as a separate state in the eastern two-thirds of the island, dispersed the church members, and postponed the commencement of the Puerto Plata mission. However, in 1845 the Society stationed E. J. Francies and M. W. Flanders at Jacmel, in French-speaking Haiti (the western third of the island).[100] Flanders soon withdrew owing to ill health, and Francies died seven months later. Until the arrival of W. H. Webley in 1847, the main activity of the mission comprised schools work, conducted by a Miss Harris and a Miss Clark. The San Domingo mission in the east was finally established in March 1852, when W. K. Rycroft settled at Puerto Plata and re-constituted the church there.[101] This station was regarded by the BMS as an offshoot of the Turks Island mission, and bore no relation to the Haiti mission at Jacmel.

When Underhill arrived in 1859, he found the Haiti mission on the verge of extinction. Webley's solitary ministry had been virtually suspended for four months owing to illness; none of the other forty-six members of the church was capable of conducting worship in his absence; and the boarding

---

97. W. Indies and Africa Sub-Committee Reports, Report of the Sub-Committee on the Bahamas mission; BMS Committee Minutes, 17 Apr. 1861, p. 51.

98. *BM* 34 (1842), 102.

99. *BM* 35 (1843), 223-5.

100. *BMS Annual Report*, 1844-5, pp. 41-2; BMS Committee Minutes, 19 June 1845, p. 160, ; cf. Underhill, *Life of Phillippo*, 224.

101. Myers (ed.), *Centenary Volume of the BMS*, 212-13; *BMS Annual Reports*, 1851-2, p. 3, 1852-3, p. 4.

school founded by Miss Harris, which had been instrumental in the conversion of a quarter of the church membership, had closed. Underhill, observing that it was surely never intended that one individual should constitute the Society's entire contribution to the evangelization of Haiti, recommended that a second missionary be appointed, to be stationed at Port-au-Prince.[102] In fact two additional missionaries, V. Bouhon and W. Baumann, were accepted in 1861 for service in Haiti.[103]

In one West Indian context, therefore, the BMS was still prepared to increase its slender missionary commitment. There was, however, an underlying lack of realism in the Society's policy of maintaining a minimal missionary presence in fields where the church was so weak. Even the sympathetic Underhill had warned Webley in 1859 that it was impossible to expect the churches of England to supply the men and means to cover Haiti with chapels and mission stations, and urged him to enforce the principles of self-extension on the Haitian church.[104] It was a counsel of perfection for a church still in its infancy. Without an investment of missionary resources on a scale at least equivalent to that seen in Jamaica, there was no prospect of the Jamaican story being reproduced in the Society's other West Indian fields. The Baptist mission in Trinidad affords further illustration of this fact.

Baptist history in Trinidad begins with the settlement in May 1815 of the first of several groups of former slaves from Virginia who had been recruited into British marine regiments during the American war of 1812-14. Many of these slaves were Baptists, converted in the revivals which swept the state of Virginia in the late 1780s. On discharge from the marines, the Virginian slaves were settled in the south of Trinidad in what became known as the 'Company villages'. The village communities were isolated and almost totally illiterate, but some form of Baptist church life on the American 'tent-meeting' pattern was organized by indigenous preachers.[105]

The first English Baptist to work in Trinidad was George Cowen, a schoolmaster employed by the Mico Charity, whose funds were used between 1835 and 1845 to promote negro education in the British West Indies. In 1841, as it became clear that the financial future of the Mico schools was uncertain, Cowen applied to the BMS for support.[106] The

102. *BM* 52 (1860), 801-6.

103. BMS Committee Minutes, 26 Feb. 1861, p. 39.

104. *BM* 52 (1860), 806.

105. Brewer, 'The Baptist churches of South Trinidad', chs. 1 to 3.

106. BMS Committee Minutes, 4 Nov. 1841, p. 11; 2 Dec. 1841, p. 23.

Jamaican decision of January 1842 increased the chances of a favourable response. The Committee, confident that the Jamaica mission would no longer be a charge on its funds, began to look for new openings in the Caribbean. In January 1843 Cowen was accepted as a missionary, to be stationed at Port of Spain.[107] At the end of the year J. M. Phillippo was sent from Jamaica to visit Trinidad, the Windward Islands and Haiti. His report advised the Committee to establish a permanent station at Port of Spain, and money from the Society's Jubilee Fund was accordingly made available to purchase the Mico premises there as the BMS headquarters on the island. Phillippo also recommended that the Society send missionaries to St Vincent (where there was a considerable Baptist population) and St Lucia, but no action was taken.[108]

Cowen planted a small church in Port of Spain, but in 1845 moved south to work in the Company villages, while a second missionary, John Law, assumed the pastorate of the Port of Spain church. Cowen, like his missionary colleagues elsewhere in the West Indies, found the existing indigenous Baptist leadership sorely deficient. He particularly deplored the Company churches' tolerance of drunkenness and debauchery at camp meetings and funeral wakes.[109] Cowen died in 1852, having seen little fruit in terms of either spiritual or numerical growth in the Company churches. Some signs of spiritual revival were evident in 1854, but there was no BMS missionary stationed in the south to channel its energies. W. H. Gamble, who arrived in the Company villages in 1856, found discipline lax and respect for the pastorate at a low ebb.[110] Underhill's deputation report on his visit to Trinidad in 1859 commented adversely on instances of 'most unseemly conduct' in public worship - 'the congregation rising up, dancing and jumping' - and complained of ignorant pastors and independent-minded people, who resisted interference by the missionary.[111] In Trinidad, as elsewhere, the problems of grafting the native Baptist plant into the British Baptist tree remained substantial.

107. BMS Committee Minutes, 12 Jan. 1843, pp. 4-5.

108. Brewer, 'The Baptist churches of South Trinidad', 97-102; Underhill, *Life of Phillippo*, 216-25; *BM* 36 (1844), 272-3, 586-8.

109. Brewer, 'The Baptist churches of South Trinidad', 110-13.

110. W. H. Gamble, *Trinidad: Historical and Descriptive* (London, 1866), 110-11.

111. *BM* 52 (1860), 798-9.

V: Prelude to Withdrawal: The West Indies Field, 1860-1892

In the course of their deputation visit to Jamaica, Underhill and Brown attended the annual meetings of the Jamaica Baptist Union, held at Montego Bay in February 1860. The statistical returns from the churches were not encouraging, and it was accordingly resolved to set aside a week of prayer for spiritual revival.[112] The Jamaican pastors were influenced by the major revival movement which had swept through the United States in 1858 and crossed the Atlantic to Ulster, Scotland and Wales in 1859.[113] In Jamaica, as in other parts of the globe in 1858-60, organized 'revival' prayer meetings were instrumental in promoting the coming of revival itself. The first to be affected, in October 1860, were Moravian congregations at St Elizabeth on the south coast. From there the current of new spiritual life flowed eastward and northward to the areas of Baptist predominance. Over Christmas, J. M. Phillippo reported packed services at Spanish Town, and predicted that the whole island would in time be affected.[114]

Phillippo's forecast was correct. During the early months of 1861 all the Baptist churches witnessed scenes of fervent public confession of sin and intense religious excitement. Some of the European pastors began to express concern at the incidence of emotional hysteria and physical excesses. Visions, prophesyings and claims of extraordinary possession by the Spirit were common. In some parts, such as St Ann, there was even a resurgence of obeahism (the private practice of magic) and myalism (an Africanist religious cult).[115] On these grounds, two historians of Jamaica, W.J. Gardner in the nineteenth century and Philip Curtin in the twentieth, claimed that the revival degenerated into a reversion to the African religious past, and identified the native Baptists as the chief culprits.[116] Phillippo, a first-hand observer, testified that, on the contrary, the revival almost eliminated obeahism and myalism, and reduced the incidence of funeral wakes. The short-term benefits to the Jamaica Baptist Union were clear: approximately 3,800 baptisms and 1,600 backsliders restored to church

---

112. Underhill, *Life of Phillippo*, 302.

113. For the revival movements of 1858-60 see J. E. Orr, *The Second Evangelical Awakening in Britain* (London, 1949). Orr's contention that England was similarly affected has been questioned by later historians.

114. Underhill, *Life of Phillippo*, 306.

115. Correspondence of East and Underhill, Underhill to East, 1 Mar. 1861.

116. Gardner, *History of Jamaica*, 465; Curtin, *Two Jamaicas*, 170-1.

fellowship were reported during 1861.[117] The revival was a reversion, not to African paganism, but to the black American Christian tradition from which the Jamaican Baptists sprang. As such, it inevitably evoked mixed reactions from European observers.

In the long term the revival failed to reverse the decline in the health of the Jamaican churches. In itself it could address neither the problem of inadequate church leadership nor the underlying economic malaise of the people. The Jamaican ministers continued in 1861 to appeal to the BMS for financial aid on a scale which threatened to sabotage the efforts of Underhill and Brown to obtain the limited measure of assistance proposed in their deputation report on Jamaica.[118] During the early 1860s distress intensified as sugar cultivation became less profitable and unemployment rose. After two years of drought in 1863 and 1864 starvation was a distinct possibility.

In January 1865 Underhill wrote a private letter to Edward Cardwell, Secretary of State for the Colonies, drawing his attention to the plight of Jamaica's poor, and criticizing the Jamaican legislature for gross neglect of the interests of the negro population. Underhill proposed a searching inquiry into the legislation passed since emancipation, and recommended that the Governor be instructed to encourage freeholders to cultivate new export crops as an alternative to sugar.[119] In reality Underhill expected little from the Governor, and less from the Colonial Office. He relied far more on the Baptist ministers to urge their flocks to grow crops for export and organize marketing co-operatives. For Underhill, small-scale capitalist enterprise by the Jamaican peasantry offered the only escape from continued impoverishment and the only hope of educational and spiritual progress. He had perceived that nothing less than the Society's investment in the creation of an autonomous Jamaican church was at stake: unless the people made the transition from a subsistence to a commercial economy, the ideal of self-support would remain an elusive one.[120]

Cardwell sent Underhill's letter to Governor Eyre with a request for his comments. Eyre circulated the letter to the local *custodes* (the chief citizen and justice of the peace in each parish). One *custos* passed the letter to the

---

117. Underhill, *Life of Phillippo*, 313-14; see also Myers (ed.), *Centenary Volume of the BMS*, 199-200.

118. Correspondence of East and Underhill, Underhill to East, 31 Aug. 1861.

119. E. B. Underhill, *A Letter Addressed to the Rt. Honourable E. Cardwell* ... (London, n.d. [1865]).

120. Correspondence of East and Underhill, Underhill to East, 30 Jan. 1865.

editor of the *Jamaica Guardian,* who published it on 21 March.[121] Underhill's letter aroused immediate and widespread controversy. So-called 'Underhill meetings' were organized by the negroes, supporting Underhill's statements and petitioning the Governor for remedial action to be taken. Amidst mounting discontent, and fearful of a popular uprising, Governor Eyre replied to Cardwell, blaming Underhill and the Jamaican Baptist ministers for stirring up the people to believe in 'imaginary wrongs'. Eyre also intercepted correspondence between the ministers and the BMS.[122]

In October the uprising which Eyre feared took place. On the 7th and 11th rioting broke out at the Petty Sessions court at Morant Bay. On the second occasion the rioters set fire to the courthouse, and eighteen lives were lost. Soon the whole area was in revolt. Retribution was swift and savage. The rising was put down within three days. Martial law was declared, 439 negroes were shot or hanged, and over a thousand negro homes plundered and burned. Many of those arrested had no conceivable connection with the events at Morant Bay. Among them were G. W. Gordon, a member of the House of Assembly who had been baptized by J. M. Phillippo,[123] and three Baptist or native Baptist ministers, J. H. Crole, Edwin Palmer, and James Service. Gordon was executed for sedition. The rising and its brutal suppression now became the subject of intense public argument in Britain. In December the Government suspended Eyre and appointed a Royal Commission of Inquiry. Underhill fed D. J. East with supplies of Blue Books and other information to enable him to defend the Baptist ministers before the Commission against Eyre's charge that they had fomented the revolt.[124] In the event Eyre did not repeat his accusations, and Underhill's contention that he was in no way responsible for the rising was vindicated. The Commission found that Eyre's suppression of the outbreak had been disproportionate to the original offence. Eyre was dismissed, although a humanitarian attempt to bring him to justice for the murder of G. W. Gordon eventually failed.[125]

---

121. Ibid., Underhill to East, 14 Apr. 1866.

122. Payne, *Freedom in Jamaica,* 92.

123. On Gordon see G. A. Catherall, 'George William Gordon: Saint or Sinner', *BQ* 27 (1977-8), 163-72. Gordon ended his religious pilgrimage as a native Baptist, though Underhill, *Life of Phillippo,* 319-20, claims that he maintained a connection with the United Presbyterian Church after his baptism by Phillippo in 1861.

124. Correspondence of East and Underhill, Underhill to East, 16 Feb. 1866.

125. On the rising and its aftermath see Payne, *Freedom in Jamaica,* 90-98; B. Semmel, *The Governor Eyre Controversy* (London, 1962); D. A. Lorimer, *Colour, Class and the Victorians* (Leicester, 1978), 178-200.

The Morant Bay rising marked a watershed in Jamaican secular history. The changes of 1833-38 had brought slavery to an end, but the political domination of the old slave-owning class remained intact. It was the 1865 rising and the ensuing controversy in Britain over Jamaican affairs which spelt the end of planter supremacy.[126] The House of Assembly was dissolved, and Jamaica became a Crown Colony, directly subject to the Westminster parliament. In 1867 a system of elementary education, financed by government grants-in-aid, was set up, followed in 1870 by the disestablishment of the Church of England, traditional ally of the planter class. William Knibb would have rejoiced to see his fondest dreams thus realized. In the Baptist history of Jamaica, however, the Morant Bay rising brought about no radical transformation. The BMS Committee remained committed to the view that any resumption of financial responsibility for the island was unthinkable. Even the thought of selective missionary extension financed from London was uncongenial to the Committee. It took personal representations to the Society's Officers from Sir Henry Storks, one of the Royal Commissioners, to persuade the Committee to commit funds to establish and support for three years mission stations in the Morant Bay region, scene of the disturbances.[127] The Society's long-term commitment to Jamaica continued to be limited to the support of Calabar College (whose Principal, D. J. East, was also, from the date of the College's removal to Kingston in 1869, the pastor of East Queen Street chapel).[128]

In the years after Morant Bay, the financial difficulties of the Jamaican churches remained, but they were not sufficient to prevent a substantial increase in church membership from the late 1870s onwards. Aggregate church membership in the Jamaica Baptist Union was 19,677 in 1869, 19,989 in 1876, 26,212 in 1880 and 34,984 in 1890.[129] The BMS Committee could reflect with satisfaction that its 'hands-off' policy, though frequently unpopular amongst the Jamaican ministers, had resulted in a vibrant church that was now self-extending, as well as self-supporting and self-governing. From the early 1880s, the most frequently stated objective

126. Curtin, *Two Jamaicas,* 178.

127. Underhill, *Life of Phillippo,* 346-7; Correspondence of East and Underhill, Underhill to East, 14 and 29 Mar., 14 Apr. and 16 July 1866. BMS support for the Morant Bay mission was later extended to seven years.

128. The BMS also owned the East Queen Street premises, and had sole legal right of nomination to the pastorate.

129. Myers (ed.), *Centenary Volume of the BMS,* 203. The total population of the island in 1891 was 646,300.

of BMS policy in the West Indies was to encourage the Jamaican Union, through its own missionary society, to assume responsibility for the other BMS fields in the Caribbean. The ultimate vision was the creation of a West Indian Union of Baptist churches, centred on Jamaica, and served by indigenous ministers trained at Calabar College. The driving momentum behind the process was, however, less idealistic: a decided majority on the Committee clearly felt that the other West Indian stations had absorbed BMS resources for too long, with precious little fruit to show for it. These stations were to be left to sink or swim, whether or not the Jamaica Baptist Missionary Society could be induced to rescue them.

Haiti, being the smallest and weakest of the West Indian missions, was the first to be discarded by the home Committee. D. J. East was sent on an investigative mission to Haiti in December 1880, and his report led to the sole remaining missionary, A. Pappengouth, being recalled to London for consultations.[130] On 21 April 1882 the BMS Committee resolved to open negotiations with the JBMS for the transfer of the Haiti mission.[131] In the course of the negotiations the BMS had to raise the level and extend the duration of its offer of financial support to the JBMS, and from 1 October 1883 the transfer began to be implemented.[132] For a variety of reasons, the process was not completed until 1885. It was not a success. George Rowe, sent by the JBMS to take over the work, had difficulties learning the colloquial French of Haiti, and at the end of 1890 was forced home by ill health.[133]

The Society's attitude to the West Indian mission was probably influenced by the pressure now being exerted by its most lavish benefactor, Robert Arthington, the originator of the Congo mission. In June 1885 Arthington offered the BMS £10,000 for the purchase and support of a missionary ship to operate in the Indonesian archipelago, on condition that the Society implemented a speedy withdrawal from all fields 'where the light of the Gospel has long been held forth and has been established in human hearts'.[134] In the course of the subsequent correspondence, the BMS secretary, A. H. Baynes, assured Arthington that the Committee had

130. BMS Committee Minutes, 17 May 1881, pp. 170-1.

131. BMS Committee Minutes, 21 Apr. 1882, pp. 330-1.

132. BMS Committee Minutes, 19 June 1883, pp. 259-64.

133. BMS Committee Minutes, 7 May 1886, pp. 98-9; Myers (ed.), *Centenary Volume of the BMS*, 213.

134. H/31, Arthington to BMS Committee, 22 June 1885. On Arthington see below, chs. IV and XII, pp. 118, 381.

already 'taken steps to withdraw from most of their West Indian missions'.[135] Although a slight overstatement of the current position, Baynes's assurance was an accurate indication of the direction which had been set for West Indian policy by the Haiti decision.

In September 1888 D. J. East wrote to Baynes, encouraging him to press ahead with his intention to administer the medicine of enforced self-support on the other West Indian missions, particularly on the Bahamas churches, which East believed to have become unhealthily dependent on BMS aid.[136] One of the obstacles to the Committee's plans for a transfer of the missions to Jamaican control was the reluctance of the Bahamian churches and their missionary, Daniel Wilshere, to accept black Jamaicans as missionary pastors. Wilshere had appeared before the Western sub-committee in June, and persuaded it that to attempt to introduce black Jamaican pastors into the Bahamas would only result in disunion and bitterness, in view of 'the strong race feeling adverse to Jamaica existing in the minds of the Bahamas peoples'.[137] This might be taken as evidence that white racial prejudice was a controlling influence in the Bahamas churches, but their membership was, in fact, overwhelmingly black. The real problem was the native ministers' jealousy of any appointment that would subject them to the authority of a non-white outsider: 'political reasons', warned Wilshere, 'make our people most apprehensive of a transfer to Jamaica'.[138] He urged the Society not to proceed with its proposed transfer without first sending Baynes on a deputation visit to the whole West Indian field. In the event, the Society sent, not Baynes, but East from Jamaica, who was strongly committed to the cause of BMS withdrawal, and no friend of Wilshere's. East visited the Turks and Caicos and San Domingo missions, and reported to the Committee accordingly.[139]

In the light of Wilshere's opposition and East's report, the Society lowered its sights somewhat, and in 1891 opened negotiations with the JBMS for the transfer of the Turks and Caicos Islands and San Domingo missions to Jamaican control. The JBMS was willing to undertake super-

135. H/31, Baynes to Arthington, 30 Sept. 1885.

136. WI/4, East to Baynes, 5 Sept. 1888.

137. Western Sub-Committee Minute Book 7, pp. 94-5, minutes for 19 June 1888.

138. WI/13, draft paper by Wilshere to BMS Committee, n.d. [1889]; see also WI/4, Wilshere to East, 4 Mar. 1889.

139. WI/4, East to Baynes, 19 Nov. 1888; *BM* 81 (1889), 187; *BM* 82 (1890), 191. It would appear that East decided that a visit to the main Bahamas mission was pointless in view of Wilshere's known opposition to the transfer.

vision for four years, but not to bear any financial responsibility. If the missions were not self-supporting at the end of the four years, further BMS aid would be expected.[140] These terms were unacceptable to the BMS.[141] As a separate matter, the JBMS had requested that the BMS send a deputation to Jamaica to interest the churches in the forthcoming BMS centenary and promote offerings for the Congo mission. On the recommendation of the Society's centenary sub-committee, it was agreed that the Jamaican request be granted, and that a deputation be sent to the United States and the West Indies with three purposes: to seek the support of the American Baptist Missionary Union for the BMS centenary appeal; to interest the Jamaican churches in the centenary; and to visit all the West Indies stations with a view to advising the Committee on the future of the Bahamas mission and the proposed transfer of the Turks Island, Caicos and San Domingo missions to the Jamaica Society.[142] At this stage there was no specific mention of the Trinidad mission. However, by 22 October, the stated objects of the deputation included the establishing of arrangements which would lead to the West Indian stations becoming 'quite independent of help from the Society'.[143] The instructions issued to the deputation in January 1892 accordingly included a paragraph requesting them to see whether a sliding scale of support could be introduced that would leave the Trinidad churches self-supporting within a few years.[144]

The deputation comprised J. G. Greenhough, minister of Victoria Road, Leicester, and John Bailey, minister of Glossop Road, Sheffield. The first stage of their tour, to the United States, proved singularly unproductive. Their hopes for contributions to the centenary fund from rich American Baptists were disappointed. Their efforts to reach an amicable parting settlement with Daniel Wilshere, who had left the Bahamas following illness and a damaging split in the Nassau church, proved unavailing. On arrival in the Bahamas, they found the Nassau church, which Underhill in 1860 had described as ripe for self-support, so weakened by the division that it was in no condition to assume independent status. Everywhere Greenhough and Bailey were staggered by the poverty of the people - 'poor in a sense which that word does not convey to us'. The Baptist congregations were almost entirely composed of blacks, and thus had no

140. Western Sub-Committee Minute Book 8, pp. 140-4, minutes for 16 June 1891.

141. Ibid., pp. 180-1, minutes for 15 Sept. 1891.

142. BMS Committee Minutes, 15 Sept. 1891, pp. 6-11.

143. Western Sub-Committee Minute Book 8, pp. 207-8, minutes for 22 Oct. 1891.

144. BMS Committee Minutes, 1891-2, pp. 145-6, minutes for 18 Jan. 1892.

hope of financial self-support in the foreseeable future. The native pastors were worthy but incompetent, and had suffered from Wilshere's inability to exercise adequate supervision over eighty-six churches. The deputation could see but two options open to the home Committee: either to abandon the work to an inevitable continued decline, or to prosecute the mission vigorously with two or three missionaries. The former course seemed heartless; the latter Greenhough and Bailey hesitated to recommend, knowing that it flew in the face of their instructions. Nevertheless, they did so.[145]

The deputation confirmed Wilshere's view that Jamaican supervision of the Bahamas mission was out of the question, in view of the universal preference of the blacks for a white ministry, and their 'strong prejudice' against Calabar College. Such prejudices did not, however, exist in the churches on Grand Turk Island and San Domingo. After consultation with the Committee of the JBMS, Greenhough and Bailey recommended that these missions be transferred to the JBMS, though endorsing the Committee's stipulation that BMS funding for seven years would be needed to bring the churches to independence.[146]

Even in Jamaica, the predominant impression made on the deputation was of the poverty of the people. The island's contributions to the BMS centenary fund were likely to amount to no more than £250, a sum made up of thousands of gifts, almost entirely in copper. English eyes, commented Greenhough and Bailey, might despise this sum, but 'we who have seen in what indigence these people live put a higher estimate upon it'.[147]

In Trinidad, which Bailey alone visited, the picture was similar. The Port of Spain church, one of the largest on the island, and certainly the wealthiest, had fewer than twenty whites in its membership of 134; the remainder were nearly all 'very poor', many of them continually seeking charity from church funds. Bailey's verdict on the sixteen churches in the south of the island was discouraging: 'our work here is very difficult and peculiar'. The missionary, William Williams, was inappropriately stationed at San Fernando, where he could exercise little influence on the churches in the Company villages. Even in these settlements, Bailey questioned how much good the Society had done. Elsewhere, the impact of the mission had been minimal. His report made no recommendations, but simply listed

145. Reports of Committee and Abstracts for 1892-3, J. G. Greenhough and J. Bailey, Report on the West Indian Missions of the BMS, pp. 3-7.

146. Ibid., pp. 8-9.

147. Ibid., pp. 9-10.

four points for the attention of the BMS Committee. Among them was a request from Williams for another missionary to be appointed to the southern district, and the need for funds for a new chapel building at Princes Town.[148] Bailey's report could be interpreted as an implicit endorsement of the case for withdrawal.[149] More plausible, however, is the supposition that Bailey, by letting the facts of the weakness of the Trinidad mission speak for themselves, was attempting to convince the Committee that the prospect of a self-supporting church was as hopelessly unrealistic in Trinidad as in the Bahamas.

Most sections of the deputation report were considered at a joint meeting of the Western and finance sub-committees on 7 October 1892. Wherever its recommendations departed from the course already decided on by the General Committee, they were repudiated or ignored. In the case of the Bahamas, the meeting expressed its inability to see why self-support was impossible for the BMS churches, when the native Baptist churches had been self-supporting for years. C. A. Dann, appointed by the Society to succeed Wilshere in the Nassau pastorate, was to be supported for two years only, after which all the Bahamas churches were to be thrown on to their own resources. Dann was authorized to inform the Bahamas churches that the Society was prepared, for the next four years, to finance the training of suitable candidates for the ministry at Calabar College, and to encourage the churches to form a connection with the Jamaica Baptist Union, with an eventual view to the formation of a West Indian Baptist Union. The recommendation that the Turks and Caicos Islands mission should be transferred to the JBMS was accepted, but the Jamaican insistence on seven years of BMS guaranteed support was rejected in favour of a four-year period of decreasing aid, terminating in complete withdrawal.[150]

Bailey's report on Trinidad was considered at a further meeting on 20 December. If, as has been suggested, Bailey had calculated on jolting the Committee into an awareness of the depressing realities of the Trinidad mission, his stratagem sadly misfired. The reaction of the joint sub-committees was to deplore the 'sad lack of spiritual force and aggressive ability' shown by the Trinidadian churches. The tonic prescribed for this deficiency in aggressive spirit was the same as for the other West Indian missions: financial support would be gradually withdrawn over a four-year period, during which the Society would again pay the expenses at Calabar

148. Ibid., J. Bailey, Report on the Mission in Trinidad, pp. 13-18.

149. As does Brewer, 'The Baptist churches of south Trinidad', 159.

150. Western Sub-Committee Minute Book 9, pp. 60-72, minutes for 7 Oct. 1892.

College of a few suitable Trinidadian candidates for the ministry.[151] This last proposal was as unrealistic in Trinidad as it was in the Bahamas.[152]

The recommendations of the Western and finance sub-committees were adopted without amendment by the General Committee at its meetings on 15 November and 20 December.[153] The decisions reached in the final three months of 1892 thus brought about the speedy and total withdrawal of the Society from the whole West Indies field, with the exception of its support for Calabar College.[154]

It is hard to imagine a more comprehensive repudiation of the report of an official deputation than was witnessed in October 1892. Greenhough and Bailey had presented the Society with a stark choice between abandoning the West Indian missions to further decline, and committing substantially increased missionary resources to those parts of the West Indian field which had no reasonable prospect of effective support from Jamaica. The second option was never seriously considered by a Committee which had long since determined that the West Indies could not be permitted to divert resources from Africa and the East. Yet the Committee persisted in adhering to the delusion that withdrawal would propel the weaker Caribbean churches to a magical and rapid maturity. Those who had visited the field and seen for themselves the poverty both of economic resources and of spiritual leadership available to those churches knew better. The nineteenth-century history of the BMS West Indian mission thus suggests that, amongst missionary policy-makers in London, a fervent belief in the creation of an autonomous church as the overriding goal of missionary activity survived right into the 1890s to a greater extent than some earlier writing on the missionary movement implied.[155] It also suggests that, if Western missions have been guilty of dominating the will of the younger churches, their failure has not always consisted in clinging to power when control should have been relinquished: the weakness of BMS policy in the Caribbean lay rather in the insistence on imposing autonomy on churches which had never received the financial and spiritual resources to make maturity possible.

151. Ibid., pp. 95-7, minutes for 20 Dec. 1892.

152. Brewer, 'The Baptist churches of south Trinidad', 149.

153. BMS Committee Minutes, 15 Nov. 1892, pp. 446-56; 20 Dec. 1892, pp. 2-5.

154. *BM* 85 (1893), 223-6.

155. To a lesser extent, the same conclusion emerges from recent writing on the CMS. See C. P. Williams, *The Ideal of the Self-Governing Church* (Leiden, 1990).

IV

Cameroons and the Congo, 1841-1914

I: Fernando Po and the Cameroons, 1841-1887

The BMS West Indian mission can claim to have been one of the progenitors of the campaign to end slavery within the British empire. Emancipation in the British West Indies did not, however, signal the end of the Atlantic slave trade or of the determination of British Christians to see it halted. The continuing humanitarian crusade against slavery became in its turn the catalyst for a new BMS mission to West Africa.

Among the liberated slaves in membership with the Baptist churches of Jamaica there rapidly developed a keen desire to bring the gospel to their native continent of Africa. BMS missionaries encouraged the Jamaican churches to think in these terms, and in 1839-40 Knibb, Burchell and other members of the Jamaica mission sought to persuade the BMS Committee to establish a new West African mission staffed primarily by West Indian Christians.[1] The Committee was initially hesitant, and it is possible that no initiative would have been taken had it not been for the wave of enthusiasm on behalf of West Africa which swept through the evangelical world in 1840. That enthusiasm had been unleashed by the plans of Thomas Fowell Buxton, successor to William Wilberforce as leader of the anti-slavery lobby, for a British expedition to the Niger River intended to extinguish the slave trade at its source. Buxton had reached the conclusion that the trade would never be eliminated solely by the activity of British naval squadrons patrolling the West African coast; rather he looked to a blend of civilization, commerce and Christianity as the medicine for Africa's sickness. The expedition would open the way for missionaries, godly traders, and agriculturalists to administer the medicine. The Bible and the plough would together regenerate Africa. Buxton held a great public meeting at Exeter

---

1. Hinton, *Memoir of William Knibb*, 275-80; BMS Committee Minutes, 11 Apr. 1839, pp. 185-6, 28 May 1840, p. 62.

Hall on 1 June 1840 to publicize his project. The attention of all the missionary societies was directed to West Africa as never before.[2] It was surely no coincidence that two days later the BMS Committee resolved, 'in compliance with the representations of our brethren in Jamaica, and following what we apprehend to be the clear indications of Providence', to commence a mission in West Africa.[3]

The Society determined to send an expedition to explore the possibilities for a mission on the Niger, and appointed for the task a Jamaica Baptist minister, John Clarke, and a doctor practising in Jamaica, G. K. Prince. Clarke and Prince sailed from London for Africa on a vessel carrying coals for Buxton's expedition, and arrived at the island of Fernando Po on 1 January 1841. Fernando Po was merely a stopping-off point en route for the Niger, but Clarke and Prince received such a warm reception from the governor of the British naval base at Clarence, and found the freed slaves who colonized the settlement so open to the gospel, that they recommended to the Society that its base station for the new mission should be located there. They also crossed to the Cameroonian mainland and established contact with the principal chiefs. After fourteen months Clarke and Prince left for home, persuaded, in the absence of any opening to proceed to the Niger according to the original plan, that the BMS should commence work in Fernando Po and the Cameroons.[4]

The vessel carrying Clarke and Prince back to England was blown off course by storms, and ended up off the West Indies. The missionaries were thus able to visit the Jamaican churches and recruit volunteers for the African mission. On returning to England in September 1842, they reported to the Committee and pressed the claims of the new mission before the Baptist public. As a result, four couples offered themselves to the Society; among them was Alfred Saker, a draughtsman at the Admiralty dockyard at Devonport, and his wife Helen. In August 1843 the Sakers and John Clarke sailed in the *Chilmark* for Jamaica to assemble the West Indian missionary party, while Prince and the other recruits sailed direct to Fernando Po. The Jamaican volunteers, with their families, amounted to forty-two persons; the better educated among them were to serve as teachers, the remainder were simply settlers, intended to form the nucleus

2. E. Stock, *The History of the Church Missionary Society* (4 vols., London, 1899-1916), i, 451-4; P. D. Curtin, *The Image of Africa* (Madison, 1964), 298-313.

3. BMS Committee Minutes, 3 June 1840, pp. 64-5.

4. Cox, *History of the BMS*, ii, 353-72; BMS Committee Minutes, 6 Aug. 1840, p. 96; 20 May 1841, pp. 192-3; 25. Nov. 1841, p. 20; 29 Sept. 1842, p. 182.

of the first Christian community. The *Chilmark* reached Fernando Po in February 1844.

The missionaries found the community at Clarence, composed as it was largely of freed slaves and other black immigrants, receptive to the Christian message. Saker's first convert at Clarence, Thomas Horton Johnson, became the first African pastor of the Bethel church in Cameroons Town (now Douala) on the mainland.[5] But the missionaries' chief concern was to reach the indigenous peoples of the Cameroons mainland, and these presented a much more formidable challenge. When Saker and Johnson took up residence at King A'kwa's town (Cameroons Town) on the Cameroons estuary on 16 June 1845, they found themselves amongst a people whose way of life contravened almost every Victorian notion of what constituted civilization and decency. Some of the tribes were cannibalistic, inter-tribal warfare was endemic, and total nudity was normal. They were, wrote E. B. Underhill in his biography of Saker, 'utterly barbarous, practising the wildest and most debasing superstitions, and given up to the practice of every vice that degrades humanity'.[6] For two years Saker preached to an audience that was at best uninterested and at worst non-existent. He had to wait till November 1849 for his first baptism and the formation of a church comprising Alfred and Helen Saker, Johnson and his wife, and the first Douala convert.[7]

Slow missionary progress was not the only discouragement to confront Saker and his colleagues. *The Times* described Fernando Po in 1848 as 'the most pestiferous land which the universe is known to contain', and its fever-ridden reputation proved well-deserved.[8] Saker lost his infant daughter in July 1844, and had to send his wife and second child home for recuperation in February 1847. By mid-1848 Saker had seen two missionary colleagues die and two others (one of them G. K. Prince) invalided home. The mission seemed on the point of collapse, and Saker was compelled to leave Cameroons Town to fill the gaps at Clarence. European mortality had, however, been anticipated. The mission had been staffed chiefly by Jamaican recruits on the basis of the then prevalent supposition that black people possessed a racial immunity to the fevers of the African climate. The discovery that this was very far from being the case proved demoralizing for

5.   On Johnson see *MH* (Aug. 1866), 526; J. van Slageren, *Les Origines de l'Eglise Evangélique du Cameroun* (Leiden, 1972), 25-6.

6.   E. B. Underhill, *Alfred Saker* (London, 1884), 31.

7.   Ibid., 36, 53-5.

8.   Cited in Curtin, *The Image of Africa*, 343-4.

the Jamaican party. Depressed spirits became dissatisfied ones as a result of poor management of the settler community. The settlers were all quartered within the mission site at Clarence, rather than being encouraged to set up their own small-holdings. Those who were teachers expected to be awarded equal status to the European missionaries, and were disgruntled when they were not. The settlers for their part 'felt that they were in the same position as the Teachers', and were similarly disappointed.[9] The outcome was that John Clarke led the majority of the Jamaicans home in 1848; the vision of a West Indian mission to Africa had failed.

Happily, the failure was not total. The Jamaican, Joseph Merrick, who, with his wife, accompanied Dr and Mrs Prince to Fernando Po in 1843, began work among the Isubu people at Bimbia in 1845. Although Bimbia proved a less productive field for church planting than Cameroons Town, Merrick made excellent progress in language work, translating Genesis, Exodus, Matthew, and John into Isubu, and preparing an Isubu dictionary. Merrick's work laid the foundations for Saker's translation of the Bible into the related Douala language, which he completed in 1872. Merrick himself died at sea on his way to England in October 1849.[10]

Merrick's contribution was brief but significant. Of more enduring importance to the survival of the Cameroons church was the work of Joseph Jackson Fuller. Fuller, born a slave in Jamaica, came to West Africa in 1845 to join his father Alexander, who had arrived with the Princes and Merricks in 1843. J. J. Fuller was accepted by the BMS as a full missionary in 1850, and served the Baptist cause in the Cameroons until his retirement in 1888. At a time when members of the Baptist public appear to have been on the point of abandoning the Cameroons mission as a lost cause, it was Fuller who pleaded with them not to lose heart at the high mortality and slow progress of the mission; the Committee was sufficiently impressed to publish Fuller's appeal in the *Missionary Herald*.[11] In a context where European missionaries came and went with some rapidity, it was Fuller, even more than Saker, who provided continuity and stability. After 1858, those qualities became needed as never before.

The British had abandoned their naval base at Fernando Po in 1845, and thereby afforded the Spanish government the opportunity to implement Spain's long-standing claim to the island. Until 1858 the Spanish authori-

9. A/5, 'Cameroons and Fernando Po. Notes by Mr Fuller and Mr Grenfell', 6-8.

10. On Merrick see *BM* 42 (1850), 197-204, 265-70; van Slageren, *Les Origines*, 21-3, 31.

11. *MH* (Mar. 1852), 185-6; cf. van Slageren, *Les Origines*, 28.

ties did relatively little to hamper BMS work at Fernando Po, but in May of that year all public worship of any religion apart from the Roman Catholic faith was prohibited. Saker therefore resolved to look for a site for a new settlement to replace Clarence in which freedom of religion could be secured. He selected a site at Ambas Bay, and named his settlement 'Victoria'. Saker's dream was that Victoria should become a haven of Protestant liberty, and a centre whence commerce, civilization and Christianity might advance into the interior.[12] The ideals which animated both Buxton's Niger expedition in 1840-2 and now David Livingstone's project to introduce commerce and Christianity to East Africa via the Zambezi, also provided the inspiration for Saker's plans for a Christian colony at Victoria. Saker hoped that Victoria would serve the British government as a naval base and in due course become a British colony. The reality of Victoria never matched his vision. Ambas Bay was unsuitable as a deep-water harbour, and the Foreign Office was content to leave Victoria as a purely nominal colony, administered by the senior BMS missionary as 'Governor' - a denial of Baptist principles on church and state which caused some embarrassment to the missionaries.[13] More seriously, many of the Fernando Po free negroes refused to follow Saker to Victoria; by 1862 only eighty-two persons had settled at Victoria, half of them school-children.[14] Nevertheless, a Baptist church was established there, and here Thomas Comber began his missionary career in 1876.

Expulsion from Fernando Po was in fact the least of the problems which faced the BMS in the Cameroons after 1858. In 1859 a new recruit arrived in the shape of Alexander Innes, a Scotsman from Liverpool and a 'Scotch Baptist' in churchmanship. Innes's coming, commented J. J. Fuller, 'was the beginning of some very dark days in the Mission and for the little church'.[15] Innes speedily fell out with Saker, accusing him of tyrannical behaviour towards his black colleagues and of excessive expenditure. The dispute was referred to the Committee, which promptly recalled Innes for consultations. A sub-committee interviewed Innes in February 1860, and

12. Underhill, *Alfred Saker,* 87-95.

13. Saker's regulations for the colony provided for a Governor as representative of the owners, who, in the absence of British annexation, remained the BMS. See Underhill, *Alfred Saker,* 170; T. Lewis, *These Seventy Years* (2nd edn., London, 1930), 44, 52.

14. Underhill, *Alfred Saker,* 117; see also H. H. Johnston, *George Grenfell and the Congo* (2 vols., London, 1908), i, 37.

15. A/5, MS Autobiography of J. J. Fuller, 73. The 'Scotch Baptists' had founded several churches in Lancashire. They were strongly opposed to an ordained, 'one-man' ministry. (See above, ch. I, p. 32).

Alfred Saker, Missionary in the Cameroons, 1844-1876.

Joseph Jackson Fuller, Missionary in the Cameroons, 1850-88.

Thomas Comber, Missionary in the Cameroons and Congo, 1876-87

Thomas Lewis, Missionary in the Cameroons and Congo, 1883-1915.

reported to the BMS Committee on 12 March.[16] As a result, Innes was dismissed, and Saker reassured that the Committee regarded Innes's charges, 'in so far as they affect Mr Saker's moral character', as 'utterly unfounded'. Nevertheless, the Committee suggested to Saker that he should consider 'whether a modification of his treatment and employment of the natives may not now have become expedient'. In communicating this resolution to Saker, Frederick Trestrail, the joint-secretary of the Society, revealed that, even before Innes's arrival in the Cameroons, he had received a letter from sixteen Africans, complaining of harsh treatment by Saker. Although dismissing Innes's more sweeping charges, the Committee had come to appreciate that Saker's position in Cameroons Town, attempting to run a Christian community 'without police, court, magistrate or judge', carried with it peculiar temptations.[17]

Unfortunately for the BMS, Innes's dismissal did not mark the end of the affair. In 1862 Innes enlisted the public support of John Clarke and C. H. Spurgeon in his campaign against Saker, and published a savage pamphlet repeating his allegations against Saker, and printing the letters of complaint from Cameroonian Christians of which the Committee was already aware.[18] The Committee published a statement in the *Missionary Herald* defending Saker, but wrote privately to Saker, requesting him to return to England for consultation.[19] He arrived home in July 1863, and had two interviews with the Western sub-committee. The sub-committee produced a nineteen-page report, which again concluded that the charges levelled against Saker were 'in the main unfounded'. However, it was clear that relationships between Saker and his fellow-missionaries were strained, and the report made various recommendations designed to diminish the exceptional authority which Saker possessed over the affairs of the Cameroons mission.[20] Saker returned to Africa in September 1864.

The Committee's hopes for improved relationships within the Africa mission were disappointed. Saker found himself repeatedly out-voted by his

16.   A/1, 'Transactions of the Committee ... with Mr A. Innes'.

17.   [F. Trestrail] to Saker, 12 Mar. 1860, in W. Indies and Africa Sub-Committee Reports (Acc. No. 219).

18.   A. Innes, *Cruelties Committed on the West Coast of Africa by an Agent of the Baptist Mission* ... (London, 1862).

19.   *MH* (Mar. 1862), 192-3; BMS Committee Minutes, 9 July 1862, p. 183; Underhill, *Alfred Saker*, 123.

20.   Report dated 15 Sept. 1863, in W. Indies and Africa Sub-Committee Reports (Acc. No. 219).

colleagues, following the implementation of a recommendation made by the 1863 report that all policy decisions should be taken by a meeting of the entire missionary staff. Disagreement focused on his concentration on 'civilizing' the Douala by encouraging industry and commerce, which his colleagues regarded as a diversion from the priority of evangelism.[21] Complaints from R. Smith and Q. W. Thomson (who, with the Jamaicans Fuller and F. Pinnock, were Saker's only remaining colleagues) compelled the Committee in November 1868 to recall Saker once more. Saker had two interviews with the Western sub-committee in July 1869, but their 'unsatisfactory' outcome determined the BMS Committee to send E. B. Underhill as a deputation to the Cameroons.[22]

Underhill and his wife accordingly accompanied the Sakers on their return to Africa at the end of the year. The course of the deputation visit was transformed by the sudden death of Mrs Underhill at Cameroons Town. The tragedy effected what Underhill would have struggled to achieve by diplomacy. Fuller's account is ungrammatical but moving: 'The differences which existed was brought to a termination by her death all agreeing to bury all the unpleasantness in the grave with her and thus ended what at first seem an unending trouble'.[23]

Underhill's report to the BMS Committee in June 1870 once again supported Saker's policy, but the heat had gone out of the controversy amidst the expectation of a happier future for the Africa mission.[24] Innes continued his personal vendetta against Saker for years to come. He responded to the publication of the BMS *Centenary Volume* in 1892 with a series of published letters hostile to the Society, which formed the basis of a vitriolic 'biography' of Saker, published in 1895.[25] Innes's credibility is certainly suspect, yet Saker cannot be wholly exonerated of those charges which were confirmed by other, more reputable sources. There is no doubt that Saker had authoritarian tendencies which were given free rein in a context where the senior missionary exercised jurisdictional authority over

21. Underhill, *Alfred Saker*, 136-9.

22. Western Sub-Committee Minutes, 23 June, 15 Sept. 1868, 28 June, 5, 12 July, 27 Sept. 1869; BMS Committee Minutes, 17 Nov. 1868, p. 500, 7 Oct. 1869, pp. 96-7.

23. A/5, MS Autobiography of J. J. Fuller, 133.

24. BMS Committee Minutes, 28 June 1870, pp. 214-16; cf. Underhill, *Alfred Saker*, 139-40.

25. A. Innes, *More Light ... The Only True Biography of Alfred Saker and his Cruelties* (Birkenhead, 1895).

the Christian community. The character who emerges with greatest credit from these years is J. J. Fuller - who clearly suffered from Saker's regime, yet refused to contemplate breaking his connection with the BMS (as Saker's opponents urged him to do), and as an old man defended Saker's memory against Innes's wilder statements.[26] The Society could have wished for no more faithful servant to guide the Cameroons church through the new challenges which confronted it in the 1880s.

On 12 July 1884 King Bell of the Cameroons signed a treaty with the German agent Nachtigal, ceding sovereignty of a large tract of the Cameroons to Bismarck's Germany. The Western powers were 'scrambling' to partition Africa amongst themselves, and by March 1885 the British government had made it plain that Germany would be given a free hand in the Cameroons. On 22 April the BMS Committee noted that the British decision had 'greatly aggravated the difficulties of the situation', and authorized Alfred Baynes, the General Secretary, to conduct such negotiations with the Foreign Office as seemed prudent.[27] The future of the Cameroons mission looked distinctly uncertain, and in late September Baynes received a letter from Friedrich Fabri, the German missionary strategist and colonial enthusiast, recommending that the BMS hand over its Cameroons mission to the Basel Mission.[28] The Basel Mission drew its support chiefly from Lutheran pietists in Wurttemberg, and already worked on the Gold Coast (Ghana). With Baynes's approval, Fabri raised the suggestion at a conference on missions to the new German colonies held in Bremen in October. The conference warmly endorsed the proposal, and asked the BMS not to negotiate with any other missionary body until the Basel Mission had come to its own decision, following the despatch of a commission of enquiry to the Cameroons. On 15 December the BMS Committee considered two reports on the matter. The first, from the finance sub-committee, urged the Committee first to decide in principle whether the BMS was prepared to transfer the Cameroons mission to a German missionary organization. The second, from the Western sub-committee, expressed the view that the completion of German control of the Cameroons and the enforced use of the German language in the colony made a transfer of the BMS mission to some evangelical German mission the wisest course, and accordingly recommended the Committee to respond in the affirmative to the question posed by the finance sub-

26.   Fuller's MS Autobiography, 132; Innes, *More Light,* 15-17, 21.

27.   BMS Committee Minutes, 22 Apr. 1885, pp. 238-9.

28.   H/25, Fabri to Baynes, 23 Sept. 1885.

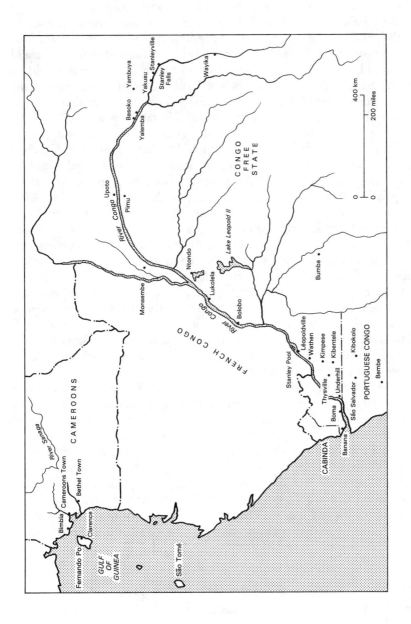

Map 3: The Cameroons and Congo Missions in the Late Nineteenth Century.

committee. The Committee accepted the recommendation.[29]

By 15 December 1885, therefore, the BMS had committed itself to withdrawal from the Cameroons, and indicated its willingness to hand over the mission to the Basel Mission, provided that adequate guarantees could be obtained that the Baptist principles of the native churches would be respected. However, some members of the Committee felt uneasy about the proposed transfer of the work to a mission so closely identified with the predominantly Lutheran state churches of Germany. Their spokesman was Alfred Tilly, pastor of Tredegarville Baptist Church in Cardiff, and founder and first secretary of the Livingstone Inland Mission to the Congo. Tilly had on his own initiative written several letters to German Baptist leaders, inquiring whether the German Baptists would be prepared to assume responsibility for the Cameroons churches, if the BMS were to offer £750 per annum in support. At its meeting on 20 January 1886 the BMS Committee considered a report from the finance sub-committee which presented three replies from German Baptist leaders to Tilly's overtures. The German Baptist Union had indicated its willingness to take over the mission, but only on condition that the BMS supplied a subsidy of at least £1,000 for ten years. The Committee accepted the recommendations of both the finance and Western sub-committees that this was too high a price to pay, and as a result the negotiations with the Basel Mission went ahead.[30] The Basel Mission undertook not to impose Lutheran convictions on the Cameroonian Baptists, and in October 1886 the two societies reached agreement in principle over the transfer.

The Society's refusal of the approach from the German Baptists might appear strange, in view of the fact that annual expenditure on the Cameroons mission had been running at between two and four times the amount of subsidy which the Germans requested. But the Baptist denomination in Germany was still very young, short of money, and without a missionary organization of any kind. It is also clear that Baynes, at least, felt that the new BMS mission on the Congo was the Society's first priority in Africa, and demanded all available resources.[31] With hindsight, however, some members of the Society may well have regretted the decision. The transfer of BMS property to the Basel Mission (at a price of £2,000) did not proceed smoothly, and proved a tricky assignment for J. J. Fuller as the senior BMS

29. BMS Committee Minutes, 15 Dec. 1885, pp. 426-35, 440.

30. H/23, Tilly to Baynes, 21 Dec. 1885; BMS Committee Minutes, 20 Jan. 1886, pp. 466-75.

31. H/25, Baynes to Ochler, 24 Mar. 1886.

representative. George Grenfell told Baynes in 1887 that 'no other man could have fought the battle as he has done'.[32] More seriously, relationships between the Baptist congregations and the Basel missionaries proved far from harmonious. The problem was not baptism in itself, but ecclesiology: congregational independency was a notion wholly alien to these missionaries. As a result, first the Bethel church in Douala in 1888, and then the Victoria church in 1889, severed all connection with the Basel Mission. In 1890, following appeals for help from the Cameroons, the German Baptists formed a committee to aid the Cameroonian churches, and in 1891 the first German Baptist missionaries arrived. The Germans formalized their work in the Cameroons in January 1898 by the formation of the *Missions-Gesellschaft der deutschen Baptisten.*[33]

For a brief period after the First World War it appeared that the BMS connection with the Cameroons might be revived. German missionaries were expelled from Germany's former colony, the BMS was asked to take over the work, and Thomas Lewis and L. C. Parkinson went to the country in 1921 on an exploratory visit. In the event, the negotiations necessary for the resumption of BMS work came to a standstill in 1922, the German missionaries were allowed to return, and were joined later by American Baptists.[34] By the late twentieth century, Baptists in the Cameroons formed one of the largest Protestant communities. Despite all the difficulties of the Saker years, a church had been planted which later grew to maturity.

II: The Origins of the Congo Mission, 1873-1880

On 1 May 1873 David Livingstone was found dead by his bedside at Chitambo in northern Zambia. In September 1877 the *Missionary Herald* carried on its front cover the stirring slogan 'Africa for Christ'. Livingstone had not lived to see the coming of Protestant missions to the Congo basin, but he was in a real sense the originator of the advance by Christian missionaries into the heart of Africa. He had been the unceasing advocate of a policy of continual missionary progress into the central African interior, believing that only thus would the slave trade be overcome and the gospel spread sufficiently broadly for African peoples at some future date to

---

32. A/19, Grenfell to Baynes, 20 Sept. 1887.

33. Van Slageren, *Les Origines*, 47-52; L. E. Kwast, *The Discipling of West Cameroon* (Grand Rapids, 1971) 81-6.

34. Lewis, *These Seventy Years*, 289-95. General Committee minutes, 22 Apr. 1921, p. 22; 13 July 1921, p. 45; 12 July 1922, p. 81; 22 Nov. 1922, p. 120.

respond en masse to Christianity. Furthermore, those who were dispatched to search for Livingstone during his final elusive years in Africa found themselves drawn by their quest into the exploration of the Congo basin. Lieutenant Grandy, sent out by the Royal Geographical Society in 1872, advanced from the mouth of the Congo river to São Salvador (Mbanza Kongo), the capital of the ancient Kongo kingdom. From the other side of the continent, Lieutenant Cameron succeeded in reaching Nyangwe on the Lualaba river, and returned convinced that the Lualaba was a head-water, not of the Nile, as Livingstone had believed, but of the Congo. Most important of all, H. M. Stanley, fired by the example of Livingstone, returned to Africa in 1875, and in 1877 successfully followed the Congo river all the way from Nyangwe to Boma, thus proving Cameron right.

Stanley arrived at Boma on 8 August 1877. The news of his success did not reach London till mid-September. On 11 July the BMS Committee had decided to accept an offer of £1,000 from Robert Arthington of Leeds for the purpose of establishing a mission on the Congo river.[35] Arthington was a wealthy recluse, a Quaker by upbringing, but by now Baptist in his leanings.[36] A passionate enthusiast for all things missionary, Arthington had followed the journeys of Grandy and Cameron with interest, and his offer to the BMS had assumed, as if it were beyond argument, that the Lualaba and Congo were one.[37] The news of Stanley's exploits thus merely set the seal on an enterprise to which the Society had already committed itself. The Committee decided as a first step to ask Thomas Comber and George Grenfell, two young missionaries who had already made their mark as pioneers of the Cameroons interior, to undertake an exploratory journey to the Congo. Arthington's £1,000 arrived in November, but the cost of Comber and Grenfell's expedition was met by a gift of £500 from Charles Wathen, a Bristol businessman.[38]

Comber and Grenfell received the Committee's request on 5 January 1878. They immediately signified their acceptance of the commission, and, without waiting for further instructions, boarded a mail steamer bound for the mouth of the Congo, which happened to arrive within the next few days. This initial flying visit lasted less than a month, as the rainy season was about

35.   BMS Committee Minutes, 11 July 1877, pp. 199-200.

36.   On Arthington see B. Stanley, 'The Miser of Headingley', in W. J. Sheils and D. Wood (eds.), *The Church and Wealth* (Studies in Church History 24; Oxford, 1987), 371-82.

37.   G. Hawker, *The Life of George Grenfell* (London, 1909), 93-5.

38.   BMS Committee Minutes, 8 Oct. 1877, pp. 257-8.

to commence and the mail steamer made its return voyage to the Cameroons at the beginning of February. The two missionaries were nonetheless able to visit Banana, Boma and Musuku, and leave a letter for the king of the Kongo at São Salvador, informing him that they would return to visit him.[39]

The BMS was not the only society concerned to penetrate the heart of Africa via the Congo river. On 28 February the first two missionaries of the Livingstone Inland Mission landed at the mouth of the Congo. The LIM owed its origins to Alfred Tilly, a member of the BMS Committee who seems to have feared that the BMS might be content to remain on the coast. The Mission was financed by a small group of businessmen known to Tilly, and was to draw many of its candidates from Henry Grattan Guinness's East London Institute for Home and Foreign Mission. Although comparable in many ways to Hudson Taylor's China Inland Mission, the LIM also owed much to the ideals of Livingstone himself. The LIM was originally intended to be entirely self-supporting, financed by the commercial activities of a series of Christian colonies along the Congo river.[40] Its first two stations, at Matadi and Palabala, antedated BMS work on the Congo, and for some years the LIM was the dominant missionary force on the Congo. By September 1882 the LIM had sent out thirty-seven missionaries, compared to the BMS total of nine.[41]

Comber and Grenfell returned to the Congo at the beginning of July 1878 for their official reconnaissance expedition, accompanied by eight African helpers. They were well received at São Salvador by the king (Ntotela), Dom Pedro V, and travelled on to Tungwa, the centre of the Makuta country. But the principal chief of the Makuta refused them leave to proceed any further towards their ultimate goal of the upper river, and they returned to São Salvador, having at least decided that this should be the site of the first BMS station.

At São Salvador on 20 August Grenfell wrote to the BMS resigning from the Society. His biographers understandably offer no explanation. Grenfell had left the Cameroons on 28 June knowing that Rose Edgerley, his young Jamaican housekeeper and a member of the Victoria church, was pregnant

39. Hawker, *Life of Grenfell*, 99-102; J. B. Myers, *Thomas J. Comber* (3rd edn, London, n.d.), 70-2.

40. F. E. Guinness, *The First Christian Mission on the Congo* (4th edn., London, n.d. [1882]), 35-41.

41. W. H. Bentley, *Pioneering on the Congo* (2 vols.; London, 1900), ii, 13; the fullest account of the LIM is in D. Lagergren, *Mission and State in the Congo: A Study of the Relations Between Protestant Missions and the Congo Independent State Authorities with Special Reference to the Equator District* (Uppsala, 1970).

and that he was the father. The affair had become known, and on 10 July Q. W. Thomson, the senior Cameroons missionary, wrote a distraught letter to Alfred Baynes giving him the news. Thomson was reluctant to believe the truth, and wrote again on 22 July, reporting that he had made further enquiries, but that no doubt was possible.[42] A letter from Comber, written from São Salvador on 9 August, provided further confirmation.[43] With this correspondence before it, the BMS Committee on 19 November accepted Grenfell's resignation and terminated his connection with the Society.[44] Grenfell had promised Rose he would return to marry her, and hence sailed direct from the Congo for Victoria, where his daughter was born. For two years he worked for a commercial concern in Victoria.

Thomas Comber returned to England to report to the Committee, saddened by the 'heavy loss' which the mission had sustained.[45] On 15 January 1879 the Committee accepted the recommendation of the Western sub-committee that Comber should return to Africa in April, if possible with two colleagues, to establish a base station at São Salvador, 'having always in view, reaching the interior of the Continent of Africa by the waterway of the mighty Congo river'.[46] In fact, the two colleagues became three: H. E. Crudgington was accepted for service at the same meeting, and a month later W. Holman Bentley and J. S. Hartland. In addition, Comber took with him his new bride, Minnie. The party sailed from Liverpool on 25 April, and landed at Banana on 9 June.

Bentley and Crudgington reached São Salvador on 14 July, and, encouraged by the Ntotela's friendly reception, set about establishing their base station. Hartland and Comber followed later. On 24 August the mission suffered the first of its many bereavements: Minnie Comber died of cerebral malaria. Within a week of her death, Comber had set out with Hartland from São Salvador on a first attempt to press inland. As in the previous year, however, it proved impossible to advance further than Tungwa. The chiefs of the Makuta were less than friendly, and refused to let the missionaries pass. This was the first of a series of thirteen fruitless attempts by Comber to establish a route between São Salvador and the beginning of navigable

42. A/6, Thomson to Baynes, 10 and 22 July 1878.

43. A/12, Comber to Baynes, 9 Aug. 1878.

44. BMS Committee Minutes, 19 Nov. 1878, pp. 508-10. Grenfell's letter of resignation is not extant.

45. A/12, Comber to Thomson, 5 Oct. 1878.

46. BMS Committee Minutes. 15 Jan. 1879, pp. 31-2.

river at Stanley Pool. On one such journey, at Mbanza Makuta in 1880, Comber and Hartland, with their Cameroonian boy companions, were attacked. Comber was shot and wounded.[47] The root cause of the chiefs' opposition was a fear that the white men had come to usurp their trading role as middlemen. Most of the lower river peoples owed allegiance to Nga Liema, a chief at Stanley Pool who had gained control both of the ivory trade descending from the upper river, and of the lower river trading network connecting the Pool with the coast.[48] Success in reaching the Pool was not to come until 1881, and then by another route and by different means.

An even higher priority than finding a route to Stanley Pool was to establish a depot at the mouth of the Congo for the receipt and forwarding of supplies from Europe. By December 1879 Comber was writing to Baynes urging that such a depot be established at Banana, and making 'earnest request' that efforts be made to secure Grenfell's services to run it. This recommendation was accepted, apparently without any disagreement, at the meeting of the BMS Committee on 23 April 1880. Grenfell was offered the post of superintendent of the proposed Banana station at a salary of £150.[49] He responded enthusiastically, but indicated that the executors of the estate of the merchant whose business he was running would have to give their consent before he could be released. The Committee meeting on 21 September heard that Baynes had approached the executors, that Q. W. Thomson at Victoria had offered to assume temporary oversight of the business, and that on these terms the executors were prepared to release Grenfell.[50]

Thus it was that by the end of 1880 Grenfell was back on the Congo with his family, erecting the mission buildings at Musuku (found to be a preferable site to Banana), and re-admitted to the mission, albeit in a role that was at first strictly defined. If there were those who felt the decision to be precipitate, they have left no record of their views. Baynes must have regarded his decision as a calculated risk, but he never had cause to regret it.

47. Myers, *Comber*, 96-109; Bentley, *Pioneering*, i, 206-11.

48. A/31, Bentley to Baynes, 12 Aug. 1882; R. M. Slade, *English-Speaking Missions in the Congo Independent State (1878-1908)* (Brussels, 1959), 41.

49. BMS Committee Minutes, 23 Apr. 1880, pp. 349-51. Comber's letters pressing for Grenfell's re-appointment have not been preserved.

50. BMS Committee Minutes, 21 Sept. 1880, pp. 458-60.

III: Mission, Church and State on the Congo, 1880-1914

Comber and his BMS colleagues were not alone in seeking to blaze a trail between the coast and Stanley Pool. While both the BMS and the LIM were attempting the south-bank route, H. M. Stanley was pushing towards the Pool on the north bank. Stanley was in the employ of Leopold II of Belgium, who in 1876 had set up his *Association Internationale Africaine*, ostensibly to pioneer international exploration of the Congo basin, but in reality as the first step towards the creation of Leopold's personal African commercial empire - the Congo Free State. Before Stanley could reach the Pool, however, the Italian Savorgnan de Brazza, working on behalf of the French government, succeeded in making the journey in the opposite direction, from east to west, and hence established French claims to the north bank of the river. News of Brazza's success prompted Bentley and Crudgington to try the north- bank route, and on 29 January 1881 they reached the Pool - six months before Stanley's party got there.

The initial reaction of the BMS pioneers to the completion of the north-bank route was to abandon São Salvador, which had thereby lost its rationale as a base station. Only the entreaties of the Ntotela, who preferred the Baptists to the Portuguese Catholic priests who had also arrived in the Kongo kingdom, persuaded them otherwise.[51] It was a crucial decision, without which the work of the Society in Angola would never have developed. Crudgington was sent home in June with a recommendation that São Salvador be maintained, but the north-bank route to the Pool be followed. On 20 July 1881 the Committee accepted his recommendations, and agreed to establish a base station on the north bank of the Pool, with intermediate north-bank stations at Isangila and Mbu. The Committee also agreed to proceed with the construction of a steamer for the upper river, and to recall Grenfell to supervise the work.[52] Robert Arthington had first offered money for a Congo steamer in December 1877, but for a joint scheme with other missions, which never materialized. In May 1880 he had revived the idea by offering the BMS £4,000 for the purchase and upkeep of a Congo steamer, on condition that the Society should endeavour to open up a route eastwards from the upper river to meet a possible extension of the LMS Tanganyika mission.[53] The BMS accepted the offer in June 1880. The

51. H. M. Bentley, *W. Holman Bentley* (London, 1907), 88-91.
52. BMS Committee Minutes, 20 July 1881, pp. 205-9; *BMS Annual Report*, 1881-2, pp. 22-3.
53. Stanley, 'The Miser of Headingley', 378.

Committee's July 1881 decision led to the launching of the *Peace* at Stanley Pool in June 1884, and signalled the completion of Grenfell's rehabilitation. He was no longer to be the warehouseman at Musuku, but the spearhead of the Society's forward policy on the upper river.

The selection of the north-bank route to the Pool proved a mistake, owing to the difficulty of the terrain. Meanwhile, Stanley had established his force at the Pool, and thereby curbed the ability of Nga Liema to block further European advance. During 1882 the BMS accordingly reverted to the south-bank route; the base station at Musuku was moved up-river to Tunduwa (near present-day Matadi), and named 'Underhill'. The last of the north-bank stations to be abandoned was Manyanga in 1884, when 'Wathen' station was moved across the river to a new site at Ngombe Lutete. It was July 1882 before sufficient recruits were available to establish a permanent station at the Pool. 'Arthington' station was located on the south bank on land leased from Leopold's agent. The draft contract agreed by Comber committed the Society to conditions which the Committee found unacceptable - such as an undertaking not to advance ahead of the Association's agents on the upper river. These were removed only after a personal embassy by Alfred Baynes to Brussels to negotiate with Leopold's officials.[54] However, in 1886 the Arthington site was moved to a more suitable location three miles to the east in Kinshasa which survives to this day as the national headquarters of the *Communauté Baptiste du Fleuve Zaire.*

The deadlock which had confronted the BMS in its first attempts to penetrate the Congo basin had been broken by Stanley's armed expedition. 'It is the feeling of us all', Bentley confided to Baynes, 'that this Expedition has been the instrument in God's hand of opening up the country, and humanly speaking ... the only hope of our ever reaching the country'.[55] From 1883 the attraction of Leopold's forces was increased by the attempts of Portugal to re-assert her sovereignty over the Congo district. These bore fruit in February 1884 in the signing of an Anglo-Portuguese treaty which would have ceded to Portugal control of the mouth of the Congo river. Experience in São Salvador was quite sufficient to convince the BMS missionaries that such an outcome would be harmful to Protestant interests and a fillip to the export of slaves to the Portuguese island of São Tomé.[56]

54. BMS Committee Minutes, 21 Nov. 1882, pp. 34-60; *MH* (Dec. 1882), 417-18.

55. A/31, Bentley to Baynes, 12 Aug. 1882.

56. A/31, Bentley to Baynes, 21 Apr. 1884.

Bentley, then home on furlough, was at the hub of a campaign to persuade parliament to refuse to ratify the treaty. The BMS lent its full support to Leopold at the Berlin West Africa Conference from November 1884 to February 1885, which thwarted Portuguese ambitions and gave Leopold precisely what he wanted: recognition by the Powers of his sovereign rights over the Congo. Of the BMS stations, only São Salvador fell within the territory given to Portugal. Baptists, in common with many others, rejoiced at a solution which seemed to preserve the Congo as a 'Free State' from annexation by anyone else, and to maintain an open door for free trade and Christian civilization.[57] They can hardly be censured for failing to perceive Leopold's true but well-disguised intentions to reap maximum profit from his acquisition.

During his furlough in 1884 Bentley also urged the Committee to implement its commitment to Arthington to commence work on the upper river. As a result of his persuasion, and a further gift of £2,000 from Arthington, the Committee resolved in July 1884 to construct a chain of at least ten stations between Stanley Pool and Stanley Falls (Kisangani), and sanctioned the recruitment of at least six additional missionaries to reinforce the mission. During 1883 the mission had lost four missionaries by death, and four more were sent home as a result of illness.[58] Also dead were the two engineers sent out to assemble the *Peace* at Stanley Pool. Grenfell had had to use his own mechanical training to assemble the vessel himself, aided by the Africans he had brought with him from the Cameroons.

By the time he received news of the July 1884 decisions, Grenfell had completed the first two of the series of voyages on the upper river and its tributaries which led to his being awarded the Founder's Medal of the Royal Geographical Society in 1887. The first voyage from January to March 1884 was undertaken in the *Peace*'s whaleboat; the *Peace* herself made six journeys between July 1884 and December 1886. The results in missionary terms were not immediately apparent: the first upper river station at Lukolela was not established until November 1886. Grenfell was conscious that some domestic supporters accorded his explorations an importance which was to the detriment of the less spectacular labours of colleagues such

---

57.   Bentley, *Holman Bentley*, 152-6; *BMS Annual Report*, 1884-5, pp. 41-5; Lagergren, *Mission and State*, 66-75.

58.   Bentley, *Holman Bentley*, 151; BMS Committee Minutes, 16 July 1884, pp. 48-52. The deaths were: W. H. Doke, J. S. Hartland, H. W. Butcher, J. Hartley. H. Dixon, W. Ross, H. G. Whitley and H. E. Crudgington were sent home because of their own or their wives' illness.

as Thomas Comber, whereas others grew impatient at the apparent neglect of evangelism.[59] He found reassurance in Livingstone's famous dictum that 'I view the end of the geographical feat as the beginning of the missionary enterprise': pioneering was essential for the construction of a coherent missionary strategy aimed at the key centres of population.[60]

The July 1884 Committee resolutions heralded the commencement of a new era in the Congo mission, which saw the BMS missionary force grow to the largest in the Congo. Five new recruits arrived on the Congo in 1884, eight more in 1885, and another eight (including Samuel Silvey from the Cameroons mission, and Martha Spearing, the first single woman to be appointed) in 1886.[61] The Committee's vision of ten stations on the upper river never materialized, but the advance Grenfell longed for was progressively achieved. Lukolela in 1886 was followed by Bolobo in 1888, which became the base for Grenfell and the *Peace*. In May 1890 F. R. Oram and W. L. Forfeitt began work at Upoto; two months later J. H. Weeks and W. H. Stapleton founded the Monsembe station.

Neither expanding recruitment nor geographical advance were in themselves guarantees of real growth. There were periods when the rate of missionary mortality equalled or even surpassed the rate of recruitment: five died between Christmas 1884 and June 1885; six in 1887, including Thomas Comber himself, whose boundless energy had earned him the Kikongo name of 'Vianga-Vianga' - 'Hurry-Hurry'. In December 1887 Grenfell warned Baynes that it might be necessary to abandon 'Arthington' and Lukolela stations, if reinforcements were not forthcoming.[62] Those who remained alive worked under increasing strain, physically overburdened and spiritually frustrated by the limitations which inadequate manpower imposed. Grenfell feared that Bentley in particular was worrying himself sick at the lack of progress. Bentley was not strong physically, and had in fact completely lost his sight while in Britain in 1885: much of the final preparation of his *Dictionary and Grammar of the Kongo Language* (1887) was accomplished by a blind man.[63] By the time he was back on the

59. Hawker, *Grenfell*, 250-1.

60. Myers, *The Congo for Christ* (London, n.d. [1895]), 86-7; Slade, *English-Speaking Missions*, 78-9.

61. Bentley, *Pioneering*, ii, 429-31. The brides of Bentley, Weeks and Darling also joined the ranks of the mission in 1886.

62. Grenfell to Baynes, 6 Dec. 1887, in Hawker, *Grenfell*, 259-60.

63. Bentley, *Holman Bentley*, 160-70.

field in November 1886, Bentley's sight was virtually restored, but frustrations of another kind were just beginning.[64]

Bentley had returned to the Congo in 1886 destined to assume responsibility for one of the projected upper river stations, and one of his first assignments was to accompany Grenfell on the sixth voyage of the *Peace* up the Kwango river. A re-evaluation of Bentley's role became necessary when Thomas Comber's death in June 1887 deprived the Ngombe Lutete station of its senior missionary. His colleagues came to the conclusion that his existing linguistic expertise should now be applied to the translation of the New Testament into Kikongo, and that he should therefore take Comber's place at Ngombe Lutete.[65] The intention was that Bentley should be freed from normal station work in order to devote himself exclusively to translation. Reality turned out to be very different. The Ngombe Lutete staff were continually being depleted by sickness, death, or relocation to fill gaps elsewhere, making it impossible for Bentley to concentrate on his biblical work. In January 1889 he pleaded with Baynes not to reinforce or further extend the upper river work at the expense of efficiency on the older stations.[66] By August he was requesting permission to be freed from all station duties in order to achieve his goal of a completed New Testament by the time of his next furlough.[67] Although his request was granted, Bentley did not reach his target: the Bentleys took their next furlough in 1892, and it was December 1893 before the Kikongo New Testament was completed.

The combined pressure induced by missionary mortality and the policy commitment to continual advance on the upper river helps to explain why progress in church-planting on the lower Congo was relatively slow. The first baptism - of Comber's 'boy', William Mantu Parkinson - did not take place till 29 March 1886. The first African church - that at São Salvador - was not formed till 4 December 1887. The majority of the earliest converts of the Congo mission were young people adopted by the missionaries as domestic servants or assistants. Nlemvo - traditionally regarded as the first Congo convert (though not the first to be baptized) - was given to Bentley in 1880 as a house boy by his uncle, chief of Lemvo village in the Kongo kingdom. Bentley sent him back to his village for the duration of the great

64. A/31, Bentley to Baynes, 2 Nov. 1886.

65. Bentley, *Holman Bentley*, 201-2, 230-2; Bentley, *Pioneering*, ii, 183.

66. A/31, Bentley to Baynes, 31 Jan. 1889.

67. A/31, Bentley to Baynes, 22 Aug. 1889; cf. Western Sub-Committee Minutes, 18 Nov. 1889.

push towards Stanley Pool, but subsequently re-engaged him. Nlemvo, though only about fourteen years old, accompanied Bentley to Britain in 1884-6 to assist him in the language work. In 1887 he settled with Bentley at Ngombe Lutete, where he was baptized on 19 February 1888.[68] Five of the six founding members of the Ngombe Lutete church formed on 1 January 1889 had been brought to Ngombe by their missionary patrons.[69] Similarly at 'Arthington' station on the Pool, the first three converts were boys from São Salvador employed by the mission.[70]

As in much of Africa, the very first Protestant converts thus tended to be individuals who had been uprooted from their own societies and placed in an environment artificially protected by missionary influence. The missionaries were not unaware of this fact, and as a result were strengthened in their conviction that the Christian education of the young held the key to the evangelization of the Congo. Bentley in particular believed that from the Ngombe Lutete school God would raise up the evangelists of the future, and was supported in this belief by Sir Charles Wathen, the station's benefactor.[71] Former pupils of Ngombe Lutete were indeed to play a crucial role in the Congo church, but Bentley himself realised the cultural dangers implicit in looking to education to mould converts into a shape acceptable for church leadership. Contrary to the views of some of his missionary colleagues, Bentley supported Nlemvo's decision to abandon his trousers when going out preaching and wear the traditional cloth, and commented:

> Personally I hope that our converts will be Christian Kongos, and not endeavour to efface their nationality, lest they thereby lose their influence. We are most anxious to see the natives get to work upon their own people. An earnest active native church is the hope of Kongo.[72]

A native church composed largely of 'boys' and other direct dependants of the missionaries had little impact on society and only limited prospects of growth. At the close of 1893 the total African membership of the BMS

68. On Nlemvo see Mrs Bentley's unpublished manuscript, '"Kiambote" Nlemvo: True Knight of the Cross' (1938).

69. Ngombe Lutete church roll, 1889-1904 (in Omedis-Nlemvo Centre de Santé, Kinshasa); and A/31, Bentley to Baynes, 24 Apr. 1888 and 31 Jan. 1889.

70. Myers, *The Congo for Christ,* 47-50.

71. *MH* (Oct. 1890), 379-81; Bentley, *Holman Bentley,* 62-5.

72. A/31, Bentley to Baynes, 24 Apr. 1888.

Congo churches was still only seventy-nine, fifty-one of whom were members at São Salvador.[73] However, 1894 saw signs of a break-through at Ngombe Lutete: during the year nineteen baptisms took place and the church membership grew from twelve to thirty-four. Steady growth was sustained for the rest of the decade.[74] Returning from furlough in February 1900, Bentley was delighted to find 400 people from the scattered churches of the Ngombe Lutete district present for communion, of whom 120 were communicants.[75] By the end of 1900 the Ngombe Lutete church and its out-stations had 280 members, nearly double the size of the São Salvador church, and more than half of the total Congo membership of 492.[76] It is not easy to identify the causes of the break-through: decreased missionary mortality may have played a part; regular itinerant preaching by both missionaries and African Christians was clearly important; the success of the Wathen school was also instrumental, in Bentley's view, in gaining acceptance for the Christian message in villages which had boys at Ngombe Lutete.[77]

As the first BMS stations to see substantial church growth, Ngombe Lutete and São Salvador were the first to confront BMS missionaries with some of the policy dilemmas which have surfaced repeatedly in modern African church history. The most acute of these concerned rules for the admission of converted polygamists. The initial policy of all missions working on the lower river was to admit to baptism and church membership anyone whose profession of faith seemed genuine, irrespective of their marital status. Since most of the first converts were youths, few problems in practice arose. A more stringent policy first appeared, significantly, at the first mission station to experience conversion en masse - the former LIM station of Mbanza Manteke - which had been inherited by the American Baptist Missionary Union (ABMU) in 1884.[78] From 1886 onwards converts at Mbanza Manteke appeared in their hundreds. Within a decade the senior missionary there, Henry Richards, had introduced a rule requiring

---

73. *BMS Annual Report*, 1893-4, p. 125.

74. Ngombe Lutete church roll, 1889-1904; slightly different figures are given in A/31, Bentley to Baynes, 7 Jan. 1897.

75. A/31, Bentley to Baynes, 6 Mar. 1900.

76. *BMS Annual Report*, 1900-1, p. 187.

77. Bentley, *Pioneering*, ii, 344-5.

78. In 1884 the LIM was compelled by financial crisis to hand over its work to the ABMU and the SMF; see E. M. Braekman, *Histoire du Protestantisme au Congo* (Brussels, 1961), 65, 90-8.

Robert Arthington (1823-1900),
benefactor of the BMS.

George Grenfell, Missionary in the
Cameroons and Congo, 1875-1906.

W. Holman Bentley, Missionary in
the Congo, 1879-1905.

Alfred Henry Baynes, Secretary of
the BMS, 1876-8; General
Secretary, 1878-1906.

all polygamists to put away all but the first wife prior to baptism. This more rigorous line became standard in the churches of both the ABMU and the *Svenska Missionsförbundet* (SMF), which had also begun work on the Congo in 1884. Influenced by these precedents, George Cameron at Ngombe Lutete wrote in September 1898 to all his BMS colleagues, seeking their approval for a change of policy to accord with the ABMU position. In December, with Bentley away on furlough, Cameron persuaded the Ngombe Lutete church to adopt new rules debarring polygamists from membership, and requiring that all but the first wife be put away.[79]

Cameron's unilateral action forced the Society to re-examine its position on the polygamy issue. Bentley was annoyed at Cameron's '*coup d'état*' and 'drastic revolutionary rules'.[80] R. H. C. Graham and the São Salvador missionaries favoured some tightening up of disciplinary procedures, but opposed the debarring of wives of polygamists from membership.[81] Grenfell observed that the issue was not yet a vexed question on the upper river, but cited Alfred Saker in support of Bentley's view that polygamists should be excluded from office-holding but not church membership.[82] Faced with such conflicting views from the field, the Western sub-committee came to the conclusion that each native church in conference with its missionaries must decide its own policy on the question. Nonetheless, it expressed the opinion that it was most desirable that missionaries should so far as possible agree on the matter, so as to avoid 'confusion and controversy' among converts and enquirers.[83]

On hearing the Committee's ruling, Bentley, now back on the field, expressed his fears for the unity of the Ngombe Lutete church if Cameron continued to press his views.[84] The Wathen missionaries tried and failed to reach agreement on the issue at a staff meeting in December 1901. They could agree only that any missionary wishing to propose a polygamist for baptism should bring the case before the staff meeting, so that all might understand the facts of the case, after which each missionary would be free to act as he thought best.[85] Nevertheless, the discussion did yield one

79. A/61, Cameron to BMS Congo missionaries, 29 Sept. 1898; Cameron to Baynes, 27 May 1899.

80. A/31, Bentley to Baynes, n.d. [May 1899].

81. A/61, Graham to BMS Congo missionaries, 15 Apr. 1899.

82. A/20, Grenfell to Baynes, 22 July 1899.

83. General Committee Minutes, 20 Nov. 1900, p. 357.

84. A/31, Bentley to Baynes, 10 Feb. 1901.

85. Ngombe Lutete archives, Wathen station minutes, 23 Dec. 1901.

conclusion of lasting significance: it was agreed that both state marriage and Christian marriage should no longer be referred to as *sompa* - the traditional Kikongo word for marriage, which implied that the man had merely 'borrowed' a woman from her family - but as *kazala* - a word meaning the union of two previously separate entities. *Kazala* eventually became the accepted word for Christian marriage in the Kikongo-speaking churches. Although the immediate issue in contention at Ngombe Lutete had not been resolved, an important step had been taken in the process of establishing within the African church a Christian concept of marriage in place of the traditional proprietary understanding which lay at the root of the polygamous system.

Church growth on the upper river followed a not dissimilar pattern to that displayed by the older churches of the lower river. After some months or years of waiting for conversions, the missionaries then entered an initial phase in which converts were drawn mostly from the ranks of their personal servants or from slaves liberated in the region of the station. The first baptismal service on the upper river took place at Bolobo in March 1889, when Grenfell baptized five young people, all of whom had worked for him or other missionaries. The first six converts at Lukolela, baptized in January 1892, were either house-boys or freed slaves. The first four converts at Upoto in October 1894 were all young people, three of them house-boys or girls of Oram and Forfeitt.[86] But the numbers were small: by the end of 1900 the upper river stations could boast only fifty church members between them, thirty-six of them at Bolobo.[87]

The number of converts gained during the first decade of work on the upper river may have disappointed some home supporters, but they had cause to be thankful that the work on the upper river had even survived. There were times when that had seemed unlikely. One Saturday evening in February 1891, F. G. Harrison, who had succeeded Grenfell as missionary in charge of the *Peace*, docked the vessel at Bolobo after a journey to Upoto, only to find the town burnt to the ground and deserted. Robert Glennie was left to tell Harrison what had happened. A Free State expedition under Captain van Kerkhoven had been heading up-river bent on extracting the riches of ivory and other resources which Stanley had brought to light. To save Leopold expense, van Kerkhoven supplied his labour needs by recruit-

---

86. A/19, Grenfell to Baynes, 22 Mar. 1889; Bentley, *Pioneering*, ii, 251, 276-7; Myers, *The Congo for Christ*, 104; box 'Congo Log Books', Upoto Log Book, 1890-1954, entries for 7-8 Oct. 1894.

87. *BMS Annual Report*, 1900-1, p. 187.

ing forced levies from the riverside towns. His pretext for intervening at Bolobo was a fight which had taken place some months before between the townspeople and the feared Bangala. To quell this 'insubordination', van Kerkhoven had imposed fines, payable principally in men, on the Bolobo chiefs. They had refused to pay, and took their people across the river to French Congo. Van Kerkhoven's men retaliated by looting Bolobo and razing it to the ground. Harrison rescued the situation by arranging a palaver between the Captain and the Bolobo chiefs, at which van Kerkhoven agreed to rescind the labour fines and reduce the other fines. As a result, the chiefs brought their people back across the river. Harrison was in no doubt that the favourable outcome of the palaver was due to his wife plying the Captain with tea and other medical attention after he had been afflicted by fever. Be that as it may, he was surely right in his supposition that his timely return may have saved the Bolobo station from extinction.[88] Similar hostile action by Free State officials at Lukolela drove most of the population permanently across the river, and forced missionaries to withdraw from the station in 1895.[89]

Upoto station also had a precarious existence in its early years. At the time of its foundation in 1890 Free State forces were still fighting for commercial and military control of the region, and the station log book for September to December 1890 contains repeated references to skirmishes between the State and the local tribes.[90] Warfare between tribes was also endemic during the 1890s. In December 1892 Ngombe men from Kalagba, knowing that Oram was alone on the station, and that the men of Upoto, with whom they had a long-standing feud, were away fishing, burnt the town, and then attacked the mission itself. Oram was driven to fire on the attackers, seriously wounding one, at which they withdrew. F. G. Harrison, who arrived on the *Peace* shortly afterwards, refused to condemn Oram in view of the fact that 'the station might have been destroyed and the future of the mission ... jeopardized'.[91]

If life at Upoto was dangerous, the prospect of work higher up the river near Stanley Falls was at this stage unthinkable. The area was dominated by

88. F. G. Harrison papers; cf. Bentley, *Pioneering*, ii, 235-6. Harrison had contributed to the trouble with the Bangala by recruiting a gang of them for service on the *Peace,* to the resentment of the Bolobo people.

89. BMS Committee Minutes, 19 Nov. 1895, pp. 380-3. Although missionaries were withdrawn, some work at Lukolela was continued from Bolobo.

90. Upoto Log Book, 1890-1954, entries for 12 Sept., 3 Nov., 1, 11, 18 Dec. 1890.

91. F. G. Harrison papers; see Upoto Log Book, 1890-1954, entries for 6, 26 Dec. 1892.

Tippu Tib, the great Arab slave-trader, and the Free State post at the Falls was a weak affair in comparison. When the *Peace* visited the Falls at the end of 1891, Harrison found the population living in fear, if not in hiding. Within a few months, however, the outlook had begun to change. The Arabs overran the State post, which the State then repossessed in force: this, commented Harrison, was 'the beginning of the end of Arab influence in Central Africa'.[92] The decline of Arab power was to be a slow process, but by 1895 the Arab stranglehold on the Falls district was broken. Earlier in the 1890s, BMS strategy for expansion had focused on the Ubangui river. The waning of Arab power now enabled the Society to revert to plans for a missionary advance towards the Falls, with the eventual goal of using the Aruwimi river to strike further east. The site for Yakusu was selected by Grenfell and Harry White in October 1895. White was left at Yakusu for a few weeks to test its suitability as a mission site, and returned in February 1896 to establish the new station.

Even more than the other stations on the upper river, Yakusu teetered on the brink of survival for its first few years. Albert Wherrett died within a month of his arrival in November 1896. Harry White died on his way home to England the following July. The State authorities had ordered the mission to evacuate Yakusu on the grounds that the Falls district was not yet sufficiently 'organized' to permit mission work, and White and J. R. M. Stephens had been sent home to confer with the Committee.[93] Representations from Baynes to Brussels eventually secured the withdrawal of the notice to quit, but some in the Society shared the view that Arab influence in the region was still too strong, and it was July 1898 before the Committee endorsed the recommendations of Stapleton and Grenfell that the station 'should by all means be permanently retained'.[94] Grenfell saw Yakusu as the crucial frontier post in the coming struggle between Christianity and Islam for supremacy in central Africa.[95] He also shared Arthington's determination to see the completion of a trans-African chain of mission stations by an advance up the Aruwimi to link up with the work of the CMS in Uganda.[96] This forward movement was held up in Grenfell's last years by the

92. F. G. Harrison papers.

93. A/20, Grenfell to Baynes, 10 Jan. 1897.

94. General Committee Minutes, 19 July 1898, pp. 48-52; Hawker, *Grenfell*, 401-2; Slade, *English-Speaking Missions*, 134-5.

95. Slade, *English-Speaking Missions*, 136.

96. A/20, Grenfell to Baynes, 6 Mar. 1901.

protracted refusal of the Free State to grant the BMS the sites it was seeking at Yambuya on the Aruwimi and at Yalemba. Only in the final year of his life, in 1905-6, was Grenfell given the necessary permission to take up residence at Yalemba and reinforce the infant church already planted by his protegé, the liberated slave, Disasi Makulo.[97]

The decision to retain Yakusu soon proved amply justified. W. H. Stapleton baptized the first three converts in 1902. By the end of 1904, he was reporting 'an extraordinary manifestation of Divine favour' throughout the Yakusu district. Fifty-three had been baptized during the year, and schools established in nine-tenths of the Lokele villages. As Grenfell had predicted, Arab influence in the area placed a high premium on education.[98] Stapleton died in 1906, but the next decade witnessed the beginnings of the most rapid church growth in the history of the Congo mission, spearheaded by a force of up to ninety evangelists: by 1914 the membership of the Yakusu church stood at 965.[99] In 1911 the BMS began work far beyond Yakusu at Wayika and Mabondo on the upper reaches of the Congo.[100]

At the same time as the foundations of the work at Yakusu were being laid, first by Stapleton, and then by William Millman (missionary at Yakusu from 1898 to 1937), less spectacular initiatives were being taken on the lower river. As early as 1893 Bentley had urged the Committee to commence work among the Zombo people of Portuguese Congo.[101] His hopes came to fruition in 1899 when Thomas Lewis, veteran of the Cameroons and São Salvador, established the Kibokolo station. Five years later, the Camerons left Ngombe Lutete to found a further station at Mabaya, south of São Salvador. Neither of the new stations flourished - reporting only ten church members between them in 1912.[102] BMS work in Portuguese Congo was overshadowed by the recruitment of forced labour for the plantations of São Tomé and Principé, which eventually provoked the Buta rebellion of 1913-15.[103] More encouraging to the Society was the opening

---

97. Johnston, *George Grenfell*, i, 447; on Makulo see Makulo Akambu, *La Vie de Disasi Makulo* (Kinshasa, 1983).

98. H. Sutton Smith, *Yakusu: The Very Heart of Africa* (London, n.d. [1912]), 217, 236, 277; Slade, *English-Speaking Missions*, 135-6.

99. C. E. Wilson, et. al., *After Forty Years* (BMS, London, n.d. [1919]), 28-9.

100. *BMS Annual Report*, 1911-12, p. 71.

101. A/31, Bentley to Baynes, printed letter, n.d. [1893].

102. *BMS Annual Report*, 1912-13, p. 162.

103. See below, ch. XI, pp.336-7.

in 1909 of the Kimpese Evangelical Training Institution, a joint venture with the ABMU designed to train evangelists and teachers for the Belgian, French and Portuguese Congo.[104]

The first twenty-five years of the BMS Congo mission were dominated by three men: Holman Bentley, translator and philologist among the Bakongo people of the lower river; George Grenfell, pioneer and navigator of the upper river; and the administrator, Alfred Baynes, master-minding the whole enterprise from his desk in London. In 1905-6, within a period of seven months, all three passed from the scene. Bentley died at home in Bristol in December 1905. Baynes finally retired from the service of the BMS on 31 March 1906. Grenfell died at Basoko on 1 July. Between them they can claim much of the credit for the fact that the Congo mission not merely survived, but to a substantial degree fulfilled the vision of its originator, Robert Arthington. But they also bear much of the responsibility for a fact which posterity has viewed with less favour - the tenacity of the BMS in believing in the essential benevolence of Leopold's Congo Free State, despite a growing body of evidence to the contrary. By the early 1890s it was clear to most impartial observers that the primary purpose of the State was to maximize Leopold's personal wealth. The profitability of the State depended on the collection of rubber and ivory by a system of forced labour, operated with considerable brutality by the agents of the State or the concessionary companies, which had been granted rights over large tracts of the country. The incident at Bolobo in 1891 was just one example of the willingness of the State to sacrifice the indigenous peoples of the Congo on the altar of the white man's profits. Yet the BMS continued to defend Leopold against the mounting volume of criticism until 1905. Such apparent myopia in a society with an honourable tradition of humanitarian protest demands explanation.[105]

In 1881-2 Stanley's expedition had opened the way for the BMS to reach Stanley Pool. From 1883 to 1885 Leopold's embryonic organization on the Congo seemed an angel of light in comparison with the dark spectre of Portuguese annexation. In 1885 the Congo Free State was set up with fine-sounding guarantees of free trade and provision for native welfare. From 1885 onwards, the prospects for missionary advance on the upper river were blighted by the growing dominance of the Arab slave-traders. Between

---

104. The SMF was involved in the planning of KETI, but finally declined to participate; see Lewis, *These Seventy Years,* 231-8.

105. For full treatments of this question see Slade, *English-Speaking Missions,* and Lagergren, *Mission and State, passim.*

1892 and 1895, that dominance was broken by the power of the Free State. All this inclined those who directed the Congo mission, and especially Baynes, Grenfell and Bentley, to support the Free State against its critics. This standpoint was quite compatible with a willingness to complain privately to higher authority whenever individual agents of the State acted in an unacceptable manner. Thus Baynes visited Brussels in October 1895 to complain at an attack on Monsembe village and mission by a State force in May. For missionaries on the spot such a stance became increasingly difficult to maintain, as the State tightened the screw in exploiting the natural resources on which its fiscal survival depended. Stapleton had warned Baynes after the Monsembe incident:

> It is becoming a grave question with me and ... with others also how long we can reconcile silence on the question of the infamous wrongs to which these people are subject, with our conscientious view of our duty towards them as missionaries ... In my judgement the State would not have dared to have committed many of the outrages that disgrace its name in the face of the moral pressure the BMS from an independent standpoint could have brought to bear.[106]

Moral pressure on the government was in fact increasing, owing in large measure to the publicity given to State outrages by the ABMU missionaries, J. B. Murphy and E. V. Sjöblöm. Leopold responded in September 1896 by appointing a Commission for the Protection of the Natives, comprising six Congo missionaries, among them Bentley and Grenfell. But the Commission's powers were limited, and none of its members came from the Equator district, where the rubber atrocities were concentrated. Grenfell himself, now convinced of the reality of the abuses, though still persuaded of Leopold's personal good intentions, regarded the Commission as little more than a farce.[107] Nonetheless, the work of the Commission in 1897 was succeeded by a lull in public interest in the Congo question, which lasted till 1902. In that year the journalist E. D. Morel began his campaign for Congo Reform, and succeeded in mobilizing the full weight of the British nonconformist conscience in opposition to Leopold's regime. The BMS Committee, however, still maintained its public profession of confidence in Leopold's rule - to the growing disquiet of the *Baptist Times* and denomi-

---

106. Stapleton to Baynes, 14 Jun. 1895, cited in Slade, *English-Speaking Missions*, 242.

107. Lagergren, *Mission and State*, 199-200; Hawker, *Grenfell*, 372-4.

national leaders such as John Clifford.[108] On 17 March 1903 the Committee issued a public statement in reply, pointing out that BMS missionaries worked in districts far removed from the scene of the alleged cruelties, and so could not bear testimony on the question.[109] Baynes's report to the annual members' meeting on 28 April included a statement prepared by the Western sub-committee, which supported the idea of a State enquiry into the allegations, but declined to associate the BMS directly with any request to Brussels.[110] This did not satisfy Clifford, who induced the Baptist Union assembly two days later to pass a resolution authorizing the Union to join in an united appeal to the British government to intervene to enforce the provisions of the Berlin Act of 1885.[111]

In August 1903 Grenfell drafted a letter to Leopold II, explaining that his conscience no longer permitted him to wear the decorations which the king had bestowed on him for his services to the State. Grenfell's action was not, however, a protest against atrocities perpetrated by the agents of the Free State. At this point he still believed that the crimes which had been committed were the action of individual officials, and, in his experience, these had been suitably punished by the authorities. Rather his protest was prompted by the continuing refusal of the State to permit the BMS to realize its plans for advance on the upper river, and so complete the chain of Protestant stations across central Africa. Grenfell sent his letter, with the decorations, to Baynes in London, leaving it to his judgment whether they should be forwarded to Leopold. Baynes deemed it wise to take no action.[112]

Despite the BMS Committee's assertion that its missionaries were not in a position to provide first-hand testimony of abuses, some, notably John Weeks at Monsembe and A. E. Scrivener at Bolobo, were soon doing precisely that, supplying Morel with accounts of the drastic impact of excessive taxation in the Equator district. What convinced many missionaries of the truth of the allegations of atrocities was a fact-finding tour in 1903 by the British consul at Boma, Roger Casement. Casement's evidence

108. *Baptist Times,* 13 Mar. 1903, cited in Slade, *English-Speaking Missions,* 268n.

109. General Committee Minutes, 17 Mar. 1903, pp. 45-6.

110. General Committee Minutes, 24 Apr. 1903, pp. 54-5; Slade, *English-Speaking Missions,* 270.

111. Slade, *English-Speaking Missions,* 271.

112. A/21, Grenfell to Leopold II, 10 Aug. 1903; Grenfell to Baynes, 11 Aug. 1903; Baynes to Grenfell, 9 Apr. 1906. These letters were discovered when the BMS vacated its Gloucester Place premises in 1989.

of the true extent of atrocities was the conclusive blow for Grenfell, causing him to resign from the Commission for the Protection of the Natives.[113] By April 1904 he was a sadly disillusioned man, admitting that he had been duped:

> I really believed the King's first purpose was to establish law and order and to promote the well being of the people, and that the development of the resources of the country was a means to that end. I regretfully, most regretfully, admit that those who have so long maintained the contrary are to all intents and purposes justified, and that I have been blinded by my wish to believe 'the best'. The recent revelations have saddened me more than I can say! [114]

Baynes himself soon reached the same conclusion. Leopold had bowed to the mounting agitation by appointing a Commission of Enquiry into the alleged atrocities. Five months before its report was published in November 1905, Baynes wrote to Grenfell, admitting that the evidence presented to the Commission 'more than justified the statements that have been made as to cruelty and oppression', and expressing the hope that the 'terrible cruelties' of the rubber-producing districts would soon come to an end.[115] Baynes still wished to delay any public statement by the Society until the Commission's report was published, but the pressure of feeling in the denomination was too strong: on 17 October the Committee at last acknowledged publicly that there was no doubt as to the reality of the Congo atrocities, and appealed to the British government to intervene under the powers of the Berlin Act to bring the present oppressive regime to a speedy termination.[116]

The publication of the report of the Commission of Enquiry led ultimately to the demise of the Free State. The Congo became a Belgian colony in 1908, although the British government withheld recognition of the Belgian annexation until July 1913, as evidence was at first plentiful that the system of heavy taxation and forced labour remained in existence in some areas. Reports from BMS missionaries on the upper river, such as D. C. Davies at Yalemba, played an important part in sustaining Foreign

---

113. Lagergren, *Mission and State,* 320-31.
114. A/20, Grenfell to Baynes, 27 Apr. 1904.
115. A/20, Baynes to Grenfell, 14 June 1905.
116. General Committee Minutes, 17 Oct. 1905, pp. 188-9.

Office pressure on Brussels.[117] Thus the BMS came to play an important, if belated, part in the Congo Reform movement. The delay was due to the cherished conviction of the mission's leaders that the Free State was to be thanked, not just for opening the way to the interior, but also for the elimination of what Grenfell called 'a state of lawlessness and misery that makes my old diaries blood-curdling and horrible'.[118] By 1905 they had realized that the lawlessness of European commercial exploitation was no better than the apparent lawlessness of the age of cannibalism and the slave trade which it had replaced.

117. Yakusu archives, 'Recent Correspondence on Congo Affairs between the BMS and the Belgian Colonial Minister...', 1911.

118. Johnston, *George Grenfell*, i, 480.

V

India and Ceylon, 1837-1914

I: Labouring in Vain? Caste and Conversion in India

'There is, dear Christian friends, something which causes great distress both to myself and, I believe, to every one in the mission: it is the fear, the almost certainty, that we are labouring in vain.' These sober words introduced an article on the BMS India mission which appeared in the *Missionary Herald* for November 1847. The author was William Robinson of Dhaka, veteran of forty years' missionary experience in Bengal and the East Indies. Robinson did not hesitate to assert that, while the Society's Jamaica mission was basking in its phenomenal success, its work in India was 'dying' - dying from lack of missionary recruits, inadequate funding and waning enthusiasm in the British churches.[1] Robinson's complaint was more than the pessimism of an old man wearied by his labours. His own ministry had indeed not been devoid of all fruit: as pastor of the Lall Bazar Church in Calcutta from 1825 to 1838 he had baptised over 250 converts, and even in Muslim-dominated Dhaka he had seen some encouragement.[2] Robinson's article reflected, not personal disillusionment, but the deep concern of missionaries of all societies about the deadening effect which the paucity of evangelistic success in India was having on the zeal of the supporting public in Britain. What success there was among mid-Victorian Protestant missions in India was concentrated in the south; societies which operated only in the north, such as the BMS, had to come to terms with the fact that the gospel had so far failed to pull down the strongholds of Hindu idolatry. Although Robinson went to his grave in the Wari cemetery in Dhaka in 1853 with his confidence in the gospel undiminished, his anxiety for the future of the India mission remained well-founded.

1. *BM* 39 (1847), 722-5.

2. IN/28, W. Robinson to J. Penney and J. Thomas, 12 Nov. 1838, and Robinson to Thomas, 2 July 1839.

At the end of 1843, fifty years after Carey and John Thomas had arrived in Bengal, the total membership of the BMS churches in the Indian sub-continent was 1,449. By way of comparison, Baptist membership in the Bahamas, where the Society had been operating for only ten years, was 2,141. Of the 1,449 members in the Indian sub-continent, 454 were in the Calcutta district, 465 in North India, and 530 in Ceylon. Nearly half the Bengal membership, and possibly a similar proportion elsewhere, were Europeans.[3] The problem which faced the Society's Indian missionaries was not that no-one would listen to their message. On the contrary, most found, as did W. W. Evans in Calcutta in 1843, that it was relatively easy to gather a crowd in a public place to hear the gospel proclaimed.[4] Thomas Phillips, writing from Muttra near Agra in the same year, could even report that 'missionary work is quite easy and delightful here'.[5] A polite reception for the itinerant evangelist was common enough, particularly from Hindus, but willingness to pay the price of conversion to Christianity was quite another matter. The social pressures militating against conversion were of an entirely different order from those faced by evangelistic preachers in Britain.

The most formidable of all these pressures throughout this period remained the caste system.[6] Whereas the early converts of the Serampore mission had included a disproportionate number of high-caste people, from the 1830s the caste system operated in such a way as to exclude nearly all who possessed means and influence from the Christian community. It will be emphasized in section III below that one fatal result of this exclusion was the growth of a dependent mentality in the Indian churches, which in turn further inhibited their growth. Since the various trades and handicrafts were the monopoly of particular castes, conversion to Christ meant for any tradesman or craftsman either complete renunciation of his employment or a severely restricted practice of it. As one Bengal missionary testified in 1870,

If a man is a barber, after his baptism, he will not be allowed to shave any but Christians. If he is a shopkeeper, there are only certain articles

3.   *BM* 36 (1844), 265, 272. These figures exclude the GBMS churches in Orissa (see section V below).

4.   Ibid., 38.

5.   Ibid., 150.

6·   On this whole subject see D. B. Forrester, *Caste and Christianity: Attitudes and Policies on Caste of Anglo-Saxon Protestant Missions in India* (London, 1980).

that the people generally will buy from him. If he is a baker or confectioner, only Christians will eat what passes through his hands ... He belongs to a sect that is everywhere spoken against, and his profession of Christianity has most likely driven him from his home[7]

The hold which caste associations exercised over economic activity ensured that few Hindus from artisan and commercial backgrounds joined the churches. Indian Christians were also almost entirely debarred from government service, although their exclusion became less comprehensive after the end of East India Company rule in 1858. As a result, churches in the urban areas tended to draw the few converts they had from those who were either at the bottom of the caste pyramid, or outside it altogether.

In the rural areas, particularly in Bengal, economic sanctions of a different kind operated to dissuade the peasantry (the *ryots*) from adhering to Christianity. In most of North India the power of the *zamindars* - the landholder class who provided the land revenue for the British, as they had done for the Mughals before them - remained intact. In Bengal the Permanent Settlement of 1793 had increased the fiscal pressure on the *zamindars*, but from the early nineteenth century they in turn further tightened the screw on the *ryots*.[8] As a Christian *ryot* was likely to be denied access to the market to sell his produce, he was a liability to the *zamindar*. Instances of open persecution of Christian *ryots* by the local *zamindar* were relatively common, notably in Bengal. *Zamindars* in the Jessore district in 1844 compelled their *ryots* to sign a bond stipulating the payment of twenty to thirty rupees to the *zamindar* if a *ryot* was found attending Christian worship, observing the sabbath, or reading Christian tracts.[9] One case which attracted much publicity both in Bengal and in England involved a group of converts at Baropakhya near Barisal in 1855. Thirteen Christians had their homes looted and were kidnapped by agents of the *zamindars*. The resulting legal action eventually went all the way to the Supreme Court in Calcutta, assisted on the Christian side by stalwart lobbying from E. B. Underhill, who was in India at the time.[10] Underhill hoped to see the Bengal

7. *Reports and Documents on the Indian Mission, Prepared for the Use of the Committee of the Baptist Missionary Society* (London, 1872), 106, also 17.

8. P. J. Marshall, *Bengal: The British Bridgehead. Eastern India 1740-1828* (The New Cambridge History of India, II.2; Cambridge, 1987), 124-5, 149-50.

9. *BM* 36 (1844), 480.

10. E. B. Underhill, *The Case of the Baropakhya Christians* (London, 1856); G. Soddy, *Baptists in Bangladesh* (Dhaka, 1984), 142-7.

BMS missionaries emulate their Jamaican brethren by working for the emancipation of the 'poor, depressed *ryot* of Bengal ... from the hand of the tyrant and spoiler'.[11] In fact the evangelical missionary conscience never became as aroused over the condition of the *ryots* as it had over West Indian slavery. Nevertheless, agitation by missionaries of several societies, notably John Wenger of the BMS, contributed to the reform of the Permanent Settlement in 1857-9, when the powers of the *zamindars* were curbed.[12] Moreover, the determination shown by BMS missionaries in defending the rights of village Christians in South Bengal was generally successful in preventing them from becoming a landless class.[13]

Where *zamindar* hostility and caste sanctions coincided, Christians could be totally excluded from community life. This happened at the village church in Chitoura near Agra in 1847. When it became clear to James Smith, the BMS missionary pastor, that the *panchayat*, the council of caste elders, still exercised control over the lives of some members, he determined to discipline those members who continued to acknowledge the authority of the *panchayat*. The result was the break-up of the church, and a decision by the *zamindars* to exclude Christians from the markets, shops and wells in the village. Smith saw no alternative but to form a Christian settlement on some sterile land half-a-mile from Chitoura. The rump of the Chitoura membership settled in Nistarpur - 'the town of salvation' - and the church began to grow again. By January 1856 there were fifty members, and a total village community of 104. With European help, employment was provided in the shape of a large weaving shop (most of the converts were weavers).[14]

The Chitoura Christian village was an obvious target in the Indian rebellion of 1857; the Christians were scattered, and many subsequently found government employment in Agra. Chitoura was the last in a series of experimental Christian settlements, whose history goes back to Jessore in the 1820s, if not to Serampore itself.[15] By the mid-1850s the Society had

11.   E. B. Underhill, *Principles and Methods of Missionary Labour* (London, 1896), 103.

12.   G. A. Oddie, *Social Protest in India: British Protestant Missionaries and Social Reforms 1850-1900* (New Delhi, 1979), 110-28. Wenger is celebrated chiefly for his work in succession to William Yates on the Bengali and Sanskrit Bible; see E. B. Underhill, *The Life of John Wenger of Calcutta* (London, 1886).

13.   See Wenger's testimony in *Reports and Documents on the Indian Mission*, 16.

14.   *BM* 50 (1858), 450-3.

15.   For the Jessore Christian village of 'Christianpore' see Soddy, *Baptists in Bangladesh*, 39.

reached the conclusion that these experiments had purchased Christian security at the price of isolation.[16] That verdict was accurate enough, but it is hard to see what alternative course of action could have been pursued by Smith in 1847, other than to tolerate the perpetuation of caste divisions within the church. Furthermore, the Christian villages did at least represent attempts to provide a genuine communal framework for the life of the individual convert, and thus fill something of the social void created by the severance of caste ties. More satisfactory in the long term were the rural churches, such as those in the Khulna area of Bengal, where a group of initial converts from the same caste and the same locality succeeded in remaining within their existing village community, and establishing a sufficiently stable communal base to attract new converts from other backgrounds. Where, however, as in the Jessore district, individual converts emerged from disparate backgrounds, they rarely had enough in common to resist the magnetic pull of the old caste associations.[17]

The combination in northern India of the economic power of the *zamindars* with the social and ideological pressures of the caste system constantly threatened to strangle the life of the infant church wherever it came to birth. Occasionally, however, the corporate identity of a caste could operate in a direction favourable to Christianity, given the right initial stimulus. Such was the case among the Nomo Sudra or Chandal caste in the Barisal and Faridpur districts of Bengal following the baptism in 1845 of the Hindu reformer and holy man, Kangal-Mohunt. Kangal began to proclaim that his quest for the *Satya Guru* - the true teacher - had been fulfilled in the person of Jesus Christ. Over the remaining twenty years of his life, Kangal lived as an itinerant evangelist, commending the gospel by his simplicity of life and devotion to prayer. His witness stimulated what has been described as a mass movement towards Christianity among his own Nomo Sudra caste, creating a strong Christian community in the Barisal and Faridpur districts which supplied many of the leaders of the Baptist churches of East Bengal well into the twentieth century.[18]

---

16.   Underhill, *Principles and Methods,* 104.

17.   Soddy, *Baptists in Bangladesh,* 64-7; *Reports and Documents on the Indian Mission,* 47.

18.   Soddy, *Baptists in Bangladesh,* 124-32; Didcot, CR 492, The Church in Bangladesh, p. 2. On mass or 'people movements' towards Christianity in late nineteenth-century India see Forrester, *Caste and Christianity,* 69-92; J. W. Pickett, *Christian Mass Movements in India* (New York, 1933).

II: The Rebellion of 1857 and its Aftermath

The story of Baptist work in Delhi in the aftermath of the great rebellion or 'Indian mutiny' of 1857 provides another example of the potential of caste ties in certain circumstances to encourage, rather than inhibit, conversion to Christianity. Although sparked off by fears among the sepoy regiments at Meerut that they were to be forcibly converted to Christianity, the rebellion was interpreted by almost all Christian opinion in India and Britain as an indication that Britain had not done enough to bring the gospel to her Indian subjects. It was a divine judgment on the East India Company for its dalliance with Hindu 'idolatry', and a warning to Britain to be faithful to the terms of her imperial stewardship in India. India was 'saved' only by the heroic exploits of Christian soldiers, pre-eminent among them being Henry Havelock, son-in-law to Joshua Marshman and formerly lay pastor of the BMS church at Agra. Havelock's military victories won him heroic status in domestic public opinion.[19]

The rebellion had relatively little impact on Bengal, although short-lived mutinies by the sepoys at Dhaka and Chittagong compelled the temporary suspension of missionary work in these two towns.[20] The BMS mission in North-West India was, on the other hand, virtually eliminated. At Agra the mission house, two chapels and their accompanying schools were plundered or destroyed; the Christian village at Chitoura was left in ruins; at Muttra the missionary, Thomas Evans, had to flee for his life.[21] In Delhi, the centre of the rebellion until its recapture by the British on 20 September, the BMS suffered its first martyrdoms. The resident missionary, John Mackay, the widow and two daughters of his predecessor, J. T. Thompson, and an Indian evangelist, Wilayat Ali, were murdered by the rebels in May.[22] Both the Baptist mission and the Anglican SPG mission (the only other Protestant mission in the city) were all but wiped out.[23]

19. B. Stanley, 'Christian responses to the Indian mutiny of 1857', in W. J. Sheils (ed.), *The Church and War* (Studies in Church History, 20; Oxford, 1983), 277-89. On Havelock see O. Anderson, 'The growth of Christian militarism in mid-Victorian Britain', *English Historical Review* 86 (1971), 46-72; W. Brock, *A Biographical Sketch of Sir Henry Havelock, K.C.B.* (4th edn., London, 1858); J. C. Marshman, *Memoirs of Major-General Sir Henry Havelock, K.C.B.* (3rd edn., London, 1867).

20. *BM* 50 (1858), 120-1; H. Bridges, *The Kingdom of Christ in East Bengal* (Dhaka, 1984), 39-40.

21. *BM* 50 (1858), 116.

22. *BM* 49 (1857), 510-11, 583; 51 (1859) 245-6.

23. J. P. Alter and H. J. Singh, 'The Church in Delhi', in V. E. W. Hayward (ed.), *The Church as Christian Community: Three Studies of North Indian Churches* (London, 1966), 20-1.

The BMS encouraged Baptists to interpret the rebellion as a desperate effort by the Brahminical caste to halt the onward march of Christian civilization in India. John Wenger believed that God had permitted the mutiny in order to overturn the powers of Hinduism and usher in the reign of Christ.[24] The BMS Committee accordingly called for an increased effort for the evangelization of India, and resolved to re-occupy the abandoned stations at the earliest opportunity. 'The cruel persecutors of Delhi claim at our hands a Christian's revenge', urged the *Missionary Herald* - 'the announcement of the gospel of peace and pardoning love'.[25] James Smith, formerly of Chitoura, was stationed in Delhi in June 1859: his experience in the city over the next four years appeared to provide indications that Wenger's prophecy might be fulfilled.

Smith was soon reporting unprecedented interest by the Hindu population in the gospel. He began nightly open-air preaching between the Red Fort and the Chandni Chowk bazar, and was astonished to gather an average audience of 250, many returning night after night to hear the gospel. Interest was keenest amongst the *chamars*, who were leather-workers, but also doers of all sorts of menial tasks, and the largest outcaste community in the city. Smith claimed that 'hundreds' of *chamars* had professed a desire to become Christians, and many had actually broken caste. He organized four meetings in different parts of Delhi to teach the serious inquirers. Delhi, before the mutiny a barren field for the Society, now seemed ripe for the harvest.[26]

The former Baptist chapel near the Red Fort had been destroyed by the rebels, and only four members of the old church remained. Smith now constituted a new church at Chandni Chowk, and planted two others at Purana Killa and Shahdra. By the end of 1859 a total of ninety-four converts had been baptized, and twenty-five preaching stations established. Twelve months later the converts numbered 250, now grouped into six different congregations. Most, but not all, were said to be from 'the poorest of the people'.[27] This was church growth at a rate without precedent in the BMS India mission, yet signs were already evident that the hoped-for gospel triumph in Delhi was not to be. The Agra missionary, J. G. Gregson, visiting Delhi in October 1859, observed that some who once came to hear Smith did so no longer, and that the Hindu gurus were vigorously

24. *BM* 50 (1858), 389.
25. Ibid., 116-17; 51 (1859), 113.
26. *BM* 51 (1859), 524, 646-7, 709-10, 773.
27. *BM* 52 (1860), 251; 53 (1861), 310.

combating the missionary influence. Gregson believed that if only a number who were currently halting between two opinions were to declare an open profession, hundreds or even thousands might follow.[28]

By 1861 the Hindu reaction which Gregson feared had become a reality. While sixty-six new converts were baptized during the year, seventy-five were excluded from membership. The missionaries explained that some had flocked to the churches in the hope of improving their temporal lot, while others 'had never entirely renounced their heathen habits' - probably meaning that they had continued to owe allegiance to the old caste brotherhoods.[29] In the wake of the failure of the 1857 rebellion, Christianity had appeared to present the Delhi *chamar* community with an attractive alternative to the continuance of a religious system which kept them firmly at the bottom of the social pile. But once it became clear that Christianity was not an automatic passport to enhanced status in the post-mutiny city, a 'people movement' towards Christianity became less likely. Nevertheless, a genuinely committed Baptist community of lower-caste converts was established in Delhi in the course of the 1860s, centred on a new church building at Chandni Chowk, opened in 1864 (Central Baptist Church). As late as 1865, Smith could report that 'the Lord is doing a great work in Delhi among the lower castes', with between 50 and 100 people attending nightly prayer meetings.[30] Both the SPG and the BMS missions opted from the early 1880s for a form of modified segregation, in which converts settled in clusters around a church and primary school, while remaining within their former localities and continuing to practise their former caste trades. Central Baptist Church had a membership of 137 by 1896, and nearly 160 by 1913.[31] Delhi's comparative strength as a Baptist centre in the twentieth century was thus built on the foundations laid in the post-mutiny era.

Other parts of the North India mission witnessed no such dramatic upturn in missionary fortunes in the aftermath of the 1857 rebellion. Missionaries were, however, of the opinion that open hostility to Christianity had moderated, at least among the Hindu population; Muslims remained generally implacable in their opposition. In Bengal missionaries read somewhat enviously of the reports from Delhi; most reported that Bengali attitudes to the gospel remained much as they had been before.[32]

28.   *BM* 52 (1860), 50.

29.   *BM* 54 (1862), 325-6; cf. Alter and Singh, 'The Church in Delhi', 29.

30.   *BM* 57 (1865), 604.

31.   Alter and Singh, 'The Church in Delhi', 29-33.

32.   See the responses to question 58 in *Reports and Documents on the Indian Mission, passim.*

However, resentment against the British presence amongst sections of the Calcutta community was now more noticeable, and in places the first stirrings of Indian nationalism could be discerned. Writing of the Entally district of Calcutta in 1870, John Wenger observed that 'Christianity is regarded as the national religion of the foreign conqueror, and the antipathy of which the latter is the object is also extended to his religion'. Meanwhile, at Serampore College John Trafford identified the rise of 'a *national* spirit' among the student body as one of the reasons for the rarity of conversions to Christianity.[33] Educated, English-speaking Bengalis were gravitating to the rational theism of the Brahmo Samaj, and rejecting the doctrine of the vicarious atonement, while remaining attracted to 'the Spirit of Christ' in an ethical and non-dogmatic sense.[34] Many who were drawn by the person of Christ found missionary Christianity alien and unpersuasive.

For the great majority of Hindus, after 1857 as before it, to become a Christian was still, in the words of John Lawrence, missionary at Monghyr, in 1870, 'the most base, disgraceful, and ruinous thing that could possibly happen to one'.[35] That conviction was, and probably still is, the greatest barrier to the spread of Christianity in northern India.

III: Missionary Strategy and the Persistence of Dependency

The Society gave James Smith's work in Delhi considerable prominence in the pages of the *Missionary Herald*. Smith was admired on the home Committee, not merely for his church-planting achievements, but even more for his resolute attempts to make the Delhi churches independent of the control and financial support of the BMS. 'I would rather the churches fell into error', proclaimed Smith, 'than keep them under the Missionary's thumb. Independence must be secured at almost any cost'.[36] His sentiments were music to the ears of a Committee that was all too accustomed to hearing its missionaries justify the continuing dependent status of the Indian churches. From the early 1850s onwards, a determination to propel its churches towards genuine financial independence was the dominant characteristic of the Society's policy in India.

33. Ibid., 13, 116.

34. Ibid., 104. The Brahmo Samaj was founded by Ram Mohun Roy in 1828, and fused elements of Christian worship with Hindu devotion to form a reformed, monotheistic brand of Hinduism likely to appeal to educated Bengalis.

35. Ibid., 149.

36. *BM* 56 (1864), 189.

The momentum behind the Committee's policy was supplied in large measure by E. B. Underhill, secretary in charge of foreign affairs since 1849. The India mission had remained static in size and limited in strategic vision since the reunion with the Serampore Mission in 1837, which had imposed considerable financial strain on the BMS. In 1852 Underhill, having secured a more stable financial basis for the Society, initiated a phase of renewed expansion and fundamental re-evaluation of strategic objectives in India.[37] For two and a half years from 1854 to 1857, Underhill (accompanied by his wife and daughter) was away in India and Ceylon seeking to revitalize the Society's first and most celebrated field.

Two concerns impressed themselves on Underhill's mind during his deputation tour. The first was the tardiness of the missionaries in implementing the Committee's policy, enunciated in resolutions passed in April 1852 and June 1853, that the Indian churches should be urged to elect and support their own pastors.[38] Underhill's second concern took shape in the course of his tour. The more he witnessed of the itinerant preaching which formed the primary evangelistic thrust of the Baptist missionaries, the less convinced he became of its effectiveness - most converts were not, in fact, the result of this method. At first he was inclined to attribute the lack of response to an insufficient emphasis by the preacher on the 'criminality of idol-worship' and the necessity of repentance, but by the end of his tour Underhill was questioning the wisdom of concentrating evangelistic effort on the bazar and the public concourse: if Christianity were to reach the middle and artisan classes, missionaries would have to follow the harder road of penetrating Indian homes with the gospel.[39]

The 1857 rebellion temporarily pushed these fundamental strategic concerns into the background, but they re-emerged in the 1860s. In July 1862 the Committee considered a paper on the subject of 'native agency' in India, which saw the solution to the disproportion between the escalating costs and meagre results of the India mission to lie in a more extensive use of native agents, and a severance of the 'leading strings' which tied the existing agents to missionary control.[40] The paper led the Committee to formulate new plans for the vernacular theological training of Indian

---

37. Underhill, *Principles and Methods,* 3-8.

38. Ibid., 94-6, 134-6; BMS Committee Minutes, 21 Apr. 1852, pp. 327-8, and 14 June 1853, pp. 16-17.

39. Underhill, *Principles and Methods,* 92, 122-4.

40. The paper, by James Webb, is preserved in rough draft form in the volume 'Sub-Committee Reports Eastern'.

preachers, and to press the missionaries to make rapid progress towards granting independent and self-sustaining status to the Indian churches.[41] However, when these resolutions were discussed at a conference of the Bengal missionaries in January 1865, the view was repeatedly expressed that the proper relationship between European missionaries and Indian preachers was that 'we direct and they obey in a Christian spirit'. The conference resolved unanimously that the Indian preachers were 'generally not fitted' to discharge pastoral and evangelistic duties without missionary superintendence, and that, as recipients of the Society's financial support, they should remain subordinate to missionary control.[42]

The response of the Bengal missionaries evoked dismay in the minds of the Committee. A pained circular letter to all Indian missionaries was sent in reply, arguing that the admitted deficiencies in the Society's Indian national agents were the result of the state of 'continuous abiding dependence' in which the churches had been maintained.[43] The Committee had been strengthened in its adherence to self-supporting principles by an interview in 1866 with the superintendent of the Calcutta Mission Press, C. B. Lewis, then on furlough, at which Lewis had presented a paper boldly identifying the heart of the problem as the payment of both Indian pastors and evangelists from BMS funds. During that same furlough, Lewis's wife, Marianne, wrote the pamphlet which led to the formation in the following year of 'The Ladies' Association for the Support of Zenana Work and Bible-Women in India, in connection with the Baptist Missionary Society' - later known as the Baptist Zenana Mission.[44]

The BMS annual report for 1867-8 contained a lengthy review of the progress made towards the establishment of independent churches in the Society's missions. While the picture in the Western missions was described as broadly encouraging, the Eastern churches presented a depressing contrast. Of the fifty-six churches in the Indian mission, few had an Indian pastor and deacons functioning independently of missionary control, and in only one, South Colinga in Calcutta, was the pastor wholly supported by

---

41. BMS Committee Minutes, 9 July 1862, p. 182; 8 Oct. 1862, pp. 199-200; 14 Jan. 1863, p. 220; Sub-Committee Reports Eastern, Report of Sub-Committee on Native Agency, 13 Jan. 1863, and circular letter dated 29 Oct. 1863.

42. Sub-Committee Reports, Miscellaneous, 1863-7, circular letter dated 10 July 1867, pp. 3, 4.

43. Ibid., p. 5.

44. Printed in *Reports and Documents on the Indian Mission*, 235-40. For the origins and history of the Baptist Zenana Mission see below, ch. VII, pp. 227-232.

the membership. Moves towards financial independence had, however, been initiated in the churches in the Delhi, Jessore and Barisal districts, which were the strongest numerically in the India mission. The report was not unsympathetic to the difficulties faced by the Indian churches. It recognized that the caste system had thrown most converts on to the missionary for protection and support, that converts had been gathered only in ones or twos, and as a result had faced bitter opposition and been deprived of their livelihood. Dependency was acknowledged as a natural consequence of the Indian social context, yet at the same time was repudiated as unacceptable for those whom Christ had made free.[45] The resolution of this contradiction was to defy the best minds in the BMS India mission for years to come.

E. B. Underhill was by now determined to effect fundamental reform in the India mission, not least because the state of BMS finances in 1868 made continuance on present lines impossible.[46] At the Committee meeting on 13 October the Officers presented a paper, written by Underhill, identifying 'two great defects' in the operation of the India mission. They were essentially the two main concerns of his 1854-7 deputation tour, in elaborated form. The first was that the Society's missionaries were touching the life of India's people 'only at its outskirts'. Anchored by institutional responsibilities or family ties to fixed places of abode (usually well removed from the indigenous population), missionaries sallied forth periodically to preach in the bazars, where they attracted only the poor, idle, curious, or ignorant. Evangelism was being conducted, not from a life lived in common with the national population, but from a life lived apart. The second defect was, once again, the dependence of almost all the Society's 130 Indian preachers on European funds. The paper made four recommendations for future policy. Educational and training institutions should be made self-supporting; the location of mission stations should be reviewed in order to give missionaries a more direct influence over the surrounding population; the Society should recruit a more mobile missionary agency, made up of men who were unencumbered by family and institutional ties, and prepared to support themselves on the field; finally, a clear distinction must be drawn between national workers in pastoral charge, who must speedily be made dependent on their churches for support, and those who were itinerant evangelists, who should be regarded as companions of their missionary brethren.[47]

45. *BM* 60 (1868), 327-33.

46. Underhill, *Principles and Methods*, 12-13.

47. 'Our Indian Mission: Its Condition and Prospects', in Underhill, *Principles and Methods*, 189-209.

The Officers' paper gave rise to 'much serious and animated discussion', and even sharp disagreement within the Committee.[48] After further discussion at the meetings on 23 December 1868 and 13 January 1869, the first, second and fourth recommendations were agreed, but a decision on the third and most controversial recommendation, relating to the creation of a more mobile and independently supported missionary agency, was postponed until the July meeting.[49] In the interim, Underhill gained influential support from William Landels, minister of Regent's Park Chapel, in a speech at the Society's annual public meeting. Landels was closely associated with Hudson Taylor's China Inland Mission, founded four years earlier on principles not dissimilar to those Underhill was now advocating.[50] Landels referred extensively to the Officers' paper, and added his own eloquent plea for missionaries who would be prepared to forego marriage and 'go out two by two, *roughing* it among the people of the land, living with them as much as possible, labouring for their own support, if necessary' and seeking by a life of self-denial to commend the gospel.[51] Landels' ideas were similar to those advanced by earlier critics of the missionary movement, such as Edward Irving; in the Indian context, they also anticipated in some respects the thinking of C.F. Andrews of the Cambridge Mission to Delhi.[52]

Landels' speech provoked considerable controversy within the denomination, and notably within the pages of *The Freeman* newspaper.[53] Many of the Society's Indian missionaries felt that their integrity and consecration were under challenge. On 14 July the Committee, after 'prolonged consideration', resolved in favour of the idea of recruiting missionaries specifically for 'an active and wandering life', though it was now stated that the Committee would be prepared to provide for 'all needed requirements and such exigencies as may arise' (a compromise formula that allowed for, but did not enjoin, self-support). It was also resolved that the rule of the Society

48. BMS Committee Minutes, 13 Oct. 1868, p. 484.

49. BMS Committee Minutes, 23 Dec. 1868, pp. 509-10; 13 Jan. 1869, pp. 6-9.

50. T. Landels, *William Landels D.D.: A Memoir* (London, 1900), 328; T. Richard, *Forty-five Years in China* (London, 1916), 28.

51. *BM* 61 (1869), 406.

52. B. Chaturvedi and M. Sykes, *Charles Freer Andrews* (London, 1949), 70-4; D. O'Connor, *Gospel, Raj and Swaraj: The Missionary Years of C. F. Andrews 1904-14* (Frankfurt, 1990), 173-83.

53. *The Freeman*, 21 May to 8 Oct. 1869, *passim*.

should in future be that 'young men sent out as Missionaries, should go forth unmarried, and remain so, for two years at least'.[54]

In order to allay the continuing disquiet in the denomination, the Officers made the next quarterly meeting of the Committee, held at Leicester on 5 October, an open meeting, which pastors of contributing churches were entitled to attend. At least 250 persons were present at the meeting. A memorial with ninety signatures was presented, requesting the Committee to reconsider its ruling on the marriage of missionaries. However, after an explanatory statement by Underhill, and a frank but 'brotherly' discussion, unanimous resolutions were passed which left the Committee's policy intact, while seeking to re-assure the anxious.[55] A potentially serious crisis of domestic confidence in the Indian policy of the Committee had been defused, but soon afterwards a document was circulated amongst Committee members, signed by a number of the Society's India missionaries, which objected strongly to the proposed changes in Indian policy. In response, and at William Landels' suggestion, a special committee was set up to inquire into the entire working of the India mission.[56]

At the behest of the special committee, a questionnaire of sixty-seven questions was sent in June 1870 to all the Society's India missionaries. Many of the questions were purely factual, but others sought opinion on the competence of native preachers, and whether their payment from missionary funds was prejudicial to the spread of the gospel.[57] The replies to the questionnaire confirmed that the majority of missionaries saw no objection to the payment of Indian workers from foreign funds. Several, including G. C. Dutt, the Bengali whose work at Khulna from 1867 was among the most fruitful in the whole mission, predicted dire consequences if payments to Indian evangelists were discontinued. Dutt saw no possibility of support from the churches, and predicted that unpaid evangelists would 'wander like fakirs' and be regarded as 'loafers and outcastes'.[58] However, a significant minority of missionaries were beginning to perceive the problem which Underhill saw so clearly.[59]

54. BMS Committee Minutes, 14 July 1869, pp. 66-7.

55. Underhill, *Principles and Methods*, 14, 212-15.

56. BMS Committee Minutes, 19 Oct. 1869, pp. 100-1; 2 Nov. 1869, pp. 104-5; 7 Dec. 1869, pp. 115-16; Landels, *William Landels*, 323-4.

57. *Reports and Documents on the Indian Mission*, 2-7.

58. Ibid., 63. On Dutt see Soddy, *Baptists in Bangladesh*, 48, 52, 58-64.

59. *Reports and Documents on the Indian Mission*, 26, 47-9, 107, 183, 203, 234.

The special committee on the India mission presented its report in April 1871. It concluded that the results of its survey were 'not favourable to the qualifications and efficiency of the native preachers', and recommended that the Society's entire force of Indian preachers be given twelve months' notice; only those who convinced a board of missionaries of their efficiency were to be re-engaged.[60] These recommendations produced a storm of protest on the field, even from supporters of Underhill's policy, such as C. B. Lewis.[61] A revised report was accordingly prepared, omitting the proposal to dismiss all the Indian preachers. It was adopted by the Committee on 21 February 1872.[62]

The report adopted in 1872 established a policy framework for the India mission which remained intact for several decades.[63] It affirmed the principle of maximum mobility for missionaries, who were to move on to new spheres of labour whenever sufficient converts had been gathered to establish a viable church, or in cases where their work had been evidently unproductive. The radical emphasis of 1868 on a brigade of self-support-ing, 'apostolic' missionaries living in simple identification with the indig-enous population had, however, disappeared (though the resolutions of 14 July 1869 remained unrevoked). In terms of church policy, the report ruled that financial support for Indian agents should be discontinued as soon as practicable. It also urged that specific provision for ministerial training be added to the existing programme at Serampore College, and a similar ministerial class be established in the North-West Provinces.[64] The first steps towards the creation of autonomous Baptist churches in India had been taken.

Deciding the policy agreed in 1872 had not been easy. Implementing it proved even more difficult. Effective autonomy for the Indian churches presupposed the existence of strong district unions of churches, and these did not exist. An association of Baptist churches in Bengal had been formed as early as 1842, but had become moribund after a few years.[65] The first effective union of Baptist churches was formed by the strong congregations

---

60. Ibid., 251-3.

61. Ibid., 264.

62. Ibid., 341-5.

63. Underhill, *Principles and Methods*, 16-17.

64. *Reports and Documents on the Indian Mission*, 342-5.

65. D. S. Wells (comp.), *Ye are My Witnesses 1792-1842: One Hundred and Fiftieth Anniversary of the Baptist Missionary Society in India* (Calcutta, 1942), 22-3.

of the Barisal district in 1890, after a decade in which they had met annually in a looser association. The union adjudicated in disputes that could not be settled by individual churches, and published a handbook printing accounts and church membership statistics. Robert Spurgeon of Barisal saw the handbook as 'a great stride forward', giving the churches a sense of corporate identity and correct ideas of self-government.[66] Other district unions were subsequently established in other parts of Bengal, laying the foundations for the formation of the Bengal Baptist Union in 1922.[67]

Amongst churches less strong than those of the Barisal district, financial dependency remained a problem well into the twentieth century. At the fifth triennial conference of all BMS India missionaries held in Calcutta in 1907, the Indian 'home missionary', B. C. Ghose, observed that dependence on foreign resources was becoming more and more distasteful to Indian Christians, yet all except two of the missionaries present voted for a motion which declared that paid native evangelistic agency was still a necessity for the Society.[68] Some progress was, nevertheless, being made. The mean annual contribution per member to church funds in the India mission rose from 2.75 rupees in 1900 to 4.72 rupees in 1913. By the latter date forty-seven Indian pastors and thirty evangelists were supported by the churches.[69]

The strengthening spirit of co-operation between Protestant missions in the wake of the World Missionary Conference at Edinburgh in 1910 now gave additional momentum to the moves towards autonomy for the Indian churches. A series of six regional missionary conferences held during 1912 under the presidency of John R. Mott gave the subject prominence, culminating in a national conference in Calcutta, which decided to set up a National Missionary Council of India; Herbert Anderson of the BMS became its first half-time secretary in 1914.[70] The Calcutta conference urged that 'all positions of responsibility made available for Indian Christians should be related to Church organisations rather than to those of Foreign Missionary Societies'. This was a clear call for an end to the

---

66. *MH* (May 1893), 159-60; see also *MH* (Nov. 1892), 437-8.

67. W. E. French, *The Gospel in India* (London, 1946), 143-4; Soddy, *Baptists in Bangladesh*, 187.

68. Minutes of the Fifth Triennial United Conference of the Bengal, North India, and Orissa Missionaries, (Calcutta, 1907), 11. Ghose himself supported the motion.

69. G. W. Macalpine and C. E. Wilson, Report on the India and Ceylon Missions of the Baptist Missionary Society (1914), 59-60.

70. H-R. Weber, *Asia and the Ecumenical Movement 1895-1961* (London, 1966), 135-7.

widespread practice by the missionary societies of employing Indian evangelists. The BMS triennial conference held in January 1914 (presided over by Sir George Macalpine, the chairman of the Society, then on a deputation tour with C. E. Wilson) agreed that 'this is the ideal for which we must strive', yet thought it probable that it would be 'many years' before the BMS could dispense with a paid national agency in some districts.[71] There was in fact considerable confusion in missionaries' minds on the subject. The Bengal and North India BMS conferences in 1912 had voted by slender majorities to recruit no more Indian evangelists to the mission staff in Bengal and North India - but the effect of these decisions was to reduce the numbers of Indians coming forward for theological training almost to nothing.[72]

Macalpine and Wilson tried to clear up the confusion in the course of their deputation tour in 1914, but without total success. The 1914 triennial conference resolved, *both* that more evangelists were needed to work in connection with, and, where possible, under the direction of district unions of Baptist churches, *and* that there was an urgent need for more Indian workers 'trained and supported by the Mission'. Macalpine and Wilson noted the 'irreconcilable discrepancy' in their deputation report, and hastened to explain that the 'real policy' of the conference was represented by the former statement, but not the latter.[73] Missionaries were still unclear as to the appropriate relationship between church and mission. All, however, were agreed that the more adequate training of pastors and evangelists was a prerequisite of the establishment of viable independent churches.

IV: Serampore College and Theological Training

Serampore College and its accompanying mission station were specifically excluded from the reunion between the Serampore Mission and the BMS negotiated in 1837.[74] After Joshua Marshman's death in December of that

---

71. Macalpine and Wilson, Report on the India and Ceylon Missions, 61, 65.

72. Minutes of the Bengal Conference, Oct. 1912, p. 5; Minutes of the North India Conference, Nov. 1912, pp. 20-1.

73. Minutes of the 7th Triennial United Conference, p. 6; Macalpine and Wilson, Report on the India and Ceylon Missions, 63, 65, 78.

74. The best account of the history of the College in this period is in Underhill, *Principles and Methods,* 245-65; see also W. S. Stewart (ed.), *The Story of Serampore and its College* (Serampore, 1961), 27-9.

year, the management of the College fell principally on John Clark Marshman and John Mack, the Scotsman who had taught at the College since 1821. Although J. C. Marshman put substantial money of his own into the College, its funding and hence its future became a source of increasing anxiety to him. In 1842 Marshman made overtures to the BMS, who agreed to provide the salary of a theological professor. W. H. Denham thus joined the teaching staff in 1844 as a BMS missionary, and became Principal on Mack's death in 1845. In 1850 Marshman, who was contemplating leaving India, made a fresh approach to the Society with a view to guaranteeing the future of the College. An agreement was reached in August 1851, whereby the Society was given use of the premises for a ministerial training class, to be financed, in part, by £500 per annum from BMS funds. The government of the College remained in the hands of its Council, but it was agreed that BMS representatives would predominate on the Council. While in India in 1855, E. B. Underhill received a letter pointing out that Marshman's imminent departure confronted the College with a stark choice between becoming a secular institution and full union with the BMS. Underhill, with the support of the Bengal missionaries, pressed the home Committee to sanction the latter course, and on 12 December 1855 his proposals were overwhelmingly carried.[75] Although the College Council remained legally responsible for the College, the effective management of the institution was now in the hands of the BMS. For the first time, the Society had the opportunity to integrate Serampore College into its overall Indian strategy.

The original prospectus for Serampore College, written by Joshua Marshman in 1818, had declared that the institution was to be 'pre-eminently a divinity school, where Christian youth of personal piety and aptitude for the work of an evangelist should go through a complete course of instruction in Christian theology'.[76] As was emphasized in Chapter Two, the breadth of the curriculum and the openness of the College to non-Christian students were conceived by its founders as integral to, rather than subversive of, its missionary character.[77] The Serampore Trio had also insisted on instruction being in the Bengali vernacular rather than English, and on a prime place for Sanskrit in the curriculum. During the 1830s this policy was progressively modified in response to the rising demand for English education in Bengal, and the growing influence of Alexander Duff's emphasis on the role of English-medium education in winning the Bengali

75.   BMS Committee Minutes, 12 Dec. 1855, pp. 346-7.

76.   Stewart (ed.), *The Story of Serampore and its College,* 21.

77.   See above, ch. II, p. 52.

élite for Christ. English now supplanted Sanskrit as the primary focus of linguistic studies at Serampore.[78] By the 1840s, training for Christian ministry had become increasingly marginal to the work of the College, in part because of the difficulty of recruiting suitable students. In accordance with the 1851 agreement, the BMS re-established a vernacular theological class, taught by George Pearce, but Pearce found the ethos of the College uncongenial to his work, and removed his class to the Alipore district of Calcutta.[79] The College's affiliation in 1857 to the new University of Calcutta further reduced the importance of theological subjects in the curriculum, and syphoned off the ablest students to degree-level study at the University.[80] From the 1850s to the 1870s the bulk of the student body were elementary students in the school department of the institution. There were very few students in whom the staff saw the potential for Christian service in their maturer years; there was no specific theological training.[81]

As currently constituted, Serampore College was doing little to forward the Society's primary objectives in India of raising a trained national agency and establishing independent churches. Pearce's vernacular class, although essential to the Society's plans for native agency, did not flourish, with eligible students proving hard to find.[82] Both the BMS Committee and John Trafford, Principal of Serampore since 1858, believed that the proper place for such a class was at the College itself - hence the ruling of the 1872 report on the Indian mission that a ministerial training course be commenced at Serampore (and a similar one in the North-West Provinces) and the Alipore class discontinued.[83] In point of fact, no such course was begun at Serampore, while in the North-West only a preparatory class, taught by James Smith in his spare time, proved possible at this stage. Alfred Baynes, sent out to India in 1881, was accordingly instructed to report on how provision could be made for the training of evangelists, pastors, and normal school teachers, either at Serampore or elsewhere. Impressed by the scale of state educational provision, and convinced of the pre-eminent need

78.   Marshman, *Life and Times of Carey*, ii, 501-2; M. A. Laird, *Missionaries and Education in Bengal 1793-1837* (Oxford, 1972), 142-5, 154.

79.   Underhill, *Principles and Methods*, 100; *Reports and Documents on the Indian Mission*, 124-5, 139.

80.   *Reports and Documents on the Indian Mission*, 127.

81.   *BM* 51 (1859), 450-1; *Reports and Documents on the Indian Mission*, 112, 123.

82.   *Reports and Documents on the Indian Mission*, 133.

83.   Ibid., 345-6.

of the churches for trained pastors, evangelists and school-teachers, Baynes recommended that Serampore College be reconstructed specifically as a 'Native Christian Training Institution'.[84] Following Baynes's recommendation, the BMS Committee resolved on 17 January 1883 to abandon the present College and school classes, and to run the College mainly and avowedly as a vernacular Christian Training Institution.[85]

The College department at Serampore was closed in December 1883, the link with Calcutta University severed, and admission to the school restricted to Christian pupils. A vernacular theological class was re-commenced. Even in its new attenuated form, the College still did not flourish, and when Baynes visited Serampore again, in 1890, he formed the still more drastic opinion that the College should be entirely abandoned by the Society. Believing that Serampore fostered in its students a life-style ill-suited to pastoral ministry among the poor, and fatal to the development of self-supporting churches, Baynes recommended to the BMS Committee that the work of theological training be removed to Barisal or some other location in East Bengal nearer to the bulk of the Baptist community.[86] He had, however, reckoned without the opposition of his predecessor, E. B. Underhill, now Honorary Secretary of the Society. Underhill regarded the 1883 decision as a 'disastrous step', and a betrayal of the liberal educational ideals of the Serampore Trio.[87] Underhill now wrote to all members of the Committee, enclosing a masterly review of the history of the College, which argued that to abandon Serampore would be a breach of the Society's obligations, both to the founders of the College and to the late J. C. Marshman.[88] When Baynes's report was considered by the Committee on 21 January 1891, Underhill moved an amendment proposing that the mission and College at Serampore be 'resuscitated on the lines laid down by its founders'.[89]

Underhill's amendment was eventually put to the vote at the February meeting of the Committee. It was lost by a considerable majority, but there

---

84. Underhill papers, 'Serampore College and the BMS, 1877 to 1892', Second Part of Report on Serampore College, 30 Dec. 1882.

85. BMS Committee Minutes, 17 Jan. 1883, pp. 114-15.

86. 'Serampore College and the BMS, 1877 to 1892', Report on Serampore College Training Institution, 1 May 1890.

87. Underhill, *Principles and Methods*, 267.

88. Ibid., 233-76.

89. BMS Committee Minutes, 21 Jan. 1891, p. 180.

was sufficient division of opinion for a vote on the original motion endorsing a move to Barisal to be postponed. This outcome was due in part to a persuasive speech in support of Underhill by G. H. Rouse, the India Secretary and distinguished successor to John Wenger in literary and translation work.[90] In fact the question was postponed indefinitely, while Underhill increased the pressure on Baynes in 1896 by publishing his case for the retention of the College in his *Principles and Methods of Missionary Labour.*

Presentation copies of Underhill's book were sent to all BMS India missionaries, including George Howells, recently arrived on the staff of the former General Baptist theological college at Cuttack.[91] Howells was impressed by Underhill's arguments, and alerted to the existence of Serampore's Danish charter of incorporation of 1827, empowering the College to award degrees, which had for long been a dead letter. In 1900 Herbert Anderson, Rouse's successor as India Secretary, invited Howells to read a paper on theological education to the Triennial Conference of Baptist Missionaries in December. Howells took the opportunity to propose that Serampore College be reconstituted as a Christian University, and that an interdenominational senate be set up to confer degrees and diplomas in theology on students from institutions throughout India. The Conference received Howells' proposals sympathetically but not uncritically, and in due course Howells was given permission by the Society to publicize his ideas more widely.[92] As a result the decennial conference of all Protestant missionaries in India, held at Madras in December 1902, appointed a committee to negotiate with the College Council regarding the revival of the charter and the formation of an interdenominational Senate to promote degree-level theological study at Serampore.

The BMS Committee had not yet expressed its mind on Howells' proposals, and there was still considerable support for Baynes's view that the Society should concentrate on vernacular theological training for its own church leaders. Nevertheless, Howells, though still a junior missionary on the staff of the Cuttack college, had the consistent support of Herbert Anderson. While on furlough in 1904, Howells was invited to meet the

---

90. BMS Committee Minutes, 17 Feb. 1891, pp. 211-12; 'Serampore College and the BMS, 1877 to 1892', 139.

91. The account which follows is based mainly on G. Howells *et al., The Story of Serampore and its College* (Serampore, 1927), 61-72.

92. Minutes of the Third Triennial United Conference of the Bengal, North-West India, and Orissa Missionaries, (Calcutta, 1900), 24-8.

Committee, and made a favourable impression.[93] The prospects for the realization of Howells' vision were further improved by the appointment in 1904 of C. E. Wilson from Serampore College, initially (from 1905) as joint-secretary of the Society, and then, after Baynes's retirement in March 1906, as General Secretary. In the same year, the health of the Principal of Serampore, E. S. Summers, failed, and Howells was appointed in his place. Howells now had both the domestic support and the position in India to make his dream a reality. In November 1907 the BMS Committee resolved to reopen the College for higher Arts and theological education, and in ✓ January 1908 an initial grant of £7,000 was made available from the Arthington Fund for new land and buildings.[94] By March 1909 £25,000 had been raised by public appeal and contributions from the Fund, but more was needed. Although determined efforts to obtain a grant from the Rockefeller Foundation proved ultimately unavailing, the immediate financial future of the reconstituted College was secured by lavish donations from G. B. Leechman, a retired Ceylon merchant, and son of a former tutor at the College.[95] In addition, a grant of £25,000 from the Arthington Fund made possible major improvements to the College premises. The higher theological department was opened in 1910, and the Arts department was revived and re-affiliated to Calcutta University in 1911. The power conferred by the 1827 charter to confer degrees in theology was utilized for the first time in 1915.

E. B. Underhill had fought and George Howells had won a protracted battle for the very survival of Serampore College. Believing that a general education on Christian principles would leaven the lump of Indian society, they argued strongly against the restriction of the College to Christian students. They were able to defend their case by appeal to the example of the founders of the College, who possessed a similar faith in the Christianizing influence of education, and had provided for the admission of Hindu and Muslim students. On the other hand, Alfred Baynes and the majority of the BMS Committee in the 1880s and 1890s did not regard the general diffusion of Christian higher education as an appropriate priority for the Society. They wished to see the College either function effectively as a training institution serving the immediate needs of the Baptist churches, or cease to be a burden on the Society's resources. Although given short shrift

93. Howells, *et al.*, *The Story of Serampore and its College* (1927 edn.), 67-8.

94. General Committee Minutes, 20 Nov. 1907, p. 192; 22 Jan. 1908, p. 5. On the Arthington Fund see below, ch. XII, pp. 381-3.

95. John Leechman was a tutor from 1832 to 1837.

by the College's historians,[96] their arguments also could (and did) claim congruence with the aims of the founders, for whom the College's role in training Indian evangelists was primary.[97] There is no doubt that Howells' victory ushered in a golden age of unrivalled influence and academic achievement at Serampore (one of his faculty was T. H. Robinson, later a renowned Old Testament scholar). Yet the vernacular theological department - the one which held the key to the creation of mature and autonomous Indian churches - remained weak, not least because the opportunity of employment on the BMS staff had apparently been closed by the decisions of 1912. In 1915 the department had only four students, none of them from Baptist churches.[98] As the focus of church growth in India moved increasingly to tribal and low-caste peoples with minimal educational provision, the need for effective vernacular theological education, at a much lower level than Serampore was fitted to provide, was to become more and more insistent.

V: The Orissa Mission, 1822-1914

The pioneer missionaries of the General Baptist Missionary Society, William Bampton and James Peggs, began work in Cuttack, the capital of Orissa, in 1822.[99] Preaching stations were also opened at Puri (1823), Berhampur (1825), and later at Ganjam and Pipli. The first profession of faith came from a Telegu weaver, Erun Senapaty, who was baptized by Bampton at Berhampur on Christmas Day, 1827. The first Oriya to be converted was Gangadhar Saringhy, a Brahmin, baptized by Charles Lacey in March 1828. The baptized membership grew quite rapidly thereafter, reaching about 200 by 1842. The great majority of converts were in the Cuttack area. The Cuttack church had 137 members in 1845, and its six out-stations a further fifty-two.[100] As in Bengal, a significant proportion of the earliest converts were of high caste, and hence promising material for evangelistic work. Gangadhar, two other early Brahmin converts, and

---

96. *The Story of Serampore and its College* (1918 edn.), 34-5; (1927 edn.), 23-5, 61; (1961 edn.) 32-3.

97. 'Serampore College and the BMS, 1877 to 1892', Second Part of Report on Serampore College, 30 Dec. 1882, pp. 1, 5.

98. *BMS Annual Report,* 1915-16, p. 20.

99. This paragraph is based mainly on J. Peggs, *A History of the General Baptist Mission* (London, 1846).

100. Ibid., 257.

Dinabandhu Mohanty, the first convert at Ganjam and a member of the writer caste, all became evangelists in the mission. In 1841 Gangadhar and two others began studying under Amos Sutton at Cuttack. By January 1846 there were eight students, and the class was formalized as the Cuttack Mission Academy (later the Cuttack Theological College, whose staff George Howells was to join fifty years later). From an early date the Orissa mission thus had the advantage of a training institution located at the heart of a geographically concentrated Christian constituency - an advantage that Serampore in the BMS mission lacked.

Many of the converts were settled in Christian villages, seven of which had been formed by 1844. The early missionaries had no doubts about the process, seeing the villages as oases of Christian truth amidst the wastes of idolatry.[101] Christian villages tended to act as a magnet for the outcaste and fellow traveller, and thus helped to inflate the total Christian community to about five times the size of the baptized membership. Also included in the Christian community were the children in the orphanages opened at Cuttack and Berhampur in 1836, and at Ganjam in 1841. Within a year of their foundation, the role and significance of the orphanages were transformed by the disclosure, following the dispatch of British forces to suppress the Goomsur insurrection, of the *Meriah* human sacrifices practised in the Kond Hills. The animistic Konds habitually appeased the spirits by the sacrifice of kidnap victims, usually children. British officials, most notably Major S. C. Macpherson, now began a campaign to rescue the *Meriah* victims and substitute buffalo sacrifices for the human ones. Most of the rescued children were taken to the Baptist orphanages. During the eighteen years of the British campaign, about 250 *Meriah* children were placed in the orphanages (including one run by the American Free Will Baptists at Balasur).[102]

Numbers of these *Meriah* orphans became committed Christians and key figures within the Baptist churches. One, Paul Singh, trained in the Cuttack Academy as an evangelist.[103] Orphanage work entered a new phase in 1866, when famine removed a quarter of Orissa's population. In response to appeals from the British authorities, the Baptist missionaries opened new orphanages at Cuttack, Pipli and Berhampur, which received about 1,300 children.[104] Again, large numbers of the children became Christians,

---

101. Ibid., 296-7, 304-5.

102. *Indian Report of the Orissa Baptist Mission,* 1871-2, 5-6.

103. S. P. Carey, *Dawn on the Kond Hills* (London, 1936), 28-9.

104. *GBMS Annual Reports,* 1866-7, pp. 7-14; 1867-8, p. 5.

Map 4: Orissa

resulting in significant growth in the churches at Cuttack, Pipli and Berhampur during the 1870s.[105] Of a total communicant membership in the Orissa mission in 1879 of 982, 452 were in the Cuttack churches, 209 at Pipli and 152 at Berhampur.[106] Church membership in the Orissa mission remained heavily concentrated in these three clusters for the rest of the century. The pattern was broken only after the mission ventured inland from the Orissa coastal plain to evangelize the aboriginal peoples of the hills.

In December 1879 J. G. Pike (grandson of the founder of the GBMS) and P. E. Heberlet began work at Sambalpur in West Orissa, a remote station which the Free Will Baptists had opened in the 1830s, but then abandoned. Sambalpur itself proved relatively unproductive, but in 1888 fourteen Mundas, an aboriginal hill tribe, were baptized.[107] The Mundas were from the village of Telanpali, forty miles from Sambalpur, where a former Lutheran from Ranchi, Prabhu Sahai, was exercising a remarkable Christian influence. Twenty more Mundas were baptized in 1889, and the total Christian community at Telanpali grew to over 100. However, in

---

105. *GBMS Annual Reports*, especially 1871, p. 36; Myers (ed.), *Centenary Volume of the BMS*, 260.

106. *GBMS Annual Report*, 1878-9, pp. 11, 14, 24, 38.

107. *Indian Report of the Orissa Baptist Mission*, 1888-9, p. 33.

January 1890 Prabhu died, and growth ground to a halt. Some who had professed faith when healed of cholera after Prabhu - reputed to be 'mighty in prayer' - had prayed for them, now fell away.[108] However, the process of conversion among the Mundas was subsequently resumed, and they were soon well represented in the Sambalpur church.[109]

Evangelists such as Prabhu played a crucial role in the growth of the church in West Orissa. Three other evangelists based at Sambalpur, Daniel Das, John Pal and Durga Charan Mohanty, were the primary instruments in a movement of conversion from 1893 which forms another example in a British Baptist field of the 'people movements' towards Christianity that became increasingly common in India from the 1860s onwards. P. E. Heberlet, itinerating with his team of Sambalpur evangelists in the cold season of 1892-3, was encouraged by the conversion of a headman of a low-caste village to concentrate future itinerations on low-caste communities. The following year Daniel Das found the response which Heberlet hoped for in Budipadar in Patna state, where the conversion of one low-caste man sparked off eager interest in Christianity in this and neighbouring villages. Das summoned Heberlet to help. Subsequently, first John Pal, fresh from the Cuttack college, and then D. C. Mohanty, spent periods at Budipadar, lodging in the very midst of the low-caste people, and thus losing caste themselves. Whilst most of the believers were low-caste, one group of forty well-to-do weavers came night after night in 1894 to hear the gospel, until Heberlet believed they were 'prepared to come out in a body'. Although Heberlet had to leave this group to baptize converts elsewhere, other groups clearly made the corporate decision to profess conversion.[110]

Over the next two decades, the low-caste movement initiated at Budipadar spread throughout the villages in the three adjoining regions of Patna state, Bargarh, and Borosambar/Phuljar.[111] On one day in 1909 in Patna state, nearly 400 were baptized: the news 'spread from village to village like an electric current'.[112] By 1914 the Balangir, Padampur and Sambalpur church districts accounted for almost half of the total Orissa membership of 3,691,

---

108. *Indian Reports of the Orissa Baptist Mission,* 1889-90, pp. 39-40; 1890-1891, p. 103.

109. Wells (comp.), *Ye are My Witnesses,* 115.

110. Wells (comp.), *Ye are My Witnesses,* 110-11, 115; *BMS Orissa Reports* for 1893, pp. 31-2; for 1894, pp. 34-6; for 1895, p. 31; for 1896, pp. 34-5.

111. See especially *BMS Orissa Report* for 1904, pp. 26-9.

112. *BMS Orissa Report* for 1911, p. 53.

and recorded 155 of the 206 baptisms in Orissa in that year.[113] The Christians were scattered in over 100 villages, and no formal churches were organized until F. W. Jarry and Gordon S. Wilkins arrived in 1913. Sixteen churches were constituted in Patna state between 1914 and 1917, and federated in a church union. From the Patna union grew the West Utkal Baptist Church Union of 1922, which in turn became an important part of the Utkal Baptist Central Church Council formed in 1933 - the first fully autonomous church body in the BMS India mission. The Orissa churches - many of them among the youngest in the entire mission - were thus the first to reach the goal of independent church life.[114]

The West Orissa mission was one example of an increasing trend throughout India for missions to concentrate their evangelistic efforts on low-caste or tribal peoples. Other examples of the same trend in the BMS mission included: the independently financed Indian Home Mission to the Santhals, founded in 1867 to minister to the Santhal people of the Suri district; the work among the Santhals, Oraons and Garos of North Bengal initiated after 1904; and, supremely, the South Lushai or Mizoram mission undertaken in 1903.[115] Although such initiatives frequently met with group responses to Christianity on an impressive scale, instant evangelistic success was not guaranteed. The mission to the aboriginal Konds of Orissa provides the clearest instance of this fact.

The first Baptist missionary to work among the Konds was John Orissa Goadby, who made regular visits to the Hill Tracts from his base at Bhanjanagar (Russellkonda) between 1862 and his death in 1868. Goadby acquired the Kui language, but was compelled by the famine of 1866 to leave the Konds and go to the aid of his missionary colleagues in Cuttack. Goadby latterly considered returning to a new base at Balliguda in the heart of the Tracts; had he lived to do so, it is possible that the Konds might have embraced Christianity almost a century earlier than in fact they did.[116] After Goadby's death, no sustained missionary contact with the Konds was made

---

113. *BMS Annual Report*, 1914-15, pp. 244-5. The first four baptisms in the Kond Hills have been added to the figure given in the Report.

114. Wells (comp.), *Ye are My Witnesses*, 116-17; French, *The Gospel in India*, 146. The Utkal Christian Church Union of Orissa had been formed at Cuttack in 1908.

115. On the Santhal mission see O. Hodne, *L. O. Skrefsrud, Missionary and Social Reformer among the Santals of Santal Parganas* (Oslo, 1966); on the North Bengal tribal work see Wells (comp.), *Ye are My Witnesses*, 28-32; on Mizoram see below ch. IX, pp. 269-76

116. B. M. Boal, 'The Church in the Kond Hills: An Encounter with Animism', in Hayward (ed.), *The Church as Christian Community*, 269.

till 1891. The Orissa Mission Report for 1889 had contained an account by P. E. Heberlet of a request from the Hindu sub-magistrate at Udayagiri for a mission to be established there.[117] This appeal was brought to the attention of two Baptist students of Cliff College in Derbyshire, Abiathar Wilkinson and Arthur Long, who offered to the GBMS for service at Udayagiri. The GBMS Committee was preoccupied by the current nego-tiations with the BMS for the merger of the two societies, and turned down their application. An interdenominational committee was accordingly set up to support the proposed mission.[118] The BMS did not assume respon-sibility for the Kond mission until 1893.[119]

Wilkinson and Long sailed for Orissa in the autumn of 1889, and were followed a year later by their fellow Cliff College student, Thomas Wood. In January 1891 the three men settled in Udayagiri. On 25 March Wood died of fever. Wilkinson survived till 1897, and translated the Gospel of Mark into Kui. Long likewise proved susceptible to the fevers of the Tracts; he also found Wilkinson a difficult colleague. In consequence, Long spent much of his missionary career either at Bhanjanagar or away from the Hill Tracts altogether, working for five years in Sambalpur and for two in Berhampur. He never became fluent in the Kui language, and died of black-water fever on 23 April 1909. Despite these several frustrations, Long's tombstone at Bhanjanagar records that 'he lived to see the desire of his heart realized in the establishment of the Khond mission'. It was Long who persuaded the Arthington Committee in 1905-6 to support the mission, and fed Alfred Baynes with all the necessary information.[120] He also accompanied Robert Fletcher Moorshead, secretary of the recently founded Medical Mission Auxiliary, on his tour of the Hills in 1906 - a tour which convinced Moorshead that the Kond mission should 'advance at the point of the lancet' and combat the priest-doctors of animism with the preacher-healers of Christianity.[121] Most significant of all, it was Long who inspired one of George Howells' Oriya students at Cuttack, John Biswas, to commence his pioneer evangelistic ministry among the Konds.

117. *Indian Report of the Orissa Baptist Mission,* 1888-9, p. 27.

118. Carey, *Dawn on the Kond Hills,* 42-3.

119. BMS Committee Minutes, 20 June 1893, pp. 275-6.

120. Arthington Committee Minute Book No 1 (1905-7), minutes for 23 Oct. 1905, 29 Jan. 1906.

121. Carey, *Dawn on the Kond Hills,* 50, 53-4; H. V. Larcombe, *First, the Kingdom!* (London, n.d.), 56-8. For the origins of the Auxiliary, and of BMS medical work in India, see below, ch. VII, pp. 233-9.

The first generation of missionaries to the Konds thus passed without seeing any fruit to their labours. The second generation included further representatives from the same evangelical stable - Peter Horsburgh from Cliff College and Edward Evans from its twin institution at Harley College, Bow - but also Oliver Millman, an educational missionary from Serampore (and brother of William Millman of Yakusu). From 1908 Millman pioneered Kui-medium schools in the Tracts, which proved immensely popular. Nonetheless, it was six years before Millman was able to report the first converts from the Kui-speaking people. On Easter Sunday 1914, Bisi and three members of his household were baptized. They were from the Domb people, Kui speakers and animists, but regarded as inferior by the indigenous Konds.[122] The Domb community was to provide the bulk of Baptist membership in the Kond Hills for the next forty years. The harvest among the Konds themselves would not be reaped until after 1956.

VI: Ceylon (Sri Lanka), 1830-1914

James Chater, pioneer of the Ceylon mission, died on his way home to Britain on 2 January 1829. His successor, Ebenezer Daniel, arrived in August 1830 to find the mission in a sad state of decline.[123] The mission's two churches, at Colombo and Hamvälla (twenty miles from Colombo), were in a weak state, and some of the village schools which Chater had founded had folded up after his departure. Daniel revived the flagging schools work, and initiated a programme of regular evangelistic preaching in 107 villages around Colombo. By 1838 the mission had 17 schools containing about 450 children, and a total church membership of 135, congregated in six church centres. Daniel was assisted from 1838 by a second missionary, Joseph Harris, and five national workers.[124]

The progress made in the villages was not matched in Colombo itself, where the nominal Christianity fostered by Dutch rule rendered the relatively substantial Christian presence largely ineffective. Under the Dutch, Christian baptism had become primarily a civil ceremony bestowing judicial status and opening the door to government service; many who became Protestants under this incentive reverted to Buddhism after the end of Dutch rule in 1796. In search of a more responsive missionary base,

---

122. Boal, 'The Church in the Kond Hills', 225.

123. *Historical Sketch of the Baptist Mission in Ceylon; From its Commencement to the Present Time* (Kandy, 1850), 12; *BM* 34 (1842), 99.

124. *Historical Sketch of the Baptist Mission*, 18-20.

Harris moved inland to the ancient capital of Kandy in 1841. Kandy was relatively unevangelized, apart from a small CMS mission established in 1817. Harris was soon joined at Kandy by C. C. Dawson, sent out to establish a printing press to produce Sinhalese tracts and school books. The press remained in Baptist hands only until 1847, when the BMS Committee ordered its abandonment to reduce expenditure; it was eventually taken over by the Kandy Religious Tract Society, and was thus the parent of the work in twentieth-century Sri Lanka of the United Society for Christian Literature.[125] The new station at Kandy also pioneered evangelism among the Tamil labourers on the coffee plantations; but the mobile nature of the labour force and its low level of literacy (below 5 per cent) proved major obstacles. The anti-British disturbances in the Kandy region in 1848 also had a lasting adverse impact on the plantation mission.[126]

By Ebenezer Daniel's death in June 1844, the Ceylon mission could boast over 500 church members and 1,257 pupils in forty vernacular elementary schools; there were ten mission stations, and about ninety-four preaching centres.[127] The Ceylon mission in the second half of the century possessed a missionary of equal calibre to Daniel in the person of Charles Carter, who served in Kandy from 1853 to 1881, and again from 1888 to 1891. Described by Bishop Copleston of Colombo as 'about the best Sinhalese scholar who has ever arisen from among European missionaries', Carter completed a fresh translation of the New Testament in 1862, and of the Old Testament in 1876. His Sinhalese Bible completely replaced the 1823 version, and went through four editions. Carter also produced a Sinhalese grammar (1862), an English-Sinhalese dictionary (1891) and a Sinhalese-English dictionary (published posthumously in 1924).[128] Yet, for all Carter's linguistic achievements, the BMS mission as a whole stagnated from the mid-nineteenth century, and hence fell far behind the Wesleyan Methodist and CMS missions in scale and influence. There were three main reasons for the Baptist decline.

125. Ibid., 24-5; D. W. M. Hanwella, 'The Educational Activities of the Baptist Missionary Society in Ceylon 1812-1912', M.A. thesis (Univ. of Ceylon, 1965), 162-5; H. J. Charter, *Ceylon Advancing* (London, 1955), 55.

126. *Historical Sketch of the Baptist Mission,* 27, 30; K. M. de Silva, *Social Policy and Missionary Organizations in Ceylon 1840-1855* (London, 1965), 270-3.

127. *BMS Annual Report,* 1844-5, p. 28; *BM* 36 (1844), 268; Hanwella, 'The Educational Activities of the BMS', 52, 55-6.

128. Hanwella, 'The Educational Activities of the BMS', 166-71; Charter, *Ceylon Advancing,* 63-4.

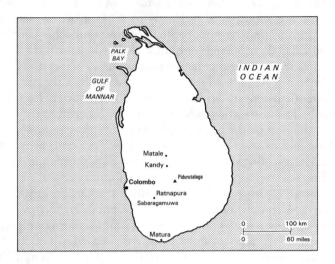

PALK
BAY

GULF
OF
MANNAR

INDIAN
OCEAN

Matale .
Kandy .
Pidurutalaga
Colombo   ▲
. Ratnapura
Sabaragamuwa

Matura

0   100 km

0   60 miles

Map 5: Ceylon/Sri Lanka

The first and chief explanation was paucity of financial and human resources. The Ceylon mission suffered with particular severity from the economies induced by the poor financial situation of the Society in the 1840s. A field staff of five in 1843 was reduced by death and sickness to a single one in 1850, and was only replenished to its former level for a period during the 1880s. By 1849 the mission had only two principal stations - Colombo and Kandy; much of the work initiated in the early 1840s, including the infant church at Matura on the south coast, was abandoned.[129] Many of the schools depended on direct contributions from individual Baptist Sunday schools in Britain, and BMS policy prevented the acceptance of any government grant aid throughout the period of the Central School Commission (1841-69). In comparison with other mission schools, Baptist schools were thus inadequately financed. With the abolition of the Commission in 1869 and introduction (as in England and Wales) of a dual system of state and grant-aided denominational schools, Baptist missionaries reconciled their consciences to the acceptance of grant aid by arguing that the grants were for secular education only, leaving

129. *Historical Sketch of the Baptist Mission,* 40-1.

freedom for Christian instruction intact.[130] Grant aid facilitated a limited revival of the Baptist schools, which now became of central importance to the Society's evangelistic strategy: of the 1,922 pupils in the thirty-five Baptist schools in the Colombo district in 1879, 1,617 were from Buddhist families.[131]

A second reason for the stagnation of the mission was the lack of provision for the training of pastors, evangelists and school teachers. Ebenezer Daniel had opened an academy in Colombo in 1843, which admitted five students, and shortly afterwards a sixth. Daniel's death dealt a serious blow to the institution. Responsibility for the academy passed, first to C. C. Dawson, then to Jacob Davies, sent out in September 1844, and finally to C. B. Lewis, who arrived in January 1846.[132] After Lewis's transfer to Calcutta in the following year, the academy appears to have faded out of existence. Although individual missionaries gave occasional tuition to trainee evangelists, regular provision for Baptist theological training in Ceylon was not resumed until 1908. Similarly, the majority of teachers in Baptist schools had little or no training before 1870. Thereafter, it was necessary to employ trained teachers in order to raise standards and procure grant aid. The result was a growing resort to non-Christian teachers, and a weakening in the Christian emphasis of the schools.[133] By 1901-2, the missionary staff was fundamentally divided, both on the principle of whether schools' work should be continued, and on the specific issue of whether state aid, with its accompanying restrictions, should be accepted.[134]

From the 1860s a third retarding influence began to affect all Christian activity in Ceylon. Buddhism, hitherto largely tolerant of the Christian presence, now developed in response an increasingly adversarial tone. The first signs were comments from missionaries in the 1860s that Buddhist apathy towards Christianity was giving way to active opposition.[135] During the 1880s this indigenous Buddhist revival received an infusion from Western sources through the theosophical movement, introduced to Ceylon by Colonel H. S. Olcott. Under Olcott's leadership, the Buddhist Theo-

---

130. Hanwella, 'The Educational Activities of the BMS', 81-4; *BMS Annual Report*, 1870-1, 12.

131. *BMS Annual Report*, 1879-80, 12.

132. *BM* 36 (1844), 673; *Historical Sketch of the Baptist Mission*, 29-30, 32-4.

133. Hanwella, 'The Educational Activities of the BMS', 127-8.

134. SRL/1, J. G. Greenhough, Report of Visit to Ceylon (1902), 4-5.

135. Hanwella, 'The Educational Activities of the BMS', 68.

sophical Society (founded in 1880) established Buddhist schools to challenge the Christian monopoly of educational provision.[136] The Buddhist revival also generated pressure for the insertion of a conscience clause into Christian schools, which would permit Buddhist parents to withdraw their children from religious instruction. Despite firm opposition from the missions, a conscience clause was imposed on vernacular schools following the report of the Wace Commission in 1905. Christian missions no longer had a free hand to use elementary schools as a proselytizing agency.[137] The time was ripe for the BMS to re-assess its whole Ceylon strategy.

That re-assessment was initiated by a paper written in November 1905 by Bruce Etherington, a young missionary stationed in Colombo. Etherington observed that, for most of the last six years, the Ceylon mission had been served by only one fully active missionary, leaving two out of its three districts (Colombo, Kandy and Sabaragamuwa) unmanned. The Baptist churches could not find pastors, evangelists were old and few in number, and school teachers untrained. Meanwhile the Buddhists had galvanized their forces, encouraged by the claims of the theosophists that Christianity was now a spent intellectual force in the West. Etherington's proposed solution was that the Society should inaugurate a Forward Movement in the island, which would increase the staff to five male and four female missionaries within seven years. He also urged the establishment of a training institution for pastors, evangelists and teachers, and advocated a much closer relationship with the India mission.[138]

The General Committee reacted positively to Etherington's proposals, and resolved to reinforce the Ceylon mission.[139] Eight new missionaries were sent to Ceylon between 1906 and 1910; Etherington himself died at the age of thirty-three in 1907. By 1911 the missionary staff comprised three men and five single women. However, this complement compared with a total of forty-one missionary staff in the CMS mission, while the Wesleyans had even more.[140] A first step towards a training institute was taken in 1908, when one of the new recruits, H. J. Charter, began training three evangelists at Matale. Charter had only two years' Sinhalese, and

136. K. Malalgoda, *Buddhism in Sinhalese Society 1750-1900* (Berkeley, 1976), 242-57.

137. Hanwella, 'The Educational Activities of the BMS', 141-50; K. M. de Silva, *A History of Sri Lanka* (London, 1981), 412.

138. SRL/1, Bruce Etherington, Concerning Ceylon.

139. General Committee Minutes, 20 June 1906, pp. 98-9.

140. H. Anderson, Report of the Deputation to Ceylon (1911), 3-4.

depended heavily on the assistance of Samuel de Saram, the most intellec-tually able Sinhalese Baptist of the period. However, this work was suspended after the Arthington Fund Committee voted £5,000 in 1910 for the building in Colombo of a complex, to include hostel accommodation for Baptist students in the city and a theological training institution.[141] This 'Arthington Institute' opened in 1913, but the Baptist community was simply too small to make a denominational theological institution perma-nently viable (in 1914 there were 954 communicant members in thirty-one churches).[142] In later years Baptist students for theological and teacher training were sent to the joint CMS-Wesleyan Methodist Missionary Society training colony at Peradeniya, established in 1915.[143]

The full realization of Etherington's vision was thus hampered by the small size of the Ceylon mission and the corresponding reluctance of the BMS to invest heavily in so small a field. Herbert Anderson, reporting on a deputation visit to the island in March 1911, took it for granted that any proposals he might make should not involve the Committee in any increased expenditure, apart from provision for a modest increase in staff. Anderson recommended that the existing policy of providing vernacular primary education for Buddhist children should be abandoned in favour of the provision of boarding schools for Christian boys.[144] This was a belated recognition that Baptist primary schools had failed in their evangelistic objectives, while the Baptist community had suffered for too long from the lack of any boys' secondary education. Girls' high schools had been founded in Colombo in 1846 and Matale in 1907. The churches had been pressing the BMS for funding for a boys' boarding school in Colombo since 1909, but in the event raised 22,000 rupees themselves to commemorate the centenary of the Ceylon mission.[145] Anderson's recommendation and the churches' generosity thus together made possible the opening of Carey College in Colombo in 1914.

The lack of facilities for boys' secondary and ministerial education had left the Ceylon churches in 1913-14 with an alarming dearth of candidates for the pastorate.[146] To some extent this weakness was offset by the fact that

---

141. Arthington Committee Minute Book No 2 (1908-10), pp. 199-204, minutes for 13 Oct. 1910.

142. *BMS Annual Report*, 1914-15, p. 249.

143. Charter, *Ceylon Advancing*, 71-3, 114.

144. Anderson, Report of the Deputation to Ceylon, 25, 27-8.

145. *MH* (Feb. 1913), 40; Charter, *Ceylon Advancing*, 100.

146. Macalpine and Wilson, Report on the India and Ceylon Missions, 7.

the churches had progressed further towards autonomy than their more disparate Indian counterparts. A Baptist Union had been formed in 1895. Ten of the fifteen principal churches in 1913 were self-supporting, while the weaker congregations were assisted by a Church Aid Sustentation Fund.[147] Given the provision of more adequate structures for leadership training, the prospects for the small Ceylon Baptist community appeared rather brighter in 1914 than they had been for most of the previous half century.

147. Ibid., 59, 61; Anderson, Report of the Deputation to Ceylon, 15-17.

VI

China, 1845-1912

I: The Origins and Early Years of The BMS Mission, 1845-1874

On 29 August 1842 the Western powers imposed the Treaty of Nanking on the imperial government of China. The treaty marked the termination of the first of the so-called 'opium wars', in which Western (and specifically British) naval power was employed to blow open the Chinese empire to Western trade, including the pernicious traffic in opium from British Bengal. Hitherto the Qing (or Manchu) rulers of China had endeavoured to restrict to the minimum the ingress of foreign influence into the 'Celestial Empire'. Their obduracy had frustrated the aspirations, not just of Western merchants, but equally of Western Christians. Apart from the translation work in Canton of Robert Morrison of the LMS, Protestant missionaries had no access to the most populous nation on earth.

The Treaty of Nanking forced the door of imperial China ajar by guaranteeing to foreigners rights of residence in five 'treaty ports', and ceding Hong Kong to Britain. British Christians, although many of them deplored the conduct of their government in prosecuting the opium war, were united in hailing the outcome of the war as a singular overruling of divine providence - God had turned human evil to the good of his purposes for the salvation of China.[1] Convinced of the call of God, a number of British and American missions rushed to commence operations in the treaty ports. The BMS was not one of them, primarily because of the indebted condition of its finances at the time.[2] The Society did, however, make a donation of £500 from its Jubilee Fund to the American Baptist Foreign

1. B. Stanley, *The Bible and the Flag: Protestant Missions and British Imperialism in the Nineteenth and Twentieth Centuries* (Leicester, 1990), 104-9.

2. *BMS Annual Report*, 1841-2, pp. 42-3, 88-9.

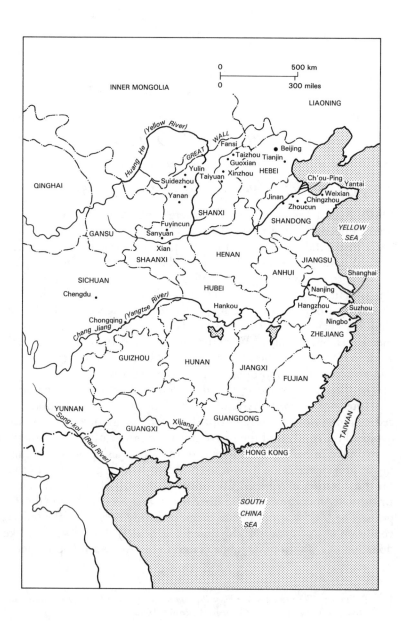

Map 6: China

Missionary Society, which had established a mission in Hong Kong.[3] The General Baptist Missionary Society went considerably further, resolving in March 1843 to commence a China mission.[4] T. H. Hudson, W. Jarrom and their wives sailed for the treaty port of Ningbo in 1845. This first missionary venture by English Baptists in China was not a great success. Mrs Jarrom died in February 1848, and her husband resigned two years later. The GBMS discontinued its China mission in 1854-5. Hudson continued to work independently in Ningbo, and in 1866 completed a Chinese translation of the New Testament, based on the version which Joshua Marshman and the Macao Armenian, Johannes Lassar, had published at Serampore in 1811.[5]

Christian enthusiasm for China, so buoyant in 1842-3, soon flagged. It revived in 1853, when first reports reached Britain of the Taiping rebellion, a massive uprising against the Qing dynasty in south China whose leaders had absorbed elements of Protestant missionary teaching. Expectations that a new day was dawning in China reached their peak in the wake of the second 'opium war' of 1856-60. The treaties which concluded the war appeared to give Europeans virtually unlimited access to inland China and to guarantee security to Chinese converts. In 1858 the veteran Congregationalist, John Angell James, published a pamphlet, *God's Voice from China*, calling on the British Protestant churches to respond to the unmistakable call of God to devote their energies to the evangelization of China. James reminded Baptists that the East had always been the principal object of their missionary zeal, and urged them not to neglect China.[6] James's appeal was taken up by several leading Baptists, among them Edward Steane, secretary of the Baptist Union. At Steane's suggestion, the BMS Committee on 20 April 1859 resolved in principle to commence a China mission, a decision confirmed by the annual members' meeting on 26 April.[7] The Society, anxious that the new field should not injure its existing missions, opened a special China fund; over the next year £2,469 was contributed to the fund.[8]

---

3.   *BM* 35 (1843), 394.

4.   *General Baptist Repository, and Missionary Observer* (Apr. 1843), 97-101, 123.

5.   H. R. Williamson, *British Baptists in China 1845-1952* (London, 1957), 18-19; *General Baptist Magazine* (Oct. 1854), 473.

6.   J. A. James, 'God's Voice from China to the British and Irish Churches', in *The Works of John Angell James* (17 vols.; London, 1862), 16, pp. 536-7.

7.   *BM* 51 (1859), 320, 333, 377.

8.   *BM* 52 (1860), 334.

The BMS was fortunate to receive offers of service from two men with Chinese missionary experience and competence in the Chinese language. Hendrik Kloekers had worked in China from 1855 to 1858, initially with the Netherlands Chinese Evangelization Society.[9] Charles J. Hall and his wife had also served with the Chinese Evangelization Society, in Ningbo. The CES had been founded in 1850 following the visit to Britain of Karl Gützlaff, a Prussian who had undertaken freelance mission work in China. The Society proved incapable of paying its agents a regular salary, and by 1859 was on the point of collapse. Hall in consequence was glad to transfer his allegiance to the BMS. Two years later the BMS sought to obtain the services of a more celebrated former missionary of the CES - James Hudson Taylor - but was disappointed.[10] The mission which Taylor went on to found in 1865, the China Inland Mission (CIM), was to exert a major influence on the BMS China mission throughout its history.

In 1859 Charles Hall moved from Ningbo to Shanghai, where Mr and Mrs Kloekers joined him in March 1860. While Hall remained mainly in Shanghai, Kloekers made exploratory visits to some of the cities on the Yangtze river which were under the control of the Taiping rebels. Accompanied by Griffith John of the LMS, he visited the Taiping capital, Nanjing (Nanking), in November. They had several conversations with the Taiping leaders. The first reports which the BMS received of this visit gave the impression that the movement, though containing much doctrinal error, adhered clearly and firmly to 'the main truths of the Gospel'. The BMS annual report for 1860-1 spoke enthusiastically of churches being built, the gospel preached and the Sabbath observed in Nanjing. On their last day in the city, John and Kloekers had been given an Edict of Toleration, guaranteeing Protestant missionaries free access to all the rebel territories. Encouraged by these reports, the Committee appealed for six more recruits for China and instructed Hall and Kloekers to establish their base in Nanjing or its vicinity.[11]

Once Kloekers' own journal of his visit reached London, it became apparent that this estimation of the Taipings was distinctly rose-tinted. Kloekers, citing evidence that Hong Xiuquan, the founder of the movement, believed himself to be the son of God in the same sense as Jesus Christ,

9.   Williamson, *British Baptists in China*, 22; A. J. Broomhall, *Hudson Taylor and China's Open Century. Book 3: If I Had a Thousand Lives* (London, 1982), 42, 496.

10. Broomhall, *If I Had a Thousand Lives*, 251-2; BMS Committee Minutes, 10 July 1861, p. 82.

11. *BM* 53 (1861), 241, 312.

concluded that the Taipings were Unitarians. The *Missionary Herald* nevertheless remained unshaken in its confidence that the rebellion was opening up China to the gospel, and expressed the hope that missionary instruction would purge the movement of its doctrinal errors.[12] Hall, who visited Nanjing in January 1861, was even more negative in his verdict than Kloekers, calling Hong an impostor and a 'very Antichrist', who claimed equality with Jesus. The *Herald* conceded that the movement must contain 'very contradictory elements' in order to elicit such varying judgments.[13] Hall accordingly moved north to Yantai (Chefoo) in Shandong (Shantung), only to find his scepticism towards the Taipings confirmed when two of his American missionary colleagues were murdered by a group of rebels.[14] Kloekers, however, continued hopeful, and spent a second period in Nanjing from September to November 1861, preaching and teaching.[15] His hopes were disappointed. The rebel authorities requested Kloekers not to return to Nanjing. The BMS annual report for 1861-2 finally accepted that there was no prospect of missionary success in Nanjing, and that Shandong in imperial north China was the most likely sphere of the Society's operations.[16]

By moving north to Yantai, Charles Hall had determined that Shandong would be the Society's first field in China. Initially his choice did not seem a happy one. Cholera raged in the Yantai district throughout 1862 and 1863. Hall himself and his baby daughter were fatal victims of the disease in July 1862. Three missionary couples - the Laughtons, the McMechans, and the Kingdons - arrived between 1863 and 1865 to reinforce the infant mission. But by the end of 1867 ill health and overwork had forced the McMechans, the Kingdons and the Kloekers to resign. The interest of the Christian public in China had tailed off since the heady days of 1858-60, and China now figured less prominently in the pages of the *Missionary Herald*. The survival of the China mission was by now so precarious that the Committee considered the possibility of withdrawal. In January 1868 it was decided to continue China operations, but on a minimum-cost basis.[17] The

12.   Ibid., 449, 454-5. The initially favourable report of the visit to Nanjing probably came from Griffith John; see J. S. Gregory, *Great Britain and the Taipings* (London, 1969), 135; R. W. Thompson, *Griffith John* (revised edn.; London, 1908), 146-8.

13.   *BM* 53 (1861), 585-6.

14.   *BM* 54 (1862), 52-4.

15.   Ibid., 273-4.

16.   *BM* 54 (1862), 328-9.

17.   BMS Committee Minutes, 17 Jan. 1867, p. 258; 15 Jan. 1868, pp. 392-3.

Laughtons comprised the sole complement of the China mission until the arrival in February 1870 of a young Welshman, Timothy Richard, fresh from his studies at Haverfordwest Baptist College.[18] China was still a minor, and possibly only a temporary, commitment for the BMS.

When Richard joined him, R. F. Laughton had gathered a church of approximately thirty-five members, scattered over three villages in the Yantai district. Although the majority were extremely poor, Laughton had in 1869 opened a pastoral support fund, with the ultimate aim of establishing a Chinese church that would be 'self-governing, self-supporting, and set free from every kind of foreign influence which tends to hinder its free, native, natural development and extension'. With the Committee's encouragement, Laughton had set his face against any payments from mission funds to Chinese agents.[19] These were bold principles for any China mission to adopt at this time, let alone a mission with such slender resources of missionary manpower and national church membership. Nonetheless, the necessity of dissociating Christian missions more clearly from other facets of the Western impact was urgent. Laughton reported that the principal difficulty confronting the mission was the 'deep and wide-spread hatred to foreigners caused by the nefarious *opium* traffic'; as a result, the officials and literati were manipulating popular feeling against Christianity.[20] Anti-foreign feeling escalated in the late 1860s, reaching a tragic crescendo in Tianjin in June 1870, when twenty-one foreigners, including twelve Catholic missionaries and a larger number of converts, were brutally murdered.[21]

The infant BMS church was at first reluctant to accept full financial responsibility for its own life, when other missions in Yantai supported their native preachers.[22] Timothy Richard, although no less committed than Laughton to the maxims of self-support, soon reached the conclusion that Yantai, a town of only 20,000 already served by six missionaries from three different Protestant missions, was not a strategic centre for BMS activity.[23]

---

18. At Haverfordwest Richard had been a student of the India missionary and gifted linguist, G. H. Rouse, whose missionary service had been suspended owing to ill health.

19. *BM* 61 (1869), 330, 620-1.

20. Ibid., 754.

21. P. A. Cohen, *China and Christianity: The Missionary Movement and the Growth of Chinese Antiforeignism 1860 -1870* (Cambridge, Mass., 1963), 233.

22. *BM* 62 (1870), 329.

23. *BM* 63 (1871), 749-50.

Richard, who had initially applied to the CIM rather than the BMS, came out to China captivated by Hudson Taylor's heroic vision of pressing beyond the security of Western influence into the densely-populated interior.[24] He accordingly took every opportunity to make journeys into the interior of Shandong and beyond, and two members of the Yantai church began their own itinerations.

R. F. Laughton died of typhus on 21 June 1870. At the end of the year Richard gained a new colleague, when Dr William Brown arrived in Yantai. The Committee had been considering sending a medical missionary to China since 1862, when Hall had pointed out that medical work had proved uniquely effective in opening the people's hearts to the gospel.[25] Brown was the first professional medical missionary to be sent by the BMS to any field.[26] He erected a small hospital and dispensary in Yantai, and in the year 1873-4 treated 2,869 persons.[27] However, as will be seen in Chapter Seven, the Society's commitment to professional medical work was still very hesitant: Brown was recalled in February 1874, because of his refusal to engage in evangelistic preaching alongside his medical work.[28] It was ten years before the next qualified doctor (J. R. Watson) was appointed to China. As late as 1880 it was the publicly stated view of the Committee that all that was required in the way of medical expertise in the China mission was for missionaries to take a much shorter course of medical and surgical training than was demanded of prospective doctors. Medical training was still regarded merely as a useful auxiliary to the one great missionary task of preaching the gospel.[29] From 1874 to March 1877 Richard was thus the sole BMS representative in China. During these years the first signs became apparent that here was an original and controversial missionary thinker without parallel in the Society's history.

24. T. Richard, *Forty-five Years in China* (London, 1916), 29.

25. *BM* 54 (1862), 461-2.

26. *BM* 64 (1872), 698-9. John Thomas, the Society's first missionary, was, of course, a surgeon, but the sending out of doctors specifically to practise medicine was a much later development; see below, ch. VII, pp. 233-4.

27. *BM* 66 (1874), 319.

28. Sub-Committee Reports, 1878-79, Extracts from Correspondence with Dr William Brown.

29. *MH* (May 1880), 153.

II: The Formation of a Missionary Thinker: Timothy Richard, 1875-1884

In January 1875 Richard handed the Yantai church into the care of the American Baptist mission, and moved 250 miles inland to Chingzhou (Ch'ing-chou-fu), the administrative capital of a populous district of eleven counties. The city also possessed an Islamic theological college, two mosques, Buddhist and Taoist temples, and an abundance of new religious sects. It was, to Richard's strategy-conscious mind, 'ripe for the harvest'.[30] As the only foreigner in the city, he adopted Chinese dress, distributed tracts and administered basic medical remedies to growing numbers of inquirers.

It was at Chingzhou that Richard's missionary principles assumed their mature form. He observed that the reforming religious sects which were now so numerous in this part of China propagated their doctrines by means of self-supporting and self-managing societies, and concluded that 'the best way to make Christianity indigenous was to adopt Chinese methods of propagation'.[31] Laughton before him had espoused the principles of self-support, but Richard went further in advocating that itinerant evangelism should be left almost entirely to the Chinese. The foreign missionary had a pioneering role, but it was a very specific one. Influenced by Edward Irving's famous sermon on 'Missionaries after the Apostolical School' preached before the LMS in 1824, Richard argued that the apostolic method of missionary work, as laid down in Matthew 10:11, was to seek out the 'worthy' as the primary audience for the Christian message. The 'worthy' included both those who gave evidence of seeking after religious truth, and those who had the power to mould public opinion. Hence at Yantai, and more particularly at Chingzhou, Richard targeted his message at two groups - the devout teachers of the different religions (especially the leaders of the reforming sects), and the highly educated scholar-officials who formed the imperial civil service.[32]

While at Chingzhou Richard used to act as host to his friend and former colleague at Yantai, the American Presbyterian missionary, John L. Nevius, on his twice-yearly evangelistic tours into the interior of Shandong. The two men discussed missionary methods together, and Richard showed Nevius some of his stations where his principles could be seen in operation. Nevius

---

30.   *MH* (Dec. 1875), 234.

31.   Richard, *Forty-five Years*, 107.

32.   W. E. Soothill, *Timothy Richard of China* (London, 1924), 77-84; P. A. Cohen, 'Missionary approaches: Hudson Taylor and Timothy Richard', *Papers on China*, vol. 11 (Harvard Univ., 1957), 35-6, 47; E. Irving, *For Missionaries after the Apostolical School* (London, 1825), 29-31.

was deeply impressed, and based his own exposition of missionary methods, published in 1886 as *Methods of Mission Work*, on Richard's pattern.[33] What became internationally known as 'the Nevius method' thus owed a substantial debt to Richard's example.[34] The basic principles of a self-supporting church were, however, professed just as clearly by Laughton and, from 1877, by Richard's new colleague, Alfred Jones. As Nevius's ideas were one of the sources within China of the 'Three-Self Principles' of self-government, self-propagation and self-support, it may be justifiably asserted that Richard and his early BMS colleagues were among the progenitors of the Three-Self Movement established in Communist China after 1951.[35]

Between 1876 and 1879 North China experienced the most devastating famine in modern Chinese history - it is estimated that nine and a half million lives were lost.[36] Shandong province was the first to be affected. Richard found himself in the midst of suffering of heart-rending proportions, surrounded by thousands dying of hunger. From the summer of 1876 the foreign press in Shanghai printed a series of graphic descriptions by Richard of the famine, in which he appealed to the foreign community for aid. As a result, prominent foreign residents in the city formed the Shandong famine relief committee in March 1877. Richard became the single most important agent for the distribution of its funds in Shandong. He was assisted by Nevius, and, from March 1877, by Alfred Jones, who kept the accounts of the relief effort.[37]

The relief work of the missionaries had a marked effect on the responsiveness of the Chingzhou people. Richard's prediction of the rich spiritual harvest to be reaped in Chingzhou now began to be realized. Jones and Richard reported in the autumn that the mission had about 300 serious adult inquirers, from all classes of society.[38] The China section of the BMS annual report for 1877-8 was able, for the first time, to tell of crowded

---

33. J. L. Nevius, *Methods of Mission Work* (new edn., London, 1898).

34. Richard, *Forty-five Years,* 107; see also Soothill, *Timothy Richard,* 92-3.

35. H. S. C. Nevius, *The Life of John Livingston Nevius* (New York, 1895), 402-5. Three-Self principles, though enunciated by Henry Venn and Rufus Anderson in the 1850s, were popularized in China by Nevius and J. C. Gibson of the English Presbyterian Mission; see G. A. Hood, *Mission Accomplished? The English Presbyterian Mission in Lingtung, South China* (Frankfurt, 1986), 135-47.

36. P. R. Bohr, *Famine in China and the Missionary: Timothy Richard as Relief Administrator and Advocate of National Reform, 1876-1884* (Cambridge, Mass., 1972), xv.

37. Ibid., 89-94; Soothill, *Timothy Richard,* 86-97.

38. *MH* (Mar. 1878), 60, 62.

services and many instances of genuine conversion.[39] Pastor Qing, trained by Laughton in Yantai, and in Richard's judgment 'one of the finest Christians ever found in China', was summoned to pastor the growing flock, which now numbered 700 members and 1,000 catechumens.[40]

By November 1877 the misery in Shandong was largely over, but signs of an even more severe famine were already apparent in other northern provinces, notably in Shanxi (Shansi). In response to a request from William Muirhead, LMS missionary and secretary of the Shandong relief committee, Richard set out for Shanxi, leaving the Chingzhou church in the hands of Pastor Qing and Jones. Richard and Jones both believed that the call to Shanxi was 'a direct leading from God to open up the interior of China'. They anticipated that Christian famine relief would, as in Shandong, 'afford unanswerable evidence' of the truth of Christianity and the purity of the motives of its representatives.[41]

At the end of November Richard arrived in Taiyuan, the capital of Shanxi. He was only the third Protestant missionary to enter Shanxi.[42] Within a month he was writing to Muirhead, reporting 'terrible suffering', with eight to nine million people in the province having been listed as eligible for relief.[43] In January 1878 Muirhead accordingly re-activated the Shanghai committee to establish the China Famine Relief Fund; a London committee was formed in February. Three missionaries - J. J. Turner of the CIM, David Hill of the Wesleyan Methodists and Albert Whiting of the American Presbyterians - were dispatched to assist Richard. Whiting died soon after, but Turner and Hill joined Richard in distributing over 120,000 of the total of 200,000 taels (then equivalent to about £60,000) collected by the Fund. The London committee raised £32,303, of which half was contributed through the missionary societies; the BMS contribution was £2,666.[44] Richard and his two missionary colleagues aided 100,641 persons in 1878, and a further 56,962 in 1879. Despite their efforts, Richard estimated that at least three to four millions died in Shanxi alone.[45]

---

39. *MH* (June 1878), 140.

40. Richard, *Forty-five Years*, 125; Soothill, *Timothy Richard*, 99.

41. Richard, *Forty-five Years*, 125.

42. J. J. Turner and F. H. James of the CIM had arrived in Nov. 1876; both later joined the BMS.

43. *MH* (Apr. 1878), 96.

44. Bohr, *Famine in China*, 95; *MH* (May 1879), 123.

45. *MH* (Jan. 1880), 6-7.

The missionary-led attempt to relieve the North China famine from 1876 to 1879 was one of the first major programmes in humanitarian relief in modern history. Its originator, and the pioneer of systematic distribution methods, was Timothy Richard.[46] Richard himself reflected that the famine had been a God-given opportunity to show the Chinese that missionaries were what they professed to be, 'the best supporters of the State'. Yet he acknowledged that the Shanxi famine had failed to draw inquirers in their hundreds to the missions, as had happened in Shandong, even though the distribution of relief had always been accompanied by an evangelistic message. Shanxi lacked both the years of missionary preparation and the army of native preachers which undergirded the current growth of the church in Shandong.[47] Nevertheless, the first Protestant church in Taiyuan was opened in 1878; until 1881 it was a united church supported by both BMS and CIM missionaries. Richard doubled the BMS staff in October 1878 by marrying Mary Martin, of the United Presbyterian mission in Yantai.

The famine was no sooner over than Richard began to turn his mind to the question of how future famines could be averted. His conclusion was that China needed what only Western civilization could bestow, namely a commitment to 'discover the workings of God in Nature, and to apply the laws of Nature for the service of mankind'.[48] He became convinced that teaching the scholars and officials the miraculous inventions of Western science offered the only hope of saving China from similar catastrophes. Already persuaded that evangelistic strategy dictated a concentration on the 'worthy', he now believed, in addition, that the practical demonstration to the 'worthy' of natural theology was crucial in order to persuade them of the Christian message. To equip himself for his task, Richard spent over the next four years the extraordinary sum of nearly £1,000 of his own money on books and scientific apparatus. From 1879 he devoted an increasing proportion of his time to lecturing on Western science to the officials and students who were to be found in large numbers in Taiyuan, a centre for the second-level civil service examinations. In 1881 he also published a Chinese tract, *Present Needs*, designed to convince the authorities of the need for scientific modernization.[49]

46. Bohr, *Famine in China*, 126-7.

47. *MH* (Jan. 1880), 8.

48. Richard, *Forty-five Years*, 158.

49. Bohr, *Famine in China*, 146-8; Richard, *Forty-five Years*, 158-9; Soothill, *Timothy Richard*, 122-8. Some of the £1,000 came from a personal legacy.

In pressing the claims of Western technology on the Chinese educational and governmental elite, Richard's immediate objective was the prevention of any repetition of the horrendous suffering of 1876-9. His ultimate goal was, however, more expansive: it was nothing less than the building of the kingdom of God in China. Richard's vision of the kingdom embraced the regeneration of both material and spiritual life. Where it was distinctive and controversial was in its assumption that spiritual regeneration was in some sense actually dependent on the prior transformation of the material.[50] The goal of the process was, nevertheless, the turning *en masse* of the Chinese people to Christ. Increasingly disillusioned with the conventional evangelistic strategy of seeking the conversion of individuals, Richard believed that his approaches to government officials and leaders of the religious sects would be the trigger for the masses of China to 'be turned to the Lord in large bodies'.[51]

III: Alfred Jones and the Reinforcement of the China Mission, 1880-1888

While Timothy Richard was developing his distinctive missionary strategy in remote Taiyuan, Alfred Jones continued to guide the remarkable growth of the Shandong church based at Chingzhou. Working alongside other missions which did not practise self-support, yet grew less rapidly, Jones saw triumphant confirmation of what he termed 'Mr Richard's bold principles'. Two letters from Jones, extensively quoted in the BMS annual report for 1880-1, proclaimed the virtues of self-support, and assured the Society that the 'necessity for nursing native Christians at the expense of foreigners, if they be sincere, is a figment of faithless fear and fancy'.[52] No doubt such assurances strengthened the resolve of the Committee to enjoin similar principles on other BMS fields, notably the West Indies. Although the universal applicability of Jones's dictum could be questioned, its validity in the Chinese context is undisputed. The Baptist insistence on these principles ensured that, for many of the people of Shandong, Christianity wore a recognizably Chinese face, rather than the transparently foreign features which characterized so much missionary Christianity in China. With a mere handful of missionaries - Jones was on his own until the arrival in 1879 of J. T. Kitts, followed in 1881 by J. S. Whitewright - the role of Chinese

50.   Bohr, *Famine in China*, 147.

51.   CH/2, Richard to Baynes, 2 Feb. 1884.

52.   *MH* (May 1881), 167.

itinerant evangelists was paramount.[53] Moreover, there was a conscious attempt, in Jones's words, to 'adapt the teaching of Scripture to Chinese circumstances, to exhibit it in Chinese forms of thought and language'.[54] Richard was quite justified in informing Alfred Baynes in 1883 that Jones's work in Shandong was one of the most promising in all China.[55] When Jones went home on furlough that year, he left behind forty-two churches, all self-supporting and with their own Chinese pastors, with an aggregate membership of over 800.[56] Although never attaining the renown of Timothy Richard, Jones deserves to be remembered as the builder of the Shandong church and the architect of one of the most notable success-stories in the Society's history.

Alfred Jones's commitment to an indigenous church did not diminish in the slightest his belief - shared by all his colleagues - that the BMS China mission desperately needed more missionary recruits. Once back in Britain, Jones asked the Committee for seven or eight men at once, and seven more to follow quickly. The Committee responded by issuing an appeal for fourteen new missionaries for China, to be sent out over the next three to four years, as funds permitted.[57] By the end of September 1883 the £2,100 required for the outfit and passage money of fourteen missionaries had been supplied, all of it from the city of Bristol. Half was promised by Charles Wathen, benefactor of the Congo mission, and the other half was raised by Richard Glover, pastor of the Tyndale church and chairman of the Society's China sub-committee. China fever once again gripped the Baptist denomination as Glover delivered a stirring address at the autumnal missionary breakfast in Leicester.[58] The annual report for 1883-4 rejoiced that 'many gifted and suitable brethren' were offering for China service; however, only four of the proposed fourteen had been accepted, simply because the Society's funds did not yet permit a larger proportion to be supported. By the autumnal Baptist Union assembly in October 1884, the figure had risen to eight.[59] Six months later the Committee was still withholding suitable candidates from going to China on the grounds of inadequate funds.[60]

53. Jones also married in 1881.
54. *MH* (May 1883), 162.
55. CH/2, Richard to Baynes, 1 Feb. 1883.
56. *MH* (Sept. 1883), 306-7.
57. Ibid., 305-11.
58. *MH* (Nov. 1883), 373-4, 376-81.
59. *MH* (May 1884), 163-4; *MH* (Nov. 1884), 392.
60. *MH* (May 1885), 175.

Although it was 1886 before the target of fourteen was reached, Jones and Glover had between them raised the profile of the China mission to a new level within the life of the Society.

Shortly before returning to China in 1884, Jones was told by Baynes that the new recruits were to be regarded as consolidating and reinforcing, rather than extending, the China mission. Baynes took the view that the India mission had squandered its strength by allowing missionaries to spread themselves out in ones and twos along the Ganges valley, and was determined that the mistake should not be repeated in China. Jones was in full agreement, on the grounds that the Chinese, once converted, needed a great deal of instruction and training: 'They do not do to be left to themselves in the sense of depriving them of spiritual nurture and oversight of *such* kind as they cannot get from one another.'[61] Indigenous principles had their limits.

Two-thirds of the new recruits sent to China between 1884 and 1887 were thus sent to Shandong rather than Shanxi, to the chagrin of Timothy Richard.[62] Richard believed that extension in Shanxi ought to take precedence over consolidation in Shandong, and felt that the Shandong mission had departed from the self-supporting principles on which it had been set up.[63] Jones and his Shandong colleagues, on the other hand, saw no contradiction between their adherence to self-support and their insistence on the continuing need for missionary instruction of prospective church leaders. The Native Training Institution set up by J. S. Whitewright at Chingzhou to train pastors, evangelists and teachers exemplified this dual emphasis. The maxims of a self-supporting church were continually drummed into the students, and the aim was to bring the Institution itself rapidly to a position of entire dependence on church support.[64] Yet the four-year curriculum, though professedly determined by local needs, in fact followed traditional British lines, including the study of Christian evidences and Joseph Butler's *Analogy of Religion*.[65]

61. CH/5, Jones to Baynes, 23 Mar. 1885.

62. CH/2, Richard to Baynes, 1 Mar. 1887. Of the fifteen new missionaries accepted between 1884 and 1887, only five were allocated to Shanxi.

63. CH/2, Richard to Baynes, 26 Dec. 1887.

64. *MH* (Apr. 1888), 137-8; *MH* (May 1888), 180-2.

65. *MH* (May 1889), 170-1; *MH* (May 1898), 209, 214-15.

IV: Timothy Richard, the Home Committee, and Discord in Shanxi, 1885-1891

In the autumn of 1884 the Richards left China for their first furlough in Britain. Once home, Timothy Richard took every opportunity to urge his views on the home Committee. He met with some encouragement. The annual report for 1884-5 included a lengthy extract from Richard, arguing that the traditional missionary methods developed in Africa or the South Seas would not do for the advanced civilization of China.[66] The *Missionary Herald* for August 1885 printed 'A Plea for China', in which Richard appealed for volunteers for China, not merely from the Baptist colleges, but from parliament, the universities, business, and literature.[67] He also distributed to members of the Committee a pamphlet, *Fifteen Years' Mission Work in China*, advocating an inter-mission scheme to establish a high-class missionary college in every Chinese provincial capital, in order to bring about the 'national conversion of China'. Some members took fright at the word 'national', fearing that Richard's intention was to create an established church in China.[68] Richard promptly issued a revised version of the pamphlet, eliminating the word 'national', under the title *A Scheme for Mission Work in China*.[69] Despite the advocacy of one member (possibly Glover), the General Committee in May 1886 finally rejected the scheme as impossibly expensive. All that Richard obtained was a declaration of intent to send out a larger number of highly qualified men to China, as the funds of the Society might permit.[70]

Deeply wounded, Richard resigned his post as secretary and treasurer of the Shanxi mission.[71] His disappointment at the refusal of the Committee to adopt any of his suggestions to meet the present needs of China brought to the surface other grounds of resentment, notably the preference given to Shandong over Shanxi in the allocation of missionary recruits.[72] Resent-

---

66.   *MH* (May 1885), 176-8.

67.   *MH* (Aug. 1885), 341-2.

68.   Richard, *Forty-five Years*, 197-8.

69.   Printed in Richard, *Conversion by the Million in China: Being Biographies and Articles* (2 vols.; Shanghai, 1907), ii, 60-73.

70.   China and Japan Sub-Committee Minute Book 1, pp. 84-7, minutes for 8 Apr. 1886; BMS Committee Minutes, 7 May 1886, pp. 84-6.

71.   CH/2, Richard to Baynes, 8 Apr. 1886. Glover and Baynes subsequently persuaded Richard to withdraw his resignation.

72.   CH/2, Richard to Baynes, 5 July 1886.

ment deepened when in August 1886 the *Missionary Herald* published a letter from Herbert Dixon, recently settled in Taiyuan after sickness had terminated his career in the Congo mission.[73] Richard regarded Dixon's letter as an attack on his missionary methods from one who had 'some missionary experience in an uncivilized country'.[74] In fact Dixon's implicit criticism of Richard reflected the views of the missionary community in Taiyuan, which for some time had been suspicious of Richard's methods and theology. This feeling went back to 1881, when Hudson Taylor had instructed the CIM missionaries to withdraw from common worship with the BMS mission, on the grounds of Richard's alleged unorthodoxy. J. J. Turner, Richard's former co-worker in the famine relief effort of 1878-9, had left the CIM in 1883 for the BMS. By 1884 Turner and Sowerby were attacking their absent senior colleague in letters to Baynes. Reports critical of Richard also reached West Street Baptist Church in Rochdale from the Baptists working for the small independent Shou-Yang Mission.[75]

Richard thus returned to Taiyuan at the end of 1886 to a situation fraught with potential for division. Perhaps unwisely, he distributed to his colleagues copies of his *Scheme for Mission Work in China*. J. J. Turner's reaction was to write a letter to the Shanxi local committee of the BMS, accusing Richard of devaluing evangelism, individual conversion, and work among the poor, and of proposing that something other than the gospel was to save the Chinese. Turner's letter was forwarded to London in March 1887. Richard wrote in reply to Baynes, protesting, with some justice, that Turner had totally misrepresented the *Scheme*.[76] Both collective and individual letters critical of Richard subsequently reached the BMS Committee from all the other Shanxi missionaries.[77] Herbert Dixon wrote first to his own pastor, T. V. Tymms (a member of the Committee), and then to Baynes. He alleged that Richard's missionary message was 'a conglomerate wherein Science, Heathenism, Roman Catholicism, and Christianity are bundled up into a new "Gospel for Nations"', and claimed that his

73. *MH* (Aug. 1886), 361.

74. CH/2, Richard to BMS Committee, 12 May 1887; see also Richard, *Forty-five Years*, 204.

75. CH/5, Jones to Baynes, 2 Jan. 1885. For the Shou-Yang Mission see Williamson, *British Baptists in China*, 52, 65.

76. CH/2, Richard to Baynes, 7 Mar. 1887.

77. Most of these letters are not preserved, but they are listed in China and Japan Sub-Committee Minute Book 1, p. 147, minutes for 19 July 1887.

missionary approach had been a complete failure. He described with horror Richard's use of chanted litanies and his hanging of a large white satin cross, flanked by yellow streamers 'exactly like those used in Buddhist temples', in the Taiyuan chapel. Dixon's final complaint was that Richard had distributed a Chinese guide to enquirers, whose provisions for a pyramidical structure of ecclesiastical offices amounted to 'most barefaced popery'.[78] It was this pamphlet in particular which had united Richard's colleagues in opposition; they enclosed an English translation with their collective letter to Baynes, written on 20 April.

The pamphlet in dispute - the *Curriculum* or *Order of Study* - had been drafted some years previously as an outline course of study for Chinese evangelists. Richard had recently revised it for distribution to devout Confucians who thought all other religions were led by well-meaning but ignorant people.[79] In this form, it sought to lead the devout seeker after enlightenment through a series of stages - inquirer, church member, student, teacher, and county teacher - which would lead ultimately to the highest good of celestial happiness. For each stage a lengthy list of moral, religious and intellectual attainments was prescribed, which would be assessed by examination at the end of a set period. Thus, to qualify for church membership, inquirers had to commit to memory Jeremy Taylor's *The Rule and Exercise of Holy Living* (1650) and Isaac Watts' *The Psalms of David*. Candidates for the office of teacher (and hence for the pastorate) were to be examined in ten subjects, including arithmetic and the natural sciences. The pamphlet contained no mention of the name of Christ, the atonement, or faith. The *Order of Study* was self-evidently designed to present Christianity in a form acceptable to the Confucian scholarly mind, with its view of society as a hierarchy of intellectual merit, measured by success in formal examinations.[80]

Richard defended his pamphlet by explaining that it was not primarily a guide to salvation, but a guide for those who wished to know the course of education necessary for Christian leadership.[81] This satisfied neither his colleagues nor the BMS China and Japan sub-committee. On 20 September the sub-committee directed that the pamphlet should be withdrawn as

78. CH/1, Dixon to T. V. Tymms, 18 Mar. 1887, and [Dixon] to Baynes, 25 Apr. 1887. Tymms evidently sent Baynes a copy of Dixon's letter.

79. CH/2, Richard to BMS Committee, 12 May 1887.

80. CH/1, 'Course of Religious Study', by T. Richard, translated from the Chinese by F. H. James.

81. CH/2, Richard to BMS Committee, 12 May 1887.

unsuitable for circulation, and suggested that the possibility of Richard being transferred to the Shandong mission be explored.[82] Richard had, in fact, already determined to leave Shanxi, finding intolerable a situation in which most of his colleagues refused to share fellowship with him. After waiting in vain for instructions from London, he made his own decision to remove to Beijing (Peking). There he received a warm invitation from the Shandong staff to join them. At first he declined, fearing that the Shandong local committee would shackle his freedom of action just as the Shanxi committee had done.[83] Richard deplored the growing power of local missionary committees as a development which tied the hands of older and more experienced missionaries, and stifled the influence of God's free Spirit. Although disillusioned with individualistic evangelism, Richard held a typically romantic belief that significant achievements were invariably the product of individual effort rather than majority rule.[84] However, a meeting with the Shandong local committee in February appeared to give Richard what he wanted - freedom to work among the official and educated classes in the provincial capital of Jinan (Tsi-nan-fu). He would run a small Christian newspaper and bookshop, and as soon as possible commence an institution of higher education.[85] Richard, believing that here was a strategic opportunity to teach national leaders rather than followers, accepted the proposal, subject to the approval of the BMS Committee.[86]

The BMS Committee knew nothing of the dispute between Richard and his colleagues until 19 June 1888. At the meeting on that date the China and Japan sub-committee presented two reports. The first, dated 19 April, briefly reviewed the history of the Shanxi divisions. No detailed reference was made to the content of the *Order of Study*. The officers of the Society were no doubt anxious that the Shanxi affair should not be allowed to add fuel to the flames of the Downgrade controversy, currently raging in the denomination. The second report, drawn up by the sub-committee on 4 June, printed the resolutions of the February meeting of the Shandong local committee, and recommended that Richard be appointed to work amongst the officials and scholars of Jinan, but that the proposal to set up a Christian

---

82. China and Japan Sub-Committee Minute Book 1, pp. 160-3, minutes for 19-20 Sept. 1887.

83. CH/2, Richard to Baynes, 26 Dec. 1887.

84. CH/2, Richard to Baynes, 12 Mar. 1888.

85. CH/1, 'Appointment of Mr Richard to Tsi-nan-fu', 22 Feb. 1888.

86. CH/2, Richard to Baynes, 12 Mar. 1888.

educational institution be rejected. The report was accepted, despite a protest from one member that he had never, in his twenty years of service on the Committee, known a like case of the rejection of an unanimous request from the field.[87]

On receipt of the Committee's decision, Richard submitted alternative proposals to Alfred Jones for work at Jinan. These were unacceptable to the Shandong committee, for Richard had reverted to an insistence that he be given 'sole control' and freedom from the committee's authority.[88] The Shandong missionaries, though more sympathetic to Richard's missionary strategy than their Shanxi colleagues, were, in the final analysis, unprepared to accept his independent spirit. With both of the Society's China missions now closed to him, the dilemma of where to station Richard now seemed insoluble. The problem was intensified by further letters from Turner and Sowerby, accusing Richard, on the basis of his writings, of substituting 'something else for the Gospel of Christ'. Richard now found himself compelled to defend his essential theology in writing to Baynes.[89] The BMS Committee, confronted with translations by Turner of Richard's Chinese publications, requested an independent translation.[90] Baynes approached James Legge, Professor of Chinese at Oxford University and a former LMS missionary, who in the event merely confirmed the general accuracy of Turner's translation, and added his own comments. Legge's verdict was that, whilst Richard's proposals for national reform to the Chinese authorities contained 'utter dreams and foolish fancies', there was little evidence in the submitted writings of theological error, principally because there was so little that was theological in them. If, however, Richard's writings were a fair specimen of what he actually taught the people (which Legge doubted), there would be reason for serious complaint.[91]

The BMS Committee delivered its judgment on the Richard affair on 18 December 1888. It supported the Shandong committee in its insistence

---

87. BMS Committee Minutes, 19 June 1888, pp. 251-67. The protesting member is mentioned, but not identified, in Richard, *Forty-Five Years*, 214. Richard (followed by Soothill) here dates the committee decision incorrectly in 1889.

88. CH/6, Jones to Baynes, 4 Oct. and 5 Nov. 1888.

89. CH/65, Turner to BMS Committee, May 1888; CH/64, Sowerby to Baynes, 18 May and 17 July 1888, and to BMS Committee, 1 Aug. 1888; CH/4, Richard to BMS Committee, 17 Oct. 1888.

90. BMS Committee Minutes, 18 Sept. 1888, pp. 339-41.

91. China and Japan Sub-Committee Minute Book 1, pp. 246-8, Legge to Baynes, 27 Sept. 1888.

that, if Richard were to pursue literary and educational work in Shandong, it could only be under the same regulations and constraints as applied to all his colleagues. It rejected Richard's alternative suggestion that he be set free to carry on such work elsewhere. Whilst expressing confidence in Richard's fidelity to the central truths of the gospel, the Committee declared its disapproval of many of his missionary aims and methods, particularly his estimate of the proportion which efforts to promote the social and material welfare of the people should bear to 'direct Gospel teaching and work'.[92]

On receiving these resolutions in April 1889, Richard concluded, understandably, that he had lost the confidence of the home Committee.[93] He seriously considered resignation. For the next three years his status in the China mission was anomalous. While remaining a BMS missionary, he was effectively his own master. On hearing the Committee's decision, Richard travelled from Beijing to Jinan to consult his Shandong colleagues, but, finding them engaged in famine relief, immersed himself in the same work. Another serious famine had struck north China at the end of 1888, and the missionary societies once again found themselves assuming much of the burden of raising and distributing relief. The BMS sent £4,000 in aid.[94] In May 1890 Richard travelled south to Shanghai to attend the second general conference of China missionaries. Shortly afterwards he was invited by Li Hongzhang, China's virtual foreign minister and a firm advocate of China's modernization, to edit the Tianjin daily newspaper, the *Shibao*. Richard eagerly accepted what seemed a providential opening to promote the cause of national reform, and the BMS Committee, faced with a *fait accompli*, agreed to countenance his appointment for an experimental period of one year.[95]

Richard's anomalous relation to the Society was not resolved until after Richard Glover and T. M. Morris had visited China in 1890-1 as the first home deputation to the China field. On arriving in China in November 1890, Glover and Morris met Richard in Tianjin, warned him that he would find no support from the Committee for any policy of an educational mission, such as he had proposed in 1888, and urged him to leave his editorial post to resume work 'more completely evangelical' in Shandong.

92.   BMS Committee Minutes, 18 Dec. 1888, pp. 469-73.

93.   CH/2, Richard to Baynes, 23 July 1889.

94.   *MH* (July 1889), 248.

95.   Richard, *Forty-Five Years*, 215, 217; CH/2, Richard to Baynes, 26 June 1890; BMS Committee Minutes, 9 Sept. 1890, pp. 455-8.

Richard replied that his heart was, and always had been, in evangelistic work, that his present post was only a second-best activity, and was 'too secular to be his choice'. Glover and Morris met Richard again at the end of their tour, in April 1891. By this time the *Shibao* was on the edge of financial collapse. Richard asked the deputation to present the Committee with a choice between taking over the newspaper as a distinctively Christian concern, and sanctioning his remaining in Tianjin to work among the scholars and members of the secret religious sects. Glover and Morris replied that neither option was likely to commend itself to the Committee, and urged Richard once more to join the Shandong mission, which he was reluctant to do except on his own terms.[96]

After the deputation had departed, Richard received a letter from Dr John Murdoch of the Christian Literature Society of India, who was currently on a visit to China, inviting him to replace the late Alexander Williamson as secretary of the Society for the Diffusion of Christian and General Knowledge among the Chinese (SDK).[97] Murdoch had in fact already suggested to Glover and Morris that Richard should assume this role, while continuing to be supported by the BMS. Although Glover and Morris made no mention of the matter in their report, Glover was enthusiastic, and put the case to the BMS. In July 1891 the Committee gave the Officers of the Society authority to negotiate with Murdoch, and to support Richard's work for the SDK to a limit of £200 per annum.[98] Until his retirement in 1915, Richard, while still supported by the BMS, fulfilled the desires of his heart in his influential role as editor and promoter of the extensive range of publications issued by the SDK (later known as the Christian Literature Society of China).

The tensions between Timothy Richard and many of his missionary colleagues never became generally known. The BMS succeeded in avoiding a 'Richard controversy' that could easily have exposed the Society to the doctrinal gunfire which C. H. Spurgeon was currently directing against the Baptist Union. Nevertheless, what took place in the China mission between 1885 and 1891 merits the full treatment which has been given to it. The missionary strategy Richard advocated during these years was, after 1900, increasingly accepted by many Protestant missions in China (though never fully by the BMS itself), and indeed set the direction of national reform in China after the Republican Revolution of 1911-12. Not until 1922-7 did

96. CH/10, Report on China Missions of the BMS, pp. 30-1.

97. CH/3, Richard to Baynes, 20 May 1891; see also Soothill, *Timothy Richard*, 170.

98. BMS Committee Minutes, 15 July 1891, pp. 382-4.

it become apparent how fragile was any apologia for Christianity which presented the faith as the guarantor of material progress and national regeneration.[99]

More broadly, the discord in the Shanxi mission in the 1880s is the first example in the BMS (and one of the first in Protestant missions as a whole) of the impact of the new theological liberalism on assumptions which had hitherto gone virtually unchallenged. Richard's liberalism did not consist in the overt denial or even reformulation of any major Christian doctrine - his opponents were unable to make the charge of unorthodoxy stick. Indeed, Richard was able to put up a strong (and remarkably modern) argument that his concept of salvation as a reality which embraced deliverance from '*all* sin and misery of the present life', including political oppression, was more biblical than that of his critics.[100] His liberalism lay rather in his application to missionary theory of the immanentist and evolutionary temper of so much late Victorian thought. Such application became most sharply controversial in reference to approaches to non-Christian faiths. Twenty-five years before J. N. Farquhar popularized the idea that Christianity should be seen as the fulfilment, rather than the antagonist, of other faiths, Richard was arguing that 'Christianity has the power of assimilating all that is good in other religions. We come here to counteract their false teaching and to fill up what is awanting just as Christ came not to destroy but to fulfil'.[101] Richard's willingness to acknowledge good in other religions was, however, less decisive for his critics than he imagined.[102] Their opposition sprang from a more broadly-based suspicion that Richard was prepared to minimize the distinctiveness of the Christian gospel by wrapping it in a package designed to appeal to the modernizing Confucian mind. Their objection was less to his theology than to his apparent substitution of natural science for theology. His strategic principles were shared in varying measure by Richard Glover, Alfred Jones, Evan Morgan and Moir Duncan, but never secured majority support in the Society. Until the Boxer rising of 1900 transformed the Chinese political landscape, Richard's place in the gallery of Baptist missionary heroes was far from secure.

99.   Stanley, *The Bible and the Flag*, 142-6.

100. CH/4, Richard to BMS Committee, 17 Oct. 1888.

101. CH/2, Richard to BMS Committee, 12 May 1887. Farquhar's *The Crown of Hinduism* was published in 1913; such views had been held by a few Indian missionaries from the 1870s.

102. Richard, *Forty-five Years*, 205, traces the opposition in Shanxi to the publication of a tract on Taoism, but the extant correspondence lends no support to this claim.

V: *Reform, Reaction and Revolution, 1892-1912*

The Glover-Morris deputation of 1890-1 made a number of recommendations, two of which were of major significance for the future of the China mission. The opening up of the Shaanxi (Shensi) field, and the sending of single women missionaries to China for the first time, were the result.

The floods and protracted famine which afflicted Shandong province between 1888 and 1890 led to the emigration of up to 40,000 people to Shaanxi province in the west. Among them were eighty-seven converts of the BMS Shandong mission, and four teacher-pastors, trained in Whitewright's Native Training Institution. The Christian emigrants established a 'gospel village' north of Xian, and appealed to the BMS for missionary help. Evan Morgan from Taiyuan made a visit to them, and submitted a report to the Committee.[103] The initial inclination of the Society was to refuse the request, and enforce a wholly self-supporting status on the Shaanxi church. Alfred Jones felt that this was to take self-support to absurd limits, and urged that the emigrants should not be abandoned.[104] This argument carried weight with Glover and Morris, who recommended that A. G. Shorrock and Moir Duncan should be removed from their work at Taiyuan and sent to Shaanxi as soon as possible.[105] An additional consideration influencing Glover was his desire to remove Shorrock and Duncan (who, while not approving of all Richard's schemes, admired him greatly) from what he called 'the stifling atmosphere of Brethrenistic associations' which characterized the CIM-dominated missionary community in Taiyuan. There the orthodoxy of a missionary who sympathized to any degree with Richard was suspect.[106] The BMS Committee accepted the deputation's recommendations, although urging Shorrock and Duncan to encourage the Shaanxi church to aim for total independence of missionary aid at the earliest practicable date.[107] Shorrock and Duncan thus became the pioneers of the Shaanxi mission. They were joined in 1895 by Evan Morgan, Richard's most committed supporter in Taiyuan.

Glover and Morris had been required by their instructions to advise the Committee on the wisdom or otherwise of sending single women mission-

---

103. China and Japan Sub-Committee Minute Book 2, pp. 119-20, minutes for 16 June 1890; BMS Committee Minutes, 21 Jan. 1891, pp. 188-9.

104. CH/6, Jones to Baynes, 20 Nov. 1890.

105. CH/10, Report on China Missions of the BMS, pp. 19-22.

106. CH/10, Glover to [Baynes], 5 Nov. 1891.

107. BMS Committee Minutes, 17 Nov. 1891, pp. 78-80.

aries to China.[108] The original view in the BMS China mission had been that the presence of single lady workers would have prejudiced the mission in the eyes of the Chinese, but this objection had collapsed in the light of the success of the CIM's policy of sending out large numbers of single women. Herbert Dixon at Taiyuan reported in 1887 that the CIM single women were not useful merely for nursing sick missionaries, but had secured a regular attendance of fifty to seventy Chinese women at their services, whereas the BMS did not have one.[109] The plain fact was, as the Shandong local committee noted in 1886, when urging the Society to revise its policy, that the women of China were unreachable either by male missionaries or by their preoccupied wives.[110] Glover and Morris, convinced by the evidence of church membership statistics, recommended that four single women be sent to Shandong, but offered no opinion as to whether they should be employed by the BMS or by the Baptist Zenana Mission.[111] The BMS Committee saw 'great advantage and propriety' in the latter course, despite the fact that the Zenana Mission was by its conception and very title a peculiarity of the Indian field.[112] The Society was not yet prepared to follow the lead of the CMS, which had in 1887 removed the barriers to the candidacy of single women - a decision which was already having a dramatic effect on CMS recruitment.[113] The BMS had, nonetheless, taken a cautious step towards recognizing that women could have an independent mission-ary vocation outside the specialized circumstances of the Indian zenanas. Agnes Kirkland, Lucy Shalders, Annie Aldridge and Annie Simpson duly took up their work in Chingzhou and Ch'ou-P'ing in 1893-4.

The 1890s, although a turbulent decade in China's political history, were marked by the sustained growth of the church in Shandong province. Total membership, 1,200 at the end of 1890, had reached 4,177 by 1900. Growth would have been still more rapid, according to Alfred Jones, if the missionary staff had been kept at a more realistic level. Jones complained that his colleagues were over-burdened with institutional responsibilities, and had little time left for evangelism or for representing the mission to the

108. CH/10, Instructions Given to Deputation to China, p. 2.

109. CH/1, Dixon to Baynes, 14 Oct. 1887.

110. CH/6, Jones to Baynes, 11 May 1886.

111. CH/10, Report on China Missions of the BMS, pp. 13-14.

112. CH/10, Copies of Resolutions Adopted by the General Committee on Report of China deputation, pp. 4-5. See below, ch. VII, p. 231.

113. E. Stock, *The History of the Church Missionary Society* (4 vols.; London, 1899-1916) iii, 367-70.

local authorities.[114] The rate of growth in the Shanxi church was actually higher, but it was from such a low base that progress seemed painfully slow. Glover and Morris had found a mere twenty-nine members in the province in 1891; by 1900 the total was 256.[115] In comparison with Shandong, Shanxi had been allocated slender (and disunited) missionary resources; Glover and Morris also believed that the prevalence of opium addiction in the province was a retarding influence.[116] The new church in Shaanxi, formed in 1890 by thirty of the eighty-seven Shandong emigrants (the remainder had died of famine, fallen prey to opium, or joined the Roman Catholic church), had 219 members by 1900, most of them from the Shandong emigré community; the impact on the Shaanxi native population was minimal.[117]

The Sino-Japanese war of 1894-5, although potentially disruptive in its effects on mission work, was apparently welcomed by most Protestant missionaries as an instrument of Providence to humble the imperial pride of the Qing regime and shake China out of her rigid conservatism. Missionaries knew that the war could lead to the overthrow of the Qing dynasty, and viewed the prospect with equanimity or even enthusiasm.[118] The BMS annual report for 1894-5 was one of a number of missionary organs to cite with approval the verdict of Griffith John that the war 'is going to be a source of great blessing to China. It is an awful chastisement, but China needed it, and will be all the better for it'.[119] Although the Qing regime survived the military defeat at the hands of Japan, the war had the anticipated effect of weakening conservative forces in China, and strengthening the advocates of reform. Thus the BMS annual report for 1897-8 was able to discern 'a most remarkable revolution' in the attitude of the Chinese

---

114. CH/7, Jones to Baynes, 27 Feb. 1895.

115. CH/10, Report on China Missions of the BMS, pp. 17, 37-8; Williamson, *British Baptists in China*, 48, 53.

116. CH/10, Report on China Missions of the BMS, p.17; see also Williamson, *British Baptists in China*, 49.

117. Williamson, *British Baptists in China*, 54-6; R. Glover, *Herbert Stanley Jenkins* (London, 1914), 31-2.

118. CH/9, Farthing to Baynes, 29 and 31 Oct. 1894.

119. *MH* (May 1895), 190. See S. C. Miller, 'Ends and means: missionary justification of force in nineteenth-century China', in J. K. Fairbank (ed.), *The Missionary Enterprise in China and America* (Cambridge, Mass., 1974), 270-1.

leadership towards foreign ideas and influences, which was clearly attributable, 'in the good providence of God', to the Japanese war.[120]

Behind the national reform movement which steadily gathered momentum during 1897-8 stood the figure and influence of Timothy Richard. Richard was in close touch with Kang Youwei, the principal reforming leader, while the SDK newspaper, the *Wanguogongbao*, fed international news and Christian opinions to the reformers. After Kang had been appointed tutor to the young Emperor Guangxu, a breathless period of one hundred days of modernizing reform ensued, from 11 June to 21 September 1898. G. B. Farthing reflected that during this period the Christian church seemed to be 'rapidly becoming the darling of the Emperor'; Christian affiliation became suddenly and dangerously popular.[121] Everything changed on 21 September, when the real power behind the throne, the reactionary Empress, executed a swift *coup d'état*. The Emperor was placed under house arrest, and the reforming leaders executed or exiled. The literati who had been cultivating Christian acquaintances now rushed to dissociate themselves from any suspicion of reforming tendencies.[122] Richard saw the reaction as a temporary set-back, being confident that soon a fresh band of reformers would rise up, 'as it were from the graves of the martyred heroes'.[123] The BMS annual report for 1899-1900 took the same optimistic view, assuring Baptists that there had been no 'real abiding reaction among the peoples of China, only a temporary arrestment of expression and action'.[124] Few in the Society had any inkling of the horrors that lay ahead.

The reaction at the imperial court unleashed a new wave of anti-foreign feeling that reached its violent peak in 1899-1900 in the Boxer rising in north China. The Boxer movement was led by devotees of heterodox sects who practised occult rites (which included boxing-like gestures). Originally they had no enthusiasm for the Qing dynasty, but the imperial administration succeeded in restricting their hatred to the foreign community, and in particular to missionaries, whom the Boxers vilified as secret agents of the Western powers. Both Catholic and Protestant churches in the North suffered severely at the hands of the Boxers. The Catholics lost nearly fifty missionaries and perhaps 30,000 national Christians. The Protestants lost

---

120. *MH* (May 1898), 207-8.

121. CH/9, annual report on Shanxi mission for 1898, appended to Farthing to Baynes, 19 Jan. 1899.

122. CH/9, Farthing to Baynes, 13 Oct. 1898.

123. *MH* (May 1899), 213.

124. *MH* (May 1900), 216.

fewer converts - approximately 2,000 - but recorded an even higher total of missionary martyrs - 135 adult Protestant missionaries and fifty-three missionary children lost their lives. The worst affected province was Shanxi, whose governor from March 1900, Yuxian, actively incited the Boxers to murder Christians; here 159 members of the Protestant missionary community were killed.[125]

Among the 159 were twelve BMS missionaries, three BMS missionary children, and fourteen members of the Shou-Yang Mission, the Society's partner in the Taiyuan area. G. B. Farthing, who had written to Baynes on 23 April, assuring him that he did not anticipate any permanent danger,[126] was one of the first BMS group to be massacred, at Taiyuan on 9 July. Farthing, his wife and three children, S. F. and Mrs Whitehouse (whose three-year old son had died only months earlier on the voyage to China), and Miss E. M. Stewart (governess to the Farthing children, and not herself a BMS missionary), were slaughtered in Yuxian's presence with thirty-three other members of the Protestant and Catholic missionary communities. Six Chinese members of the BMS church died at the same time. One month later, eight more BMS missionaries were captured by the Boxers and imprisoned at Xinzhou, forty-five miles to the north of Taiyuan. On 9 August they were all beaten to death. Those who died were the Congo veteran, Herbert Dixon, and his wife; two younger missionary couples, the McCurrachs and the Underwoods; and two recent arrivals in China, S. W. Ennals, and Bessie Renaut of the Baptist Zenana Mission.[127] Within a month the Society had lost the whole staff of the Shanxi mission.

On 19 July the first rumour of the Taiyuan massacre reached Timothy Richard in Shanghai, but no confirmation followed.[128] As the gravity of the threat to the BMS staff became clear, Richard took what steps he could to protect his former colleagues (and critics) by communicating with the British consular authorities.[129] In reality there was little he could do, and even the missionaries who were daily pouring by the score into Shanghai

---

125. There is some uncertainty over the precise totals; see K. S. Latourette, *A History of Christian Missions in China* (London, 1929) 512-17; Williamson, *British Baptists in China*, 69-70.

126. CH/9, Farthing to Baynes, 23 Apr. 1900.

127. H. Dixon papers, telegram from J. P. Bruce, dated 8 Nov. 1900; Williamson, *British Baptists in China*, 65-7; *MH* (Dec. 1900), 540-3, 572-4.

128. CH/3, Richard to Baynes, 21 July 1900.

129. Soothill, *Timothy Richard*, 249-50.

were being advised to leave. He accordingly left for Japan on 25 July.[130] From Yokohama he reflected on events which many would have seen as the destruction of all his ambitions; Richard, however, clung to the hope that 'out of this terrible darkness and suffering and moral chaos ... there will soon arise Divine Order - the Kingdom of God'.[131]

Order of a kind was soon imposed on China - by the military might of the Western powers, who captured Beijing on 14 August. The settlement which they enforced on the Chinese government provided for the punishment of the chief perpetrators of anti-foreign outrages, and the payment of substantial indemnities as compensation to foreign institutions for lives lost and property damaged. Most Protestant societies declined to accept any indemnity for lives lost. At Richard's suggestion, however, the compensation due to the Protestant missions for the damage done to their Shanxi property was devoted to the establishment of a Western university in Taiyuan. His original vision was for an institution that would build the kingdom of God through the imparting of Christian values to the Shanxi intellectual élite. Richard, as Chancellor, possessed full control, and appointed Moir Duncan from Shaanxi as Principal. When, however, plans were revealed for a rival Chinese university in Taiyuan, Richard entered into negotiations with the governor of Shanxi for an amalgamation of the two into a single institution with separate Western and Chinese departments. This proposal was eventually accepted, but at the price of abandoning an overtly Christian basis. Hence theology could not be taught at Shanxi University. Missionary influence remained strong, initially through Duncan, and from 1907 by his successor as Principal, W. E. Soothill, the Methodist missionary and Richard's biographer. Although Shanxi University itself failed to survive the Revolution of 1911-12, numerous other Western-style institutions of higher education (mostly modelled on the American Christian colleges) were established in Republican China.[132]

Of more immediate relevance to the building of the kingdom of God in China was the condition of the church. The small BMS church in Shanxi had been all but wiped out by the Boxers. Of the 100 church members in Xinzhou, forty-four had been killed; in the small church at Fansi, twenty-two out of twenty-four had died. Furthermore, some Christians had survived only by publicly renouncing their allegiance to 'the foreign Church'. The BMS missionaries who re-entered the province in 1901 dealt gently with these apostates by treating the entire church roll as having been

130. CH/3, Richard to Baynes, 25 July 1900.

131. CH/3, Richard to Baynes, 2 Aug. 1900.

132. Soothill, *Timothy Richard*, 253-68.

erased, and requiring all to make a new declaration of faith before being admitted to membership. Only five per cent of the surviving Shanxi members failed to renew their faith in this way. When W. Y. Fullerton and C. E. Wilson visited the province in 1907, they found membership had recovered to 219: the church had been 'born again'.[133]

In Shandong over 120 church members had been killed in the rising, and many more drifted away under the force of persecution. Membership plummeted from 4,177 in 1900 to about 3,400 in 1904. However, by 1907 the losses had nearly been made good, and the church had made renewed progress to self-supporting status: within three years the number of pastors, wholly supported from church funds, had been increased from seven to eighteen.[134] Even more encouraging to the 1907 deputation was the rapid expansion since the Boxer rising of the young church in Shaanxi: Fullerton and Wilson witnessed the baptism of forty-three converts at the quarterly church assembly in October, which brought the total membership to 1,010.[135] On the debit side, the deputation found that in the BMS mission, as generally throughout China, over-burdened missionaries had neglected evangelism in favour of pastoral, medical and educational work, and called for renewed attention to winning 'the present generation of the heathen'.[136]

Perhaps the most remarkable feature of Fullerton and Wilson's report was their support for Timothy Richard's work with the Christian Literature Society and their unqualified endorsement of his missionary vision. They spoke with reverence of 'the prophetic insight of this man of God, whose one aim is to glorify Jesus Christ, and whose one ambition is to see China brought to His feet'.[137] Richard, now Protestant adviser to the Chinese government on foreign missions, obtained an audience for Fullerton and Wilson at the Chinese Foreign Office. At this and similar interviews with leading officials the two men surprised themselves with the enthusiasm with which they urged public works and currency reform as among 'the means God would use for the redemption of China'. They found a ready response to all such suggestions, though less willingness to talk about spiritual

133. W. Y. Fullerton and C. E. Wilson, Report on the China Missions of the Baptist Missionary Society (1908), pp. 22, 54-6.

134. Ibid., 53, 55; Williamson, *British Baptists in China*, 48, 63.

135. C. E. Wilson to Amy Wilson, 20 Oct. 1907 (private letter in possession of Mrs E. M. Vicary).

136. Fullerton and Wilson, Report on the China Missions, pp. 32-3, 72.

137. Ibid., p. 42.

Alfred G. Jones, Missionary in China, 1876-1905.

Timothy Richard, Missionary in China, 1870-1915.

W.Y. Fullerton, Home Secretary of the BMS, 1912-27.

C.E. Wilson, Missionary in Bengal, 1894-1905; General Secretary of the BMS, 1906-12; Foreign Secretary, 1912-39.

matters. The deputation report urged that Richard be set free from office responsibilities in Shanghai and given a roving commission to take whatever opportunity he wished to advance the kingdom of God in China; and accordingly recommended that the BMS should for two years support an office manager in Shanghai.[138] After the years of hesitation with which the Society had greeted Richard's plans, this was a strange conversion. Even the theologically conservative Fullerton seems to have accepted Richard's strategy of seeking after the 'worthy', persuaded that it was no more than an application of 'the great doctrine of election'.[139] The strengthening current of sentiment in favour of reform in China had swept away the theological and strategic reservations which had hitherto hedged the Society's attitude to its leading China missionary.

The 1907 deputation thus advocated both increased evangelistic effort in China, and the investment in higher education which Richard believed to be so crucial. The implicit tension between these two emphases could be resolved only through a substantial increase in missionary resources, as the General Committee recognized in accepting the deputation report's recommendations in April 1908.[140] These included the appointment of thirty new workers to China, seven more men for each of the three provinces, plus nine additional workers for the Zenana Mission. The new recruits would enable a line of new stations to be opened, stretching northwards into Shanxi from Xian (Hsi-An-Fu) in Shaanxi, all financed by the Arthington Fund.[141] These plans came to fruition in 1910-11, when missionaries were stationed at Yanan (Yen-An-Fu), Suidezhou, and Yulin, and a hospital building was commenced at Sanyuan, to be staffed by Dr and Mrs Andrew Young. Richard Glover later reflected that if the Society had known what was to take place in the closing months of 1911, it would have hesitated to adopt this expansive policy in Shaanxi.[142] It was now the turn of the Shaanxi mission, the only part of the BMS China field to escape unscathed during the Boxer troubles, to pass through the fire.

The authority of the alien Qing regime crumbled steadily after the almost simultaneous deaths in November 1908 of the Emperor and Empress Dowager had left an infant, Pu-yi, on the imperial throne. On 1 October

138. Ibid., pp. 12-13, 43-4.

139. W. Y. Fullerton, *At the Sixtieth Milestone* (London, 1917), 152-3.

140. General Committee Minutes, 24 Apr. 1908, pp. 106-7.

141. Fullerton and Wilson, Report on the China Missions, pp. 61-8.

142. Glover, *Herbert Stanley Jenkins*, 81.

1911 rebellion against Qing rule broke out in the far western province of Sichuan. It was followed by uprisings in Wuchang and Hankow. On the 22nd the rebellion spread to Xian. Within a few days over 10,000 Manchus were slaughtered in Xian city. Two Swedish missionaries and six missionary children were killed. The BMS staff in Xian survived, thanks to the intervention of members of the Guomindang (Kuomintang), the nationalist and pro-Western wing of the revolutionary movement. Andrew and Charlotte Young, returning to Xian from medical work in the north, ran into the thick of the fighting, and took refuge in a cave near Zhongbu for ten days. Later they joined their two doctor colleagues, George Charter and Cecil Robertson, and one nurse, Helen Watt, in Xian, treating about 600 seriously wounded patients a day in the small BMS hospital. Further north, in the remote new stations of Yanan and Suidezhou, five other BMS staff and their children waited anxiously, in constant danger from the revolutionaries of the Elder Brother Society, the secret society that now controlled the northern section of the province.[143]

The lives of the Shaanxi missionaries remained in real danger until the arrival in December of an eight-man armed relief expedition, organized by J. C. Keyte, recently returned from furlough. Two other BMS missionaries, H. D. Fairburn and P. D. Evans, joined Keyte on the expedition. Mercifullly these missionary warriors never had to fire a shot. On the return journey from Xian to Beijing, the party crossed between the warring imperialist and revolutionary armies, which had agreed to suspend hostilities to allow the foreigners to pass. The expedition finally reached the safety of Beijing on 17 January 1912.[144]

By this time the revolution was nearly complete. The leader of the Guomindang, Sun Yat-sen, had been installed in Nanjing as provisional President of the new Chinese Republic on 1 January. On 12 February the boy emperor, Pu-Yi, abdicated, and Sun resigned, to make way for Yuan Shikai, protégé of Li Hongzhang and protector of the BMS Shandong missionaries during the Boxer rising. Yuan assumed the Presidency on 12 March. Sun, the product of an American missionary education and a man of vaguely Christian ideals, became for a while Vice-President. He wrote to Timothy Richard that he hoped to be able to 'establish a kingdom of God on earth and make the Government of the Republic pure and righteous'.

143. Williamson, *British Baptists in China*, 84-7; E. F. Borst-Smith, *Caught in the Chinese Revolution* (2nd edn.; London, 1913), 17-79.

144. On the Shaanxi Relief Expedition see Borst-Smith, *Caught in the Chinese Revolution*, 83-129; J. C. Keyte, *The Passing of the Dragon* (London, 1913), Book III.

The BMS annual report for 1911-12 cited his words, and reflected in hyperbolic vein on how 'the most conservative of all nations' had carried out 'in an incredibly brief space of time the greatest revolution in history ... There is now an opportunity such as we never witnessed before for the advance of the Kingdom of God in China'.[145] The months and years to come were indeed to see the heyday of Christian missions in China. But they would also witness the gradual disintegration of the Republic into a political chaos that was a far cry from the new order of the Kingdom of God.

145. *BMS Annual Report*, 1911-12, pp. 59, 69.

VII

The Domestic Life and General Policy of the Society, 1817-1906

I: The Era of John Dyer, 1817-1841

1. Systematization

James Hinton of Oxford, elected joint-secretary of the BMS with John Ryland at the Northampton committee meeting in October 1815,[1] found the pressure of combining his office with his pastoral responsibilities too great, and resigned his post at the annual meeting at Oxford on 1 October 1817. The Society then appointed as 'assistant secretary' John Dyer, pastor of Hosier's Lane, Reading, and a member of the BMS Committee since 1812.[2] For a year Dyer combined his secretarial duties with his Reading pastorate, but he too found the load impossible to bear, and after the 1818 annual meeting Dyer relinquished his pastorate to become the first salaried, full-time secretary of the Society.[3] John Ryland remained the nominal secretary until his death in 1825, but it was Dyer who staffed the London office of the Society, opened in October 1819, and steered the BMS through the troubled waters of the Serampore Controversy in the 1820s.[4]

John Dyer was chiefly responsible for overseeing the transition of the BMS from the loosely-structured fellowship of Andrew Fuller's day to the more formal pattern of philanthropic organization characteristic of evangelical voluntary societies in the nineteenth century. Hence, during his period of office, the *Periodical Accounts*, the bulletin of missionary informa-

---

1. See above, ch. I, p. 33.

2. *PA* vi, 243; on Dyer see E. A. Payne, *The First Generation* (London, n.d.), 120-6.

3. *PA* vi, 344; F. A. Cox, *History of the Baptist Missionary Society from 1792 to 1842* (2 vols.; London, 1842), i, 279.

4. See above, ch. II, pp. 61-7.

tion begun by Fuller, evolved into a conventional annual report of the kind issued by other societies. The former function of the *Periodical Accounts* was increasingly taken over by the monthly periodical, the *Missionary Herald,* which first appeared in 1819, and has been published without interruption ever since.[5] A written constitution for the Society, first adopted at the Oxford annual meeting in 1817, was revised following representations from Joseph Gutteridge and other London supporters, and adopted at the Cambridge annual meeting in October 1819. According to this 'Plan of the Society', which remained in force (with limited amendments) until 1843, a General Committee of not more than fifty members was given responsibility for circulating missionary 'intelligence' and promoting the interests of the BMS in the country. The General Committee normally met annually. From this body, a Central Committee of twenty-one persons (plus the treasurer and secretaries) was elected to conduct the affairs of the Society by means of monthly London meetings. Twelve of the twenty-one were required to be resident in London or its immediate vicinity, thus guaranteeing the metropolitan control of the Society's management which Joseph Gutteridge had made his objective.[6]

Both the General Committee and the Central Committee were usually presided over by the treasurer of the Society, who, since the resignation of Reynold Hogg in 1795, had been a layman. Of the five treasurers with whom Dyer worked, three deserve particular note. Benjamin Shaw, treasurer from 1821 to 1826, had been Member of Parliament for Westbury from 1812 to 1818 - the first Baptist M. P. since 1784. Shaw, a prominent London merchant and insurance director, was associated with Francis A. Cox, the Society's first historian, in the founding of University College, London.[7] His appointment as treasurer is evidence of the concern of the Committee to give the Society a more assured social standing than had been the case under Andrew Fuller. John Broadley Wilson, who held office from 1826 to 1834, had been an official in the ordnance department at Devonport dockyard, but, 'on becoming truly pious', abandoned his career

5. From 1819 the BMS Committee published regular annual reports; these were described as a 'continuation' of the *Periodical Accounts* until the early years of the twentieth century.

6. *PA* vii, 4, 6, 26-8. In 1826 the General Committee was increased to eighty members, and the Central Committee to twenty-five (of whom sixteen were to be resident in London). The General Committee was further increased to 100 members in 1838.

7. R. G. Thorne (ed.), *The House of Commons 1790-1820, vol. 5. Members, Q-Y* (The History of Parliament, London, 1986), 132-3. Shaw is omitted from Dr D. W. Bebbington's list of Baptist M. P.'s in the nineteenth century in *BQ* 29 (1981-2), 3-24.

and retired to Clapham.[8] Although baptized as a believer by Isaiah Birt in Plymouth, Wilson had retained his original Anglican connections, and in London attended Rowland Hill's Surrey Chapel, strictly speaking an Anglican proprietary chapel, but a church which welcomed preachers from a wide spectrum of denominations. Wilson thus provided a strategic link between the BMS and the wider and more fashionable evangelical world beyond the Particular Baptist denomination. He was succeeded in office by William Brodie Gurney of Denmark Hill, official short-hand writer at the Houses of Parliament and founder of the Sunday School Union.[9] Gurney's employment gave him access to Members of Parliament, which must have been a valuable resource for the Society, particularly in relation to West Indian affairs in the aftermath of slave emancipation.

The growing systematization of the Society's affairs, whilst it contributed to the estrangement between the Serampore missionaries and the home Committee, bore undoubted fruit in a significant increase in the level of Baptist support. E. B. Underhill estimated that the total number of Baptist churches in Britain contributing to the Society rose from a maximum of 180 in 1817 to about 750 in 1842.[10] In part the increase was due to the planting of new Baptist churches, particularly in Wales, but the BMS had also won the support of congregations which previously had stood aloof. The Society's total annual income grew from a mere £6,648 in 1816-17 to £26,548 in 1840-1. In real terms giving to the BMS increased very significantly in the last few years of Dyer's secretaryship.[11]

Nevertheless, the rising level of ordinary contributions to the general account of the mission had failed to keep step with the accelerating expenditure occasioned by the expansion of the Jamaica mission and the reunion with the Serampore Mission in 1837-8. In fact, ever since 1820, the BMS had balanced its books only by repeated additional appeals for special objects and by loans from a few wealthy supporters. In March 1839 Dyer had to warn the Committee that the BMS could not survive for much longer on the basis of such temporary expedients. W. B. Gurney similarly informed the Committee that the financial condition of the Society was

8.   Cox, *History of the BMS*, i, 435. On Wilson see *BM* 30 (1838), 199-200.

9.   On Gurney (1777-1855) see *DNB*; *BM* 47 (1855), 529-33, 593-600; A. C. Underwood, *A History of the English Baptists* (London, 1947), 147.

10. E. B. Underhill, *Christian Missions in the East and West* (London, 1873), 128. B. Stanley, 'Home Support for Overseas Missions in Early Victorian England, c. 1838-1873' Ph.D. thesis (Cambridge, 1979), 210, estimates the total of contributing churches in England in 1850-1 at 655.

exposing him to an 'amount of outlay and risk of loss to which one individual ought not to be subjected', and talked repeatedly of resignation.[12]

2. Tragedy

The BMS Committee responded to these warnings from its officers by appointing a three-man sub-committee to consider measures to increase the regular voluntary income. The principal recommendation of the sub-committee was that the Society should appoint a home secretary to promote domestic support, leaving Dyer to concentrate on foreign affairs. This recommendation was adopted by the Central Committee on 27 March 1839.[13] The search thus began for a colleague for John Dyer. Since September 1825 he had had the assistance of Eustace Carey, invalided home from Bengal, as a deputation agent, but Carey continued in poor health and had no administrative responsibilities.[14] Dyer was indeed anxious to be relieved of the burden of managing the Society's finances, but for some time resisted the notion of a co-secretary, partly out of a concern to save money, but partly from a reluctance to share the control which had for so long been his alone.[15]

On 5 December 1839 the BMS Committee voted, by a slim majority, to invite Joseph Angus, the young pastor of the historic church at New Park Street, Southwark, to become co-secretary of the Society, with responsibility for home affairs.[16] The division of opinion reflected, not any opposition to Angus personally, but uncertainty over the wisdom of proceeding with a course about which Dyer had expressed reservations. Angus took some time to make his decision. His church was reluctant to release him, and suggested that the Society should make use of Angus's services on a part-time basis only. In the event Angus himself concluded that the uncertain

---

11. J. B. Myers (ed.), *The Centenary Volume of the Baptist Missionary Society 1792-1892* (London, 1892), 333; Stanley, 'Home support for overseas missions', 70-1. Myers's figures are misleading as an index of the level of regular voluntary support for the BMS. Contributions for the general purposes of the Society in 1840-1 were only £18,097 (*BMS Annual Report*, 1840-1, p. 82).

12. BMS Committee Minutes, 7-14 Mar. 1839, pp. 164-75.

13. BMS Committee Minutes, 7, 14, 27 Mar. 1839, pp. 169-70, 175-6, 180-1.

14. Mrs E. Carey, *Eustace Carey: A Missionary in India* (London, 1857), 407-54, 479-89.

15. BMS Committee Minutes, 27 Feb. 1840, p. 37; *BM* 33 (1841), 438; Cox, *History of the BMS*, ii, 380-1.

16. BMS Committee Minutes, 21 Nov. 1839, p. 5; 5 Dec. 1839, p. 9.

prospects of the Society allowed 'no time or place for half-measures or half-men', and accepted the post on its original terms.[17] His appointment was announced at the Society's annual meeting in Exeter Hall on 30 April 1840.

John Dyer apparently accepted Angus's appointment with good grace, and for a year the two men worked together. However, by early July 1841 Dyer was showing unmistakable signs of mental strain. He attended the weekly Committee meeting on 8 July, but the next day collapsed in his office at Fen Court. He insisted on returning to work in time for the Committee on 15 July, but was persuaded to remain in another room during the meeting. Over the next week he alternated between periods of tranquility and bouts of intense depression. On the morning of Thursday, 22 July John Dyer's body was found drowned in a cistern at his Sydenham home. Unaware of the tragedy, the BMS Committee that day passed a resolution expressing its hope of a speedy recovery. The following week a shocked Committee recorded its desire 'with humility and profound submission to the will of God to bow to the inscrutable and heart-rending Providence' which had deprived the Society of its senior secretary.[18] The man who had carried almost alone the burden of implementing the administrative revolution in the life of the BMS had lost his life in the process.

II: The Era of Joseph Angus, 1841-1849

1. Crisis and Celebration

John Dyer's suicide left the BMS in the hands of Joseph Angus, then only twenty-five years old. The sense of crisis was intensified by the growing disproportion between the Society's income and expenditure. The severe economic depression of 1841-2 was beginning to affect all the missionary societies to an alarming extent.[19] On 8 September the Committee decided that the crisis warranted a three-day conference of the General Committee, to be held from 5 to 7 October.[20] The October conference was marked by a note of sombre realism. After a warning by Angus that expenditure for the current year was likely to exceed projected income by up to £6,000, the Committee adopted the goal of raising the annual income to £25,000, and

---

17. BMS Committee Minutes, 23 Apr. 1840, pp. 50-1.

18. BMS Committee Minutes, 8, 15, 22, 29 July 1841, pp. 208, 210, 211, 215-16; *BM* 33 (1841), 437-8.

19. Stanley, 'Home support for overseas missions', 29-30.

20. BMS Committee Minutes, 8 Sept. 1841, pp. 234-5.

appointed a sub-committee to consider how this might be done. As a means of reducing expenditure, the question was raised for the first time of whether the Jamaican churches were ready for financial independence from the BMS; although Joshua Tinson, who was present, gave the opinion that the Jamaica mission as a whole was not yet ripe for self-support, the seed had been sown of the decision that was to be taken in Kingston in January 1842.[21] On the question of the secretaryship, there was agreement that two persons were needed, but again there was a division between those who favoured the old Dyer-Eustace Carey pattern of one central and one travelling secretary, and those who insisted that a co-secretary to work with Angus at Fen Court was necessary. The latter opinion narrowly prevailed, and by secret ballot William Brock of Norwich (a member of the Central Committee) was chosen to be Angus's colleague.[22]

William Brock, who was happily settled in his pastorate, declined the Society's invitation. From November 1841 to June 1843 the Committee made repeated attempts to find a colleague for Joseph Angus.[23] The quest proved fruitless, and Angus had to carry sole administrative responsibility for the BMS during a period which included the celebration of the Society's jubilee, the granting of financial independence to the Jamaica mission, and the establishing of the West Africa mission. Almost incredibly, until 1844 Angus combined these duties with being one of the secretaries at Stepney College.[24] The highlight of the jubilee celebrations was a public meeting in Kettering on 1 June 1842, when an estimated four thousand people gathered on the lawn of the house in which the Society had been founded to hear some of the leading Baptist orators of the day applaud the achievements of the past fifty years. However, the tone of the meeting was not one of pure self-congratulation. On the contrary, the opening address by the chairman, W. B. Gurney, pulled no punches in its insistence that Baptists had failed to give sacrificially to the missionary cause - 'the only men who have made sacrifices have been our missionaries'.[25]

Gurney and Angus were clearly determined to use the jubilee to place the Society's finances on a more stable footing. They succeeded only to a limited extent. A jubilee fund of £32,000 was raised, which enabled the Society to extinguish its debt and build new headquarters in Moorgate. However, the

21. See above, ch. III, p. 83-4.

22. BMS Committee Minutes, 5-7 Oct. 1841, pp. 249-56.

23. BMS Committee Minutes, 4 Nov. 1841 - 22 June 1843, *passim.*

24. E. A. Payne, *The Great Succession* (London, n.d.), 19.

25. *BM* 34 (1842), 374.

remainder of the 1840s saw no significant increase in regular income, which fluctuated around a static mean until the late 1850s. The goal of a regular annual income in excess of £25,000 was not attained until the 1860s.[26] Without the curtailment of expenditure produced by the cutting free of the Jamaica mission, the BMS would have been in desperate straits during the 1840s; as it was, a deficit was recorded in every year from 1842 to 1849.[27] The support of the churches remained inconsistent from year to year and geographically patchy. Of the 900 churches which supported the BMS in 1847, over 200 had not done so in 1846; and of the 900 which contributed in 1846, over 250 did nothing in 1847. The Society remained weak in certain parts of the country, notably in the east of England - the stronghold of high Calvinism. In 1850-1 it is estimated that less than 44 per cent of Particular Baptist churches in England contributed to the Society.[28]

2. The Colonies and Europe

Since the adoption of a formal constitution for the Society in 1817, the object of the BMS had been defined as follows:

> The great object of this Society is the diffusion of the knowledge of the religion of Jesus Christ through the heathen world, by means of the preaching of the Gospel, the translation and publication of the Holy Scriptures, and the establishment of Schools.[29]

In contrast to the Society's practice in Andrew Fuller's day, when the BMS supported evangelistic work within England,[30] this form of words theoretically ruled out activity in the British Isles, Europe, or those British colonies which were not generally regarded as being part of 'the heathen world'. Thus a proposal in 1831 to commence operations in France was rejected 'after considerable discussion' by the Committee, on the grounds that it did not fall 'within the limits originally prescribed by the Society'.[31] Since 1832 the BMS had supplied one missionary pastor to the church established by

---

26. Stanley, 'Home support for overseas missions', 70-1; Myers (ed.), *Centenary Volume of the BMS*, 333.

27. E. B. Underhill, *Principles and Methods of Missionary Labour* (London, 1896), 3.

28. *BM* 40 (1848), 314, cited in Stanley, 'Home support for overseas missions', 194-5.

29. *PA* vi, p. 245.

30. See above, ch. I, pp. 18-19.

31. BMS Committee Minutes, 22 Apr. 1831, p. 30.

British settlers at Grahamstown in the Cape Colony (William Davies from 1832 to 1838, and George Aveline from 1838 to 1843). The Grahamstown mission was, however, viewed by the Committee as an exceptional venture, whereby the Society paid passage money and offered support for missionary work among the surrounding Xhosa population, but declined any further responsibility. The Cape Colony was the preserve of the LMS and the Wesleyan Methodists, and there was no question of South Africa becoming a distinct BMS field.[32]

It was not long before the appropriateness of the limitation of the BMS to work among the 'heathen' was questioned. One result of the critical situation which faced the Society in the early 1840s was a willingness within the Committee to consider whether any modification of its constitution was required by its present circumstances.[33] Two plans for reforming the constitution were considered in 1842-3. When the second of these was introduced, in January 1843, Edward Steane, joint-secretary of the Baptist Union, gave notice that he intended to submit a modification of the Rules so as to enable the Society 'to include in its operations the British Colonies and Foreign Parts'.[34] Steane's modification, which substituted for the phrase 'through the heathen world' the words 'throughout the whole world beyond the British Isles', was accepted by the annual meeting of the Society in April. At the same time, the old Central Committee and General Committee were replaced by a single Committee of thirty-six persons.[35]

The change in the objects of the Society was made with the primary intention of enabling the BMS to take over the work of the Baptist Colonial Missionary Society in Upper Canada. The latter was a small venture, begun in November 1836; it established a Baptist college in Montreal, and sent out Benjamin Davies to assume the presidency in 1838. The new society struggled financially, and its Committee, which was dominated by BMS men, saw a merger with the older society as the obvious solution.[36] In August 1843 the BMS Committee accordingly accepted the incorporation of the Colonial Society within the BMS, which thus assumed responsibility for the Montreal college and also established connections with the home

32. BMS Committee Minutes, 1 Dec. 1831, pp. 76-8; 23 Aug. 1838, pp. 81-3.

33. BMS Committee Minutes, 26 Apr. 1842, pp. 116-17.

34. BMS Committee Minutes, 19 Jan. 1843, pp. 10-11.

35. BMS Committee Minutes, 2 Feb. 1843, pp. 17-19; *BMS Annual Report*, 1842-3, pp. ix-x.

36. J. D. Bollen, 'English-Australian Baptist Relations 1830-1860', *BQ* 25 (1973-4), 294-6.

missionary work of the churches in this part of Canada.[37] When Benjamin Davies returned to England to become president of Stepney College, the BMS sent out J. M. Cramp in his place.[38] For a brief period in the 1840s, Canada thus occupied a regular place in the pages of the *Missionary Herald.* However, the involvement of the BMS in Canada was on a small scale, and hence vulnerable to financial pressures. The Montreal college closed in 1849, and the Society withdrew from Canada in the following year.[39]

The enthusiasm shown in 1842-3 for commencing BMS work in the colonies of British settlement thus proved short-lived. Between 1856 and 1860 the Society gave limited support to Baptist work in Victoria, Australia, in response to pressure from its Birmingham auxiliary, but there was never any question of the BMS adopting Australia as a field.[40] Ironically, the constitutional change made in 1843 turned out to have greater significance for work in Europe, despite the fact that the Society's report for 1842-3 intimated that the Committee had no immediate plans for that continent.[41] Within a matter of months the Society was in fact considering its first venture into Europe. In August 1843 the Committee received a request to take over a mission at Morlaix in Brittany, commenced in 1834 by the Baptist churches of Glamorgan. After a visit to Brittany by Joseph Angus, the Committee agreed to the proposal, accepted John Jenkins, the worker at Morlaix, as a BMS missionary, and sent out John Jones of Pontypool to join him.[42] Jenkins laboured until his death in 1872, when he was succeeded by his son, Alfred. The Brittany mission remained small, but a source of particular interest to Welsh Baptists, on account of linguistic and cultural affinity. When the BMS Committee resolved in 1885 to phase out all support for the work in Brittany, the Welsh churches protested with such vigour that the decision was modified to ensure that Alfred Jenkins's work at Morlaix continued to receive BMS funding.[43]

37. BMS Committee Minutes, 17 Aug. 1843, 107-8.

38. *BM* 36 (1844), 262-4.

39. BMS Committee Minutes, 3 July 1849, p. 297-9, 12 July 1849, p. 306; *BMS Annual Report,* 1849-50, p. 34.

40. Bollen, 'English-Australian Baptist relations', 298-301.

41. *BMS Annual Report,* 1842-3, pp. 53-4.

42. BMS Committee Minutes, 17 Aug. 1843, p. 109; 7 Dec. 1843, pp. 150-1; *BMS Annual Report,* 1843-4, pp. 66-7.

43. *MH* (May 1885), 209; Myers (ed.), *Centenary Volume of the BMS,* 219-20; T. M. Bassett, *The Baptists of Wales and the Baptist Missionary Society* (Swansea, 1991), 21-2.

In the longer term, the 1843 constitution acquired a significance of a different kind. Its statement of the objects of the Society, although simplified in 1915, remained without essential alteration until 1992. Since the late 1970s the phrase 'throughout the whole world, beyond the British Isles' - introduced in order to widen the Society's horizons - had paradoxically come under question for its exclusion of the BMS from assuming any missionary responsibility within its own home-land.[44]

III: The Era of E. B. Underhill, 1849-1876

1. Consolidation

In 1849 Joseph Angus accepted an invitation to become president of Stepney College. The BMS Committee now seized the opportunity to fulfil its long-standing intention of having two joint-secretaries. Two of the Committee's own members were appointed. Frederick Trestrail, Baptist minister and secretary of the Baptist Irish Society since 1843, was given primary responsibility for home affairs; in 1845 Trestrail had declined an earlier unofficial invitation to become Angus's colleague at the BMS.[45] The onerous task of managing the foreign correspondence of the Society was given to a layman, Edward Bean Underhill. Underhill had been a member of the Committee for only a few months, but his familiarity with the BMS stretched back to his school-days in Oxford as a pupil and member of the congregation of James Hinton, pastor of New Road Baptist Church and BMS assistant secretary from 1815 to 1817. A grocer by trade, Underhill had left Oxford in 1843 owing to the ill health of his wife, and had devoted himself to the study of Baptist history. He was destined to become the most learned and most widely influential secretary ever to serve the Society, with the possible exception of Andrew Fuller himself. After Frederick Trestrail's retirement in 1870, Underhill was assisted by Clement Bailhache. In 1876 Underhill himself retired, but continued to serve the Society in an honorary capacity until his death in 1901.[46]

---

44. See below, ch. XVI, pp. 522-3. In 1915 the phrase 'the great object' was amended to 'the object', and the words 'by the preaching of the Gospel, the translation and publication of the Holy Scriptures, and the establishment of Schools' were removed (reflecting, by implication, the acceptance of medical work as a proper activity of the Society).

45. *The Short Story of a Long Life: Memorials of Frederick Trestrail D.D., F.R.G.S. ... edited by his widow* (London, 1892), 135, 139-40. The BMS Committee Minutes for 1845 contain no record of this invitation.

46. On Underhill see *DNB*; *MH* (July 1901), 347-53; Payne, *The Great Succession*, 29-39.

The greatest challenge confronting Underhill and Trestrail in 1849 was the continuing financial weakness of the Society, which was itself a reflection of what Underhill in retrospect termed 'a general distrust throughout the churches'.[47] To save money, the services of paid deputation agents, such as Eustace Carey, were dispensed with, throwing most of the burden of public advocacy of the BMS on to its two secretaries.[48] For their first five years in office, each spent six months annually touring the country on the Society's behalf. The fruits of their efforts gradually became evident. During the 1852-3 financial year, the long-standing deficit on the accounts was substantially reduced, and at the 1853 annual meeting it was announced that 'an old friend' had cancelled the remaining debt of £1,813.[49] The 'old friend' was none other than Samuel Morton Peto, co-treasurer of the Society since 1846. Peto, a highly successful building and railway contractor, had been elected M. P. for Norwich in 1847, and was the most influential Baptist businessman of his day. On W. B. Gurney's death in 1855, Peto became sole treasurer of the BMS; in the same year he was made a baronet. With Underhill and Trestrail, Peto must share the credit for the improvement in the financial position of the Society during the 1850s. His period as treasurer came to a sad end in the aftermath of the failure of his business in May 1866. He resigned his office in March 1867 on the grounds that he considered it inappropriate to hold responsibility for the Society's finances at a time when bankruptcy proceedings were about to be instituted against his firm.[50] He was succeeded as treasurer by Joseph Tritton of Norwood.

Underhill's secretaryship, although happily free of the bitter divisions which made John Dyer's task so difficult in the 1820s, was not without periods of lively internal debate within the Society. One of the most significant of these related to a sustained attempt by the young C. H. Spurgeon between 1863 and 1866 to secure changes in the BMS constitution. Spurgeon was concerned to see a closer relationship between missionaries on the field and their sending churches, and defined the role of a missionary society in terms which recalled the pristine days of Andrew Fuller. For Spurgeon, the BMS had become 'an interposing medium',

47. Underhill, *Principles and Methods of Missionary Labour*, 3-4.

48. Carey, however, continued to travel for the BMS for 3-4 months a year until his death in 1855; see Mrs E. Carey, *Eustace Carey*, 530-1.

49. Underhill, *Principles and Methods of Missionary Labour*, 5.

50. *BM* 59 (1867), 327-9; see B. and F. Bowers, 'Bloomsbury Chapel and Mercantile Morality', *BQ* 30 (1983-4), 210-20.

distancing the home churches from direct participation in the missionary enterprise. In particular, he objected to the terms of membership of the BMS, which were purely financial in nature, and made no reference to church membership or even Christian profession. On this last point Spurgeon gained influential support from, amongst others, Morton Peto and William Landels, the minister of Regent's Park Chapel. A protracted debate on the terms of membership resulted in a change to the constitution being passed at the 1866 annual meeting, which added the words 'all Christian persons concurring in the objects of the Society' to the existing formula which prescribed the level of donations and subscriptions qualifying a contributor for membership.[51] This wording remained in the constitution until 1915.[52]

E. B. Underhill's primary contribution to the BMS lay in his shaping of its overseas policy. His views were fashioned by three extended visits to the field. His tour of the Indian sub-continent from 1854 to 1857 bore fruit in the new policy on 'native agency' and missionary strategy in India, formulated from 1862 onwards. As was seen in chapter five, this policy aroused considerable controversy, during which Underhill's attempts to break the pattern of missionary location in India were widely criticised, but also strongly supported by William Landels.[53] Underhill's visit to the West Indies in 1859-60 provided the inspiration for his letter to Edward Cardwell in 1865, which brought the BMS back into the public eye as the champion of the rights of the former slave population of Jamaica.[54] Finally, his journey to the Cameroons in 1869-70, though marked by personal tragedy, brought peace to a divided mission.[55] These protracted absences threw a heavy burden on Frederick Trestrail, who had to carry both the home and the foreign portfolios while Underhill was away. The strain of working inordinately long hours told on Trestrail (who frequently slept at the Mission House during these periods), and led to his decision to retire in May 1870.[56]

51. *BMS Annual Report,* 1865-6, p. xii; I have written on this episode more fully in 'Spurgeon and the Baptist Missionary Society, 1863-1866', *BQ* 29 (1981-2), 319-28.

52. *BMS Annual Reports,* 1913-14, p. 156; 1914-15, p. 202.

53. See above, ch. V, pp. 149-54. Landels' stance in both the constitutional debate of 1863-6 and the Indian controversy of 1869 is consistent with his support for the China Inland Mission, founded in 1865.

54. See above, ch. III, pp. 88-9, 97-8.

55. See above, ch. IV, p. 113.

56. *The Short Story of a Long Life,* 189-91.

2. Norway and Italy

Underhill's secretaryship saw two further ventures by the BMS into Europe, one of which lasted longer than the other. From 1863 to 1885 the Society supported the evangelistic work of Gottfried Hubert, a native Norwegian, at first in the Krageroë district on the west coast of Norway, and then more widely. Although Hubert's labours were not unsuccessful in promoting the growth of the small Baptist community in Norway, the Norway mission was one of the casualties of the Society's decision in 1884 (under pressure from Robert Arthington) to devote an increasing share of its resources to expansion on the upper Congo. BMS support for the Norway churches was phased out by 1892.[57]

The BMS Italy mission was of more enduring significance. It was no accident that it originated in 1870-1, at a time when the First Vatican Council had stiffened the resolve of British Protestants to reclaim Italy from Roman Catholic domination. During the autumnal assembly of the Baptist Union in 1868 a small independent committee had been formed to support two English Baptist ministers, James Wall and Edward Clarke, who had begun evangelistic work in Bologna and Spezia respectively. In March 1870 William Landels, a prominent supporter of this venture, raised in the BMS Committee the possibility of the BMS making a grant to James Wall. On 22 April it was agreed to grant £100 to the Italian committee on Wall's behalf. Landels and others pressed for a more substantial commitment. A motion to give Wall £200 a year for two years was unsuccessful, but the Committee eventually agreed that contributions for Wall's work could be received by the treasurer, and that information on the Italy mission could be printed from time to time in the *Missionary Herald*.[58] In September 1870 Rome fell to Victor Emmanuel's Italian nationalist army, virtually extinguishing the temporal power of the papacy. James Wall speedily took advantage of the new measure of religious liberty and settled in Rome, where he constituted the first Baptist church in the city in January 1871. Soon afterwards Sir Morton Peto visited Italy, and on his return gave an enthusiastic report to the BMS Committee on the work of both Wall and Clarke. In the light of Peto's report, and in response to the consistent

57. *BM* 56 (1864), 370; *MH* (May 1885), 206-8; *MH* (May 1892) 233-4; Myers (ed.), *Centenary Volume of the BMS*, 220.

58. T. D. Landels, *William Landels, D.D. A Memoir* (London, 1900), 324-5; BMS Committee Minutes, 29 Mar. 1870, p. 168; 5 Apr. 1870, p. 169; 22 Apr. 1870, p. 176; 20 Sept. 1870, p. 243; 18 Oct. 1870, pp. 254-5.

encouragement of William Landels, the BMS adopted Wall as a missionary in September 1871.[59]

The new opportunities presented by the unification of Italy also seized the imagination of Thomas Cook, the Leicester General Baptist and founder of the firm of travel operators. In 1872-3 Cook persuaded the General Baptist Missionary Society to begin a work of its own in Rome.[60] Initially the Society worked through an Italian evangelist, Paolo Grassi, a former Catholic priest baptized by James Wall in September 1873. Grassi's links with Wall meant that from the beginning there was a close working relationship between the two Baptist missions in Rome. In fact, in April 1872 James Carey Pike, secretary of the GBMS, had written to the BMS suggesting that the two societies consider 'united action' in the Rome mission. The response of the BMS Committee had been friendly but cautious, and nothing came of Pike's overture at this stage.[61] Nevertheless, close co-operation of an informal kind was established, although the two missions remained formally distinct until the fusion of the two societies in 1891. In 1878 the GBMS sent its first missionary, N. H. Shaw, to Rome, and opened a chapel in the Via San Maria Maggiore (allegedly on the site of the house of Pudens, the converted Roman senator mentioned in the New Testament) to house the congregation planted by Grassi.[62] The cost of the chapel was met principally by Thomas Cook, who organized a party from Britain to attend the opening services in March.[63]

The Landels family made a pre-eminent contribution to the Italy mission. William Landels paid regular visits to the country. In 1875 his second son, W. K. Landels, was appointed by the BMS to work in Naples, where an evangelist had already commenced work. Premises for a chapel and missionary residence were purchased in 1881 with funds raised by William Landels. In 1877 his elder son, John, a Baptist minister in Kirkcaldy, was accepted by the Society. After short periods working with Wall in Rome and with his younger brother in Naples, John Landels moved to Genoa in December 1878, where he planted a church which survived his

59. Landels, *William Landels*, 325; *BM* 63 (1871), 54-5, 196 -7; BMS Committee Minutes, 9 May 1871, pp. 327-8; 25 Sept. 1871, pp. 367-8.

60. *General Baptist Missionary Observer*, Jan. 1872, 30-2; Feb. 1872, 66-7; Nov. 1873, 443-5.

61. BMS Committee Minutes, 7 May 1872, p. 450; 21 May 1872 pp. 458-9.

62. Pudens is mentioned in the New Testament in 2 Timothy 4:21.

63. *MH* (July 1878), 153-5; *MH* (May 1879), 128.

death from typhoid in November 1879.[64] During the 1880s Baptist work was developed in Turin, Florence, and other centres. By 1892 the united BMS mission in Italy was served by six missionaries (including James Wall's sister-in-law, Miss Julia Yates) and twelve Italian evangelists.[65]

The churches planted by the BMS in Italy after 1870 formed the basis of the Baptist denomination in twentieth-century Italy, which remains one of the smaller Protestant communities. Active BMS involvement came to an end in 1921, when the Society handed over its Italian mission to the Southern Baptist Convention. However, direct links between British and Italian Baptists were re-established in 1991, following an invitation from the Italian Baptist Union to the BMS and the three Baptist Unions of Great Britain, to co-operate in sending personnel to engage in pastoral and evangelistic work in Italy.[66]

IV: The Era of A. H. Baynes, 1876-1906

1. Expansion

On E. B. Underhill's retirement in 1876 the Society appointed in his place two co-secretaries, both of them already on the BMS staff. One was the Association Secretary, Clement Bailhache, who was a Baptist minister and was responsible for liaison with the home churches. The other was the Minute Secretary and accountant, Alfred Henry Baynes. Baynes's career as an accountant had begun in 1858 with employment in Sir Morton Peto's firm of Peto, Brassey and Betts. In February 1861 Peto sent him to the BMS to assume responsibility for the Society's accounts. When Trestrail retired in 1870, Baynes assumed the additional role of Minute Secretary. The extensive knowledge of the Society's affairs which he built up through the exercise of these duties made him an obvious candidate in 1876 to succeed Underhill. Following the death of Clement Bailhache in December 1878, Baynes was appointed General Secretary, with sole responsibility for overall policy. The appointment of J. B. Myers as Association Secretary enabled Baynes to concentrate on foreign affairs for the remainder of his period of office.

Although lacking Underhill's intellectual qualities as a scholar and missionary strategist, Alfred Baynes possessed exceptional managerial abili-

---

64. Landels, *William Landels*, 257-8, 325-6; W. Landels, *Memorials of a Consecrated Life: A Biographical Sketch of John Landels, Missionary in Genoa* (London, 1881), *passim*.

65. *MH* (May 1892), 235.

66. *BT*, 28 Mar. 1991, pp. 1, 13.

ties and a soundness of judgment which enabled him to preside over a remarkable expansion in the scale and geographical scope of the Society's activities.[67] His years of office, reflected J. G. Greenhough on Baynes's death in 1914, commenced 'a wonderful extension which fills us with amazement today and continually'.[68] When Baynes became General Secretary in 1879, there were thirty-five male missionaries in India, and only two in China; the Congo mission was still in its infancy. By his retirement in 1906, there were seventy-three male missionaries in India, thirty-six in China, and thirty-five in Africa.[69] The Congo mission, though originating in Robert Arthington's mind, was Baynes's first love and principal achievement. He also directed the evolution of the China field from a minor and possibly temporary commitment into a major sphere of operations. So far as India was concerned, he presided over the incorporation of the Orissa mission within the BMS and the commencement of work in the Lushai Hills (Mizoram). The expansion which marked the 1880s and 1890s was not peculiar to the BMS, but rather one expression of a revolution of scale, mood, and geographical penetration which affected all British Protestant missions during these years of 'high imperialism'. Baynes, therefore, deserves to be remembered, not as the sole instigator of the transformation which affected the BMS, but as the man who successfully managed a process of growth whose origins lie in the complex amalgam of social, political, and religious forces that shaped the missionary dynamic of late Victorian Protestantism.

Not all of the initiatives taken during the Baynes years were of lasting importance. The BMS undertook two short-lived ventures into Japan (1878-90) and Palestine (1886-1905). The Japan mission was the result of the application to the Society of W. J. White, who had lived in Japan for some years and wished to return as a missionary. White and his wife laboured alone in Tokyo until 1885, when G. Eaves was sent to join them. However, Eaves's health collapsed, and in 1890 the Society transferred the Japan mission to the American Baptist Missionary Union. The Palestine mission similarly consisted of just one missionary couple, Mr and Mrs Y. El Karey, who worked at Nablous. The mission had originated in 1867 as

67. On Baynes see B. R. Wheeler, *Alfred Henry Baynes, J.P.* (London, n.d.); *MH*, Dec. 1914; and Payne, *The Great Succession*, 43-53.

68. *MH* (Dec. 1914), 350-1.

69. Payne, *The Great Succession*, 51-2. Until 1897-8 the *BMS Annual Report* give figures for male missionaries only. The *Annual Report* for 1905-6, p. 127, lists 61 'wives and lady helpers' in India, 20 in China, and 24 in the Congo.

an ecumenical venture, but had become increasingly dependent on Baptist support. El Karey was a member at Regent's Park Chapel, and William Landels and his wife kept the mission going until the BMS assumed responsibility in 1886.[70]

2. Fusion and Centenary Celebration, 1891-2

The secretaryship of A.H. Baynes witnessed two significant landmarks in the Society's history. On 30 June 1891, as part of the wider amalgamation of General and Particular Baptists, the General Baptist Missionary Society fused with the BMS. On 2 October 1892 the BMS celebrated its centenary. Thus within a hundred years of the formation of the 'Particular Baptist Society for propagating the gospel among the heathen' the spirit of evangelical activism and co-operation engendered by the Evangelical Revival had led Baptists from an originally Calvinistic tradition to embrace within their fellowship those who remained firmly committed to Arminian principles. The GBMS was the overseas missionary arm of the General Baptist New Connexion. The BMS, on the other hand, was a voluntary society, wholly autonomous of the Baptist Union. Hence, whilst any moves towards the Particular Baptists by the Connexion would inevitably impel the GBMS towards closer association with the BMS, there was no necessary constitutional reason (although compelling practical reasons) why the initiatives taken by Particular Baptists in the 1880s to bring about a rapprochement with their General Baptist cousins should prompt the BMS to consider amalgamation with the GBMS.

The constitution of the GBMS, adopted in 1819, laid down that the annual meeting of subscribers and friends should take place on the Wednesday evening of the Association week (the Connexion's annual assembly), at the place where the Association was held.[71] When in 1855 the Society found itself confronted with the need to elect a new secretary to replace J. G. Pike, secretary for the first thirty-eight years of its history, the final decision to appoint Pike's second son, J. C. Pike, was made by the full Association meeting. 1855 at first seemed likely to be as clear a watershed for the GBMS as 1815 had been for the BMS. J. G. Pike had combined his secretarial duties with the pastorate of the church at Mary's Gate, Derby, and had administered the Society from his pastor's study. After his death, the GBMS Committee felt that the time had come for the secretaryship to be regarded as a full-time, salaried post, but this ideal proved easier to assert

70. Landels, *William Landels*, 328-9.

71. GBMS Committee Minutes, 23 June 1819, p. 14.

than to implement, when funds were critically short.[72] J. C. Pike remained in pastoral charge in Leicester throughout his period as secretary, and the financial and organizational basis of the Society continued to be slender throughout its separate history.[73] Thus, whilst the prospect of loss of General Baptist identity by amalgamation with the Particular Baptists caused disquiet in parts of the Connexion in 1890-1, to the GBMS Committee the vastly greater financial resources available to the older missionary society had always constituted a magnetic attraction.

The process which led to the amalgamation of the General and Particular Baptist traditions has been fully described by John Briggs.[74] The question of a union of the two missionary societies was first discussed within the BMS Committee in May 1889, following resolutions passed at the spring assembly of the Baptist Union on the subject of amalgamation. A joint conference of delegates from the two societies met on 18 September 1889 and reached the conclusion that union was legally practicable. Fortified by this verdict, Charles Williams of Accrington, one of the leading advocates of amalgamation within the Baptist Union, moved in the BMS Committee that the union of Particular and General Baptists in foreign missionary work was 'desirable'. On 18 March 1890 the BMS Committee gave unanimous approval to an amended version of Williams's motion, declaring that union was 'in the interest of the Church of Christ and the furtherance of Christian missions'.[75] At the BMS annual general meeting on 29 April Williams gave notice of a motion, to be moved the following year, specifying the name of the Society as 'the Baptist Missionary Society, including the Particular Baptist Missionary Society for Propagating the Gospel amongst the Heathen ... formed in 1792, and the General Baptist Missionary Society ... formed in 1816'.[76] On 11 June 1890 a further joint conference of the two societies reached unanimous agreement that the two societies should be completely united. The recommendations of this conference were adopted

---

72. GBMS Committee Minutes, 20-22 June 1855, pp. 490-3; 25 June 1856, p. 504; 19 May 1857, p. 518; 24 June 1857, pp. 522-3.

73. Pike was pastor of the Dover Street church until 1859, and subsequently assistant pastor and then pastor of the church at Friar Lane, Leicester. On his death in 1876 he was succeeded as secretary of the GBMS by William Hill.

74. 'Evangelical ecumenism: the amalgamation of General and Particular Baptists in 1891', *BQ* 34 (1991-2), 99-115, 160-79.

75. BMS Committee Minutes, 21 May 1889, pp. 100-1; 17 Sept. 1889, pp. 176-7; 7 Oct. 1889, pp. 223-5; 19 Nov. 1889, pp. 237-8; 18 Mar. 1890, pp. 307-8.

76. *BMS Annual Report*, 1889-90, p. xvi.

unanimously by both the BMS Committee and the GBMS Committee, and 'almost unanimously' by the General Baptist Association.[77] Final approval of the merger was given by the BMS annual members' meeting on 28 April 1891 and the General Baptist Association on 25 June.[78]

Under the terms of the fusion agreement, six members of the GBMS Committee (including Thomas Cook and the GBMS treasurer, W. B. Bembridge) became honorary members of the BMS Committee. The former secretary of the GBMS, William Hill, was appointed secretary of the Bible Translation Society, which since 1840 had supported all translation work undertaken by the BMS.[79] On the field, the union of the two societies made little difference, although the Orissa missionaries now had access to the wider resources of fellowship and finance offered by the BMS India mission as a whole.

The successful outcome of the union negotiations gave added lustre to the centenary celebrations of 1892-3. John Clifford, the brightest star in the General Baptist firmament, was invited to preach the missionary sermon at Nottingham on 31 May 1892 in commemoration of Carey's sermon of 100 years earlier.[80] Clifford preached on Carey's text of Isaiah 54:2-3, and delivered a rousing message on Carey's new vision of the universality of God's fatherly love for the family of mankind. It was a sermon which appeared to make Carey into an honorary member of the General Baptists, but few among Clifford's hearers would have perceived any incongruity.[81] The commemorative gatherings in Nottingham on 30-31 May were followed by further celebratory meetings in Leicester and Kettering in early June, in London in October, and finally in Northampton in March 1893.

The Society set a demanding three-fold target for its centenary appeal. An attempt was to be made to raise a thanksgiving fund of £100,000 and to increase the annual income of the Society by about £30,000 to £100,000.

---

77. BMS Committee Minutes, 17 June 1890, pp. 350-6; 16 July 1890, pp. 391-3.

78. *BMS Annual Report*, 1890-1, pp. xv-xvi; BMS Committee Minutes, 15 July 1891, pp. 395-410.

79. The Bible Translation Society was formed in 1840 as a result of the refusal of the British and Foreign Bible Society to accept the insistence of the BMS that the Greek word *baptizo* should be translated by a word meaning 'immerse', as had been the practice in the Serampore versions.

80. Carey's sermon was in fact delivered on 30 May 1792. The organizers of the centenary mistakenly observed the wrong date; see J. B. Myers (ed.), *The Centenary Celebration of the Baptist Missionary Society, 1892-3* (London, 1893), v.

81. Myers (ed.), *Centenary Celebration of the BMS*, 20-32.

The thanksgiving fund was to be devoted to seven specified objects. Of these the most ambitious was the proposal to finance the outfit, passage and probation expenses of one hundred new missionaries.[82] The first objective, the raising of the fund itself, was met with remarkable ease. By 31 March 1893 £113,500 had been received in cash or promises. The other two objectives proved elusive. The Committee would not contemplate sending out large numbers of missionary recruits (even assuming that they could be found) unless the regular income were raised to a level sufficient to sustain them. In fact the ordinary receipts for general purposes in 1892-3 were substantially down on the previous year, doubtless as a result of the centenary appeal, and the year closed with a deficit of £15,874, leaving the Society with a total debt of £30,515.[83]

By the close of the 1893-4 financial year the BMS had been able to accept only twelve of the hoped-for new recruits. Ordinary receipts from the churches had risen slightly, despite the impact of severe agricultural and commercial depression and the collapse of the Liberator Building Society, in which many Baptists had invested.[84] It appears that over £46,000 of the centenary fund was eventually used to wipe out the massive deficits incurred by the Society during the early 1890s.[85] Although the clearing of debt was one of the original objects of the fund, the allocation of so much of it to this purpose must have been deeply disappointing to the Committee. For the BMS, the 1890s, whilst they saw an escalation in British imperial enthusiasm, witnessed neither the great influx of recruits nor the massive increase in regular giving which had been anticipated in 1892. By 1897-8 total BMS income had reached £78,546, the largest total ever recorded, but still well below the stated goal of £100,000.[86] The Baynes era closed with the BMS still struggling to achieve a stable equilibrium between income and expenditure.

3. *Women missionaries and the Baptist Zenana Mission*

One of the more gradual of the transformations which affected the BMS during Baynes's secretaryship related to the developing role of women in the Society. Although missionary wives had been essentially involved to varying

82. The objects are listed in full in Myers (ed.), *Centenary Volume of the BMS,* 339.

83. *BMS Annual Report,* 1892-3, pp. 3-4, 92-3.

84. *BMS Annual Report,* 1893-4, pp. 93-4.

85. *BMS Annual Report,* 1894-5, p. 98.

86. *BMS Annual Report,* 1897-8, p. 120.

degrees in the work of the BMS from the beginning, their contribution was rarely acknowledged and hence has left little historical record. The active role of Hannah Marshman in the Serampore mission may have been unique in its day, but it is possible that later missionary wives did as much, but without the public acknowledgment that she received.[87] Similarly, in the home life of the Society, women played an indispensable role as missionary collectors and organizers. From the early 1840s they were particularly involved in managing the fund-raising activities of children in Sunday Schools and juvenile missionary associations - a new source of support which all the missionary societies began to cultivate assiduously: by 1849 the BMS was hoping to receive about £3,000 a year from these juvenile sources.[88] Yet women had no representation on the Society's committees and no voice in its public meetings, despite the fact that they probably formed the majority of the audience. Thus William Brock could tell the female element of the audience at the jubilee meeting at Kettering in 1842, without any fear of contradiction:

> Ladies, it is not yours to be supreme, it is ours. It is yours to obey. But though it is ours to be supreme, yet it is a supremacy in which there is to be nothing capricious, nothing tyrannical. You are not to be our drudges today, and our toys tomorrow. You are our companions - you are our helpmates.[89]

Brock was in fact seeking to make the point that Christian nations accorded women a dignity which was denied them by the social ethics of Islam or Hinduism. It was the spiritual and social plight of women in the Indian zenanas[90] which provided the motivation for a movement which was to give women an assured (though still subordinate) place in the missionary movement and sow the seeds of an eventual challenge to the assumptions of exclusively male control.

Occasional attempts to penetrate the zenanas in Bengal had been made by missionary wives of various societies since the early 1820s, including Mrs

---

87. On Hannah Marshman see S. K. Chatterjee, *Hannah Marshman: The First Woman Missionary in India* (Hooghly, 1987) and *MH* (Feb. 1991), 10-12.

88. *Juvenile Missionary Herald* (June 1849), 92, cited in F. K. Prochaska, *Women and Philanthropy in Nineteenth-Century England* (Oxford, 1980), 81. The *Juvenile Missionary Herald* first appeared in January 1845, and soon attained a circulation of 45,000.

89. *BM* 34 (1842), 385.

90. The zenanas (a word derived from the Persian *zan* = woman) were those parts of high-caste Hindu dwellings from which all males outside the immediate family were excluded.

W. H. Pearce of the BMS Calcutta mission. The first to achieve any lasting success in this regard was Elizabeth Sale, wife of John Sale of the BMS, who was granted admission in 1854 to a zenana in Jessore to teach needlework and other crafts. When the Sales moved to Calcutta in 1858, Elizabeth began regular teaching visits to zenanas in the Entally area. She became a close friend in Calcutta of Marianne Lewis, wife of C. B. Lewis, then superintendent of the Calcutta Mission Press.[91] From this point on, zenana visiting became an increasing feature of the lives of missionary wives and daughters in the Calcutta mission. In 1866 Marianne Lewis, then on furlough in England, wrote a pamphlet, *A Plea for Zenanas,* to publicise the vision which she and Elizabeth Sale had developed. It was a plea for Baptists to follow the example of other missions by setting aside ladies to work as full-time, paid agents in the zenanas. Lewis argued that the Christian education of high-caste women and girls offered unrivalled opportunities for evangelism and for strengthening the growing feeling in favour of social reform in Bengal.[92]

The BMS Committee had already given its approval in principle to developing zenana work on the lines suggested by Mrs Lewis, and received her pamphlet with enthusiasm.[93] A circular was then issued, inviting ladies to a meeting at the mission house on 22 May to consider acting on Mrs Lewis's paper. The meeting, which was attended by twenty-five ladies, but presided over by E. B. Underhill, resolved to establish an Association, 'in connection with' the BMS, to 'aid its operations among the female population of the East'. The funds of the Association were to be devoted to the work of zenana visitation and Bible women in India. At the first meeting of the Committee of the new Association, it was agreed to call the new body 'The Ladies' Association for the support of Zenanah [*sic*] work, and Bible women in India in connection with the Baptist Missionary Society'. Lady Peto was invited to be treasurer; after some hesitation, she accepted the

---

91. On the origins of the Baptist Zenana Mission see Payne, *The Great Succession,* 101-12; Myers (ed.), *Centenary Celebration of the BMS,* 44-5; *Jubilee 1867-1917: Fifty Years' Work among Women in the Far East* (London, n.d.).

92. Baptist Zenana Mission papers (bound vol.), Mrs C. B. Lewis, *A Plea for Zenanas.* Mrs Lewis referred to the example set by the Free Church [of Scotland] and 'Church of England' missions; by the latter she probably meant the interdenominational Society for Promoting Female Education in the East, which assisted CMS work.

93. BMS Committee Minutes, 18 Apr. 1866, pp. 120-1; 19 Feb. 1867, pp. 278-9.

Joseph Angus, Secretary of the BMS, 1841-9.

Amelia Angus, Foreign Secretary of the Ladies' Association for the Support of Zenana Work and Bible Women in India, in Connection with the Baptist Missionary Society, 1869-93.

Elizabeth Sale (1818-98), pioneer of Baptist Zenana work in Bengal.

Marianne Lewis (d. 1890), instigator of the Ladies' Association for the Support of Zenana Work and Bible Women in India, in Connection with the Baptist Missionary Society.

invitation, despite her husband's recent resignation from the same office in the parent Society.[94]

The new Association began work in Calcutta and Delhi with two European agents (both recruited in India) and a small group of Indian Bible women. By February 1868 about 300 zenanas in Calcutta and 35 in Delhi were being reached.[95] The first missionary to be recruited from Britain - a Miss Fryer of Bristol - was sent out in 1871. During the 1870s the Association extended its work to Dhaka, Monghyr, Agra, Serampore, Suri, and Allahabad. By 1880 the Association employed a total of twenty-seven European or Eurasian women and forty-four Indian Bible women, engaged in school-teaching and work among the poor women of the villages, as well as in zenana visitation.[96] In that year the name of the Association was altered (by the addition of the words 'and China' after 'India') to permit it to support the work of Bible women in China. This experiment proved short-lived, chiefly owing to the opposition of Timothy and Mary Richard to the principle of paying Chinese nationals from mission funds; by 1883 the words 'and China' had been dropped from the title of the Association.[97] The Association finally began work in China in 1893-4, after the Glover-Morris deputation of 1890-1 had drawn attention to the opportunities for single women missionaries in China.[98] China thus re-appeared in the title of the Association until 1897, when the name was changed to the briefer (though now misleading) 'Baptist Zenana Mission'. The work of the Association was publicised through a series of periodicals, culminating in the monthly *Baptist Zenana Magazine*, which was published from 1904 to 1911, when it was incorporated within the *Missionary Herald*.

Although a separate body, the Ladies' Association was joined to the BMS by the closest possible ties, many of them of a family nature. The Angus family provides the most striking example. From 1869 to 1893 the Foreign Secretary of the Association was Mrs Amelia Angus, wife of Joseph Angus and daughter of W. B. Gurney. Her youngest daughter, Isabel, served the Association as a missionary in Delhi (1882-7), Bhiwani (1887-1907), and

---

94. BZM Minutes, 22 and 31 May 1867, pp. 1-4.

95. *Report of the Ladies' Association...in connexion with the BMS* (London, 1868), 5, 7.

96. *Report of the Ladies' Association...in connexion with the BMS for 1879-80* (London, 1880), 4-5.

97. BZM Committee Minutes, 23 Apr. 1880, pp. 241-2; 16 and 25 June 1882, pp. 57, 61; *Report of the Ladies' Association...in connexion with the BMS for 1882-3* (London, 1883), 9-10.

98. See above, ch. VI, pp. 198.

finally in Calcutta as India General Secretary (1907-19). On Mrs Angus's death in 1893, Isabel's two elder sisters assumed responsibility for the Association: Miss Amelia Angus (who had served since 1884 as Honorary Finance Secretary) became Foreign Secretary, and Edith Minute Secretary. Both Amelia and Edith Angus remained in office in the Zenana Mission (from 1914 the Women's Missionary Association) until 1919.[99]

The formation of the Baptist Zenana Mission created welcome opportunities for missionary service for Baptist women, but, if anything, made it even harder for single women to secure a recognized autonomous role within the BMS itself. The first two women missionaries in the Africa mission seem to have been accepted on an exceptional basis on the strength of family connections. The first, Emily Saker, youngest daughter of Alfred Saker, was accepted in September 1879 in view of her existing school-teaching experience in the Cameroons mission and her knowledge of the Dualla language, obtained from a childhood and youth spent in the country.[100] The second, Carrie Comber, elder sister of the three Comber brothers who served in the Africa mission, met an initial rejection from the BMS Committee in November 1879 when she offered as a school-mistress for Victoria, Cameroons, but, on trying again a year later with the backing of 'strongly commendatory letters', was accepted.[101] The successful service of Emily Saker and Carrie Comber apparently gave the Committee confidence to accept other single women candidates for teaching roles in the Cameroons, for in 1882 two more were accepted - Gertrude Fletcher (who later served with the Zenana Mission in India) and Gwen Thomas (who later became Thomas Lewis's second wife). A few similar openings for single women teachers were created in the early years of the Congo mission. The first single woman missionary on the Congo, Martha Spearing, was accepted in 1886, but as late as 1917 only three Congo stations had single women missionaries: São Salvador, Ngombe Lutete, and Bolobo.[102] Throughout the period of this chapter, the BMS remained a predominantly male society, staffed and controlled almost entirely by men.

99. D. Angus, *The Favour of a Commission: The Life of Isabel M. Angus 1858-1939* (London, n.d.), *passim; BMS Annual Report,* 1918-19, p. 41.

100. E. B. Underhill, *Alfred Saker Missionary to Africa* (London, 1884), 59-60; BMS Committee Minutes, 2 and 16 Sept. 1879, pp. 230-1, 233-4.

101. BMS Committee Minutes, 4 Nov. 1879, p. 257, 16 Nov 1880, pp. 12-13. Carrie Comber married R. Wright Hay of the Cameroons mission (subsequently of Bengal), but died in 1884.

102. *Jubilee 1867-1917,* 30; *BMS Annual Report,* 1916-17, pp. 132-3. Martha Spearing died at Stanley Pool in 1887.

4. Medical missionaries and the Medical Mission Auxillary

For the first sixty years or more of the nineteenth century the medical missionary had no assured place in the missionary movement. The work of missions was understood to be, in the words of the BMS constitution, 'the preaching of the Gospel, the translation and publication of the Holy Scriptures, and the establishment of Schools'. The practice of medicine in Britain was as yet unregulated and lacking in professional respectability. The offer of medical care by missionaries who might possess some skill in this area was not, therefore, given a high priority by the ministers who dominated missionary society committees. Thus, although John Thomas, the first missionary to be accepted by the BMS, was a surgeon, his medical skills were viewed by the Society's founders as largely incidental to his primary commission. Later, individual missionary candidates occasionally studied medicine as part of their training - for example, William Bampton of Orissa and John Mack of Bengal- but they were not thereby categorized as 'medical missionaries'.[103]

The gradual transformation in attitudes to medical missions which began to affect all British societies and denominations from the 1860s had various causes. At the domestic end, the crucial factor was the coming of professional regulation to medical practice following the Medical Act of 1858. On the field, there was the stark fact of devastating levels of missionary mortality, as well as the abundant evidence from certain countries, China especially, that Western medical expertise was a powerful magnet attracting people to the missionary message.[104] Attitudes changed most rapidly in Scotland, whose ancient universities had strong faculties of medicine and where the Edinburgh Medical Missionary Society (formed in 1842) facilitated the training of medical missionaries for many different societies.

It is thus no surprise that the first application to the BMS from a candidate offering himself specifically as a 'medical missionary' came in November 1869 from a student at the training institution of the Edinburgh society, William Brown. After careful consideration of his application by the BMS Committee and its candidates' sub-committee, Brown was

---

103. F. S. Piggin, *Making Evangelical Missionaries 1789-1858* (Sutton Courtenay Press, 1984), 238-9.

104. C. P. Williams, 'Healing and evangelism: the place of medicine in later Victorian Protestant missionary thinking', and A. F. Walls, '"The heavy artillery of the missionary army": the domestic importance of the nineteenth-century medical missionary', in W. J. Sheils (ed.), *The Church and Healing* (Studies in Church History 19, Oxford, 1982), 271-85 and 287-97.

accepted 'as a medical missionary' in April 1870, and appointed to Yantai.[105] The *Missionary Herald* for October 1872 proudly described him as 'the first medical missionary supported by the Society'.[106] However, as was noted in Chapter Six, Brown was recalled in 1874 because of his insistence on devoting himself wholly to medical work, leaving evangelistic preaching to others.[107] A separate and little-known episode in 1874-5 made it abundantly clear that the BMS Committee did not yet regard medical work as an integral part of Christian mission to be pursued in its own right.

On 29 September 1874 the BMS Committee considered an offer of missionary service from a Mr William Carey of Edinburgh, member of the Royal College of Surgeons, and a student of medicine at Edinburgh University.[108] Carey, a great-grandson of the founder of the Society, was asked to defer his application until the conclusion of his college course in August 1875. However, Carey wrote to the Society again in November, forwarding a memorial from himself and three other Baptist students studying medicine under the auspices of the Edinburgh Medical Missionary Society. The memorial sought to know the mind of the BMS on the value of medical missions, and in particular on whether the Society anticipated employing a distinct medical missionary agency, whose sphere of labour should be 'in the dispensary and hospital ... to co-operate with their ordinary missionaries in carrying on the work of the Lord in heathen lands'.[109] A sub-committee was set-up to consider the memorial. Its report re-iterated the accepted missionary wisdom that, whilst medical skill was to be valued for its evangelistic potential, a missionary's sphere of duty could not be 'like that of the Medical man, chiefly or wholly confined to the Dispensary or the Hospital'. The BMS, declared the report, was not prepared to accept any candidate 'who does not possess the primary qualifications for preaching of the gospel, and who is not prepared to make that his primary duty'. Though there might be a legitimate role for mission dispensaries, the sub-committee took the view that mission hospitals would constitute 'a diversion of funds that would better be applied to the direct ministry of the word'. Significantly, however, the wording of this section has been amended, probably as a result of discussion within the full BMS

105. BMS Committee Minutes, 23 Nov. 1869, pp. 112, 128-9; 1 Mar. 1870, p. 155; 22 Apr. 1870, p. 177; 7 June 1870 p. 203.

106. *BM* 64 (1872), 698.

107. See above, ch. VI, p. 81.

108. BMS Committee Minutes, 29 Sept. 1874, pp. 246-7.

109. The memorial is to be found in the bound volume, Sub-Committee Reports, 1874-5.

Committee, to allow for the possibility that mission hospitals should be established at the Committee's discretion.[110]

E. B. Underhill and C. M. Birrell were sent to Edinburgh to explain the Committee's views on the subject. Despite the virtual rejection of the memorial, William Carey subsequently submitted his formal application to the Society, and was accepted as a medical missionary on the basis set out in the sub-committee's report. It was thus as a medical missionary - but on the understanding that this meant evangelist first, and doctor second - that William Carey, M.D., was allocated to Delhi at the Committee meeting on 7 September 1875.[111] The low prominence which he gave to medical work in Delhi was the result, not of any lack of personal commitment to the task (as Mary Causton implied in her history of BMS medical missions), but of strict adherence to the brief given him by the Committee.[112]

The next fully qualified doctor to be recruited by the BMS was Sidney Comber, also a student at the Edinburgh Medical Missionary College, who was accepted by the candidates' sub-committee for service on the Congo on 8 June 1883.[113] Comber was followed to the Congo by William Seright in 1886 and Sidney Webb in 1893. Of the three, only Webb survived long enough to exercise a medical role of any significance.[114] In each case it is likely that the BMS Committee envisaged their role as medical missionaries as falling within the limits laid down by the 1875 report: their medical expertise was auxiliary to their primary evangelistic role.

On 14 January 1884 the candidates' sub-committee interviewed James Russell Watson and his fiancée, Agnes Russell. Both were in their final year of medical training, James at Charing Cross Hospital, and Agnes at the London School of Medicine for Women. The sub-committee recommended, not merely that the couple be accepted for service in north China, but also that they be permitted to marry before departure (contrary to the

---

110. Sub-Committee Reports, 1874-5, Report of Sub-Committee on Medical Missionary Students' Memorial.

111. BMS Committee Minutes, 29 June 1875, pp. 353-4; 14 July 1875, pp. 356-7; 7 Sept. 1875, p. 374; Candidates Sub-Committee Minutes, 8 July 1875, pp. 73-4. I have seen no evidence that the other three memorialists - J. A. Howard, R. P. Simpson, and E. G. Carey - applied to the BMS.

112. M. I. M. Causton, *For the Healing of the Nations: The Story of British Baptist Medical Missions 1792-1951* (London, 1951), 44-5, 48.

113. Candidates Sub-Committee Minutes, 8 June 1883, pp. 7-8.

114. Webb served at Ngombe Lutete from 1893 to 1895; see W. Brock, *From Mill Hill to the Congo* (London, n.d. [1908]).

Society's normal rule, adopted in 1869).[115] James and Agnes Russell Watson thus sailed for Shandong in January 1885, where they inherited the dispensary work at Chingzhou pioneered by earlier BMS missionaries, and developed it into the first in-patient hospital run by the Society (although not housed in purpose-built premises). Agnes Russell Watson's status as the first female doctor to be employed by the Society has not been generally recognized, primarily because the BMS from the outset tended to regard her as a well-qualified helpmeet to her husband rather than as a doctor in her own right.[116]

The minutes of the candidates' sub-committee meeting which accepted James Watson and his fiancée do not contain the usual stipulation that their medical work was to be viewed as auxiliary to the work of evangelism. The omission may be significant as an indication that in the special circumstances of the China field the Society was beginning to regard professional medical work in a more favourable light. Ten years later, when the candidates' sub-committee accepted an application for service in India from F. Vincent Thomas, a medical graduate of the University of Edinburgh and son of J. W. Thomas, BMS India missionary, the minutes still record the qualification:

> Mr Thomas desires to make his medical work auxiliary to his work as a Christian missionary, and he has assured the Sub-Committee that his one great desire in connection with his offer for work in India, is to take to the peoples of India the Gospel of the Grace of God.[117]

Behind this minute lay the reality of a difficult interview in which Thomas had argued that medical missionaries could not do their work adequately without the support of full hospital facilities, whilst the majority of the committee held to the view that the BMS possessed no mandate from the churches for such an expensive undertaking as the financing of mission hospitals. The committee's refusal to provide any commitment to develop a hospital almost led Thomas to withdraw his candidacy, but he was persuaded not to do so.[118] Vincent Thomas served at Kharar, Muttra and Kosi before moving to Palwal in 1901, where eventually, in 1905, he saw his desire fulfilled in the construction of the Florence Toole Memorial Hospital for men.

---

115. Candidates Sub-Committee Minutes, 14 Jan. 1884, pp. 17-18.

116. See the comment in BMS Committee Minutes, 16 Jan. 1884, p. 426; but cf. *MH* (Jan. 1912), 27.

117. Candidates Sub-Committee Minutes, 19 Nov. 1894, p. 48.

118. R. F. Moorshead, *'Heal the Sick': The Story of the Medical Mission Auxiliary of the Baptist Missionary Society* (London, 1929), 20-3.

By 1894 Baptist attitudes to medical missions were beginning to change Richard Glover and Samuel Vincent had taken Thomas's side in the debate in the candidates' committee, but had been outnumbered. Furthermore, there is evidence that the ladies of the Baptist Zenana Mission already held a more progressive view than their male counterparts in the BMS. On 20 February 1891 the BZM Committee, having already accepted for medical missionary service Edith Brown, subject to the completion of her medical studies, considered an application from Ellen Farrer, who had already graduated from the London School of Medicine for Women and the Royal Free Hospital. Farrer had indicated in her papers that 'she hoped she would be allowed to develop medical mission work - even to having a Hospital if it seemed admirable'. Before she was admitted for the interview, Mrs Angus urged the Committee to be clear in their intentions for their medical work, and warned them not to accept Farrer 'unless we were prepared to give her what was needed in future years to carry on her work'. The Committee had no hesitation in recognizing that to send out Brown and Farrer implied a commitment 'to maintain the work properly'. Ellen Farrer was then admitted, and found the interview 'less terrible by far than my fears'. The minutes record that she 'made a very pleasant impression', and was accepted unanimously.[119]

Edith Brown and Ellen Farrer sailed for India in October 1891. Brown went to Palwal, and built up a small zenana dispensary commenced by Gertrude Fletcher and Miss N. Rocke (who had received some medical training) into a women's hospital.[120] She resigned from the BZM in 1894 to devote herself to what became the North India School of Medicine for Christian Women at Ludhiana, one of the two premier Christian medical institutions of twentieth-century India.[121] Farrer went to Bhiwani, and took over a dispensary started by Isabel Angus and Annie Theobald. In March 1899 she had the pleasure of seeing the first hospital buildings at Bhiwani opened, financed by contributions raised during her first furlough in 1897. Although Bhiwani hospital had to close for a time after Farrer was invalided home in 1900, it re-opened in December 1901 following her return with a colleague loaned by the LMS. Her remarkable career at Bhiwani lasted till 1933 and twice earned her the award of honours from the Indian imperial

119. BZM Committee Minutes, 20 Feb. 1891, pp. 102-4; IN/149, diary of E. M. Farrer for 20 Feb. 1891.

120. In *Jubilee 1867-1917*, 51, Miss Rocke is listed as the first doctor in the BZM, but I have not seen confirmatory evidence of her having qualified as a doctor.

121. S. G. Browne, *et. al.* (eds.) *Heralds of Health* London, 1985), 317; C. Reynolds, *Punjab Pioneer* (Bombay, 1968).

government for distinguished public service.[122]

The trio of James Russell Watson, Vincent Thomas and Ellen Farrer supplied the crucial stimulus which led to medical missions being given an assured place in BMS thinking through the formation of the Medical Mission Auxiliary in 1901. As early as 1887, Russell Watson had written to A. H. Baynes, urging the Committee to abandon its reliance on the role of medical amateurs in the China mission and accept no lower a professional standard for those undertaking medical work than was needed to be placed on the British Medical Register at home.[123] In 1894, while on furlough in Britain, he had discussed with Dr Percy Lush, a Baptist general practitioner in London, the idea of forming a medical mission auxiliary to the BMS, similar to that established by the CMS two years earlier.[124] Reluctantly Russell Watson and Lush had concluded that there was as yet insufficient support in Baptist circles for such a step.

Russell Watson's next furlough in 1901 coincided both with Ellen Farrer's period of sick leave in Britain and with a report from the India field by Vincent Thomas urging the necessity of a more structured approach to BMS medical work. Armed with Thomas's report, Russell Watson, Farrer and Lush agreed to approach the officers of the BMS and BZM with the assistance of Lush's brother-in-law, the distinguished Baptist surgeon, Alfred Pearce Gould. They received a favourable response, and a joint meeting of interested people from the two Committees was held on 17 September 1901, when Dr Herbert Lankester, the honorary secretary of the CMS Medical Mission Committee, spoke.[125] The meeting expressed its opinion that a Medical Mission Auxiliary to the BMS and BZM jointly should be formed. Percy Lush then prepared a draft scheme for an organization 'on generally similar lines to the "Medical Committee" of the CMS'. At the BMS General Committee meeting in Edinburgh on 8 October, members received copies of a leaflet describing the CMS Medical Mission Committee and of its magazine, *Mercy and Truth*. Lush's draft scheme was referred to a special committee under his chairmanship.[126] At the next meeting of the General Committee, on 19 November, the special committee's report was adopted, setting up a Medical Mission Auxiliary

122. IN/145, *Fifty Years for Bhiwani Hospital: The Farrer Jubilee;* IN/148, Funeral address for Dr E. M. Farrer (1959).

123. CH/13, J. R. Watson to A. H. Baynes, Jan. 1887.

124. The CMS had taken the first steps towards forming a medical auxiliary in 1885, but they came to fruition only in 1892; see E. Stock, *The History of the Church Missionary Society* (4 vols, London, 1899-1916), iii, 309-10, 661.

125. Moorshead, *Heal the Sick,* 31-2.

(MMA) to the BMS and BZM. The objects of the Auxiliary were defined as the creation and maintenance of interest among Baptist churches in the medical work of the two societies, the raising of funds to support the hospitals run by the two societies (and ultimately their entire medical agency), and to recruit fully qualified medical missionaries. Stress was laid on the fact that the Auxiliary was to be viewed, not as a rival organization but as a handmaid to the existing societies.[127] The fear that the MMA might introduce competition and confusion in the minds of Baptist missionary supporters was present from the beginning, and was to dog the history of the MMA throughout the years of its separate existence. Dr Percy Lush was appointed chairman of the MMA committee.

In 1902 Robert Fletcher Moorshead, a young Baptist doctor from Bristol who had originally hoped to serve in China, was appointed as honorary secretary of the MMA. Moorshead's appointment was initially for one year only. In fact he was to remain as secretary until the MMA ceased to exist as a separate organization in 1925, when he became the first Medical Secretary of the BMS. He continued to his death in 1934 to be the leading advocate in British Baptist life of the cause of medical missions.[128]

The founding of the MMA in the closing years of Alfred Baynes's period of office marked the belated acceptance by the BMS that alleviation of physical suffering was in some sense an integral part of the overseas missionary commission of the Church. Other societies - notably the LMS, and somewhat later the CMS - had reached that conclusion first, and their example was a potent influence behind the formation of the MMA.[129] Baptists, with their strong evangelical insistence on the priority of conversion as the goal of missionary activity, had been slower than some to concede that care of the body was more than a secondary means to a spiritual end. They had also been held back by the massive financial implications of commitment to the erection and maintenance of mission hospitals. The next half-century of BMS history was to prove that their hesitations on this point were well founded.

126. General Committee Minutes, 8 Oct. 1901, pp. 42-5.

127. General Committee Minutes, 19 Nov. 1901, pp. 58-9; *BMS Annual Report,* 1901-2, pp. 123-4.

128. H. V. Larcombe, *First, the Kingdom! The Story of Robert Fletcher Moorshead Physician* (London, n.d.). Moorshead received an honorarium equivalent to an unmarried missionary's allowance.

129. The LMS had nineteen doctors in service in 1895, and over twice as many by 1905; see N. Goodall, *A History of the London Missionary Society 1895-1945* (London, 1954), 509.

VIII

The West Indies, 1892-1992

I: The BMS and Jamaica, 1892-1944

1. Baptist poverty and the support of the ministry

At the time of the BMS Centenary in 1892 there seemed every indication that the Society's 1842 decision to withdraw from Jamaica (except from involvement in Calabar College) had finally been justified through the establishment of a self-supporting and expanding indigenous Baptist community. However, the steady growth which the Jamaican Baptist churches had experienced since the late 1870s was not sustained into the early years of the new century. In 1897, for the first time for twenty-one years, Baptist membership declined. By 1904 membership had fallen from its 1890 level of 34,984 to 32,763.[1] There was a brief and spectacular recovery in the aftermath of the great Kingston earthquake of 14 January 1907, when 1,400 lives were lost and most of the city, including all its Baptist chapels, was destroyed. The calamity of the earthquake appears to have drawn many to the churches in search of spiritual security. During 1907 6,217 persons were baptized, and at least 7,444 joined enquirers' classes. By 1908 membership of the churches in the Jamaica Baptist Union (JBU) had risen to 38,946.[2] Yet the Baptist churches failed to retain this flood of new adherents, and Baptist membership resumed its decline after 1908, falling to 31,442 in 1917 and 30,350 in 1920. A BMS deputation in 1921 suggested that many of those thus lost had made an insincere profession of faith in 1907, but also recognized that responsibility lay with

---

1. WI/6, *Annual Report of the Jamaica Baptist Union for 1917,* 18; Report by the Rev. Charles Williams on a Visit to Jamaica, Trinidad and the Bahamas (1904), p. 2.

2. *MH* (Mar. 1907), 71-2; *MH* (Apr. 1907), 109-10; *BMS Annual Report,* 1907-8, p. 68; WI/6, *Annual Report of the JBU for 1917,* 18.

the Jamaican ministers, who had been unable to disciple the new converts.[3]
The 1921 deputation concluded, as had two earlier BMS deputations in
1904 and 1909, that the most serious problem facing the Jamaica Baptist
Union was the inability or reluctance of the churches to give adequate
support to the pastoral ministry. The issue of financial provision for the
ministry dominated the Society's relationships with Jamaica in this period,
and led eventually to the resumption by the BMS of major involvement in
the island in 1944.

In 1904 the 202 churches in the Jamaica Baptist Union were served by
sixty-three pastors. By 1909 there were two fewer churches, but the number
of working pastors had fallen to fifty-five. A decreasing proportion of the
pastors was European: twenty-four out of fifty-six in 1899, eighteen out of
fifty-five in 1909, and only fifteen out of fifty-five in 1921. With some
pastors holding responsibility for a circuit of as many as six churches, the
burden of pastoral care fell on the deacons and class leaders, many of whom
were women, and most of whom were wholly untrained. The class leaders
were also largely responsible for the maintenance of public worship and for
the collection of contributions towards the support of the pastor. The
'ticket' system continued to function, and all communicant members were
expected to contribute sixpence or a shilling on presentation of their tickets
at the monthly communion service. In theory, the system should have
ensured adequate remuneration for the pastors. The 1909 deputation of
T. S. Penny and C. E. Wilson calculated that if every member contributed
only sixpence a month, the average annual stipend would have been £204.
In fact it was only £97, and a mere £86 for the indigenous Jamaican pastors.
Out of this meagre total, most pastors had to expend at least £40 per annum
on travel within their extensive circuits. By 1921, the average stipend had
risen to £130, but in the meantime the cost of living had more than doubled.
Baptist ministers in Jamaica were poor, and becoming poorer.[4]

The impoverished condition of the Jamaican Baptist ministry can be
attributed to three causes. First and most fundamental was the poverty of
the denomination as a whole. Baptists in Jamaica were almost all drawn
from the black population, descended from the former slaves. Most were

3.   Centenary of the Jamaica Baptist Mission, 1914. Report of the Deputation by Mr F.
     J. Godden, J.P., Canterbury, p. 3. Western Sub-Committee Minute Book No. 17, p.
     5, Report of Visit to Jamaica Feb.-Mar. 1921 by T. S. Penny.

4.   Report by the Rev. Charles Williams, p. 2; T. S. Penny and C. E. Wilson, Report of
     the Deputation to Jamaica October-December, 1909 , pp. 11-13; Western Sub-
     Committee Minute Book No. 17, pp. 3-4.

landless day labourers, with a weekly income in 1909 of only six or seven shillings a week. Many church members, the 1909 deputation was assured, had 'practically no money most of their time'.[5] A second and derivative factor was the reluctance of Baptist members to give generously of such meagre resources as they did possess towards the support of a pastor with whom they had only intermittent contact under the circuit system. Many churches saw their pastor only on communion Sunday, and average attendance at communion was only about 40-45 per cent of total member-ship.[6] Baptists freely volunteered their labour to help construct chapel buildings, but were less willing to contribute their monthly dues to a distant minister who, by their standards, was rich. Their reservations were, no doubt, increased by the fact that the minister was ultimately responsible for the management of the church finances: since educated, middle-class Baptists were virtually non-existent, ministers normally had to act as their own treasurers.[7] In the third place, the Baptist predicament was aggravated by the absence of the financial support from Britain which other denomi-nations enjoyed: the Methodist church, for example, had in 1909 the benefit of an annual subsidy of £2,000 from the Wesleyan Methodist Missionary Society, plus ten fully supported missionaries.[8]

Thomas Penny and C. E. Wilson observed in 1909 that 'if there is any place in the world where a new scheme of ministerial settlement and sustentation seems to be needed it is in Jamaica'.[9] The JBU and Jamaica Baptist Missionary Society (JBMS) had in fact already resolved to set aside a percentage of their annual income to create a denominational reserve fund, and Penny and Wilson proposed that the BMS should assist in the raising of this fund. However, the idea failed to get off the ground in Jamaica, and both the 1914 and the 1921 BMS deputations to the island repeated the recommendation that a ministerial sustentation fund be established.[10] The 1921 deputation, the second of three visits to the island undertaken for the Society by Thomas Penny, a leading Baptist layman

---

5.   Penny and Wilson, Report of the Deputation, p. 15.

6.   WI/6, *Annual Report of the JBU for 1917*, 19.

7.   Ibid., 15, 20; Report of the Rev. Charles Williams, p. 4; Centenary of the Jamaica Baptist Mission, p. 9; Western Sub-Committee Minute Book No. 17, p. 5.

8.   Penny and Wilson, Report of the Deputation, p. 16.

9.   Ibid., p. 17.

10. Centenary of the Jamaica Baptist Mission, p. 9; Western Sub-Committee Minute Book No. 17, p. 10.

from Taunton who had considerable experience of the Baptist Union's own sustentation scheme, bore fruit in action. Penny travelled to Jamaica via New York in the company of two officials of the American Baptist Home Mission Society, whose board was considering financial aid to the Jamaican Baptists. Later that year Penny returned to New York, accompanied by Ernest Price, the principal of Calabar College, to further the negotiations. The outcome was an undertaking from the American Society to provide $2,000 a year for the support of the Jamaican ministry, plus further substantial aid to Calabar College. The BMS for its part agreed to provide a grant of £2,000 from the Baptist United Fund to form the nucleus of a sustentation fund, on condition that the Jamaican Baptists themselves raised a sum of £3,000, thus creating an initial capital fund of £5,000.[11]

The BMS grant of £2,000, although essential, was not the Society's most important contribution to the sustentation scheme. T. I. Stockley, a former BMS missionary in Colombo and pastor of West Croydon Tabernacle since 1901, had decided in January 1921 to resign his pastorate in order to accept an invitation from the secretary of the Keswick Convention to visit Jamaica to hold a series of conventions on behalf of the Keswick movement. On 13 July the BMS General Committee agreed to invite Stockley to remain on the island for twelve months, with a view to 'the encouragement of the ministers and the spiritual quickening of the churches'.[12] Stockley accepted the invitation. His itinerant ministry in Jamaica was much appreciated, and in March 1922 the General Committee, on Ernest Price's recommendation, agreed to invite Stockley to continue in Jamaica as the first superintendent of the sustentation scheme.[13] Stockley initially declined, but then changed his mind. In January 1923 he began work as a BMS 'representative' in Jamaica; he was not technically a missionary, as his support was a first charge on the new fund, and was in practice dependent on the grant from the American Baptists.[14]

11. General Committee Minutes, 22 Apr. 1921, pp. 22-3; 13 July 1921, pp. 34, 45-6; 16 Nov. 1921, p. 83; WI/19, *Jamaica Baptist Union and Jamaica Baptist Missionary Society: New Forward Movement* (Mar. 1923). The Baptist United Fund was raised jointly by the Baptist Union and the BMS after World War I.

12. West Croydon Baptist Church, Deacons' Minutes, Jan.-Feb. 1921; *West Croydon Baptist Magazine* (July 1921), 3-6; General Committee Minutes, 13 July 1921, p. 34. Stockley's two sons, Clement and Handley, were both BMS doctors in China, and his grandson, David, served as an agricultural missionary with the Society in Bangladesh (1952-84) and Brazil (1985-92).

13. General Committee Minutes, 22 Mar. 1922, p. 39.

14. General Committee Minutes, 20 Sept. 1922, p. 101; 22 Nov. 1922, 120-1.

Thomas Stockley set himself the goal of raising the £3,000 Jamaican contribution to the sustentation fund within two or at the most three years. At his own expense he printed 30,000 copies of a personal letter to all JBU members, urging them to contribute a shilling each to the scheme in its first year.[15] Stockley's enthusiasm and industry in visiting the circuits met a good response, although his time scale proved optimistic. The target of £3,000 was not in fact reached until early 1927. However, once it was attained, Stockley regarded his work as done, and promptly submitted his resignation to the BMS, explaining that he had accepted an invitation from the Canadian fundamentalist leader, T. T. Shields (who was a personal friend of Stockley's) to assist him in the staffing of a new seminary which he had opened in Toronto.[16] To the Society's regret, Thomas Stockley's major contribution to Baptist life in Jamaica was thus brought to a close (although he spent a further and valued period in Jamaica from 1936 to 1939, ministering in an unofficial capacity).

The sustentation scheme established by Thomas Stockley survived until 1945. It undoubtedly eased the hardship of the most needy Jamaican pastors as the Jamaican economy worsened after 1929 in the wake of the world depression and resulting slump in the sugar trade. Nonetheless, the sustentation scheme was an incomplete and inadequately funded solution to the problem of ministerial support. It was not a comprehensive scheme (it merely supplemented the lowest stipends) and contained no provision for annuities. As will be emphasized in section 3 below, the scheme proved unable to staunch the decline in both the numbers and the quality of the Jamaican Baptist ministry. The inadequacy of ministerial provision in turn contributed to a continued decline in Baptist membership, which had fallen to 21,452 by 1942.[17]

2. Calabar College and High School

The economic difficulties of the Jamaican Baptist ministry had an inevitable effect on the health of Calabar College. The size of the student body had in any case been severely curtailed following the decision of the colonial government to concentrate teacher training at the Mico College. The normal school department at Calabar was closed in 1901, leaving the College with only six students at the time of its move from the East Queen

---

15. WI/19, T. I. Stockley to C. E. Wilson, 10 May 1923, with enclosures.

16. WI/19, Stockley to Wilson, 25 Mar. 1927. Stockley was Dean of Shields' Toronto Baptist Seminary from 1927 to 1931.

17. General Committee Minutes, 8 July 1942, p. 174.

Street premises to Chetolah Park in 1904.[18] A further limitation on the numbers at Calabar in the first decade of the century was the suspicion with which some of the churches regarded Arthur James, who had succeeded D. J. East as President (Principal) of the College in 1893. James saw it as his task to introduce his students to modern critical approaches to the Bible, and as a result some pastors discouraged their promising young men from applying to Calabar. James decided in 1909 to retire (at the age of fifty-eight), partly because of the ill health of his wife, but also, no doubt, influenced by the lack of whole-hearted support from the churches.[19]

When Thomas Penny and C. E. Wilson visited Calabar in 1909, they found only four students in residence, and learnt that in four of the last ten years no candidates had been accepted for entry. Understandably they concluded that Baptist ministerial training would be far more efficiently and satisfactorily conducted within the context of a united theological college. Penny and Wilson accordingly put to an interdenominational meeting in Kingston on 1 December proposals for a united college involving Presbyterians, Congregationalists, Methodists, Moravians, and Baptists. The scheme was subsequently broadened to encourage Anglicans also to participate. The meeting agreed to remit the idea to the consideration of the respective denominational synods and church conferences.[20]

At first only the Moravians gave enthusiastic assent to the 1909 proposals, and the JBU accordingly dropped the idea of a united college. However, in 1913 the Methodists expressed interest in a co-operative venture, and in September their first students came into residence at Calabar. Teaching was conducted jointly with the Baptists, and a Methodist tutor, J. T. Hudson, joined the Calabar staff. This arrangement came to an end in 1918 because of practical difficulties occasioned by the World War.[21] Co-operation on a broader front seemed likely following negotiations in 1923 with the Wesleyan Methodist Missionary Society, Moravian Missionary Society and Colonial Society of the Congregational Union, but in the event only the Methodists resumed a partnership in theological training with Calabar, participating in united classes, while having their own residential college, Caenwood.[22] In 1937 they were joined by the Presbyterians from St Colm's

18. Report by the Rev. Charles Williams, p. 2; Penny and Wilson, Report of the Deputation, p. 19.

19. Penny and Wilson, Report of the Deputation, p. 33-5.

20. Ibid., pp. 25-31.

21. Western Sub-Committee Minute Book No. 17, pp. 2-3.

22. General Committee Minutes, 21 Nov. 1923, p. 105.

College, who supplied one, and subsequently two, tutors.[23] Thus, whilst the 1909 vision of a single united college was not realized during this period, Baptists were involved in a growing measure of ecumenical co-operation in theological training, which prepared the ground for the more fundamental innovations of the 1960s.

The 1909 deputation had also recommended that consideration be given to setting up a boys' secondary school to provide a good standard of education at a price which the sons of Baptist ministers could afford. Suitable provision for girls already existed in the form of Westwood High School, founded in the previous century by Frederick Trestrail, joint secretary of the BMS, and his wife. The absence of any such provision for boys was a further factor restricting recruitment of ministerial candidates to Calabar College, and inhibiting the development of a Baptist middle class.[24] The deputation's suggestion was taken up with enthusiasm by Ernest Price, previously minister of Cemetery Road Baptist Church, Sheffield, whom the Society appointed as president of Calabar in succession to Arthur James in 1910. Price lost no time in 1911 in securing the support of the BMS Committee for a scheme for a boys' boarding school in connection with the College, and intended chiefly for the sons of pastors. Calabar High School opened in September 1912, with sixteen boarders and thirteen day boys. By 1915 the numbers had grown to eighty, of whom twenty-one were sons of ministers of various denominations.[25]

Under the leadership of Ernest Price and his Australian colleague, David Davis, who joined the Calabar staff in 1911, Calabar High School gradually established a reputation as one of the leading boys' schools on the island. Some of its pupils later attained prominent positions in Jamaican public life, among them Sir Philip Sherlock, first Principal of the University of the West Indies (formerly the University College of the West Indies). Its success was achieved in spite of severe limitations of premises, resources and personnel. The school shared not only its site but also its teaching staff with the College. Until 1942 the President of the College was also the headmaster of the High School, in addition to his wider responsibilities in the life of the denomination.

The later years of Ernest Price's long tenure as President of Calabar (1910-37) were marred by a bitter and damaging controversy with leading

---

23. *BMS Annual Report*, 1937-8, p. 31; WI/12, *Report of Calabar College and Calabar High School for the year 1938*, 4.

24. Penny and Wilson, Report of the Deputation, pp. 19-20.

25. *MH* (Feb. 1912), 44; *MH* (July 1915), 177; General Committee Minutes, 22 Nov. 1911, p. 247.

figures in the JBU. A major dimension in the dispute was the clash between two dominant personalities - Price and Cowell Lloyd, the English minister of East Queen Street Church, Kingston. Control of the management and finances of Calabar College was the substance of the argument. The trust deed of the college specified that its affairs should be managed by a general committee, 'but subject nevertheless to such stipulations as the Committee of the Baptist Missionary Society should determine'. The deed did not dictate the constitution of the general committee, but it became accepted that all Baptist ministers on the island had a right to membership.[26] Given such lack of definition, conflict between Price, who saw himself, understandably, as responsible to the BMS for the affairs of the college, and some of the ministers represented on the Calabar general committee was inevitable.

At the end of May 1931 the Calabar general committee and JBU executive committee voted, by slim majorities, to ask the BMS to recall Ernest Price. Both parties amongst the Jamaican ministers urged the Society to send out a deputation to deal with the matter.[27] Thomas Penny and Dr J. H. Rushbrooke (a member of the BMS General Committee since 1927) were appointed to this delicate task. Penny and Rushbrooke visited Jamaica in November, and, it would appear, were successful in clarifying the issues at stake, though less so in reconciling the warring parties. After the submission of their report to the BMS Committee, a letter was sent to the members of the Calabar general committee, apportioning blame for the dispute fairly evenly between Price and Lloyd, but refusing to recall Price.[28]

From this point on, matters went from bad to worse. Garbled and partial extracts from the Society's letter were published in the Jamaican newspaper, *The Daily Gleaner*. One of the Jamaican pastors who supported Lloyd sued both Price and David Davis for libel. The BMS drew up in July 1932 a scheme for the administration of the college and High School on a new basis, but in the divided state of opinion in Jamaica there was little chance of its early acceptance. Sixteen Baptist ministers who supported Price were suspended by the JBU. In December 1934 the Calabar general committee declared its final refusal to co-operate with the current President of the

---

26. General Committee Minutes, 20 July 1932, p. 90.

27. Western Sub-Committee Minute Book No. 18, p. 56.

28. General Committee Minutes, 2 Feb. 1932, p. 1; Western Sub-Committee Minute Book No. 18, p. 82-8. The deputation's report was not allowed out of the Mission House, and it appears that no copies have been preserved.

college, and reported that ministers and churches had declined to contribute funds to the work of the college under the present regime. As a result,
the BMS General Committee gave authority in January 1935 for all
theological classes at Calabar to be discontinued.[29] Calabar College as such
thus ceased to function early in 1935, although united lectures were
continued at Caenwood.[30]

Although Price and Davis won their libel case, the damage done to the
Baptist reputation on the island could not be easily remedied. What became
generally known in Jamaican Baptist circles as 'the impasse' was resolved
only through the reluctant decision of Ernest Price to retire from missionary
service in July 1937.[31] The Society appointed Dr Gurnos King, pastor of the
church at Union Street, Kingston-on-Thames, to succeed him, and sent out
a senior deputation, comprising Seymour J. Price and Thomas Powell (a
former Congo missionary), to install King and restore peace to the troubled
Jamaican churches. The deputation proved generally successful in effecting
reconciliation, and obtained agreement on a new basis of management for
Calabar College.[32] The college re-opened under Gurnos King, who rapidly
made a great impression on the churches.[33] Tragically, however, King died
on 30 January 1939. A. S. Herbert of Berkhamsted was appointed in his
place, but found the three-fold responsibility of being President of the
college, headmaster of the High School, and *de facto* superintendent of the
churches too much for him. In 1942 the offices of President and headmaster
were separated, and David Davis, who had served continuously on the
college staff since 1911, was appointed headmaster of the High School.

3. A new relationship: the BMS and Jamaica, 1941-4

The protracted difficulties at Calabar during the 1930s inevitably
aggravated the already serious problems of ministerial supply which faced
Jamaican Baptists. By 1941 the ministerial shortage had reached critical

29. WI/19, C. E. Wilson to Jamaica Baptist ministers, 29 Sept. 1933. General Committee
    Minutes, 22 Apr. 1932, p. 28; 7 Nov. 1934, p. 122; 30 Jan. 1935, p. 17; 26 Apr. 1935,
    p. 45.

30. *BMS Annual Reports,* 1934-5, p. 20; 1935-6, p. 48.

31. General Committee Minutes, 1 July 1936, p. 88. Price was not officially recalled, but
    it is clear that his decision to retire was made unwillingly (information from Rev. D.
    W. F. Jelleyman).

32. General Committee Minutes; 20 Jan. 1937, p. 20; 3 Nov. 1937, pp. 121-5.

33. B. G. Griffith and E. A. Payne, Report of the Deputation to Jamaica, July, 1939, p. 11.

proportions. In response to the increasingly urgent appeals for help from the JBU, the BMS agreed in April 1941 to give financial assistance to enable up to three British ministers to settle in Jamaica. Only one such minister, P. S. Bragg, came forward, and difficulty was then experienced finding a pastorate capable of paying a stipend sufficient to support him. In the end the Society had to assume entire financial responsibility for Mr and Mrs Bragg, who thus became the first full missionaries of the BMS to be sent to Jamaica, other than to Calabar, since 1842.[34] In addition, the BMS sent two retired China missionaries, Henry and Helen Stonelake, to Jamaica to give general assistance to the Baptist churches. On their return to Britain at the end of 1942, the Stonelakes gave the West Indies sub-committee a disquieting impression of the state of the denomination:

> For the 200 Churches there were 50 ministers, about half of whom were thoroughly reliable. 25% wanted help in various ways; 25% ought not to be in the Ministry at all, for various reasons, including old age. There was something seriously wrong with many of the Churches; there was no adequate sustentation scheme.[35]

Henry Stonelake suggested that a BMS 'Commissioner' be sent out for a period of perhaps three years to assess the situation, secure the confidence of the ministers, and discuss the way ahead. This suggestion was endorsed both by the JBU executive, and by A. S. Herbert, who was sending equally depressing reports to the Society about the condition of the churches and the poor quality of their ministry. The BMS Committee adopted the proposal in July 1943, and set up a sub-committee to nominate the Commissioner.[36] One member of the sub-committee was Thomas Powell. Powell submitted a memorandum to the West Indies sub-committee, which concluded as a result that the BMS ought to re-instate Jamaica as one of its fields. For his pains, Powell then found himself nominated, and appointed, as the BMS Commissioner to Jamaica.[37]

Independently of Powell's appointment, it had been arranged for H. R. Williamson to visit Jamaica as part of a major tour of BMS fields planned for 1944. Williamson was on the island from 2 February to 5 March, and

---

34. General Committee Minutes; 24 Apr. 1941, p. 98; 8 July 1941, p. 129; 4 Nov. 1941, pp. 203-4; 20 Jan. 1942, p 15. The Braggs resigned in 1945.

35. General Committee Minutes, 20 Jan. 1943, p. 30.

36. General Committee Minutes, 7 July 1943, pp. 164-5.

37. General Committee Minutes, 19 Jan. 1944, pp. 131-4.

had extensive consultations with JBU leaders regarding their request for renewed help from the Society. He was told that the 1842 decision was a 'mistake', which had left the Jamaican churches with problems of finance and organization that remained unsolved a century later.[38] He found the ministers almost unanimous in welcoming the prospect of Powell's arrival as Commissioner, in desiring a new relationship with the BMS, and in urging the necessity of a reorganization of the JBU in order to achieve centralized control and funding. There was even a considerable body of opinion in the churches in favour of the Society's assuming a large measure of control over JBU affairs. Williamson recognized that any such move would be opposed by influential members of the JBU executive, and was careful to emphasize that the BMS was interested only in extended co-operation, not in the resumption of control. On the other hand, increased control by the JBU over questions of church property and finance, ministerial settlement and stipends, seemed to Williamson essential, although admittedly at odds with 'Baptist procedure as commonly understood'.[39]

Thomas Powell left for Jamaica in December 1944, in the company of E. C. Askew, newly appointed as tutor at Calabar College. A. S. Herbert had resigned the presidency of the college earlier in the year, and Powell was appointed acting president in addition to his primary role as Commissioner.[40] He found the condition of the churches quite as serious as he had been led to expect. There were only thirty-five working pastors, ten of whom Powell judged inadequate; eighteen circuits had no ministers at all; 'scores' of churches were in danger of extinction. His initial recommendation was that, unless the BMS could speedily supply six non-Jamaican ministers, the Society ought to consider handing over responsibility for Jamaica to a Baptist missionary agency from the USA.[41] In 1942 the Southern Baptist Convention had first expressed interest in entering Jamaica. The Baptist denomination on the island was at a critical turning-point, and it was by no means certain that the revised relationship between

38. CH/67, Memorandum to H. R. Williamson from [-] Dyer and M. E. W. Sawyers, 3 Feb. 1944.

39. CH/67; Williamson to Chairman and Officers of BMS, 1 Mar. 1944; Report on Jamaica, part 1, 5 Mar. 1944. This is the original and confidential version; for the official printed report see H. R. Williamson, *Fresh Ventures in Fellowship* (London, 1944), 6-11.

40. General Committee Minutes, 5 July 1944, pp. 177-9.

41. WI/20, Report by T. Powell to BMS, [19 May] 1945; Report by Thomas Powell to Officers and Members of BMS Committee, 16 March 1946, p. 26.

the JBU and the BMS which Powell had been commissioned to establish would prove either permanent or successful.

II: Baptists in Trinidad, 1892-1945

The Society's decision in December 1892 to withdraw from Trinidad was implemented in the face of sustained pressure from Baptist leaders on the island, who succeeded only in securing a slight extension of the timetable for withdrawal. William Williams, missionary to the southern churches, resigned at the end of 1893 in protest at the decision to discontinue financial support, and returned to Britain. In 1894 R. E. Gammon, minister of St John's, Port of Spain, appealed to the BMS to send a replacement missionary to the southern district. The BMS Committee declined, but asked Gammon to exercise a general superintendence over the churches, and indicated its readiness to make some financial recompense to the St John's church.[42] With BMS support for Gammon's own stipend due to come to an end at the close of 1898, the church secretary at St John's warned the Society that the congregation could not guarantee to pay more than £225 of his stipend of £260. The Committee agreed as a temporary measure to make up the difference, but treated the subsidy as the promised remuneration for Gammon's work in the southern churches. At the same meeting the Committee refused earnest requests from various sources, including Gammon himself, to appoint a missionary for five years to supervise and train the southern pastors.[43]

In view of the Society's repeated refusal to commit funds to the southern work, the St John's church decided to accept the Ecclesiastical Grant, offered by the colonial government to all denominations in proportion to their numbers. This acceptance of the principle of concurrent endowment, which the BMS had always opposed, made possible the appointment in 1902 of J. J. Cooksey, previously a missionary in the Sudan, as superintendent of the southern churches. Gammon retired in 1900, and was succeeded by B. E. Horlick, a minister who had filled the St John's pastorate during Gammon's furlough in 1898. Horlick was recognized by the BMS Committee as its representative on the island, but had no financial connection with the Society.[44]

---

42. BMS Committee Minutes, 19 June 1894, pp. 242-6.

43. General Committee Minutes, 15 Nov. 1898, pp. 157-64.

44. P. D. Brewer, 'The Baptist churches of South Trinidad and their missionaries', M.Th. thesis (Glasgow, 1988), 165-6; WI/20, J. H. Poole, 'The Baptist Church in Trinidad: Historical Sketch', 2-3.

J. J. Cooksey reacted strongly to the prevalence in the Company churches of practices inherited from the 'native' Baptist tradition. In particular he set his face 'like a flint' against the wild 'All Night Meetings' which, he believed, encouraged immorality. Cooksey, with the full support of Horlick and his deacons at Port of Spain (and of some of the leaders of the Company churches), prohibited the holding of such meetings on premises owned by the BMS. The Baptist Union of Trinidad (formed in the 1860s) virtually severed fellowship with those churches that sanctioned 'All Night Meetings'. When Charles Williams of Accrington visited the island on behalf of the BMS in 1904, he found Cooksey 'in great trouble', and the churches seriously divided over the issue.[45] Williams tried to effect a reconciliation, but was unable to prevent a complete breakdown of relationships, which led eventually to Cooksey's resignation, and a declaration of independence from all connection with the BMS by a number of churches, including those at Third Company, Fifth Company and Sixth Company. Those churches that remained loyal to the original mission were included in a reformed constitution for the Baptist Union, drafted by Horlick in 1907, which vested ownership of all property in the BMS. Although some of the seceding churches eventually rejoined the Union (in the case of Third Company, not until 1943), others have remained in separation until the present day, grouped in a body known as the Union of Independent Baptist Churches (which itself subsequently split into two).[46]

In 1906 Horlick asked the BMS to recruit a young man from one of the Baptist colleges to serve as his assistant. J. H. Poole, a student at Bristol College, who had applied for missionary service in China, but had been declined on health grounds, was appointed for a period of three years. The assistantship was not a success, partly because Poole could not live on the allowance paid to him, and he left for an English pastorate in 1909. However, in January 1912 Poole returned to Trinidad at the request of the BMS, to succeed Horlick as minister of St John's and superintendent of the Baptist mission. Like Horlick, Poole was recognized by the Society as the BMS representative on the island, but was supported by his church, and hence not regarded as a BMS missionary. Poole now began a remarkable ministry in Trinidad, the final phase of which was not terminated until 1970. His main period of service at St John's lasted until his retirement in 1946, apart from three years in the 1920s, when he worked, initially for the

45.	Report by the Rev. Charles Williams, pp. 4-5.

46.	Poole, 'The Baptist Church in Trinidad', 3-4; Shelf VI/2, *1816-1966: The Baptist Church in Trinidad and Tobago*, 3.

YMCA in Trinidad, and then in the Bahamas. Poole was active in civic affairs and further education in Trinidad, and influenced a number of figures who became prominent in public life, among them Eric Williams, the future Prime Minister of Trinidad and Tobago. To Poole, more than any other individual, belongs the credit for keeping the weak Baptist cause in Trinidad from extinction, and, eventually, for persuading the BMS to recommence work on the island in 1946. 'Rarely', pronounced Thomas Powell in panegyric mood after a brief visit to Trinidad in December 1945, 'has the West Indies witnessed a ministry more wonderful'.[47]

Poole's greatest problem was the persistence and indeed multiplication on the island of the 'native' Baptist groups now known as 'Bush-Baptists' or 'Shouters'. Although firmly opposed to many of their practices, Poole believed that, given adequate pastoral supervision, these groups could have been formed into orderly Baptist communities. The same lack of pastoral leadership was woefully evident in the southern churches which had remained loyal to the Baptist mission, many of whose 'pastors' were manifestly unsuited for Christian leadership. In 1917 Poole grasped the nettle and dismissed them all. The Ecclesiastical Grant, which had previously been divided to provide the pastors with meagre allowances, was now put to the support of an 'assistant superintendent', to be responsible for the southern district. The man appointed was a lay worker from the Methodist Church in Barbados, T. S. Payne. Payne already held Baptist views, and was baptized at St John's on taking up his appointment as assistant superintendent and pastor of the Fourth Company church. Payne served the southern churches with distinction until his retirement in 1945. His son, S. E. E. Payne, served with the BMS in Orissa from 1940 to 1960, when he returned to Trinidad, where he and his wife worked as BMS missionaries until 1965.[48]

In 1943 a fund of £6,000 was launched to mark the centenary of the Baptist mission on the island. The money was to be devoted to the construction of a new church and community centre at Fourth Company. The BMS made a grant of £500, the first financial contribution made by the Society to Trinidad since 1900.[49] There is no indication, however, that the

---

47. Poole, 'The Baptist Church in Trinidad', 3-4; *Baptist Union Directory*, 1979-80, p. 304; WI/20, Report by Powell dated 3 Jan. 1946.

48. Poole, 'The Baptist Church in Trinidad', 4-5; *BMS Annual Report*, 1953-4, p. xxiv.

49. BMS Committee Minutes; 3 Nov. 1943, p. 230; 19 Jan. 1944, pp. 31, 33; Williamson, *Fresh Ventures in Fellowship*, 12. The location of the new church was subsequently transferred to Fifth Company.

BMS Committee regarded the donation as signifying any commitment to renewed involvement in the island. H. R. Williamson set off on his tour of the fields in December 1943 with no more than a 'vague hope' that he might be able to include Trinidad on his itinerary. In the event, Williamson spent a fortnight on the island, and was greatly impressed by Poole's work at Port of Spain. More importantly, he was convinced by Poole that the time had now come for the Society to reconsider its policy and enter into a new partnership with the Trinidad churches. If nothing were done, Williamson feared that the impending retirement of both Poole and Payne would lead to a rapid deterioration of the work in the southern churches. He accordingly recommended that the Society appoint (and initially support) a successor to Poole, that two missionary couples should be appointed to the southern district, and that two deaconesses be supplied to engage in women's work.[50]

The Society's committees gave lengthy consideration to Williamson's report, and also to a historical survey prepared by Poole, which pulled no punches in its assertions that BMS policy in the West Indies had been 'inept and short-sighted', and that Baptists in Trinidad, who should by rights have formed the largest Free Church denomination, had been left to the ravages of lawlessness and 'old African superstitions'. It was eventually decided to appoint just one missionary couple to the southern district, and initially only one woman worker. Sydney and Muriel Poupard were appointed to the former role in November 1945, and Eva Waggott to women's work in the following year.[51] The Macedonian call of J. H. Poole had led the Society to recognize that its withdrawal from Trinidad in 1892 had failed to achieve the desired invigorating effect, and must now be reversed.

III: The BMS and the Bahamas, 1892-1947

The Society's withdrawal from Trinidad after 1892 had exposed the magnitude of the problems of leadership and discipline which faced the weak Baptist cause on the island. In the Bahamas, a similar process can be discerned, but the much greater size of Baptist membership in this group of islands ensured that the survival of the Baptist denomination was never in any doubt. Probably for this very reason, the arguments which were put to the Society in favour of a resumption of work in the Bahamas failed to carry the irresistible force which proved decisive in the case of Trinidad.

---

50. Williamson, *Fresh Ventures in Fellowship*, 11-16.

51. Poole, 'The Baptist Church in Trinidad', 9. General Committee Minutes; 5 July 1944, p. 178; 3 July 1945, p. 134; 6 Nov. 1945, pp. 195-7, 228-9; 3 July 1946, pp. 137, 139.

When Charles Williams visited the Bahamas on his 1904 deputation to the West Indies, the initial signs were that the Society's progressive withdrawal of financial support from the islands after 1892 had proved justified. Admittedly the Baptist family was divided into four. In addition to the BMS mission churches under C. A. Dann, and two groups of 'native' Baptist churches which had never identified themselves with the BMS, there was now a 'Bahamas Baptist Union' of twenty-eight churches, founded by the former BMS missionary, Daniel Wilshere, who had returned to the islands after his dismissal by the Society. Yet the state of health of the churches was encouraging: the number of Dann's BMS churches had grown from sixty-seven in 1892 to seventy-three in 1904, and membership had increased from 3,371 to 3,842. Total Baptist membership was nearly one in five of the population.[52]

The limited surviving evidence suggests that this rising trend was not sustained after 1904. The BMS annual report for 1905-6 (the last to print statistics for the Bahamian churches) recorded a total of 3,711 members in the seventy-three churches.[53] No further evidence of the state of the churches is available until 1923, when Thomas Stockley visited the Bahamas from Jamaica, at the request of the BMS Committee, in order to pave the way for the settlement of J. H. Poole as superintendent of the BMS mission and pastor of the main BMS church, Zion, Nassau. Stockley reported that the Zion congregation had almost fallen to pieces after Dann's death in 1917, and now had a membership of only 200, rather than the 500 he had been led to expect. Stockley did not visit the out-islands, but interviews with a number of the leaders of their seventy-one BMS churches indicated that they were sorely in need of pastoral supervision, and in danger of drifting off into the wild extravagances of the 'Holy Jumpers', one of the more extreme groups of 'native' Baptists in the islands. Stockley repeatedly urged the BMS, to send, at the very least, one good man to supervise the out-island churches.[54]

The BMS did not respond to Stockley's pleas, though the Society did agree to make a single grant of £150 towards Poole's removal expenses from Trinidad and the first year of his stipend.[55] On the conclusion of Poole's

52. Report by the Rev. Charles Williams, 5-6, cited in P. D. Brewer, 'British Baptist missionaries and Baptist work in the Bahamas', *BQ* 32 (1987-8), 298-9.

53. *BMS Annual Report,* 1905-6, p. 117.

54. WI/19; T. I. Stockley, Report of a visit to the island of New Providence [1923]; Stockley to C. E. Wilson, 10 Sept. and 19 Oct. 1923.

55. General Committee Minutes, 21 Nov. 1923, pp. 93, 104.

ministry in Nassau in January 1926, he submitted a report to the BMS, apparently recommending increased involvement by the Society, but it was not brought before the Committee.[56] The BMS advised the Zion church to invite T. S. Payne of Trinidad as Poole's replacement. This the church did, but evidently with some reluctance, and on financial terms which Payne was eventually compelled to decline.[57] Leonard Tucker, who had served as a tutor at Calabar College from 1891 to 1901, and subsequently on the home staff of the Society, was called to the pastorate instead, and thus became the BMS representative in the Bahamas. Tucker's pastorate was marked by disputes with his church officers, and came to an acrimonious end in March 1931. Talmage Sands, a Bahamian Methodist trained at Calabar and Caenwood, was called to succeed him. Tucker's pastorate had left a legacy of resentment in the church against the BMS, and all connections with the Society were now severed. Sands took the church (and with it the BMS mission as a whole) into membership with the National Baptist Convention of the USA.[58]

The tangled story of BMS involvement in the Bahamas reached its final chapter in 1947 with a deputation visit by Thomas Powell from Jamaica. The Society's attention had been drawn to the sad state of the Baptist denomination in the Bahamas by a letter written to Dr J. H. Rushbrooke by Mr Kenneth Howard, a Baptist then serving with the Royal Air Force in Nassau. Confirmation of Howard's reports was provided by J. H. Poole, who had 'retired' to Nassau as minister of St Andrew's Presbyterian Church.[59] Powell's written report to the Society on his visit painted an equally dark picture. Division, rivalry and scandal abounded, especially at Zion church, where some members still looked to the BMS to intervene. The condition of the out-island churches was 'deplorable', with unfit leaders and declining membership. Powell urged the necessity of external help to redeem the situation. His preference was for the BMS to re-enter the field, but the Society took no action other than to refer the matter to the Baptist World Alliance.[60]

---

56. WI/22, Report by Thomas Powell on Origin, Development and Present Condition of the Baptist Churches, 5 Oct. 1947, pp. 6, 15.

57. General Committee Minutes, 16 Mar. and 22 Apr. 1927, pp. 43, 57.

58. WI/22, Report by Thomas Powell, pp. 5-8. The National Baptist Convention was formed by black Baptists in the USA in 1895.

59. General Committee Minutes, 3 July and 6 Nov. 1945, pp. 134, 195.

60. WI/22, Report by Thomas Powell, pp. 4, 15-16; General Committee Minutes, 5 Nov. 1947, p. 215.

By 1947 it was, perhaps, too late for the BMS to attempt to recoup a situation which had been steadily moving beyond the Society's control ever since 1917. Nonetheless, it is hard to escape the conclusion that the Bahamas mission represents one of the most notable missed opportunities of the Society's history. After 1947 the different groups of Bahamas churches strengthened their several connections with various Baptist bodies in the USA. Most of the churches came together in 1971 to form the Bahamas United Baptist Convention, thus healing the division created in 1892 between the BMS mission and Wilshere's Bahamas Baptist Union.[61] The only indirect connection between the BMS and this part of the Caribbean since the Second World War was the service with the JBMS in the Turks and Caicos Islands in the early 1970s of a British minister who had previously served in Jamaica, Michael Woosley.[62] More recently, however, Bahamian Baptists have expressed interest in renewing their historic links with the BMS, creating the possibility that this chapter in the Caribbean history of the Society may not yet be closed.

IV: The BMS in Jamaica, 1945-1992

1. Ministerial support and the American connection

A number of specific assignments faced Thomas Powell when he arrived in Jamaica in 1945. Possibly the most demanding was the task of establishing a comprehensive central fund for ministerial sustentation and superannuation to replace Stockley's 1927 scheme. Powell's discussions with the JBU on this matter were complicated by the lack of clarity which surrounded the extent of his authority as 'Commissioner', and also by a misunderstanding which had arisen during H. R. Williamson's visit. The Union was under the impression that Williamson had committed the BMS to provide £4,800 a year for twenty years to get such a scheme established, whereas he had in fact merely indicated that a single grant of this sum might be possible. Some leaders of the JBU felt that the BMS had reneged on its promises, and were not slow to argue that the Jamaican churches would do better to look to the rock from which they were hewn, and seek help from Baptists in the USA. For the next decade Jamaican Baptists, whilst never abandoning their partnership with the BMS, found the much greater

---

61. M. C. Symonette and A. Canzoneri, *Baptists in the Bahamas: An Historical Review* (El Paso, 1977), 70.

62. *BMS Annual Report,* 1974-5, p. 29.

financial resources of the Southern Baptist Convention of the USA an almost irresistible attraction.[63]

Hampered by these difficulties, Powell failed to set up a permanent scheme. He did, however, succeed in introducing an interim scheme, to which the BMS contributed a sum of £1,500. The interim scheme was less than satisfactory. Churches were at first slow to contribute, the allowances paid were insufficient to live on, and not all ministers were included.[64] In 1949 the JBU invited two of its ministers, D. E. Allen and D. A. Morgan, and the new president of Calabar, Keith Tucker, to draw up plans for a permanent scheme. Allen and Morgan visited Britain in the autumn to discuss the plans with the BMS. The resulting agreement led to the inauguration of a new comprehensive scheme on 1 April 1950. The BMS supplied nearly £2,500 for the first three years of the scheme, but the central fund could not have been established without lavish donations from the Southern Baptist Convention, and also some aid from Canadian Baptists. The success of the scheme also owed a great deal to the vision and industry of Keith Tucker, who combined his duties at the College with the roles of secretary-treasurer of the fund and treasurer of the JBMS. In its final revised form, inaugurated on 1 December 1953, the scheme provided for the payment of all ministerial stipends and superannuation benefits from a central fund. It was decided that the first two British Baptist ministers recruited by the BMS for Jamaica in response to Powell's pleas for additional ministerial help - Noel Clarke and Sidney Bastable - should be included in the scheme.[65]

The Southern Baptist input to Jamaica was not limited to finance. From 1953 the Foreign Mission Board of the Convention had a permanent representative on the island, who assumed the pastorate of a recently formed independent Baptist congregation at Half Way Tree in Kingston. This church (which took the name Bethel) became a centre of Southern Baptist influence, not least among the students at nearby Calabar College. The Southern Baptists also brought over pastors for short-term evangelistic campaigns, and students for vacation Bible schools for children and young

63. WI/20, Report by Thomas Powell, pp. 2-3, 31; General Committee Minutes, 16 Jan. 1946, pp. 29-32.

64. General Committee Minutes, 5 Nov. 1947, p. 213; WI/21, Tucker to Williamson, 17 May 1949.

65. WI/21: Tucker to Williamson, 17 May 1949; 'Recommendations resulting from discussions between...the BMS and...the JBU'. *BMS Annual Reports*, 1952-3, pp. xxvii-xxviii; 1953-4, p. xxii.

people. Keith Tucker and David Jelleyman, the BMS tutorial staff at Calabar, had some misgivings about the nature and intent of the Southern Baptist influence, but fears of an American take-over were relieved from the end of 1955 by the Foreign Mission Board's decision to withdraw its representative. Elements in the JBU continued to look to the Convention for major financial aid until September 1959, when a tripartite conference between representatives of the Convention, the JBU and the BMS, led the Southern Baptists to scale down their involvement in the island. The Foreign Mission Board maintained a limited presence in Jamaica until the late 1970s.[66]

In the long term, the Southern Baptists contributed less by their dollars than by their teaching on stewardship. Even during the 1950s the level of giving from the Jamaican churches to the central fund showed a steady increase. Nonetheless, the financial difficulties of the denomination were not at an end. As the Southern Baptist grant to the central fund was progressively reduced from $5,000 in 1955 to nil in 1960, the fund fell into difficulties, and drastic cuts had to be made in the grants paid to ministers.[67] Yet the fund stayed afloat, not least because of the continuing support of the BMS, which contributed £1,000 per annum throughout the 1950s. The Society's financial assistance to the JBU as a whole has continued to the present day.[68] The process of reorganization of the JBU reached a decisive stage on 31 March 1969, when the Union at last became an incorporated body (a step which had been on the agenda since 1903), and trusteeship of Baptist property in Jamaica passed from the BMS to the JBU.

2. From Calabar to the United Theological College of the West Indies

Thomas Powell's second major assignment as BMS Commissioner in 1945 was to investigate some major questions surrounding the future of Calabar High School and College. The High School was short of cash for capital development, short of space on its shared site with the college, and short of pupils. The lack of a science department and the location of the school in an 'undesirable' area were discouraging applications, and the low pupil numbers meant low levels of government grant. When he arrived in Jamaica, Powell had serious doubts about the wisdom of the BMS continu-

66. Didcot, D. W. F. Jelleyman file. Interviews with Rev. D. W. F. Jelleyman, 1.3.90, and Rev. D. Monkcom, 24.4.90. *BMS Annual Report*, 1959-60, pp. xxviii-xxix.

67. *BMS Annual Reports*, 1955-6, pp. xxvi-xxvii; 1957-8 p. xxvii; 1958-9, pp. xxv-xxvi.

68. In 1989-90 the BMS gave £1,600 to the JBU, £400 to Calabar High School, and £2,000 to UTCWI in support of a tutor.

ing to run the High School, but the experience of living on the premises convinced him that the school was worth preserving. A new and more attractive site at Red Hills Road had been under consideration for some time. Powell was soon persuaded of the advisability of moving both the High School and the college to the new site, but opinion on the BMS Committee was still hesitant about the viability of the school. Eventually, however, Powell's arguments prevailed, and the new site was purchased. The BMS advanced the required capital of £8,379, and the loan was repaid from the proceeds of the sale of the Chetolah Park site. The new premises for the college and High School were formally opened in September 1952.[69]

Enrolment at the new school increased rapidly, reaching nearly 350 in 1953 and 1,700 by the mid-1980s. Although Baptist pupils were only a small minority in the new school, the denomination now had a strong base on which to build the educated leadership in both church life and public affairs which Jamaican Baptists had conspicuously lacked for so long. Throughout the 1950s and 1960s the leadership of the school was dependent on staff who (though not technically BMS missionaries) were recruited through the Society: such as Murray White, headmaster from 1949 to 1959, Cecil Woodyatt, second master from 1947 to 1963, and Walter Foster, a member of staff since 1940 and headmaster from 1962 to 1972. Foster was succeeded by the first Jamaican headmaster, Arthur Edgar. BMS personnel continued to teach at the school until 1984, when Mrs Christine Jelleyman retired from the staff after thirty-one years of missionary service at Calabar with her husband, David.

Those in the 1940s who doubted the wisdom of moving Calabar College to the proposed new location were influenced by a concern to see the existing co-operation in theological training with the Methodists and Presbyterians preserved, and indeed extended. A move to Red Hills Road would, they feared, make the existing arrangements for shared teaching between Calabar, Caenwood and St Colm's more difficult to maintain. (It did so, but the strong general will to preserve the co-operative relationship ensured that joint classes continued after 1952). More fundamentally, proposals were afoot, under the British government's programme of Colonial Development and Welfare, to establish a University College of the West Indies, with the prospect of a united theological college forming at least part of its theological faculty.[70] In 1946 informal discussions took place

69. WI/20, Report by Thomas Powell, pp. 36-43. WI/21, 'Recommendations resulting from discussions...', pp. 2-3. General Committee Minutes, 7 Apr. 1945, pp. 86-9; 3 July 1945, pp. 135, 137.

70. CH/67, H. R. Williamson, Report on Jamaica, part 2, 13 Mar. 1944, pp. 3, 8-9.

in the Conference of British Missionary Societies about the possibility of a united college. Majority opinion in the JBU, however, was in favour of the continuance of Calabar as a Baptist denominational college.[71] Alone of all the Free Churches on the island, Baptists did not participate directly in the Union Theological Seminary, formed by the merger of Caenwood and St Colm's in 1955, although joint classes between Calabar and the seminary continued as before.

From 1959 negotiations on the formation of a united theological college in Jamaica were held between the Union Seminary, the Baptists and the Anglicans (who had their own St Peter's College in Kingston). A major incentive was the promise of substantial funding from the Theological Education Fund of the International Missionary Council (from 1961 part of the World Council of Churches). The main hesitations came from the Baptists, who were fearful that participation would lead to a dilution of their denominational identity. When in May 1964 the decision was taken to proceed with a united college, the JBU made its agreement to participate conditional upon Baptist students being given separate residential accommodation.[72] The United Theological College of the West Indies (UTCWI) came into formal existence in 1966, but for its first two terms functioned on the existing sites at Calabar, Caenwood, and St Peter's. In 1967 the new premises adjacent to the Mona campus of the University of the West Indies were opened, and the Red Hills Road site was taken over in its entirety by the High School. Donald Monkcom, president of Calabar since 1959, became Dean of Studies in the UTCWI. His Calabar colleagues, David Jelleyman, New Testament tutor since 1948, and Horace Russell, tutor in Church History since 1958, went on to exercise key roles in the new institution. Jelleyman succeeded Monkcom as Dean of Studies in 1968. Russell, a Jamaican and former Calabar student who had undertaken postgraduate research at Regent's Park College, Oxford, became the third president of UTCWI from 1972 to 1976.

In association with the neighbouring Roman Catholic seminary (St Michael's), another Catholic seminary in Trinidad, and the Anglican Codrington College in Barbados, the UTCWI functions as the theology department of the Faculty of Arts and General Studies of the University of the West Indies. Seven Protestant traditions are directly involved in

71. General Committee Minutes, 3 July 1946, p. 138; WI/20, Report by E. A. Bompas on visit to Jamaica, 1949.

72. Interviews with Rev. D. W. F. Jelleyman, 1.3.90, and Rev. D. Monkcom, 24.4.90.

sponsoring the college.[73] The JBU continued until the 1980s to look to the BMS for assistance in maintaining Baptist representation on the UTCWI faculty. After a three-year gap following the retirement of David Jelleyman in 1984, the Society again supplied a tutor at UTCWI in the person of Keith Riglin, a member of staff from 1987 to 1989.

3. A revived denomination

In the 1940s Jamaican Baptist life was at a low ebb. Church membership was in decline, the standard of pastoral ministry was often low, and the divisions created by the 'impasse' of the 1930s had left their mark. Most Baptists were poor and uneducated, and the denomination had low public esteem. Church life continued in places to be dogged by the hold of 'obeah' occult practice, and by the influence of cults which blended Christian revivalism with animistic belief - such as that known as 'pocomania'. Christian standards of family life were hard to maintain in a society whose pattern of sexual relationships still bore the chaotic imprint of slavery: about 70 per cent of all Jamaican births in the first half of the twentieth century were illegitimate.[74]

By the end of the 1980s much had changed. Some of the old problems had been largely overcome. Others - such as the strains on Christian marriage - remained, while new challenges had arisen. The pastoral ministry was now better trained, better paid, and more fully staffed. There was still, however, a shortage of ministers: in 1989 there were ninety pastors serving a total of 288 churches.[75] The role of lay leaders (many of them women) in the circuits continued to be crucial, and the need to train them more adequately remained urgent.

The protracted decline in Baptist membership was reversed in the 1950s. Church membership rose steadily during the decade, despite the emigration to Britain of 200,000 Jamaicans. The problems encountered by Christians among the Jamaican immigrant community in British church life became a matter of concern both to the JBU and to the BMS. Three Jamaican ministers, M. E. W. Sawyers, C. H. L. Gayle, and C. S. Reid, spent periods in Britain working in London, Birmingham, and Manchester, mainly among immigrant communities. It was no fault of theirs that they were

---

73. Anglicans, Baptists, Disciples of Christ, Lutherans, Methodists, Moravians, and the United Church of Jamaica (formed by the Presbyterian and Congregational churches).

74. F. Henriques, *Family and Colour in Jamaica* (2nd edn., London, 1968), 90.

75. Statistics supplied by the Jamaica Baptist Union.

largely unsuccessful in facilitating black integration into Baptist churches.[76] In Jamaica itself, Baptist membership stagnated during the 1960s, but rose again thereafter, reaching a peak of 41,394 in 1985. Up to that point, Baptists, though not the largest denomination on the island, had more than held their own in numerical terms in contrast to the other historic denominations. After 1985 Baptists themselves experienced a serious decline: JBU membership had fallen to 34,498 by 1989.[77] This latest change in Baptist fortunes probably reflected the renewed importance of American cultural and religious influences in Jamaica. The most flourishing Protestant communities were now those with the strongest links with the USA: Seventh Day Adventists and Pentecostalists of various kinds, only minor forces in the 1940s, had to some extent taken over the former Baptist role amongst the lowest socio-economic groups in Jamaica.[78]

Nonetheless, Baptists retained very considerable support among the poorer sections of society, and hence were affected directly by the vicissitudes of the Jamaican economy. The late 1970s and early 1980s were a particularly difficult period, as the sugar trade declined into virtual extinction, and the banana trade experienced a protracted depression. Yet Baptists no longer carried the reputation of being a denomination composed exclusively of the poor and uneducated. They gained heightened prestige after Jamaica won her national independence on 5 August 1962. Three out of the seven declared 'national heroes' of Jamaican history were Baptists or had strong Baptist connections - Sam Sharpe, Paul Bogle and G. W. Gordon.[79] Two leading Baptists served in the Senate (the upper house of the Jamaican parliament) for periods during the 1970s and 1980s: C. S. Reid, pastor of Calvary Baptist Church, Montego Bay, and Errol Miller, Professor of Education in the University of the West Indies. Reid in particular attracted prominence as an independent senator during the late 1970s, by writing and broadcasting against the violence perpetrated in the name of the

76. *BMS Annual Reports*, 1960-1, p. xxxiv; 1961-2, p. xxxviii; interview with Rev. D. Monkcom, 24.4.90.

77. Statistics supplied by the Jamaica Baptist Union.

78. H. O. Russell, 'An overview of the Church in Jamaica during the past twenty-five years', *The Fraternal* 223 (July 1988), 18, 20-1.

79. Sam Sharpe was declared a national hero in 1975. Of the two heroes of the Morant Bay rising, Bogle was a deacon of a 'native' Baptist church, whilst Gordon moved from Presbyterian allegiance through Anglicanism to affiliation to the 'native' Baptist churches. See ch. III above, p. 98, n. 123.

warring political parties at a time when democracy in Jamaica was under serious threat.[80]

It would clearly be false to attribute the degree of transformation that took place in Jamaican Baptist life wholly to the decision by the BMS in 1945 to resume a more active involvement in the island. After 1945 the Society neither flooded Jamaica with missionaries nor poured in vast quantities of money. Thomas Powell was not replaced on his retirement in 1948. The BMS continued its policy of supporting missionary personnel only at Calabar College, whilst actively encouraging the settlement of gifted British ministers in key Jamaican pastorates (such as that of Leslie Larwood at East Queen Street from 1953 to 1958). The Society also made a direct contribution to the training of lay leaders through the service of William and Nora Porch at Calabar from 1969 to 1974. The increased commitment of the Society to Jamaica after 1945 was strategic, making a major contribution to the improvement in the provision for, and quality of, pastoral leadership. Although Jamaican Baptists do not owe their origin to the BMS, and although the Society's involvement in the island was on a relatively minor scale from 1842 to 1945, the BMS has played an important part in establishing the JBU as one of the more active and vibrant Christian communities in modern Jamaica. It should also be noted that the JBU was the prime mover in the formation in 1970 of the Caribbean Baptist Fellowship (a constituent body of the Baptist World Alliance), which unites approximately 200,000 Baptists in the Caribbean region.

V: The BMS in Trinidad, 1946-1992

The field which the BMS re-entered in 1946 soon confirmed the warnings of J. H. Poole and others about the immense difficulties which confronted Baptist work in Trinidad. Sydney Poupard, originally appointed to work amongst the southern churches, was in fact called to succeed J. H. Poole in the pastorate of St John's, Port of Spain. The Poupards did not take up their intended work at Fifth Company until 1948, when the BMS sent a British Baptist minister, J. P. Hickerton, to assume the St John's pastorate as a minister serving 'under the auspices' of the BMS. The former BMS Home Secretary, B. Grey Griffith, visited Trinidad later that year, and reported that the Poupards and Eva Waggott faced in the southern churches 'as difficult a task as there is anywhere in our Society'. Superstition, illiteracy, and suspicion of white persons were among the obstacles they faced. In Port of Spain Griffith found the St John's church

80. Interviews with Rev. D. W. F. Jelleyman, 1.3.90, and Rev. D. Monkcom, 24.4.90.

already seriously divided.[81] Hickerton was a gifted preacher who had been President of the Oxford Union while a student at Regent's Park College. As a pastor, however, he was not a success, and his five years at Port of Spain were marked by controversy. By January 1953, when his pastorate was discontinued, the St John's congregation was in a parlous state, and the Baptist reputation on the island decidedly low.[82]

The restoration of peace at St John's was initiated by the appointment in June 1952 of the former China missionary, Amos Suter, first as moderator of the church (while Hickerton was on furlough), and then as its pastor. By March 1957 the church secretary was able to report that Amos and Nellie Suter had been mainly responsible for transforming St. John's from 'a bewildered, fractious and anxious community' into a unified and forward-looking fellowship.[83] In the south, progress proved much harder to achieve. The Poupards devoted their energies to running training courses for pastors and church leaders, but frequently met with an indifferent and complacent response.[84] The churches remained heavily dependent on the government Ecclesiastical Grant to pay their pastors, but its level was barely sufficient to cover travelling expenses. Many church members contributed to church funds on the basis of monthly dues, determined according to the cost of living of several decades previously; freewill offerings were still an unconventional method of giving in 1960.[85] Recognizing that the base for producing trained indigenous leaders was still slender, the BMS gradually increased its input of missionary resources. By December 1955 the Society had three missionary couples and one deaconess on the island, serving an aggregate church membership of only 620. There is some evidence of limited church growth during the late 1950s, but the published membership statistics are notoriously unreliable.[86]

On 31 May 1962 the abortive Federation of the West Indies (formed by the British in 1958) ceased to exist, following the withdrawal first of Jamaica and then of Trinidad. Three months later, on 31 August, Trinidad and

81. WI/20, Report of B. Grey Griffith on visit to Trinidad, 6 Nov. to 9 Dec. 1948.

82. WI/Misc, G. C. Cooke to V. E. W. Hayward, 29 Jan. 1953.

83. WI/Misc, Cooke to Hayward, 4 Mar. 1957.

84. *BMS Annual Report,* 1954-5, p. xxv.

85. *BMS Annual Report,* 1960-1, pp. xxxv-xxxvi.

86. WI/Misc, Insert in 'BMS Work in Trinidad', compiled by S.G. Poupard, June 1954. The *BMS Annual Report,* 1955-6, p. 11, recorded church membership as 500. The *BMS Annual Report,* 1956-7, p. xxxii, reported forty-nine baptisms during 1956, yet gave a membership total of 990 (p. 12).

Tobago became an independent member of the British Commonwealth. The small Baptist denomination faced the new political era with rather greater resources than it had possessed twenty years earlier. By 1962 the missionary complement had risen to nine, and the published church membership to 1,160.[87] A Baptist secondary school, the Cowen-Hamilton Secondary School, was opened north of St Mary's village in January 1962. The Trinidad churches also had the benefit during the 1960s of the uninterrupted service of some experienced missionaries. William and Eileen Bell, another ex-China mission couple, replaced the Poupards in the South in November 1956, and served the southern churches continuously until their retirement in 1972. Eva Waggott - known in the churches as 'Sister Eva' - remained active in women's work throughout the island, as well as holding pastoral responsibility in the Fourth Company church. In 1972 she was instrumental in establishing a Baptist centre to provide practical training for girls who had received no secondary education. She retired in 1974.[88] Most venerable of all, J. H. Poole, at the age of seventy-nine, returned to Trinidad in 1961 to resume the pastorate at St John's, initially as a *locum tenens* during Amos Suter's furlough, then from January 1963 as pastor in his own right. Deteriorating health finally compelled Poole to resign the pastorate on 1 January 1970, though he continued to live on the island until his death, at the age of ninety-six, in 1978.[89]

Expatriate leadership of the quality provided by Cranston Bell, Waggott and Poole was an asset, yet also something of an imported luxury in an independent Caribbean nation in the 1960s. J. H. Poole was the last European to pastor the Port of Spain church. The BMS suggested the name of a British minister (Peter Brewer) to succeed him, but the church felt that growing nationalist consciousness made it unwise to appoint a Briton to the island's leading Baptist church, and instead called the principal of the Cowen-Hamilton School, Allan Parkes, to the pastorate.[90] Parkes was Jamaican by birth but a naturalized Trinidadian. A few BMS missionaries continued to serve as pastors of individual southern churches throughout the 1970s, but the emphasis of the Society's contribution was increasingly on assisting the Baptist Union of Trinidad and Tobago with its own

---

87. *BMS Annual Report*, 1961-2, p. xxxviii.

88. *BMS Annual Report*, 1974-5, pp. 29, 44.

89. WI/Misc, J. H. Poole to G. C. Cooke, 1 Jan. 1970; *Baptist Union Directory*, 1979-80, p. 304.

90. WI/Misc, Correspondence on Port of Spain pastorate.

administrative structures and programmes of leadership training. The Union tended to evolve over-elaborate structures which the churches were unable to maintain. Peter Brewer, whom the BMS had, in any case, appointed to its Trinidad staff in 1970, played a part in the reduction of the Union's committee structure from a bewildering seventeen committees to four main divisions in 1978.[91] Brewer's primary role was as Director of Training and secretary of the Ministerial Recognition Committee.

By 1970 the BMS was no longer the only missionary body working with the Trinidadian Baptists. From 1970 to 1976 the Foreign Mission Board of the Southern Baptist Convention worked with the Baptist Union, but not on a fully integrated basis. The size of the Board's financial input to the Union gave rise to fears of American domination. The resulting tensions led to a policy statement from the Union in 1976, ruling that all foreign missionaries should be fully integrated into the life of the Union. In response, the Southern Baptists withdrew their missionaries, and four churches which they had founded withdrew from the Union. These events contributed to a process of fragmentation of Baptist life in Trinidad which continued into the 1990s.[92]

In 1980 Trinidad possessed three fully trained Baptist ministers and one trained deaconess.[93] Their presence marked a partial fulfilment of a goal which the BMS had first sought to attain as early as the 1890s, even though it has to be said that the Baptist churches still possessed neither the means nor the will to support these ministers on a full-time basis. Nonetheless, with other Trinidadians in training at UTCWI or elsewhere, the Union was emboldened in 1980 to resolve that no more BMS missionaries would be invited to serve as pastors of churches.[94] Within two years of the Baptist Union's decision there were no BMS missionaries left in Trinidad. In more recent years, two BMS couples have been involved in the Union's lay training programme: Michael and Valerie Bonser served from 1985 to 1987; and in 1989 Peter and Sheila Brewer returned to Trinidad to undertake similar work. The Baptist community in 1992 remained numerically weak (the Baptist Union of Trinidad and Tobago had an active membership of less than 2,000), relatively poorly educated, and internally divided. The Southern Baptists had resumed work in Trinidad on a free-

91. *BMS Annual Reports,* 1975-6, pp. 40-1; 1976-7, p. 27; 1977-8, p. 28; 1978-9, p. 20.

92. Information from Rev. Peter Brewer, 17.7.90.

93. The ministers were V. A. Cadette, S. Dewsbury, A. Parkes; the deaconess was Sister J. Placide.

94. *BMS Annual Report,* 1980-1, pp. 26-7.

lance basis, working with any Baptist group prepared to use their services. By 1992 the Baptist Union as a body was able to command the support of only a minority of the Baptist ministers on the island. Southern Baptist influence, exercised through the Caribbean Baptist Fellowship and the Trinidad and Tobago Baptist Fellowship (an 'umbrella' body providing informal links between the various Baptist groups) was once again a significant element in a confused denominational situation.

A serious question mark must remain over the wisdom of the Society's nineteenth-century policy in Trinidad, culminating in the 1892 decision to throw the churches on to their own scanty resources of leadership. Since 1946 the BMS had worked hard to repair the damage, and propel this small part of Trinidad's Protestant community towards self-supporting life and growth in what was now a religiously plural island, with large Hindu and Muslim populations in addition to the majority Catholic community. That these objectives had not been achieved by 1992 is evidence of the persistence of the weaknesses in the tradition of folk-religion which BMS missionaries had struggled to rectify ever since 1843.

IX

India and Ceylon, 1914-1947

I: The New Tribal Harvest: The Example of Mizoram

Protestant missions in nineteenth-century India had devoted much of their efforts to reaching the higher-caste Hindus through the diffusion of Christian education. By 1914 many missionaries were contrasting the relative failure of this strategy with the spectacular evangelistic results being witnessed among low-caste and tribal peoples. Educational work was not abandoned - indeed, for some missionaries it gained new significance as a means of infusing the gathering forces of Indian nationalism with Christian principles - but it no longer commanded the consistent enthusiasm of all sections of the Protestant missionary movement.[1] If the supreme aim of BMS work was 'not a nebulous Christianisation of the people's ideas, but definite conversions to God', argued T. W. Norledge of the Society's Calcutta secretariat in 1919, a diversion of resources from higher-caste work to low-caste and tribal groups was imperative.[2] There was a feeling that the BMS had escaped the main currents of the so-called 'mass movements' taking place in various parts of India (although West Orissa and the Barisal district of East Bengal could be cited as notable exceptions).[3] In part this was purely an accident of geography, but some missionaries also sensed a tension between Baptist church polity - with its emphasis on the individual confession of faith expressed in believer's baptism - and the collective nature of conversion in the people movements.[4] W. E. French, who served

---

1. A. Mathew, *Christian Missions, Education and Nationalism: From Dominance to Compromise 1870-1930* (New Delhi, 1988), ch. 6.

2. *BMS Annual Report*, 1918-19, p. 11.

3. *BMS Annual Report*, 1916-17, p. 13.

4. Minutes of Indian Missionaries, 1911-17, H. Anderson, The National Missionary Council and BMS Mission Policy (1917), 8-9.

269

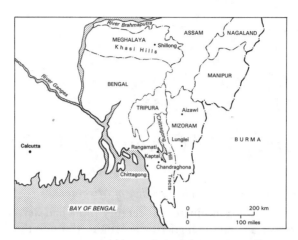

Map 7: Mizoram and the Chittagong Hills

continuously in Bengal from 1911 to 1950, went so far as to declare that 'our Baptist methods will never produce mass movements, for our emphasis is essentially on the personal salvation of individuals and the weeding out of the sheep from the goats'. Baptist principles, proclaimed French, guaranteed church growth that was solid, if slow.[5]

In view of the challenge which movements of mass conversion posed to any rigid transference of Baptist ecclesiology to the Indian context, it may be significant that the formative influences on the BMS Mizoram mission - the most notable people movement in the BMS in this period - were not consistently Baptist in character. J. H. Lorrain and F. W. Savidge first arrived in this remote hill territory in North-East India in January 1894 under the auspices of the 'Arthington Aborigines Mission', founded by Robert Arthington in 1889.[6] F. W. Savidge was originally a Wesleyan, but was baptized in 1890 at Highgate Road Baptist Church, North London, where he became a member. His friend Lorrain came from a Congregational background, but was also baptized at Highgate Road; his church membership throughout his later service with the BMS was at Lansdowne

---

5. W. E. French, *The Gospel in India* (London, 1946), 132-3.

6. On the origins of the Mizoram mission see A. M. Chirgwin, *Arthington's Million* (London, n.d.), 74-86; C. L. H minga, *The Life and Witness of the Churches in Mizoram* (Serkawn, Mizoram, 1987), 43-56.

Hall in West Norwood.[7] Within four years Lorrain and Savidge learnt the Mizo (Lushai) language, translated Luke, John and Acts, and published a Lushai grammar and dictionary. However, following the decision of the Welsh Calvinistic Methodists to extend their work in the Khasi hills to Lushai (Mizoram), Arthington withdrew his workers in 1897 to avoid duplication of missionary resources. Lorrain and Savidge then formed their own mission, the Assam Frontier Pioneer Mission, and returned to North-East India in 1899 to Arunachal Pradesh. Meanwhile, the Welsh mission began work in the north of Lushai, building on the linguistic foundations laid by Lorrain and Savidge. The Calvinistic Methodist mission to the north was to be the most powerful influence on the Baptist life and polity of Mizoram.

In July 1900 D. L. Donald, BMS missionary at Chittagong, received a letter from Edwin Rowlands of the Calvinistic Methodist mission, inform-ing him that the Welsh mission intended extending their work to south Lushai. Donald replied that he had for some time been seeking, with the full backing of the BMS Committee, to extend his own work to south Lushai. Donald sent a copy of his reply to the BMS India Secretary, Herbert Anderson, who raised the matter with Alfred Baynes. Baynes then opened negotiations with the Welsh mission, which agreed in January 1901 to cede the south Lushai field to the BMS, provided the Society undertook to occupy the field within twelve months.[8] The BMS accepted this condition, and sent George Hughes (Donald's replacement at Chittagong) on a prospecting journey in September 1901 through the Chittagong Hill Tracts into south Lushai. Hughes's report urged the Society to enter both the Tracts and south Lushai without delay. Meanwhile Anderson wrote to Lorrain and Savidge, suggesting that they return under BMS auspices to the Lushai field. In December the Committee agreed to a permanent occupa-tion of the Hill Tracts. George and Edith Hughes settled at Rangamati, pioneering a work among the tribal peoples of the Hill Tracts which had gathered 1,000 enquirers in twenty-five villages by the end of 1914.[9] A

7.   H. Anderson, Report of a Visit to the South Lushai Mission in January and February 1913, p. 7; *BMS Annual Reports*, Directory of Missionaries; General Committee Minutes, 5 Nov. 1935, memorial resolution for F. W. Savidge; and 4 July 1944, pp. 130-1, memorial resolution for J. H. Lorrain. Highgate Road was not in the mainstream of Baptist life; see J. Wilmot and J. H. Pizey, *God's Work in God's Way* (London, 1934). Lansdowne Hall was an independent evangelical church formed by a secession of members from Chatsworth Baptist Church, West Norwood.

8.   General Committee Minutes, 12 Feb. 1901, pp. 415-20.

9.   *BMS Annual Report*, 1914-15, p. 161.

hospital was opened at Chandraghona on the edge of the Tracts in 1908, and substantially extended in 1925.

The only obstacle to a similar entrance to south Lushai was finance. There was no immediate prospect of Robert Arthington's massive bequest to the BMS becoming available for distribution; an extension of the agreed deadline was therefore obtained from the Welsh mission.[10] Finally, in December 1902, the General Committee resolved to meet the cost of the new mission by a loan, until such time as the Arthington money became available, and accepted Lorrain and Savidge as missionaries of the Society.[11] The two men arrived at Lunglei on 13 March 1903.

The Mizo people were animists and nomadic cultivators, living on hill-top village sites which were periodically rotated as the soil became exhausted. Numerous sacrifices were offered to appease the spirits and ensure the fertility of the land. Head-hunting was still practised occasionally, but was being suppressed rapidly by the British, who had imposed their rule on the territory in 1893. When Lorrain and Savidge arrived in Lunglei, they found an existing Christian community of 125, the fruit of annual visits by the Welsh missionaries from the north. Only thirteen were baptized church members.[12] Lorrain and Savidge began by preaching a traditional evangelical message of salvation from the penalty of sin, but found that the Mizos had 'no sense of sin and felt no need for such a Saviour'. They changed their approach to one which proclaimed Jesus as the vanquisher of the Devil and all his powers, and found a radically different response. Once it was emphasized that the salvation which Jesus offered in the name of *Pathian* (the Mizo High God) brought both freedom from the power of evil spirits in this life and entrance into the Mizo paradise - *Pialral* - in the life to come, further conversions began to take place.[13] Lorrain in particular spoke of heaven, hell, and spiritual battles with Satan and the powers of darkness with a frankness more characteristic of an earlier missionary generation. He did so in his official reports to the BMS as much as in his preaching to the Mizos, for this was a theological vocabulary native to Lorrain's background in revivalistic evangelicalism, even if it was given a new accent in the animistic context.[14]

---

10. General Committee Minutes, 17 Dec. 1901, pp. 78-81, 18 Feb. 1902, pp. 162-3. For Arthington's bequest see below, ch. XII, pp. 381-3.

11. General Committee Minutes, 16 Dec. 1902, p. 460.

12. Hminga, *The Churches in Mizoram,* 61.

13. Ibid., 57, 62-3.

14. See, for example, IN/113, Lushai Hills Log Book, 1903-47, 13, 18, 22.

Expectations of 'revival' were instilled into the infant Mizo Christian community from an early date. Since 1905 news of the revival which had swept Wales and spread to the Welsh mission field of the Khasi hills had encouraged prayers for a similar 'revival' in Mizoram. In March 1906 a group of evangelists from both halves of the Mizoram field travelled north to attend an assembly of 10,000 Khasi Christians, and saw, in Lorrain's words, 'the Holy Spirit so marvellously poured forth, that the scenes there were described as being unmatched by anything witnessed since Pentecost'. Although the Khasi movement was thereby spread to northern Mizoram, no such results were seen in the Baptist field in 1906, apart from the conversion of some of the boys in Savidge's school at Lunglei.[15] Lorrain positively discouraged any attempt to work up revival excitement, but in April 1907 saw his prayers answered at the annual church gathering at Lunglei, when at the close of the proceedings 'the whole audience seemed to be taken possession of by the Holy Spirit, and everyone began to pray or weep or confess'.[16] In most of the villages with groups of Christians, prayer meetings were now established, meeting four or more nights a week to pray systematically for a few villages at a time. The pace of conversion quickened noticeably, with some chiefs now professing Christianity, and whole villages turning to Christ.[17]

The Welsh Revival of 1904-5 thus produced a distant echo in the hills of south Mizoram. However, other aspects of the Welsh inheritance were of even greater significance for the future development of the Baptist churches. Worship followed Methodist lines, with an emphasis on song, spontaneity, and individual testimony. Still more crucial was the adoption of the Welsh practice of the all-age Sunday school. Until 1913 there was no organized church life, for believers were scattered in over eighty different villages. Lorrain therefore adopted the practice of appointing the most mature Christian in each village as 'Sunday school superintendent', charged with teaching believers of all ages simple Christian doctrine, hymns, and reading skills. The Sunday school became the key agent both of Christian education and of evangelism, and the 'superintendent' the chief link between Lorrain and each village. The duty of every convert to bring others to Christ was stressed from the outset. All converts were similarly taught to tithe their crops to the church, which was supporting four evangelists as

---

15. Lushai Hills Log Book, 26-7.

16. *MH* (Aug. 1907), 250.

17. Lushai Hills Log Book, 34; Hminga, *The Churches in Mizoram*, 87-9.

early as 1905. Once a year the whole Baptist community gathered at Serkawn for communion, baptisms, teaching and business. When Herbert Anderson visited Mizoram in 1913, he was able to report that a church which was as yet unorganized was already self-propagating and self-supporting.[18]

After Anderson's visit steps were taken to organize churches and celebrate communion in the larger Christian villages. It was decided to reproduce in the south the presbyterian church polity of the northern Calvinistic Methodist churches. 'We are not here', explained Lorrain in the Society's annual report for 1913-14, to make the Mizo Christians

> Eastern duplicates of Western Baptists, but to bring them to Christ and to so guide them that they shall develop along their own national lines into a strong Lushai Church of God, a living witness of the Power of the Gospel to change savages into saints and head-hunters into soul-hunters.[19]

The annual gathering became the church assembly, and a presbytery was formed, comprising seventy-seven leading church members; effective control of all Christian work in the BMS field was immediately vested in the presbytery. The first Baptist pastor, Chuautera, was ordained in 1914. The Sunday school superintendents evolved into the presiding elders in charge of the village congregations, for whom annual summer schools of instruction were instituted in 1915. A training class for pastoral and evangelistic ministry was begun in 1918. General education was not neglected: by 1921 Savidge had under his supervision fifteen boys' schools, with 421 pupils.[20] Girls' education and women's work were pioneered by two long-serving missionaries - Edith Chapman (1919-52) and Marjorie Clark (1922-54). In a society which originally regarded girls as not worth educating, Chapman and Clark had by 1953 trained nearly eighty Christian girls as certificated teachers and leaders of the women's work in the villages. All education in Mizoram until 1947 was conducted by the two Protestant missions, which can thus claim most of the credit for the fact that by the

18. Anderson, Report of a Visit to the South Lushai Mission, 8-11; Lushai Hills Log Book, 13, 28, 36.

19. *BMS Annual Report*, 1913-14, p. 122, cited in Hminga, *The Churches in Mizoram*, 100.

20. *BMS Annual Reports*, 1915-16, p. 108; 1921-2, p. 21.

mid-1970s Mizoram had the second highest literacy rate of any Indian state.[21]

The clear-sighted and coherent church-planting strategy adopted in Mizoram attracted the admiration, but not the imitation, of the rest of the BMS India mission. It is hard to resist the conclusion that the imaginative nature of Mizoram's church policy was the product of the infusion into the BMS mission of ideas and influences which passed by those whose experience remained narrowly denominational. It is perhaps providential that the presbyterian polity of the Baptist churches was in place before the First World War removed 500 men from South Mizoram to serve in France with the Indian Labour Corps, among them Baptist Sunday school teachers, evangelists and elders; Lorrain himself spent four months in France ministering to the Mizo volunteers.[22] Despite the absence of Lorrain and several of the leading Christians, the church continued to grow during the war years. Indeed, it was soon after the exiles returned that the movement began which was to make Mizoram the most spectacular example of church growth in any BMS field in the twentieth century.

The first signs of heightened spiritual intensity appeared in July 1919; by the close of the year Lorrain could describe 'a wave of Revival sweeping over the Lushai country', with 'companies of joyful, Spirit-filled young men and women ... going up and down the land proclaiming by word and song the Gospel of the Cross'.[23] Worship was characterized by continuous singing and dancing, accompanied for the first time by drums; many indigenous hymns were composed. Between 1919 and 1924, the years of most rapid growth, the total Baptist community grew from 3,670 to 8,770, and church membership from 1,017 to 3,198. The rate of growth in the larger Presbyterian community to the north was slightly less, but converts there were baptized more readily, resulting in a closer correspondence between total Christian community and communicant membership. In the midst of such an influx into the churches, BMS missionaries were fearful of nominal professions and cautious in their baptismal policy - over-cautious in the judgment of Mizoram's church historian.[24] Even in Mizoram, concern that

---

21. E. Chapman and M. Clark, *Mizo Miracle* (ed. M. Sykes, Madras, 1968), 79; Hminga, *The Churches in Mizoram*, 277.

22. Hminga, *The Churches in Mizoram*, 112-13; *BMS Annual Report*, 1917-18, p. 14.

23. *BMS Annual Report*, 1919-20, pp. 18-19.

24. Hminga, *The Churches in Mizoram*, 123-4; Hminga's view is influenced by his impression that the rate of growth was lower in the south than in the north, whereas his own graphs and statistics suggest the contrary.

the church should comprise none but true believers remained uppermost in BMS policy.

Some converts did, in fact, fall away in the post-revival period in the later 1920s under the impact of what Lorrain termed 'a great tidal wave of old-time sin'.[25] An additional retarding influence may have been the impact of cut-backs in BMS expenditure following the financial crisis of 1925-6, which contributed to a decline in Sunday school attendance - apparently because funds no longer existed to buy the safety pins and other articles used to reward attendance and diligence in Scripture reading![26] The period was also a transitional one in missionary personnel: Savidge retired in 1925, and the Lorrains in 1932. W. J. L. Wenger, who arrived at the height of the revival in 1922, was hindered by his wife's illness, and was transferred to the Chittagong Hills in 1932. These BMS pioneers were replaced by two couples who were to serve the Mizo church continuously almost to the close of the missionary era, Horace and Bessie Carter (1930-59), and Frank and Florence Raper (1932-61). Edith Chapman and Marjorie Clark provided continuity between the two missionary generations.

The Baptist churches continued to grow during the 1930s and 1940s, attaining by 1949 a total Christian community of 31,079 and a church membership of 12,133. However, increasing emphasis was now placed on the maintenance of spiritual life, with many members being placed under church discipline in some years. Sporadic outbursts of revival fervour were now greeted with less enthusiasm by missionaries and church leaders alike. A new wave of 'revival' swept north Mizoram from 1935 to 1939, marked by speaking and singing in tongues, and intense emotionalism. Baptist leaders, aware of the problems being caused in the Presbyterian churches, firmly resisted the spread of the revival to the south.[27] When a group of Mizo church leaders submitted a memorandum in May 1946 to a visiting committee concerned with the political status of the territory after Indian independence, they pointed out as 'a simple statement of fact' that 'this is a Christian country'.[28] It was a legitimate assertion, but the new political consciousness implied new problems for the churches in the years ahead, for political divisions in a genuinely Christian country tend to become ecclesiastical ones.

25.   Lushai Hills Log Book, 112.

26.   Ibid., 122-3; Hminga, *The Churches in Mizoram*, 146-7. For the financial crisis of 1925-6 see below, ch. XII, pp. 383-5.

27.   Hminga, *The Churches in Mizoram*, 161-5.

28.   Ibid., 184.

II: Christian Approaches to Indian Faiths

Lorrain and Savidge were not the only BMS missionaries in early twentieth-century India who still conceived of their work in terms of a spiritual battle with the satanic forces of heathenism: such a theological perspective was shared by others, particularly those who had been trained at C. H. Spurgeon's Pastors' College or Henry Grattan Guinness's Harley College in Bow. Such missionaries tended to be attracted to the front-line work of pioneer evangelism among animistic tribal peoples. However, most of the Society's India missionaries worked in the context, not of 'primitive' animism, but of sophisticated Hinduism, and amongst them (as amongst Protestant missionaries as a whole) an alternative theological emphasis was becoming more common. It was the missionary encounter with Hinduism which placed the re-evaluation of the relationship between Christianity and other faiths on the theological agenda of the whole Christian church, and thus opened a debate that still continues today.

The sixty-five Indian missionaries who submitted opinions in advance to Commission IV of the 1910 World Missionary Conference on Christian approaches to other religions were unanimous in their view that a sympathetic attitude to India's most ancient religion was now an indispensable requirement for missionary service in India. There was less unanimity, however, on just how far sympathy should go. Some simply regarded the highest points of Hinduism as useful jumping-off points for Christian proclamation, but many went further, using the language of 'fulfilment': Christ should be presented, not as the destroyer of Hinduism, but as the one who fulfilled its noblest aspirations.[29] The new theological accent was paralleled by a gradual shift in evangelistic method from attempts to prove the truth of Christianity by rational argument to a conviction that the most powerful witness to the Hindu was a transparently holy life. As one BMS missionary pointed out in 1928, this transition was exemplified by the contrast between the emphasis at Edinburgh 1910 on 'the Missionary Message in relation to Non-Christian Religions' and that adopted by the International Missionary Council (IMC) at its Jerusalem conference in 1928 - which considered 'the Christian Life and Message in relation to Non-Christian Systems of Thought and Life'.[30]

29. *World Missionary Conference, Edinburgh 1910: Report of Commission IV* (Edinburgh and London, 1910), ch. VI; E. J. Sharpe, *Faith Meets Faith* (London, 1977), 35-6.

30. Minutes of Indian Conferences, 1924-30, paper by J. I. Hasler on 'The Christian Life and Message in Relation to Hinduism', 1.

Dr Ellen Farrer, Medical Missionary in North India, 1891-1933.

R. Fletcher Moorshead, Honorary Secretary of the Medical Mission Auxiliary, 1902-25; Medical Secretary of the BMS, 1925-34.

J. H. Lorrain, Missionary in the Lushai Hills (Mizoram), 1903-32.

George Howells, Missionary in Orissa, 1895-1906; Principal of Serampore College, 1906-29.

The advocates of 'fulfilment' were usually missionaries engaged in higher educational work rather than rural evangelism. It is no surprise, therefore, that the principal exponent of this approach within the BMS should be George Howells, Principal of Serampore College. Howells held the highest academic qualifications of any BMS missionary in this period. After his initial training at Regent's Park College in London, where he obtained both a B.A. and a B.D., he undertook Semitic studies at Mansfield College, Oxford, under G. B. Gray and S. R. Driver, and earned a B. Litt. Subsequently, while on furlough from India, he obtained the Cambridge M.A. and the Tübingen Ph.D. He received one honorary D.D. from St Andrews on his appointment as Principal of Serampore in 1906, and a second from the University of Wales in 1930 on his retirement.[31] While in Oxford, it is likely that Howells was influenced by the ideas of Monier Monier-Williams and Max Müller, the founders of comparative religion in Britain and the primary architects of the 'fulfilment' theory. His Principal at Mansfield, A. M. Fairbairn, also took a keen interest in comparative religion.[32]

In the academic year 1909-10, Howells delivered the Angus lectures at Regent's Park College on the theme of 'The Soul of India: An Introduction to the Study of Hinduism, in its Historical Setting and Development, and in its Internal and Historical Relations to Christianity'. The lectures were published in expanded form in 1913.[33] Howells' chief concern was to stress the points of similarity and contact between Christianity and Hinduism. Arguing that Semitic and Indian religion alike taught both the transcendence and the immanence of God (though Semitic religion emphasized the first, and Indian religion the second), he criticized previous missionary teaching in India for its preoccupation with the transcendence of God, to the almost total exclusion of a message more congenial to the Hindu mind - his immanence in creation and the human spirit.[34] The Hindu three-fold way of salvation through work (*karma*), knowledge (*jñāna*), and faith (*bhakti*) was paralleled within the New Testament by the respective writings of James, John, and Paul. Hence it should not be rejected as worthless, but

31. E. W. Price Evans, *Dr George Howells: Missionary Statesman and Scholar* (Baptist Union of Wales, n.p., 1966), 16.

32. E. J. Sharpe, *Not to Destroy but to Fulfil: The Contribution of J.N. Farquhar to Protestant Missionary Thought in India before 1914* (Uppsala, 1965), 43-55, 129-30.

33. According to A. de M. Chesterman, the BMS considered publishing the lectures, but decided against it (H/62).

34. G. Howells, *The Soul of India* (London, 1913), 400-2, 463-9.

purified and incorporated within the more perfect plan of salvation realised in Jesus Christ.[35] The human spirit was essentially religious, and the task of the Indian missionary was to commend the person of Jesus Christ as the one who fulfilled all the aspirations of Hindu devotion and supplied what Hinduism lacked - redemption from the power of sin.[36]

The *Missionary Herald* gave Howells' book an enthusiastic review, though it placed more stress on Howells' identification of the 'fatal defects' of Hinduism than on his positive exposition of its religious values.[37] Later the same year the *Herald* gave an equal welcome to J. N. Farquhar's *The Crown of Hinduism,* which rapidly acquired much wider renown than *The Soul of India* as an apologia for the 'fulfilment' approach.[38] After only nine months in India, Percy Bushill of the BMS Delhi mission had reached the conclusion that behind the diverse faiths of India there lay a 'religious unity' that suggested that all had, to some degree, heard the voice of God. On vacation at Simla in September 1915, Bushill read Farquhar's book in the intervals between tennis at the YMCA club, and thought both the book and the standard of play very good.[39]

Although *The Soul of India* caused scarcely a ripple on publication, it became in the more polarized theological climate of the early 1920s the chief ammunition for critics of the Society's stance on questions of biblical inspiration and higher criticism.[40] However, the issue of the relationship between Christianity and Indian faiths was hardly addressed during the ensuing controversy. A more liberal evaluation of Hinduism was espoused by a growing number of BMS missionaries during the 1920s, but more traditional views retained considerable support. In March 1928 J. I. Hasler of Agra read a paper to the BMS North India conference in which he acknowledged that he had seen 'the impress of the Divine Spirit' in the lives of devout Hindus and Muslims, and confessed that he had joined in prayer with adherents of both faiths. The missionary message to the Hindu, argued Hasler, should be founded on the superiority of Christian spiritual experi-

35. Ibid., 413-14.

36. Ibid., 404, 489.

37. *MH* (June 1913), 204-5.

38. *MH* (Nov. 1913), 48.

39. Bushill papers: circular letter VII, 6 Aug. 1915, and diary of P. N. Bushill, pp. 75, 85. On the Bushills of Coventry see C. Binfield, *Pastors and People: The Biography of a Baptist Church Queen's Road, Coventry* (Coventry, 1984), *passim.*

40. See below, ch. XII, pp. 378-9.

ence rather than credal authority.[41] Although the conference minutes record that some members took exception to Hasler's views, these were now sufficiently widely accepted for the *Missionary Herald* in 1929 to print an article by Hasler endorsing the view that both Christian and non-Christian faiths should be regarded 'not so much as bodies of doctrine as complexes of experience'.[42]

Most missionary debate within India on these issues was concerned with the Christian message to Hindus. Of the estimated 5,000 Protestant foreign missionaries in India in 1924, only twelve were engaged in work among Muslims.[43] The BMS was one of the few societies so involved. In 1914 the BMS set aside William Goldsack of Jessore, Lewis Bevan Jones of Dhaka, and Joel Lall of Delhi (an Indian home missionary learned in Arabic and Persian literature) for Muslim work.[44] Believing that knowledge of the 'tongue of the angels' was indispensable for a missionary to Muslims,[45] Bevan Jones learnt Arabic, and soon became recognized as an authority on missions to the Muslim population of India. In 1924 he attended the third international conference of missionaries to Muslims organized by the IMC in Jerusalem. The conference recommended that Islamic study centres be established in all major Muslim mission fields. The National Christian Council of India (NCC) took up the idea, with the strong support of its secretary, William Paton, and in 1926 approved the proposal to establish such a centre in India. In 1928 the NCC committee on Muslim work drafted a constitution for the centre, and appointed Bevan Jones as Principal. Financial difficulties delayed the opening of the centre till 1930, when the 'Henry Martyn School of Islamics' opened in Lahore. The name of the school was chosen by Bevan Jones in honour of the celebrated Anglican Evangelical who went to India as an East India Company chaplain in 1805. Bevan Jones served as Principal until 1941.[46]

The Henry Martyn School exercised a significant role, both through the training of missionaries from many societies for Muslim work in the Indian

---

41. Hasler, 'The Christian Life and Message', 2, 4, 12.

42. Minutes of the North India Conference, 1-7 March 1928, p. 77; *MH* (Nov. 1929), 256-8.

43. E. M. Jackson, *Red Tape and the Gospel: A Study of the Significance of the Ecumenical Missionary Struggle of William Paton (1886-1943)* (Birmingham, 1980), 111.

44. On Lall see *MH* (1924), 243-4.

45. *BMS Bengal Report*, 1915-16, pp. 48-9.

46. C. Bennett, 'A Theological Appreciation of the Reverend Lewis Bevan Jones (1880-1960): Baptist Pioneer in Christian-Muslim Relations', *BQ* 32 (1987-8), 238, 240-1.

sub-continent, and more particularly through Bevan Jones's publications, *The People of the Mosque* (1932), *Christianity Explained to Muslims* (1938) and *Woman in Islam* (written with his wife, Violet, in 1941). Through his writings Bevan Jones pioneered a theological approach to Islam which paralleled the approach to Hinduism developed by Farquhar and others in the early years of the century. Criticizing previous missionaries to Muslims for their combative and prejudiced propaganda, Bevan Jones insisted that:

> our concern as followers of Christ when dealing with Islam and Muslims should be to seek to discover and fulfil, not to destroy and supplant. We should rejoice in every evidence we can find of the presence of God's Spirit in Islam, and in every witness it makes to His Being and Majesty.[47]

The many fragments of truth in other religions were, for Bevan Jones as for Howells, evidence that 'God's Spirit is quietly at work in the hearts and minds of men'. Rejecting the pessimism of those who saw no hope of progress within the system of Islamic orthodoxy, he affirmed his faith that a 'Power' was at work within Islam that would one day confound the calculations of its most rigidly orthodox leaders and rebuke the little faith of many a Christian evangelist.[48] Nevertheless, Bevan Jones did not hesitate to assert the defects of Islam. The greatest of these was its lack of a sense of sin and of a remedy for sin: for Bevan Jones, as for Howells, Calvary remained the heart of the gospel. The missionary must preach Christ crucified, even though the Cross is a stumbling block to Muslims, no less than Jews. Pre-eminently, however, Christ would be uplifted by the Christlike spirit of his disciples, rather than by their words.[49]

The People of the Mosque was warmly reviewed by C. E. Wilson in the *Missionary Herald*.[50] In contrast, Wilson's review a few months later of the controversial American report, *Re-Thinking Missions*, was scathing in its criticism of the report for reducing the missionary motive to a concept of seeking the love and knowledge of God in fellowship with those of other

---

47.　L. Bevan Jones, *The People of the Mosque* (London, 1932), 244; cited in Bennett, 'Lewis Bevan Jones', 243.

48.　Jones, *The People of the Mosque*, 245-6.

49.　Ibid., 259, 308-9.

50.　*MH* (Dec. 1932), 294.

faiths.[51] The extreme liberalism represented by the American report never gained support in the BMS. The spectrum of views within the Society, though broader than it had once been, was narrower than the theological diversity which now characterized the Protestant missionary movement as a whole, and which had been strikingly revealed at the Jerusalem meeting of the IMC in 1928.[52] The experiential approach to other religions, so widely supported at Jerusalem, itself came under strong challenge at the Tambaram meeting of the IMC a decade later. Hendrik Kraemer's *The Christian Message in a Non-Christian World*, written for the Tambaram conference, marked a re-affirmation of the radical discontinuity between the Christian revelation and other faiths: revealed truth, not subjective religious experience, was the heart of the missionary message. The review in the *Missionary Herald* commended Kraemer's book without qualification, but also without any acknowledgment that Kraemer's missiology stood in essential contradiction to the 'fulfilment' theory, as expounded by Farquhar, Howells or Bevan Jones.[53] It is hard to discover how widely Kraemer's views gained acceptance among BMS missionaries. Undoubtedly diversity of opinion remained, but it is worthy of note that by the early 1950s Kraemer's book was being recommended to missionary candidates by Dennis Northfield (then warden of St Andrew's College, Selly Oak).[54]

III: From Mission to Church in India and Ceylon

It was the Indian mission field which first compelled Baptists to re-examine their theological convictions about the status of non-Christian religions. It was similarly in India that BMS missionaries began to grapple for the first time in the twentieth century with the process whereby power was devolved from foreign mission to indigenous church. The motive power behind this process was four-fold. In the first place, the BMS Committee, as has been seen in earlier chapters, had been seeking ever since the 1850s to move BMS work in all fields, and in India especially, towards the goal of autonomy. A second factor was the rise of Indian nationalism, which stimulated the desire of educated Indian Christians of all denomina-

51. *MH* (Apr. 1933), 80-1; see W. E. Hocking (ed.), *Re-Thinking Missions: A Laymen's Inquiry After One Hundred Years* (New York and London, 1932), 58-9.

52. *MH* (June 1928), 140-2; Jackson, *Red Tape and the Gospel*, 158-9.

53. *MH* (June 1938), 129; see H. Kraemer, *The Christian Message in a Non-Christian World* (London, 1938), 142-7, 328-32; Jackson, *Red Tape and the Gospel*, 160.

54. Information from Mr Stanley Mudd, 8.7.90.

tions to gain control of the structures of decision-making from which had they hitherto been excluded. A third and related influence was the pressure applied on all Protestant missions by the IMC, particularly after the Jerusalem conference of 1928, to take indigenization seriously. The fourth and arguably the most decisive consideration in the late 1920s and 1930s arose from the disproportionate share of BMS field expenditure taken by the India mission: the need of the Society to curtail overseas expenditure was a powerful and constant under-current assisting the flow of devolution.

1. War, nationalism and the 'church centric', 1914-25

The First World War disrupted the India mission to a considerable extent, but not disastrously. Thirty-seven BMS missionaries from all fields had enlisted for war service by 1918, and substantial numbers of Indian Christians served in the Indian Labour Corps in France, Flanders, or Mesopotamia.[55] Two BMS missionaries of German provenance, Mr and Mrs A. T. Teichmann of Chittagong, were interned.[56] Many missionaries who remained at their posts seem to have had no qualms about instructing their flocks with the 'true facts' about British war aims: T. D. Williams at Naryanganj saw such work as 'doing our bit for the Empire', but also likely to have an abiding effect in the advancement of Christ's kingdom.[57] In fact the war broadened the political horizons of many Indian Christians, particularly those who served in the forces, and hence intensified the pressure in the churches for devolution: the Society's annual report for 1918-19 welcomed the growing challenge to missionary authority as a sign of maturity, but hinted at some of the tensions which were arising as a result.[58]

The decisions taken in 1912 by the Bengal and North India conferences to terminate the recruitment of Indians to the BMS staff were soon reversed once it became clear that the flow of students for theological training had virtually dried up.[59] By 1916 the BMS had only six Indians in theological training, compared with thirty in 1901; numbers in the vernacular theological department at Serampore had plummeted from seventeen in 1912 to one. These statistics caused George Howells to warn the BMS triennial

---

55. *BMS Annual Report*, 1917-18, pp. 8, 10-11.

56. *BMS Annual Report*, 1915-16, p. 13.

57. Ibid., pp. 25-6.

58. *BMS Annual Report*, 1918-19, pp. 11-12.

59. *BMS Annual Report*, 1914-15, p. 42.

conference in 1917 that, unless something drastic were done, Indian agency would be extinct in the BMS mission within thirty years. The fundamental problem, in Howells' view, was that the bulk of the Society's Indian agency - the evangelists and assistant missionaries - were wholly dependent on the word of European missionaries for their status, security of employment, and promotion. The answer, proclaimed Howells, lay in the formation of a united Baptist church, 'and that as an indispensable preliminary to a larger United Free Church'. What J. H. Shakespeare had done, and was still seeking to do, for the Baptist Union in England, was the model to be followed in India. The BMS could set an example by becoming organically one with the Baptist Union.[60]

Howells' audience in 1917 did not need to share his penchant for dreaming ecumenical visions to perceive the force of his central point that the fatal weakness of the India mission was the disjunction between the Indian churches on the one hand and the Society's Indian agency on the other. The same point was made still more forcibly at the same conference by William Carey of Barisal, great-grandson of the founder of the BMS, and by now one of the most senior and respected missionaries on the Indian field. The mission, complained Carey, educated, employed, paid, and controlled its Indian agents without reference to the churches, thus withdrawing the natural leaders from the churches, and constituting them as a separate body of professional evangelists under a foreign organization. Carey drew on his own church-planting experience in East Bengal to affirm that the solution was not to send more men to College for training for the full-time pastorate - which would merely preoccupy the churches with questions of financial support - but rather the promotion of 'voluntary effective evangelism on a large-scale, by the local membership of the Church'. If this were encouraged, the churches would in time grow their own pastors and evangelists from the spiritual root of this common effort.[61] The conference resolved in response 'that we do now and henceforth proceed on the principle of making the church centric in all our plans'.[62]

---

60. Minutes of Indian Missionaries, 1911-17, G. Howells, 'Our Indian Agency and the Theological Student Problem', pp. 1, 2, 7, 13, 15-16. On Shakespeare see R. Hayden, 'Still at the Crossroads? Revd J. H. Shakespeare and Ecumenism' in K. W. Clements (ed.), *Baptists in the Twentieth Century* (London, 1983), 31-54.

61. Minutes of Indian Missionaries, 1911-17, W. Carey, 'The Indian Church', pp. 2, 4. Rev. William Carey of Barisal (1861-1935) was a grandson of Jabez Carey, and is not to be confused with Dr William Carey of Delhi (1850-1932), a grandson of Jonathan Carey.

62. Minutes of the Eighth Triennial Conference, 1-6 Mar. 1917, p. 9.

The phrase 'church centric' became a slogan of the India mission for the next two decades, but Carey's views on lay ministry as the key to the problem were never widely adopted; if they had been, the process of making the 'church centric' would have been a shorter and less tortuous one.

The years 1919-20 were marked in India by general political unrest, which the British authorities met with often ruthless force. The effect on Indian politics was to bring to the fore a new generation of nationalist leaders, led by Mahatma Gandhi, and to unleash the campaign of non-violent non-co-operation of 1920-22. At first the impact of the unrest on the BMS mission seemed to be limited to some student centres and Muslim districts: the BMS annual report for 1920-1 reflected with satisfaction that the Society's educational institutions in India 'deal largely with young life, and benefit a community which has not at present mixed itself up with the vital public movements of the day', while Baptist evangelism 'does not concern itself with social or political questions'.[63] This very guarded attitude to Indian nationalism, which was held by Herbert Anderson in particular, was fairly typical of Protestant missions in India at this time.[64] 1921 proved a much more difficult year in the history of the BMS mission, with major disruption to the Society's schools in the Dhaka area. Anderson's response was to dismiss non-co-operation as 'the complete denial of our missionary ideals', and the demands of some Indian Christian leaders for the merging of missions within the church and an immediate transfer of control to Indian hands as 'not practicable'.[65] Anderson has received a bad press for expressing such views as these in his role as secretary of the National Missionary Council (NMC), and in particular for opposing the replacement of the NMC by the National Christian Council in 1923.[66] In fairness to Anderson, it should be said that his own experience of Baptist churches in India convinced him that the structures necessary for effective autonomous church life were simply not yet in existence: an era of partnership between mission and church was required to develop these structures to bear the strain of complete devolution.

The Baptist experience in Bengal provides some confirmation of Anderson's views. The movement towards Baptist church union initiated

63.   *BMS Annual Report*, 1920-1, p. 11.

64.   Mathew, *Christian Missions*, 169-76; G. Studdert-Kennedy, *British Christians, Indian Nationalists and the Raj* (New Delhi, 1991).

65.   *BMS Annual Report*, 1921-2, pp. 9, 11, 16, 17.

66.   Jackson, *Red Tape and the Gospel*, 104, 106. Jackson's description of Anderson as 'devious' (apparently citing S. K. Datta) is not substantiated.

by the formation of the Bakarganj and Faridpur union in 1890 bore fruit in the formation of the Bengal Baptist Union at Barisal in May 1922. Its leading architects were William Carey and B. A. Nag of Calcutta. Nag was a convert of the Dhaka missionary, R. Wright Hay, and, as a prominent figure in Calcutta municipal affairs, became the most articulate Indian voice advocating the transfer of responsibility from the BMS to the Indian churches. The 1922 union, however, never fulfilled the hopes of its founders. There had been disagreement in the preparatory discussions over whether a union or a united Baptist church was the more appropriate goal. Attempts to involve the churches planted by the Australian and New Zealand Baptist Missionary Societies, and by the American Baptists, proved unavailing.[67] One missionary felt in retrospect that the union had been 'almost sterilized' from the beginning by wrangling over its name and constitution.[68] It was hampered by the lack of full-time officers, and even more by the unwillingness of Indians serving as BMS assistant missionaries and evangelists to transfer their allegiance from the Society to the union. They felt that to do so, while European missionaries remained independent of church authority, would merely exacerbate the sense of a racial divide between church and mission. J. D. Raw of Barisal, reviewing the problem in a paper to the Bengal conference in 1926, had to admit that, despite all the efforts since 1917 to make the church 'centric', church and mission still stood in sharp antithesis.[69]

2. Orissa, 1926-33, and Bengal, 1926-31

The financial year 1925-6 closed with an alarming deficit on the Society's accounts of £34,565. A special commission of enquiry was appointed, which made recommendations for the reduction of overseas expenditure by £18,000 a year; the lion's share of the cuts were to be borne by the India mission.[70] Closure of stations was inevitable. The commission recommended that closure should be considered wherever stations were manned by a single missionary, or restricted to one type of work, or were capable of being run from another station. The triennial conference of India missionaries, reviewing the proposals in August 1926, felt that the primary

---

67. Minutes of the Bengal Conferences, 22-28 Feb. 1922, pp. 63-5, and 19-22 Dec. 1922, pp. 5-6.

68. IN/49, anonymous fragment of letter to William Carey from Shiltong, 30 Sept. [192?].

69. Minutes of the Bengal Conference, 14-19 Feb. 1926, pp. 53-4.

70. *BMS Annual Report*, 1925-6, p. 5. See below, ch. XII, p. 384.

emphasis should rather be placed on withdrawal from stations in favour of Baptist church unions, with the BMS assisting the process where necessary by subsidies or loans of personnel. The conference saw greatest scope for such withdrawal in Bengal, and looked to the Bengal Baptist Union to step into the gap.[71] The General Committee endorsed the triennial conference's recommendations. The financial crisis thus brought about a considerable reduction in BMS work in Bengal, notably in evangelistic work and primary education. Some areas were transferred to the Union, but this was piecemeal action which failed to deal with the real issues of structure and control. Within five years the decisions taken in 1926 were being described as 'precipitate devolution'.[72]

The emergence of a more wholesome and coherent devolution policy in the India mission between 1928 and 1935 owed a good deal to the stimulus provided by the Jerusalem conference of the IMC. John Reid, successor to Herbert Anderson as India Secretary, returned from the conference fired with zeal for more rapid progress towards the creation of autonomous churches. Orissa, where a church union of limited scope had been in place since 1908 (the Utkal Christian Church Union co-ordinated evangelistic work) was again the first field to move. A special joint church and mission conference was called at Puri from 29 March to 1 April 1929 to consider how the findings of the Jerusalem conference and the ensuing NCC meeting at Madras could be applied to the Orissa field. The meeting resolved that the formation of a United Christian Council was necessary for the evangelization of Orissa, and that, to achieve this end, the mission should be 'merged in the Indian Church so that the latter may be centric in all Christian activities'.[73]

The vision delineated at Puri took four years to take flesh. The two leaders of the Puri conference - John Reid of the BMS and M. L. Jachuk from the Cuttack church district - were both dead within a year. By the Orissa missionary conference in February 1930 district church unions had been formed in all six districts of the Orissa field, but the conference judged that some of the infant unions were not yet ready to define their attitude towards the proposed united council; time was needed for both churches and conference to grasp all that would be involved in the step.[74] Hesitation

71. Minutes of the United (Tenth Triennial) Conference, 14-21 Aug. 1926, pp. 4-9.

72. Minutes of the Church and Mission Conference, Serampore, 2-6 April 1931, p. 2; see *BMS Annual Report*, 1926-7, p. 10.

73. Minutes of the Special Joint Conference held at Puri, 29 Mar.-1 Apr. 1929, pp. 1-3.

74. Minutes of the Orissa Conference, 19-24 Feb. 1930, p. 19.

was greater on the part of the Orissa churches than within the BMS: as late as March 1931 the majority of the district unions were opposed to the immediate formation of a central council. Nevertheless the unions were prepared to co-operate with the BMS in setting up a joint committee to prepare proposals on the subject for the 1932 Orissa conference.[75]

The 1932 conference, meeting at Balangir in February, accepted the proposals of the joint committee for the formation of a Central Church Council (or *Sangha*), to integrate the work of the BMS and Utkal Christian Church Union. However, the nature of the churches' hesitation was revealed in the provision that initially the Council should be responsible only for church work, the training of workers, and elementary education, leaving the mission in charge of the major institutional commitments, such as the Stewart School in Cuttack and the women's hospital at Berhampur.[76] However, the scope of the Central Church Council as eventually adopted by the 1933 conference was significantly broader. The work of the Council was to be divided into two sections: the first to deal with church affairs, defined as the primary business of the Council; and the second to cover missionary and property matters, education, medical work and all items that required the sanction of the BMS Committee. Although all BMS work in Orissa was thus in principle placed under the authority of the Utkal Baptist Central Church Council, the mission retained much of the responsibility for the day-to-day running of medical and educational work.[77]

Jerusalem 1928 gave a similar push to the process of devolution in Bengal. The Bengal missionary conference in February 1930, influenced by a report prepared by B. A. Nag for the Bengal and Assam Christian Council, resolved that 'definite steps should now be taken to frame proposals for the merging of the Baptist Mission with the Baptist Churches of Bengal'.[78] At the resulting conference between BMS and Bengal Baptist Union representatives at Serampore in April 1931, S. K. Chatterji of the LMS reported on the Jerusalem discussion on the older and younger churches, and subsequent developments within the NCC. Chatterji, one of the twelve

75. Minutes of the Orissa Conference, 6-11 Mar. 1931, pp. 10-11.

76. Minutes of the Orissa Conference, 3-7 Feb. 1932, pp. 22-4. The Stewart School for the Anglo-Indian community was founded as the Protestant European School in 1880, and later became the responsibility of the BMS. The Berhampur hospital was opened in 1907.

77. Minutes of the Orissa Conference, 24-30 Jan. 1933, pp. 22-5. Cf. French, *The Gospel in India*, 146-8.

78. Minutes of the Bengal Conference, 9-13 Feb. 1930, p. 8.

Indian delegates at Jerusalem, was the Principal of the Union High School at Bishnupur, an outstanding boys' boarding school founded in 1926 jointly by the BMS and LMS. Also present at Serampore in an advisory capacity was William Carey, veteran campaigner for church autonomy, and now officially retired. The meeting decided that the time had come for all the Baptist churches in Bengal to unite in a single body, and for the BMS to merge with that body, and cease to operate as a separate entity in Bengal.[79]

3. C. E. Wilson and the transfer of power in Ceylon and Bengal, 1931-5

The spectre of further financial crisis now re-appeared to accelerate, but also complicate, the transfer of power. On 6 October 1931 the General Committee considered the critical financial position of the Society, and approved a grant allocation to the India mission for 1932 of only £31,500, £8,500 less than the sanctioned expenditure for 1931. The allocation to Ceylon was halved from £5,000 to £2,500; it was intended that the grant would be reduced annually thereafter, to disappear entirely within ten years.[80] C. E. Wilson was despatched to the East to bring and explain the bad tidings. His first port of call was Ceylon, where he had the privilege of presiding over the most rapid and least painful transfer of control experienced by any of the Society's Eastern missions.

At a series of meetings in Colombo in the first week of December, Wilson outlined the gravity of the financial situation, and prepared the ground for the formation of the Ceylon Baptist Council. The aim was to bring under one Baptist body the distinct activities in the island of the BMS, the Ceylon Baptist Union (1895), and the Lanka Baptist Mission, the indigenous mission founded in 1887. Integration was not accepted without reservation. W. M. P. Jayatunga, who had followed his father and grandfather into the Baptist ministry, and was the first Sinhalese to train at Serampore College, favoured a bipartite arrangement, whereby the Baptist Union would be responsible for all church affairs, and the Lanka Baptist Mission for all mission station work.[81] Nevertheless, the principle of integration was accepted, albeit in a less than total form. The constitution of the Ceylon Baptist Council, adopted on 22 February 1932, assumed the continuing separate existence of the Baptist Union and Lanka Baptist Mission, and

79. Minutes of the Church and Mission Conference, Serampore, 2-6 Apr. 1931, p. 2.
80. General Committee Minutes, 6 Oct. 1931, pp. 77-8; H. J. Charter, *Ceylon Advancing* (London, 1955), 145, wrongly describes these events as taking place in 1924.
81. Ceylon Baptist Council Minutes, 1932, Appendix, pp. vi-vii.

provided for the annual election of fifteen members to the Council by a joint meeting of the assemblies of the two bodies; the BMS would nominate ten members.[82] At the first full meeting of the Council in August, J. A. Ewing, the senior BMS missionary in Ceylon, was elected chairman, and Jayatunga secretary.[83]

The mixed structure created in 1932 did not prove ideal. The churches felt inadequately represented on the Council (the Union had only ten delegates), and by 1935 it was clear that a single body responsible for all Baptist work in the island was desirable. Accordingly in July 1935 the Baptist Union and Lanka Baptist Mission were deemed to cease to exist, and the membership of the Council was broadened to comprise all missionaries, pastors, and women evangelists, plus one lay member from each church.[84] W. M. P. Jayatunga's secretary's report for the year ending August 1936 was able to reflect with satisfaction on the achievement of complete integration, and on the success of the churches in assuming so rapidly the financial burden which the BMS had thrust upon them.[85] Although the Society's original goal of total independence in finances and personnel for the Ceylon mission within ten years proved impracticable, by the 1950s the drastic reduction imposed in 1932 appeared, in Howard Charter's words, as 'a blessing in disguise'.[86] Jayatunga went on to become chairman of the Ceylon Baptist Council for many years, the first national Principal of Carey College (in 1946), the sole Ceylon delegate at the IMC meeting at Whitby (Canada) in 1947, and a keen advocate of the plans for a united church of Lanka.[87] From many angles, therefore, the devolution process in Ceylon must be judged a success. Yet the autonomous churches proved no more successful than their predecessors in terms of numerical growth. In his chairman's address to the Council in 1946, Jayatunga noted with regret that, for the last fifty years, Baptist membership had increased at an average rate of only ten new members per annum.[88] In terms of spiritual life and

82. Ibid., pp. vii-ix.

83. Ceylon Baptist Council Minutes, 1932, pp. 2, 13.

84. Ibid., 1935, pp. 16-18. However, the Ceylon Baptist Union in fact survived in some form until 1958; see below, ch. XIII, p. 429.

85. Bound with Ceylon Baptist Council Minutes, 1932-8.

86. Charter, *Ceylon Advancing,* 145-6.

87. Ibid., 104; *MH* (Aug. 1947), 70; H-R. Weber, *Asia and the Ecumenical Movement 1895-1961* (London, 1966), 230n.

88. H. R. Williamson, *The Christian Challenge of the Changing World* (BMS, London, 1946), 117.

evangelistic vision the Baptist churches were little stronger on the coming of national independence in 1948 than they had been in 1914.

Wilson's next major assignment on his 1931-2 tour was the united conference of all BMS India missionaries at Serampore in January. It was not an easy task. The European missionaries were sore at the severity of the cuts being imposed, while the Indian home missionaries, led by B. A. Nag, objected to the Society's plans to transfer them, but not the Europeans, to the authority of the Baptist unions.[89] Reports were given on the present state of church-mission relationships in Bengal, Orissa and North India. Both at Serampore, and in the provincial BMS conferences which followed, the financial crisis threw such a shadow over the discussions that Wilson found it necessary to stress that 'our concern for Indian Church organisation and for Church and Mission partnership is not merely the present result of our reduced income and a hasty desire to cast the burdens of the BMS upon other shoulders'.[90] It was a valid disclaimer, yet Wilson himself was quite explicit in telling the home Committee on his return that 'the only way ... in which the desired financial retrenchment could be achieved would be by relating all the Mission expenditure to the Church'.[91]

Wilson's tour imparted new momentum to the movement to establish a genuinely authoritative Baptist Union in Bengal. At the end of March 1932 a joint meeting of representatives of the BMS, Bengal Baptist Union, and churches not affiliated to the Union, enunciated the vital principle that all BMS missionaries as well as Indian workers should become subject to the authority of the new church body.[92] The period of engagement between the two parties that followed was not free of mistrust. When the Bengal Baptist Union voiced its suspicions in December 1933 that the BMS might not submit to the authority of the new Council, the Bengal conference minuted its regret, and drew the lesson that negotiations had centred 'too much in policies and too little in Christian faith and fellowship'.[93] Despite the tensions, the marriage went ahead. The Council of the new Bengal Baptist

89. Minutes of the (Eleventh) United Conference, 7-12 Jan. 1932, p. [17]; Visit of the BMS Foreign Secretary to Ceylon and India November, 1931-March, 1932, pp. 9-11.

90. Visit of the BMS Foreign Secretary, p. 7.

91. General Committee Minutes, 21 Apr. 1932, p. 42.

92. Minutes of the Joint Meeting of Bengal Baptist Union Executive Committee..., 26-28 Mar. 1932, p. 4.

93. Minutes of the Bengal Conference, 15-21 Feb. 1934, p. 36.

Union held its first meeting at Serampore College in October 1935. One of its first items of business was to pass a memorial resolution for William Carey, who had done so much to bring the Union into being; Carey had died in August, after fifty-one years' service in India.[94] B. A. Nag was present to see the cause into which he had latterly put his whole strength come to fruition, but by the first meeting of the General Assembly of the Union, in March 1937, he too was dead.[95] The first president of the Union was J. N. Rawson, who had served the BMS, initially at Dhaka from 1905, and since 1910 as tutor and then vice-principal of Serampore College.

4. From Mission to Church in North India

The North India mission lagged well behind in the process of devolution. Its two principal constituent areas, the Delhi-Agra district and Bihar, were hundreds of miles apart, the Baptist community was relatively small and fragmented, and few churches had pastors. BMS missionaries fulfilled demanding institutional roles in the high schools in Delhi, Agra, and Bankipore near Patna, or in the hospitals at Palwal and Bhiwani. Most were necessarily limited in their ability to participate in the life of the churches. Although district church councils were set up as early as 1916-17, the Baptist Union of North India (BUNI) was not formed till January 1948. Its first president was Alfred Haider Ali, whose personal history is a classic example of how some of the most promising 'mission boys' of the pre-1914 period became the heirs to the new era in church-mission relations inaugurated in the 1930s and 1940s.[96] Haider Ali's father (who died before he was born) was a Baptist evangelist, and his mother a teacher in the BMS Gange Girls' School in Delhi. Alfred found a foster father in the person of Stephen Sylvester Thomas, BMS missionary for thirty-six years, and warden of the Baptist hostel in the Civil Lines compound, where Alfred grew up. With a childhood so shaped by Baptist influences, it was not surprising that Haider Ali should enter Serampore College after the First World War and later be appointed as a home missionary of the Society. A broader ecumenical perspective must also have come naturally to someone reared in the Delhi mission under S. S. Thomas and C. B. Young, who

94. Minutes of the First Meeting of the Council of the Bengal Baptist Union, 3-7 Oct. 1935, p. 3.

95. Minutes of the First Meeting of the General Assembly of the Bengal Baptist Union, 25-29 Mar. 1937, p. 4.

96. *MH* (Sept. 1947), 79.

taught at the Anglican St Stephen's College and was a personal friend of the celebrated Anglican missionary, C. F. Andrews. Monthly prayer meetings with the Cambridge Mission were a regular feature of Baptist missionary life in Delhi at this time.[97] As pastor of Central Baptist Church, Delhi, in the late 1930s, Haider Ali was one of the three BMS Indian delegates to the IMC conference at Tambaram; another was Philip John, pastor at Patna and the first vice-president of the BUNI.[98] The infant BUNI thus had the benefit of able leaders of broad experience, but the problems which had delayed its formation until 1948 had not been removed, and were to re-appear in its future history.

IV: Serampore College, 1910-1949

Relatively few Serampore students demonstrated such an unambiguous return on the Society's major investment in their future as did Alfred Haider Ali. The fulfilment of George Howells' aspirations for a wider ecumenical and educational role for Serampore College necessarily made it more difficult to justify continuing Baptist responsibility for the entire financial support of the College. Following the re-opening of the higher theological department in 1910, Christian students from all denominational back-grounds were drawn to Serampore, whilst the College's re-affiliation to Calcutta University in 1911 attracted a growing number of Hindu students to the Arts Department. By 1920 the student body numbered 351, of whom only ninety-two were Christians. Almost half of those ninety-two came from the Syrian churches of South India.[99] One of the Syrian students, and the first to obtain a B.D. Honours degree from the University in 1920, was C. Eapen Abraham of the Mar Thoma Church of Travancore. Abraham joined the teaching staff at Serampore in 1925, and in 1949 became the first Indian Principal of the College. He was the founder and first secretary of the Church History Association of India, Burma, and Ceylon.[100] Abraham was a fine example of the high-calibre theological students produced by Serampore in this period. What caused alarm in the BMS Committee,

97. B. Chaturvedi and M. Sykes, *Charles Freer Andrews* (London, 1949), 70; D. O'Connor, *Gospel, Raj and Swaraj: The Missionary Years of C. F. Andrews 1904-14* (Frankfurt, 1990), 184-5, 283-5; Bushill Papers, diary of P. N. Bushill, 55, 93.

98. The other delegate was Dr Benjamin Pradhan of Cuttack.

99. *BMS Annual Report,* 1919-20, p. 12.

100. K. V. Mathew, *Walking Humbly with God: a Biography of the Rev. C.E. Abraham* (Kottayam, 1986).

however, was the lack of Baptist theological students, in both the higher and, especially, the vernacular theological departments: 'we must all realise', C. E. Wilson warned Herbert Anderson in 1916, 'that the development upon the Arts side would not compensate for the loss of men trained for the ministry of the Gospel'.[101]

The increasingly interdenominational character of the College was reflected in the revision to the Serampore Charter enacted by the Bengal Act of 1918, which brought to fruition the plans agreed at the Madras conference of 1902.[102] The old Council of five members (four of whom had to be Baptists) gave way to a new Council of thirteen members, of whom only four (plus the Principal) were Baptists. The Council met, as before, in London. Academic matters were placed under the control of a Senate, meeting in India, whose membership was so constructed as to reflect the main Protestant denominations represented in India.[103]

Almost all of the voluntary income of Serampore College derived from Baptist sources, but these were now inadequate to support the expanded scale of the institution. Protracted attempts were made to broaden the financial base of the College to parallel the changes in its governmental structure, but without success. The financial problems at Serampore grew ever more serious. In 1922 the school department was closed; it re-emerged in 1923 as the William Carey High School at Bishnupur, which amalgamated three years later with the LMS Bhowanipore school to form the Union High School (later known as the Siksha Sangha High School). In 1926 the vernacular theological department was also closed, having consistently failed to attract sufficient students to be financially viable. It was proposed to establish in its place a joint institution, serving all the Baptist churches of Bengal, and situated in a centre 'in close touch with village life'.[104]

Despite this curtailment of Serampore's activities, by December 1924 the College was in debt to the BMS to the amount of £3,000. J. H. Oldham, Secretary of the IMC and newly appointed as Master of the College, wrote a paper for the Council on the future of Serampore, which concluded that

---

101. IN/92, Wilson to Anderson, 23 Nov. 1916.

102. See above, ch. V, p. 161.

103. *BMS Annual Report,* 1920-1, p. 13; W. S. Stewart (ed.), *The Story of Serampore and its College* (Serampore, 1961), 114-15.

104. Minutes of the Bengal Executive Committee, 19-20 Nov. 1926, pp. 108-12. Vernacular theological training was later conducted initially at Barisal, then at Khulna, and finally on an interdenominational basis at Krishnagar.

only three options were available. The closure of the College and suspension of the Charter Oldham rejected as unthinkable, unless a more attractive site could be found to establish a centre of interdenominational higher theological education. The second possibility was to fulfil the terms of the Charter by continuing theological courses at some other location, probably Bishop's College, Calcutta. Although such a move might attract funding from other societies, it would be unsatisfactory from a Baptist viewpoint, and could only be a temporary solution. The third option was for the BMS to undertake full financial responsibility for maintaining the College on its present basis (which now included a science department in addition to arts and theology).[105] The Council then submitted Oldham's paper to the BMS Committee. In January 1925 the General Committee accepted the joint recommendation of the India and Ceylon and finance sub-committees that the Society should assume the entire responsibility for the maintenance of the full range of courses at Serampore.[106]

The Society was now committed to finding an extra £2,500 a year to finance the work of the College. The prolonged financial crisis into which the BMS, along with most Protestant societies, entered in the financial year 1925-6, played havoc with these plans. While drastic cuts were being imposed on the rest of the India field, the logic of the 1925 decision implied that the allocation to Serampore should, at the very least, be maintained intact. Although some reduction was in fact made to the Serampore grant, the impression was created in the India mission that the College was immune from the sacrifices demanded of the rest of the work. Those who felt that the College was doing little to serve the needs of the Baptist churches now had more tangible grounds for resentment. Their spokesman was Percy Knight, superintendent of the Calcutta Mission Press (the largest single enterprise of the India mission), who circulated a letter on the subject to all BMS India missionaries in the summer of 1927.[107]

In response to Knight's pressure, the future of the College figured prominently on the agendas of field conferences and committees held in 1928. It was now clear that the additional income hoped for in 1925 had not materialized. The nature of the dissatisfaction with the College had

105. IN/130, [J. H. Oldham], 'The Future of Serampore College: A Review of the Position, Adopted by the Council of Serampore College, December 19th, 1924'.

106. General Committee Minutes, 21 Jan. 1925, pp. 9-10.

107. M. E. Bowser, Report of a Visit to Ceylon and India October 8th, 1927-April 1st, 1928, p. 16. In 1917 the Calcutta Press employed 250 workers (*BMS Annual Report*, 1916-17, p. 159).

changed little since the 1880s: it was said that the College was impossibly expensive, wrongly located, and largely irrelevant to the life of the churches. John Reid, the India Secretary, raised the possibility of the arts and science departments being closed, and Serampore becoming a United All-India Theological College, but the College staff felt the suggestion to be impracticable.[108] At the Bengal conference in February the College faculty responded to criticism of Serampore with a re-statement of the case for 'Christianising' higher education in India, and insisted that the BMS must be prepared to put more resources into the College if it were to continue.[109] The new BMS Women's Secretary, Eleanor Bowser, touring the field at the time, heard both sides of the argument repeatedly; though impressed by the defence mounted by Serampore, she felt that the staff had failed to appreciate the volume of the criticism and the need to relate the work of the theological department to church life in the villages.[110]

The uncertain future of Serampore threw a shadow over the search for a replacement for George Howells, who wished to retire. A Council meeting held in October 1928 had to decide both whether to continue the attempt to run the College on its present lines at Serampore, and whom to nominate to the Senate to succeed Howells. The meeting resolved to carry on at Serampore, and to invite C. B. Young of Delhi to be the new Principal. Young declined the invitation, and Dr G. H. C. Angus of the College staff (and a grandson of Joseph Angus) was appointed instead.[111] For twenty years Angus had the difficult task of leading Serampore College through a period of staff shortages, political unrest in the student body, and fundamental questioning of the future of the institution.

The debate over Serampore was symptomatic of a wider questioning of the place of Christian colleges in Indian missionary strategy. In January 1929 a conference of missionary educators and Indian Christians at Agra, chaired by William Paton (successor to Oldham as Secretary of the IMC), proposed that a commission of inquiry into Christian higher education in India be appointed. The Lindsay Commission, chaired by A. D. Lindsay, Master of Balliol College, Oxford, toured the Christian colleges from November 1930 to April 1931, and published its report in September 1931. The report made various recommendations calculated to restore the

---

108. Minutes of the Serampore College Standing Committee, 20 Jan. 1928, pp. 2-5.

109. Minutes of the Bengal Conference, 10-15 Feb. 1928, pp. 20-22.

110. Bowser, *Report of a Visit to Ceylon and India*, p. 17.

111. IN/49, S. P. Carey to W. Carey, 7 Oct. 1928; Minutes of the Serampore College Standing Committee, 12 Dec. 1928, p. 8.

Christian influence of the colleges, and bridge the frequent gulf between college and Christian community.[112] It said relatively little about Serampore, even though the four other Indian colleges offering degree-level theological education were dependent on Serampore as the degree-awarding institution. The report did urge that the staff at Serampore be strengthened sufficiently to enable entirely separate arts and theological faculties to be established, and recognized that this could be done only if other denominations contributed funds and personnel. If no such support proved forthcoming, the report recommended that the BMS 'accept no further responsibility for the maintenance of the theological faculty at Serampore', and that the theological department should become a purely examining body.[113]

Many Indian Christian leaders made it plain that they regarded the idea of closing the theological department at Serampore as unthinkable.[114] In the light of such strongly expressed Indian opinion, the triennial BMS conference of January 1932 supported the continuance of the arts, science and theological departments at Serampore, provided that the Lindsay recommendations for strengthening the staff and improving the efficiency of the College met with 'a reasonable measure of success' by the end of the 1933-4 session. If this condition were not met, the conference favoured the closure of the arts and science departments. More controversially, the conference refused, in view of the serious reduction in the India allocation for 1932, to recommend that any part of it should be devoted to the College beyond 30 June 1932, but requested the College Council, in consultation with the BMS Committee, to devise means for supporting the College for the rest of the year.[115] C. E. Wilson, reporting on the meeting to the BMS Committee, deplored the proposal to cut off all supplies, and expressed the hope that somehow means would be found to keep the College going to the end of the 1933-4 session.[116]

In August the executive committee of the India conference expressed its concern that the home Committee had rejected the recommendation of the missionary staff that the College should cease to be a charge on the India

112. *Report of the Commission on Christian Higher Education in India: An Enquiry into the Place of the Christian College in Modern India* (London, 1931). For a summary and analysis see Mathew, *Christian Missions*, 202-18.

113. *Report of the Commission*, 311, 342-3.

114. Information from Rev. E. L. Wenger, 18.7.90.

115. Minutes of the (Eleventh) United Conference, 7-12 Jan. 1932, pp. 6-7, 12.

116. Visit of the BMS Foreign Secretary, pp. 14-16.

allocation, and reiterated the opinion that, 'in spite of the immense value of Serampore College to the Christian Church in India', the BMS could not afford to bear, unaided, practically the entire burden of the missionary support of the College.[117]

It was thus against the background of very real hesitation on the field as to the continued viability of the College that the BMS General Committee in July 1933 accepted the proposal of William Paton that Serampore should be one of the six colleges to benefit from a united public appeal, launched under the presidency of Lord Halifax as a result of the Lindsay Report. Inclusion in the India Colleges Appeal depended on Serampore becoming a genuinely co-operative enterprise, and for a while hopes were high of a substantial measure of co-operation from the Church of Scotland, the English Methodists, the CMS and the SPG.[118] However, by July 1934 it was clear that the Anglicans in particular were deterred by the close connection between the theological and arts departments, and that the price of co-operation in advanced theological education could be the closure of the arts department - a price which the Council conceded it might have to pay.[119] In fact, though Serampore received short-term aid from the India Colleges Appeal, only two missions in this period translated their professions of goodwill for Serampore into serious long-term support: the Church of Scotland provided one member of staff, J. F. McFadyen, from 1938 to 1946; and the Canadian Baptists contributed towards the support of another from 1947 to 1953.[120] The American Baptists and Welsh Presbyterians provided small-scale financial assistance, but nothing more. C. E. Wilson acknowledged in 1948 that 'the hope, so often expressed, of a worthy response in interdenominational support of the College has been sadly disappointed'.[121]

Other missionary societies had failed to fulfil the hopes of the BMS for more broadly based support for Serampore. A secure future for the College in post-independence India could be built only on the foundation of direct

117. Minutes of the United Conference Executive Committee, 17-18 Aug. 1932, p. 4. G. H. C. Angus voted against the resolution.

118. General Committee Minutes, 5 July 1933, p. 68; see *MH* (Jan. 1935), 16; Jackson, *Red Tape and the Gospel*, 118-20.

119. Serampore archives, Serampore College Council minutes, 10 July 1934.

120. Stewart (ed.), *The Story of Serampore and its College,* 61, 83; IN/130, Serampore College Council minutes, 14 Apr. and 9 July 1947.

121. IN/130, Serampore College Council minutes, statement by Wilson dated 6 Dec. 1948.

support from the Indian churches. That possibility could not be realized while the government of the College remained in the hands of a select group of mission executives in London. In April 1947 the College Council reached the conclusion that 'on grounds of principle and expediency, it was desirable that the Council should be transferred to India as soon as was practicable'.[122] The BMS raised no fundamental objection, although C. E. Wilson voiced his fears to the Council that the move would weaken the ties of the College to the Society whose support had more than once saved it from extinction. George Howells (who served on the Council in his retirement) had no such reservations about the dilution of the denominational basis of the College, and indeed wished to see the removal of all credal restrictions from appointments to the College staff.[123]

The question of the relocation of the Council now became closely connected with the appointment of a successor to G. H. C. Angus as Principal. Strong representations issued from the Senate in India in favour of C. E. Abraham, but there was some hesitation in BMS circles about appointing a non-Baptist. In the event, the Council agreed to leave the appointment to the newly constituted Council in India. On 2 June 1949 the old Council held its last meeting in London; seven members of the old Council resigned, and eight new members representing the Indian churches were elected in their place. Later that month the new Council met at Serampore, for the first time in ninety-four years, and elected Abraham as Principal and Angus as Master. The BMS had committed itself to continuing, for at least five years, to support the College by the provision of its annual grant of £1,000 and four members of staff.[124] The links with the Society had thus been preserved, but there could be no doubt that the College, like India itself, was entering into a new and different era in its turbulent history. However lively the debate within the BMS over the difficulty of relating the College to the needs of the Baptist churches of northern India, there can be no gainsaying the major contribution which Serampore had already made, and would continue to make, to the theological education of the leadership of the Indian churches as a whole. It is significant that in 1970 the four newly consecrated bishops of the Church of North India had all received their theological education at Serampore.[125]

122. Ibid., minutes for 14 Apr. 1947.

123. Ibid., statements by Howells, dated 23 Nov. 1948, and Wilson, dated 6 Dec. 1948.

124. Ibid., minutes for 4 and 20 Mar., 2 and 28-29 June 1949.

125. Information from Rev. E. L. Wenger, 18.7.90.

V: The Second World War and Indian Independence

The India field of the BMS was more directly affected than any other by the Second World War. Disruption was most severe in the sphere of medical work. In Mizoram and the Chittagong Hill Tracts hostilities came uncomfortably close, as the Japanese advanced through Burma and reached the borders of Assam. Considerable numbers of Royal Air Force casualties were brought in to Chandraghona hospital.[126] In 1941 Dr Hilda Bowser, returning to the women's hospital at Palwal (opened in 1914), lost her life when her ship was torpedoed and shelled. Three BMS doctors were called up for military service - R. W. Thomas of the men's hospital at Palwal (built in 1905), G. O. Teichmann of Chandraghona, and Stanley Thomas of the Moorshead Memorial Hospital at Udayagiri in the Kond Hills, newly opened in January 1939. By April 1942 a Japanese invasion of India seemed a distinct possibility, and the decision was taken to close the Berhampur women's hospital for three months; the hospital did not return to full activity until the arrival of Dr Muriel Rigden Green in 1943.[127]

The coronation of George VI in May 1937 had been celebrated at Udayagiri with a splendid procession led by three elephants from Bhanjanagar; the mahout of the middle elephant held aloft a framed portrait of the royal couple, and the missionaries proudly wore rosettes of red, white and blue. Eight years later, one of those missionaries, Gordon Wilkins, on his way home for furlough, was greeted on the platform of Khargpur station by cries of 'Quit India! Down with the British!' from a crowd awaiting the arrival of a prominent Indian National Congress politician.[128] The change in political climate that followed the end of the war was rapid, radical and unexpected. No less unexpected by most missionaries was the fact that independence on 15 August 1947 was won at the price of partition.

The greater part of the BMS field in Bengal now found itself in the new nation of Pakistan. The Bengal Baptist Union resolved to disregard the new frontier, and continue as one body for the present. Baptist work in Baraut, Bhiwani, Delhi and Palwal was caught up in the sectional violence that followed partition. In Bhiwani Hindus massacred almost the entire Muslim

126. Williamson, *The Christian Challenge*, 66; M. I. M. Causton, *For the Healing of the Nations* (London, 1951), 150.

127. Berhampur Christian Hospital archives, station committee minutes, 1938-47, and *Christian Hospital Berhampur: Souvenir Programme, November 4th 1967*.

128. E. G. Wilkins, *By Hands, Bullocks and Prayers: Building the Moorshead Memorial Hospital Kond Hills, Orissa, India* (n.p., 1987), 66, 162.

population; many villages around Palwal were destroyed, and their inhabitants killed; in Delhi, Hindus and Sikhs united in attempts to drive the Muslims out. BMS missionaries in the affected areas were involved in medical care and humanitarian relief to refugees: at Bhiwani hospital staff operated round the clock and performed 300 dressings a day.[129] There was as yet no suspicion that the foreign missionary era in the Indian subcontinent might be drawing to its close: an article in the *Missionary Herald* for October 1946 by the India Secretary, D. Scott Wells, outlined the need for eighty-one new 'European or Indian' missionaries required for India, most of whom were clearly expected to come from Britain.[130] Nevertheless, the months and years that followed independence were to prove a severe test of the capacity of the newly-autonomous Baptist churches to meet the challenges of the post-colonial era.

129. *BMS Annual Report,* 1947-8, pp. 12-15.
130. *MH* (Oct. 1946), 82-5.

X

China, 1912-1952

I: Building the New China, 1912-1925

The Revolution of 1911-12 appeared to herald a new day for Christian missions in China.[1] For the first time in modern Chinese history, there was unlimited freedom to propagate Christianity, and a general receptivity to its teaching. 'The very air seems charged with opportunity for the presentation of the Christian message', observed Harold Balme of Jinan in 1913.[2] The change in public attitudes to missionaries since 1900 was 'a moral miracle of the first magnitude', agreed E. W. Burt in 1916.[3] China had turned its back on reaction and isolation, and stood ready to appropriate all that the West had to offer to facilitate national reconstruction and progress. These were years in which mission funds were in ample supply, at least from the American societies. As a result, the Protestant missionary force in post-1912 China invested massively in major institutional projects intended to shape the new China in the image of the Christian West. The BMS had neither the resources of the biggest institutional spenders nor the inclination (displayed by some other missions) to neglect traditional evangelism. Yet the Society undoubtedly participated in the shift of strategic emphasis. The Arthington Fund enabled the BMS to fund major new projects on a scale matched in no other period in its history. Moreover, the missionary strategy for the national regeneration of China marked the adoption of ideas which derived in part from the Society's most senior China missionary - Timothy Richard. In the spheres of education, women's

1. For a much fuller account of the BMS China mission, 1912-52, readers are referred to the excellent book by H. R. Williamson, *British Baptists in China 1845-1952* (London, 1957). Williamson's account underpins most of what follows.

2. *MH* (Feb. 1913), 57.

3. *MH* (Sept. 1916), 199.

work, Christian literature and medicine, the BMS greatly expanded its activities during this period.

The Republican Revolution created an insatiable hunger for education at all levels. Elementary schools sprang up in thousands of villages. Enrolment in the BMS village schools and the boarding schools at Chingzhou, Taiyuan, Xian and Fuyincun increased tremendously, and there was no resistance to compulsory attendance at Christian worship and religious instruction. Girls' education in particular expanded as women began to seek emancipation from their oppressive domestic seclusion and an entrance into the public sphere. From a Christian perspective the danger, warned Miss M. E. Shekleton of the BMS Shaanxi mission, was of an uncritical espousal of what was imagined to be a Western model of womanhood and a repudiation of all 'home duties and joys'.[4] For the first time girls received government encouragement to gain access to higher education, and mission schools for girls proliferated. The small number of Baptist Zenana Mission workers now came into their own, especially in Xian, where a centre for women's work enjoyed great success under the leadership of M. E. Shekleton, Jennie Beckingsale, and others. Miss Beckingsale is typical of the highly qualified single lady missionaries whom the advances in women's higher education in Britain were now making available to the missionary movement: a scholar of Somerville College, Oxford, and a graduate of Trinity College, Dublin, her work as Principal of the BMS girls' boarding school in Xian was cut short by her death from peritonitis in June 1913.[5]

The greatest challenge and opportunity for the missions in Republican China lay at a higher educational level. 'How is it that there are so few men of learning in the Christian Church?' was a disturbing question constantly being posed amongst Chinese students. The obvious answer was that under the Qing regime all holders of government office (which meant almost all educated people) had to participate in Confucian ceremonies; Christianity had offered little attraction for the student class.[6] Now that educated attitudes to Christianity were so much more favourable, Protestant missions held high hopes of winning the intelligentsia for Christ through Christian colleges and such agencies as the Christian Literature Society (CLS) and the YMCA. The strategic vision of Timothy Richard was now widely shared.

---

4.   *MH* (Sept. 1913), 289-90.

5.   *MH* (Aug. 1913), 257-8. Women could not matriculate at the University of Oxford until 1920.

6.   See H. R. Williamson in *MH* (Oct. 1914), 299-300.

Co-operation between China missions in higher education was largely a by-product of the Boxer rising. Missionaries thrown together by evacuation to the safety of the treaty ports conferred on what needed to be done to counteract what they regarded as the 'ignorant superstitition' of the Boxers, and fastened on co-operative enterprise in higher education as the principal answer.[7] The first union institution to be founded as a result was the Shandong Christian University (SCU), established in 1904 by the BMS and the American Presbyterian Mission.[8] Other missions joined later.

Until 1917 the SCU was a federal institution, comprising a theological school at Chingzhou (formerly the BMS Gotch-Robinson Institute for the training of pastors, evangelists and school-teachers), an arts college at Weixian, and, from 1910, the Union Medical College at Jinan. In 1917 the three departments were brought together on one ample site at Jinan, known as Cheloo University. The former premises at Chingzhou were converted into a high-grade middle school, to feed pupils into the SCU. The purchase of the Jinan site and erection of the medical college were made possible through Arthington Fund grants: C. E. Wilson observed wryly in 1926 that Arthington himself 'would perhaps have been more surprised than pleased' if he knew that his money had laid the foundations for a Christian university.[9] 'Institutional' mission - which Arthington certainly deplored as a diversion from mobile evangelism - was now accepted as an indispensable ingredient of a common strategy for the conversion of China: 'China must be won by Chinese' was the title affixed to an article by E. W. Burt in the *Missionary Herald* in 1917 describing the planned relocation of the SCU at Jinan.[10]

To some extent these high ideals for the SCU were realized. Years later Burt was able to reflect on his own twenty years of service in the university (1905-25), and draw satisfaction from the knowledge that many of his former students were indeed exercising influential roles in Christian leadership throughout China.[11] In 1925 the SCU received a charter from the Canadian government to confer degrees in arts, science, medicine and theology. It was an achievement which indicated the stature of the univer-

---

7.   CH/56, MS autobiography of E. W. Burt, p. 36.

8.   The close co-operation between the BMS and the American Presbyterian mission in Shandong originated in the deep friendship between Timothy Richard and J. L. Nevius.

9.   *MH* (Nov. 1926), 254.

10. *MH* (Jan. 1917), 13-15.

11. CH/56, MS autobiography of E. W. Burt, p. 43.

sity's influence, but also symbolized the entrance of the institution into a new era in which the missionary societies could no longer dictate policy. Wilson and R. F. Moorshead wrote to the BMS staff at SCU in 1928, warning that the greatly increased scale of the university was in danger of undermining its missionary purpose and saddling the Chinese church with a burden it could never support.[12]

Arthington money also made possible the two most notable examples of BMS involvement in what might be called 'educational evangelism.' The Taiyuan student institute, museum and preaching hall, erected in 1910, was a co-operative venture between the BMS and the YMCA. Under the leadership of H. R. Williamson, this evangelistic ministry was aimed at the students of Shanxi University and the higher officials in the provincial capital.[13] Still more influential were the museum and institute, founded by J. S. Whitewright at Chingzhou in 1887, and re-located at Jinan in 1905. The Whitewright Institute and Museum typified the new missionary confidence that Western science and natural history had a part to play in reaching educated Chinese for Christ. Scientific demonstration was, however, regarded as a *praeparatio evangelica,* rather than (as in Richard's more fanciful moments) spiritually efficacious in its own right. The visitors who flocked to the Museum, soon averaging a thousand a day, were welcomed into the neighbouring preaching hall for evangelistic preaching and spiritual counselling.[14] From 1917 the Institute and Museum functioned as the extension department of the SCU, earning the praise of the American mission leader, Robert E. Speer, as 'the most effective piece of university extension work which can be found in Asia, if not in the world'.[15] Whether it was effective in strictly evangelistic terms is harder to establish. H. R. Williamson, who succeeded Whitewright as director following his death in 1925, certainly believed that the Institute did much to break down anti-Christian prejudice in Jinan, and thus prepare the way for the Christian message.[16]

Literature was no less important than educational work as a means of disseminating Christian principles in the new China. The connections between the BMS and the CLS remained extremely strong after 1912.

---

12. CH/64, Wilson and Moorshead to BMS staff at SCU, 17 Feb. 1928.

13. J. B. Middlebrook, *Memoir of H. R. Williamson* (London, 1969), 22.

14. See obituary of Whitewright in *MH* (Feb. 1926), 35-6; Williamson, *British Baptists in China,* 201-2.

15. Middlebrook, *Memoir of H. R. Williamson,* 33.

16. Williamson, *British Baptists in China,* 202-3.

Richard served as secretary of the CLS until his retirement in November 1915; during the twenty-four years of his period of office it published over 300 Chinese titles. Evan Morgan, who had joined Richard in 1906, continued to work for the CLS until his retirement in 1935. Another BMS missionary, Albert Garnier, served the CLS from 1926 to 1937, and was joint general secretary from 1929 to 1930. Whereas Richard had seen Christian literature primarily as an evangelistic agency directed at the scholar-official class, the accent under his successors fell more on the production and translation of works that would promote theological and Christian education - such as James Hastings' *Dictionary of the Bible, Encyclopedia of Religion and Ethics,* and *Dictionary of Christ and the Gospels,* which all appeared in Chinese translation between 1923 and 1935.[17] After the Communist revolution, the Baptist tradition in the production of Chinese literature was maintained by two former BMS China missionaries through two "special projects" which the Society adopted in 1953: Hubert Spillett was based in Hongkong as general secretary of the Council on Christian Literature for Overseas Chinese; while Jim Sutton worked from Kuala Lumpur as the distribution secretary for Christian literature of the Malayan Christian Council.[18]

The years after 1912 also saw the coming to fruition in China of the strengthened commitment of the BMS to medical work expressed by the formation of the Medical Missionary Auxiliary in 1901. Although the old rationale for medical missions as a wedge to gain an entrance for the gospel into hostile territory now appeared redundant, the evangelistic potential of mission hospitals as 'an object lesson in aggressive altruism' was greater than ever in the new climate.[19] BMS strategy from 1913 aimed at the centralization of medical work in six centres in the three provinces: at Chingzhou, Zhoucun, and Jinan in Shandong; at Taiyuan in Shanxi; and at Xian and Sanyuan in Shaanxi. Major hospitals were already in existence at Chingzhou and Taiyuan (the Schofield Memorial Men's Hospital from 1907, and the Arthington Women's Hospital from 1912). At Xian there was a small, mud-walled hospital. The hospital at Sanyuan was as yet uncompleted. In 1913 the MMA launched an appeal to fund the construction of major new hospital premises at Xian, Zhoucun and Jinan. It was a bold move at a time when the Baptist Union was seeking to raise £250,000 for a Sustentation

---

17. Ibid., 254, 256-7.

18. A third 'special project' adopted in 1953 was the experimental Brazil mission; see below, ch. XV.

19. H. Balme, 'The mission hospital and the Christian church', *MH* (Feb. 1913), 57-9.

Fund.[20] Nonetheless, enthusiasm among British Baptists for China medical missions was buoyant, in part because of the tragic deaths in March-April of two of the Society's best-known China doctors - Cecil Robertson and H. Stanley Jenkins, who both died of typhus in Xian.[21] Their deaths proved powerful sources of inspiration. Within a few months the required sum of over £9,000 was raised. Substantial additional funds were once again provided by the Arthington Fund.

The new hospital at Xian, which Robertson and Jenkins had planned, was opened in their memory in 1917. The Foster Hospital at Zhoucun, financed to a large extent by the family of Charles F. Foster of Cambridge, was completed in 1915. In the same year the teaching hospital at Jinan was opened as an adjunct to the Union Medical College, established in 1910 as a branch of the SCU. The prime mover in the building of the hospital and the leading figure in the Medical College was Dr Harold Balme, an associate missionary of the BMS, author of *China and Modern Medicine* (1921), and President of the University from 1921 to 1927.[22] Under Balme's leadership, and with the financial assistance of the Rockefeller Foundation, the College expanded to become one of the two premier centres of Christian medical education in China.[23] The College included a nurses' training school from 1914. After the closure in 1916 of the medical schools at Hangzhou and Nanjing, the College became a much broader inter-mission enterprise, and began to train medical personnel for mission hospitals throughout north, east and central China. In 1923 the Beijing Union Medical College for Women was merged into the SCU College, which thus became responsible for the training of Christian women doctors.

Being a missionary doctor in China in this period was a hazardous business. Six BMS doctors died from disease between 1913 and 1923. Robertson and Jenkins in 1913 were followed by John Lewis at Taiyuan in 1916 (from typhus), Thomas Scollay at Xian in 1918 (from pneumonia), G. K. Edwards at Taiyuan in 1919 (from typhus) and Andrew Young at Sanyuan in 1922 (again from typhus).[24] Edwards' death came only a year after he and H. R. Williamson had escaped unscathed from a period at

20. *MH* (Nov. 1913), 362-5; R. F. Moorshead, *'Heal the Sick': The Story of the Medical Mission Auxiliary of the Baptist Missionary Society* (London, 1929), 84-8.

21. R. Glover, *Herbert Stanley Jenkins* (London, 1914); F. B. Meyer, *Memorials of Cecil Robertson F.R.C.S. of Sianfu* (London, 1913).

22. Balme was affiliated to the BMS, but supported independently.

23. The other being the Beijing Union Medical College.

24. On Young see J. C. Keyte, *Andrew Young of Shensi* (London, 1924).

Taizhou in North Shanxi assisting the authorities in combating an epidemic of pneumonic plague.[25] The problems of filling missionary ranks decimated by typhus were compounded by some disastrous episodes in the history of the hospitals themselves: the Memorial Hospital at Xian was damaged by an earthquake in 1921, and more severely by the explosion of the nearby government powder magazine in 1922; a year later the men's hospital at Taiyuan was burnt down and had to be rebuilt. Despite these cumulative blows, the China medical mission continued to expand up to 1925, when there was a complement of fourteen British and seven Chinese doctors, and ten British nursing sisters.[26]

This level of medical staffing was never again reached. The diminished financial resources of the Society after 1925, and the further deterioration in political stability in northern China were two of the reasons. The Republican Revolution had signally failed to bring the anticipated new order to China. The death of Yuan Shikai in 1916 was followed by a decade of civil war, when most of northern China fell into the hands of warlords and brigands; only in the south did Sun Yat-sen's Guomindang government exercise any real authority. In Shandong the problems of lawlessness were compounded by the presence from 1915 to 1929 of Japanese armies, staking their claim, as the Germans had done before them, to informal imperial influence. As the 1920s proceeded, Baptist work in parts of the province became impossible to sustain. By 1929 Chingzhou struck a visiting BMS deputation as like 'a dead city', controlled by bandits, with almost all BMS work closed.[27] The heady idealism with which most Protestant missionaries had greeted the Republican regime in 1912 was no more, not least because anti-foreignism, apparently expunged from Chinese national consciousness in 1911-12, was now once again rampant - in a more sophisticated and dangerous guise than ever before.

II: Anti-Foreignism and Missionary Education, 1922-1934

During 1922 a wave of anti-foreign and anti-Christian sentiment swept through the universities and colleges of China. For the first time, Christian missions were denounced, not just as tools of foreign influence, but in specifically Marxist-Leninist terms as handmaidens of the forces of capitalist imperialism. At the same time, Sun Yat-sen was turning from a

25. *MH* (Aug. 1918), 95-9.

26. Williamson, *British Baptists in China*, 245-6.

27. CH/12, Duplicate Book of C. E. Wilson's 1929 Deputation Tour, p. 9; CH/46, Wilson to BMS colleagues, 17 May 1929.

pro-Western orientation to a pro-Communist stance. Opposition to Western imperialism now became the dominant motif of Chinese nationalism, and mission schools and colleges were repeatedly attacked over the next few years as instruments of cultural aggression. The primary means which the missions had adopted to build the new China now bore the brunt of nationalist antipathy.[28]

The anti-foreign movement entered a second and more militant phase after 30 May 1925, when twelve Chinese demonstrators were killed by British police in the Shanghai international settlement. Nationalism - especially its left-wing variant expressed by the infant Chinese Communist Party - now acquired an appeal that many educated Chinese found almost irresistible. The impact on all institutions of higher education was serious. In the middle of their examinations the students at SCU went on strike, and joined the anti-British demonstrations in Jinan. The university senate agreed not to penalize the students, re-scheduled their exams, and expressed sympathy with their demands for an impartial investigation into the Shanghai incident. Some of the missionary staff were deeply unhappy with this policy. H. H. Rowley of the BMS, who taught biblical studies in the School of Theology, was appalled that supposedly Christian students and a professedly Christian institution should appear to condone demonstrations which incited people to murder foreigners. Rowley submitted his resignation to the university, but was persuaded to withdraw it after the senate passed a more reflective resolution. This warned students that the legitimate expression of patriotism could not be permitted to interfere with the educational objectives and best interests of the university.[29]

On occasion the heightened political tensions imposed considerable strain on relationships between missionaries. The bulk of missionary opinion now favoured an explicit repudiation of 'extraterritoriality' and any reliance on treaty rights. However, a minority of Protestant missionaries - of whom Rowley was one - regarded such a view as pure sentimentalism, and held some form of treaty protection to be a necessary guarantee of religious liberty in a nation which had no effective governmental authority.[30] Similar disagreements surfaced in 1927, following serious anti-foreign riots in Nanjing and the rapid northward advance of the Nationalist armies.

28.   B. Stanley, *The Bible and the Flag* (Leicester, 1990), 14-15, 142-3.

29.   CH/64, Rowley to Wilson, 12 June and 14 Aug. 1925; Paper by Rowley on 'Mission schools and Chinese politics'; Minutes of Special Meeting of Senate of SCU, 29 July 1925.

30.   CH/64, Rowley to Wilson, 8 Mar. and 1 May 1926.

Most BMS missionaries, along with many from other Protestant societies, were withdrawn from inland China on British consular advice. The SCU continued to function, but with only about one-third of its students, and just two foreign members of staff. Some missionaries felt that the withdrawal was premature, cowardly, and liable to misinterpretation by the Chinese. Henry Payne of Jinan wrote an article to this effect in the *Missionary Herald,* commending Catholic missionaries for staying put.[31] However, others in the Society regretted Payne's article, and felt that consular advice should be respected.[32]

The most serious problem posed by the anti-foreign movement to the missions was the demand that all mission schools and colleges should submit to government registration. Pressure for registration mounted from 1926, and became intense after the unification of most of China under the new Nationalist government set up by Chiang Kai-shek in Nanjing in 1927-8. The price of registration was the elimination of all Christian teaching from the curriculum in primary schools, and the making of all such teaching voluntary in higher-level schools. For Christian colleges and universities, registration would mean the removal of any explicit reference to Christian objectives from an institution's statement of purpose. The initial attitude of the BMS Committee was to resist registration at such a high price. 'The schools and colleges which a missionary Society maintains must be *missionary* in the fullest possible sense', insisted C. E. Wilson in the *Missionary Herald* for January 1928; one of their purposes was unashamedly to win converts for Christ.[33] However, the growing numbers of Chinese Christians who sympathized with nationalist aspirations saw the matter differently: for them, to refuse to register was a betrayal of national loyalty. The issue first came to a head in relation to Shandong Christian University.

In November 1928 both the senate and the field management board of SCU voted in favour of registration. They were influenced by the lobbying of the new acting President of the university, Li Dianlu, who had the strong support of the Chinese staff and students.[34] Confronted with this evidence,

31. *MH* (July 1927), 157-8.

32. E.g. CH/64, Rowley to Payne, 11 July 1927, and Rowley to Wilson, 13 July 1927.

33. *MH* (Jan. 1928), 7; see also CH/64, Wilson to Rowley, 20 Sept. 1927.

34. CH/64, Rowley to Wilson, 11 Nov. 1928. The field board contained representatives of the supporting missions; it was subject to the Board of Governors, which met in two sections, in London (the BMS section) and New York (the American Presbyterian Mission section).

first the British section of the board of governors and then the BMS China sub-committee dropped their earlier opposition to registering SCU, and accepted the university's new statement of purpose, which spoke only of maintaining the 'spirit of love, sacrifice, and service' of its Christian founders. The China sub-committee was not unanimous in its decision: T. M. Bamber, pastor of Rye Lane Chapel, Peckham, voted against.[35] Bamber saw the decision as 'a death blow ... to the vital spiritual work in China', and warned Wilson that 'those whose hearts are keen on evangelism and not on higher education will give even more than now to the CIM at the expense of the BMS'.[36] Those like Bamber who had never been keen on higher educational work were hardly likely to approve the change of policy. More worrying to C. E. Wilson was the consequent resignation, both from the university and from the BMS, of one of his most promising young missionaries, H. H. Rowley. Rowley, a member of Melbourne Hall, Leicester, had been increasingly unhappy with the pro-Nationalist stance of his Chinese colleagues; he objected strongly, for instance, to the decision of the senate in November to introduce the Nationalist memorial service to Sun Yat-sen as a regular substitute for morning prayers.[37] To Rowley the issue raised by registration could be put with stark evangelical simplicity:

> Either this University stands for a definitely and aggressively Christian purpose, or it does not. If it does, then it seems to me to be the only honest thing to say so clearly and unashamedly, when the Government asks us to define our purpose. If it does not, then it ought to, since it is supported with funds subscribed specifically for aggressive Christian work.[38]

Political realities were compelling the Society and its missionaries to engage in a fundamental re-examination of the objectives of Christian involvement in education. In view of the seriousness of the questions currently confronting the China mission, the Society sent C. E. Wilson and a senior member of the Committee, W. Parker Gray of Northampton, out to China in March 1929. Wilson cabled Rowley to delay the implementation of his resignation

35.   China Sub-Committee Minute Book No. 10, Minutes for 12 Dec. 1928, pp. 181-3. The voting was 16 to 1, with 5 abstentions.

36.   CH/46, Bamber to Wilson, 20 Dec. 1928.

37.   CH/64, Rowley to Wilson, 11 Nov. 1928.

38.   CH/64, Rowley to Li Tien-lu, 7 Jan. 1929; see also Rowley to Wilson, 4 and 7 Jan. and 9 Aug. 1929.

until he arrived, but in vain. Rowley left China in February, and in October 1930 was appointed Assistant Lecturer in Semitic Languages at University College, Cardiff, the first stage in what proved to be a glittering career in British biblical scholarship.[39] The SCU finally registered with the Nationalist government in 1931, although the School of Theology was excluded.

The decision to register reached in December 1928 applied only to SCU; the question of whether BMS schools should be registered was left to the deputation to investigate. The issue dominated the whole deputation tour. Wilson and Parker Gray found Chinese Christian opinion unanimous in favouring registration as a means of removing from BMS schools any suspicion of being subversive in their purpose; church leaders saw no difficulty in carrying on religious instruction in the schools on a voluntary basis.[40] Missionary opinion was less enthusiastic. At the inter-provincial conference at Taiyuan in May it was clear that a minority of missionaries still opposed registration, whilst the majority saw it as regrettable, but to be preferred to closure.[41] The conference decided to recommend that the home Committee approve registration of Baptist middle schools for a trial period of one year. This recommendation was approved by the China sub-committee in September (by a vote of 29 to 2), and by the General Committee in October. An explanatory article in the *Missionary Herald* stressed that the Society was prepared to close its China schools if registration proved to inhibit 'the missionary effectiveness of the schools in winning young life to Christ'.[42]

Registration of the BMS schools in Shanxi and Shaanxi followed. In Shandong, events took an unexpected turn. When application was made to the provincial education authority to register the boys' and girls' high schools at Chingzhou, the applications were rejected, apparently because religion still appeared on the school curricula, albeit on a voluntary basis (as the central government in Nanjing specifically allowed).[43] When the Council of the Shandong Baptist Union met in December 1929, opinion had hardened significantly against registration. Baptist leaders now saw no

39. CH/64, telegram from Wilson to Rowley, Jan. 1929; Rowley to Wilson, 9 Oct. 1930. See G. W. Anderson, 'Harold Henry Rowley 1890-1969', *Proceedings of the British Academy* 56 (1970), 309-19.

40. CH/46, Wilson to BMS colleagues, 17 May 1929, separate letter on registration.

41. CH/12, C. E. Wilson, Diary of China Deputation Tour, 7 May 1929.

42. China Sub-Committee Minute Book No. 10, minutes for 17 Sept. 1929, pp. 203-4; *MH* (Nov. 1929), 253-6.

43. CH/57, F. S. Drake to C. E. Wilson, 8 Oct. 1929.

hope of squaring the Christian character of their schools with the government regulations, and recommended that the schools be closed. A few days later the assembly of the Union accepted the Council's recommendation, despite the violent irruption into the meeting of a crowd of protesting students, who kidnapped eight of those present and dragged them off to the local National Party headquarters. Missionaries welcomed the Union's action as a sign of the maturity and integrity of the Shandong church. F. S. Drake of Chingzhou even claimed the outcome as one which missionaries had sought all along: the rejection of registration had to be a spontaneous expression of Chinese Christian opinion, rather than imposed from London.[44]

The Shandong decision led to the closure of all Baptist schools in the province except for a few kindergarten and elementary schools. The Baptist Union put its energies instead into a rural education and literacy scheme, which made about 2,000 Baptists literate over the next four years. However, missionaries and the Shandong Baptist Union both soon came to regret the closure of the Shandong schools. With the boys' middle school at Taiyuan having shut down in 1928 for lack of staff, there was now no post-primary education for boys anywhere in the China mission. As a senior middle school certificate was the entrance qualification for SCU, the effect on Baptist recruitment to the university was serious. By early 1934 only twenty-one out of 575 students at SCU were Baptists; in 1925 one-third had come from Baptist schools.[45] The institution which had been commended to British Baptists in 1917 as the means of training Chinese leaders to win China for Christ had been cut off from its roots in Baptist church life.

III: Church, Mission and Politics, 1922-1935

'The central and practical problem which attracts me in China as in the International Council in Jerusalem last year', commented C. E. Wilson at the end of his deputation tour in 1929, 'is the growth of the Indigenous Church and its relation to the Older Churches through which the Christian faith has been received'.[46] Visiting China after an interval of twenty-two years, Wilson had been much impressed by the remarkable growth of the Chinese church and the quality of its leadership.[47] But he had also been

---

44. Williamson, *British Baptists in China*, 135-6; *BMS Annual Report*, 1929-30, p. 12; CH/57, Drake to Wilson, 23 Dec. 1929.

45. Williamson, *British Baptists in China*, 136; General Committee Minutes, 20 July 1932, pp. 57-8, and 6 Feb. 1934, pp. 6-8.

46. CH/12, Duplicate Book of C. E. Wilson, p. 92.

disturbed by the amount of institutional 'luggage' which now seemed to be regarded as essential to the missionary enterprise in China. His visit to SCU at Cheloo left him with decidedly mixed feelings: 'It is the most uncomfortably fine place I was ever in. Serampore is a modest villa beside this palace - or group of palaces'. Hearing of the current American plans to pull down the existing teaching hospital and build another of 200-250 beds at vast expense left Wilson 'very sceptical and disquieted as to the effect of all this display of wealth to the Chinese'. He seriously questioned whether such a lavish outlay of foreign money was helping or hindering the growth of a truly indigenous Chinese church.[48] In the new political climate created by the anti-foreign movement, the splendid institutions constructed by the missionary expansion of 1910-25 began to seem more of a liability than an asset. Christianity in China now had to travel light or not travel at all.

1922 - the year in which antiforeignism again reared its head in China - also saw the first and decisive steps taken towards the establishment of an indigenous Chinese Protestant church. The China Continuation Committee set up in the wake of the Edinburgh World Missionary Conference had prepared the way for the meeting in Shanghai in May 1922 of a National Christian Conference. 'The one burning issue of the Conference', reported the *Missionary Herald*, 'was Chinese leadership', and its chief outcome was the creation of the National Christian Council of China, comprising fifty-one Chinese and forty-three missionary members. Its first Baptist members were Harold Balme, Frances Coombs of Taiyuan, and Zhang Sijing, the senior Shandong pastor who later became General Secretary of the Shandong Baptist Union.[49] Although the Council was to be a central agency serving the various Protestant churches, rather than an authoritative ecclesiastical body, its establishment was widely interpreted as 'the founding of the Church of China'.[50]

The coming together between 1922 and 1927 of the 'Church of Christ in China' was a distinct but related development.[51] Originating in the Presbyterian communion, the Church of Christ in China was formalized in October 1927 as a federation connecting churches mainly of Presbyterian or Congregational background. Two of the Shandong Baptist pastors

47. General Committee Minutes, 9 Oct. 1929, p. 157.

48. CH/12, Duplicate Book of C. E. Wilson, pp. 28-30, 97; Diary of China Deputation Tour for Apr. 1929.

49. *MH* (Apr. 1923), 107.

50. *MH* (Aug. 1922), 155-8.

51. Bob Whyte, *Unfinished Encounter: China and Christianity* (London, 1988), 157.

attended the inaugural assembly, and returned home 'convinced that the union was in the Divine plan'. As a result, the Shandong Baptist Union in December decided unanimously to affiliate. 'It is surprising to us who have been brought up in a denominational atmosphere', observed Henry Payne in the *Missionary Herald,* 'to see how little the Chinese care for these distinctions'.[52]

Payne welcomed the decision of the Shandong Baptist Union as a sign that the general withdrawal of BMS missionaries in 1927 had not left the Chinese church 'like a man stumbling aimlessly in a dense fog'. Although missionaries were able to return during 1928, the losses of 1927 were never wholly made good: the total BMS China staff in May 1929 was only ninety-five, compared with 142 in 1925. E. W. Burt, who had been appointed as the Society's first full-time China Secretary in 1925, saw the evacuation of 1927 as a blessing in disguise. It had weaned the Chinese church from its total dependence on the foreigner, and elicited 'the unsuspected latent powers of our Chinese leaders'. Nevertheless, Burt still appealed to the home constituency to send the recruits needed to plug the yawning gaps in missionary staffing.[53] Similarly, the overwhelming impression which Chinese leaders themselves left on C. E. Wilson during his 1929 tour was that, if the China mission were to be saved from rapid decay, it must have more missionaries, especially those with theological and educational training.[54] There was as yet no suspicion that the days of the foreign missionary in China might be numbered. 'Need for adjustment of our plans and relationship with the Chinese Church there certainly is', Wilson concluded, 'but no less need for keen and earnest evangelistic men with the pastoral spirit.'[55] However, whilst BMS numbers did recover slightly after 1929, the peak level of 1925 was never surpassed: the total missionary force fluctuated around the 100 mark during the 1930s, and declined sharply in 1939 and again after 1945.[56]

The participation of the Shandong Baptist Union in the Church of Christ in China had been secured on the understanding that the Baptist churches could retain their distinctive character and autonomy.[57] Anxiety

---

52. *MH* (Feb. 1928), 32-3. Some Methodist churches also joined.

53. *MH* (May 1929), 104-5; CH/56, MS Autobiography of E. W. Burt, pp. 83-4.

54. CH/12, Duplicate Book of C. E. Wilson, pp. 52-3.

55. CH/46, Wilson to BMS colleagues, 17 May 1929.

56. Williamson, *British Baptists in China,* 276.

57. CH/12, C. E. Wilson, Diary of China Deputation Tour for 20 May 1929.

on this score was probably the reason for the less than enthusiastic response of BMS home officials to the new united body. C. E. Wilson felt that the Church was 'too much engineered by foreigners', but was happy to leave the Baptist churches free to determine their own attitude to the organization.[58] The Shaanxi veteran, A. G. Shorrock, now retired in England, viewed with alarm the prospect of the Shanxi and Shaanxi Baptists following the Shandong example, fearing that the aim of the Church of Christ was 'to absorb and to abolish all distinctive principles'.[59] However, those currently serving in Shanxi and Shaanxi appear to have had no such fears. Thomas Lower from Shanxi and James Watson from Shaanxi both wrote home after the Baptist churches of the two provinces had decided to join the Church of Christ in 1933, giving assurances that Baptist principles and liberty had been safeguarded in what was 'really a federation rather than an organic Church union'.[60] The participating churches of each province were organized into synods. The Baptist preponderance in Shanxi and Shaanxi ensured that here the synods were almost entirely Baptist in character; in Shandong the synod comprised associations of both Baptist and Presbyterian churches.

From 1932 the progressive devolution of responsibility to the Chinese church had the benefit of the experienced hand of H. R. Williamson as China Secretary. Williamson was enormously popular with the Chinese. In 1929 Wilson and Parker Gray found that Williamson received 'something like an ovation at every meeting we had with the Chinese', and had to resist the clamour of the Shanxi Christians that he be restored to his former sphere of labour rather than remain in Shandong to be groomed as E. W. Burt's successor.[61] Evidence of Williamson's qualities as a Chinese scholar and linguist was supplied in 1936, when he declined the offer of the Chair of Chinese Studies in the University of London.[62] To Williamson must belong much of the credit for the fact that relationships between the BMS and the Chinese church were so generally free of tension even amidst the turbulent changes of the 1930s. His recall in 1938 to assume the Foreign Secretary-ship was a serious loss to the China mission.

58. CH/12, Duplicate Book of C. E. Wilson, p. 64; see E. W. Burt's comment in CH/56, MS Autobiography, p. 80.

59. CH/64, Shorrock to Wilson, 8 May 1933.

60. General Committee Minutes, 8 Nov. 1933, p. 99.

61. CH/46, Wilson to BMS colleagues, 17 May 1929.

62. Middlebrook, *Memoir of H. R. Williamson,* 40; CH/67, [C. E. Wilson] to Williamson, 10 Dec. 1936.

In China, as in other fields after 1925, the process of devolution was driven, not merely by rising nationalist sentiment, but also by the financial needs of the Society. The China mission, dependent as it was on the Arthington Fund for the new commitments undertaken after 1912, was affected with particular severity by the virtual exhaustion of the Fund by the close of 1927.[63] The BMS allocation to China was reduced by about twelve per cent between 1925 and 1928. From 1927 Chinese Christians replaced BMS personnel in a growing number of key leadership positions. Progress towards a trained indigenous ministry was most substantial in the mature church in Shandong, which still accounted for over two-thirds of Baptist membership in 1930, even though the young church in Shaanxi had grown more rapidly from the beginning.[64] The Baptist churches remained at their weakest in Shanxi, affected by the rival attractions of Pentecostal and Adventist groups, and by a general enervation of spirit which C. E. Wilson in 1929 could only attribute to the climate and high altitude of the province. The strong Catholic presence in Shanxi was possibly a more pertinent factor.[65] In 1931 the Society declared its intention to withdraw completely from Shandong within the foreseeable future. The Shandong and inter-provincial conferences asked for a transitional period of fifteen years. The BMS Committee felt this was too long, and decided in February 1932 to reduce its allocation to Shandong by ten per cent annually, thus setting the goal of withdrawal by 1942. However, after two years the period of devolution was extended to fifteen years.[66]

China's unification under Chiang Kai-shek and the Guomindang in 1927-8 had been accomplished at the price of the ruthless suppression of the Chinese Communist Party, whose membership fell from about 60,000 to 20,000 in a matter of months. Chiang was hailed by most missionaries as a man raised up by God to save China from the menace of godless Communism; their enthusiasm increased after he was baptized into the Methodist Episcopal Church in 1930.[67] Communism was driven underground, or, more accurately, into the mountains of Jiangxi province, where

63.   *MH* (Nov. 1926), 253-5; *MH* (Jan. 1927), 13-16.

64.   Williamson, *British Baptists in China*, 219-20, 276. In 1930 Shandong had 7,122 members, Shanxi 1,067, and Shaanxi 2,418.

65.   CH/12, Duplicate Book of C. E. Wilson, p. 54.

66.   General Committee Minutes, 3 Feb. 1932, pp. 13-14; 20 July 1932, p. 60; 6 Feb. 1934, p. 7.

67.   G. A. Young, *The Living Christ in Modern China* (London, 1947), 53.

Mao Zedong (Mao Tse-tung) began to construct a new power base among the peasantry, animated by a new indigenized Chinese brand of Marxist ideology. As the Guomindang government consolidated its military strength and curbed anti-foreign excesses, the Communist threat to the Christian cause seemed to many missionaries to fade into comfortable oblivion. A more immediate cause of anxiety to them was the imperial aggression of Japan, whose occupation of Manchuria in 1931 was the first step in a process which culminated in the full-scale invasion of 1937. For the Guomindang government, missionaries, with their continuing extraterritorial rights, were influential allies against Japanese power.[68]

If, for the missionary movement as a whole, the years from 1928 to 1937 marked something of a lull in the storm, for most BMS China missionaries they were far from peaceful. Indeed, 1928 added another name to the roll of Baptist missionary martyrdoms in China: Grace Mann, a young recruit to the Shanxi mission, was murdered by bandits on the road between Taiyuan and Xinzhou on 12 November. In Shaanxi from 1928 to 1931 the worst enemy was famine. For three successive years from 1928 both the May wheat harvest and the September cotton and millet harvest failed. The paralysis of China's railway network, and the fact that Shaanxi was still in rebel warlord hands, aggravated the province's suffering. Once again, BMS missionaries became heavily involved in famine relief. John Shields and George Young fed up to 800 people a day in Sanyuan in early 1929, until Shields was invalided home after having been trampled under foot by a crowd desperate for food. The end of the famine in 1931 ushered in a period of sustained spiritual and numerical growth in the Shaanxi church. In the five years from 1931 to 1935 1,662 new converts were baptized.[69] The growth in Shaanxi was largely responsible for the fact that the decade from 1931 to 1940 recorded the highest average annual total of baptisms (715) in the history of the China mission.[70]

IV: China Divided, 1935-1945

Two inter-related themes dominate Chinese history in this period. The first is the escalation of Japanese aggression into a full-scale invasion of north China, launched in July 1937. The second is the emergence of the Chinese

---

68. J. K. Fairbank, *The Great Chinese Revolution: 1800-1985* (London, 1987), 196, 215-27.

69. Young, *The Living Christ in Modern China*, 61-6, 77-8.

70. Williamson, *British Baptists in China*, 278.

Communist Party (CCP) from the apparent failure and seclusion of 1928-35 into a position of mass support and political influence, and the corresponding collapse of the prestige and moral authority of the Guomindang government. From 1937 to 1945 China was once again a divided nation. The Japanese controlled the coastal and northern provinces, including Shandong and Shanxi. The Guomindang government, exiled to Chongqing in Sichuan, ruled over 'Free China' in the west and north-west, including some of Shaanxi. Finally, the Communists controlled an initially small but highly significant area around Yanan in north Shaanxi; by 1945 their authority extended to large tracts of rural China. The BMS mission, located as it was in the north, had to cope both with the perils of Japanese occupation and with the very different challenge of a close encounter with China's version of the atheistic faith of Communism. A few BMS personnel also had experience in other parts of Free China: some of the missionaries withdrawn from Shanxi in 1939 were transferred to south-west China, where they served in evangelistic, relief and student work: Victor and Eva Hayward, for example, worked from 1940 to 1944 in Guizhou province, where the Church of Christ in China had initiated its own home mission.[71]

The BMS mission in Shanxi was the first to be affected by the Japanese invasion. At Guoxian in the north of the province, twelve Baptist members were among the estimated 4,000 civilians murdered after the Japanese captured the city; many others had fled. At Xinzhou a deacon was shot, and two Baptist workers imprisoned and tortured. After a prolonged period of bombing during October 1937, Taiyuan fell to the Japanese on 8 November.[72] The eight remaining BMS missionaries in the province struggled to keep the two Taiyuan hospitals going.[73] The senior missionary, F. W. Price, was much involved in negotiating with the occupying authorities on behalf of his colleagues and church members. In February 1938 the situation had stabilized sufficiently for the northern stations of Xinzhou, Guoxian and Taizhou to be re-occupied. Ernest and Edna Madge, newly married, were able to return to Shanxi from Hankou (Hankow). They found Taizhou itself peaceful, but the province as a whole full of 'fleeing multitudes,

71. Ibid., 172-3; *Through Toil and Tribulation: Missionary Experiences in China during the War of 1937-1945* (London, 1947), 166-78. Victor Hayward subsequently became secretary of the National Christian Council of China.

72. Williamson, *British Baptists in China,* 161-2; *Through Toil and Tribulation,* 45-6.

73. The eight were F. W. Price, Dr Ellen Clow, Dr H. G. Wyatt, Dr C. V. Bloom, Victor and Eva Hayward, Beulah Glasby and S. R. Dawson.

running they know not whither, but ever running from danger'.[74] The reality of the danger was brutally demonstrated on 4 May, when Harry Wyatt and Beulah Glasby (and their driver) were murdered near Guoxian by Chinese guerrillas, who mistook them for Japanese.[75] Within the cities, however, the risks were small, and the missionaries were keen to stay. 'The Shansi church never has been strong', commented Ernest Madge in June, 'but it might easily collapse completely if we withdrew, under the present pressure'.[76]

A missionary withdrawal from Shanxi finally became necessary in August 1939, after a period of intensified anti-mission activity, during which sixteen members of the Taiyuan church were falsely charged by the Japanese with complicity in Chinese guerrilla activities. One of those imprisoned, Wang Chinzhang, a senior evangelist, was eventually killed. During the six years when missionaries were absent the Shanxi church did not flourish, but neither did it collapse. The church at Taiyuan met under the capable leadership of the matron of the Baptist orphanage, Mrs Xu Lingzao, who built up a new, youthful, and zealous congregation to replace the many members who had left the city. The problem came after the war when the older members returned to find a very different church, which had severed its former links with the Church of Christ in China. The returning exiles consequently formed a congregation of their own, which restored the connection with the Church of Christ in China, and had little to do with the younger and more separatist group. At Xinzhou, Gouxian and Taizhou worship continued regularly, often in private homes, throughout the six years. At the outstations of Yuanping and Fansi the church maintained a precarious existence in the face of many obstacles.[77]

The Japanese invaded Shandong in the course of December 1937. Despite the occupation, BMS work continued in the main urban centres of Chingzhou, Zhoucun and Jinan until August 1942, when all missionaries were removed to Shanghai or other internment centres. Thirty-four BMS missionaries and eighteen of their children were interned. The Chingzhou hospital remained open throughout the Japanese occupation, under the leadership of Dr Jing Yihui. The Foster hospital at Zhoucun, despite being bombed when the Japanese invaded, functioned till August 1939, and again

74. CH/62, E. G. T. Madge to C. E. Wilson, 28 Feb. 1938.

75. On Wyatt see E. A. Payne, *Harry Wyatt of Shansi 1895 -1938* (London, 1939).

76. CH/62, Madge to Wilson, 7 June 1938.

77. Williamson, *British Baptists in China*, 165-9; idem, *The Christian Challenge of the Changing World* (BMS, London, 1946), 39; CH/62, Madge to Williamson, 18 Mar. 1946; H. W. Spillett papers (in possession of Mr A. H. Spillett), p. 55.

from December 1939 to March 1942. The university hospital at Jinan remained open until December 1941. The university itself survived in much attenuated form, first at Jinan, then in exile in Shanghai and subsequently at Chengdu in Sichuan province. Church life remained strong in the major cities; in many of the smaller urban centres and rural villages services were suspended, although Zhang Sijing worked hard as secretary of the Shandong Baptist Union to maintain contact.[78]

Japanese occupation thus inflicted severe disruption, but not irreversible damage, on the work of the mission and the life of the Baptist churches in Shanxi and Shandong. Indeed, in some respects, the enforced missionary withdrawal actually strengthened the churches by further weakening the ties of dependence which the missions had been loosening ever since 1927. Ernest Madge reflected in December 1943 that if missionaries were to return to Shanxi and Shandong, it should be in a merely advisory capacity, and not to re-create dependence on missionary leadership.[79] There was never any serious doubt within the Society about the wisdom and necessity of its missionaries returning to the two occupied provinces at the end of the war. H. R. Williamson, who visited China on a deputation tour from October 1945 to February 1946, heard a few Chinese voices saying that they had managed for so long without foreign help, and could continue to do so. However, the vast majority of church opinion was in favour of a speedy restoration of missionary aid.[80] The Society's original intention to withdraw completely from Shandong by 1947 no longer appeared relevant. Nevertheless, relationships between church and mission could never be the same again. In this respect the lessons of the Japanese war and the challenge which Communism posed to other parts of the China mission in the same period were fundamentally the same.

In late 1935 the Communist 'Red Army' arrived in Shaanxi after the epic 6,000-mile 'Long March' from Jiangxi. Dislodged from Jiangxi by Nationalist troops, Mao Zedong's forces now set about establishing a new territorial base beyond the reach of effective Nationalist control. The Communist presence in Shaanxi, centred on Yanan, cut off the 200-strong Baptist church in Yanan from the rest of the Shaanxi field. No BMS missionaries had resided at Yanan since 1922. The Communists soon took over the Baptist hospital, school and church building, compelling the

---

78. Williamson, *British Baptists in China*, 157-61; idem, *The Christian Challenge*, 33-5; *Through Toil and Tribulation*, 101-110.

79. CH/62, Madge to Williamson, 6 Dec. 1943.

80. Williamson, *The Christian Challenge*, 37, 47.

congregation to worship in a cave in a nearby village. The Communist intention was to advance from Shaanxi into Shanxi, and thence to strike through to Hebei and Japanese-occupied territory on the coast. In February 1936 some 30,000 Communist troops crossed the Yellow River into Shanxi. The Red Army was now close enough to Taiyuan to have an immediate impact on the Shanxi mission - casualties of the fighting were treated at both BMS hospitals in Taiyuan, and for a time BMS staff were evacuated.[81] In the event, the arrival of the Japanese in 1937 presented Shanxi with problems of a different kind. It was the missionaries in Shaanxi who faced the closest encounter with Communism.

On the morning of 12 December 1936 George and Nora Young in Xian were awoken by the sound of gunfire and of exploding bombs. Chiang Kai-shek, having flown to Xian in an attempt to extinguish dissent in the Manchurian forces who were supposed to be fighting the Communists on his behalf, had been captured by the conspirators. For two weeks Chiang was a prisoner, finding solace in his Bible and his Christian faith. His release on Christmas Day was hailed by the Xian missionaries as a miracle. In political terms it signified the imminent rapprochement of Communists and Nationalists in a common front against the Japanese. Within weeks the Communists were in control of the country just to the north of Xian, and had infiltrated Xian itself. Most foreigners were evacuated from Shaanxi on 18 January. Four BMS missionaries chose to remain in Xian - James Watson, F. S. Russell, H. G. Stockley and George Young. They were agreeably surprised that the Communists, who had brought with them the reputation of having murdered thousands in Jiangxi, were now friendly and peaceable. The CCP political leader, Zhou Enlai (Chou En-lai), came to Xian to address a meeting of church and mission leaders in 1937, and stressed that the CCP now stood for religious freedom and wished the missionary doctors and teachers to stay. Young, though still convinced that Christianity and Communism were mortal enemies, found the social idealism, dedication, and sacrificial spirit of the Communists deeply impressive and humbling.[82] Many missionaries who came into first-hand contact with Communism over the next fifteen years were to find their fundamental antipathy to Communist ideology qualified by the incontrovertible evidence of the high social morality of the Communist political programme.

81. Williamson, *British Baptists in China*, 145; CH/64, H. W. Spillett to C. E. Wilson, 14 Apr. 1936.

82. CH/67, prayer letter from G. Young dated 24 Mar. 1937; Young, *The Living Christ in Modern China*, 175-88.

The formation of the united Communist-Nationalist front in April 1937 removed the threat of a Communist military take-over in Shaanxi, although the CCP contined to build up its power base at Yanan in the north. In Xian Christian concern focused instead on the mounting extremism of the Nationalist authorities, who employed secret police and concentration camps in their attempt to re-educate the young in sound political principles.[83] Xian was also bombed repeatedly by the Japanese between 1939 and 1944; the Jenkins-Robertson Memorial Hospital was destroyed in March 1939, but medical work was transferred to another location in the eastern suburbs. Throughout the war, the Shaanxi church was both strengthened and tested by a Pentecostal renewal movement, known as the 'Spiritual Gifts Society', introduced to the province in 1937 by three evangelists from Nanjing.[84] The movement produced deep conviction of sin, heightened fervour in worship, and a new zeal in evangelism. Yet it was also characterized by a misuse of the gift of tongues, and an emphasis on 'jumping', swooning, and other ecstatic experiences. George Young welcomed the new spiritual life, but sought to counteract the tendency to devalue biblical truth and ethics in favour of visionary experience. A Bible Training Institute was opened in Xian in March 1942 to train ordinary church members and provide refresher courses for pastors and church workers; 300 students from all the Protestant churches in Xian attended courses in its first three years. A more advanced theological class to train men for the ministry was begun in 1944 in an attempt to remedy the continuing dependence of the Shaanxi church on an ageing leadership, many of whom had, as children, been among the original Shandong emigrants.[85] The war years in Shaanxi were thus, for all their instability, a period of spiritual life and growth in the church. As one pastor remarked, 'Those who had been dead in prosperity, had become alive again in adversity'.[86]

V: The Church and the Communist Revolution, 1946-1952

As Japanese fortunes in the Second World War declined from 1943, the influence of the CCP increased. The Japanese occupation and the devastat-

---

83.   Young, *The Living Christ in Modern China*, 166-7.

84.   Similar movements affected other provinces in the 1930s, including Shandong; see Whyte, *Unfinished Encounter*, 176-7.

85.   Young, *The Living Christ in Modern China*, 86-95, 223-30; CH/67, prayer letter from Young dated 30 Dec. 1947; CH/62, Madge to Williamson, 6 Dec. 1943.

86.   Williamson, *British Baptists in China*, 172.

ing effects of the war on the Chinese economy enabled the CCP to present itself to the peasantry of north China as the only hope of economic reform and national salvation. Membership of the Party grew from about 40,000 in 1937 to 1.2 million in 1945. On the ending of the World War and the renewal of open conflict between the Communists and the Nationalist government, the CCP was strongly placed through its hold of the north China countryside to wage a war of attrition against the Guomindang.[87] The Nationalist government soon gained a reputation for gross economic mismanagement (resulting in hyper-inflation) and shameless corruption. In October 1946 Ernest Madge observed that the veteran warlord governor of Shanxi, Yan Xishan, was 'nothing more than a feudal despot of the worst type'. The rapid success of the Communists in Shanxi was attributable to the fact that they, for all their faults, at least defended the poor against the rich, whereas Yan's officials were 'just battening on the poor to keep their own system going'. Madge commented that the church in Corinth 'could hardly have faced a worse environment' than the corrupt atmosphere which now surrounded the church in Taiyuan.[88]

Taiyuan city was now full of refugees, with a population of 313,700 crammed within its medieval walls. Those who had come in from the surrounding Communist territory were subjected to two weeks of interrogation by the government's 'Pacification Commission'; the alternative, for those who remained in the countryside, was forcible re-education at the hands of the CCP. It was no wonder that the people, in the words of Hubert Spillett (the Shanxi provincial secretary), were 'sad-looking' and ill-nourished. 'You may wonder', wrote Spillett to his prayer supporters in November 1947, whether it is worthwhile sending missionaries at great expense by air 'into this tense, tragic city'. Spillett was in no doubt as to the answer - the Chinese church still wanted missionaries, and their supportive role was more than ever needed. With missionary encouragement the divided Taiyuan church was now drawing together again, and even engaging in joint evangelistic ventures: 221 signed decision cards at a 'Youth for Christ' campaign run by two American evangelists in September 1947.[89]

Within months such a campaign would have been unthinkable. These were in fact the last days of the missionary presence in Shanxi. During 1948

87. Fairbank, *The Great Chinese Revolution*, 245-8, 258.

88. CH/62, Madge to Williamson, 20 and 30 Oct. 1946.

89. CH/64, Spillett to Williamson, 27 Sept. 1947, and circular letter from Spillett dated 5 Nov. 1947; CH/65, H. G. Stockley to C. C. Chesterman and H. R. Williamson, 10 Oct. 1947.

the Communists rapidly consolidated their hold on the province. On 19 July the eight remaining BMS staff were evacuated to Beijing, although later in the year Dr Handley Stockley and Hubert Spillett returned to Taiyuan for a short period. They concluded that there was no possibility of a missionary return to the city. Taiyuan eventually fell to the Communists on 23 April 1949.[90] Ernest and Edna Madge were transferred to work with the Chinese Border Mission in the city of Xichang (now part of Sichuan province), where they joined William and Winifred Upchurch, formerly of Sanyuan, in pioneer work amongst the aboriginal border tribes. The two couples remained in Sichuan until the Communist take-over compelled them to leave in 1951.[91] The Shanxi church entered the new era with scant resources of national leadership. The only ordained pastor, Chinliang, was held in solitary confinement by the Communists for several months, then sent to slave labour in the mines and finally killed. At least six other church leaders also lost their lives.[92] At the close of the missionary era Shanxi remained the weakest link in the BMS China mission.

In Shandong the unsettled conditions in the countryside soon confined the BMS missionary presence to Jinan, where work in the university, hospital and theological school continued throughout the civil war, and even after the inauguration of the Chinese People's Republic on 1 October 1949. In 1951 the Communist government took over the university premises and transferred the theological school to Nanjing, where it became part of the new union seminary opened in November 1952 as part of the government's programme of rationalization of theological education. Despite the turbulent political context, the Shandong Baptist Union made progress in this period, in terms of both numerical growth and self-sufficiency. Over 100 baptisms were recorded by the Union during 1948. In November 1948 the Shandong synod of the Church of Christ in China met for the first time in thirteen years, and by 1950 BMS missionaries could report that the Shandong synod had at last become 'a really united church'. When the last BMS missionaries left the province in the spring of 1951, the Baptist churches were in the care of a force of twenty-three pastors and about fourteen evangelists. Although some of the rural churches then ceased to

90.   CH/64, H. R. Williamson to members of BMS China sub-committee, 20 July 1948; H. W. Spillett papers, pp. 66-8. Williamson on p. 191 of his book mis-dates the evacuation at 19 July 1949.

91.   Williamson, *British Baptists in China*, 175-6, 197-8; information from Rev. E. G. T. Madge, 11.7.90.

92.   Williamson, *British Baptists in China*, 190-1, 338.

hold services, the general trend in Shandong seems to have been a favourable one for some years thereafter: between 1953 and 1956 the membership of the synod increased by twenty-two per cent.[93]

Shaanxi - which seemed for a time in early 1937 to be on the brink of Communist rule - was paradoxically the last of the three provinces in the BMS mission to experience the change of regime. As late as March 1948 there were still thirty BMS missionaries in the province. The Communist armies then began their spring offensive and made a sudden push across the Xian plain. Missionaries faced the agonizing decision of whether or not to leave. On the one hand, a decision to remain would impose a financial burden on the church members, and possibly expose them to danger. Yet to leave seemed like cowardice in what many regarded as 'a spiritual struggle between the Kingdom of God and Satan'.[94] In the event it was decided that those missionary families with children, and probationer missionaries, should be evacuated, leaving seventeen missionaries to stay on in Xian and three in Sanyuan. On 8 June 1948 ten adults and eleven children were evacuated to Chengdu in Sichuan province. Here the evacuated missionaries engaged in pastoral work, school-teaching, and theological education under the auspices of the Sichuan synod of the Church of Christ. Most of this group left Sichuan in mid-1949, but some remained until late 1951.[95]

The Easter of 1948 supplied abundant evidence that the Shaanxi church possessed very considerable spiritual resources with which to meet the coming challenge. At a packed united communion service in Xian on Maundy Thursday a Lutheran pastor and Bishop Liu of the Episcopal Church received the elements from A. K. Bryan of the BMS - it seemed to George Young like a 'foretaste of heaven'. On the Saturday 10,000 people thronged the city square for a 'Youth for Christ' rally, and scores made commitments to Christ. During the first week of May, Wang Mingdao, the Beijing evangelist, spoke to 1,500 people daily at the spring assembly of the Shaanxi synod. His messages were full of prophetic fire, warning of coming judgment and calling for repentance. Young took heart that God was raising up men of such spiritual stature 'to save China'.[96] Wang Mingdao was indeed destined to be a key figure in the years to come, although not quite

93. Ibid., 186-9, 338-9; V. Hayward, *Christians and China* (Belfast, 1974), 60.

94. CH/67, prayer letter from G. Young dated 16 Mar. 1948.

95. Information from Rev. J. Sutton, 30.5.90. The group comprised B. F. and M. Price, A. E. and J. Bastable, S. L. and D. Henderson Smith, J. and E. Sutton, Miss V. Harrison and Miss W. Harkness.

96. CH/67, prayer letter from G. Young dated 22 July 1948.

in the sense that Young envisaged. As perhaps the most outspoken opponent of the Three-Self Patriotic Movement Church and its theology, Wang was bitterly attacked by the Three-Self leaders and finally arrested in August 1955; he remained in prison until his release at the age of seventy-nine in 1979.[97]

In November 1948 two Shaanxi pastors - Wang Daosheng and Sun Zhiyi - returned from the national assembly of the Church of Christ in China, held in Suzhou (Soochow) in October. They spoke with realism and urgency of the gravity of the crisis now facing the church in China. Wang preached a stirring sermon in the city church in Xian, warning that Communism was God's judgment on the nation for its corrupt systems and sinful living. At the Shaanxi synod in December Wang was elected president of the church for the coming year. There was also a frank discussion on whether missionaries should stay or go: the church leaders were unanimous in urging them to remain. At the missionary conference which followed eleven BMS staff elected to stay.[98]

The Chinese People's Liberation Army entered Xian on 20 May 1949. The church was initially fearful, but soon set about organizing itself for the new era. At the Xian district church council in August ten pastors and evangelists were appointed. The churches accepted responsibility for their support, but the pastors also undertook to engage in productive work to satisfy government requirements.[99] When the council met again in December to elect officers for the coming year, the Chinese chairman announced that George Young, the current vice-chairman, would automatically become chairman in 1950. Young then rose to protest, explaining that the missionaries were united in feeling that the new age demanded that all appearance of foreign control should be eliminated from the church. Despite the reservations of some church leaders, the missionaries then gave up their positions as office-holders and an all-Chinese council was elected for 1950. The change was not merely from European to Chinese control but also from ministerial to lay preponderance: for the first time lay persons held a majority of church offices.[100] With hindsight it is easy to assert that such reforms were long overdue. There is no doubt that the pressure of political

97. Whyte, *Unfinished Encounter*, pp. 243-4; P. L. Wickeri, *Seeking the Common Ground: Protestant Christianity, The Three-Self Movement, and China's United Front* (Maryknoll, 1988), 164-70.

98. CH/67, prayer letter from G. Young dated 31 Dec. 1948/15 Jan. 1949.

99. CH/67, prayer letter from G. Young dated 26 Aug. 1949.

100. CH/67, prayer letter from G. Young dated 3 Feb. 1950.

events was decisive in convincing both missionaries and church leaders of the necessity of devolution. Nevertheless, foreign control of the church in Shaanxi cannot be depicted in simplistic terms either as an imposition on unwilling Chinese or as a prize jealously guarded by power-hungry missionaries: whether rightly or wrongly, it had been perceived, even by many Chinese Christians, as a necessary but temporary instrument of spiritual growth.

At first the church in Shaanxi enjoyed an unexpected degree of liberty under the new regime, and missionaries reacted with enthusiasm to the Communists' achievements in land, economic and social reform. Within three months of the 'liberation' of Xian, corruption, prostitution, and poverty had been almost eliminated from the city.[101] In May 1950 a visiting team of national church leaders - comprising Y. T. Wu, Liu Liangmo, Y. C. Tu (Tu Yujing) and Ai Niansan - were surprised by the absence of church-state tensions in Shaanxi, such as were common in other parts of China. The explanation they offered was the existence in north-west China of a large Muslim population, which had been granted freedoms that the Christian church was able to share.[102] The team had come to Xian to report to a meeting of delegates from all the north-western provinces on the series of interviews which they and other Christian leaders had had with Zhou Enlai earlier in May to discuss the place of the Protestant churches in Communist China. Although the eventual fruit of these interviews - the 'Christian Manifesto' of July 1950 - was not yet available in its final agreed form, the team brought with them the essential message of the Manifesto, namely that there was a future for the church in China, but on condition that it severed all links with foreign imperialism, became genuinely indigenous, and supported the government's reforming programme.[103]

The same message was communicated to the Shaanxi synod in July 1950 by Dr H. H. Tsui (Cui Xiangxiang), General Secretary of the Church of Christ in China, who had also been present at the meetings with Zhou Enlai. The synod accordingly saw the BMS hand over all control over finance, property and personnel to the Church of Christ. A resolution was passed expressing appreciation of the fifty-eight years of BMS work in Shaanxi, accepting the new responsibility devolved on the Chinese church,

---

101. CH/67, prayer letter from G. Young dated 26 Aug. 1949.

102. CH/67, prayer letter from G. Young dated 31 July 1950.

103. On these interviews and the Manifesto see Whyte, *Unfinished Encounter*, 215-19; Wickeri, *Seeking the Common Ground*, 95-6, 127-33; Hayward, *Christians and China*, 48-51.

and affirming the ecumenical nature of the Church of Christ. The missionaries present received the resolution with joy as a sign that the goal of all missionary endeavour had been achieved. There was no hint of anti-missionary feeling. Dr Tsui, pointing out that there were some missionaries whose devout piety concealed superior and domineering attitudes, asked the synod to express its views frankly on whether missionaries should be asked to leave. In response the synod resolved that all the Shaanxi missionaries were 'genuine friends of the Chinese people', and invited them to remain as long as possible.[104]

The honeymoon period of Christian-Communist relationships in north-west China (which applied to a lesser extent in the nation as a whole) was brought to an end by the Chinese entry into the Korean War in October 1950. Communist China was now in open conflict with the United States of America, the unflinching ally of the Nationalists throughout the years of civil war. The long-accumulated resentment against American imperialism in China overflowed in a passionate denunciation of all things foreign and Western. The Protestant churches in China now paid the price for the American domination of China missions since 1912; the Catholic Church suffered in equal measure as retribution was exacted for the consistently anti-Communist policy of the Vatican.

The National Christian Council officially endorsed the Christian Manifesto in October 1950. Intense pressure was now placed on all Protestants to sign it. 180,000 did so within the next six months. Eventually 417,389 signed the Manifesto - almost half the total membership of the Protestant churches.[105] A new law passed in February 1951 to enable the suppression of 'anti-revolutionaries', led to the arrest and execution of thousands. In Xian 146 persons were executed, many of them tried by a people's court and put on show before a crowd of 20,000. In April Zhou Enlai summoned 151 Protestant leaders to a conference in Beijing, whose purpose was 'to sever all relations between Chinese Churches and American imperialism and to help patriotic Chinese Christians to become independent, self-governing and self-propagating'. It was the crucial step in the establishment of the Three-Self Patriotic Movement Church. At the conference delegates made bitter accusations against fellow ministers and missionaries of being 'spies' and 'secret servants of Imperialist Power'. The Beijing denunciations set the pattern for a nation-wide movement of 'denunciation meetings', in which Christians were encouraged to denounce

---

104. CH/67, prayer letter from G. Young dated 31 July 1950.

105. Whyte, *Unfinished Encounter*, 218; Wickeri, *Seeking the Common Ground*, 131.

their leaders and fellow-members, as well as criticize themselves, for imperialistic tendencies and thoughts. The conference also issued regulations for 'dealing with Christian organizations receiving financial assistance from America', which required the immediate severance of all relationships between the Chinese churches and the American mission boards. Although aimed specifically at American missions, the regulations were soon applied to all. The missionary era in China was about to be brought to an end.[106]

Seven delegates from Xian attended the Beijing conference. They reported to the Shaanxi synod in May, which 'sorrowfully' asked the BMS missionaries to terminate their work immediately. The missionaries left Xian on 5 June 1951, and arrived in Hongkong on the 10th.[107] The last BMS missionary remaining in west China, Jim Sutton, left Chengdu in November 1951. Thereafter the sole BMS representative in China was Hubert Spillett, the Field Secretary since 1949, who endeavoured from his base in Shanghai to wind up the affairs of the mission and maintain what contact he could with the Baptist churches. Spillett finally left Shanghai on 9 September 1952.[108]

VI: Postscript: The BMS and the Church in China since 1952

It would be inappropriate for a history of the Baptist Missionary Society to contain an extended treatment of the life of the former Baptist churches in the period after missionaries had been withdrawn. Readers who wish to pursue the story of the church in China after 1952 are referred to the standard books by Bob Whyte and Philip Wickeri.[109] Nonetheless, in so far as China remained a pressing concern of the Society after 1952, some brief concluding comments are in order. Direct contact with Chinese people was maintained through the literature work of Hubert Spillett in Hong Kong and Jim Sutton in Malaya. For twenty years from 1962 the Society also maintained a Chinese link in the medical sphere, through the allocation of medical missionaries to the Junk Bay Medical Relief Council in Hong Kong.

106. CH/67, prayer letter from G. Young dated 5 July 1951; Whyte, *Unfinished Encounter*, 221-7; Wickeri, *Seeking the Common Ground*, 133-40.

107. CH/67, prayer letter from G. Young dated 5 July 1951.

108. H. W. Spillett papers, pp. 104-5.

109. Whyte, *Unfinished Encounter*, and Wickeri, *Seeking the Common Ground*. See also G. Hood, *Neither Bang Nor Whimper: The End of a Missionary Era in China* (Singapore, 1991).

The China experience had a profound effect on the BMS, as on the missionary movement as a whole. Missionary activity after 1949 had to be conducted with a much greater sensitivity to the political context of the non-Western world. Throughout Asia, and increasingly in Africa, nationalism and hostility to Western imperialism became the dominant forces shaping relationships between national church and foreign mission. BMS missionaries who had served in China took with them to other fields certain convictions about the pre-eminent importance of establishing a church that was self-supporting and not encumbered with institutions that depended on foreign funds. Two BMS China missionaries subsequently assumed positions of leadership in the Society which gave them the opportunity to apply the lessons of the China experience to BMS policy as a whole. Victor Hayward, General Foreign Secretary from 1951 to 1959, was the primary architect of the Society's "special project" in Brazil, where he sought to create a mission which self-consciously avoided the institutional bias which had helped to render the Chinese church so dependent on Western aid.[110] Ernest Madge, who was transferred to India after the evacuation from China, succeeded Hayward as General Overseas Secretary from 1959 to 1976. In 1972 Hayward became the first Project Officer of the China Study Project of the Conference of British Missionary Societies (later the Conference for World Mission).

Contact with the church in China after 1952 was intermittent, and almost non-existent during the years of the Cultural Revolution (1966-76). Such contacts as did remain possible, were maintained largely through the medium of the China Study Project, of which the BMS was a founder member. Western denominational distinctions became increasingly redundant within China after the official establishment of the Three-Self Patriotic Movement Church in 1954. From 1958 unification of worship services under the authority of the local Three-Self committee became the norm in all major centres. The Church of Christ in China thus lost its separate identity. The regulations adopted for unification in Taiyuan in 1958 suggest that the approach to the elimination of distinctive denominational principles and 'negative and pessimistic doctrines' was frequently heavy-handed.[111] During the period of the Cultural Revolution, when China turned its back on the policy of an United Front incorporating an ideologically purified Christianity, almost all organized church life was suppressed, and worship was driven underground into the privacy of Christian homes.

110. See below, ch. XV, pp. 471-8.

111. Wickeri, *Seeking the Common Ground*, 219-22.

During the 1980s China adopted a more open policy towards contact with the West and hence also towards organized religion. Christianity re-surfaced into accepted public existence, although worship continued in many cases to be conducted in private homes rather than on church premises. The policy of the BMS was to encourage the improved climate for Christianity by refraining from public criticism of the Three-Self Patriotic Movement Church, and utilizing to the full the opportunities afforded by occasional contact with officials such as Bishop K. H. Ting, president of the China Christian Council since its inception in 1980. This policy reflected the historical links of the Society with churches which, for the most part, had joined the Church of Christ in China, and hence were more likely after 1954 to be associated with the Three-Self Movement. Those missions whose partner churches during the Nationalist period had remained independent of wider associations tended, conversely, to espouse the cause of the unregistered, 'underground' churches, and to be more openly critical of the China Christian Council: the Overseas Missionary Fellowship - successor to the CIM - was the most notable example.[112]

Evidence emerged during the 1980s of the remarkable growth of the church in many parts of China, even during the hidden years of the Cultural Revolution. In the three provinces where the BMS once worked, the trends of the first half of the century had been sustained. In Shandong and Shaanxi the church had experienced very substantial growth. The total Protestant community in Shandong in 1985 numbered some 250,000, five times the number in 1949; in Jinan three churches had re-opened following the Cultural Revolution, serving a Protestant community of 3,000.[113] In Xian in 1983 the number of Protestants was double that in 1949, attending two churches and fourteen home meetings; total membership in 1985 was over 6,000. The Protestant church in Shanxi remained comparatively weak, although there was some recovery from the 1960s onwards: by 1985 the united church in Taiyuan had a total Christian community of about 1,000 and a membership of over 300; in 1946 Baptist membership in Taiyuan had been 400.[114]

---

112. For a recent analysis from the perspective of the unregistered churches and the Overseas Missionary Fellowship see T. Lambert, *The Resurrection of the Chinese Church* (London, 1991).

113. *MH* (Apr. 1986), 63.

114. Whyte, *Unfinished Encounter*, 428-31; *MH* (May 1986), 85-6; General Committee Minutes, 25 Apr. 1946, p. 91. Whyte's figure of 100 Protestant members in Taiyuan in 1949 seems too low.

By the mid-1980s occasional visits from Western Christians to China were once again possible. In December 1983 Reg Harvey, BMS General Secretary, participated in one of the first of these, organized by the British Council of Churches, and saw abundant evidence of lively and growing Christian communities.[115] In 1986 Angus MacNeill, BMS Overseas Secretary, took part in a China tour organized by the American and British Councils of Churches. Although the primary object of the tour was to attend an ecumenical conference in Nanjing, MacNeill was able to make an independent visit to Xian. He worshipped with the main Protestant congregation in the city, and found 500-600 people gathered on a Saturday morning for one of the three main services of the week. He also made contact with the former BMS hospital in Xian (now the government Fourth Hospital) whose senior staff were anxious to renew links with the Society.[116]

Another result of the more favourable climate to religion obtaining in the 1980s was the establishment in 1985 of the Amity Foundation. The Foundation was set up by a group of Chinese Christians and non-Christians to promote educational, health and social welfare work in China. Sympathetic overseas church agencies were invited to assist Amity programmes through the provision of financial assistance, equipment and foreign language teachers. In 1987 the Foundation also established, in co-operation with the United Bible Societies, a printing press in Nanjing, with the primary object of producing large amounts of Bibles and Christian literature.[117] The BMS gave financial support to the Foundation, and in 1986 the first British Christian teachers supported by the Foundation arrived in China. However, up to 1992 none of them had been recruited under the auspices of the BMS.

1989 was a year of extraordinary turmoil throughout the Communist world. President Gorbachev's programme of *perestroika* within the Soviet Union triggered off a remarkable series of popular revolutions which overthrew the old regimes throughout Eastern Europe. China's democratic ferment had independent origins, although it was influenced to some extent by ideological trends in Europe. The death on 15 April of Hu Yaobang, former General Secretary of the Chinese Communist Party and an unre-

---

115. *BT*: 2 Feb. 1984, p. 4; 9 Feb. 1984, p. 6; 16 Feb. 1984, p. 4; 23 Feb. 1984, p. 4; 1 Mar. 1984, p. 4; 8 Mar. 1984, p. 4.

116. BMS Overseas Department, Report on Visit to China by Rev. A. T. MacNeill, May 1986. Saturday services are organized primarily for the benefit of those whose weekly day off is Saturday.

117. Whyte, *Unfinished Encounter*, 420-2.

pentant champion of political modernization, was the spark which ignited the protest movement. During the six weeks that followed, growing numbers of students in Beijing, Shanghai and other major cities demonstrated in favour of the introduction of democratic reforms in China. For a time it seemed that in China also the Communist monopoly of power would be broken. The massacre of Tiananmen Square in Beijing on 4 June, when government troops killed several hundred demonstrators, broke the back of the democratic movement, and brought these hopes to a bloody end. The reactions of the Chinese church to these events were mixed. Bishop Ting publicly supported the students' campaign as 'patriotic activity'. Although some 'leftist' church leaders supported the government, many within the TSPM demonstrated openly in favour of democracy. The majority of Christians, particularly those in the unregistered churches, kept their heads down, and stayed out of trouble.[118]

The brutal suppression of the democratic movement had an ambiguous effect on church-state relations in China. On the one hand, the religious policy of the CCP tightened as hard-line leftism re-asserted itself. On the other hand, the support given to the students by Bishop Ting and other TSPM leaders created a distance between the TSPM and the government which had not previously been present. Moreover, evidence suggests that all strands of the Chinese Church have continued to grow since 1989.[119] The events of Tiananmen Square revealed the existence beneath the surface of Chinese society of powerful ideological currents that may yet produce a very different political order in the years ahead. What can be said is that the Chinese church faces this uncertain future with much greater numerical strength and more truly indigenous spiritual resources than it possessed forty years earlier when confronted by the upheaval of the Communist revolution.

---

118. Lambert, *Resurrection of the Chinese Church,* 214-15; *MH* (Oct. 1989), 205; *Friends of the Church in China*, minutes of AGM, 25 Nov. 1989, chairman's report.

119. Lambert, *Resurrection of the Chinese Church*, 214-58.

XI

The Congo Mission, 1914-1959

I: Protest, Prophecy and Schism

In China the period from 1911 to 1927 was crucial in alerting Christian missions to the implications for their work of nationalism and the growing reaction to Western imperialism - implications that became fully apparent only in the tumultuous years from 1949 to 1952. Events in Congo between 1913 and 1925, although less obviously momentous, were also overshadowed by two major surges of indigenous protest and initiative, which similarly can be seen, in retrospect, as anticipations of the more fundamental political transformation of the 1960s. In both of these movements of African protest BMS missionaries played major (though contrasting) roles, and both had serious consequences for the life of the Baptist churches. At the heart of the first of the two was the Buta rising in Angola (Portuguese Congo) from 1913 to 1915.

1. The Buta Rising

In June 1913 J. Sidney Bowskill, BMS missionary in Angola since 1899, returned to São Salvador after furlough to find the country in a state of extreme unsettlement. Throughout Angola resentment had been aroused by the imposition of a hut tax, but in the São Salvador district the principal cause of the trouble was the forcible recruitment by the Portuguese of labourers for the cocoa plantations at Cabinda.[1] Reports abounded that the Portuguese agents had perpetrated rape, robbery and other forms of oppression. Feelings were thus already running high when on 13 October a Portuguese official arrived at São Salvador to see Paulo Moreira, the *chef de poste*, demanding another 1500 workers, this time for the cocoa plantations on the islands of São Tomé and Princípe. Moreira summoned the

---

1. For the wider disturbances of 1913-15 see R. Pélissier, *Les Guerres Grises: Résistance et Révoltes en Angola (1845-1941)* (Orgaval, 1977), 232-6; *MH* (1913), 156.

336

principal chiefs of the district, but they refused to supply any more men. Moreira threatened any chiefs who refused with a fine of 30 dollars, or six months' imprisonment for those who declined to pay. He also applied pressure on individual chiefs, and in particular on Kiditu, king of the Bakongo. Kiditu and one other chief, Tangi, gave in, and a substantial number of men left under escort for the coast.[2]

Most of the chiefs regarded Kiditu's submission as betrayal, and on 21 November news reached São Salvador that a Catholic chief from Nsongola, Tulante Buta, had raised the standard of revolt against Kiditu. At dawn on 10 December Buta's forces attacked São Salvador, burning the Catholic section of the town but leaving the Protestant section untouched. Moreira, with no more than half a dozen troops at his disposal, appealed to Bowskill to go out and treat with Buta. Somewhat reluctantly, Bowskill agreed. He took with him Haldane Gilmore (doctor at São Salvador hospital), Mantu Parkinson (the first of the Bakongo to be baptized), Miguel Nekaka (another early São Salvador convert, baptized by Thomas Lewis on 23 May 1889),[3] and Daniel Ngyuvula.[4] To Bowskill's relief, Buta greeted them warmly, and arrangements were made for a grand palaver with Moreira on 11-12 December.[5]

On 11 December Bowskill, accompanied by all the BMS staff, arrived at the great square in São Salvador to be greeted by what he later described as 'the most impressive sight I have seen in the Congo'. Gathered under the acacia trees around the perimeter were over 700 of Buta's warriors; by the end of the day their number had grown to 2,000. In the centre of the square 'a little knot of white folks' assembled - the BMS missionaries, two Catholic priests, three nuns, and Moreira - to hear Buta recount his grievances. Buta's long speech accused Kiditu of having 'sold the country' by his collaboration with Moreira and the Portuguese labour atrocities. It reached its dramatic climax with the pronouncement 'Therefore, Kiditu we dethrone', a conclusion immediately echoed on the lips of all the warriors. As a result of the two-day palaver, Kiditu and two of his chief advisers were forced into exile

2. R. H. Carson Graham, *Under Seven Congo Kings* (London, n.d.), 133-6; *San Salvador: Mr Bowskill's Letters on the Native War of 1913-4, and Other Documents* (London, n.d. [1914]) 15-21; A/122, São Salvador Log Book, 1897-1920, pp. 159-60.

3. A/122, São Salvador Church Minute Book, 1887-1903, minutes for 20-23 May 1889.

4. Ngyuvula had been baptized by W. Wooding on 1 Aug. 1900; A/122, São Salvador Church Minute Book, 1887-1903.

5. Graham, *Under Seven Congo Kings,* 136-8; *Mr Bowskill's Letters,* 21-7; São Salvador Log Book, 1897-1920, pp. 160-4.

in the Belgian Congo. Official accounts of the palaver were kept by G. C. Claridge for the BMS and by one of the priests, and were sent off to the Portuguese Governor for adjudication. First reports of his reaction reached São Salvador on 18 January 1914: it seemed that the Portuguese had acquiesced in Kiditu's deposition, and that peace had been restored. However, that very morning Moreira arrested Nekaka, Mantu, and two other Protestants, Pedro Lombo and José Nlandu. From that moment the survival of the BMS São Salvador mission was in jeopardy.[6]

News of the arrests spread 'like wildfire'.[7] Buta's armies re-assembled, this time in open revolt against the Portuguese. During the following week the BMS missionaries made two attempts to dissuade the rebels from launching a renewed attack on São Salvador. Buta, however, was not to be mollified, and on 25 January attacked the town. Protestant as well as Catholic houses were burnt, but no attempt was made to enter the BMS compound. Moreira's few soldiers were soon besieged in the *Mbongi* (fortress) at one end of the town, and desultory fighting continued for some weeks.[8] On 27 January, in response to Bowskill's urgent plea for help, Thomas Lewis arrived from Kibokolo after a perilous journey. 'The whole country', Lewis reported to London, 'is like a powder-mine at present'.[9] Two days later Bowskill managed to leave for Matadi in order to alert the Governor to the desperate situation at São Salvador. The Governor told him that troops were already on their way, and Bowskill returned to São Salvador, arriving on 13 February. On 19 February he was summoned to the fortress and placed under arrest pending the arrival of the Governor and his force. At Bowskill's request, Gilmore at once sent word to Matadi to cable the news to London, with instructions to publish Bowskill's regular letters to the Society narrating the course of the rising.[10] The Society proceeded to do so, and lost no time in making the news public: Bowskill's arrest was first reported in the British press on 27 February, and questions were soon being asked in parliament.[11] Not for the last time, the BMS found itself embroiled in public controversy with Portugal over Angolan affairs.

Bowskill had in fact been released on parole on 26 February, pending a trial which was not to take place: the Bowskills left São Salvador in

6.   *Mr Bowskill's Letters*, 28-54; São Salvador Log Book, 1897-1920, pp. 164-7.

7.   São Salvador Log Book, 1897-1920, p. 167.

8.   Ibid., pp. 167-73; *Mr Bowskill's Letters*, 55-62.

9.   *Mr Bowskill's Letters*, 57, 65.

10. São Salvador Log Book, 1897-1920, pp. 173-6.

11. A/123, Scrap Book on Bowskill's arrest and imprisonment, 27 Feb. 1914-1916.

November, never to return to Portuguese Congo. Nevertheless, his arrest, and that of the four Protestant Africans, signified that the Portuguese administration had concluded that the BMS mission was the true instigator of the Buta rising. That conclusion was false, but understandable. Almost all of Kiditu's closest advisers had been Catholics. Buta's first attack on São Salvador had pointedly left the Protestant community well alone. Nekaka and Mantu had accompanied Bowskill in his negotiations with Buta on 10 December, and, as the Protestant interpreters at the grand palaver, had repeatedly questioned the translation offered by the Catholic interpreters. Buta put no faith in his own Catholic priests, and had insisted on Bowskill being present at the palaver as the only acceptable intermediary with Moreira.[12] Circumstantial evidence of this kind was sufficient to convince the Portuguese that the BMS missionaries were not merely in collusion with Buta but even obsessed with the craving for British rule in Congo.[13] Buta was still at large with a Baptist, Simão Seke, as his chief lieutenant. As what was originally a localized outbreak grew into a conflagration affecting the entire Bakongo people, the Protestant community was made to pay dearly for this alleged disloyalty. Nekaka was kept in prison until 12 August and Mantu until the 27th.[14] Portuguese soldiers burnt at least seven Baptist chapels, destroyed and looted the farm plots of Baptist church members, and shot a number of Zombo women and children in the Kibokolo area.[15] Besides all this, the damage to the life of the Baptist churches was incalculable.

After the second attack on São Salvador in January 1914, almost all the male Protestant church members fled the town. Deacons' meetings and church meetings were suspended. Eventually Bowskill summoned a deacons' meeting for 30 September, but none of the São Salvador male deacons nor any of the outstation deacons were present. The church meeting which followed on 5 October was attended by a mere thirty-three members, only five of them men. Regular deacons' and church meetings were not resumed until March 1915. It then became evident how serious had been the break-down in church discipline and pastoral care caused by the war: 'very formidable' lists were presented of church members who had lapsed by indulging in immorality, prohibited dances, and the drinking of palm

12. *Mr Bowskill's Letters*, 32-3, 51-2, 55.

13. A/123, G. C. Claridge to C. E. Wilson, 22 June 1914.

14. São Salvador Log Book, 1897-1920, pp. 200, 204. Nlandu, dying of sleeping sickness, had been set free earlier; Lombo was not released till 30 November.

15. São Salvador Log Book, 1897-1920, pp. 183, 189, 193-6.

wine.[16] Church membership fell from 1,058 at the end of 1912 to 530 at the end of 1916.[17] Church funds were severely affected by the declining membership, the damage inflicted on church members' property, and the demands of the Portuguese hut tax.[18]

The primary responsibility for the rebuilding of the shattered Angolan churches fell to R. H. Carson Graham, missionary at São Salvador since 1886. Graham played a key role in negotiating an amnesty between the rebel chiefs and the Portuguese authorities, but felt sadly betrayed in July 1915 when the Portuguese arrested Buta, Seke, and the other leaders of the revolt.[19] Despite this betrayal, Graham continued to urge the São Salvador church to respect biblical teaching on the duties of subjects to obey their rulers.[20] Although an uneasy peace returned to the region during the reign of Alvaro Nezingu, king of the Bakongo from 1915 to 1923, Portuguese suspicion of the BMS mission remained for decades to come. In 1921 the colonial government issued Decree 77, which prohibited the use of the vernacular languages in all Protestant schools. All Baptist teacher-evangelists had to obtain a certificate of proficiency in Portuguese to continue to operate, and over two hundred BMS village schools had to close as a result. Happily the churches had had a Kikongo hymnbook for some years, and a complete Kikongo Bible since 1916, and many members had already been taught to read.[21] In July 1923 the authorities even threatened to prohibit all use of Kikongo in public worship and enforce the withdrawal of the Bible and hymnbook.[22] Despite such opposition, the Angolan churches soon resumed their growth. Amongst the hitherto indifferent Zombo people the growth was spectacular. The membership of the Kibokolo church grew from eight in 1916 to 1,734 in 1933. A similar pattern of rapid growth in a previously unfruitful area emerged amongst the Mbamba people after the

16. A/122, Deacons' Meeting Minutes, 30 Sept. 1914, 3 Mar. 1915, 31 Mar. 1915; Church Meeting Minutes, 5 Oct. 1914, 8 Mar. 1915, 5 Apr. 1915, 17 May 1915, 5 July 1915.

17. Graham, *Under Seven Congo Kings*, 236; A/122, Deacons' Meeting Minutes, 2 Jan. 1918.

18. Graham, *Under Seven Congo Kings*, 176; A/122, Church Meeting Minutes, 5 Apr. 1915, 17 May 1915.

19. Graham, *Under Seven Congo Kings*, 167-9.

20. A/122, Church Meeting Minutes, 2 Aug. 1915.

21. C. E. Wilson, 'The BMS and Bible Translation', *BQ* 10 (1940-1), 162-3.

22. Graham, *Under Seven Congo Kings*, 194-7, 206; C. J. Parsons, 'The BMS in Africa: The years of latency, 1919-1939' (BMS MS), p. 7.

re-opening of the old Mabaya station on a new site at Bembe in 1932.[23] Bowskill's readiness to risk confrontation with the Portuguese state in 1914 had alarmed his more prudent colleagues, and for a time the survival of the Baptist churches in Angola was indeed in question.[24] By the 1930s there could be little doubt that the churches were reaping the spiritual benefits of Bowskill's moral courage.

2. The 'Prophet Movement'

The second great stirring of African protest to affect the Congo mission in this period was more specifically religious in character, although its political implications were ultimately no less serious than those of the Angolan risings of 1913-15. The movement's origins can be traced to the failure of a certain Simon Kimbangu to get himself appointed as evangelist in the BMS out-station church at Nkamba in the Ngombe Lutete district. Kimbangu had been baptized at Ngombe in 1915 by S. F. Thompson, and since 1917 or 1918 had felt a call to preach. The night after his rejection by the Nkamba congregation (probably in March 1921), Kimbangu claimed to have received a vision, giving him direct authority to become an apostle or missionary to his people and engage in a ministry of healing. Kimbangu traced the source of his spiritual authority through his mother to G. R. R. Cameron, on the grounds that he had once 'blessed' her after she had protected him from attack. The readiness of the Bakongo to attribute to the first missionaries a spiritual power uniquely derived from God now enabled Kimbangu to claim such direct spiritual authority for himself.[25]

Kimbangu's apparent spiritual powers rapidly attracted attention. People flocked to Nkamba, bringing their sick for healing, and even their dead to be raised. By 6 April 1921 news of his miracles had reached Ngombe Lutete. The next day a delegation comprising many of the senior deacons of the Ngombe Lutete church visited Nkamba to form their own judgment. Most were convinced that 'the prophet', as Kimbangu had become known, was indeed doing the work of God in apostolic power, and as such was a sign of the restoration of New Testament Christianity. They accordingly gave Kimbangu the official status within the church which he had been seeking.

23. A/98, MS book on Kibokolo, 1899-1935; Parsons, 'The years of latency', pp. 9, 11; *MH* (Feb. 1933), 39-40.

24. A/123, Thomas Lewis to C. E. Wilson, 22 July 1914; A/122, São Salvador Staff Meeting Minutes, 30 Mar. 1915.

25. D. J. Mackay, 'Simon Kimbangu and the BMS tradition', *Journal of Religion in Africa* 17 (1987), 113-71.

Two, Kuyowa and Mbandila, became his closest lieutenants. Only two of the Ngombe deacons - Nlemvo and Masakidi - remained unpersuaded.[26] At this stage, however, there was no question of the prophet and his supporters leaving the BMS church. On 17 April R. L. Jennings, the senior missionary at Wathen, wrote to Kimbangu, inviting him to the station for a consultation. Their meeting two days later left Jennings and his colleague A. W. Hillard unimpressed, believing the man to be deluded.[27] From this point on the situation gradually deteriorated.

On 18 May Jennings and Hillard visited Nkamba, having been urged to see the prophet's wonders for themselves. They left unconvinced that any genuine cures had taken place, and said so publicly. Furthermore, Jennings was in close touch with M. Morel, the Belgian administrator at Thysville (Mbanza Ngungu), who had already reached his own conclusion that firm action must be taken against Kimbangu. Morel summoned Jennings to a conference at Thysville on 1 June. Jennings pleaded with him to refrain from military force, but to no avail. On 5 June Morel arrived at Nkamba with a small force to arrest Kimbangu. The prophet urged his supporters not to resist, and gave himself up. But stones were thrown, and the soldiers opened fire, causing at least one fatality. Amidst the ensuing uproar, Kimbangu himself slipped away. Morel had lost his catch. However, ten days later nine Baptist deacons and other supporters of the prophet were arrested. Word spread rapidly that Jennings had 'betrayed' Kimbangu to the state, despite the repeated protestations of the missionaries to the contrary. 'Our leaders are in prison, and our Teachers [Missionaries] put them there' ran the chorus of one popular hymn composed by the prophet's followers. The movement was now set firmly on the road towards separation from the BMS, even though Kimbangu himself continued to resist this conclusion for some time.[28]

Kimbangu himself was now in hiding, but a host of 'minor prophets' had appeared throughout the Ngombe district and beyond as far as São Salvador, proclaiming their prophetship by speaking in tongues and 'a

26. Mackay, 'Simon Kimbangu', 132-5, 148; C. Irvine, 'Birth of the Kimbanguist movement in the Bas-Zaire 1921', *Journal of Religion in Africa* 6 (1974), 36.

27. Irvine, 'Birth of the Kimbanguist movement', 37; Ngombe Lutete archives, Wathen station minutes, 1900-25, J. S. Bowskill, 'Notes on the "Prophet" movement'.

28. Irvine, 'Birth of the Kimbanguist movement', 37-44; Mackay, 'Simon Kimbangu', 149-53; Bowskill, 'Notes'. In all, twelve deacons were arrested, of whom two (Kibangudi and Wavanduka) died in prison (Ngombe Lutete archives, Church Meeting Minutes, Apr. 1922).

mighty shaking-trembling of the whole body'.[29] The São Salvador church meeting on 7 June, though unconvinced that any complete cures had taken place, rejoiced that the prophets were bringing 'multitudes within the sound of the Gospel' and agreed to send an investigative deputation to the Ngombe church.[30] However, by early July Carson Graham's attitude to the movement was more cautious, not least because the Portuguese authorities had taken fright and arrested many of the prophets and their alleged followers - among them fourteen church leaders. Graham had his work cut out convincing the Portuguese that the prophets were simply 'good people carried away by a foolish enthusiasm'.[31] Theologically, Graham remained perplexed. A movement which, according to New Testament accounts of false prophecy, ought to have exhibited genuine signs and wonders in support of false teaching, seemed in fact to combine spurious wonders with a genuine commitment to biblical truth.[32] The São Salvador church leaders remained in prison till 9 December, but Graham succeeded in containing the impetus of the movement within the Angolan church: there were no substantial losses in church membership.[33]

Across the border in the Belgian Congo the impact on the church was infinitely more serious. Hardly anybody came to the annual meetings of the Ngombe church in July 1921. Later that month J. S. Bowskill returned from furlough to replace Jennings as senior missionary at Ngombe. He found himself in the midst of a crisis no less alarming than the one he had faced at São Salvador. On 11 September the morning service (now attended only by station children and a few workmen) was interrupted when Kimbangu himself arrived outside the church with a vast crowd, and called on all present to follow him or face the fire of God's wrath. Terrified, most of the children joined the prophet's procession, leaving the missionaries with a mere handful of worshippers.[34] Kimbangu had broken cover, and troops were again sent to Nkamba to arrest him. Again he gave himself up, and was escorted to Thysville with about 125 of his supporters under arrest. Martial law was declared, Kimbangu was tried for treason, and sentenced

29. Bowskill, 'Notes'.

30. A/122, Church Meeting Minutes, 7 June 1921.

31. A/122, São Salvador Log Book, 1920-54, 9 July 1921.

32. *MH* (Oct. 1921), 192-3. Graham had in mind 2 Thessalonians 2:9.

33. Graham, *Under Seven Congo Kings*, 182-94; A/122, São Salvador Log Book, 1920-54, station report for 1921.

34. Bowskill, 'Notes'.

to death. After urgent appeals for clemency by the Society and its missionaries, King Albert commuted the sentence to life imprisonment. Kimbangu was sent to Katanga, where he died in 1951. Many of his followers were exiled to the upper river. BMS church, educational and medical work in the Ngombe district remained at a fearfully low ebb until the early months of 1922, when the first signs appeared here and there of a return to the mission. But the damage was serious and permanent. In August 1923 Bowskill deleted the names of over 900 church members from the roll for having 'turned their backs on the church of Christ', thus reducing the membership in one stroke from 1,500 to below 600.[35] The Ngombe church never recovered its former position as the strongest church of the BMS Congo mission.

On 8 September 1921 Bowskill wrote home expressing his regret that the Belgian government had so got 'the wind up' about the prophet movement:

> If they had acted less severely the whole thing might have been over by now, as it is, I'm afraid they are sowing a lot of trouble for themselves for the future. The bitterness in the people's minds won't die out very quickly. Perhaps this unrest is only the counterpart of what is happening all over the world.[36]

Bowskill was right. The attempt to suppress Kimbangu by force had transformed a politically innocuous movement into a powerful challenge to the colonial state.[37] Thirty years later it was to re-surface to haunt the closing years of Belgian rule. Jennings, Hillard, and Bowskill had approached the issue as a pastoral rather than a political problem. It was Morel who sought *their* co-operation in dealing with Kimbangu, rather than vice-versa; and their advice was consistently against the use of force. However, once force was exercised, all previous missionary contact with the Belgian authorities became in the mind of the prophet's Baptist supporters conclusive evidence of conspiracy. The missionaries became branded in African eyes as traitors to their own church and scriptural teaching. They thus unknowingly watered the seeds of schism that eventually bore fruit in the *'Eglise du Jésus Christ sur la terre par le prophète Simon Kimbangu'* - the largest independent church of modern Africa.

35. Ngombe Lutete archives, Church Meeting Minutes, 8 Jan. 1923; *BMS Annual Report*, 1923-4, pp. 71, 160.

36. Ngombe Lutete archives, Bowskill to Mr Thomson, 8 Sept. 1921.

37. Mackay, 'Simon Kimbangu', 147-8.

II: The Life of the Church

Church life on the lower river in the 1920s, though overshadowed by the prophet troubles, was not all gloom. Chief among the encouragements was the remarkable growth of the church in the Kibentele (now known as Nlemvo) district. Kibentele derived its name from Holman Bentley, who used to make regular itinerations there from Ngombe Lutete, although it was not formally constituted as a mission station until 1920, when W. B. Frame settled there. In December of that year the church membership stood at 567. Twelve months later it had reached 1,010. Growth continued at a less spectacular rate to the end of 1924, when membership reached a peak of 1,535. Such rapid numerical expansion outstripped the capacity of the church for nurturing its new converts, and membership declined over the next four years, as many were excommunicated for moral lapses or irregularity in attendance at church meetings or communion. In 1929 a renewed period of rapid growth began, which took the membership to a peak of 2,017 in 1934. The church fell back again thereafter; over the next twenty years membership fell to a figure of 1,200 in January 1954.[38]

The experience of Kibentele was in some measure representative of the Congolese church as a whole. Numerical growth was at a far higher level than before the First World War, most notably during the early and mid-1930s. Total communicant membership for the whole Congo mission rose from 5,495 in 1914 to 9,059 in 1920, 13,129 in 1930, 31,196 in 1940, 33,256 in 1950 and 50,336 in 1960. But membership fluctuated sharply from year to year as phases of rapid growth were followed by years in which excommunications outnumbered baptisms.[39] Church discipline was exercised most frequently in relation to marital offences and the use of alcohol. In both areas, missionary moral standards cut clean across indigenous cultural norms, resulting in continual difficulty in enforcing a consistent standard of church discipline. A ruling from a missionary conference at Kimpese in 1940 that any church member found trading in, using, or even possessing strong drink after January 1941 would be suspended from church fellowship aroused reservations among some church leaders. The Thysville deacons urged P. H. Austin to move slowly on the matter, anticipating particular difficulties if the ban on 'holding' strong drink were applied to weddings.[40] Their caution was justified, for fourteen years later

38. Mbanza Ngungu archives, Kibentele Church Minute Book, 1918-59.

39. *BMS Annual Reports.*

40. Mbanza Ngungu archives, Thysville Church Minute Book, c. 1919-54, Church Meeting Minutes, n.d. [Oct.-Dec. 1940]; see also Wathen Minute Book, 1925-53, minutes for 18 June 1940.

the Thysville church had to admonish its own pastor for permitting strong drink at his daughter's wedding.[41]

Difficulties of this nature were characteristic of all parts of the Congo field, but some churches and missionaries faced in addition problems peculiar to particular localities. For many years secret initiation ceremonies associated with ancestor worship presented the Yakusu church with repeated policy dilemmas. During William Millman's early service at Yakusu, when the church was as yet unformed, the mission held back from any open attempt to forbid Lokele mission boys from participation in these *libeli* ceremonies. But by 1910 Millman and H. Sutton Smith were convinced that the cult must be resisted as evil, and accordingly made public renunciation of the ceremonies a test for continuance in church membership.[42] The price paid by the church for its support for the hard line pioneered by its missionaries remained high into the 1920s and beyond. The officially reported total of members in good standing in the Yakusu church fell from 3,931 in December 1923 to 2,431 in December 1924, after a meeting of the elders of the village churches had ruled that those who had been through *libeli* earlier in the year could not yet be re-admitted to communion. The elders advised that a letter be sent to the BMS explaining that 'the Church was wounded not dead'. In 1925 Millman returned from a 'sad and painful' tour of the Lokele villages, having largely failed in his efforts to encourage the men to renounce the *libeli* ceremonies.[43] The station log book for the following year paints a similar picture with regard to the Baena tribe to the east of Yakusu, with church members being suspended for participation in the *kabile* initiation ceremonies in the forest.[44] The uncompromising missionary stance towards these rites could be criticized as culturally myopic, but it was endorsed from the beginning by African church leaders who believed that essential Christian morality was at stake. By the 1950s, *libeli* rites were fast disappearing from the Yakusu district; in the late 1980s they were practised only by the Bakumu and possibly one or two of the other isolated tribes on the south bank of the river.

In January 1923 J. H. Marker, writing a station report for Upoto for the past year which recorded 101 baptisms but 140 suspensions from membership for moral lapses, posed the question: 'Can it be that numerical

41. Thysville Church Minute Book, c. 1919-54, Church Meeting minutes, Mar. 1954.

42. H. Sutton Smith, *Yakusu: the Very Heart of Africa* (London, n.d. [1912]), 61-8.

43. Yakusu archives, Yakusu Log Book, 1923-38, entries for 24 June, 1 Aug., 31 Dec. 1924, 3 Feb. 1925.

44. Ibid., entries for 3, 7 Apr., 3, 12-14 May, 21 Aug. 1926.

ascendancy has again proved to be the ally of spiritual degeneration?'[45]
Marker was not alone in his concern. The Bolobo station report for 1929,
which similarly recorded 139 baptisms but 149 suspensions, interpreted the
losses as an index of a materialistic and carnal spirit in the church, especially
amongst the young, 'who are growing up around us and are being led away
by the glamour and error of a false civilisation. We have had to pay the price,
and pay heavily, for the ever rapidly increasing development of our
District.'[46]

As in other parts of Africa in the 1930s, the conjunction of rapid
numerical growth with an increasing penetration of the cash economy into
village life led missionaries to pray for true spiritual renewal. The Anglican
Church in East Africa was indeed transformed over the next three decades
by the revival movement which began in Rwanda in December 1933.[47] The
BMS Congo mission experienced a similar movement, but on a smaller
scale and for a much shorter period.

On 28 February 1935 Andrew MacBeath sat in a motor-boat en route
from Bolobo to Lukolela, attempting to type a prayer letter containing the
news that 'revival has come to Bolobo'. MacBeath reported widespread
weeping over sin leading to public confession and restitution, unprecedented fervour in prayer and hymn-singing, and a new passion for
evangelism. The revival had begun a month previously when Botendi, one
of the station carpenters, had been convicted, first by reading a booklet by
MacBeath about the fulness of the Holy Spirit, and then by a dream in
which he saw a vast multitude of sheep, all lost. Although some feared that
he was trying to start a prophet movement, Botendi's experience of total
surrender to Christ and new spiritual fervour rapidly spread to others,
including the pastor of the Bolobo church. Soon the training school for
teacher-evangelists was 'transformed into an apostolic upper room of prayer
and praise and witness-bearing', and the atmosphere of the boys' school
changed beyond recognition.[48]

As he wrote his prayer letter, Macbeath was taking Botendi and six others
with him to Lukolela for the monthly communion at the beginning of
March. The revival fire thus spread to Lukolela. By 24 April R. T. Tyrrell

45. A/65, Upoto Log Book, 1890-1954.

46. A/95, Bolobo station report for 1929.

47. B. Stanley, 'The East African Revival: African Initiative within a European Tradition',
    Churchman 92 (1978), 6-22.

48. A/95, Bolobo misc. corresp. 1931-55, Letter from A. MacBeath, 28 Feb. 1935. See also
    A/118, Ann M. Wilson to Elsie [West?], 9 Apr. 1935; and *MH* (July 1935), 161-3.

was able to report that over two hundred in the Lukolela district had professed 'conversion or re-conversion'.[49] A score of other young men most affected by the revival had also gone out to other parts of the Bolobo district, urging church members to consecrate themselves wholly to Christ and receive 'the fulness of the Holy Spirit'. Many were converted at Tshumbiri, which the BMS had taken over from the American Baptists as recently as January 1931. The station log book recorded that not a few lethargic Christians had 'their little world turned upside down by the dynamic of the Holy Spirit', although there were also cases of possession by spirits being 'mistaken for possession by the Holy Spirit'.[50]

The revival had a discernible impact on the Baptist churches of the middle river. Church membership at Bolobo rose from 2,177 in December 1934 to 3,437 three years later. 727 persons were baptized at Bolobo during 1936 - the highest total yet recorded - and a further 104 at Lukolela and 127 at Tshumbiri. Missionaries also reported that 'the break with heathenism is much more definite and the Christian standard is of a higher order'.[51] Yet twenty years later a document produced by the Bolobo staff commented that the high expectations fostered by the revival remained largely unful-filled. The document pointed in explanation to the inability of the BMS church to occupy except in a superficial way the huge area of 12,000 square miles inland from Bolobo, and also to the advent of 'competition for the allegiance of the people' (presumably referring to Roman Catholic mis-sions).[52] The revival failed to affect the Congo field as a whole: the geographical isolation of the middle river stations prevented the East African pattern of teams of renewed Christians spreading the revival message to new locations from being widely applied in the Congo. Deprived of the stimulus of geographical expansion, the Bolobo revival gradually lost its momentum.

The great majority of BMS churches in the Congo thus had to face the challenges of growth whose qualitative depth did not always match its quantitative dimensions, without the exceptional spiritual resources that a revival movement could have supplied. These challenges were frequently

49. A/118, Lukolela Log Book, 24 Apr. 1935.

50. A/127, Tshumbiri Log Book, 1930-49, Tshumbiri station report for 1935.

51. *BMS Annual Reports*, 1934-5, p. 31; 1935-6, p. 29; 1936-7, p. 12; 1937-8, p. 116; A/ 95, draft station report for Bolobo for 1937. See also A. MacBeath, 'The Revival in Bolobo, Belgian Congo', *International Review of Missions* 27 (1938), 415-23.

52. A/95, document produced for BMS deputation and Middle River Regional Confer-ence, 1956.

heightened by shortages of missionary staff. J. H. Marker's question of 1923 had been raised at the end of a twelve-year period at Upoto during which church membership had increased from thirty-five to 800 and the number of village schools from twelve to 116, while the missionary staff had actually decreased from eight to three.[53] Such circumstances accentuated the dependence of the village churches on the capabilities of the teacher-evangelists. At Upoto in 1928 the staff instituted a six-month course of training for prospective teacher-evangelists. The first fourteen students completed the course in April 1929. By the end of 1930 sixty students had been trained. The 1938 Upoto station report was able to record that the evangelization of the Upoto district was in the hands of a total of 129 teacher-evangelists, serving eighteen villages and 180 church members on the north bank of the river, and 102 villages and 1153 members on the south bank. However, the number of teacher-evangelists had in fact declined from 208 in 1934, owing in part to many having been 'tempted by the more lucrative employment of traders and companies'. The 1939 report took a more favourable view of the same process, observing that the teacher-evangelists were able to make use of the trade routes and roads now traversing the Upoto region to lift many above the 'new commercial atmosphere'.[54]

Missionaries thus perceived that the economic development of the Congo carried major implications for the churches. On the one hand they saw trade undoubtedly opening doors for the entrance of the gospel, yet on the other they deplored the impact on the church of proliferating and lucrative opportunities in commercial employment. At Upoto even primary school attendance suffered as children were lured away from school by the prospect of earning ready money from the gathering of copal, ebony, and palm nuts.[55]

Perhaps the most far-reaching consequence of the commercialization of the Congo was the transformation of Kinshasa from its status at the turn of the century as a transit station for river traffic into the city of Léopoldville and the capital of the Belgian Congo. Even before the First World War the potential of the town was apparent to the discerning eye. The industrialist

53. A/65, Upoto Log Book, 1890-1954, station report for 1922. The most notable loss to the staff was that of W. L. Forfeitt and his wife, who left Upoto in October 1922 after more than thirty years' service on the Congo.

54. A/65, Upoto Log Book, 1890-1954, station annual reports for 1928, 1930, 1938, 1939.

55. A/65, Upoto Log Book, 1890-1954, station annual report for 1938.

and active Congregationalist, Sir William Lever, made a point of visiting the BMS Kinshasa mission during his tour of the Congo in 1912-13. The following year he gave £1,000 towards the building of a new BMS church at Kalina (now the International Protestant Church). The same mail that brought news of his donation also contained details of Sir William's proposal to purchase a large section of the mission's valuable waterfront site at Kinshasa. The Kalina church was duly opened by a director of Lever Brothers in August 1915, and the sale of the BMS property to their new Congo subsidiary, the *Huileries du Congo Belge* (HCB) was concluded in December 1916. Sir William's shrewd philanthropy thus secured a prime location on which to found Lever Brothers' (subsequently Unilever's) massive palm-oil empire in the Congo. The BMS for its part gained £8,500 from the deal, and the right to use HCB vessels for the transport of goods and passengers on the Upper River.[56] Thus came to an end the era of the Congo mission steamers - the *Peace* (1884-1908), the *Goodwill* (1893-1915), and the *Endeavour* (1906-15), although for some years the Society retained a smaller vessel, the *Grenfell*, for use on the Upper River.[57]

Sir William Lever was not alone in his appreciation of the potential of Kinshasa. C. E. Wilson returned from his Congo deputation of 1919 convinced that Kinshasa, as the likely future capital of the colony, was of vital strategic importance for the BMS.[58] H. Ross Phillips was accordingly instructed to move the Congo secretariat from Matadi to Kinshasa, and D. Christy Davies and his wife were immediately brought down from Yalemba to minister to the growing Lingala-speaking population in Kinshasa. Until 1933 Davies employed his excellent Lingala to good effect in building up a strong Bangala congregation alongside the older work amongst the Bakongo people.[59] From 1924 both congregations worshipped in a new church building erected at Itaga in the African quarter of the city, with the Kalina church now being reserved for English services. A third church centre was opened in 1930.[60] The city grew in population from 25,000 in 1926 to 410,000 in 1959. The rapid growth of Kinshasa-Léopoldville was

56. A/102, Kinshasa Log Book, 1881-1956, entries for 8 Dec. 1912, 8-10 Feb. 1913, 22 Apr. 1914, 18 Aug. 1915, 11-16 Dec. 1916. Cf. C. Wilson, *The History of Unilever* (2 vols.; London, 1954), i, 167-79.

57. W. Y. Fullerton, *The Christ of the Congo River* (London, n.d.[1928]), 78-9.

58. C. E. Wilson *et. al., After Forty Years* (BMS, London, n.d. [1919]), 15-20.

59. J. W. Hughes, *D. Christy Davies: A Brief Memoir* (London, 1962), 44-51.

60. Parsons, 'The years of latency', 15-16.

instrumental in the evolution of Lingala towards its current status as the *de facto* national language of Zaire. It was a Kinshasa BMS missionary, Malcolm Guthrie, who in 1935 published the first full grammar and dictionary of the Lingala language, followed in 1939 by a revised French edition, which soon became a standard reference work.[61] The 1919 decision to augment the Society's presence in Kinshasa thus proved amply justified.

III: Education and Training for Christian Leadership

The involvement of the Society in educational work in the Congo stemmed in large measure from its concern to establish an autonomous African church. In the absence of any state system of elementary education (either in Belgian Congo or Angola), mission primary schools were the necessary foundation of a programme of Christian education and in themselves evangelistic instruments. The village teacher was usually also the village evangelist. As late as 1950, at least half of the enquirers seeking baptism into the BMS churches came from the mission's own schools.[62] No clear division could be made between evangelistic and educational work.

Yet the Society found, just as the British churches had found in the previous century, that the resources of voluntary Christian effort were unequal to the demands of the task of mass elementary education. 'There is no doubt that the children in the class rooms learn about God', acknowledged Ellen Clow, BMS Associate Foreign Secretary, in her report on her Congo deputation visit of 1951-2, 'but schools are costly. Like a whirlpool they suck in an increasing amount of missionaries' strength and time'.[63] Schools work tended to suffer with disproportionate severity whenever BMS finances were in a critical state. Such was the case in 1926 when, following a deficit of £34,565 on a total BMS budget of £240,000 in the financial year 1925-6, the Congo field was asked to contribute £1,000 towards drastic savings in overseas expenditure: the Wathen staff could

---

61. The spread of Lingala was also assisted by the work of missions; see W.J. Samarin, 'Protestant missions and the history of Lingala', *Journal of Religion in Africa* 16 (1986), 138-63. Guthrie's work was based on Frank Longland's 1914 revision of W. H. Stapleton's *Suggestions for a Grammar of Bangala* (1903). In later life, as Professor of Bantu Languages in the University of London, Guthrie began work on a complete revision of his *Grammaire et Dictionnaire*, which was continued after his death by Dr John Carrington, and published by the BMS in 1988. On Guthrie see *Proceedings of the British Academy* 59 (1973), 473-98.

62. H/100, E. M. Clow, 'Impressions of Congo visit', p. 2.

63. Ibid., p. 2.

meet their own share of that reduction only by dismissing thirty-nine of the 129 boys at the Wathen boarding school.[64]

Without more staff, reflected Dr Clow in 1952, the BMS had no hope of providing more boarding schools, which were the most profitable in terms of the formation of Christian character. Women's work in particular could be strengthened by the provision of boarding education for girls.[65] Popular demand ensured that boys far outnumbered girls in the mission schools, with the result that for most of this period women lagged far behind men both in literacy rates and in church membership. At Upoto in 1924 less than ten per cent of the church membership were women; in 1930 women accounted for only twenty per cent of the total membership of the Congo churches.[66]

Ellen Clow saw the provision of state education as the only ultimate solution to the Society's dilemma, in which great educational opportunities were becoming an increasing burden to its missionaries. Given current resources, she observed, the BMS could not undertake even to provide primary schooling for the children of all church members. The remainder would either remain illiterate or go to Roman Catholic schools, where a 'high proportion' would become Roman Catholics.[67]

The village school was indeed the point at which the competition between Protestant and Roman Catholic missions was most sharply focused. Yakusu missionaries complained in 1930 that the Catholics had taken advantage of the temporary absence of BMS teachers from two village schools (caused by their need to raise money to pay state taxes) to persuade the villagers to construct Catholic schools. Three years later the local priest, Père Tack, protested to the Belgian administrator that A. G. Mill at Yakusu had forcibly removed the tin medals which Tack had given children in order (according to Mill) to entice them away from the BMS school.[68] In 1935 the Wathen staff reminded the home Committee that the station needed teaching staff more than any others, 'as we are up against a growing opposition from the Roman Catholics'. The Catholic school at neighbouring Ngombe Matadi had been established as a deliberate counter to the

64. *BMS Annual Report,* 1925-6, pp. 5-6, 168-9; Mbanza Ngungu archives, Wathen Minute Book, 1925-53, minutes for 21 June, 8 July 1926. On the financial crisis in the mid-1920s see ch. XII below, pp. 383-4.

65. H/100, E. M. Clow, 'Impressions of Congo visit', p. 2.

66. A/65, Upoto Log Book, 1890-1954, station report for 1924; A/95, Bolobo Minute Book, 1929-39, minutes for 2 Sept. 1930.

67. H/100, E. M. Clow, 'Impressions of Congo visit', p. 2.

68. Yakusu archives, Yakusu Log Book, 1923-38, entries for 12 Feb. 1930, 20 Mar. 1933.

influence exercised by Wathen's superior educational facilities.[69] The growing appeal of Roman Catholicism, according to the Upoto station report for 1938, was two-fold: older Christians were attracted by the Catholics' preparedness to baptize after only a short probationary period; whilst the young were drawn by the educational advantages which the Catholic missions now offered:

> Ten years ago there was practically no Roman Catholic educational work in village schools throughout the district but that is not the case today. They have realised that our village schools were strong evange-listic centres and have made great efforts to follow the same lines. The recent dedication of a number of native priests at a neighbouring Catholic mission shows how far behind we are.[70]

Baptist complaints about what was still termed 'Roman Catholic aggres-sion' thus reached a peak during the 1930s in response to an apparently concerted Catholic endeavour to counteract Protestant influence on the young. From the 1940s a gradual and sustained improvement in Protestant-Catholic relations can be discerned. In 1931 and 1933, partly in response to the growing Catholic challenge, the Protestant missions working on the lower river convened two educational conferences at Kimpese. The first recommended the creation of a three-tier system, comprising preparatory schools in village catechetical centres, regional schools of an intermediate standard, and station high schools of a more advanced standard. Even the last-named, however, such as the Wathen boarding school, were not recognized as secondary schools. From 1930 the senior class at Wathen was designated as an *école française,* in which all teaching was done in French. The hope was that the best pupils from Wathen would go on to Kimpese to the inter-mission Evangelical Training Institution (KETI), renamed at the 1933 conference as *L'École de Pasteurs et d'Instituteurs* (EPI), when it was resolved to establish an *école normale* to run alongside the evangelists' course.[71]

69. Mbanza Ngungu archives, Wathen Minute Book, 1925-53, minutes for 18 July 1935; interview with Kathleen Brain, 13.11.87.

70. A/65, Upoto Log Book, 1890-1954; cf. T. B. Adam, *Africa Revisited: A Medical Deputation to the Baptist Missionary Society's Congo Field* (BMS, London, n.d. [1931]), 94-6.

71. *Report of Second Education Conference Kimpese, Congo Belge 25 July-2 August, 1933* (Kimpese, 1934), 1-3; Parsons, 'The years of latency', 16-17; EPI was staffed jointly by the BMS, the American Baptist Foreign Missionary Society, the Christian and Missionary Alliance, and (from 1937) the Svenska Missions Förbundet.

From this point on the emphasis at the Kimpese institution, founded originally to train village *catéchistes* who would be both evangelists and teachers, began to shift towards professional teacher-training. As late as the 1950s, Kimpese missionaries continued to deplore the trend, but found that the more able candidates increasingly opted for the teachers' course, leaving the pastoral course undersubscribed and with few students of real ability.[72]

Nonetheless, over the next two decades EPI Kimpese produced a number of men who assumed key leadership positions in the Protestant community. Within the BMS sphere, two of the most celebrated were two sons of Masakidi, former houseboy to Holman Bentley, and one of the two faithful Ngombe deacons during the prophet troubles. The elder son, Jacques Nzakimwena, studied for the pastorate at EPI and later returned for the advanced theological course. After his ordination in 1944 - as the first ordained pastor of the BMS Congo mission - Nzakimwena ministered at Kingemba in the Ngombe Lutete church district. In 1955 he visited Britain with another Kimpese graduate, Samuel Koli of Upoto, for the Jubilee Congress of the Baptist World Alliance. Koli had been identified in the EPI annual report for 1952 as destined to become 'an outstanding leader in the Church at Upoto'.[73] In fact his destiny was higher still: Koli (ordained in 1954) eventually became the second General Secretary of the *Communauté Baptiste du Fleuve Zaire*. Nzakimwena died of cancer in 1956. His younger brother, Emile Disengomoka, took the teacher training course at EPI, taught for a time at Ngombe Lutete, then, like his brother, returned to Kimpese for further study. After a period as headmaster of the BMS primary school at Mbanza Ngungu, Disengomoka became the first Congolese to study in Belgium for the three-year teaching diploma, the *Régent littéraire*. On his return to Congo in 1955, he was appointed headmaster of the Ngombe Lutete school. He became actively involved in the consultative structures of the colonial government, serving as a member of the Commission for the Protection of Native Rights, and after independence was appointed president of IPOC, the Protestant-sponsored institute for the furtherance of technical education in the Republic. He died, also of cancer, in 1965.[74]

72. A/100, Prayer letter of R. C. Salmon, 6 Jan. 1952; A/105, Report on higher theological training at Kimpese, Nov. 1954.

73. A/100, Kimpese Annual Report, 1952.

74. Information from Ruth W. Page and Kathleen Brain.

By national independence in June 1960, eight more Congolese had followed Nzakwimwena and Koli in being ordained as pastors in BMS churches.[75] All ten had received their advanced theological training at EPI Kimpese, which until 1946 remained the only secondary-level educational institution in which the BMS was involved. In that year the Society opened a training institute for teacher-evangelists at Kibokolo in Angola. The intention was to use the Society's Terjubilee Celebrations Fund to provide each of the four areas of the Congo mission with its own institute. Accordingly in 1947 the *École Grenfell* was established at Yalemba to train church leaders and primary school teachers for the upper river.[76] However, the proposed fourth institute for the middle river never came into being, whilst the Angola institute had an intermittent history, initially at Kibokolo and later at Calambata near São Salvador, as a joint enterprise with the Canadian Baptists. The *École Grenfell,* on the other hand, flourished under the leadership of John Carrington - educationalist, linguist, botanist, and one of the Society's most gifted missionaries - who was Principal from 1951 to 1958. The *École* continued to function until forced to close by the Simba rebellion of 1964.

Before the Second World War all Protestant schools in Belgian Congo were denied government subsidies and hence official recognition. Repeated protests by the Protestant missions, voiced through the Congo Protestant Council, bore fruit in 1946, when the door was opened to apply for state funds from 1948 onwards. The Congo Field Council accordingly agreed a list of schools to be presented to Government as ready for inspection and subsidy.[77] The effort required to meet government standards of inspection was considerable: Kinshasa missionaries reported 'a very serious withdrawal of time and effort from essential church and pastoral work'.[78] This was the backcloth for Ellen Clow's observation in 1952 that schools work was demanding more and more missionary time and energy. State recognition had been pursued in the interests of a long-term strategy for leadership training, but its coming brought short-term costs which some found hard to pay. The availability of state funding also made BMS involvement in general secondary education a possibility for the first time. A six-year secondary school at EPI Kimpese was opened in 1953, and plans were

---

75. The eight were André Dioko, Antoine Wantwadi, Daniel Mompoko, Jacques Nkosi, Bethuel Tunga, Georges Tomatala, Maurice Mondengo, and Samuel Lilemo.

76. *BMS Annual Report,* 1947-8, pp. 36-7.

77. A/69, Congo Field Council minutes, 13-21 Sept. 1948.

78. A/102, Kinshasa Station Log Book, 1881-1956, station report for 1948.

formed to open a *latin-humanités* secondary school at Ngombe Lutete in 1958. However, the necessary state funding was not forthcoming, and Ngombe did not receive its secondary school until the 1960s.[79]

In 1931 Dr T. B. Adam had summed up BMS educational policy on the Congo by declaring:

> It is no part of our intention, as it is no part of our Commission, to educate the country, nor yet do we seek to compete either with Government, with the Catholics, nor with any other Mission. Our educational system must be firstly evangelical, secondly evangelical, and finally evangelical.[80]

Adam's declaration was blunt, but accurate enough as a description of the Society's educational objectives on the Congo. Reality, however, was a little more complex. In a situation in which Catholic missions had been awarded most, if not all, of the resources which the colonial state was prepared to make available for education, Protestant missions were compelled to play the game according to rules not of their choosing. As a result, even if their increasing investment in education did not always yield the anticipated benefits in terms of the life of the church, they contributed more to the general education of the country than Adam could have expected.

IV: Medicine: Defining a Policy

BMS medical work on the Congo was pioneered by three doctors who did not survive their first term of service: Sidney Comber and William Seright who each served for a brief period in the 1880s, and Sidney Webb, who exercised a significant medical role at Ngombe Lutete from 1893 to 1895.[81] However, no consistent policy on the sending of qualified medical personnel to the Congo was apparent until after the formation of the Medical Mission Auxiliary in 1901. The first two doctors sent out under the auspices of the Auxiliary were Mercier Gamble, who arrived at São Salvador in 1907, and E. C. Girling, who began work at Bolobo in 1908. Under their supervision the first hospitals were opened at Bolobo in 1912 and São Salvador in 1913. On the upper river at Yakusu rudimentary medical care

---

79. A/69, Congo Field Council minutes, 20-27 Aug. 1957, minute 559.

80. Adam, *Africa Revisited*, 76-7.

81. *MH* (Aug. 1907), 243-4; on Webb see W. Brock, *From Mill Hill to the Congo* (London, n.d. [1908]). See also above, ch. VII, p. 235.

was first provided by William Millman and W. H. Stapleton, and later by H. Sutton Smith and A. G. Mill, who had received some training in tropical medicine. A small hospital building had been erected between 1908 and 1911. However, Yakusu had no resident doctor until Clement Chesterman's arrival in 1920. Under his supervision a new hospital was erected, and Yakusu secured government recognition as a centre for the training of *infirmiers* (medical auxiliaries).[82]

Clement Chesterman's principal achievement was, however, in his pioneering of a new approach to tropical medicine which became influential far beyond the Society's own sphere. By 1924 he had established that, in some parts of the Yakusu region, thirty per cent of the population were infected with sleeping sickness, and would die within two years if not treated. By 1927 he had reduced the incidence of infection to 0.3 per cent by means of a comprehensive programme of chemotherapy (using a new drug, tryparsamide), administered in the villages by nursing auxiliaries trained at Yakusu. He built up a network of eighteen health centres and thirty-five dispensaries, covering a total area of 10,000 square miles. Axiomatic in Chesterman's medical philosophy was the belief that prevention is better than cure, and that co-operation with government was essential for an effective community health programme. The work of registering and treating sleeping-sickness patients was conducted in the name of, and largely financed by, the colonial government.[83] He also believed that a community emphasis in health policy was imperative if evangelistic opportunities were to be seized and Roman Catholic influence in the villages thwarted.[84] Chesterman subsequently employed the same strategy that had proved so effective in virtually eradicating sleeping sickness from the Yakusu region to combat yaws, and with striking success.[85] It was also the basis of the programme of leprosy treatment initiated by his distinguished successor at Yakusu, Dr Stanley Browne.

Stanley Browne's interest in leprosy had first been aroused while studying tropical medicine in Antwerp in 1935-6. Arriving at Yakusu in May 1936, Browne had little idea of the true extent of leprosy in the area.

82. *Yakusu Notes* 149 (Feb. 1953), 2-4; M. I. M. Causton, *For the Healing of the Nations* (London, 1951), 114-23.

83. A/41, C. C. Chesterman to W. Y. Fullerton, 30 July 1927; S. G. Browne *et al.* (eds.), *Heralds of Health* (London, 1985), 110-12, 122-3, 309.

84. A/41, Chesterman's report on Yakusu for 1932-3.

85. Browne (ed.), *Heralds of Health*, 123; C. C. Chesterman, *In the Service of Suffering* (London, 1940), 126.

However, on journeys into the Topoke forest with Dr Raymond Holmes, undertaken for sleeping sickness control purposes, he was horrified to find sufferers from leprosy in its advanced stages, living in appalling conditions as exiles from their village communities. Browne and Holmes accordingly decided to employ the existing district public health programme to conduct a leprosy census. They were astonished to discover that in some villages over half of the population were infected. It was decided to establish a leprosarium for the most advanced cases across the river from Yakusu at Yalisombo. The early years at Yalisombo were frustrating: no effective treatment was available, and patients kept drifting back to their villages. The breakthrough came with the introduction in the late 1940s of the newly developed drug, dapsone, which was eventually to replace hydnocarpus injections as the primary treatment for leprosy in tropical Africa. Dickie Likoso, a brilliant Yakusu *infirmier* who was seriously infected, volunteered for treatment with dapsone and became the first leprosy sufferer in Central Africa to be cured. Within two years the population at Yalisombo grew from 118 to 1,025. More significant still, dapsone was soon available in sufficient quantities to be administered by the auxiliaries in the district health centres to all registered leprosy sufferers. Clement Chesterman's district health programme thus became the basis in the 1950s for a remarkably successful onslaught on leprosy.[86]

By the early 1950s Yakusu had acquired an international reputation for its community health work. Fame carried with it an apparent ability to secure resources of men and money that were denied to the other Congo hospitals. The feelings of resentment against Yakusu entertained by some missionaries came to a focus over the issue of *recensement* - the government-sponsored annual public health census which Stanley Browne, like Chesterman before him, had come to regard as essential to the community health programme. Browne had to some degree sacrificed his original ambition of pursuing a hospital-based role as a missionary surgeon for a community health emphasis which he now defended against all criticism.[87] Financially, *recensement* work was indispensable to the survival of the Yakusu hospital and medical school. Ever since the financial crisis of 1925-6, BMS policy had been that the Congo hospitals should be self-supporting; by 1952, São Salvador was the only Congo hospital to receive a direct grant

86. E. E. Sabben-Clare *et al.* (eds.), *Health in Tropical Africa During the Colonial Period* (Oxford, 1980), 75-8; P. Thompson, *Mister Leprosy* (London, 1980), *passim.* For the history of leprosy treatment in tropical Africa see J. Iliffe, *The African Poor: A History* (Cambridge, 1987), 214-29.

87. Pimu archives, S. G. Browne to Stephen [Henderson-Smith], 1 July 1954.

from the BMS. Spiritually, *recensement* afforded strategic opportunities for evangelism in the villages surveyed. Medically, argued Browne, an accent on community health was the only way forward for tropical Africa.[88]

This view of Congo medical policy was not shared by all. From 1952 it was strongly opposed by the Congo Field Secretary, Leslie Taylor, who regarded *recensement* work as a distraction from hospital and station duties, and was sceptical of its evangelistic potential.[89] Taylor, like his predecessor, W. D. Reynolds, found relations with Yakusu difficult. The issue of who should sign the legal contracts engaging medical missionaries to work for the government was hotly debated in 1952. Taylor believed that his status as the Society's legal representative required him to draft and sign the contracts; whereas Browne felt that a vital principle of professional ethics was breached if anyone other than a doctor signed a medical contract. A similar disagreement surfaced over whether the subsidies granted by the government to individual missionary doctors should be pooled amongst all the Congo hospitals. A deputation visit to the Congo field in 1951-2 led by Dr Ellen Clow had revealed the extent to which Yakusu was out of step with the rest of the field on these matters.[90] By 1953 the differences between Leslie Taylor and Stanley Browne were so serious that they overshadowed the Brownes' furlough in that year. For some months their return to Yakusu was in question. The BMS faced a delicate situation. Not only was Stanley Browne married to the daughter of H. R. Williamson, only recently retired as Foreign Secretary; he was also widely known in the Baptist constituency and beyond, and greatly in demand as a deputation speaker.[91] On the other side, Taylor had the active support of Ellen Clow and Victor Hayward as Foreign Secretary. In December 1953 Clement Chesterman agreed to mediate between the parties, but met with limited success: nonetheless the Brownes agreed to return to Yakusu in March 1954.

Leslie Taylor's attitude was influenced by the problems which the Society was experiencing in keeping the younger doctors who joined the Yakusu staff. Stanley Browne was a brilliant doctor but a demanding and at times inflexible colleague. Browne's personality and style of leadership also

88. Ibid.; see also H/100, Paper by S. G. Browne to Conference of BMS Medical Advisory Sub-Committee, Hemel Hempstead, 2 May 1953.

89. A/135, L. J. Taylor to BMS Officers, 7 July 1953 and to C. C. Chesterman, 7 Jan. 1954.

90. H/100, E. M. Clow, 'Impressions of Congo visit', pp. 6-8; A/134, Yakusu Sub-Committee Minutes, 19 Sept. 1957, pp. 12-13.

91. A/135, Hayward to Taylor, 2 Sept. 1953.

aroused resentment among a group within the Yakusu church, led by Samuel Lokangu from the Yakusu printing press. When Victor Hayward, accompanied by Taylor, visited Yakusu during his Congo deputation visit in May 1956, this group presented a letter requesting that Browne should be withdrawn from Yakusu, and made various verbal accusations against him. Browne appealed to the Chairman of the Society for a commission of enquiry to investigate the charges against him. The divisions at Yakusu itself were partly of a personal nature, but more fundamentally reflected the dissatisfaction of some church workers with the privileged financial position which the medical staff enjoyed as a result of government funding. From this point on, the broad divergences within the Congo field over medical policy were hard to disentangle from the internal tensions at Yakusu.[92]

Since June 1955 the Society had been considering a proposal from the colonial government that the Yalisombo leprosarium should be upgraded to become the principal government centre for leprosy treatment on the Upper Congo. The government would supply all funds for staff and buildings, if the BMS undertook to recruit the necessary medical personnel. Stanley Browne found the idea of serving as medical director of the new centre attractive, but the BMS hesitated, conscious that it would be hard pushed to meet its staffing commitments should Browne feel obliged to resign from the Society's service. By early 1957 the Society's consideration of the matter was complicated by the existence of the commission of enquiry which had been set up into the Yakusu difficulties.[93] When the General Committee in April 1957 indicated the Society's willingness to co-operate with the project, it did so under conditions which proved unacceptable to Browne and failed to elicit a favourable response from the government.[94] The Yalisombo project was not yet dead, but was about to be submerged in a wider argument from which it would never recover.

The three-man commission of enquiry into the Yakusu problems reported in May 1957. Its report concluded that the allegations made against Browne were unfounded, and accused Taylor of prejudice against him. The report was accepted by the Society's Honorary Officers, but not by the General Purposes sub-committee. The sub-committee, conscious of Victor Hayward's unhappiness with the report, recommended that a

---

92. Interviews with Samuel Lokangu, 30.9.87, and Mrs Mali Browne, 13.2.89.

93. General Committee Minutes, 5-6 July 1955, p. 72; 24-25 Jan. 1956, p. 12; 6-7 Nov. 1956, p. 149; Minutes of Officers Meetings, 3 Nov. 1955, 5 Jan. 1956, 3 Jan. 1957.

94. General Committee Minutes, 25-26 April 1957, p. 78.

further sub-committee be set up 'to enquire into the policy of the Society both medical and general at Yakusu, and to review its application and working'. The Yakusu sub-committee held its first meeting in August 1957.[95]

The Yakusu sub-committee interviewed a number of former Congo missionaries in addition to Ellen Clow and Victor Hayward. Strangely it neither sought any written submission from Leslie Taylor nor sent a representative to Yakusu, although W. H. Ennals, a former Yakusu missionary of thirty years' experience, did report to the sub-committee on an investigative visit made at the Society's request in the summer of 1957. The sub-committee reported on 13 February 1958. Although not uncritical of Dr Browne, the report generally supported his policies, and reserved its strongest criticisms for Leslie Taylor; it recommended that he be transferred to some other post within the Society. One member of the sub-committee, Gwenyth Hubble (the Principal of Carey Hall), was unable to attend the meetings at which the report was drafted, and submitted a minority report supporting Taylor and Hayward.[96]

The Yakusu report was adopted (by a majority vote) by the General Purposes sub-committee on 20 March. Furthermore, the committee proceeded to accept Leslie Taylor's resignation, which he had originally offered in April 1957 in response to the report of the commission of enquiry, but had agreed to hold in abeyance pending the outcome of the Yakusu sub-committee report. In response Ellen Clow tendered her resignation, and it was announced that Victor Hayward had already resigned.[97] The decisions taken on 20 March caused immediate consternation on the field. Three missionaries resigned on the spot, and at least seven more threatened resignation. The Chairman of the Society (Dr G. H. C. Angus) received representations from the Lower River Regional Conference and most other parts of the Congo field, urging the retention of Leslie Taylor. By the date of the next meeting of the General Purposes sub-committee on 10 April it was evident that the BMS was facing a grave crisis. At that meeting Dr Ernest Payne, the General Secretary of the Baptist Union (who had not been present on 20 March), criticized the action of the sub-committee in

95. A/134, Minutes of Officers Meeting, 7 May 1957; Chairman's Report from the General Purposes Sub-Committee to General Committee re Yakusu Matters [1959]; Yakusu Sub-Committee Minute Book.

96. A/134, Yakusu Sub-Committee Minute Book.

97. A/134, Minutes of General Purposes Sub-Committee, 20 Mar. 1958.

accepting a resignation tendered a year previously.[98] Payne was clearly influential in inducing the committee on 17 April to rescind its acceptance of Taylor's resignation, and he and Angus drafted a joint statement on the crisis for presentation to the General Committee.[99] Damage limitation was now the principal object in view. At the General Committee on 24-25 April resolutions were framed which persuaded Hayward and Clow to withdraw their resignations, and also enabled Taylor and a number of his Congo colleagues to follow suit. The Brownes' response to these resolutions was, however, to tender their resignations.[100] The Brownes returned home in the summer of 1958. Persistent but ultimately unavailing efforts were made to secure the withdrawal of their resignations: these were finally accepted in April 1959. Moreover, the withdrawals of resignation by Hayward, Clow and Taylor proved merely temporary. Hayward, feeling that the General Committee had tried so hard to conciliate Browne that his own position was again rendered impossible, finally resigned at a special meeting of the General Committee on 9 March 1959. The resignations of Ellen Clow and Leslie Taylor were finally accepted by the General Committee in April.[101]

Thus ended probably the most divisive and damaging dispute to affect the Society and its constituency since the Serampore controversy of the 1820s. As in that controversy, failings of human temperament and relationship played their part, but do not provide a total explanation. The issue beneath the surface of the argument was the degree of policy autonomy to be permitted to the medical work. The major administrative reorganisation of the Society between 1946 and 1948 had terminated the separate existence of the medical department. Clement Chesterman had been unhappy with the change at the time, and in consequence had discontinued his secretarial role within the Society, although continuing as Medical Officer.[102] The Yakusu medical staff felt that the new administrative regime threatened to sacrifice their unique professional achievements for the sake of non-medical concerns. Stanley Browne was undoubtedly correct in his

---

98. A/134, Minutes of General Purposes Sub-Committee, 10 Apr. 1958; A/70, Minutes of Lower River Regional Conference, 8-12 Apr. 1958.

99. A/134, Minutes of General Purposes Sub-Committee, 17 Apr. 1958.

100. General Committee Minutes, 24-25 Apr. 1958, pp. 35-7, 56-7; 1-2 July 1958, pp. 95-6.

101. General Committee Minutes, 4-5 Nov. 1958, pp. 111-13; 20-21 Jan. 1959, pp. 4-6; 9 Mar. 1959, pp. 34-9; 23-24 Apr. 1959, pp. 42-6.

102. A/134, Yakusu Sub-Committee Minute Book, pp. 5-6, evidence of V. E. W. Hayward. See below, ch. XII, pp. 388-9.

perception of future trends in tropical medicine: the Zairean community health service today owes a considerable debt to the pattern pioneered at Yakusu. On the other side of the controversy, Leslie Taylor believed that Yakusu's commitment to government work was a liability which must be broken for the good of the whole Congo field. The events of 1958-9 revealed that most Congo missionaries agreed with him.

The divergence in medical perspectives between Yakusu and other parts of the Congo field reflected the less favourable conditions obtaining in most of the other BMS hospitals, which lacked the regular government funding that Yakusu enjoyed, and also adequate medical staff. The Society aimed to maintain a minimum complement of two doctors at each of its hospitals, but this goal was achieved only intermittently. There were times in the 1950s when the new hospital at Pimu (commenced in 1932 but not opened till 1936) had no doctor, in contrast to Yakusu's two or even three. In the absence of a doctor, state subsidies were reduced, and standards inevitably dropped. Throughout the 1950s Pimu was regarded by the Society as the medical department of Upoto station, and not as a station in its own right. At Ntondo hospital on the Middle River the problem of sustaining medical cover was even more acute than at Pimu. The BMS had assumed responsibility for Ntondo from the American Baptist Foreign Missionary Society (ABFMS) in 1946, but never had sufficient doctors available for the Congo to staff the Ntondo hospital on a stable basis.[103]

One solution to the perennial problem of resourcing mission hospitals was co-operation with other societies. In December 1930 a meeting took place at KETI, Kimpese, between representatives of the ABFMS and the BMS to discuss a proposal from the ABFMS for a united hospital and training centre for *infirmiers* to be located at Kimpese.[104] However, the report to the BMS from Dr T. B. Adam, whom the Society had sent out to review the medical work of the whole Congo field, was discouraging. Adam estimated that a sum of £40,000 would be required to construct and endow the hospital, and concluded that 'in the circumstances of an unprecedented world depression' it was impossible to ask mission boards for such a sum.[105] The idea of a united mission hospital on the Lower River thus lapsed, although as a first step the ABFMS proceeded to set up its own nursing school at Sona Bata, with some assistance from Dr Ernest Price and other

---

103. I. S. Acres, 'Partners in Healing' (unpublished BMS MS, 1983), 82-3, 89-91.

104. For the history of IME see G. W. Tuttle, 'IME: Institut Médical Evangélique: The First 25 Years' (unpublished MS, 1983, in BMS archives).

105. Adam, *Africa Revisited*, 63.

BMS personnel. The scheme was revived in July 1946 at a meeting of the West Central African Missionary Conference in Kinshasa, which set up a committee to investigate possible sites. The committee reported to the interested societies in April 1947, recommending a site not far from EPI, Kimpese. The problem of initial funding was largely overcome in 1948, when a sum of 16,000 Belgian francs was offered by the *Fonds du Bien-Etre Indigène*, the native welfare fund set up by the Belgian government in recognition of the service given by the Congolese during the Second World War. Even so, in September the BMS Congo Field Council voiced its grave concern that the project was too ambitious.[106] Despite such reservations, the final decision to go ahead with the *Institut Médical Evangélique du Bas Congo* was taken at a meeting on 28 February 1949, attended by representatives of the BMS, ABFMS, SMF, Disciples of Christ Mission, and Christian and Missionary Alliance. IME (as the new hospital soon became known) admitted its first patient in July 1952 and was formally opened on 5 June 1953.

IME rapidly became known throughout the lower river and beyond for the high standards of its nursing school and hospital. Two BMS surgeons, Ernest Price and (from 1958) David Wilson, were largely responsible for IME's success in establishing a distinguished reputation in orthopaedic surgery. By independence in 1960 IME had laid the foundations for its own distinctive and substantial contribution to the creation of the Zairean health service. Although the BMS had found the formulation of a consistent and workable medical policy on the Congo difficult, the Society had played a vital role in setting patterns of medical provision and education which would endure into the post-colonial period.

V: The Road to Independence - Church and Mission in the Congo, 1954-60

'The time seems to have come, or to be dawning, when our African brethren will expect to share with their missionary colleagues in joint Missionary and Church Councils, which will have at least consultative and advisory powers on all matters of common interest and concern'. Those perceptive words of H. R. Williamson's were written as early as 1944, at the conclusion of his visit to the Congo field.[107] Ten years later, Victor Hayward's 'Review of BMS Work Overseas' issued a prophetic call for a transformation of a more radical kind in missionary policy in the Congo:

---

106. A/69, Minutes of Congo Field Council, 18-21 Sept. 1948.

107. H. R. Williamson, *Fresh Ventures in Fellowship* (BMS, London, 1944), 32.

It is surely only a question of time before the cries of 'Imperialism' and 'exploitation' are taken up against the Colonial Government in Belgian Congo ... The impact of the rising tide of revolutionary feeling in Asia, as well as rapidly-mounting racial tension in several different parts of Africa itself, all hasten a day of sudden change in Congo. It is just as imperative here as elsewhere that ... we plan our work along lines of policy designed to leave the African Church in as strong a position as possible when conditions of foreign missionary work become far more difficult or impossible.[108]

Following Williamson's visit in 1944, an administrative structure for the Congo mission had been set up, comprising four regional missionary conferences, and, from 1948, a Congo Field Council. The responses of the regional conferences to Hayward's paper are revealing. The Lower River Regional Conference declared that 'while so far the Congo Church has not reached the required standard for it to assume full responsibility', every effort must be made to promote the process of devolution, in particular by increasing the number of ordained pastors (which in turn required the development of secondary education).[109] The middle river missionaries agreed that full spiritual authority should be given to the African, but only gradually, on account of 'the African mentality', and the Africans' own desire for a gradual process of devolution. Devolution was to be pursued for its own sake, not out of fear of Communism or an enforced missionary exodus, which were unlikely in the Congo. The Upper River Conference similarly warned against hasty devolution of power, and felt that 'the note of urgency audible throughout the Review and probably sounded because of recent experiences of the Society in the East and South-Asia fields, may be somewhat exaggerated when heard in Congo'. The Angola Conference expressed the view that 'Africans are far less willing to accept responsibility than are missionaries to relinquish it', and doubted whether there were enough church members of 'assimilated' status in Angola to enable the church to have a legal existence independently of the mission.[110]

108. H/100, 'Review of BMS Work Overseas', Jan. 1954, p. 11.

109. Jacques Nzakimwena and Samuel Koli were then the only ordained pastors in the BMS Congo mission.

110. A/69, Minutes of Regional Conferences: for Lower River, 10- May 1954; for Middle River, 15-22 Apr. 1954; for Upper River, 20-25 Mar. 1954, for Angola, 17-23 May 1954. 'Assimilated' Africans under Portuguese colonial rule were those (a tiny minority) deemed by their education to qualify for civil rights and equal status to a Portuguese national.

The consensus of BMS Congo missionaries in 1954 was thus that devolution of authority to the African churches was a vital long-term goal, but was neither urgently necessary nor immediately practicable. The China experience, whose imprint was so clearly seen in Hayward's paper, seemed of minimal relevance to the Congo. Missionaries of other societies took much the same view. In February 1956 there was still not one African delegate present at the meetings of the Congo Protestant Council, the body representing all Protestant missions in the Belgian Congo. The BMS took the first steps towards incorporating Africans into its decision-making processes at the Lower River Regional Conference in July 1956, when Jacques Nzakimwena and Emile Disengomoka were invited to attend the final day's sessions, when church and education matters were discussed. In response to prompting by Victor Hayward, who was present at the Congo field conferences that year, it was also decided to set up African Church Councils in the four main church districts of the Lower River Region, each of which would nominate one candidate for the election of a representative to the 1957 meetings of the Congo Protestant Council. A single Church Council was also established for the whole of the lower river. Similar steps were taken later on the Middle and upper river, where Church Councils already existed at local station level.[111]

Thus from 1956 to 1960 embryonic church structures were developed at district and regional levels in uneasy parallelism with the existing mechanisms of autonomous decision-making within the BMS mission.[112] At the national level, missionary control over policy, exercised through the Field Council, remained absolute. Yet considerable progress in the transfer of local power was made. Control of financial affairs passed from mission to church in most districts early in 1958. Under Samuel Koli's chairmanship, the Upoto-Pimu Church Council began to exercise significant responsibility, although some missionaries felt that it was long-winded in its deliberations and reluctant to take decisions.[113]

The Upoto-Pimu Church Council was a joint body on which missionaries sat. The Lower River Council was an entirely African body, and here

111. A/68: Minutes of Lower River Regional Conference, 6-12 July 1956; Minutes of Middle River Regional Conference, 12 -15 June 1956; Minutes of Upper River Regional Conference, 16-19 May 1956.

112. P. J. Manicom, 'Light and shadows in Congo' (unpublished MS), 69, 123.

113. *BMS Annual Report,* 1960-1, p. xxviii. Upoto archives, Log Book of Upoto-Pimu station, entries for 3 Jan. 1958, 1-3 Jan. 1959, 28 Dec. 1959-10 Jan. 1960. At Yakusu, missionaries retained control of church finances until 1960.

relations with the mission were more strained. In July 1958 the Council complained that some missionaries were ignoring its decisions, and seeking to maintain control over church affairs on their stations. Political conscious-ness was more highly developed on the lower river, and church life was deeply affected by the re-emergence of the old 'prophet movement' of the 1920s, now assuming a more formal shape as 'Kimbanguism'. Almost 700 names (out of a total of about 2,400) had to be taken off the church roll in the Ngombe Lutete district during 1958 because of adhesion to Kimbanguism.[114] At the Field Council in August 1958, Harold Casebow of Ngombe Lutete presented a paper reflecting on the gravity of the crisis. Casebow warned that the new tolerance of the Belgian authorities towards the movement was being interpreted as evidence that the government had at last recognized Kimbangu's claims to be a prophet, thus leaving the BMS as 'enemy number one'. The refusal of R. L. Jennings and A. W. Hillard in 1921 to believe in the authenticity of Kimbangu's 'miracles' had not been forgotten. Casebow believed that the secret of the movement's attraction was the desire for freedom from white domination. Unless speedy action were taken to hand over all authority to the African churches, there was, in his opinion, a real danger of the churches breaking away from the mis-sion.[115]

Casebow had perceived that the political climate in the Belgian Congo - as in Africa as a whole - was changing rapidly. When Dr David Wilson left Pimu hospital for furlough in 1957, he and his colleagues were still persuaded of the essential benevolence of Belgian colonial rule. When he returned in 1958, to IME, Kimpese, he found a totally different atmosphere prevailing. Later that year Holden Roberto, who was grandson of Miguel Nekaka and named after Robert Haldane Carson Graham of São Salvador, came to see Wilson at Kimpese. Roberto wished to obtain medical clearance to attend Kwame Nkrumah's All-African People's Conference at Accra as representative of the newly-formed Bakongo political party, the *União das Populações do Norte de Angola* (UPNA). Also a delegate to the December conference was Patrice Lumumba, president of the first nationalist political party in the Belgian Congo, the *Mouvement National Congolais*, founded in October 1958. More serious as a political force in the Lower Congo was the Bakongo tribal party, ABAKO, led by Joseph Kasavubu. In January 1959 major riots broke out in Léopoldville, during which several hundred were

114. *BMS Annual Report*, 1958-9, p. xxi; see also A/103, prayer letter from Eva Davis, 1 Apr. 1957.

115. A/69, Minutes of Congo Field Council, 19-27 Aug. 1958, pp. 28-32.

killed. Kasavubu and some of his supporters were arrested, and the country was thrown into political ferment.[116] The pace of political change had quickened to an extent that seemed inconceivable in 1954. The revolution in church-mission relationships then advocated by Victor Hayward could not be delayed for much longer.

In 1959 the BMS asked the various regional missionary conferences to express an opinion on the extent to which the church should have a say in the location of missionaries, a matter currently determined by the Field Council alone. The conferences responded by raising no objection in principle to the idea, but all pointed out that it could not be implemented until there was some central church body covering the whole Congo field.[117] In August the Field Council ruled that African opinion at the regional level could be consulted in deciding the location of existing, but not of new, missionaries. More fundamentally, the Council recognized that a choice would have to be made between alternative pathways of church-mission relationships: the existing church and mission conferences could either fuse into a unified structure (possibly with provision for some domestic matters to be withdrawn for separate discussion by the missionaries), or could continue in parallel, with a joint conference being set up to discuss matters of common interest. The Council offered no opinion on the relative merits of these options, commenting that it could not yet foresee the steps by which the Church would one day come to the goal of maturity and independence of mission aid.[118] A distinctly leisurely timetable for devolution was still in view. Political events in 1960 were to enforce a radical revision of these assumptions.

116. Interview with Dr David Wilson, 23.1.89; see A. Hastings, *A History of African Christianity 1950-1975* (Cambridge, 1979), 92-4, 131.

117. A/68, Minutes of Regional Conferences, 1959.

118. A/69, Minutes of Congo Field Council, 25-31 Aug. 1959, p. 9.

XII

The Domestic Life and General Policy of the Society, 1906-1962

I: The Era of C. E. Wilson

1. An 'All-Round' Man

In 1905 C. E. Wilson was recalled from Serampore College to succeed A. H. Baynes as General Secretary of the BMS. On assuming office in 1906, Wilson had only eleven years of missionary service behind him and was just thirty-four. In these circumstances to step into the shoes of Alfred Baynes, who had been in office for thirty-five years, was an awesome task. The transition was eased by the experienced leadership of George Macalpine, the first chairman of the Society (until 1903 the treasurer presided over meetings of the Committee). Macalpine, a wealthy businessman and engineer from Accrington, was re-elected to office for fifteen successive years.[1] Also in Wilson's favour was the fact that he was the first secretary of the Society to have had field experience. Trained for the Baptist ministry at Regent's Park College, he was an accomplished writer and linguist, whom G. H. Rouse had once had in his sights as an ideal successor in his own literary work in Calcutta.[2] When Wilson sought Rouse's advice on whether he should accept the invitation to the secretaryship, Rouse was in no doubt as to what he should do, and wrote home to Baynes in lavish praise of his qualities:

> Wilson is one of the most 'all-round' men whom I know. He can take a wide view of a subject, and also consider details carefully. He is both

---

1. C. E. Wilson, *Sir George Watson Macalpine, J.P., LL.D.* (London, n.d.), 8-9. Macalpine was knighted in 1910.

2. IN/44, G. H. Rouse to A. H. Baynes, 21 Feb. 1899.

intellectual and spiritual, with sound heart and head. He is judicious and enthusiastic, a good writer and a good speaker, a universal favourite and an attractive personality. His whole heart is given to the mission cause, and his one aim is the extension of the Redeemer's kingdom.[3]

Rouse's expectations were not disappointed in what proved to be another long secretaryship of thirty-four years, during which the BMS grew substantially in size, complexity of domestic organization, and diversity of operation. Wilson's years marked the summit of Protestant missionary expansion.

2. The Home Life of the Society

C. E. Wilson was appointed initially as the General Secretary of the BMS. Home affairs were handled by an experienced assistant, J. B. Myers, who had served the Society as Association Secretary since 1879. At a time of rapid increase in the missionary force, particularly in China, where the number of BMS personnel doubled between 1901 and 1910, it soon became apparent that it would be wise for the Society to revert to the pattern of the Underhill-Trestrail years of two senior secretaries, one with responsibility for foreign affairs and one for the home constituency. On Myers' retirement in 1912, the BMS accordingly appointed a Home Secretary of senior status, with Wilson modestly accepting a reduction in his brief from General to Foreign Secretary.

The new Home Secretary was to many a surprise appointment. William Young Fullerton, pastor of Melbourne Hall, Leicester, since 1894 was well known in the Baptist denomination and beyond it as a gifted evangelist and pastor, but seemed less obviously fitted for the complex administrative task of running a large missionary society.[4] He was an Ulsterman, originally of Presbyterian loyalties, whose Christian life had been deeply affected by D. L. Moody and, since coming to London in 1875, by C. H. Spurgeon. Fullerton studied at Spurgeon's Pastors' College, and ever afterwards gladly acknowledged Spurgeon as 'the master influence of my career'.[5] From 1879 to 1894 Fullerton exercised an itinerant evangelistic ministry in connection with the Metropolitan Tabernacle.

---

3 . IN/44, Rouse to Baynes, 16 Aug. 1904.

4 . H. L. Hemmens, *Such Has Been My Life* (London, 1953), 60; *BT*, 25 Aug. 1932, 590.

5 . W. Y. Fullerton, *At the Sixtieth Milestone* (London, 1917), 65-72.

Fullerton's appointment proved an inspired choice. As a colleague, Wilson knew he would be wholly dependable. While still in his Leicester pastorate, Fullerton had accompanied Wilson on a deputation tour to China in 1907-8, a journey that made the two men firm friends and established a mutual knowledge and trust which laid the foundations of their subsequent working relationship. It is clear that the China visit sowed in Wilson's mind the thought of bringing Fullerton to the Mission House as his colleague.[6] As an administrator Fullerton proved to be 'the soul of brevity', holding to the laudable maxim that almost every letter could be answered on one side of a sheet of note-paper, yet his letters rarely lacked personal warmth or concern.[7] As a denominational leader his evangelistic zeal and clarity of theological conviction appealed to the strong evangelical loyalties of most Baptists. Within the Mission House, his spirituality and devotion to prayer left a lasting impact. In 1913 he instituted the practice (which continues to this day) of the 'Noon Tryst', when the work of the office comes to a halt and prayer is offered for the Society's missionaries. His moving hymn, 'I cannot tell why He whom angels worship', sung to the Londonderry Air of his native Ulster, became a classic feature of countless missionary meetings in Baptist circles and beyond.[8]

Even before Fullerton's arrival at Furnival Street, C. E. Wilson was responsible for giving a new impetus to the home affairs of the BMS. Soon after his appointment in 1906, Wilson recruited W. E. Cule from the Sunday School Union to be editor and publication manager, a post which he held for thirty years with great distinction. Cule updated the format and image of the *Missionary Herald*, replaced the *Juvenile Missionary Herald* by *Wonderlands* (the title was Fullerton's) in 1909, and introduced a new imprint for the Society's publications - the Carey Press. Under Cule's expert hand, *Wonderlands* soon became one of the most popular and widely circulated children's missionary magazines in Britain. Cule was also largely responsible for building up a strong reputation for the Carey Press as the publisher of numerous Baptist missionary biographies and surveys of aspects of the history of the BMS, many of which remain valuable secondary sources for the historian today.[9]

Under the leadership of H. L. Hemmens, a young layman appointed in 1907 to co-ordinate young people's work, the first BMS summer school was

---

6 . Ibid., 16-17, 154; *BT*, 25 Aug. 1932, 588.

7 . *BT*, 25 Aug. 1932, 590.

8 . Hemmens, *Such Has Been My Life*, 62-3.

9 . Ibid., 51-2, 57-8.

organized at Folkestone in 1910. In the inter-war years summer schools became immensely popular, attracting at their peak more than one thousand Baptists each year to seaside locations for a mixed diet of Bible study, missionary education, and general hilarity. Many BMS missionaries recruited in this period owed their call to the mission field to attendance at a summer school.[10] It should further be noted that many Baptist marriages can trace their origins to friendships first made at BMS summer schools. Wilson's secretaryship also saw the organization of an impressive range of missionary auxiliaries, designed to galvanize differing constituencies in the service of the missionary cause. One of the most successful was the Girls' Auxiliary, established in Glasgow in 1903. By 1916 the 'GA' had become national in scope, with over 6,000 members in more than 300 branches. The enthusiasm of Sunday School children throughout the country was orchestrated by the League of Ropeholders, formed in 1911. London children had the added attraction of vast annual rallies, held in the Metropolitan Tabernacle from 1910 till 1939.[11] The combined influence of the summer schools, the Girls' Auxiliary and the League of Ropeholders enabled the cause of foreign missions to capture the imagination of the younger generation of Baptists in the inter-war years in a way that has never been repeated.

The most enduring of the new auxiliary organizations founded in the Wilson era was the Baptist Laymen's Missionary Movement, formed in 1917. The World Missionary Conference at Edinburgh in 1910 had recommended the general adoption throughout the sending countries of the Laymen's Missionary Movement, which was formed in the USA in 1906.[12] John Mott, the principal advocate of laymen's missionary organization, later described the movement as 'the most significant development in world missions during the first decade of the present century'.[13] As a result of the pressure from Edinburgh, a National Laymen's Missionary Movement was formed in Britain in 1912. One of those who became involved in this body was W. Parker Gray, a Baptist from Northampton, who conceived the idea of setting up a Baptist branch of the wider movement. With the active support of W. Y. Fullerton and the BMS treasurer, Sir Alfred

10 . Ibid., 52, 124-31.

11 . Ibid., 50, 90-6.

12 . *World Missionary Conference, 1910. Report of Commission VI: The Home Base of Missions* (Edinburgh, 1910), 181-201. According to Wilson, this Report was largely written by George Macalpine; Wilson, *Sir George Watson Macalpine,* 10.

13 . C. H. Hopkins, *John R. Mott 1865-1955* (Grand Rapids, 1979), 281.

Pearce Gould, the Baptist Laymen's Missionary Movement held its inaugural meeting during the Baptist Union Assembly in April 1917. The objects of the Movement were defined as 'the dissemination of information about missions and the promotion of prayers for missions among Baptist Laymen, in order that they may be aroused to take their share in claiming the kingdoms of this world for the Lord Jesus Christ'.[14] The Movement published its own journal, *The Baptist Layman*, from 1918. Although laymen's missionary organizations never flourished in Britain to the extent that they did in North America, the Baptist Laymen's Missionary Movement survived to became an enduring feature of twentieth-century Baptist church life. In 1944 the objects were broadened and the name changed to the Baptist Men's Movement.

A further conclusion of the Edinburgh 1910 Conference was that the rationale for separate women's missionary societies was fast disappearing. The Report of Commission VI commented that the existence of autonomous women's societies was causing rivalry and confusion at home, while on the field, even in the East, 'the old hard and fast lines' dividing women's work from general missionary work were being obliterated.[15] The issue was discussed at a conference held in York in June 1911 of representatives of British missionary societies, including the BZM and the BMS. Reports from this conference were presented to a special joint meeting of the committees of the BMS, BZM, MMA and Bible Translation Society in September, when papers were read reviewing the relations of the BMS and BZM. A joint sub-committee was set up to consider the matter in more detail.[16] A decision had already been taken, in response to a 'strongly expressed desire among missionary workers in the churches' to amalgamate the magazines of the BMS, BZM and MMA; the first united *Missionary Herald*, covering the work of all three bodies, appeared in January 1912.[17] The joint sub-committee proceeded cautiously and did not find agreement easy. Its report, presented in March 1912, recognized that the current division between the BMS and the BZM was no longer sustainable, yet argued that, whilst the creation of a single united fund was ultimately 'inevitable', for the moment it was 'most important' that the present mode

---

14 . K. W. Bennett, *Men in the Service of God: Seventy Years of the Baptist Men's Movement* (London, 1987), 7-8; C. T. Le Quesne, *Sir Alfred Pearce Gould K.C.V.O.* (London, 1946), 17.

15 . *Report of Commission VI*, 228.

16 . General Committee Minutes, 16 May 1911, p. 127; 19 Sept. 1911, p. 172.

17 . General Committee Minutes, 19 July 1911, pp. 169-70; *MH* (Jan. 1912).

of collecting funds for the different departments of Baptist missionary work should be continued.[18]

The incorporation in 1914 of the BZM within the BMS as its Women's Missionary Association (WMA) reflected the cautious compromise proposed by the sub-committee in 1912. Former BZM missionaries in India and China and single women missionaries working with the BMS in Ceylon, Europe and the Congo were brought together within one department of the BMS. The constitution of the BMS was amended to provide for the appointment to the General Committee of thirty members elected by the committee of the WMA. The assumption was that those elected in the normal way by the Baptist churches and associations would continue to be men. The WMA - like the MMA - retained its own committee, treasurer and separate finances.[19] In retrospect this was an unsatisfactory half-measure which could not survive for long. At the time, however, the compromise was almost certainly the result of insistence by the women that a degree of autonomy should be maintained: those who had become accustomed to almost total independence of action in running the BZM were loath to see their freedom disappear completely within a society where the reins of power were still in male hands.

The Edinburgh Conference had also drawn attention to the need for training institutions that would prepare women for missionary service.[20] As a direct response to this expression of concern, the BMS, the LMS and the Women's Missionary Association of the Presbyterian Church of England co-operated in setting up Carey Hall in association with the Selly Oak colleges in Birmingham in 1912. The Baptist WMA was given six representatives on the managing committee, but there was no Baptist member of staff in the early years of Carey Hall's history. Whereas most male candidates for the BMS applied to the Society in the course of, or on completion of, their ministerial training in one of the Baptist colleges, the majority of female applicants had received no theological preparation. The majority of those accepted after 1912 were sent to Carey Hall, although some continued to be trained at the United Free Church College in Edinburgh, whilst others attended Havelock Hall in London, a Baptist Union institution for the training of deaconesses.[21]

18 . General Committee Minutes, 20 Mar. 1912, pp. 75-8.

19 . *BMS Annual Reports,* 1913-14, p. 156; 1914-15, p. 15; *Baptist Zenana Mission Report,* 1913-14, pp. 6-7.

20 . *World Missionary Conference, 1910. Report of Commission V: The Training of Teachers* (Edinburgh, 1910), 82-94, 146-54.

21 . Candidates' Board Minutes, 13 Nov. 1923, pp. 175-8.

3. Global Fellowship and Ecumenical Co-operation

To a greater degree than A. H. Baynes, C. E. Wilson was able to benefit extensively from the enormous improvement in global travel brought about by the advent of the steamship and the opening of the Suez canal in 1869, which had reduced the length of the voyage to India by over 5,000 miles. During his period of office, Wilson made six visits to the field: to China in 1907-8 (with W. Y. Fullerton); to Jamaica in 1909 (with T. S. Penny); to India in 1913-14 (with Sir George Macalpine); to the Congo in 1919 (with the Rev. and Mrs L. C. Parkinson and Mr W. Parker Gray); to China in 1929 (with Mr Parker Gray); and finally to India/Ceylon in 1931-2. These tours gave him an unrivalled understanding of the complex problems of mission-church relationships, particularly in Asia. His visit to the Indian sub-continent in 1931-2, though motivated initially by the need to explain and implement major financial savings being imposed on the India field, was crucial in accelerating the process of devolution from mission to church in both Bengal and Ceylon.[22] In addition to his field visits, Wilson travelled extensively in connection with the Baptist World Alliance (BWA - founded in 1905) and the International Missionary Council (IMC - formed in 1921). He attended the BWA Congresses in Berlin (1908 and 1934), Philadelphia (1911), and Stockholm (1913 and 1923).

C. E. Wilson's period of office witnessed not only the development of strong confessional links within the global Baptist family, but also the growth of the modern ecumenical movement. In the early years of his office, Baptists were already actively involved in the Student Volunteer Missionary Union (SVMU - introduced to Britain in 1892) and, to a lesser extent, in its younger partner, the Student Christian Movement (SCM). By 1917 the BMS had sent out no fewer than 156 missionaries who as students had taken the SVMU pledge to devote themselves, 'if God permit', to foreign missionary service.[23] The impact of the SVMU must be partly responsible for the rapid expansion in the total missionary force of the BMS during the first fifteen years of the Wilson era from 363 in 1905-6 to 515 in 1921-2, the highest figure in the Society's entire history.[24] Baptist participation in the SCM was promoted by Martyn Trafford, son of John Trafford of

---

22 . See above, chap. IX, pp.290-3.

23 . *MH* (Feb. 1917), 37.

24 . H/96-7, BMS Details of Missionary Staff 1900-1949. These figures include both single (BZM and BMS) and married women missionaries. It should be noted that the increase of 26.5% in male missionaries (from 155 to 196) was substantially lower than that of 53.4% in all women missionaries (from 208 to 319, of whom 153 were single).

Serampore, who became secretary of the Theological College department in 1908 and within two years made the SCM a force to be reckoned with in British theological colleges. Sadly, Trafford died in August 1910, shortly after being accepted by the BMS for service in India.[25] In 1914 another Baptist of considerable theological ability, Hugh Martin, joined the staff of the SCM. Martin served the organization initially as Educational Secretary, then as Assistant Secretary, and from 1929 as managing director and editor of the SCM Press.[26] Whilst not fully representative of the theological outlook of the denomination as a whole, men such as Trafford and Martin were influential in forging links between the BMS and the SCM which ensured that the Society remained firmly within the ecumenical mainstream, despite attempts in the 1920s to align the Society with a more independent evangelical standpoint.

C. E. Wilson was fully committed to the participation of the BMS in the ecumenical structures which were established in the Protestant missionary movement in the years after 1910. His enthusiasm for ecumenical missionary co-operation, wrote B. Grey Griffith, 'won over many who were doubtful', although it must be said that many Baptists remained wary of ecumenism, at least in its domestic context, and viewed with particular suspicion J. H. Shakespeare's willingness as General Secretary of the Baptist Union to contemplate reunion with the Church of England on an episcopal basis.[27] Wilson was present at the historic World Missionary Conference at Edinburgh in 1910, and also participated in the consequent formation of the Conference of Missionary Societies in Great Britain and Ireland in June 1912. For several years he served as joint honorary secretary of the Conference, and in later years as chairman of its influential standing committee.[28] In 1928 he was one of three BMS delegates to the IMC conference at Jerusalem (the other two being Charles Pugh, the Congo Field Secretary, and John Reid, the India Secretary). It was above all his attendance at Jerusalem which convinced Wilson of the pre-eminent importance of the issue of devolution of control from Western missions to the younger churches.[29]

25 . T. Tatlow, *The Story of the Student Christian Movement of Great Britain and Ireland* (London, 1933), 355-63; *MH* (Sept. 1910), 269.

26 . Tatlow, *Story of the SCM*, 546-7, 902.

27 . *MH* (Feb. 1957), 210; R. Hayden, 'Still at the Crossroads: J. H. Shakespeare and Ecumenism', in K. W. Clements (ed.) *Baptists in the Twentieth Century* (London, 1983), 31-54.

28 . *MH* (Apr. 1939), 65.

29 . See above, ch. X, p. 314.

Under Wilson's leadership, the BMS saw no contradiction between whole-hearted ecumenical involvement and an unequivocal commitment to the absolute imperative to preach Christ to the world. When Mahatma Gandhi met a group of British missionary leaders in 1931 to discuss the vexed question of Christian 'proselytism' in India, it was Wilson who pressed Gandhi (without success) to concede that it must be right for Christians to preach to Indians 'the highest thing we know'.[30] During a period in which much of Protestant theology veered towards an extreme and undoctrinal liberalism, before swinging back in a neo-orthodox direction, Wilson's influence played its part in holding the BMS to a course which lay within the middle ground of the increasingly diverse landscape of evangelicalism.

4. Theological Controversy

The BMS in the nineteenth century, although sorely troubled at times by disputes over policy, had been almost entirely free of controversy on theological questions. This freedom came to an unhappy end in the early 1920s, when the Society, in common with other Christian organizations, found itself caught up in the parting of the ways within British evangelicalism between those who wished to embrace at least some of the findings of modern critical scholarship of the Bible, and those who repudiated such conclusions as subversive of the historic evangelical faith.[31] In 1892 a group of British evangelicals, mainly Baptists, had founded a 'Bible League' with the principal object of defending biblical authority against the inroads of the new 'higher criticism'.[32] From 1912 the secretary of the League was Robert Wright Hay, who had served the BMS, firstly in the Cameroons from 1884 to 1887, then from 1887 to 1896 in Dhaka, and finally from 1897 to 1901 as secretary of the Young People's Missionary Association. An Indian branch of the League was formed in 1921, with another former BMS

---

30 . E. M. Jackson, *Red Tape and the Gospel: A Study of the Significance of the Ecumenical Missionary Struggle of William Paton (1886-1943)* (Birmingham, 1980), 133.

31 . Regent's Park College faced similar attacks in the early 1920s over H. Wheeler Robinson's views on Old Testament criticism; see E. A. Payne, *Henry Wheeler Robinson* (London, 1946), 74. Later, in 1932, the Baptist Union itself was embroiled in controversy over the liberal views of T.R. Glover.

32 . D. W. Bebbington, *Evangelicalism in Modern Britain* (London, 1989), 187; idem, 'Baptists and Fundamentalism', in K. Robbins (ed.), *Protestant Evangelicalism* (Studies in Church History, Subsidia 7, Oxford, 1990), 305.

missionary, J. I. Macdonald, as secretary.[33] From November 1917 the Church Missionary Society found itself under attack from the Bible League, and from many CMS supporters, for its alleged toleration of higher critical views among its missionaries and candidates. The campaign soon broadened to other societies. A meeting of the League held in June 1920 warned missionary societies against the sending out of any who 'deny or doubt that every writing of the Old and New Testaments is God-breathed'. This resolution was sent to all the British Protestant societies, with a request for an assurance that no such candidates would be sent out.[34] The BMS Candidates' Board, although it declined to provide this assurance, authorized W. Y. Fullerton to tell Hay that 'no missionary is ever sent to the field who does not accept the unique and final authority of the Bible for the missionary message'.[35]

For nearly two years it seemed as if the controversy which was now tearing the CMS in two would pass the BMS by. However, the *Bible League Quarterly* for April-June 1922 published a list of all the missions which had supplied the unqualified assurance asked for in 1920, with a renewed appeal to those societies which had failed to do so. H. Tydeman Chilvers, pastor of the Metropolitan Tabernacle, noting the absence of the BMS from the list, then wrote to Fullerton asking why the BMS had declined to accept the League's formula. Fullerton's reply explained the difficulty faced by any society governed by an elected committee in accepting an addition to its constitutional basis. Nevertheless, he indicated to Chilvers that the Society was happy to accept the doctrinal statement produced by C. H. Spurgeon during the Downgrade controversy, which affirmed belief in the 'divine inspiration, authority and sufficiency of the Holy Scriptures'. Fullerton then assured Chilvers that he knew of 'no BMS missionary who is untrue to the Bible, its inspiration and authority'.[36]

This letter, with its explicit appeal to Spurgeonic authority, satisfied the elders and deacons of the Metropolitan Tabernacle, who published it in *The Sword and the Trowel* for August 1922. However, R. Wright Hay (who had been shown Fullerton's letter) now took up his challenge, and in a letter to

33 . Macdonald served in Orissa from 1903 to 1917. Before becoming a Baptist, he had been a CMS missionary.

34 . H/62, R. Wright Hay, *Untrue to the Bible: A Reply to a Pamphlet issued by the Baptist Missionary Society*, n.d. [1923], 19.

35 . H/62, [W. Y. Fullerton] to R. Wright Hay, 15 Oct. 1920; Candidates' Board Minutes, 5 Oct. 1920, p. 84.

36 . H/62, printed in R. Wright Hay, *Untrue to the Bible*, 16-17. Spurgeon's formula was that adopted by the Pastors' College Evangelical Association in 1888.

Fullerton made detailed charges against the most prominent representative of advanced theological views within the Society - George Howells, on the basis of *The Soul of India*.[37] Apart from the general complaint that Howells' thought was dominated by evolutionary concepts, Hay said surprisingly little about Howells' primary concern, namely the attempt to re-define the relationship between Hinduism and Christianity. He fastened instead on a number of statements which appeared to subvert biblical authority, most notably on Howells' assertion that 'positively no headway can be made if we confront the Hindu theory of an infallible Veda by a Christian theory of an infallible Bible'.[38] Fullerton sent Hay's attack to Howells, who complained in his reply to Hay that quotations from his book had been torn out of context.[39]

Under increasing pressure from conservative elements in the churches, expressed in letters of concern sent to the Mission House, the General Committee on 22 November 1922 issued a full statement, prepared by the Candidates' Board, affirming that the Society, though determined not to subject candidates to any credal statement, required them to show 'loyalty to the evangelical faith, including a reverent acceptance of Christ's witness to the Scripture and the Scripture's witness to itself'.[40] Nevertheless, the anxious letters from supporting churches continued. Three missionaries resigned and a missionary trust fund was set up to divert funds from the BMS and support one of those who resigned, D. T. Morgan, in his work in India.[41] Early in 1923 Hay made his attack on Howells public in a pamphlet entitled *The Baptist Missionary Society and Destructive Criticism of the Bible*. C. E. Wilson replied to this and another hostile pamphlet with a published defence of Howells' statements in their original context.[42] Hay later countered with a further pamphlet.[43] In some churches persistent rumours circulated about the alleged heterodoxy of Carey Hall.[44]

37 . See above, ch. IX, pp. 279-80.

38 . H/62, R. Wright Hay to W. Y. Fullerton, 25 Sept. 1922; G. Howells, *The Soul of India* (London, 1913), 400.

39 . H/62, G. Howells to R. Wright Hay, 31 Oct. 1922.

40 . General Committee Minutes, 22 Nov. 1922, p. 106; Candidates' Board Minutes, 14 Nov. 1922, pp. 140-2.

41 . Bebbington, 'Baptists and Fundamentalism', 319.

42 . H/62, *Bible League Criticism and the Baptist Missionary Society: Reprints and Parallels With an Introductory Note by C. E. Wilson* (London, 1923).

43 . H/62, Hay, *Untrue to the Bible* [June 1923].

44 . H/62, T. C. Jones to C. E. Wilson, 21 Apr. 1923.

In the face of such sustained pressure, the Society felt compelled to issue a further statement on 20 April 1923, giving renewed assurance that the BMS, while refusing to be bound to 'any particular theory of inspiration', 'stands for and teaches the Divine inspiration, authority and sufficiency of the Holy Scriptures'.[45] The annual report for 1922-3 declared in an emphatic and newly confident vein that the BMS 'continues in its old faith, bounded on one side by evangelical fidelity and on the other by evangelical liberty'.[46] There were signs that the Society was weathering the storm, and that its critics were far outnumbered by its supporters. At the annual meeting on 24 April a spontaneous resolution of confidence in the Officers and Committee was moved amid general applause, and passed.[47] As a footnote to the controversy, in November 1923 a special sub-committee of the Candidates' Board presented a report on the relation of the Society to the missionary training colleges. The report was concerned especially with the prevalent doubts about the orthodoxy of Carey Hall. Although denying that there was any evidence that any Baptist student at Carey Hall had been expected to accept any opinion contrary to her conscience, the report did suggest that Baptists ought to be represented on the teaching staff, and that the managing committee might be elected directly by the subscribers rather than by the sponsoring societies, to save the BMS from any appearance of endorsing any one school of theological opinion.[48]

These were difficult and divisive days in British evangelicalism. The parallel and much larger-scale controversy within the CMS led to the formation of the Bible Churchmen's Missionary Society on 27 October 1922.[49] A month later, Fullerton wrote to Howells, warning him that it was 'quite possible' that a similar secessionist society would be formed among Baptists.[50] That no such damaging split took place was due in considerable measure to Fullerton's role as Home Secretary in persuading many who shared his own Spurgeonic loyalties within the denomination that the Society remained committed to the evangelical faith. Fullerton viewed with acute distaste the heresy-hunting spirit displayed in the controversy, yet his

---

45. General Committee Minutes, 20 Apr. 1923, p. 37; *MH* (May 1923), 101.

46. *BMS Annual Report*, 1922-3, p. 5.

47. Ibid., 84; *BT,* 4 May 1923, 323-4.

48. Candidates' Board Minutes, 13 Nov. 1923, pp. 173-9.

49. G. Hewitt, *The Problems of Success: A History of the Church Missionary Society 1910-1942* (2 vols, London, 1971), i, 461-73; W. S. Hooton and J. S. Wright, *The First Twenty-Five Years of the Bible Churchmen's Missionary Society* (London, 1947), 1-16.

50. H/62, [W. Y. Fullerton] to G. Howells, 29 Nov. 1922.

own orthodoxy as a conservative evangelical within the tradition of F. B. Meyer and the Keswick Convention was unassailable.[51] Nonetheless, the controversy lost the BMS the support of a number of influential churches (for example, Porth Tabernacle, Glamorgan, and Trinity Road Chapel, Tooting).[52] How far giving to the Society was affected is not easy to judge. Receipts for the general fund declined sharply from £80,257 in 1920-1 to £73,890 in 1921-2. However, the controversy would have had its greatest impact on the 1922-3 financial year, when general income continued to fall, but in fact less rapidly than in the previous year; in the London area and in Wales, parts of the constituency where criticism of the BMS was particularly fierce, there was only a marginal decline in giving from 1921-2 to 1922-3.[53] Theological argument had relatively little effect on the financial condition of the Society in the 1920s.

5. The Arthington Fund, Financial Crisis and Retrenchment

On 9 October 1900 Robert Arthington, eccentric recluse, originator and benefactor of the Congo mission, died in Teignmouth.[54] His will left five-tenths of his residuary estate to the BMS, and four-tenths to the LMS. The remaining tenth went to his first cousins. The will did not contain adequate provision for its administration, and it was August 1910 before the actual distribution of the estate could take place. By that time it had grown to over one million pounds, of which the BMS received £466,926 11s. 6d. Arthington's stated wish (though it was not to be binding on the legatees) was that his estate should enable every tribe of mankind to be given the gospels of Luke and John and the Acts of the Apostles in their own language. However, the will required only that the money should be used 'for the purpose of spreading the knowledge of God's word among the heathen (excluding Mohammedan populations)'. The High Court, in fidelity to Arthington's commitment to pioneer evangelism, also laid down in 1904

---

51 . See the memorial tributes in *BT*, 25 Aug. 1932, 588-9; *MH* (Oct. 1932), 231-2, 238-9.

52 . A selection of correspondence from protesting churches is preserved in box H/62. A. de M. Chesterman comments that the selection represents about one-tenth of the original volume.

53 . *BMS Annual Reports.*

54 . For Arthington's relationship with the BMS in his life-time, see B. Stanley, 'The Miser of Headingley' in W.J. Sheils and D. Wood (eds), *The Church and Wealth* (Studies in Church History 24, Oxford, 1987), 371-82.

that all the money should be used for the development of new mission work, and that the whole sum should be expended within twenty-five years.[55]

The BMS placed the responsibility for the disbursement of its share of the money, denominated Arthington Fund No. 1, in the hands of a special committee. The challenge facing the BMS was how to fulfil the terms of the will without expanding the work of the Society to such an extent that financial disaster beckoned once the twenty-five years had elapsed. Four officers of the Society played a particular role in ensuring that the Fund was administered prudently: Sir George Macalpine, chairman until 1918; Edward Robinson, J.P., of Bristol, BMS treasurer from 1904 to 1914; Sir Alfred Pearce Gould, treasurer from 1914 to 1922; and, in the final stages of the Fund's life, his brother, Harry Pearce Gould, treasurer from 1922 to 1927. It was the Arthington Fund which made possible the three new pioneer ventures undertaken by the BMS in India: the assumption by the BMS of responsibility for the Kond Hills mission; the commencement of work in the Chittagong Hill Tracts (including the building of Chandraghona hospital); and the opening of the Lushai (Mizoram) mission. In the Congo, Arthington money financed the construction of the *Grenfell* steamer (to replace the *Peace*), the building of the hospital at São Salvador, and BMS participation in KETI, the evangelists' training institute at Kimpese. A good deal of the Arthington money was in fact devoted to large institutional projects, such as the women's training college at Ballygunge, Calcutta, or the Whitewright Institute and Shandong Christian University at Jinan in China. Whilst some of these projects - such as the Whitewright Institute - could legitimately be described as evangelistic in character - the relation of others to the terms of Arthington's will was less immediately apparent. C. E. Wilson's wry comment on how Arthington might have reacted to the devotion of his money to the university at Jinan was noted in chapter ten.[56] Wilson's own growing sense that the missionary movement was accumulating too much institutional baggage was a sign that the pendulum of policy was soon to swing back decisively towards the more primitive approach to evangelism that Arthington had so ardently espoused.

The loss of value suffered during the First World War by the securities in which the Arthington Fund was invested meant that in fact the money was spent by 1928, two years before the limit set by the High Court elapsed. From the early 1920s, the missionaries and other charges on the Fund were

---

55 . H/29-30, Last Will and Testament of R. Arthington; A. M. Chirgwin, *Arthington's Million: The Romance of the Arthington Trust* (London, n.d.), 38-41.

56 . See above, ch. X, p. 305.

progressively transferred to the general fund of the Society. The fact that no important BMS project initiated with Arthington money had to be abandoned after the Fund was exhausted is evidence of the care with which this, the largest legacy ever received by the Society, had been administered.[57]

The gradual exhaustion of the Arthington Fund was one reason, though not the principal one, for the protracted financial difficulties experienced by the BMS during the 1920s. The First World War itself had remarkably little adverse impact on the Society's finances, but the malaise which afflicted the British economy in the 1920s had profound effects on the finances of all the major missionary societies. The most obvious source of difficulty was the heavy losses incurred by the societies on foreign exchange rates for sterling. However, the root of the problem was their inability to sustain in less buoyant economic conditions the vastly increased scale of the missionary enterprise initiated during the late Victorian and Edwardian years. The growth in the BMS missionary force - from 311 in 1900-1 to 515 in 1921-2 - placed enormous demands on the generosity of Baptists.[58] The greater emphasis on institutional work - particularly the hospitals necessitated by the new commitment to medical missions - intensified the accumulating strain on the Society's budget. Overseas expenditure thus escalated at a pace which the domestic constituency, much of it affected by depression and unemployment, could not match. The effect of these trends on the BMS, though critical, was in fact less grave than on some of its sister societies: the CMS, for example, recorded deficits in every year between 1910 and 1941.[59]

The large deficits incurred by the BMS in the early and mid-1920s had three far-reaching consequences. The first was to add weight to the strengthening case for a simplification of the tripartite structure created by the formation of the MMA in 1901 and WMA in 1914. A commission of inquiry set up in 1924 by a united meeting of the three committees of the BMS, MMA, and WMA recommended, despite evidence of 'wide differences of opinion' within the constituency, that the three branches of the Society should become three departments, responsible to a single General Committee, and with an integrated set of finances.[60] The General Commit-

57 . Chirgwin, *Arthington's Million*, 41, 151; *MH* (Apr. 1926), 79; General Committee Minutes, 27 May 1926, p. 47.

58 . H/96-7, BMS Details of Missionary Staff 1900-1949.

59 . Hewitt, *The Problems of Success*, i, 431; see also N. Goodall, *A History of the London Missionary Society 1895 -1945* (London, 1954), 549-52.

60 . *BMS Annual Report*, 1924-5, p. 86; General Committee Minutes, 18 Mar. 1925, p. 25; Various Sub-Committees Minute Book 2, pp. 134-6.

tee, meeting in May 1925 under the shadow of an outstanding deficit of over £23,000 on the previous year's accounts, therefore resolved, with virtually no dissent, that there should a single financial system for the Society, one integrated home department, and one integrated foreign department.[61] At the annual general meeting in 1926 the Society's constitution was accordingly amended to provide for a single mode of election to the General Committee in place of the former provision for thirty members nominated by the WMA. In future the General Committee would comprise not more than 120 persons, 'of whom at least thirty shall be men, and at least thirty shall be women'. Ninety members would be elected by the associations of Baptist churches, fifteen members by ballot at the annual general meeting, and fifteen would be co-opted. At the same meeting Lady Pearce Gould, widow of Sir Alfred, was elected chairman of the Society, the first woman to hold that office.[62] It had taken financial crisis to ensure acceptance of the principle that 'whatever other differences may inevitably exist', in the government of the Society there should be 'no distinction based on difference of sex'.[63]

The second implication of the financial crisis of the mid-1920s was that the BMS accepted that it had no option but to impose drastic cuts in its field expenditure. Following the declaration of an even larger deficit for 1925-6 of £34,565, a further commission of inquiry was appointed.[64] The commission drew up proposals (endorsed by the General Committee in May 1926) for the reduction of annual expenditure by £18,000 and an increase in annual income by a similar amount. Missionaries were to be withdrawn from eighteen stations, all except five of them in India, which was still by far the most expensive of the Society's fields. BMS hospitals were to be required to raise locally at least eighty per cent of their running costs. Missionary allowances were to be reduced by five per cent, and strict controls were to be applied to the sending out of new missionaries.[65]

It was argued in chapter nine that these decisions precipitated the first serious moves by the BMS towards devolving its work in the Indian subcontinent to the indigenous churches. Although in retrospect these steps were seen to be hastily-conceived, they set in motion a process towards

61 . Finance Committee Minutes, 7 May 1925, pp. 221-2; General Committee Minutes, 13 May 1925, pp. 55-7.

62 . *BMS Annual Report*, 1925-6, pp. 22, 25.

63 . *MH* (Apr. 1926), 95.

64 . General Committee Minutes, 28 Apr. 1926, pp. 32-3.

65 . General Committee Minutes, 27 May 1926, pp. 45-8.

autonomy for the national churches which was accelerated by the impact of the Jerusalem IMC conference in 1928 and soon became irreversible.[66] By 1931 the BMS was drawing an explicit connection between its continuing financial difficulties and the need to thrust a larger amount of responsibility on to local unions of Baptist churches on the field.[67] Similarly, in the Congo mission the introduction of self-supporting status to the BMS hospitals strengthened the case for a medical policy oriented more towards community health and co-operation with the colonial government in preventive medicine.[68] Some of the most fundamental shifts in twentieth-century mission policy were thus initiated, at least in part, in response to urgent financial necessity.

A third and related consequence of the financial crisis was a gradual decline in missionary numbers from the peak year of 1921-2. By 1932-3 the BMS missionary force had fallen to 397. Although numbers recovered somewhat later in the decade, the levels of missionary staffing of the early 1920s have never been repeated. One contributor to the falling numbers in the late 1920s was the impact of the anti-foreign movement in China in 1927, but in the longer term the most significant decline was in the number of India missionaries, as retrenchment began to bite and devolution gathered pace. How far the level of candidate applications declined also, in response to falling church attendance and a diminution in the old missionary confidence, is unknown and must await further research. What is beyond dispute is that in the BMS, as in the Protestant missionary movement as a whole, the early 1920s, followed as they were by a decade of worsening economic depression, marked the watershed in the life of the Asian and African churches between the age of pioneer missionary expansion and a new era in which Western missionary personnel were to play a decreasing part.

One member of the commission of enquiry which reported in May 1926 was B. Grey Griffith, pastor of Tredegarville Baptist Church, Cardiff, and a member of the General Committee since 1921. Griffith in fact had a large share in the writing of the commission's report. Having thus come to prominence at a critical period in the Society's affairs, it is not surprising that he was chosen to become BMS Home Secretary on W. Y. Fullerton's retirement in 1927. Griffith, a man of great business ability and financial acumen, had the primary responsibility for ensuring that the new integrated

66 . See above, ch. IX, pp. 287-290.

67 . General Committee Minutes, 6 Oct. 1931, p. 77.

68 . See above, chapter XI, pp. 358-9.

structure of the Society agreed in 1925 proved workable in practice. Strategic in this regard was a new sub-committee, the home organization sub-committee, set up to co-ordinate the work of the three departments, which rapidly became one of the Society's more important committees. As a Welshman, Griffith was able in addition to cultivate better relations between the BMS and the Baptist churches of Wales, which had reached a particularly low ebb under Fullerton, owing to tensions which were partly national and partly theological in character.[69] Griffith, who remained Home Secretary until 1942, possessed a keen mind, and his inspiring preaching did much to bolster morale within the BMS during the 1930s, when deficits became an annually recurring feature and Baptist churches first became fully aware that denominational membership was declining.[70] Stirring reports of continuing church growth on the mission field were a needed tonic to drooping Christian spirits in the 1930s, as Griffith openly acknowledged in the annual report for 1937-8 in language that carries a disturbing resonance in the light of the global war which was soon to engulf Europe:

> Some of our churches are fighting a hard battle, some are in areas still depressed, but when the deputation comes they realise once again that the battle fought in their immediate neighbourhood is part of the great campaign of God in the world. To some of our churches the tide seems to be receding, but the word of the missionary assures them that it is coming in full power in far-off lands, and they rejoice that they have a share in it all.[71]

6. The BMS and the Baptist Union

In the nineteenth century the Baptist Union had seemed very much the junior partner to the Baptist Missionary Society. The Union was younger, had no full-time staff, and was less clearly defined in its functions. Until the opening of Baptist Church House in Southampton Row in 1903, the Union was actually a tenant of the Society in rooms at the Mission House in Furnival Street, home of the BMS since 1870. This disparity was greatly

---

69 . IN/92, C. E. Wilson to H. Anderson, 18 May 1916; T. M. Bassett, *The Baptists of Wales and the Baptist Missionary Society* (Swansea, 1991), 24. This was despite the appointment in 1916 of Thomas Lewis as the first full-time BMS Welsh representative.

70 . See the tributes in *MH* (Apr. 1942), 34-5; (Feb. 1962), 19-20; and Hemmens, *Such Has Been My Life*, 67-70.

71 . *BMS Annual Report*, 1937-8, p. 8.

eroded in the course of J. H. Shakespeare's seminal period of office as secretary of the Baptist Union (1898-1925). Under Shakespeare, the Union became more organized and centralized, and gained a much higher prominence in ecumenical affairs. Even in Alfred Baynes's day, Shakespeare's initiatives had been viewed with some concern by the Mission House.[72] When the issue of a closer relationship between the BMS and the Union came to a head, in 1938, it was inevitable that some of the suppressed fears which the older body entertained with regard to the younger should come to the surface.

The issue was first raised on the initiative of C. E. Wilson and B. Grey Griffith, when uncertainty over the future of the Furnival Street premises sowed in their minds the possibility of finding new joint headquarters to house both the BMS and the Baptist Union.[73] A joint committee of the two bodies was set up in December 1937, and recommended that it was desirable that the two organizations should share a new and common set of premises.[74] Robert Wilson Black, a leading Baptist layman, was instructed to look for a suitable site. Black found premises in Russell Square which seemed suitable in many ways. They were, however, leasehold, and considerably larger than was required to house both organizations. These two features proved sufficient to bring about the downfall of the scheme when the matter came up for final decision in April. At the BMS General Committee on 22 April 1938, the finance committee brought a recommendation that the Society go ahead with the Russell Square scheme. However, the treasurer, H. L. Taylor, then made clear that he could not support the recommendation of his own finance committee. He objected to the leasehold nature of the site, and more particularly to the size of the building, which 'he feared very much' might introduce 'a business element into the Society's work'. Despite his pleas, the finance committee's recommendation was passed with four dissentients. Taylor then intimated that he was not prepared to allow his name to go forward for re-election at the forthcoming annual meeting.[75] In the event, Taylor was able to withdraw

72 . E. A. Payne, *The Baptist Union: A Short History* (London, 1959), 167-8.

73 . Fuller accounts of the joint headquarters scheme are contained in Payne, *The Baptist Union*, 208-11; W. M. S. West, *To Be a Pilgrim: A Memoir of Ernest A. Payne* (Guildford, 1983), 50-3; idem, 'The Reverend Secretary Aubrey: Part II' *BQ* 34 (1991-2), 263-81.

74 . General Committee Minutes, 19 Jan. 1938, pp. 4-5.

75 . General Committee Minutes, 22 Apr. 1938, pp. 46-50.

his notice of resignation, for, three days later, the Baptist Union Assembly, influenced by the declared opposition of the treasurers of both the BMS and the Union, voted decisively against any leasehold scheme.

J. C. Carlile's editorial in the *Baptist Times* on the failure of the Russell Square scheme expressed concern that the episode should not cause any bad feeling between the BMS and the Union.[76] It was a legitimate warning, in view of the fact that the proposal had been approved by the BMS General Committee but rejected by the BU Assembly. The feelings stirred up by the affair did indeed prevent much progress being made towards a closer relationship of the two bodies for at least the next two decades. Another fifty years would have to pass before a scheme for joint headquarters obtained the approval of both bodies. For C. E. Wilson, the 1938 episode was a disappointing conclusion to a long and distinguished secretaryship. For Ernest Payne, who had succeeded W. E. Cule as Editorial Secretary of the BMS in 1936, the failure caused deep distress and was one reason why in the immediate post-war period the Union (under Payne's leadership) and the Missionary Society 'moved somewhat farther apart'.[77]

II: The Era of J. B. Middlebrook

1. A Master of the Platform

If the dominating personality in the history of the BMS during the first forty years of the twentieth century is C. E. Wilson, the history of the Society over the next two decades is held together in considerable measure by the commanding figure of John Bailey Middlebrook, Home Secretary from 1942 to 1962. Wilson's successor as Foreign Secretary in 1939 was H. R. Williamson, recalled in the previous year from his influential post as China Secretary. Although Williamson set the strategic goals of the Society during the 1940s, he was already fifty-five years of age when he succeeded Wilson, and the disruption of the war years prevented him from seeing an early realization of his policy objectives. At the Society's urgent request, he stayed on beyond normal retirement age to lead the BMS through the post-war years of momentous political change in Asia before eventually retiring in 1951.

It was J. B. Middlebrook who provided the essential continuity of leadership between Williamson's secretaryship and the even briefer foreign secretaryship of his successor, Victor Hayward (1951-9). He also presided

---

76 . *BT*, 28 Apr. 1938, p. 334.

77 . West, *To Be a Pilgrim*, 53; Payne, *The Baptist Union*, 229. Payne had been Young People's Secretary of the BMS from 1932 to 1936.

over the fundamental re-structuring of the Society's senior management in 1946 which saw the final elimination of the functional women's and medical mission departments inherited from the era of the autonomous existence of the WMA and MMA: Eleanor Bowser, Women's Secretary since 1925, became India Secretary, and Clement Chesterman, who had succeeded Fletcher Moorshead as Medical Secretary in 1936, assumed the title of Medical Officer. The re-organization had awkward implications for Bowser and Chesterman, who, in theory, had hitherto possessed equal status to the Home and Foreign Secretaries. Middlebrook now became General Home Secretary and Williamson General Foreign Secretary. It was Middlebrook, too, who was the crucial determinant of the continuing delicate relationships between the BMS and the Baptist Union of Great Britain and Ireland. From the perspective of Ernest Payne as General Secretary of the Union, Middlebrook was at times an obstructive influence, appearing to block every attempt to forge closer relationships or make progress towards a joint headquarters.[78] From the point of view of the BMS, however, Middlebrook's firmness of resolve in resisting Payne's pressure for a closer relationship was the guarantee that the Society would not in any sense be taken over by a dominant Union or become simply a tenant of premises owned and controlled by the Union.[79]

For many Baptists in the 1940s and 1950s, J. B. Middlebrook, on account of his unrivalled gifts as a master of public advocacy of the missionary cause, became almost the personification of the BMS.[80] In committee he could be doggedly and devastatingly critical of poorly thought-out ideas. On his feet in the pulpit or on the platform, he could attain heights of eloquence, a passionate expositor of the New Testament message of the uniqueness and supremacy of Christ. Middlebrook was every inch a Yorkshireman, trained for the ministry at Rawdon College (near Leeds), and whose only pastorate was at New North Road, Huddersfield, from 1923 to 1942. He had been severely wounded in the First World War, losing his left arm. At Huddersfield he had preached sermons with a keen social dimension to large congregations, and became intimately involved in civic affairs, particularly in concern for the unemployed; he had been greatly influenced by the COPEC conference of 1924.[81] He served as president of

78 . West, *To Be a Pilgrim*, 102, 117-20.

79 . Didcot, J.B. Middlebrook papers.

80 . On Middlebrook see *MH* (Aug. 1962), 114-17 and (Feb. 1978), 18, 30.

81 . J. B. Middlebrook, *The High Places of the Field* (London, 1959), 20. On COPEC (Conference on Christian Politics, Economics and Citizenship) see E. R. Norman, *Church and Society in England 1770-1970* (Oxford, 1976), 279-313.

B. Grey Griffith, Home Secretary of the BMS, 1927-42.

J. B. Middlebrook, General Home Secretary of the BMS, 1942-62.

H. R. Williamson, Missionary in China, 1908-38; Foreign Secretary of the BMS, 1938-51.

Victor E. W. Hayward, Missionary in China, 1934-50; General Foreign Secretary of the BMS, 1951-9.

the Yorkshire Baptist Association, and became an active participant in both the Student Christian Movement and the Baptist World Alliance. In the late 1930s he was one of the influential younger members of the Baptist Union Council who formed the 'Focus' group, a discussion group which gained a reputation for progressive views and its willingness to challenge the denominational *status quo*.[82] With these credentials, Middlebrook seemed to many an obvious choice to succeed B. Grey Griffith. When in 1941 H. L. Taylor showed H. L. Hemmens the short-list of candidates for the home secretaryship being considered by the selection committee, Hemmens had no doubt that his own choice would be J. B. Middlebrook; as it turned out, members of the committee were equally certain that he was the right man.[83]

2. War-time Constraints and Ter-Jubilee Celebration

Middlebrook assumed office in April 1942 at a time when the domestic life of the BMS was severely dislocated by the extraordinary constraints of war-time. Somehow a deputation programme was maintained throughout the war, albeit on a much reduced scale and with greater reliance on headquarters staff rather than missionaries, for most of whom furloughs became impossible. Perhaps the greatest difficulty facing the Society during the war was the lack of an integrated headquarters. On the outbreak of war in September 1939, the Society had briefly evacuated the Furnival Street office and occupied the Sunday school premises of Union Baptist Church, High Wycombe. On completion of an air-raid shelter in the basement of Furnival Street in December 1939, the BMS moved its offices back to London. However, on the night of 9-10 September 1940 the Mission House suffered a direct hit from a high explosive bomb. The library and several offices were wrecked. Many records were lost. Although some staff continued to work at Furnival Street in extremely difficult conditions, others were removed to premises in Kettering. Until 1944, when the Mission House was again hit and rendered unusable, a skeleton staff was maintained at Furnival Street, while the majority worked in Kettering until 1946. On the abandonment of Furnival Street, temporary accommodation was found at 93-5 Gloucester Place. This 'temporary' accommodation turned out to be permanent, becoming, with the later addition of 97 Gloucester Place, the home of the Society until 1989.

82 . West, *To Be a Pilgrim*, 49.

83 . Hemmens, *Such Has Been My Life*, 70.

The year of Middlebrook's assumption of the home secretaryship was also the ter-jubilee year of the BMS. Most of the preparations for the anniversary had been undertaken by Grey Griffith, but Middlebrook contributed a good deal to the success of the celebrations, which were launched at the Baptist Union Assembly in the spring of 1942. As in 1892, it was decided to mark the anniversary with a three-pronged attempt to raise a special fund, increase the ordinary income, and recruit additional candidates. A target figure for the special fund of 150,000 guineas was set and reached with comparative ease. By the close of 1943, the time set for the termination of the celebrations, the sum of £157,677 had been raised. Giving was especially buoyant in Wales and Scotland, which both exceeded their original targets: Wales, set a target of 15,000 guineas, eventually raised £28,324; Scotland, set 10,000 guineas, reached £13,413.[84] Inevitably, raising the regular income in war-time conditions proved a harder task. Nevertheless, although giving to the Society (excluding legacies) had fallen sharply from the pre-war figure for 1938-9 of £133,112 to £111,485 in the dark days of 1940-1, thereafter a steady recovery was achieved, with income rising at first gradually, and then more steeply; by 1945-6 total contributions had reached £169,647.[85] This rising trend continued in the immediate post-war period, stimulated by a special campaign to recruit 100,000 new subscribers.[86] Although these results reflect credit on the home staff and the Society's treasurers (H. L. Taylor until 1946 and the Rt. Hon. Ernest Brown thereafter), they also point to the disproportionate role in the raising of BMS funds played by women. At a time when most Baptist men of earning potential were away in the forces, it was the women of the Baptist churches who, to an even greater degree than usual, shouldered the burden of missionary support.

The third object of the ter-jubilee campaign was to recruit 150 new volunteers for missionary service. Within the eighteen months of the campaign in 1942-3, 257 young people signified a firm interest in missionary service, 107 of whom were interested in medical missionary work. How many of these inquirers eventually became BMS missionaries is not known, but the impact on recruitment was clearly significant. Quite independently of the ter-jubilee campaign, six of the eleven students who completed their

84 . *Baptist Missionary Society: Ter-Jubilee Celebrations: 1942-4* (London, 1945), 14-16.

85 . *BMS Annual Reports;* 1938-9, p. 210; 1941-2, p. 113; 1945-6, p. 117.

86 . *BMS Annual Report,* 1949-50, p. xliii.

training at Spurgeon's College in 1943 went out with the BMS.[87] BMS recruitment remained at a fairly high level throughout the 1940s: 154 candidates were accepted by the Society during the decade from April 1940 to April 1950.[88]

Despite war-time restrictions on the use of paper and shortage of labour, the BMS was able to mark the ter-jubilee by a series of commemorative publications. The most notable of these was the popular history of the Society written by F. Townley Lord, minister of Bloomsbury Central Baptist Church.[89] It was the first attempt at a comprehensive history of the BMS since F. A. Cox's jubilee history in 1842. A decision was also taken in November 1942 to commence preliminary research work on a standard history of the Society. Ernest Payne, who had been appointed Senior Tutor of Regent's Park College in 1940 and possessed an unrivalled knowledge of Baptist missionary history, was commissioned to undertake this task. He compiled a register of missionaries from 1792 to 1942 (which remains in the Society's archives to this day) and a bibliography, but apparently got no further with his researches. The standard history remained unwritten.[90]

3. H. R. Williamson and the BMS in a Changing World

The centrepiece of H. R. Williamson's tenure as Foreign Secretary was two extended overseas journeys, which between them covered all the major fields of BMS activity. Between December 1943 and October 1944 Williamson visited first North America (primarily to attend the jubilee conference of the North American Missionary Societies), and then Jamaica, Trinidad, and the Congo. It was a journey of 25,000 miles accomplished in difficult and sometimes dangerous war-time conditions. The second tour lasted from September 1945 to April 1946, and encompassed China, India, and Ceylon. This too was a journey involving considerable risk, notably in China, where the authority of the Nationalist government was crumbling in face of the rapid Communist advance. Yet 'Dr Wei', whose Chinese name stayed in affectionate use among his friends throughout his life, was at no time happier than when on his travels. He never fully adjusted to the

---

87 . The six were Cyril Austen, Fred Drake, Walter Fulbrook, Bruce Henry, Harold Kitson, and Jim Sutton.

88 . *BMS Annual Report*, 1949-50, pp. xxxviii, xliii; *BMS: Ter-jubilee Celebrations*, 16.

89 . F. T. Lord, *Achievement: A Short History of the Baptist Missionary Society* (London, n.d. [1942]).

90 . *BMS: Ter-Jubilee Celebrations*, 14; General Committee Minutes, 4 Nov. 1942, 201-3; *BQ* 11 (1942-5), 295-8; West, *To Be a Pilgrim*, 63.

more humdrum routines of office and committee life in London.[91] His primary and lasting contribution to the life of the Society as a whole was the strategic thinking which was formulated on his two global tours. The two reports which he wrote on his journeys were printed by the Society under the titles *Fresh Ventures in Fellowship* and *The Christian Challenge of the Changing World,* and were given a wide circulation within BMS circles. As essential sources for the work and policy of the Society in its several fields in the mid-twentieth century, they have already been extensively cited in the course of chapters eight, nine, ten and eleven.

H. R. Williamson was a born optimist. The tremendous political changes which were unfolding during the 1940s in Asia, and less obviously in Africa, he saw primarily as opportunities for new advances and fresh patterns of missionary enterprise. Williamson's second report, presented to the General Committee in September 1946, concluded with a list of recommendations on future policy for all fields. At its heart was a paragraph which summed up his perception of the challenge confronting the BMS in the immediate post-war era:

> Unless lack of finance so determines, I cannot recommend withdrawal from any of our overseas fields. The reports already in your hands indicate the great need that exists in them all for our continued and indeed increased co-operation with the Churches in India, Ceylon, China, the Congo and the West Indies. The opportunity is also there, varying in degree in different countries and in different parts of them. But by and large, I estimate that an enhanced opportunity for evangelism will face us everywhere. In any case the heart hunger of these myriads of individual Indians, Ceylonese, Chinese, Africans and West Indians is there, which only the grace and hope of the Gospel of Christ can satisfy, and that represents a need of such intensity and extent that will challenge our faith and resources to the utmost. So I feel impelled to recommend that ADVANCE and not retreat is the note that we should sound in the face of this challenging need.[92]

With the cheap benefit of historical hindsight, Williamson's confident expectation of further advance by Western missions appears misplaced.

91 . J. B. Middlebrook, *Memoir of H. R. Williamson: In Journeyings Oft* (London, 1969), 54; Didcot, J.B. Middlebrook papers.

92 . H. R. Williamson, *The Christian Challenge of the Changing World* (London, 1946), 135.

Within the BMS, the shrinkage in the missionary force which had begun in the 1920s continued unabated in the post-war era: the total missionary staff fell from 410 in 1946 to 327 in 1961.[93] More specifically, Williamson did not anticipate the impending termination of the missionary era in China, and (less immediately) in India. As did many Christian observers of China in the early and mid-1940s, Williamson placed a good deal of faith in Chiang Kai-shek and the ability of the Nationalists to rebut the Communist challenge.[94] The rapidity and finality with which events in China moved to a very different outcome proved deeply disturbing for Williamson. To preside in his closing years of office over the evacuation of all BMS missionaries from his beloved China was the 'most trying and tragic experience' of his life.[95] Similarly, in commenting on the Indian political scene, Williamson was quite sure that the contemporary slogan 'Quit India' did not apply to missionaries and that a future place for them in an independent India was secure. Yet Williamson qualified his prediction of continuing missionary freedom by the remark that it was conditional upon the assumption that India would not be partitioned on religious lines. If partition were in fact to take place, 'the prospects of religious freedom would be definitely less promising'. In this respect, the recent religious riots in Calcutta and other parts of India were portents of a future that looked 'dark and menacing'.[96]

Williamson's optimism was thus neither uninformed nor untempered by sober political analysis. If he failed to foresee the extent of the implications for the Western missionary movement of the gathering anti-colonial storm, he was in good company. Nevertheless, as was seen in chapter eleven, Williamson had perceived that, even in the less politically charged context of the Congo, the day was dawning when African Christians would demand at least an equal share with their missionary colleagues in holding the reins of power.[97] In the final analysis, Williamson's serene optimism was more than just a reflection of the mood of the age in which he had been nurtured; it derived from a deep Christian faith which held that the destiny of the world - for all its current upheavals - lay securely in the hands of Jesus Christ,

---

93 . Didcot, CR 193, Missionary Staff, 1929-61.

94 . Middlebrook, *Memoir of H. R. Williamson,* 50; H. R. Williamson, *China among the Nations* (London, 1943).

95 . Middlebrook, *Memoir of H. R. Williamson,* 65.

96 . Williamson, *The Christian Challenge of the Changing World,* 55, 103-4.

97 . H. R. Williamson, *Fresh Ventures in Fellowship* (London, 1944), 32, cited above in ch. XI, p. 364.

its only Saviour.[98] On Williamson's retirement in 1951 the Baptist denomination marked its appreciation by electing him to the presidency of the Union - curiously the first former BMS missionary to have been given the honour since the inception of the Union in its revised form in 1831.[99]

4. Victor Hayward - A Prophet of Change

Victor Hayward, a China missionary like Williamson before him, took office in 1951 at a delicate point in the Society's history. J. B. Middlebrook was away from the Mission House, seriously ill. Moreover, Hayward had not been the first name to surface within the secretariat committee convened to consider Williamson's successor. Ernest Payne, chairman of that committee, had come under pressure to allow his own name to be nominated, but had declined, influenced in part by an awareness that a partnership between himself and Middlebrook was unlikely to be an entirely harmonious one.[100] Nevertheless, Victor Hayward soon made his mark on the Society in a manner which aroused mixed reactions. At the General Committee meeting in January 1952, he delivered a major policy statement, entitled 'Prophetic View and Apostolic Spirit'.[101] He did so against the advice of J.B. Middlebrook, who had warned him 'that it was not the sort of thing we did'. Hayward was indeed disappointed by the lack of response to his paper from members of the General Committee.[102] Although clearly too radical for the ears of many Baptists at the time, it was a searching and remarkably perceptive address which set the tone and direction for his eight years as General Foreign Secretary. The prophetic view which Hayward urged on the BMS encompassed three elements.

The first was a realistic grasp of the contemporary situation. The revolution which had just overwhelmed Western missions in China was, in Hayward's opinion, a sign that Communism was a growing force in the world. In India the new Congress government faced difficulties not dissimilar to those faced a few years earlier by the Nationalists in China, and a similar outcome was conceivable. Communism was not, however, the only danger. Everywhere nationalism was in the ascendent, and only too ready to use the resurgent religions of Hinduism, Islam, or Buddhism for its own ends. Missionary work in India, East Pakistan and Ceylon could not

---

98 . Middlebrook, *Memoir of H. R. Williamson*, 73.

99 . Ibid., 72. Later, H. H. Rowley and S. G. Browne were elected to the BU presidency.

100. Ibid., 72; West, *To Be a Pilgrim*, 72-3.

101. H/100, Central Registry, document 'G'.

102. Didcot, J.B. Middlebrook papers.

afford to ignore this rising militancy. Even in Africa, there were indications of a new anti-Western spirit: 'it may not be long', warned Hayward, 'before the cry of "Imperialism!" is taken up in Congo'.

Realism of political perception should lead, secondly, to an acceptance of God's word of judgment. 'We missionaries in China', conceded Hayward, 'have learned to recognise that there is a real measure of truth in the charge of imperialism that has been brought against us by the enemies of the Church.' Ever since the 'unequal treaties' Christian missions in China had been unhelpfully yoked to the protection of Western governments. More fundamentally, missionaries had generally failed to distinguish Christianity from a purely Anglo-Saxon expression of it, with the result that Christian theology had not become indigenous in China in the same way as Marxist philosophy had done. The Church had been saddled with top-heavy institutions. Christians had been taught to receive, but not to give. Furthermore, India and East Pakistan, which Hayward had toured before taking up his new post, displayed the same disconcerting features. To an even greater extent than in China, Baptist institutions were far stronger than the Church itself, which was poorly led, heavily dependent on external funding, and lacking in missionary spirit.

This was a radical and sober assessment. Many of Victor Hayward's hearers may have felt it to be unduly pessimistic. But Hayward's third point was that the true prophet, for all his insistence on the reality of judgment, also possesses an utter confidence in God's purposes. The God who acts in and through history was leading the Church into a new era of partnership in obedience to the missionary mandate. What was now required was a renewed apostolic spirit appropriate to the contemporary context. Its ingredients were urgency, mobility and flexibility, reliance on spiritual rather than material resources, cultural identification with the people, the building up of dedicated churches as the primary objective, a recognition of the liberty of the Spirit, and finally an emphasis on Christian unity as vital to the proclamation of the gospel.

Many of the ideas outlined in this address took their mature shape in the policies pursued by Victor Hayward throughout his secretaryship. Two years later, a more detailed examination of all the BMS fields, entitled 'Review of BMS Work Overseas', sought to make specific application to each field of the principles set out in 1952.[103] As was seen in chapter eleven, Hayward's perceptions were not fully shared by all BMS missionaries, especially on the Congo, where predictions of a Communist-inspired anti-

103. H/100, Review of BMS Work Overseas, January 1954.

colonial backlash seemed, even in 1954, wide of the mark. Nevertheless, the steps taken by the BMS between 1956 and 1960 to begin to shift the balance of power in the Congo from mission to church were a logical, if cautious, response to Hayward's prophetic vision.[104]

In India, East Pakistan, and Ceylon it proved far easier to identify the problem of a financially dependent and institutionally encumbered Church than to rectify it. Hayward's plea in 1951 for a mobile missionary strategy less tied to institutional commitments thus had to await the opening of the Brazil field for its realization. As we shall argue in chapter fifteen, the Brazil mission was fundamentally important to Hayward as an opportunity to construct a new pattern of missionary work which attempted to avoid the pitfalls into which Western missions in Asia had fallen.[105] It was also - and Hayward was quite open about this - a means of rejuvenating Baptist missionary enthusiasm depressed by the China experience. One of the most significant passages in 'Prophetic View and Apostolic Spirit' was Hayward's statement that

> we must have some new work to off-set a feeling in the Churches of disappointment at [the] closing of the China field ... we must be in a position to present to the Churches, with reality and inspiration ... the sense that one door is closed but we are opening others and going into them.[106]

Although the Brazil mission undoubtedly provided the fillip which Hayward anticipated, the general trend in recruitment to the BMS during this period was a static or downward one. In 1960 the Society received applications from only twenty-six candidates, of whom just six were men. In 1961 the total was seventeen, of whom only seven were men.[107] Enquiries from women were relatively plentiful, but many of the applicants possessed insufficient educational qualifications for the posts which the overseas churches had available. The most serious shortages were of theologically trained men and doctors. To some extent, the lack of ministerial candidates for the mission field was simply a reflection of falling levels of recruitment

104. See above, ch. XI, pp. 364-8.

105. See below, ch. XV, pp. 471-8.

106. H/100, 'Prophetic View and Apostolic Spirit', 7.

107. Didcot, CR 317, 318, 319. 2 of the 17 in 1961 were from New Zealand. Slightly different totals are indicated by the minutes of the Candidates' Board, which record the interviews of 18 candidates in 1961.

for the Baptist ministry as a whole. It may also have been a response to the gradual replacement of missionaries by national pastors in key positions on the field. However, the BMS was also beginning to express its concern about the number of Baptist missionary candidates who were choosing to serve with other missions of an evangelical and interdenominational kind.[108] In some of the more theologically conservative churches in the denomination there was a perception that the BMS was no longer a consistently 'evangelical' society, and hence a tendency to direct missionary candidates to other missions. The divergence which first appeared in the 1920s between 'ecumenical evangelicals' and 'conservative evangelicals' had widened over the years, and by the late 1950s the BMS was finding some difficulty in defending its credentials as both an evangelical and an ecumenical society.

One of the most deeply held convictions expressed by Hayward in 'Prophetic View and Apostolic Spirit' was his belief that 'a divided Church will never be able to preach Christ's Gospel properly to a divided world'.[109] The commitment of the BMS to whole-hearted participation in the ecumenical missionary structures developed since 1910 was for Hayward a cardinal rule of policy. He thus lent his consistent support to the reunion negotiations in both North India and Ceylon. He was an active participant in the International Missionary Council, attending its assemblies at Willingen in 1952 and in Ghana in December 1957-January 1958. The decision taken at the Ghana meeting to integrate the IMC with the WCC was one which many in the BMS, as in other societies, viewed with considerable reservations. Hayward, himself in fundamental sympathy with the principle of integration, had to represent at the Ghana meeting the concerns of the Society as a whole about aspects of the integration scheme.[110] Both Hayward and Ernest Payne as General Secretary of the Baptist Union found that their ecumenical enthusiasm was not matched by the more conservative theological sentiments of the Baptist denomination as a whole.

Hayward predicted in 'Prophetic View and Apostolic Spirit' that in future the younger churches of the non-Western world would find it easier to relate to Western churches on equal terms as partners in mission than to Western missionary societies as recipients of their funds and personnel. For this reason above all, Hayward was committed to seeing a resolution of the continuing ambiguity surrounding the relationship between the BMS and

108. H/100, CR 160, Meeting of Secretarial Staff to Consider Candidate Needs.

109. H/100, 'Prophetic View and Apostolic Spirit', 8.

110. Didcot, CR 170, IMC and WCC Integration; see *BMS Annual Report*, 1958-9, p. xxxvii.

the Baptist Union. Believing that the Baptist churches planted by the BMS would increasingly be seeking relationships as spiritual equals with the Baptist Union in Britain, and persuaded also that the Union needed the aid of the BMS in prosecuting its own missionary task at home, Hayward was unequivocal in his support for Ernest Payne's endeavours to bring the two bodies closer together.[111] That J. B. Middlebrook did not share this enthusiasm must have been a cause of some sorrow to Hayward, and may have contributed to Hayward's disenchantment with the Society in 1958, when a protracted series of conversations between the BMS Officers and representatives of the Union took place, but to little effect.[112] The primary cause of Hayward's unhappiness was, of course, the Yakusu controversy discussed in the previous chapter. This distressing affair was a further source of tension between Hayward and Middlebrook. The former tended to see Stanley Browne as representative of an older and more paternalistic approach to mission-church relationships. Middlebrook, on the other hand, was keenly aware as Home Secretary of Browne's importance to the BMS as a focus of loyalty and enthusiasm for much of the home constituency, yet felt powerless to intervene in a matter which clearly fell outside the limits of his office.[113]

After his resignation from the Society in March 1959, Victor Hayward went to Geneva to pursue his wide-ranging missionary and ecumenical interests as Executive Secretary of the Department of Missionary Studies of the WCC. He had been too far-sighted in his prophetic vision and too liberal in his sympathies to be fully acceptable within the most conservative of the British Free Churches. Moreover, as is often the case with prophets, tact was not his greatest virtue. A great deal of what Hayward said in his paper of January 1952 - with a bluntness which did not help to secure a ready hearing at the time - has now become accepted missiological dogma even in conservative evangelical circles. His departure was a serious loss to the Society at a time when the rapid political transformation in the Congo, which he had consistently prophesied, was about to dawn, with its immense implications for BMS work in Africa.

---

111. H/100, 'Prophetic View and Apostolic Spirit', 7, 9.

112. West, *To Be a Pilgrim,* 118; Didcot, CR 166, Interim Report on Discussion between the Officers of the BMS and Baptist Union, from February 1958, in the Matter of Closer Relationships between the Two Bodies.

113. Didcot, J.B. Middlebrook papers.

XIII

The Indian Sub-Continent, 1947-1992

I: Indian Partition and the Church in East Pakistan, 1947-1971

The partition of British India on 15 August 1947 into the two independent nations of India and Pakistan unleashed a torrent of religious migrants, flowing in both directions across the newly erected frontiers. Thousands of Hindus trekked from East to West Bengal, and from Pakistan in the West into the Indian territory of East Punjab. At the same time, Muslims poured into East Bengal[1] from West Bengal and Assam, and westwards across the border between East and West Punjab. This two-way exodus had multiple effects on the life and work of the Baptist churches and their BMS missionaries. In the short term, as was stressed at the end of chapter nine, there were victims of sectional violence to be treated, and large numbers of refugees to be fed. There was an immediate and marked change in the origins, language, and dress of many of the patients attending the BMS men's hospital at Palwal in India: about half of those treated in 1948 were now refugees from the Pakistani side of the frontier. The greatest problem for the Palwal hospital was the shortage of manual labourers to draw water, cook, and wash bed-linen, caused by the departure of most of the hospital servants for Pakistan. There was a similar exodus of Hindu servants from East Bengal. Prices of food and essential supplies soared, creating additional strains for the mission hospitals.[2]

In the medium term, partition created a sense of acute insecurity amongst the Christian community of East Bengal. Under British rule, the

---

1. The present territory of Bangladesh was officially known as East Bengal from 1947 to March 1956, and as East Pakistan from 1956 to 1971.

2. IN/107: Report on BMS Men's Hospital, Palwal, 12 Jan. 1949, by Edna Throup; W. [Davis] to John [H. E. Pearse], 14 Mar. 1950.

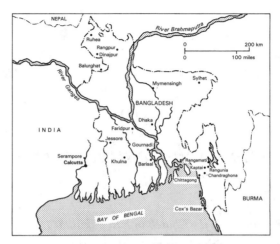

Map 8: Bangladesh

rights of religious minorities had been generally respected, but there was now a national feeling that Pakistan was for Muslims only. Despite the declaration of the Pakistani state that all citizens, irrespective of their religion, were equal before the law, Christians found great difficulty in securing government employment, and a considerable amount of mission property was requisitioned by the state. Insecurity bred insularity: the natural reaction of the tiny Christian minority in East Bengal was to keep their heads down and plan for survival rather than growth.[3] Christian schools faced particular challenges under the Islamic regime. In August 1949 an order was issued requiring all secondary schools to give daily readings, with explanation, from the Qur'ān, and the following February saw the publication of a new history syllabus, containing large amounts of Islamic history. Protestants and Roman Catholics united in protest against both measures, and were successful in securing the replacement of the August 1949 order by a new one more favourable to Christian interests. A more serious threat, affecting all Christian primary schools, was raised in 1951, when the government proposed that teaching of the Islamic faith should be made compulsory in any school in which there was a single Muslim pupil. The newly-formed East Pakistan Christian Council made a strong protest, and the proposal was put in abeyance.[4]

3.   G. Soddy, *Baptists in Bangladesh* (Dhaka, 1984), 197.

4.   Minutes of BBU Working Committee, 9-10 Aug. 1950, p. 12. IN/107: Davis to Pearse, 14 Mar. 1950; 1951 file, typescript annual report for E. Pakistan, n.d.

Initially the Bengal Baptist Union (BBU) determined to ignore the artificiality of partition, and as far as possible maintain unitary structures for the whole of Bengal. In practice, it soon became evident that the BBU must at least have a representative office in the East. It was decided in 1949 to open a BBU office for East Pakistan in Chittagong. This plan was frustrated by the requisitioning of the BMS property in Chittagong by the Pakistan government, and it was 1953 before the office was opened, located first in Barisal, and later in Dhaka. Missionaries, however, had to operate within the constraints imposed by the continued insistence of the churches that the BBU should remain undivided. In north Bengal, for example, Paul Rigden Green found himself responsible for administering from Dinajpur the new West Dinajpur Baptist Union on the other (Indian) side of the border, an arrangement that looked increasingly anomalous after the introduction of passport and visa controls at the end of 1952. Nevertheless, partition appeared to forward the progess of conversion among the aboriginal Santals of the region, partly as a result of the migration of a Christian village from East Bengal to Balurghat in India, which led to the conversion of others in the vicinity.[5]

As late as October 1955 the BBU Assembly, whilst recognizing that a growing measure of separate administration might become necessary, continued to resist any proposal to divide the Union itself.[6] To the BMS Officers, however, the case for division now seemed unanswerable. Travel between the two countries was becoming more and more difficult, and in 1956 the Indian government ruled that church and mission bodies must sever all connections with their constituent groups in Pakistan. On 17 October the South Asia committee agreed that, as from 1 April 1957, East Pakistan should become a separate BMS field.[7] Gordon Soddy, an experienced Bengal missionary who had served as acting secretary and as treasurer of the BBU, was later appointed as the first Field Secretary, based in Chittagong. The BBU now recognized the inevitable, and at its Assembly from 28 to 30 December 1956 agreed that the 'Baptist Union of Pakistan' (BUP) should be constituted as a separate body. R. N. Baroi, previously BBU secretary for East Pakistan, was appointed secretary of the new union, whose headquarters were in Dhaka.[8]

5. IN/107, W. Dinajpur Baptist Union: Annual Report 1952.

6. Minutes of the 8th Assembly of the BBU, 26-28 Oct. 1955, p. 4.

7. Didcot, CR 86, Memorandum by E. G. T. Madge on making East Pakistan a separate field of the BMS; General Committee Minutes, 7 Nov. 1956, p. 143.

8. Minutes of BBU Working Committee, 11-13 July 1956, pp. 9-10; Minutes of the 9th Assembly of the BBU, 28-30 Dec. 1956.

In the long term, the most serious implication of partition was that most of the Baptist churches of Bengal found themselves in Pakistan, and were hence separated, both from the most highly educated leaders of the Baptist community (who tended to reside in Calcutta or its environs), and from the institutions of secondary and higher education open to Baptists, which were all in West Bengal. In 1947 the BBU had Middle English schools for boys and girls in Barisal, a similar school in Khulna, a mixed school in Dinajpur which had failed to reach Middle English standard, and a school at Chandraghona which had once been of Middle English standard, but had been degraded to Upper Primary level in 1932. Baptists who desired high school education had been compelled to go to Calcutta - boys to the Siksha Sangha High School, and girls to the United Missionary Girls' High School (a joint BMS-LMS-Methodist Missionary Society enterprise). Beyond secondary level, Serampore was the only opportunity open to men, and the United Missionary Training College at Ballygunge the sole option for women.[9] The strength of the case of those, from A. H. Baynes onwards, who had warned of the dangers inherent in the geographical separation of Serampore from the bulk of the Baptist community in East Bengal, was now revealed.

One of the first tasks faced by the BBU after partition was, therefore, to improve the educational provision for the Baptist community in the East. By 1955 the two Barisal schools had been raised to High School standard, and the Dinajpur school to Middle English level. The Khulna school had, however, collapsed, and the Chandraghona school remained at primary level only. The greatest problem faced by the Baptist schools was how to find sufficient trained Christian staff. The solution to that problem depended on the access of the Baptist community to higher education. Since the introduction of visa and passport controls, it had become increasingly difficult for Baptist boys from the East to go to Serampore. College education in Dhaka was of inferior standard, and often anti-Christian in its atmosphere. The BMS had for many years run a boys' hostel in Dhaka, but it was not intended primarily for Christian students, and was run on a self-supporting basis. For Christian girls, there was no provision at all. The BBU believed that the ultimate answer lay in the foundation of a Christian College in East Pakistan, but baulked at the prospect of asking the BMS for the vast funds that would be required. In the event, the Society had to settle

9. *BMS Annual Report*, 1949-50, p. xvii; Didcot, CR 70, Christian Higher Education in East Pakistan, by G. Soddy, 25 Aug. 1955.

for the solution of making generous grants to Baptist young people for higher education in Dhaka.[10]

The provision of theological training remained the most intractable educational problem created by partition. Some young men from the BMS mission were sent during the 1950s to a Bible School in Birisiri, run by the Garo Baptist Union (which linked churches established by the Australian Baptist Missionary Society), but the training was not found to be wholly satisfactory. To meet this need, a Pastors' Training School was opened in Dhaka in July 1963, under the principalship of A. A. Somerville. Specialized tuition in Islamics was provided by Irene West, a BMS missionary who had served on the staff of the Henry Martyn Institute of Islamics, first in Aligarh from 1947 to 1959, and since 1962 in its Eastern branch in Dhaka. Most of the initial group of eight students were mature men and former primary school teachers. Somerville was succeeded as Principal in 1965 by E. Leslie Wenger, previously on the staff of Serampore College. A more ambitious project was begun in 1968, when the College of Christian Theology of East Pakistan was founded in Dhaka by ten co-operating churches and missions, with the aim of providing correspondence courses for those unable to commit themselves to full-time pastoral service. Wenger was Principal of this College also. The two institutions worked in close association until 1970, when a clear separation was made between the Pastors' Training School as a residential college for ministerial training, and the College of Christian Theology as an interdenominational institution providing theological education by extension.[11]

Partition brought many problems, but also some benefits, to the work of the BMS in East Pakistan. Chittagong developed rapidly into the main port of East Pakistan. Its Baptist church, reduced to three members after the Second World War, when the city was heavily bombed by the Japanese, gradually recovered its numbers as some Baptists from the surrounding area moved into the city.[12] Industrialization even reached the Chandraghona district, where a large paper mill was erected in the early 1950s. Further up the Karnaphuli river, at Kaptai, a major hydro-electric scheme was commenced, which necessitated the re-location of the Society's work at Rangamati. Whilst the increased population of the area placed new

10. Didcot, CR 70; and CR 163, Memorandum on E. Pakistan field prepared by G. Soddy for S. Asia Sub-Committee, 22 June 1959.

11. *BMS Annual Reports:* 1963-4, p. 15; 1964-5, pp. 19-20; 1968-9, pp. 11-12; 1969-70, p. 12.

12. Interview with Mr Chaudhuri, Chittagong Baptist Church, 21.12.88.

demands on the BMS staff at Chandraghona, the Christian hospital derived several benefits from the proximity of the paper mill. An electricity supply was installed, via the mill, in 1953, and in 1955 the mill-owners generously provided a new operating theatre. Under the supervision of Dr J. W. Bottoms, who had worked at Chandraghona since 1928 (since 1939 as medical superintendent), the hospital continued to expand its services. At the suggestion of the Pakistan government, and with its active financial support, the adjacent leprosy colony (begun by G. O. Teichmann in 1913) was also developed after 1949 into the premier centre for leprosy research and treatment in the country. By the 1960s Chandraghona hospital stood in urgent need of rebuilding, especially after cyclone damage, sustained in 1960 and 1962. The BMS made a grant of £35,000 towards the modernization and extension of the hospital, which was completed in 1971.[13]

A succession of BMS medical personnel at Chandraghona played an invaluable part in the provision of health care in one of the poorest nations in Asia. Possibly of no less significance to the long-term welfare of the country was the contribution of one BMS missionary couple, David and Joyce Stockley, to the transformation of village agriculture. At the Khulna Agricultural and Village Uplift Centre from 1954 to 1965, David Stockley taught the use of new crops and methods to students who subsequently became pioneers of agricultural innovation in many different parts of East Pakistan. In 1965 the Stockleys were transferred to Chandraghona, to develop self-sufficiency in food for the leprosy centre, and promote more productive farming methods in the district as a whole. By the late 1960s David Stockley was in demand as a consultant to church and government agricultural projects throughout East Pakistan. During the 1970s Stockley promoted irrigation schemes and modern methods of rice cultivation amongst co-operatives in the Rangunia area; by 1974 yields per acre had been raised by over 300 per cent. The Stockleys finally worked for the National Christian Council of Bangladesh Agricultural Project at Gournadi in the Barisal district, before being transferred to Brazil in 1985. David Stockley was awarded the OBE in 1977 for his contribution to agricultural development in Bangladesh.[14]

13. Minutes of the BBU Working Committee, 17-19 Aug. 1949, pp. 9-10; I. S. Acres, 'Partners in Healing' (unpublished BMS MS), 10-13; J. W. Bottoms, '"I'd no idea": A study of medical missionary work' (unpublished MS in possession of Professor A. E. Bottoms). Dr J. W. Bottoms retired in 1960.

14. *BMS Annual Reports*: 1959-60, pp. xv-xvi; 1962-3, p. 17; 1964-5, p. 19; 1965-6, p. 12; 1967-8, p. 16; 1968-9, pp. 14-15. Didcot, CR 473, Report of Regional Representative for Asia on a Visit from 9 Jan. to 26 Feb. 1974. *MH* (Mar. 1977), 42. David Stockley is the son of Dr H. G. Stockley of the China mission, and grandson of T. I. Stockley, BMS missionary in Ceylon and Jamaica.

The nation of Pakistan had been created on the false assumption that a common religion would hold together a country whose two wings were separated by geography, language, and culture. In fact, East Pakistan soon began to resent West Pakistan's near-monopoly of the structures of power and its appropriation of the lion's share of economic resources. After the Indo-Pakistan war of September-October 1965, the Awami League, under the leadership of Sheikh Mujibur Rahman, emerged as the champion of Bengali interests and provincial autonomy. Tension between the two halves of Pakistan mounted during the late 1960s, and came to a head in the wake of the devastating cyclone of 12-13 November 1970, which caused the deaths of 250-300,000 East Bengalis. The government of President Yahya Khan received strong criticism for its dilatory and inadequate response to the disaster. In the elections which followed on 7 December, the Awami League won 288 of the 300 seats in the East Pakistan provincial assembly, and 160 of the 300 seats in the Pakistan National Assembly. Sheikh Mujib now mounted a campaign for the autonomy of East Pakistan, which culminated a year later in the birth of the nation of Bangladesh.[15]

II: Orissa: Church Growth in West Utkal and the Kond Hills

Until the 1960s Baptist membership in Orissa was at its strongest in the West, in the Balangir district. The influx of Mundas and low-caste groups which had begun at the end of the 1880s was maintained well into the twentieth century. As late as the 1950s the West Utkal District Union was regularly cited in the Society's annual reports as the most encouraging instance of spiritual vitality in the India mission. A 'Forward Movement in Evangelism', initiated by the Utkal Christian Central Church Council, made its greatest impact in the western part of the State. Non-Christian villages, some of them Hindu communities, requested Christian preaching teams at a rate which surpassed the capacity of the churches to respond. The Union reported 1,384 baptisms in the two years 1953 and 1954, of which 599 were converts from outside the Christian community.[16] However, conversion growth in new villages was evidently offset to some extent by seepage from the older Christian communities, as Hinduism consolidated its hold on Orissa: church membership in the Balangir district grew from

---

15. C. P. O'Donnell, *Bangladesh: Biography of a Muslim Nation* (Boulder and London, 1984), 67-89.

16. Cuttack, Diocesan archives, joint report presented to the 17th annual meeting of the Utkal Christian Central Church Council, 1955, p. 1.

3,775 in 1937 to 4,250 in 1954, but the total Baptist community remained static at about 10,000.[17]

In comparison, the church in the Kond Hills seemed small. In fact its rate of growth since its beginnings in 1914 had been impressive, especially during the twenty years from 1927 to 1947. The first church at Mallikapori had thirty members in 1920; by 1930 there were over 400 baptized believers in sixteen village centres; in 1937 membership totalled 1,300; by 1950 there were about 4,300 members in forty-nine churches. The great majority of the converts continued to be from the Domb community, rather than from the Konds themselves, the objects of the original evangelistic vision of Wilkinson, Long, and Wood. The churches were grouped into the Kond Hills District Church Union in 1931, but missionary leadership remained firmly entrenched until after the retirement of Edward Evans, a missionary of patriarchal style and authority, in 1948. Two years later a constitution was adopted for the Union. This marked the watershed between an era in which the word of the missionary was the final arbiter in church discipline, and one which offered genuine opportunities for indigenous leadership. The first Indian national to become president of the Union, Jagannath Naik, a gifted Domb headmaster, assumed office in 1955.[18]

In 1952 the BMS concluded an agreement with the United Christian Missionary Society of the American Disciples of Christ, whereby the two missions agreed to co-operate in serving the Baptist churches of Orissa. As a result, the Utkal Baptist Central Church Council changed its name in February 1953 to the Utkal Church Christian Central Council (UCCCC).[19] In April 1956 the joint planning committee of the UCCCC received a report on the mission opportunities of the Kond Hills and West Utkal from Dr Donald McGavran, then a senior India missionary of the United Christian Missionary Society, and later renowned as the primary architect of 'church growth' theory. McGavran's analysis of the prospects in the Kond Hills, where he had spent only a few days, had a disconcerting impact on the BMS missionaries and their national colleagues. McGavran pointed out that the Kond Hills church was composed very largely of Dombs, and argued that the persistent hope of the missionaries that the Konds would

---

17. *BMS Annual Reports* 1937-8, p. 19; 1954-5, p. xii.

18. B. Boal, *The Konds: Human Sacrifice and Religious Change* (Warminster, 1982), 183-6, 191; idem, 'The Church in the Kond Hills', in V. E. W. Hayward (ed.), *The Church as Christian Community* (London, 1966), 273-5; *BMS Annual Reports* 1937-8, p. 19; 1949-50, p. xv.

19. Cuttack, Diocesan archives, Minutes of the UCCCC, 1951-8.

one day turn to Christ had deflected effort from the 'responsive community', namely the Dombs. He advised that, if, during the next few months, a few scattered baptisms were all that occurred among the Konds, the missionaries should abandon their 'Kond hope', and focus all evangelistic effort on the Dombs. McGavran's report was given further consideration by the UCCCC executive committee in July. Meanwhile the monsoon rains fell. The response of the BMS missionaries to McGavran's recommendations was cautious, and in any case no change in evangelistic strategy could be implemented until the next cold, dry season.[20]

During this same rainy season of 1956 two separate groups of Konds began to show an interest in Christianity. One was in the village of Pokari, where three brothers and their wives had been baptized in 1951. This small nucleus of believers was now joined by others, first from within the village, then from relatives in the neighbourhood and from other trading contacts living along the old East India Company road to Balliguda, which passed through Pokari. The second group was centred on the village of Teravadi, where the men of four closely-related Kond households had been converted in 1950. These also now began to influence their surrounding kin and neighbourhood groups, as well as travellers on another trading route, to Raikia market, eighteen miles from Teravadi. From these two isolated clusters of Kond Christians grew a movement that confounded McGavran's predictions, and transformed the strength and tribal composition of the church in the Kond Hills. Kond villages now begged for teaching about the new 'Jesus-God'. In 1958 Bruce and Joyce Henry, missionaries at Udayagiri since 1945-6, moved west to Balliguda in response to the new movement. The significance of these events was not fully apparent to the BMS home staff. The Society's annual report for 1958-9 was the first to observe that the numbers now flocking to the church in the Balliguda area were from 'groups previously untouched', but there was no overt recognition that the prayers of the Victorian pioneers of the Kond Hills mission were at last being answered. The fifty-eight churches in the Kond Hills District Union in 1955 had grown to 168 by the end of 1964 - a year of 'phenomenal advance', in which twenty-seven new churches were recognized by the Union. Dombs still provided the bulk of the educated church leadership, but no longer constituted the majority of the Christian community. Far from marking the abandonment of the 'Kond hope', 1956 thus witnessed the first-fruits of its realization.[21] By 1983 the total Christian community in the

20. Ibid., Minutes of Executive Committee of the UCCCC, 4-6 July 1956, p. 19. Boal, *The Konds*, 188-9.

21. Boal, *The Konds*, 189, 191. *BMS Annual Reports*, 1958-9, p. ix; 1964-5, p. 10.

CNI diocese of Cuttack (which is dominated numerically by the Kond Hills churches) numbered 33,250, with a communicant membership of 15,131 in 403 churches.[22]

From an anthropological perspective, the 'people movement' among the Konds constitutes a revealing example of processes of religious change in an animistic community increasingly affected by 'modern' cultural influences. It may not be coincidental that it was the Konds living along the routes of commercial penetration who were the first to gravitate to Christianity. Decisions to become Christians were rarely taken on an individual basis, but were made collectively by households or by the elders of whole village communities. The attraction of the Christian gospel did not lie primarily in its promise of individual salvation from sin. Rather it derived from the proclamation that the Great Creator God was utterly good, immediately accessible through prayer, and sufficiently powerful to thwart the malignity of the evil spirits, whom the Konds had hitherto sought to placate through sacrifices, originally of humans, and more recently of buffaloes. The conversion of the Konds was a spontaneous movement of indigenous initiative, taken at the very time when missionary strategy might have turned away to apparently more responsive groups.[23] As such, their story is, from the perspective of Christian faith, a salutary reminder of the unfettered sovereignty of the Holy Spirit, who refuses to conform to human patterns and predictions of his activity.

The rapid growth of the Baptist churches, first in West Utkal, and then in the Kond Hills, had a number of implications for church work and missionary policy. Amongst the illiterate Konds, adult literacy programmes became an urgent priority. Missionary itinerations from Udayagiri or Balliguda combined Christian teaching with literacy work, elementary public health education, and basic medical care. As late as the mid-1960s the basic literacy level in the district was only ten per cent.[24] For Christians, the ability to read became doubly important after the publication in 1975 of a new Kui version of the New Testament, the work of Bruce Henry, Joan Sargent, and a team of Kui-speaking translators. The new translation replaced an older imperfect one produced in 1954 by Mrs Helen Evans, wife of Edward Evans.

As the church in Orissa grew, the demand for Christian education increased. Middle English schools were available at Balangir and Diptipur

---

22. Cuttack, Diocesan archives, Report for 1980-3.

23. Boal, *The Konds*, 193-8.

24. *BMS Annual Report*, 1964-5, pp. 9-10.

in West Utkal, and at Gudripori (Udayagiri) in the Kond Hills. In 1973 Protestant secondary education for boys became available through the foundation of the Millman High School. Hostels for boys and girls at Gudripori enabled the schools to cater for boarding pupils from throughout the Kond Hills. Christian educational provision for the Oriya peoples of the plains was similarly increased by the opening in 1961 of a second Stewart School in the new state capital of Bhubaneswar. The new school was controlled by the older foundation of the Stewart School, Cuttack, until 1963, when it gained its autonomy. Christian education for girls was provided by the Buckley Girls' High School in Cuttack.

The progress of conversion among the Konds also imparted added significance to the Moorshead Memorial Christian Hospital at Udayagiri, whose opening in January 1939 marked the posthumous fulfilment of R. F. Moorshead's vision of the Kond mission advancing 'at the point of the lancet'.[25] Drs Gordon and Honor Wilkins had been responsible for the founding and early development of the hospital. After their departure in 1951, the role of senior doctor at Udayagiri passed to Stanley Thomas, who had been considerably influenced as a young man by Moorshead, and was a firm believer in the concept of 'medical evangelism'. Thomas's skill as a surgeon gained increasing renown throughout Orissa. One reason advanced by Christian Konds to explain their new allegiance has been the efficacy of Christian medical care in treating sickness, compared with the dubious results achieved by sacrifices to the spirits.[26] The high surgical reputation of the hospital was also essential to its financial viability. The inadequate level of grants from the state government made the hospital heavily dependent on income from operations. This dependence tended to limit the capacity of the hospital to meet the massive needs of the Kond people, as more money was to be earned by treating the relatively affluent Oriya people of the plains. As in many other mission hospitals, the staff were caught in a dilemma between the competing demands of human need and financial realities.

Stanley and Joyce Thomas returned to England in 1969. Sadly the subsequent history of the hospital was marked by staffing difficulties and disputes. Standards in surgery fell in the 1970s, and income decreased accordingly. Government restrictions forced the last missionary member of staff, Joan Smith, to leave in 1985. As in Zaire, there has been a tendency for the national church to view the medical work inherited from the BMS

25. See above, ch. V, p. 000.

26. Boal, *The Konds*, 194.

more as a facility for the use of the Christian community than as an integral part of the witness of the church.[27]

III: The Road to Church Union in North India and Sri Lanka

India stood in the vanguard of the movement towards Protestant church union which gathered strength in the wake of the World Missionary Conference of 1910. There was a growing feeling amongst Indian Christians that the dividing line between Christian and non-Christian in India was 'so deep that every barrier separating Christian from Christian must be overcome'.[28] Although it is progress in the South, culminating in the formation of the Church of South India in 1947, which has received most attention, parallel developments in North India can be seen from the 1920s onwards. In 1924 Presbyterian and Congregationalist churches joined together to form the United Church of Northern India. This church invited others to consider the possibility of a wider union. As a result, a series of Round-Table conferences was organized, the first two being held at Lucknow in April 1929 and Delhi in November 1930. Baptists were represented at Lucknow by J. D. Raw, and took some part in the subsequent conferences, which led to the issue of a 'Basis of Negotiation' in 1939.[29] Meanwhile, quite separate negotiations had taken place between Baptists, the Methodist Episcopal Church, and the United Church, within the framework of a 'Joint Council'. The Joint Council issued a Plan of Union in 1940 which avoided any commitment to the historic episcopate. Preferring this scheme, Baptists withdrew from the Round-Table discussions in 1940. By 1951 it was clear to the other participants in the Joint Council that the Round-Table 'Basis' offered the better prospect of progress towards union, and the Joint Council was accordingly suspended. In 1954 Baptists resumed participation in what had now become an actual negotiating committee. The committee had issued a first edition of a Plan of Union in 1951.[30]

27. E. G. Wilkins, *By Hands, Bullocks and Prayers* (n.p., 1987), 215-16. Interview with Dr and Mrs Stanley Thomas, and Rev. and Mrs Bruce Henry, 18.7.90.

28. Dr G. H. C. Angus's words to the BMS South Asia Church Union Conference, 20-21 Dec. 1956.

29. Minutes of the Executive Committee of the United Conference, 10-11 Dec. 1929, p. 7.

30. *Plan of Church Union in North India and Pakistan* (3rd revised edn.; Madras, 1957), iii-vii. The North India plan embraced Pakistan, but on the understanding that two autonomous united churches, with a common constitution, would be formed.

In Ceylon the initial impetus of the movement towards Protestant church union was supplied by the involvement of the island's Congregationalist, Methodist, and Anglican churches in the South India negotiations. The first significant step in Ceylon itself was taken at a conference of Christian teachers at Trinity College, Kandy, in 1932 on the theme of 'The Church in Ceylon in the year 2000'. The conference predicted that, by 2000, British rule would be no more, the Buddhist ascendancy would be stronger than ever, and Christian unity would be essential. A second conference for clergy and ministers in 1934, on the theme of unity, led to the formation of a Ceylon branch of the 'Friends of Reunion'. In 1940 the secretary of this body, Basil Jackson, proposed at the South Ceylon District Synod of the Methodist Church that invitations be issued to the main Protestant churches to appoint representatives to a joint committee to discuss the possibility of church union. The joint committee met for the first time in November 1940, and a negotiating committee began work in May 1945. The Ceylon Baptist Council was a full participant in these discussions from the beginning. The first edition of the Scheme of Church Union in Ceylon was issued in July 1949.[31]

The BMS adopted the consistent view throughout the negotiations in North India and Ceylon that the Baptist churches there must be left to make their own decisions on church union matters. In theory, the Society's support for the principle of a united Protestant witness in the Indian sub-continent was clear. As early as April 1930 the General Committee had resolved that 'the attempt to realise the real fellowship in the Church of Christ of all believers is a movement in accord with the Will of God, and an answer to the Master's own prayer that all His disciples may be one, that the world may believe'.[32] In practice, however, the responses of the BMS Committee were qualified by the great variety of convictions held by British Baptists on ecumenical questions. In 1947 the Society set up an India and Ceylon (later South Asia) church union sub-committee, which regularly expressed its view to the field on the various proposals made by the North India and Ceylon negotiating committees. The sub-committee's reports to the General Purposes sub-committee and General Committee ensured that, particularly during the crucial years of the mid-1950s, church union

31. G. Hewitt, *The Problems of Success: A History of the Church Missionary Society 1910-1942* (2 vols.; London, 1977), ii, 168-9; D. K. Wilson, *The Christian Church in Sri Lanka: Her Problems and Influence* (Colombo, 1975), 51-2; *Scheme of Church Union in Ceylon* (3rd revised edn.; Madras, 1955), iii-v.

32. General Committee Minutes, 30 Apr. 1930, p. 35.

matters were the subject of constant debate and disagreement within Baptist circles in Britain.

On the field some BMS missionaries played an influential part in the church union negotiations. Prominent among them were D. S. Wells and Ernest Madge, successive India Secretaries of the Society, R. C. Cowling, Ceylon Secretary from 1954 to 1959, and, most notably, E. Leslie Wenger, who sat on the negotiating committee in North India from 1954, and acted as convenor of the Baptist delegation from 1955 to 1964. Indian Baptist leaders were also involved in the negotiations. Among them were Dr Benjamin Pradhan of Cuttack and Probhudan Adhikari, an accountant from the Johnagar church, Serampore, who succeeded Wenger as convenor of the Baptist delegation in 1964, and served in that capacity until inauguration in 1970.

It was a necessary presupposition of both church union schemes from the beginning that each united church would encompass episcopal elements of church order, though it was stressed in both cases that no particular theological interpretation of episcopacy was implied or required.[33] The general readiness with which Baptist leaders in India and Ceylon accepted this precondition is indicative of the fact that a purist concept of congregational independency had never taken root in the Indian Baptist context. Church leaders who had witnessed BMS missionaries wielding quasi-episcopal superintendence over Indian churches, and who themselves had often exercised pastoral authority over groups of congregations, were unlikely to find the prospect of bishops in name as well as substance unduly threatening. Provided that participating churches were free to adopt a purely functional attitude to episcopacy, and also that there were some guarantees that episcopacy would be exercised in a constitutional fashion, the Baptist negotiators argued that there was little to fear from absorption into an episcopal church.[34]

In both church union schemes the provision for the unification of the ministry at the inauguration of the united church was another aspect which seems to have posed fewer worries to national Baptist leaders than it did to elements of Baptist opinion in Britain. Both schemes adopted the principle

---

33. W. J. Marshall, *A United Church: Faith and Order in the North India/Pakistan Unity Plan* (Delhi, 1987), 65-8; *Scheme of Church Union in Ceylon* (3rd edn.), 19. The solution of accepting the *fact* of episcopacy, without being thereby committed to any particular theological interpretation of it, was first put forward by Bishop Whitehead of Madras in 1910.

34. E. L. Wenger, 'A Baptist View on Church Union', *Church Union News and Views* (Feb. 1956), 6.

that the unification of the ministry must follow, rather than precede, the unification of the church. The first act of the united church would be an act of unification of ministries, at which the bishops and representative presbyters of the new church should receive the mutual laying-on of hands. This rite was to be understood as conferring on each minister whatever grace and authority he might need to fulfil his new commission, and not as implying any defect in his original ordination. Although some members of the BMS Committee undoubtedly felt that this conceded too much to sacerdotalism, most Baptists involved in the negotiations seemed to accept this assurance as sufficient. Indeed, their confidence was such that they accepted the deletion (in deference to Anglo-Catholic scruples) from the fourth and final edition of the North India plan of the statement that this rite was 'not ordination or re-ordination'.[35]

A further aspect of the reunion schemes which caused more disquiet in Britain than in the East was the adoption by both schemes of the South India principle that it should be 'a rule of order' of each united church that the celebration of communion should be restricted to those so authorized by ordination as bishops or presbyters.[36] The exclusion of lay celebration was a matter of anxiety to the BMS church union sub-committee from as early as 1947, when it first appeared as a feature of the proposed Ceylon scheme. The question was one of several points of concern identified by a conference on South Asia church union convened by the sub-committee in December 1956. However, the church union sub-committee of the BMS 'United Committee' responded by pointing out that Baptist churches in India had, 'in the interests of good order', generally refrained from appointing laymen to celebrate communion.[37] On this issue, as on a number of others, British Baptists needed to appreciate that Baptist practice in India and Pakistan had already 'moved from traditional principles in Britain in a direction nearer to that of other churches'. However, the Baptist representatives on the North India negotiating committee did ask for a two-year interim period, in which lay pastors might be permitted to celebrate communion, until it could be seen whether it was necessary for them to be officially ordained as 'presbyters with limited authorization'. Despite the rejection of this suggestion, Leslie Wenger was satisfied that the provision

35. Marshall, *A United Church,* 90-103; *Scheme of Church Union in Ceylon* (3rd edn.), 20-5; information from Rev. E. L. Wenger, 4.8.90.

36. Marshall, *A United Church,* 43-4; *Scheme of Church Union in Ceylon* (3rd edn.), 15.

37. The 'United Committee', a body representing the various BMS fields in India, became the Council of Baptist Churches in Northern India in April 1957.

made in the plan for such limited ordinations to take place was a sufficient guarantee that communion would be properly administered in all of the formerly Baptist areas.[38]

These were ultimately secondary issues in comparison with the question of baptism, on which the whole outcome of the negotiations, for Baptists, turned. Participation in the church union process necessarily required of Baptists a *de facto* suspension of their disbelief in the validity of infant baptism: a united church that bridged the baptist-paedobaptist divide could be formed only on the premise that both modes of baptism would be practised, and at least tolerated by all. With some significant exceptions, Baptists both in the BMS General Committee and in India/Ceylon were willing to make this limited and pragmatic concession in the interests of a united Christian witness. The difficulty lay rather with the potential case of a member of the Christian community baptized as an infant, who in adult life became convinced of the invalidity of his or her infant baptism, and accordingly requested baptism as a believer. The paedobaptist majority on both negotiating committees steadfastly refused to countenance the possibility of such a 're-baptism', for to do so would imply a denial by the church of the sacramental reality of the earlier rite. For most Baptists, however, provision for such a case was essential if liberty of conscience and the nexus between faith and baptism were to be preserved.

The issue was first raised in relation to the proposed Church of Lanka. The absence of such provision in the first edition of the Ceylon scheme was the chief item of concern raised by the General Committee in a letter sent to the Ceylon Baptist Council in July 1950. When no such provision was made by the second edition, published in June 1953, both the BMS church union sub-committee and the Ceylon Baptist churches voiced their objections. The Council felt obliged to warn the negotiating committee that, if this point were not conceded, Baptists might be unable to continue to share in the negotiating process. A small group from the other negotiating churches, including D. T. Niles, the Methodist who was the prime mover of the Ceylon scheme, met the Baptist delegates to try to break the deadlock. The result was a revised section on baptism, which was intended to safeguard the principle, fundamental to Baptists, that the Church is a body comprising believers only. The revised section stated that a person baptized

---

38. Didcot: CR 75, Church Union Proposals for Ceylon and N. India [1956]; CR 124, Report of S. Asia Church Union Conference, 20-21 Dec. 1956; CR 132, Reply ... to Report of S. Asia Church Union Conference, n.d. [1957]; CR 138, E. L. Wenger to W. C. Eadie, 12 Apr. 1957. *Plan of Church Union in N. India* (3rd edn.), 15-16.

in infancy would not become a full member of the Church until after a service of confirmation which would include 'witness before the congregation by the candidate of his belief in Jesus Christ as Lord and Saviour'. Although 're-baptism' was still prohibited, the Baptist delegates felt that their essential concerns had been safeguarded. The Ceylon Baptist Council accordingly commended to the churches the third edition of the Lanka scheme, incorporating this revised wording.[39] R. C. Cowling wrote an article for the *Missionary Herald,* setting out the new provisions on baptism. The article aroused the alarm of the Baptist Revival Fellowship, whose committee sought an interview with J. B. Middlebrook and V. E. W. Hayward. Following this meeting, held in February 1956, the *Bulletin* of the Fellowship published an article, protesting that Baptists were 'agreeing that the sprinkling of a baby is in all respects a valid Christian Baptism', and warning that the Ceylon scheme would form a dangerous precedent for the future of church union in Britain.[40]

Although the anti-ecumenical stance of the Baptist Revival Fellowship received little support from denominational leaders, it appealed to the large number of British Baptists who viewed the ecumenical movement with suspicion, if not hostility. Within the BMS there were influential persons who, whilst in no sense anti-ecumenical, feared that essential Baptist principles were being placed in jeopardy. These included the treasurer, the Rt Hon. Ernest Brown, and the chairman for 1956-7, William Davies, who insisted that the Society's regret at the failure of the Ceylon scheme to include provision for the baptism as believers of those baptized in infancy should be clearly communicated to the Ceylon Baptist Council.[41] Domestic pressure from the BMS was hence decidedly in favour of a firmer line being taken on the 're-baptism' question in the later stages of the North India negotiations. The Baptist delegation on the North India negotiating committee had indeed already pressed for provision to be made for the case of those compelled by conscience to seek believer's baptism, though baptized in infancy. One response, seriously entertained by the negotiating

39. Didcot: CR 75, Church Union Proposals for Ceylon and N. India; CR 77, Scheme of Church Union in Ceylon. General Committee Minutes, 27-28 June 1950, pp. 123, 157-8. *Scheme of Church Union in Ceylon* (3rd edn.), 12-14.

40. *MH* (Nov. 1955), 170-1; *Baptist Revival Fellowship Bulletin* 48 (Jan./Mar. 1956), 1-4. The Baptist Revival Fellowship emerged in the 1930s as a focus of conservative opposition to liberal and ecumenical tendencies in the Baptist Union.

41. Didcot, CR 75; see S. Asia Church Union Sub-Committee Minutes, 15 Mar. 1956, pp. 243-4, and 29 Oct. 1956, pp. 31-6. E. A. Bompas also took the same view.

committee in 1954-5, was to propose a service of total immersion of the believer, which would not be termed baptism, but would clearly be interpreted as such by the person immersed. This ingenious suggestion mercifully failed to attract general support in India.[42]

The third edition of the North India plan, drafted at Pachmarhi in April 1957 and remitted to the churches for their final decision, affirmed categorically that baptism was 'unrepeatable in the life of any one person, no matter by which practice it was administered'. The person baptized in infancy who came to his minister seeking baptism as a believer was to be helped to find the remedy of what he saw as a grave lack in his own baptism, 'not by re-baptism, but by some other means which effectually re-affirms his Baptism'. If he should persist in requesting believer's baptism, his minister was to refer the matter to the bishop 'for pastoral advice and direction'.[43] These statements, made in Appendix B to the plan, were subject to varying interpretations. Anglicans interpreted them as meaning that re-baptism would never be permitted. Many Baptists, on the other hand, took the appendix to mean that, in the final analysis, the bishop would permit believer's baptism in cases of genuine conscientious conviction. Leslie Wenger was more pessimistic, but 'clung to a shred of hope' that the issue was not finally closed. But correspondence with Canon T. D. Sully, secretary of the negotiating committee, seemed to indicate the contrary, and brought Wenger to the brink of abandoning his advocacy of the plan of union.[44] However, an element of doubt over the correct interpretation of Appendix B remained for some years. The publication in 1961 of a note of clarification, which stated that the Appendix did not 'imply or forbid any particular interpretation of the method of conscientious relief for a person baptized in infancy and afterwards desiring Believer's Baptism', tipped the balance of interpretation towards the Baptist view, but not conclusively.[45] Eventually, in 1965, the notorious Appendix B was omitted altogether from the fourth and final edition of the plan. The decision to remain silent on the 're-baptism' question was in effect a decision to leave the united church to frame its own policy on the issue. The

---

42. Didcot CR 83, Church Union and Believer's Baptism (1956).

43. *Plan of Church Union in North India and Pakistan* (3rd edn.), 42-3.

44. IN/143, Extract from Wenger to Sully, 8 Nov. 1957; *Church Union News and Views* (May 1958), 22-6, and (May 1959), 21-2.

45. *Church Union News and Views* (May 1961), 28.

door appeared to be left open for the special case, which was ultimately all that the Baptist negotiators had been holding out for.[46]

While the uncertainty over the meaning of Appendix B continued, the Baptist Union of Pakistan decided to repudiate the North India/Pakistan plan. In Sri Lanka, on the other hand, there was little hesitation about the union scheme on the part of Baptist ministers, two of whom, S. J. de S. Weerasinghe and W. G. Wickramasinghe, acted as successive secretaries of the negotiating committee. Some BMS missionaries, however, felt that the clear prohibition of 're-baptism' made it impossible for them to contemplate serving in the anticipated united church. The obstacles thrown in the path of the proposed Church of Lanka have come from other denominations, and have generally been more legal than theological in nature. After the Methodist Synod failed to approve the third edition of the scheme in 1962, negotiations were resumed, and a revised version of the third edition appeared in 1964.[47] By November 1971 all the negotiating churches had voted in favour, and all seemed set for the inauguration of the Church of Lanka on Advent Sunday 1972. It was anticipated that one of the five bishops would be a Baptist. However, three members of the Church of Ceylon (the legal continuation of the Church of England in the island) challenged the validity in law of the Anglican vote in favour of the scheme, and the prospects for church union receded. In 1975 the scheme again failed at the final hurdle, when a group of churches succeeded in obtaining a legal judgment that the provision of the church union bill for the assumption by the united church of all property held by the uniting churches was unconstitutional. At the end of the 1980s, the Sri Lanka Baptist Sangamaya initiated informal discussions about the possibility of re-opening negotiations, but the prospects for church union in Sri Lanka remain remote.[48]

IV: Baptists and the Church of North India since 1970

Voting in the negotiating churches on the fourth edition of the North India plan took place during 1968 and 1969. The Church of North India (CNI) was formally constituted at Nagpur on 29 November 1970. Although the presiding minister at the inaugural ceremony listed the Council

---

46. Marshall, *A United Church*, 38-40; *Church Union News and Views* (May 1965), 24.

47. H-R. Weber, *Asia and the Ecumenical Movement 1895-1961* (London, 1966), 211-12.

48. Wilson, *The Christian Church in Sri Lanka*, 53-7. Didcot, CR 437, Visit of General Overseas Secretary to Asia Field, Report by E. G. T. Madge, Mar. 1972. Overseas Sub-Committee Minutes, 19 Feb. 1976, p. 66.

of Baptist Churches in Northern India as one of the six churches which were thereby uniting, only one of the Council's constituent bodies, the Utkal Christian Central Church Council, had in fact decided unanimously to join the united church.[49] The BMS General Committee had made it clear that, for the immediate future, the Society's support would continue to be available, both to Baptist churches which voted to enter the CNI, and to those who opted to stay out.[50] The Baptist Church of Mizo District had withdrawn at an earlier stage from the CNI negotiations, partly on theological grounds, and also because of the prospect of a separate church union scheme in North-East India, which has not yet been realized. Neither the Bengal Baptist Union nor the Baptist Union of North India was able to reach a united decision either for or against the CNI: their member churches made individual decisions to join or stay out.

By 1975 about three-quarters of the former Baptist churches of West Bengal, and about half of the churches of Bihar, Delhi, Baraut and Simla had entered the CNI. In both parts of northern India a rump of Baptist churches remained, out of fellowship with those churches that had entered the CNI, and sometimes accusing the BMS of having betrayed the Baptist cause. What was worse, both the BBU and the BUNI fell prey in the mid-1970s to bitter internal divisions, which continued almost without interruption thereafter. Church union has sadly left the churches of a Baptist tradition in northern India more, rather than less, divided than before. Similar trends can be observed among those of other denominations who stayed aloof from the CNI. It would be unfair to blame the process of church union for the failings of those who have withdrawn from it, but the end result of the fragmentation of church life has been to weaken, if not to nullify, the principal argument advanced for the ecumenical movement in India as elsewhere: that it would remove the scandal of disunity from the public face of Christian witness. The problems encountered by the BBU and BUNI have naturally gave BMS strategists much heartache and food for thought. One paper presented to the overseas sub-committee by Frank Wells in 1975 attributed the lack of spiritual leadership so evident in the recent history of the two bodies to the shift in emphasis in Indian missions from education to evangelism following the Tambaram conference of 1938: the withdrawal of missionary involvement from many schools and

---

49. Marshall, *A United Church*, xi. The other five uniting bodies were: The Church of the Brethren; the Disciples of Christ; the Church of India (Anglican); the Methodist Church under the British and Australasian Conferences; and the United Church of Northern India.

50. General Committee Minutes, 5 Nov. 1969.

colleges in the 1940s, suggested Wells, had led to a dearth of younger church leaders after the 1950s.[51]

Ironically the issue of 're-baptism', which so dominated the Baptist attitude to the church union negotiations, proved only an occasional problem after 1970. The alleged refusal of the Bishop of Patna to baptize as believers those baptized in infancy was cited as one reason for the decision in 1978 of many of the former Baptist churches of Bihar to leave the CNI and re-join the BUNI. However, Dr Eric Nasir, Moderator of the CNI at the time, confessed that he had no personal objection to giving believer's baptism to those baptized in infancy. Nasir was more concerned that those in Patna diocese who had argued most strongly for a Baptist position had proved the most disagreeable and quarrelsome.[52] Church politics in North India after 1970 centred on issues more financial and ethical than theological. Decisions to join or re-join the CNI, or to stay out, were influenced more by considerations of money, property, and status, than by serious discussion of the theological issues. Control of the educational institutions and other properties inherited from the BMS was hotly disputed, often by resort to law.

Only in Orissa did Baptists enter the CNI in sufficient numbers to exert a decisive and creative influence on the united church. The Cuttack diocese was one of the largest in the CNI, extending over 300 miles from east to west, and containing 25,562 members, most of them former Baptists. J. K. Mohanty, previously secretary of the UCCCC, became the first Bishop of Cuttack.[53] In 1972 the diocese was split in two, and a separate diocese of Sambulpur created in West Orissa. Two BMS missionaries, Wilma Harkness and Carole Whitmee, occupied key positions as the first two treasurers of the Sambulpur diocese during the 1970s.

Even in Orissa those of a Baptist tradition were not wholly united in their attitude to the CNI. Many Christians in the more remote parts of the state had never heard of any bishops other than Roman Catholic ones, and viewed their new bishop with suspicion. Bishop J. K. Mohanty's first appearance in the Phulbani district, resplendent in purple cassock and cross, caused considerable offence and alarm. The Bishop invited Bruce Henry

51. Didcot, CR 485, Description of the Churches in India; Overseas Sub-Committee Minutes, 12 June 1975, p. 44.

52. Didcot: CR 514, S. Mudd, Report on Asia Visit Feb./Apr. 1978; CR 517, A. S. Clement, Brief Report of Visits to India, Nepal and Hong Kong, 17 July to 18 Aug. 1978.

53. *BMS Annual Report,* 1969-70, p. 8.

back to Orissa in 1972 to help in allaying such fears. He found about twelve of the 253 churches in the Phulbani district, most of them in the Balliguda area, wholly or partially involved in a movement to secede from the CNI.[54] Although the independent Baptist movement was fed as much by ignorance as by theological conviction, it drew a minority of churches - including some in important urban centres, such as Cuttack and Bhubaneswar - away from the CNI into a re-formed Utkal Baptist Central Church Council. Anti-CNI feeling was also stimulated by the role of the CNI leadership in allocating (and seeking eventually to eliminate) grants from Western agencies; the extremely poor dioceses of Cuttack and Sambulpur felt that their interests were suffering at the hands of the ecclesiastical bureacracy in Delhi.[55] From the perspective of the Kond Hills, even the diocesan headquarters, some 200 kilometers away in Cuttack, seemed remote, and the amount of the bishop's time taken up by CNI business in Cuttack or Delhi could appear a diversion from pastoral work. A young and still growing Kui church, faced by increasingly militant opposition from the Hindu community, did not find incorporation into the formalized structures of the CNI easy, even though at the congregational level 'Baptist' church life continued very much as it did before 1970.[56]

V: The End of an Era in India

Perhaps the most noticeable change in Baptist church life discernible from the late 1960s onwards was the decreasing role played by foreign missionaries. In 1945 there were 162 BMS missionaries serving in India. As missionaries returned to the field after the war, numbers picked up to a post-war peak in 1955 of 174 (including 36 in Pakistan). The next decade saw some decline, but also considerable fluctuation: the total for 1965 was still as high as 168 (123 in India and 45 in Pakistan).[57] From 1966, the picture changed rapidly as government opposition to the involvement of expatriates in the Indian Church hardened. In November of that year the Indian

54. Didcot, CR 439, Report by B. C. R. Henry on Visit to Orissa, Sept. 1972. It should be said that Bishop Mohanty usually wore non-episcopal dress when visiting the villages. I owe this point to Rev. E. L. Wenger.

55. However, the CNI Related Missions Committee has provided a forum in which CNI partner missions and CNI leaders have sought to develop an agreed and equitable approach to the allocation of overseas funds.

56. These tensions led to a further secession of some Kui churches from the CNI in 1989. Interview with Rev. Bruce Henry, 18.7.90.

57. Didcot, CR 385, India/E. Pakistan Missionary Statistics, 1935-1966. The figures include those on furlough.

government introduced new regulations requiring new or returning missionaries to obtain special endorsements to gain entry to the country.[58] During 1967-68 two state governments, one of them being Orissa, passed legislation forbidding conversion from one religion to another by 'the use of force or by inducement or by any fraudulent means'. Numbers of church workers in the Phulbani district were arrested under the Orissa 'Freedom of Religion Act', but were subsequently released.[59] In West Bengal, the BMS itself came under attack from the government during the 1970s, falsely accused of violating exchange control regulations. A lengthy legal case ended with the Society being vindicated in the Calcutta High Court.

Ernest Madge returned from a visit to India in November-December 1967 with the clear impression that 'we are witnessing the closing stages of missionary participation in the work of the churches'.[60] One implication of the process was the need to reduce the continuing reliance of the Baptist churches on missionary personnel for key administrative roles. At the hub of Baptist organization was the post of BMS India Field Secretary, which survived until 1966. Even after the post was replaced in that year by the new post of Administrative Secretary, its holder, Neil McVicar, remained both treasurer of the Council of Baptist Churches in Northern India and secretary of the Baptist Church Trust Association, in which most Baptist church property was vested. However, in 1968 Indian nationals were appointed to both these posts, making the administration of the Council wholly independent of the BMS for the first time. When McVicar left for furlough in 1969, no missionary was appointed in his place. Miss Joy Knapman, a Calcutta missionary since 1960, became Secretary for Missionary Personnel, with responsibility for the diminishing number of BMS India missionaries and for the Society's legal affairs in India.[61] In 1979 the indigenization of the Society's affairs in India was completed with the creation of the post of Secretary for Missionary Affairs, which was filled by an Indian, John Peacock, from 1979 to his death in 1991. Both Neil McVicar (from 1981 to 1988) and Joy Knapman (from 1988) later served the Society as its Overseas Representative for Asia.

58. *BMS Annual Report,* 1966-7, p. 2.

59. *BMS Annual Report,* 1968-9, pp. 2-3, 7.

60. Didcot, CR 389, India: Report on the General Overseas Secretary's Visit in Nov.-Dec. 1967.

61. Didcot, CR 397, General Overseas Secretary's Visit to Asia, Nov.-Dec. 1968; *BMS Annual Report,* 1969-70, p. 2.

The new climate of hostility to missionary influence was partly responsible for the rapid decline of some of the most venerable institutions
founded by the BMS in India. Perhaps the most celebrated was the Calcutta
Mission Press. The Press, whose history goes back to the translating and
publishing work of the Serampore Trio, exercised a wide influence in
twentieth-century India, printing for the Bible Society and a wide range of
Christian and secular organizations. Many universities and colleges used
the Press for their examination papers, on the grounds that its compositors
could be trusted not to sell papers to the candidates.[62] However, by the late
1960s, the Press faced growing financial difficulties. Equipment was
antiquated, and the Bengali labour force, now unionized, became increasingly militant. In 1971 the BMS reluctantly decided to close the Press. This
delicate task, involving the compensation of much of the labour force, was
accomplished in 1972 by G. Koshy, the last superintendent of the Press, and
Brian Windsor, a BMS Calcutta missionary.[63]

Another institution which went into decline in this period was the
Christian hospital at Palwal, formed by the amalgamation of the men's and
women's hospitals in 1954. In 1965 Dr Dorothy Medway retired as medical
superintendent, after thirty-three years of service, twenty-seven of them at
Palwal. Over the next few years anti-missionary attitudes among the local
people strengthened, and by 1969 there were no missionaries left. The
hospital continued under BUNI management, but with increasing difficulty. However, Palwal hospital still survives today, and receives annual
financial aid from the BMS.[64]

The Christian medical institutions least affected by the tightening
restrictions on missionary personnel were the large co-operative ventures at
Ludhiana in the Punjab and Vellore in Tamil Nadu, whose prestige enabled
them to obtain missionary visas with relative ease. Although the Ludhiana
Hospital and Medical College owe their origins in 1894 to the vision of Dr
Edith Brown of the Baptist Zenana Mission, no BMS staff worked at
Ludhiana until 1949. From 1949 to 1973 BMS personnel were well
represented on the Ludhiana staff. Jean McLellan, who worked almost
continuously at Ludhiana throughout this period, was primarily responsible for raising the standard of nursing training to degree level. The BMS

62. I owe this information to Rev. Donald Monkcom, citing the late Rev. K. F. Weller.

63. *BMS Annual Reports.* 1972-3, p. 9; 1973-4, p. 10. General Committee Minutes, 2 Nov.
    1971, p. 48.

64. Acres, 'Partners in Healing', 39-43. Dorothy Medway was awarded the MBE in 1966
    for her work in India.

contributed members of staff to the Christian Medical College and Hospital at Vellore from 1947 onwards. Ann Bothamley, a member of staff since 1967, filled influential roles both in the hospital itself and in nursing education.[65]

The other major co-operative institution involving BMS missionaries in this period was Serampore College. The transfer of the College Council to India in 1949 did not bring about any immediate weakening in the ties linking Serampore to the BMS. At the end of the five-year period of support to which the Society had committed itself in 1949, the BMS grant to the College was raised to £1,250 per annum. The re-location of the Council did, however, have the desired effect of broadening the financial base of the College, as other missions and Indian churches began to make significant contributions.[66] Throughout the 1950s and early 1960s the staffing of the College, particularly of its theological department, continued to be heavily dependent on BMS personnel. Two missionary couples may be selected as symbolic of the strength of the Society's connection with Serampore in this period. Donald and Miriam Hudson served continously at Serampore from 1942 to 1965, when Donald was appointed secretary of the Board of Theological Education for India. Leslie and Winifred Wenger, having already served on the staff from 1934 to 1941, returned to Serampore from Barisal in 1955, and stayed till 1964.

After 1965 the number of BMS missionaries at Serampore fell, until by 1969 there were none left. The change was indicative of the growing indigenization of the Serampore faculty, but also a reflection of the grave problems which the College was again facing. Student unrest was endemic, and the inbalance in staff, student numbers, and academic purpose between the small theological and vast arts/science departments had become a major source of tension. There was also a lack of clarity in defining the relationships between the Council (the ultimate governing authority), the Senate (representing the interests of the family of Indian theological institutions which award Serampore degrees), and the Faculty (the body exercising real executive power). These problems led to the appointment in March 1969 of a commission, chaired by Bishop Lesslie Newbigin, charged with making recommendations to achieve the more harmonious and effective operation of the College. The commission's report, presented in January 1970, recommended that the theological department be moved from Serampore

65. Acres, 'Partners in Healing', 55-9.

66. W. S. Stewart (ed.), *The Story of Serampore and its College* (Serampore, 1961), 85, 89.

to form part of a larger and stronger centre of theological teaching in Calcutta, in a federal relationship with Bishop's College. Newbigin argued that the vision of the founders of the College of a single educational institution, in which theology took its place at the centre of a broad Christian education, founded on a unified framework of biblical truth, was no longer viable in a secularized system of national education. It was a bold and radical report, whose recommendations were viewed favourably by the BMS but rejected by the Council.[67]

The contribution of BMS personnel to Serampore College was not yet concluded: Edward Burrows taught New Testament from 1975 to 1979, and Keith Skirrow Pastoral Studies from 1978 to 1984. Yet the College's links with BMS did weaken from the late 1960s onwards. By 1979 the primary overseas support for Serampore, both in funds and personnel, came from the Lutheran churches.[68] Many of the problems which the Newbigin Commission endeavoured to solve remained. The College was no longer held in the universal veneration in Christian circles in India which had once been its privilege, and its continuing control of degree-level Indian theological education caused resentment in some circles. The institution which had done more than any other to educate the leadership of the Protestant Church in North India in the post-independence era faced a challenge of educational reform and spiritual renewal possibly more profound than any of those which had marked its distinguished history.

By 1974 the number of BMS missionaries in India had fallen to twenty-eight.[69] In 1991 there were just four, all of them missionaries of over twenty years' standing.[70] It seems a safe prediction that within a few years there will be no BMS missionaries left in India. The first part of India to see the door close on the Western missionary presence was the North-East. In the Mizo District the rebellion of the Mizo National Front against rule from Delhi, which began in February 1966, made the Indian government extremely sensitive to foreign influence in the territory, and the last two BMS missionaries, Edith Maltby and Joan Smith, nurses at Serkawn Christian

67. Commission on Serampore College: Report presented to the Council and Senate of Serampore College on 28 Jan. 1970; L. Newbigin, *Unfinished Agenda: An Autobiography* (London, 1985), 228-9; BMS Officers' Meeting Minutes, 5 Mar. 1970, p. 24.

68. Didcot, CR 524: Report of Stanley Mudd's Visit to Asia from 7 Mar.-23 Apr. 1979.

69. *BMS Directory and Financial Report,* 1974, p. 30.

70. The four were Ann Bothamley at Vellore, Betty Marsh at Berhampur Christian Hospital, Carole Whitmee in Balangir, and Sheila Samuels, working with the CNI in Delhi.

Hospital, had to leave early in 1968. The establishment of the State of Mizoram in 1972 restored stability to the territory, and enabled Joan Smith to return to the hospital for a final period from 1972 to 1977.[71] Nevertheless, the Western missionary era in Mizoram effectively came to an end in 1968 - just seventy-four years after it began.

By a strangely significant co-incidence, that same year the Zoram Baptist Mission was formed to co-ordinate the missionary outreach of the Baptist Church of Mizo District. For over twenty years Mizo Baptists had conducted evangelistic work among Chakma and Riang immigrants into western Mizoram. Some 2,100 of the Riangs, an animistic people from Tripura, had been baptized by 1965. Progress among the Buddhist Chakmas was much slower, with only thirty converts by 1965.[72] Then came an invitation in 1967 from the Australian Baptist Missionary Society to take over their work in the Goalpara district of Assam, where a young church, planted among the Rabha tribe, was about to be left without external help on account of the inability of the Australian missionaries to renew their visas. The first two missionaries of the Zoram Baptist Mission began work among the Rabha people in June 1968. Similarly, when the New Zealand Baptist Missionary Society had to withdraw from Tripura in 1971, the Zoram Baptist Mission responded to an invitation to take up work with the Tripura Baptist Church Union. By 1989 the Mission had eighty-eight home missionaries working among non-Mizos in Mizoram, fifty missionaries working in other parts of India, and a further eighteen in training. If pastors and other church workers in Mizoram are included, a Baptist communicant membership of 41,076 in 1989 was fully supporting 581 full-time Christian workers.[73] In a poor, rural community, Mizo Baptists have made their own the principles of Christian stewardship and evangelistic responsibility so carefully inculcated from the beginning by J. H. Lorrain and the other pioneers. The Mizo Church is the most powerful illustration from a former BMS field of the truth that the closing of the Western missionary era in India heralds, not the end of Christian mission, but its entry into a new and potentially creative phase.

71. The Serkawn hospital was opened in 1955 as a development of the earlier dispensary at Lungleh. Acres, 'Partners in Healing', 44-7. *BMS Annual Reports.* 1966-7, p. 8; 1967-8, p. 14; 1973-4, p. 8.

72. *BMS Annual Report,* 1965-6, pp. 16-17.

73. C. L. Hminga, *The Life and Witness of the Churches in Mizoram* (Serkawn, 1987), 249-55; General Secretary's Report on the Life and Witness of the Baptist Church of Mizoram [1989] (given to the author by Dr H. Hrangena).

VI: Ceylon/Sri Lanka, 1948-1992

On 4 February 1948 Ceylon became an independent nation within the British Commonwealth. Political independence gave a further stimulus to the Buddhist revival which had been gathering strength in the island ever since the 1860s: Buddhist opposition to Christian influence became more militant. The greatest challenge which the new era posed to the BMS was in the sphere of education. As late as the 1940s, about 6,000 children were being educated in the forty Baptist schools. During the 1950s numbers increased, reaching 14,368 by 1959.[74] From the early days of the Ceylon mission, the BMS had seen schools work as a primary means of evangelism. A concerted effort had been made to preserve Christian influence by employing Christian teachers wherever possible. In intention it was a laudable policy, but it ran the risk of encouraging those seeking teaching posts to make a nominal Christian profession. Independence signalled the beginning of the end of the churches' freedom to use schools to teach the Christian faith to Buddhist children. Carey College, Colombo, was one of only sixteen schools in Ceylon to opt out of the government's scheme of free education in 1951, believing that it was only a matter of time before the price of state aid would be a requirement to teach the Buddhist religion.[75]

In fact it was December 1960 before the Director of Education assumed direct control of all state-aided schools, and even then the elimination of Christian influence from the former church schools was not immediate.[76] In exceptional cases, that influence was sustained under the new educational regime: Vera Armond, headmistress of the former BMS Girls' School at Matale, was granted special status by the government to enable her to remain on the staff, though no longer as a BMS missionary. More generally, there was some decline in Baptist church membership as Christianity lost its status as a passport to greater employment opportunity. Although the Baptist community in the 1960s benefited from the pruning away of dead wood, there was also a loss of evangelistic confidence and a tendency to adopt a defensive mentality.[77]

The educational changes compelled a re-evaluation of mission strategy in Ceylon. The small force of BMS missionaries - limited by government quota to six (later five) single or married couple visas - adopted a more

---

74. *BMS Annual Reports*: 1949-50, p. xix; 1959-60, p. xvi.

75. IN/107, Carey College, Colombo, Annual Report for year ending 30 Sept. 1951.

76. *BMS Annual Reports*: 1960-1, p. ix; 1961-2, p. xxiii.

77. Interview with Rev. and Mrs G. R. Lee, 31.7.90.

explicitly evangelistic profile. Work among the Hindu Tamil community of the Ratnapura area was developed by Colin and Margaret Grant. Eric Sutton Smith, the former China missionary who served as pastor of the English-speaking congregation at Cinnamon Gardens Baptist Church, Colombo, from 1959 to 1974, encouraged his members to engage in open-air evangelism and Christian drama, performed in authentic Sinhalese style.[78]

In parallel with this re-deployment of missionary resources, the process of devolution of responsibility to the national church, initiated in the early 1940s, was brought to completion. The changes made to the Ceylon Baptist Council in 1935 had been only partially successful.[79] The Ceylon Baptist Union, in theory merged into the Council in 1935, in fact retained some kind of independent existence until 1958, when the Council was re-formed as the Sri Lanka Baptist Sangamaya (SLBS). Perhaps more seriously, BMS missionaries continued to meet separately from the Council until 1952, and retained their own source of autonomous authority until the office of BMS Field Secretary was abolished on the retirement of H. T. D. Clements in 1973. As late as 1967-8, the SLBS remained heavily dependent on financial help from the BMS. From this date on, BMS financial support was phased out, and in 1974 the process of devolution reached its terminus when all property formerly held by the BMS was vested in the SLBS.[80] After 1974 the links between the BMS and the SLBS remained strong, with BMS missionaries serving as co-workers within the Sangamaya. In 1991 the Society had two couples serving in Colombo, contributing particularly to the SLBS Lay Training Institute and the Community Service Centre run by Cinnamon Gardens Baptist Church.

Throughout this period Sri Lankan Baptists had the benefit of some highly gifted leaders (many of them trained at Serampore) who occupied prominent positions in the island's Christian community. The role played in the 1930s and 1940s by W. M. P. Jayatunga was paralleled in later decades by the contributions to Sri Lankan church life made by C. H. Ratnaike, S. J. de S. Weerasinghe, and Dr W. G. Wickramasinghe. Ratnaike was for many years secretary of the National Christian Council

---

78. Sutton Smith was third son of Herbert and Ethel Sutton Smith, BMS missionaries in Yakusu and China; see *MH*, (July 1977), 110-11.

79. See above, ch. IX, p. 291.

80. Didcot: CR 164, BMS Work in Ceylon, A Memorandum by Rev. R. C. Cowling [1958]; CR 388, Ceylon, A Report on the General Overseas Secretary's Visit in Nov. 1967. *1812-1987: Baptists in Sri Lanka, Heirs of a Noble Heritage* (SLBS, n.d.), 7.

(formed in 1912). Weerasinghe, in addition to his work in church union negotiations, was secretary of the Bible Society for nearly twenty years, and chaired the translation team which produced the first fully ecumenical Sinhala Bible (the New Testament appeared in 1973, and the Old Testament in 1982).[81] Wickramasinghe, president of the SLBS at its formation in 1958, and more recently its first full-time president, has been a key figure in ecumenical relationships and in Christian education, having been Principal both of Carey College, Colombo, and of Trinity College, Kandy. Several Baptists also served on the staff of the Theological College of Lanka, established by Anglicans, Methodists and Baptists at Pilimatalawa in 1963. The College has largely replaced Serampore as the main agency of training for the Baptist ministry.[82]

By the 1980s the generation of church leadership which had served the Sri Lankan Baptist community with such distinction since the coming of national independence was passing away. There were few obvious successors, for some of the most gifted of the younger Baptist ministers had sought greater freedom of opportunity in ministerial and teaching positions in Britain or North America. In comparison with North India, the Sri Lankan Baptist community has been capably led, highly literate and well endowed financially. These assets have tended to obscure a weakness of evangelistic vision and an inability to penetrate the depressed sectors of Sri Lankan society. The SLBS membership of about 2,000 at the end of the 1980s represented a doubling of the figure for 1914, but there were still few conversions from the Buddhist population. Apart from their ministry among the Indian Tamils of the Ratnapura area, and some work among Tamils in Colombo, Baptists have had little contact with the Tamil population, and have thus been limited in their capacity to act as agents of reconciliation in the conflicts between Sinhalese and Jaffna Tamil peoples which have driven the north and east of the island into a state of chronic civil war since 1983.[83]

In 1958 R. C. Cowling, then BMS Ceylon Secretary, gave the pessimistic verdict that 'the main thing that keeps the Baptist cause going in Ceylon is the link with the West'. He saw two opposing tendencies gnawing away at the cohesion of the Baptist churches: amongst some a ritualistic orientation prevailed, which was inclining them towards uncritical support for the

---

81. In 1986 Weerasinghe was honoured by the Sri Lankan government for his work on the Sinhala Bible; see *MH* (July 1987), 132-3.

82. *Baptists in Sri Lanka*, 31-3; interview with Rev. and Mrs G. R. Lee, 31.7.90.

83. However, for a recent SLBS statement on ethnic violence see *MH* (Jan. 1991), 17-18.

church union scheme, and away from their Baptist roots; whilst others gravitated towards the simple, enthusiastic faith of the Pentecostal sects. Both groups were in fact seeking a more numinous and overtly supernatural expression of Christian faith than the moderate, unemotional and rational ethos inculcated by British Baptists.[84] To some extent the tendencies identified by Cowling in 1958 still co-existed within Sri Lankan Baptist life at the beginning of the 1990s. Whilst there was no sign of the imminent Baptist demise which he feared, the challenge undoubtedly remained before Sri Lankan Baptists to discover a distinctive and more confident missionary identity amidst the continuing restraints of a Buddhist society.

VII: Bangladesh, 1971-1992

On 25 March 1971 the Pakistan army clamped down on the campaign of civil disobedience and labour unrest organized by the Awami League in East Pakistan. Martial law was in force, and the army began killing students and intellectuals in Dhaka. By the end of the month, the reported death toll had reached 15,000. The Pastors' Training School had to be closed, and all women BMS missionaries and children were evacuated. Many Bengali refugees crossed the border into West Bengal. On 11 April a clandestine radio broadcast announced the formation of a provisional government of the independent republic of Bangladesh, under the presidency of Sheikh Mujib. From exile in Calcutta the provisional government began to direct a war of liberation against the Pakistani forces. Bengali troops absconded from the Pakistani army, and joined the civilian population in the independence struggle. In the Chittagong area, Bengalis massacred Urdu-speakers, while rumours circulated of equivalent atrocities inflicted by the advancing Pakistani army on the Hindu population. On 13 April the army re-took Rangunia. They found David and Joyce Stockley, and a colleague in the Farmers Co-operative, to be the only inhabitants: the others, many of them Hindus, had all fled. The next day the army advanced on Chandraghona, where Bengali troops were reported to be entrenched. The Pakistani major had orders to reduce the hospital to the ground, but decided to investigate the situation first. He encountered no resistance, and the hospital was saved, though a mortar shell killed one patient in the leprosy centre. Although the hospital continued to function throughout the emergency, many innocent Bengalis in the area lost their lives as the army inflicted reprisals for the atrocities committed against Urdu-speakers.[85]

---

84. Didcot, CR 164, BMS Work in Ceylon, A Memorandum by Rev. R. C. Cowling.

85. O'Donnell, *Bangladesh*, 89-96; *BMS Annual Report*, 1971-2, pp. 14-16; Prayer Letters series, D. and J. Stockley file, newsletter from D. Stockley, July 1971.

The logic of Indian support for the Bengali cause brought India and Pakistan into open conflict by 3 December. Within twelve days the superior Indian forces had reached Dhaka and forced the surrender of the Pakistani army. Sheikh Mujib was brought home from jail in West Pakistan to become the Prime Minister of the Republic of Bangladesh. The new state, born out of an inter-Muslim conflict, and nursed into existence by the Indian government, naturally assumed a clearly secular stance, emphasizing Bengali national identity rather than the Islamic faith. Many of the ten million Bengali refugees had been assisted by Christian relief agencies while in India, and now received similar aid on their return to Bangladesh. The BMS Relief Fund gave £40,000 to assist in the work of rehabilitation. Hopes of increased opportunities for Christian service and witness were high.[86]

Under the government of Sheikh Mujib (1971-5), these hopes were in some measure realized. Among Hindu communities which had suffered at the hands of the Pakistan army during the war, there was a significant movement towards Christianity. BMS missionaries were cautious in their baptismal policy towards the new converts, yet saw a number of new churches planted. In the Ruhea area five new churches, with a total membership of 145, were formed in 1973 from Hindu converts whose first contact with Christians had been in the refugee camps in India. Similarly, Hindus in the southern part of the Faridpur district, whose villages had been destroyed by the Pakistani army in 1971, had come across Christian agencies in exile in India, and were now seeking Christian teaching. By January 1975, 130 had been baptized, and many more (including sixty-eight Muslims from one village) were enquirers. Overall, as many as 6-7,000 new converts may have been added to the Christian churches by 1975. However, in places the lack of mature Bangladeshi Christians able to teach the new converts proved fatal. By 1979 virtually all the Baptist churches formed in the Barisal and Faridpur districts from the Hindu converts had reverted to Hinduism.[87]

The new opportunities attracted a flood of foreign aid and missionaries to Bangladesh. The influx of overseas aid has been a mixed blessing, apparently benefiting the urban middle-class more than the peasant farm-

86. C. J. Gulati, *Bangladesh: Liberation to Fundamentalism* (New Delhi, 1988), 67; Didcot, CR 492, The Church in Bangladesh; *BMS Annual Report*, 1971-2, p.12.

87. Didcot: CR 462, Report of Regional Overseas Representative for Asia on a Visit from 10.2.73 to 31.3.73; CR 480, Report by Rev. F. Wells on a Tour from 6 Jan. to 26 Feb. 1975; CR 492, The Church in Bangladesh; CR 527, Report by D. W. and J. King to BMS Overseas Committee, June 1979. *BMS Annual Report*, 1973-4, p. 11.

ers. Most of the population remain impoverished and extremely vulnerable to the impact of cyclones and chronic flooding, the latter caused largely by deforestation beyond the nation's borders in the upper reaches of the Ganges and Brahmaputra river systems. The Bangladesh Baptist Sangha or BBS (successor to the Baptist Union of Pakistan) responded to the continuing poverty of the country by establishing a Social, Health, Education, and Development Board (SHED) to promote rural development projects. However, the availability of overseas aid tended to perpetuate an unhealthy dependence of the BBS on external sources of finance: in 1984 68 per cent of the central budget came from the BMS, and very little from local sources. Some - both missionaries and national Christians - felt that priorities were distorted as a result, and funds used to bolster power and status, rather than meet human need. 'The biggest crime in this Sammilani (district union)', exclaimed one Bangladeshi Baptist in 1985, 'is that we took Jesus away and concentrated all our energies on relief'.[88]

The new missionary agencies which entered Bangladesh after 1971 also posed some problems for the BBS and BMS. The new missions were conservative evangelical in their theology, and tended to criticise the BMS and other older missions for being too subservient to a generation of church leaders whose zeal for evangelism had been sapped by the years of Muslim supremacy from 1947 to 1971. Nevertheless, one of the newcomers, the Liebenzeller Mission, concluded a partnership agreement with the BBS in 1975, which has endured with profit into the 1990s, despite the initial reservations of some within the BMS that the Mission might be too conservative in its theology for the relationship to be a success.[89] Relationships between the BBS and other church groups were less close than many in the BMS would have wished. The BBS stood apart from the expanding Bangladesh Baptist Union, supported by the Australian and New Zealand Baptist Missionary Societies and the Southern Baptist Convention Foreign Mission Board. After 1984 the BBS was the only substantial Christian body represented on the National Christian Council of Bangladesh, following the withdrawal of the Church of Bangladesh (Anglican/ Presbyterian).

In August 1975 Sheikh Mujib was assassinated, and the Awami League government overthrown. From that date until late 1990 Bangladesh was

88. Didcot: CR 583, Bangladesh 1984, by A. T. MacNeill; CR 600, Asia Report for 1985, by N. B. McVicar.

89. Didcot: CR 492, The Church in Bangladesh; CR 521, Report of Stanley Mudd's Visit to Asia from 9 Nov. to 23 Dec. 1978. The Liebenzeller Mission is a Lutheran pietist body whose origins are to be found in the formation in 1899 of the German branch of the China Inland Mission.

governed by military regimes, the most enduring of which - that of General H. M. Ershad - survived from March 1982 to December 1990. These regimes progressively diluted the original emphasis on Bangladesh as a secular state, and cultivated a much more pronounced Islamic orientation. Under Ershad, the Islamization of national life posed a number of problems for the small Christian community. Government restrictions on missionary involvement in the churches tightened in the late 1980s. Principally because of the changing political climate, the number of BMS missionaries in Bangladesh fell from twenty-seven in 1974 to only five in 1990, and there were signs that the decline might continue. The BBS remained one of the largest Protestant denominations, with a membership in 1984 of 9,013 in 194 churches.[90] Its problems were characteristic of a small second- or third-generation Christian community in a Muslim land. Yet the opportunities open to the Sangha for Christian witness through word and deed in a desperately poor nation remained large, and it seemed likely that the role of the BMS in supporting that witness would continue.

VIII: The BMS and the United Mission to Nepal, 1954-1992

The coming of independence to India in 1947 had an inevitable effect on the ancient Hindu kingdom of Nepal.[91] Previously impervious to almost all external influence, the kingdom was now confronted by the first stirrings of democratic protest, orchestrated by the Nepal National Congress in exile in India. The mounting pressure for political change in Nepal culminated in the revolution of February 1951, when King Tribuvan, who had been deposed by the Prime Minister, was restored to the throne with Indian help, and the traditional regime of the Ranas brought to an end. For the remainder of the decade, Nepal was in a state of political flux, in which first King Tribuvan, and then, from 1954, King Mahendra, experimented with various models of 'democratic' rule. However, from 1962 the mould of Nepali politics was set in the form of an absolute monarchical government which claimed to permit democratic expression through a structure of *panchayat* village councils. Political parties were proscribed.

The revolution of 1951 opened the door for Christian missions to enter Nepal. A small group of American missionaries had already been granted access to the kingdom in late 1949, purely for the purposes of an ornitho-

---

90. Didcot, CR 586, Asia Report, Nov. 1984, by N. B. McVicar.

91. The account which follows is dependent on J. Lindell, *Nepal and the Gospel of God* (Kathmandu, 1979), *passim*.

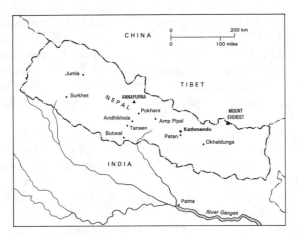

Map 9: Nepal

logical expedition. The group, led by two doctors, Robert Fleming, a Methodist, and Carl Taylor, a Presbyterian, made two further expeditions to Nepal in 1951 and 1952, which combined ornithology with some clinic work. As a result, Robert Fleming wrote to the Nepali government, offering to open a mission hospital at Tansen and establish maternity and child welfare centres in villages in the Kathmandu valley. In May 1953 this offer was accepted. Meanwhile Fleming and his colleagues pressed their mission boards in the United States to take action in response to the new opportunity.

The American Presbyterian and Methodist mission boards believed that the new opening in Nepal demanded a united response from the Protestant missionary community, and not from their communions alone. At a meeting in Allahabad in August 1953 it was accordingly proposed to form a united Protestant medical mission to Nepal. The idea was then taken up by the National Christian Council of India (NCC). On 4-5 March 1954, at Nagpur in central India, the United Christian Mission to Nepal (known from 1956 as the United Mission to Nepal, or UMN) was formed. The first missionaries had already begun work, opening clinics at Bhatgaon and Kathmandu, and a dispensary at Tansen as a first step towards the planned hospital.

The BMS was not among the eight missions and churches approved as founding members of the UMN at a meeting in Delhi in September 1954, when a constitution for the Mission was adopted. Although invitations to participate in the new mission were widely circulated, it appears that the

BMS originally viewed the venture as a matter involving its Indian partner churches rather than the Society itself. This was a logical consequence of the status of the UMN in its early years as a project of the NCC; until 1959 the headquarters of the Mission were in Bihar, where its executive secretary, Ernest Oliver, also worked as a missionary of the Regions Beyond Missionary Union. The early links between the BMS and the UMN were hence indirect, in the person of Philip John, who represented the BUNI on the UMN Board.

In 1959 Ernest and Edna Madge visited Nepal on behalf of the BMS, and reported both to the Society and to the Council of Baptist Churches in Northern India (CBCNI) that BMS participation in the United Mission seemed appropriate. In response, the executive committee of the BUNI resolved to make enquiries of the UMN regarding the Mission's requirements and conditions of service for both Indian and European personnel. As a consequence of these enquiries, the annual meeting of the CBCNI in December 1960 requested the BMS to send a nursing sister to work with the UMN. It was thus on the recommendation, and under the auspices, of the CBCNI that the first BMS missionary in Nepal, Margaret Robinson, was appointed in June 1962.[92]

After language training in Kathmandu, Margaret Robinson worked in the Shanta Bhawan hospital - the direct descendant of one of the first clinics established by the UMN in 1954. She was joined in late 1966 by a second BMS missionary, Sylvia Slade, who was allocated to the hospital at Tansen. The third BMS missionary allocated to Nepal, Margaret Kingsley, was a teacher, sent out in 1968. By this time the original concept of a purely medical mission had broadened to include educational and agricultural work. In 1963 the BMS Officers had declined a request from the UMN to provide one of twelve agricultural missionaries needed for Nepal, mainly because it was felt that the needs of other BMS fields should be given priority in the allocation of any candidates for agricultural work (who were scarce at that time).[93] The hesitation perhaps stemmed from the fact that Nepal was not yet regarded as a primary field of BMS activity. The BMS did not become a member body of the UMN until 1968, when the Society responded to the request of the CBCNI that it should take its place in the Mission, and Neil McVicar was appointed to represent the BMS on the UMN Board.[94] The annual report for 1970-1 was the first in which Nepal

---

92. Information from Rev. E. G. T. Madge, 25.9.90. South Asia Sub-Committee Minutes: 17 Oct. 1956, p. 65; 24 Jan. 1961, pp. 37-8, 43-4; 19 June 1962, p. 131.

93. Officers' Meeting Minutes: 9 May 1963, p. 44; 9 July 1964, p. 89.

94. General Committee Minutes, 25 Apr. 1968, p. 16.

appeared as a field in its own right, rather than as a sub-section of the India mission.[95] Since the early 1970s BMS participation in the UMN has increased enormously. By 1979 the Society was the third largest contributor of foreign personnel.[96] In 1990 Nepal was the third largest BMS field in terms of personnel, with twenty-three missionaries serving in a great variety of capacities, ranging from dentistry to the promotion of rural development through the Andhikhola hydro-electric project.[97]

In a number of respects Nepal constitutes a unique case in the Society's experience. No member body of the UMN has any independent existence in Nepal. Mission policy and the allocation of workers are determined by the UMN headquarters in Kathmandu rather than by the BMS. More fundamental still is the distinctive nature of the context in which the UMN operates. The UMN constitution defines the purpose of the Mission as 'to minister to the needs of the people in Nepal in the Name and Spirit of Christ, and to make Christ known by word and life, thereby strengthening the universal Church in its total ministry'[98] This task has to be fulfilled in a country where it is against the law to seek to convert anyone from their ancestral religion. From the beginning the UMN had to commit itself to refrain from all 'proselytizing' activity as the precondition for its continuing approval by the government. The establishing and discipling of a national church has necessarily played no part in the Mission's objectives - a fact which may explain the remarkable absence of theological or denominational tensions in the Mission's history. The freedom of the UMN to work in Nepal has always been of a temporary nature, depending on short-term agreements negotiated with the state; the Mission has also espoused the goal of making all its projects indigenous within as short a time-span as possible. Despite the severe restrictions on religious freedom, the Protestant Church in Nepal grew from a mere handful of believers in the 1950s to perhaps 25,000 or more by 1992. The committed service and private witness of missionaries of the UMN and other missions clearly contributed to this result, although the evangelistic role of Indian Christians was probably even more significant. The major contribution made by the UMN to the improvement of the quality of life of thousands of Nepalis is undeniable.

Nepal thus presents the anomaly of a nation in which evangelism has had to be removed from the heart of Christian mission, and foreign missionary

95. *BMS Annual Report,* 1970-1, p. 36.

96. Didcot, CR 524, Report of Stanley Mudd's Visit to Asia, 7 Mar.-23 Apr. 1979.

97. *MH* (May 1990), 19, 22.

98. *United Mission to Nepal; Constitution and Bye-Laws* (Apr. 1983), 1.

activity carried on in almost total disjunction from the life of the national church. As such, the story of the UMN departs from the conventional wisdom of missionary theory, yet with remarkable success. During 1990 Nepal faced renewed ferment, as the growing pressure for genuine democratic reform compelled the King to dissolve the government and move the country towards multi-party politics. The resulting political upheaval delayed for six months the signing of a new five-year agreement between the UMN and the government, due to be concluded in May 1990. Whatever the future might hold for Nepal, there could be little doubt that the Christian church that had taken root since 1951 would continue, not just to survive, but to grow.

XIV

Zaire and Angola, 1960-1992

I: Independence and its Aftermath: Zaire, 1960-1972

The 1960s were a decade in which the work of the Baptist Missionary Society and its associated churches in the Congo Republic (formerly Belgian Congo) and Angola was affected as never before by the rapidity and turbulence of political change. These were years which demanded of missionaries and African Christians alike courage, adaptability, and a readiness to question long-established assumptions about the relationship between foreign mission and national church. In no year was the pace of change greater than in 1960.

In January 1959 King Baudouin had made a speech promising independence to the Congo. At the Round Table conference in January 1960 the Belgians committed themselves to granting full independence to the Congo on 30 June 1960. Even before the conference took place, enthusiasm for independence was running high. As early as September 1959, reports from locations as diverse as the *Ecole Grenfell* at Yalemba on the upper river and EPI Kimpese on the lower river indicated that the passion for *indépendance* was affecting both the student body of the two institutions and church life. Margaret Bäckman at Kimpese observed that missionaries were neither as welcome nor as trusted as once they were.[1] For the first time church delegates were present at two (middle and upper river) of the four regional conferences held between April and June 1960. The Lower River Church Council chose not to send representatives to the regional conference. The question of integrating church and mission was uppermost on the agenda of the three meetings held in the Belgian Congo. Few doubted the necessity of integration, but missionary and African opinion diverged on its

---

1. P.J. Manicom, 'Light and Shadows in Congo' (unpublished MS), 131-6; A/100, prayer
    letter from D. M. Bäckman (née Tivey), 25 Jan. 1960.

extent: missionaries wished the BMS to retain control of matters such as their salaries, housing, and transport, whilst most church leaders argued that integration should be total. In Angola progress towards devolution was severely hampered by the fact that the Portuguese would have regarded any attempt to make the church independent of the mission as politically subversive; indeed, according to Portuguese law, no Protestant church could exist independently of a foreign mission.[2] Nevertheless, the Angola regional conference agreed to invite African representatives to attend the following year's conference for certain items on the agenda.[3]

Political events soon placed these discussions into a wholly different perspective. Within a week of Independence Day on 30 June, the Congolese army had mutinied against its white officers, both at Léopoldville and at Thysville (Mbanza Ngungu). Fighting broke out between Congolese and Belgian troops, and on 11 July Moise Tshombe announced the secession of Katanga province from the Congo Republic. In some places the unrest assumed a specifically anti-white form. Some American Baptist missionaries on the lower river were beaten up or raped, and on the 15th most BMS missionaries on the lower river rural stations were evacuated by helicopter to Léopoldville. Many of their colleagues on the upper river were compelled to follow two days later, though Leslie Moore and Stanley Anslow at Upoto, and Russell and Rachel Warden at Pimu hospital insisted on staying put, contrary to the strong advice of Harold Casebow, now Congo Field Secretary. Only on the middle river, at Bolobo and Ntondo, was it possible for full missionary complements to be maintained, and even here tension was high.[4]

Few missionaries in July 1960 sensed any danger from the local populace, but British consular advice urged evacuation, prompted by the fear of a Soviet invasion of the country, and a consequent escalation of the conflict to international proportions. When Patrice Lumumba's government made a direct appeal to the Soviet Union to send its troops to the Congo immediately to force the withdrawal of all Belgian forces, Anslow, Moore, and the Upoto deacons hurriedly drafted and signed a document

2.   Information from Rev. F. J. Grenfell, 29.1.91.

3.   A/68: Minutes of Upper River Regional Conference, 5-12 Apr. 1960; Minutes of Angola Regional Conference, 31 May-4 June 1960. General Committee Minutes, 1 Nov. 1960, pp. 128-30. *Yakusu Notes* (July 1960), 2-4.

4.   *BMS Annual Report*, 1960-1, pp. xxvi-xxxi; Upoto archives, Log Book of Upoto-Pimu station, 1955-82, entries for July 1960; Personal diary of F. Stainthorpe for July 1960 (in possession of Rev. F. Stainthorpe).

making over all BMS property and effects to the Upoto church. The station log book, written by Moore, records that the missionaries went to bed on the night of 20 July 'wondering if we'll be in Russian hands tomorrow'. Their fears were not realized, but Moore's concluding comment for that day was both accurate and perceptive: 'Thus policy that was being implemented slowly through the year, has, by emergencies, been carried out here in a matter of days'. The next day he re-painted the old mission station sign to read *'Eglise du Christ au Congo, BMS Upoto'*. Amidst the chaos of the Congo Republic's first few weeks of national independence, the previously gradual transfer of control from mission to church had accelerated to near frenetic pace.[5]

Within six weeks the BMS force in the Congo had been reduced from ninety-seven to fifty-five missionaries. However, the restoration of a measure of stability following the dispatch of United Nations troops to the Congo ensured that the interruption to missionary activity was short-lived. By August missionaries were beginning to return to their stations. IME hospital at Kimpese was without doctors for only three weeks, and had continued to function throughout. During his absence from Kimpese, Dr David Wilson was instrumental in establishing (under the auspices of the Congo Protestant Council) the Congo Protestant Relief Agency. The Agency was originally set up to replenish mission hospitals affected by the emergency with medical staff and supplies - but later broadened its objectives to become a major channel of international aid to refugees and victims of famine in the Congo.[6]

On 30 July - two weeks later than originally planned - a BMS delegation, comprising the Society's vice-chairman, Professor H. H. Rowley, and Foreign Secretary, Ernest Madge, left for the Congo. The events of the last month dictated that church-mission relationships were uppermost on their agenda. From 1 to 9 August Rowley and Madge met in Léopoldville with representatives of the Lower River Church Council and missionaries of the Lower River Regional Conference to draft a constitution for an integrated Lower River Church. The middle and upper river regions were less far advanced, but their own later constitutions followed the lower river pattern in many respects. In Angola, as has been seen, the process of devolution had scarcely begun, as there was no church body other than at local level. It was

---

5. Upoto archives, Log Book of Upoto-Pimu station, entries for 18-21 July 1960; information from the late Rev. L. H. Moore. The Upoto pastor, Samuel Koli, had been away at the BWA Congress in Rio de Janeiro, and did not return to Upoto till 1 August.

6. *BMS Annual Report*, 1960-1, pp. xxvi, xxix-xxx.

therefore judged necessary in November to sever Angola from the rest of the Congo mission, and make the territory a separate field, responsible directly to London. Rowley was compelled by illness to return home on 18 August, leaving Madge to attend the Field Council from 13 to 19 September, when provision was made for the transfer of all BMS work in the Congo Republic to church control.[7] From 1 January 1961 BMS missionaries in the Republic became members of, and answerable to, one of the three regional Baptist churches - *L'Eglise Baptiste du Bas Fleuve, L'Eglise Baptiste du Moyen Fleuve,* and *L'Eglise Baptiste du Haut Congo.*

BMS missionaries on the Congo now operated on a totally different basis, being allocated to their stations by the new church councils set up in each region, under the overall authority of a Central Council of Baptist Churches covering the three regions. In a few instances their return after the troubles of mid-1960 evoked mixed reactions, even from the church. At Yalemba, some of the BMS teachers supported the *Mouvement National Congolais,* and wished the missionaries to stay away, leaving them to run the teacher training department of the *Ecole Grenfell* as a purely lay institution. There was serious unrest before the majority party in the church succeeded in appointing a school director in favour of retaining links with the BMS.[8] In most places, however, returning missionaries found a warm welcome, not least because their presence was, paradoxically, more urgently needed than before independence. This was most notably the case in the field of medicine.

On the eve of independence there were between 700 and 800 doctors in the country, all of them expatriates, making a ratio of about one doctor to 25,000 people. Within a month, the number had shrunk to between 150 and 200, reducing the ratio to approximately 1:100,000. Almost all those who remained were missionaries - about fifty of them Protestants. The four BMS hospitals at Yakusu, Pimu, Bolobo, and Ntondo, and the inter-mission hospital at Kimpese, carried almost the entire burden of community health care in their respective areas. In the eastern Congo, it is estimated that *infirmiers* (medical auxiliaries) trained at Yakusu were responsible for about half of all the general medical work that continued to function in the immediate post-independence period. Even in the 1980s many of the nurses who staffed the Zairean health service had been trained at Kimpese

7.   General Committee Minutes, 1 Nov. 1960, pp. 120, 125-6, 133; A/70, Minutes of Angola Regional Conference, 2-8 June 1959; Report on Visit of Dr H. H. Rowley and Rev. E. G. T. Madge to Congo and Angola Aug./Sept. 1960.

8.   Didcot, J. F. and N. Carrington file, J. F. Carrington to C. J. Parsons, 14 Oct. 1960.

or Yakusu. In recent years nursing schools have also been established at Pimu and Bolobo. The administration of the hospitals was a source of some confusion and controversy in the aftermath of independence. Medical staff, both missionary and national, feared that control by church leaders with no medical competence would lower professional standards and narrow the range of those benefiting from medical services to church members only. Nevertheless, in 1962 overall control of the BMS hospitals and dispensaries passed from the Society to the Central Council of Baptist Churches; IME remained unattached to any one church.[9]

For medical missionaries, independence posed problems of management and human relationships, but made little difference to their everyday work. On the other hand, some missionaries whose work had previously included church responsibilities now found their patterns of life radically different. As early as September 1960, John Carrington at Yakusu had been amazed (and delighted) to find himself left without interruption for six hours at a stretch, to work on his Lingala translation of the Old Testament.[10] Other missionaries, however, found the adjustment to more narrowly defined specialist roles difficult, especially when they could see their former spheres of responsibility suffering at the hands of inexperienced and untrained Congolese. Church rules which missionaries had drawn up were now sometimes ignored, church finances were poorly kept and rarely audited, and pastoral work appeared at times to be neglected out of a preoccupation with the creation of centralized structures.[11]

The insistence of the new era on indigenous leadership in church and state placed a high premium on education, particularly among the educationally disadvantaged Protestant community. In June 1960 there were only two Protestant six-year secondary schools in the country, one of them being the Kimpese school, opened in 1953. By the close of 1960 the BMS had opened two new secondary schools (initially of a three-year type only) at Ngombe Lutete and Bolobo. The Lower River Church opened two others - at Thysville and Léopoldville - in 1962. By 1963 the number of

9. *BMS Annual Report*, 1960-1, p. xxx; Didcot, CR 305, Report by C. J. Parsons on Africa Visit, 4 Feb.-14 May, 1963; I. S. Acres, 'Partners in Healing' (unpublished BMS MS, 1983), 67, 112. E. E. Sabben-Clare *et. al.* (eds.), *Health in Tropical Africa During the Colonial Period* (Oxford, 1980), 78.

10. Didcot, J. F. and N. Carrington file, N. Carrington to C. J. Parsons, 23 Sept. 1960.

11. Didcot, CBFZ Lower River file, Kinshasa station annual report for 1961; CR 305, Report by C. J. Parsons.

Protestant secondary schools had grown to over fifty.[12] Initially the staffing of the Baptist secondary schools depended heavily on BMS personnel - a fact which reinforced the trend for missionaries to be confined to institutional roles.

The demand of the Protestant churches for increased educational opportunities was not limited to secondary schooling. In February 1962 the Congo Protestant Council (which had passed into Congolese hands in 1960) decided to establish a Protestant University at Stanleyville, to rank alongside the existing Catholic University of Lovanium in Léopoldville and the State University at Elizabethville. Many missionary observers, including the BMS Africa Secretary, Clifford Parsons, regarded the decision as premature, in view of the paucity of Protestant secondary education. Nevertheless, the Free University at Stanleyville (Kisangani) was opened in November 1963 with some fifty students.[13] The BMS made a major contribution to the life of the new university through the service of John Carrington as Professor of Botany, Ethnobotany, and Linguistics from 1966 to his retirement in 1979, and for a time as Vice-Chancellor for Academic Affairs and Dean of Faculties.

Most United Nations forces were withdrawn from the Congo at the end of June 1963. It soon became evident that the country was no more a unified nation than it had been in 1960. President Kasavubu's dissolution of parliament at the end of 1963 provoked the eastern provinces of Kivu and Kwilu into rebellion early in 1964. After Moise Tshombe's return from voluntary exile in Spain to form a new government on 10 July, the revolt spread rapidly to the Oriental province. On 4 August 1964 the *'simba'* rebels took Stanleyville. There were no BMS missionaries in the town at the time, Peter and Eileen Briggs having returned to Britain a few weeks previously. At Yakusu, however, five missionaries (James and Maimie Taylor, Lyn and Joan Collis, and Doreen West), and a visiting Methodist, June Moors, found themselves in rebel hands, and apparently in real danger. The rebels pursued the administrative director of the hospital, Pierre Lifenya, to his home village and killed him and his son. Despite this alarming beginning, the rebels generally adopted a tolerant attitude to the Yakusu staff, perhaps because two of their own officers were former Yakusu students. However, by the last week of November, as Belgian paratroops and white mercenaries fought the rebels for control of Stanleyville, any white face was in grave danger. Over the next few weeks on the upper river over eighty Europeans

---

12. *BMS Annual Report,* 1960-1, p. xxxii; Didcot, CR 305, Report by C. J. Parsons.

13. Didcot, CR 305, Report by C. J. Parsons; *BMS Annual Report,* 1963-4, pp. 25-6.

were murdered, including both Protestant and Catholic missionaries. At Yakusu on the night of 25 November Doreen West and June Moors were attacked by a group of *simba*'s; Doreen West received serious machete cuts to her arm. The next day all the Yakusu missionaries, with their four children, and some of the student nurses, were rescued by the mercenaries, and airlifted to Léopoldville.[14]

Elsewhere on the upper river, BMS missionaries narrowly escaped first-hand encounters with the rebel forces. On 6 August the *Ecole Grenfell* staff evacuated Yalemba and left by canoe for Bandu, where they met Cyril and Jeanne Austen, on safari from Lingungu. It was agreed to move the women and children immediately to safety in Léopoldville, while Ray Richards and Cyril Austen stayed on at Bandu. On 11 August, on advice from the church, they too departed, and made the 200-kilometer journey by canoe to Bumba, and thence to Upoto.[15]

At Upoto three weeks of mounting tension culminated in what the station log book described as a 'Day of Panic' on 22 August, after the government troops abandoned their base at Lisala during the night. As most of the local population fled in anticipation of a rebel take-over, Pastor Samuel Koli urged the remaining missionaries - David and Janet Claxton, Joan Greenaway, and Ray Richards (Cyril Austen had left on the 19th) to leave for their own safety. They left on an American plane for Léopoldville the next day. The rebels occupied Lisala on the morning of Sunday, 29 August. When the sound of rifle fire reached the Upoto church at worship, the entire congregation got up and fled. Samuel Koli and his family spent the night on an island on the river. On Monday morning, Koli, his son Jason, and four others returned to the mission to investigate the situation, but were surprised by two armed rebels. One of Koli's companions was shot dead, and Koli and his son had to fight for their lives, before fleeing into the forest. The mission was looted and much property damaged. After only two weeks, the Congolese National Army re-took the area. Within a month, Joan Greenaway, Stanley and Mary Anslow, and Derek and Brenda Rumbol were back in Upoto, assisting the church in rebuilding its shattered life.[16]

At Pimu hospital Russell and Rachel Warden stayed at their posts throughout the emergency, as they had done in 1960, although most of the

14. *BMS Annual Report,* 1964-5, p. 40; Didcot, H. F. Drake file, Drake to Congo colleagues, 30 Nov. 1964.

15. *BMS Annual Report,* 1964-5, pp. 40-2. Lingungu station was opened in 1948.

16. Ibid., p. 38; Upoto archives, typescript log for 1-23 Aug. 1964, and Baptist Church of the Upper River at Upoto and Binga: Annual Report 1964.

nurses and patients fled. The rebels never reached Pimu, but the near-deserted mission was seriously threatened by a group of local toughs out to steal what they could. Pastor Maurice Mondengo and his wife, Malata (the only Congolese woman left on the station) remained with the Wardens protecting church property against the constant threat of theft and looting. By the beginning of October, the danger from the rebels had lifted, and the wards were full again.[17]

For the missionaries and Congolese Christians who lived through them, these were traumatic months which will never be forgotten. The events of the rebellion also had longer-term implications for the future of the country and of Baptist work in it. Rebel activity continued in the upper river region for some years. Doreen West and another nurse, Mary Fagg, returned to Yakusu in January 1967, but it was February 1975 before the BMS was again able to station a doctor at Yakusu. It proved impossible to recommence the *Ecole Grenfell* at isolated Yalemba, and in 1966 the decision was taken to transfer theological training on the upper river from Yalemba to Yakusu, and concentrate Protestant secondary education at Upoto and Kisangani. Missionaries did not return to Yalemba. Tragically it was in Kisangani that David Claxton, who had been involved in church and secondary school work in the city, was murdered by armed robbers in June 1967. A month later renewed fighting broke out in the city. Some of the foreign mercenaries left in the area following the suppression of the *simba* rebellion mutinied and turned on the Congolese army, necessitating a further withdrawal of missionary staff from Kisangani and Yakusu.[18]

On 24 November 1965 the leading army general, Joseph (Sese Seko) Mobutu, deposed President Kasavubu in a bloodless coup, and installed himself in power. Impatient with the government's inability to hold the country's disparate elements together, Mobutu set himself the goal of creating one nation in the Congo. In May 1967 all power was concentrated in the hands of a single political party, the *Mouvement Populaire de la Révolution* (MPR). From October 1971 the dominant feature of Mobutu's MPR regime was the pursuit of *authenticité* in all areas of national life. *Authenticité* implied the creation of a distinctive national identity that would eclipse all tribal and sectional loyalties, and obliterate the cultural vestiges of the colonial era. Nomenclature and even styles of dress were changed: the Congo Republic became Zaire; Christians had to cease using

17. Pimu archives, Annual Report for 1964 on Pimu Hospital.

18. Didcot, R. F. and B. Richards file, R. F. Richards to H. F. Drake, 24 July 1967; Acres, 'Partners in Healing', 100-3.

their European baptismal names, and adopt authentic Zairean names instead. For the Baptist churches, perhaps the greatest significance of the campaign was the stimulus it gave to the existing movement to create a united Baptist community in place of the existing regional bodies.

In close parallelism with the drive for national unification was the determination of the secretariat of the Congo Protestant Council to amalgamate all Protestant groups within a united Protestant church. These efforts came to fruition in 1970 in the formation of the *Eglise du Christ au Congo* (from October 1971 the *Eglise du Christ au Zaire*- ECZ). The various Protestant bodies now became known as communities of the one church. Thus the three Baptist churches became the *Communauté Baptiste du Bas-Fleuve* (CBBF), the *Communauté Baptiste du Moyen-Fleuve* (CBMF), and the *Communauté Baptiste du Haut-Congo* (CBHC). Closely associated with the movement towards Protestant unification was a demand for all foreign missions working in the country to cede their *personnalité civile* (legal status), and fuse with their partner churches. For the BMS, the question was complicated by the fact that the Society was associated with three autonomous churches, rather than one.[19] This arrangement (whose appropriateness had never been seriously questioned in 1960) now appeared increasingly anomalous, and would appear even more so once *authenticité* came in vogue.

During 1970 a sub-committee of the Central Council of Baptist Churches prepared a draft constitution and statutes for the proposed Baptist Church of the River Congo, together with a convention to govern the new church's relationship with the BMS. The proposals were approved by the BMS Africa sub-committee in October, and were also submitted to the executive committees of the three Baptist communities. Their responses were presented at a special meeting of the Central Council in January 1971. The CBHC and CBMF approved the proposals as they stood, but the CBBF (which was closely identified with the Bakongo people) insisted on two amendments, the more important of which was that the General Secretary and his assistant should be elected in turn from each of the three regions. This was unacceptable to the other two regions, and over the next few months deadlock was reached. The matter acquired new urgency after Mobutu, as part of the *authenticité* campaign, issued a 'Law Regulating Public Worship', to come into force on 1 April 1972. The law stipulated that the only Protestant bodies to possess legal status and government

---

19. Didcot, CR 407, Report on General Overseas Secretary's Visit to Congo Nov./Dec. 1969.

Sir Clement C. Chesterman, Medical   *Dr John F. Carrington, Missionary*
Missionary in the Belgian Congo,   *in Zaire, 1938-79.*
1920-36; Medical Secretary of the
BMS, 1936-46; Medical Officer
1946-63.

W. David Grenfell, Missionary in   *H. F. Drake, Missionary in Zaire,*
Angola, 1933-69.   *1945-66; Associate Overseas*
                                          Secretary of the BMS, 1966-75;
                                          Overseas Secretary, 1975-82;
                                          Missionary in Angola, 1982-4.

recognition would be those duly registered as member communities of the ECZ. The law appeared to imply that, after 31 December 1972, the BMS would no longer possess a legal entitlement to its property in Zaire. With the CBBF still holding out against the desire of the CBMF and CBHC for full union, the BMS was accordingly compelled to investigate ways of achieving 'separate fusion' with each of the three communities. This course involved the delicate task of dividing the Society's valuable Kalina property in Kinshasa between the communities: the CBMF and CBHC strongly resisted any suggestion that Kinshasa (which was originally Bateke rather than Bakongo territory) should be regarded as the preserve of the CBBF. At the Central Council at Upoto in July 1972 H. F. Drake, the BMS Associate Overseas Secretary, eventually secured the agreement of the three communities for such an arrangement, and separate conventions between the Society and each community were actually signed.[20]

The conventions agreed at Upoto were ratified by the BMS General Committee and by the CBBF, but not by the CBMF or CBHC, which continued to press for full integration. The resulting stalemate was resolved only by the intervention, at the request of the three communities and the BMS, of Dr I. B. Bokeleale, President of the ECZ. Initially Bokeleale sought a solution which retained the separation of the three communities, whilst vesting the Kalina land in a unified secretariat. When this solution failed, Bokeleale referred the matter to the executive committee of the ECZ. The eventual outcome of negotiations between the committee, the General Secretaries of the three Baptist communities, H. F. Drake, and Angus MacNeill, Field Secretary of the BMS, was a formal decision by the executive committee on 1 December that the three communities should be unified into one *Communauté Baptiste du Fleuve Zaire* (CBFZ). The problem of Kinshasa was overcome by making Kinshasa a fourth region, independent of the Lower River. The ECZ decision was not technically an imposition, but the CBBF was left with little alternative but to acquiesce, not least because the decision cited the 1960 creation of three communities as an instance of the shameful 'balkanisation of the country according to clans and tribal regions', which the Zairois people, in the age of *authenticité*, had now repudiated. On 3-4 December the three General Secretaries, Drake, and MacNeill met to agree statutes for the CBFZ and elect its legal representatives. After protracted negotiations, Bakongo sensitivities were

---

20. Didcot, CR 421, Report on Visit to Congo by Associate Overseas Secretary, 11 Jan. to 4 Mar. 1971. General Committee Minutes; 22 Mar. 1972, p. 17; 5 July 1972, p. 39. H. F. Drake file, Drake to Madge, 19 and 24 July 1972.

eventually mollified by the appointment as General Secretary of a gifted Mukongo, Nlongi Mfwilwakanda, rather than the leading upper river candidate, [Samuel] Koli Mandole Molima, who became Regional Secretary for Kinshasa. Mfwilwakanda had worked as an education secretary for the ECZ before undertaking further study in Europe, so was well qualified for his new post. Ninety-three years and six months after the pioneering missionary party of Holman Bentley, Crudgington and Hartland had landed at Banana, the BMS Congo mission had borne fruit in the establishment of a single, fully autonomous Baptist community in Zaire.[21]

II: Revolt and Repression: Angola, 1960-1975

The years 1959 and 1960 saw an influx from across the Congo border into the Kibokolo area of various 'prophet' figures, who drew Christians away from the Baptist churches and caused the missionaries some anxiety. São Salvador was less affected, except in the Nkanda Hill church district (adjacent to the Kibokolo area), where over half the church membership were placed under church discipline in 1960 for following the prophets and taking their 'cures'. Problems with prophet movements were nothing new for the Angola missionaries, but by late 1960 this latest resurgence displayed a novel and perplexing feature: whole village populations were being taken into the bush to participate in secret ceremonies. W. David Grenfell, senior missionary at Kibokolo and soon to be appointed Field Secretary, suspected that these involved the swearing of oaths; only later were his suspicions confirmed, when it became clear that the oaths had sworn the people to secrecy about a mass movement of civil disobedience (and possibly also, violent action) against Portuguese rule, planned to commence on 15 March 1961. An incident of a different kind increased Grenfell's sense of unease. One night towards the end of 1960 someone left four copies of the newspaper of Holden Roberto's UPA (successor to the UPNA) Angolan nationalist movement on the front steps of the house of Avelino Ferreira, Grenfell's Portuguese missionary colleague. It was the first time Grenfell had heard of the UPA or the name of its leader. Suspecting an attempt to implicate the mission in some form of subversion, the two missionaries decided to hand the newspapers to the secret police, the PIDE. The episode demonstrates the absurdity of the subsequent accusation by the Portuguese that BMS missionaries had instigated the revolt which proved the begin-

---

21. General Committee Minutes: 31 Oct. 1972, p. 58; 1 Nov. 1972, pp. 66, 68; 28 Mar. 1973, pp. 14, 17-19. Didcot, CR 446, 447, 452. H. F. Drake file, Drake to Madge, 30 Nov. and 6 Dec. 1972. Interview with Rev. A. T. MacNeill, 8.6.90.

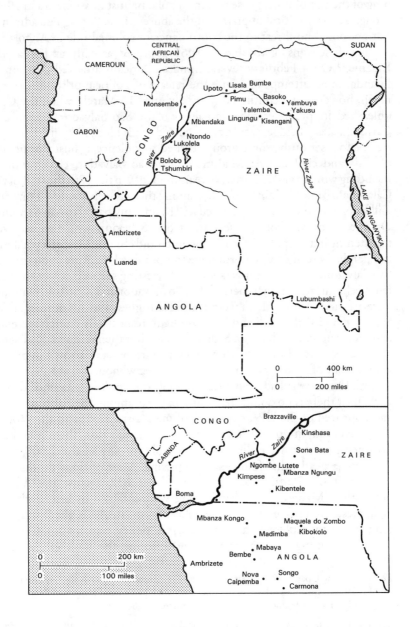

Map 10: Zaire and Angola in the Twentieth Century

ning of the end of Portuguese rule in Angola. Baptist missionaries in 1960, though severely critical in private of the abuses of the Portuguese administration, posed no threat to the continuance of colonial rule in Angola.[22]

The first signs of trouble in 1961 appeared as early as January in Kasanje.[23] On 4 February several hundred Africans attacked a prison in Luanda, in an attempt to secure the release of political prisoners. In the north, however, life continued normally until 15 March, when the UPA unleashed its premeditated campaign on the São Salvador, Songo and Carmona areas. Bridges were destroyed and roads blocked by the felling of trees. More seriously, some groups turned to violence against Portuguese officials and civilians. At Madimba, near São Salvador, eleven whites, including women and children, were murdered. On the 17th the staff of the Calambata Bible Training Institute, among them Eileen Motley, Tony and Gill Boorne of the BMS, were evacuated by an army patrol to São Salvador. On the 20th, the Portuguese staff at São Salvador, who had received threatening letters, plus all the BMS women and children, were flown down to Luanda. Next morning Portuguese troops raided the African quarters of São Salvador, searching for weapons and arresting suspects. Over the next few weeks, numerous members of the São Salvador and Kibokolo churches were arrested. Among them were Pedro Rodrigues, a senior deacon at São Salvador, and Pedro Sadi and Eduardo Bedi, respectively church secretary and senior nurse at Kibokolo. Sadi was beaten but then released. Rodrigues and Bedi were less fortunate. Rodrigues died from maltreatment in prison. Bedi was one of a group of about twenty executed without trial at Kibokolo on 4 April. Others who had been arrested simply disappeared, presumed dead.

Whilst there is no doubt that many Baptists among the Bakongo knew and approved of the UPA campaign of mass disruption, and then found themselves caught up in its escalation into violent action, there is no hard evidence that they were directly responsible for any of the 2,000 or so Portuguese deaths that followed the uprising. Most of these deaths took place *after* the Portuguese had initiated reprisals against the African population. Many of the early reprisals were inflicted by armed civilian vigilantes, given a free hand by the police. From late April, the Portuguese army began to implement a 'scorched earth' policy, napalm bombing and machine-gunning African villages, and burning the bush grass. These

22. F. J. Grenfell papers (in possession of Rev. F. J. Grenfell), São Salvador station reports for 1959 and 1960; University of York, Borthwick Institute of Historical Research, W. D. Grenfell papers, box GR3, file 1, and microfilm 66.

23. For the general political context of the 1961 revolt see J. Marcum, *The Angolan Revolution. Volume I: The Anatomy of an Explosion (1950-1962)* (Cambridge. Mass., and London, 1969), 123-58.

measures were taken indiscriminately, even amongst the Bazombo people of the Kibokolo district, who did not support the UPA, and where there had been only one Portuguese death. It was precisely this lack of discrimination in the Portuguese reaction which transformed an initially sporadic outbreak into a massive and united movement of popular protest throughout northern Angola.

The Portuguese onslaught had an immediate effect on the church and mission, as Africans abandoned their homes for the relative safety of the forest, and then crossed the border into the Congo. At Kibokolo the Sunday congregation, several hundred strong for a baptismal and communion service on 1 April, had dwindled to twenty by the end of the month. By mid-May there was only one patient left in the hospital. On 2 June David Grenfell was ordered by the Portuguese administrator at Maquela to close the mission. Grenfell refused to do so without written confirmation of the order, and travelled to Luanda to see the British Consul. Despite the Consul's best efforts, the Luanda authorities confirmed the order, and Grenfell returned to Kibokolo to implement the closure of the station. David and Margaret Grenfell were the last to leave, on 17 June. David returned once more, on 19 July, and found only four people, and a 'terrible silence'.

BMS staff were evacuated from Bembe on 18 April; the mission was subsequently bombed and sacked by the Portuguese. At São Salvador, ninety per cent of the population had fled by the end of March, but the BMS hospital continued to function on a diminishing scale until the end of September. After two attacks by rebel forces, the Portuguese burnt the Protestant half of the town on 27 June in an attempt to flush out the 'terrorists'. Those rendered homeless (mostly the old and sick, 179 in all) squeezed into six classrooms in the BMS school until 12 July, when the Portuguese commandeered most of the mission premises for their military headquarters. The refugees were then moved back to the hospital. On 9 August Dr Rodger Shields was arrested on suspicion of treating with terrorists, and taken to Luanda. He was never charged, but was expelled from the country seventeen days later. With the São Salvador mission now little more than an army garrison, there was little point in continuing to staff the station. On Sunday 29 October the last two missionaries to leave, F. J. Grenfell (David's nephew) and G. B. Merricks, baptized two women by aspersion - there being no baptistry as the church was in the hands of the army - and received them into church membership. It was a pledge of faith that the devastated Angolan church would not die, but live again. Two days later Grenfell and Merricks left by air for Luanda.[24]

24. The above account of events at São Salvador and Kibokolo is based on *BMS Annual Report*, 1961-2, pp. xxiv-xxviii; F. J. Grenfell papers, diary of F. J. Grenfell, and São Salvador station report 1961; W. D. Grenfell papers, box GR3, file 1, and microfilm 66.

Perhaps as many as 50,000 Africans were killed in the course of the Portuguese suppression of the Angolan revolt. The exposure of the magnitude of this atrocity to public opinion in Britain was in large measure the work of Clifford Parsons, Associate Foreign Secretary of the BMS, and of other Baptists who rallied to his support. On 17 March 1961 the Foreign Missions Conference of North America invited the BMS to join a delegation to Angola to investigate the crisis which had just broken in the country. The Society sent Parsons, himself an Angola missionary from 1939 to 1959, to accompany T. L. Tucker of the Foreign Missions Conference on a two-week visit. Although Parsons was unable to visit the BMS stations in the north, he held extensive interviews in Luanda with BMS missionaries and others. On his return, Parsons gave a full report to the Society's Congo sub-committee on 19 April, emphasizing that the revolt was an indication of the exhaustion of African patience after many years of Portuguese repression - a view which closely reflected an analysis of the causes of the revolt made by F. J. Grenfell. The General Purposes sub-committee suggested that the Society should issue a public statement on the situation, but the General Committee decided instead to seek the permission of the Baptist Union to present a resolution to the public session of the Baptist Union Assembly on 2 May.[25] On that day, after a moving speech by Clifford Parsons, the Assembly passed unanimously a resolution which repeated the conviction that the revolt was 'largely due to the lack of justice and charity in relationships between the races', registered 'grave disquiet at the reports of large-scale terrorism by the armed European community', and appealed to the Portuguese authorities to exercise restraint.[26]

Although considerable attention had been given by the world media to atrocities committed by the rebels, the Portuguese had successfully suppressed almost all information about their repression of the revolt. Some of those who had heard Parsons speak at the Assembly determined that action must now be taken to alert public opinion to the gravity of the situation. Among them were two young ministers from Southend, E. L. Blakebrough of Ferndale Road Baptist Church and L. E. Addicott of Earls Hall Baptist Church. On 25 May Blakebrough and Addicott submitted a protest letter, signed by twelve local ministers, to the Portuguese Embassy. With a third Southend minister, George Thompson Brake of Avenue Baptist Church, Blakebrough and Addicott formed an Angola Action Group, which issued a statement warning British Baptists, in decidedly un-Baptist language, that

---

25. General Committee Minutes, 28 Apr. 1961, pp. 51, 66-8, 71-2; F. J. Grenfell papers, 'Some Causes of the Revolt in the North of Angola in 1961'.

26. L. E. Addicott, *Cry Angola!* (London, 1962), 143.

'we are bastards if we do nothing about Angola; we repudiate our Baptist forefathers'.[27] The statement was soon in great demand throughout the country. The Group obtained the active support of both J. B. Middlebrook, Home Secretary of the BMS, and Ernest Payne, General Secretary of the Baptist Union. However, opinion at a lower level within the denomination, and even within the Group's own Eastern area of the Baptist Union, was less sure about the tone of the campaign: there were those who felt that protest should be confined to official channels, and not orchestrated by individual ministers.[28]

The Southend Action Group spawned similar groups in other parts of the country, most notably in Manchester, where the leading organizers of protest were Malcolm Purdy, minister at Newall Green, Wythenshawe (and secretary of the Manchester BMS Auxiliary) and J. F. V. Nicholson, pastor of Union Chapel, Fallowfield, and also ecumenical officer of the Manchester Council of Churches. The current chairman of the BMS, H. H. Rowley, Rylands Professor of Biblical Criticism and Exegesis in the University of Manchester, also became involved, writing an introduction to a Manchester edition of the Southend statement, which came to the attention of *The Guardian* newspaper. *The Guardian* was impressed by the evidence contained in the statement, and by Rowley's support. On 19 June *The Guardian*'s leading article, headed 'Angola Protest by Missionaries', was based largely on the statement. A series of forthright articles, many drawing on information supplied by David Grenfell, followed. It was these articles which transformed the Angola question from a purely Baptist concern into a topic of general political debate in Britain.[29] On 27 June, the Labour M.P., George Thomas, a well-known Methodist, presented to the House of Commons a petition protesting against the 'harsh and oppressive policy' of the Portuguese government. Organized by the Action Group, the petition was signed (on a single Sunday) by 37,524 members of various churches.[30] The following day Ernest Payne led a high-ranking delegation from the British Council of Churches to the Foreign Secretary, Lord Home. The campaign reached its peak with a full debate in the House of Commons on 5 July, when the Leader of the Opposition, Hugh Gaitskell, repeatedly

27. Ibid., 43.

28. Interview with Rev. L. E. Addicott, 17.4.90.

29. *The Guardian,* 19, 20, 21, 22, 23, 27, 29, 30 June; 3, 4, 5, 18 July; 16 Oct. 1961. Information from Rev. M. V. Purdy and Rev. J. F. V. Nicholson.

30. *Parliamentary Debates (Hansard),* 5th ser. vol. 643, 27 June 1961, cols 171-2. Addicott, *Cry Angola!,* 144.

used the testimony of BMS missionaries to confront the Macmillan government with the evidence of Portuguese atrocities in Angola.[31]

The Portuguese government continued to dismiss all reports of atrocities committed against the African population as 'fantastic and tendentious', and was able to count on the support of the Conservative administration in Britain. At the end of July, in an attempt to counter the growing volume of Portuguese propaganda, the Angola Action Group dispatched Eric Blakebrough and George Thomas on a fact-finding mission to the Angolan-Congo frontier. Although denied entry to Angola itself, Blakebrough and Thomas were able to interview some of the refugees (then numbering about 130,000) who had fled into the Congo. David Grenfell acted as their interpreter. They found no evidence of the revolt being inspired (as Portugal alleged) by Communist agitators. Their report followed F. J. Grenfell's analysis in attributing the revolt to the incidence of contract (forced) labour, the denial of African political rights, and other grievances, and declared the Salazar regime 'guilty of the exploitation and massacre of Africans in Angola'.[32]

British Baptist agitation over the Angola question made an undoubted contribution to the mobilising of international humanitarian opinion to demand that Portugal take immediate steps to satisfy the political aspirations of the Angolan people. Resolutions to this effect were passed at the New Delhi Assembly of the World Council of Churches in November 1961, and by the United Nations General Assembly in January 1962. In the history of British nonconformity, the campaign marks the most recent (and arguably the last) example of the power of 'the nonconformist conscience' to affect political events. In the history of the BMS, the Angola agitation stands in a line of tradition stretching back to William Knibb and the emancipation campaign. As in the anti-slavery movement, Baptist missionaries who had hitherto avoided public criticism of the colonial regime now found themselves compelled by the savage repression of an anti-colonial uprising to speak out openly against the social system which had fueled the flames of revolt. The Blakebrough-Thomas report observed that it was when the Portuguese initiated their brutal reprisals that BMS missionaries 'broke their usual silence on political matters and proclaimed that the revolt

---

31. *Parliamentary Debates (Hansard)*, 5th ser. vol. 643, 5 July 1961, cols 1457-1531.

32. *Congo-Angola Border Enquiry: Report on the Visit of Mr George Thomas, M.P. and the Rev. Eric L. Blakebrough to the Congo-Angola Border, August, 1961* (Southend-on-Sea, n.d.), 12-19; Addicott, *Cry Angola!*, 90-1.

had been provoked by years of repression and injustice'.[33] For them, the issue was one of humanitarian and Christian principle, rather than party politics. However, as in 1832, some domestic Baptist opinion expressed unease about the active involvement of the BMS in a controversy which soon followed party political lines. On arrival in Britain in August, David Grenfell was 'very distressed to find that the Angola tragedy had become a Party issue instead of a humanitarian concern'.[34]

By mid-1961 the first BMS missionaries evacuated from Angola were engaged in medical and relief work among the refugees in the Lower Congo. In November the BMS Committee sent David Grenfell back to Africa to report on the refugee situation. He found Kimpese hospital overflowing with Angolans needing treatment, some of them suffering from napalm burns. Jean Comber and Edna Staple of the Bembe staff, and Walter Fulbrook at Moerbeke, were heavily involved in feeding the refugees who had settled in the Kibentele district - of whom there were some 58,000 by the end of the year. Grenfell's principal task, in a series of meetings held in Léopoldville from December 1961 to February 1962, was to negotiate the allocation of the Angola missionaries to work amongst the refugee population. It was a delicate assignment. The lower river churches, themselves unsettled by the resurgence of Kimbanguism, were now confronted by an overwhelming influx of up to 10,000 Angolan Baptists. The Angola missionaries had to adjust to a field in which the mission now worked under the authority of the church. Grenfell himself, as Angola Field Secretary, had to be sensitive to the feelings of Harold Casebow, about to retire as Congo Field Secretary, who did not view with enthusiasm the settlement of a contingent of Angola missionaries on his patch. Grenfell was grateful for the unflinching support of Clifford Parsons in London.[35]

Despite the difficulties, the foundations were laid during 1962 of the Angolan church in exile. Baptist refugees were, on the whole, successfully integrated into the lower river churches, and did not establish their own congregations. BMS missionaries were involved in establishing sixty village schools among the refugee population, distributing relief supplies, and in medical work. In Angola the fighting and atrocities continued, and so did

33. *Congo-Angola Border Enquiry,* 1. Some Catholic critics made capital out of this fact. See H. Kay, 'A Catholic View', in P. Mason (ed.), *Angola: A Symposium* (London, 1962), 88.

34. W. D. Grenfell papers, box GR3, file 1.

35. W. D. Grenfell papers, box GR3, file 1; F. J. Grenfell papers, BMS Angola Report for 1962; *BMS Annual Report,* 1961-2, p. xxvii.

the flow of refugees across the border: by September 1962 there were an estimated 215,000 Angolan refugees in the Congo; by the end of 1964 the total was at least 400,000.[36] Increasingly the Angolan exiles gave their political support to the agents of Holden Roberto's UPA, which now set up a revolutionary government in exile. David Grenfell first established contact with the UPA leadership in Léopoldville in December 1961, and maintained close links with the revolutionary government throughout the remaining years of his work at Kibentele amongst the Angolan exiles. On his retirement in 1969 Grenfell was awarded the MBE in recognition of his refugee work - a fitting conclusion to thirty-four years of missionary service among the Bazombo and Bakongo people.

For fourteen years from 1961 to 1975 the Baptist community of northern Angola was in hiding or exile. The great majority of church members were refugees in Zaire, or in the Angolan forests. Only small numbers of elderly Christians remained in their homes, cut off from all contact with the wider church, and in many cases suffering considerably for their faith. To be a Protestant was to be suspected of involvement in the struggle for independence, and specifically of complicity with the *Frente National de Libertação de Angola* (FNLA), the military wing of the UPA. Some Baptists did indeed play a prominent part in the FNLA. One such was Pedro Vide Garcia, freedom fighter and leader of the Christians at Nova Caipemba (where there was as yet no organized church), who always carried Bibles, Christian literature and school material for his people in the forest on his secret incursions across the frontier from Zaire. In São Salvador, about 130 Christians remained behind, worshipping in secret in the home of Ilena Rodrigues, widow of Pedro, the deacon killed in 1961. Meanwhile their son, Alvaro, completed his secondary education in exile at Sona Bata and Kimpese. Feeling a call to the ministry, Alvaro went in the early 1970s to study theology at the University of Yaoundé in Cameroon. In 1974 he returned to Zaire to teach in the CBFZ secondary school at Ngombe Lutete.[37] For Alvaro, and for thousands of his compatriots, these were long years of waiting for a future that could only be hoped and prayed for.

III: The BMS and the CBFZ, 1973-1992

The first General Assembly of the CBFZ was held in Kinshasa from 14 to 21 May 1973. The Assembly ratified the statutes and constitution for the

36. Didcot, CR 307, C. J. Parsons, The Situation in N. Angola 15 Sept. 1962. *BMS Annual Report*, 1964-5, p. 27.
37. Didcot, CR 479, Report of BMS Delegation's Visit to Angola Feb./Mar. 1975.

Community drawn up at the meeting on 3-4 December 1972, and confirmed the nominations of office-holders made at that time. The Assembly also adopted unanimously a convention to govern the relationship between the CBFZ and the BMS, which was modelled on a number of similar documents produced at earlier stages in the fusion process. Under the terms of the convention, the BMS recognized the CBFZ as 'an autonomous church, governing its own life and work under the inspiration of the Holy Spirit', whilst the CBFZ for its part recognized BMS missionaries as those sent by the British Baptist churches for the purpose of collaborating with the Church of Christ in Zaire for the evangelisation of Zaire. The position of BMS Field Secretary - with its implications of autonomous executive power - ceased to exist. The pastoral care of missionaries now became the responsibility of the General Secretary of the CBFZ, and of his regional superintendents. The only parts of the Field Secretary's former responsibilities to remain in missionary hands were the personal affairs and travel arrangements of BMS missionaries, which were to be handled by a missionary nominated by the Society, and elected by the CBFZ General Assembly. Derek Rumbol, formerly missionary at Upoto and Binga, was, however, elected as assistant general secretary and treasurer of the Community.[38] From this point on, the history of the BMS in Zaire becomes only one theme within the wider history of the CBFZ.

The work of the CBFZ in its early years was conducted within the rigorous confines laid down by the *authenticité* policy of the MPR government. By May 1973 the government had compiled a list of banned religious periodicals, prohibited all uniformed youth organizations, and compelled the discontinuance of religious broadcasting. All religious gatherings other than regular church services and meetings were forbidden. The degree of rigour with which this last prohibition was enforced varied from area to area, but it prevented the holding of the Middle River Regional Assembly that year.[39] During 1974-5 the government took control of all schools from the churches. Again, the impact of this change varied widely. In Lower Zaire and on the upper river (apart from in Kisangani), many headmasters were moved. The secondary school at Ngombe Lutete found itself with a Roman Catholic headmaster. Elsewhere, changes in personnel were kept to a minimum. No BMS missionary teachers were moved by the government. In some places, strong informal links were maintained between the local Baptist church and its former school, with most children continuing to

38. Didcot, CR 442, 471; Minutes of CBFZ Assembly, 1973.

39. General Committee Minutes; 28 Mar. 1973, p. 20; 4 July 1973, p. 36.

attend morning worship on a voluntary basis. Elsewhere, nationalization did result in the almost total secularization of formerly Baptist schools.[40]

As was the case in other states in post-colonial Africa, the Zairean government found it had bitten off more than it could chew, and soon came to the conclusion that the resources of the churches were an indispensable ally in the attempt to make primary education available to all. On 26 February 1977 the Department of Education signed a convention with the ECZ which gave the communities the option of resuming responsibility for the nationalized schools. On 1 September 1977 the CBFZ resumed control of all of its former schools. Under the terms of the February agreement, the government retained responsibility for the payment of teachers, running costs, maintenance of premises, curriculum and school inspection; the communities now took over the internal administration of the schools, and were given the right to nominate and suspend members of staff (appointments and dismissals remained the prerogative of the Department).[41] Although the number of BMS missionaries involved in secondary education declined from the high levels of the 1960s, as more Zairean teachers became available, BMS personnel continued during the 1980s to teach in CBFZ secondary schools in Mbanza Ngungu, Kinshasa, Bolobo, Upoto, and Kisangani, and in the CECO (formerly EPI) school at Kimpese.

Authenticité also affected the medical sphere. All pharmacies were taken over by the state, and there was talk of nationalizing the hospitals also. Initially the medical work of the CBFZ was entirely dependent on the ability of the BMS to supply missionary doctors. Yet the Society was currently receiving very few offers from qualified doctors for missionary service in Zaire. Indeed, in 1972 there was only one BMS doctor in the country - David Masters at Pimu. The shortage of missionary doctors delayed the resumption of a full medical service at Yakusu until 1975, and was largely responsible for the fact that Ntondo hospital had no doctor between 1965 and 1978. Most serious of all, the BMS in 1972 was compelled for the same reason to abandon responsibility for Bolobo hospital, at the very point when a new hospital building, under construction since 1967, was opened. The hospital was leased for a ten-year period to FOMECO (*Fonds Médical de Co-opération*), a semi-autonomous body largely financed by President Mobutu. A clause of the agreement allowed the BMS to maintain nursing sisters at the hospital, and BMS missionaries

---

40. Didcot, CR 494, Report on Overseas Secretary's Visit to Angola and Zaire, Sept./Oct. 1975.

41. Didcot, CR 507, Report of H. F. Drake's Visit to Zaire from 8 May to 7 June 1977.

- notably Joan Parker and Georgina Mackenzie - continued to serve the hospital under the FOMECO regime, the latter as director of the nursing school until 1976. Nevertheless, the FOMECO decade was an unhappy chapter in Bolobo's history. The Christian witness of the hospital was marred, not only by the enforced discontinuance of ward services, but even more by the unsuitability of some of the Zairean doctors allocated by FOMECO. Bush hospitals such as Bolobo were unlikely to attract the best of the few Zairean doctors now graduating, and standards of medical care dropped. In 1981 the CBFZ General Assembly decided not to renew the lease to FOMECO. Bolobo hospital reverted to the CBFZ in December 1982, when David Masters was transferred from Pimu to be medical director.[42]

By 1990 the hospitals at Bolobo and Ntondo had Zairean medical directors; at Pimu and Yakusu the medical directors were still missionaries, although both hospitals now had Zairean doctors on the staff. The training and reference hospital at IME, Kimpese, was under the direction of Zairean nationals, but still depended to a considerable extent on its sponsoring missions for the provision of specialists in paediatrics, obstetrics, ophthalmology and surgery. Financing an independent hospital of this standard in a poor rural location remained perhaps the greatest problem. Although IME derived considerable financial assistance from government grants and from its supporting ECZ communities (either in the form of direct grants, or in the form of missionaries, whose salaries were paid from overseas), an increasing proportion of the hospital's income had to come from patient fees (65-70 per cent by 1987). The dilemma was how to maintain both the hospital's reputation for medical excellence, and its role as a Christian institution serving the needs of the poor.[43]

Medical work has been one area where the BMS contribution to the life and witness of the CBFZ has remained a major one until very recent times. BMS missionaries have also been involved in theological education at various levels. Probably the most pressing need of the CBFZ in recent years has been for programmes of theological education by extension, with appropriate supporting literature in Lingala, aimed at the catechists and deacons who form the leadership of the great majority of local congregations. BMS missionaries - notably Deanna Clark in the Kinshasa Secretariat and Christopher Spencer in Mbanzu Ngungu - have served the Christian

42. Acres, 'Partners in Healing', 70, 77-81, 91-3.

43. Didcot, IME Kimpese file, Consultation on the future of the Evangelical Medical Institute (IME) Kimpese, 25-27 Nov. 1987.

Education department of the CBFZ in its attempts to raise the general level of Christian understanding in the churches. At an intermediate level, BMS personnel have consistently been involved in staffing the Bible Schools at Bolobo and Yakusu, training pastors to diploma standard. The *Ecole Baptiste de Théologie* at Yakusu, successor to the *Ecole Grenfell* at Yalemba, was up-graded in 1988 to become the *Institut Supérieur Théologique de Yakusu* (ISTY). At degree level, the BMS has played some part in the Protestant Faculty of Theology in Zaire since its foundation in 1959 as part of the University of Elisabethville (Lubumbashi). Political pressures gave the Faculty a peripatetic and disturbed history in its early years, during which the institution moved from Elisabethville to the Catholic University of Lovanium, back eastward to Kisangani in 1967 as part of the Free University of the Congo, then returned to Kinshasa in 1973. When the Zairean government announced in December 1974 that both Catholic and Protestant Faculties of Theology were to be excluded from the National University of Zaire, the ECZ assumed control of the Protestant Faculty, which was at last able to enjoy a stable existence. The Faculty gained its own purpose-built buildings in 1985. In recent years the BMS has supplied the Vice-Principal and head of the Old Testament department, Dr T. Bulkeley.[44]

Most BMS missionaries in Zaire between 1972 and 1991 were involved either in medicine or in some sphere of educational work. Others participated in agricultural projects at Kimpese, Ngombe Lutete and Ntondo, or in women's literacy and Bible training work. The Society's aid was also crucial to the operation of the CBFZ secretariat in Kinshasa, where missionaries (Derek Rumbol, David Norkett, and Owen Clark) filled the post of assistant secretary and treasurer. On the middle river, a few BMS missionaries were allocated specifically evangelistic roles by the CBFZ - a comparatively rare occurrence in the modern Christian history of Zaire.

The great majority of the evangelistic work of the CBFZ in this period was, very properly, in Zairean hands. The church experienced substantial growth between 1960 and 1989: aggregate membership of the BMS Congo churches in 1960 was 39,378; by 1989 CBFZ membership was about 202,000.[45] The most rapid growth was in Haut-Zaire, while membership in the old Bakongo churches of Bas-Zaire remained relatively static. Growth was most spectacular in Kisangani. In 1932 the BMS church in

44. Munayi Muntu-Monji, *Les Vingt-Cinq Ans de la Faculté de Théologie Protestante au Zaire 1959-1984* (Kinshasa, 1984).

45. *BMS Annual Report,* 1960-1, p. 12.

Stanleyville had a baptised membership of only fifty-eight.[46] By 1987 the CBFZ had 12,000 members in what was still a relatively small city of half a million people. The increase in the Upper River churches necessitated the sub-division of the old upper river region in 1976-7; a further division took place in 1980, when the Middle River Region was split in two. Even in its reduced form, the Upper River Region remained much the largest of the six CBFZ regions, with a membership in 1989 of 77,338. As a result of the regional disparity in church growth, the weight of influence within the CBFZ had shifted away from the Bakongo towards the Bangala peoples of the middle and upper river. The first General Secretary of the CBFZ, Nlongi Mfwilwakanda, had experienced some difficulty as a Mukongo in retaining the support of church leaders on the upper river, and had been replaced by Koli Mandole Molima in 1977.

The long-established rural churches of Bas-Zaire continued to suffer from the strength of Kimbanguist competition, and from the constant exodus of younger people to Kinshasa. The population of Kinshasa grew phenomenally after independence, rising from 410,000 in 1959 to about five million by 1990. Sects of all descriptions mushroomed within this exploding population, and the Protestant communities of the ECZ struggled to keep pace with the increasing evangelistic and pastoral challenge presented by the influx of rural migrants. Nonetheless, the CBFZ witnessed significant growth in many of its Kinshasa parishes. Of the 7,775 baptisms recorded by the four CBFZ regions which made returns in 1986, 2,273 were in the Kinshasa region. By 1989 CBFZ membership in Kinshasa totalled 29,395.[47] The extent of population movement within Zaire was tending to break down the old comity agreements between the Protestant missions, and hence between the constituent communities of the ECZ. The port of Matadi in Bas-Zaire, although the headquarters of the BMS Congo mission for its first half-century, fell within the territory of the *Communauté Evangélique de Zaire* (CEZ) founded by the work of the *Svenska Missions Förbundet* (SMF). However, many of the Angolan refugees who poured into Matadi during the civil war that followed independence in 1975 came from the former BMS churches, and did not feel at home within the CEZ congregations. After repeated requests, the CBFZ eventually agreed in 1983 to plant a church in Matadi. Under the leadership of Zinu, a gifted

---

46. Yakusu archives, Yakusu station log book, 1923-38.

47. Didcot; Report of Rev. Koli Mandole Molima to 13th General Assembly of CBFZ, Ngombe Lutete, 25-29 May 1987; D. A. Rumbol, Report of a Visit to Zaire, 1 May-5 June 1990.

pastor trained at the Protestant Faculty of Theology, the church grew rapidly. By September 1987 the membership numbered 559 (about 100 being new baptised converts), and a site had already been purchased for a second congregation.

The continued growth of the CBFZ took place against the backcloth of a state of chronic crisis in the Zairean economy. Mobutu's Zaire, potentially one of the wealthiest nations in modern Africa, and undoubtedly one of the largest recipients of Western aid, witnessed only very uneven economic development. While a small élite close to the structures of government prospered, most Zairois experienced a substantial drop in their standard of living after independence. It is estimated that the real wages of unskilled workers in 1980 were between four and six per cent of their 1960 level.[48] Although not all sections of the population suffered to this extent, the country's economic malaise had an inevitable effect on the life of the church. Levels of giving to church work were low, with the result that the CBFZ remained more heavily dependent on financial assistance from the BMS than either party would have wished. In 1990 30 per cent of the income of the CBFZ secretariat came from the BMS, and only 2 per cent from church contributions.[49] Low ministerial stipends continued to deter promising young people from pastoral training, and hence aggravated the continuing educational problem of how to supply the churches with sufficient leaders of high quality. Church members with pitifully low wage levels could find it hard to resist participation in the corruption which was endemic in society as a whole. Some Christians in the impoverished regions tended to resent the amounts of church funds which seemed to be absorbed by the Kinshasa secretariat. Competition for the power and rewards of office too easily infected the spiritual life of the church.

BMS missionaries in modern Zaire, though insulated to some extent from the economic hardship experienced by their national colleagues, found working under the authority of a church faced by challenges of this nature a demanding experience. Their work in CBFZ institutions was often hampered by inadequate resources and administrative support, and roles were not always clearly defined. Only rarely, in contrast, did they have the opportunity to be involved personally in those situations where the church was vibrant and growing. Their location in often isolated rural stations was an additional problem, especially for young single missionaries. Postal

48. Nzongola-Ntalaza (ed.), *The Crisis in Zaire: Myths and Realities* (Trenton, N.J., 1986), 4.

49. Didcot, D. A. Rumbol, Report of a Visit to Zaire, 1 May -5 June 1990. 46 per cent came from rented property.

deliveries were intermittent, and visits by compatriots few and far between. Transport and communications in Zaire deteriorated to the point where missions and churches again became reliant on their own networks in order to continue to function: the work of the Missionary Aviation Fellowship (MAF) in transporting missionaries, church leaders, and medical supplies became essential, and particularly so for the CBFZ, whose work was so far-flung geographically. The MAF plane in fact fulfilled the function of the mission steamer of an earlier generation.

Circumstances of this nature intensified the problems of cultural adjustment which face any European missionary working in a non-Western environment. Missionaries who experienced difficulties in defining their role and relationship to the Zairean church did not find it easy to seek pastoral help from CBFZ pastors, as the 1973 convention stipulated. It had been an abiding concern of the Society since 1972 to devise means of pastoral care for its Zaire missionaries appropriate to the era of the autonomous church. When, as part of the re-structuring of the Society's secretariat in 1981-2, the BMS proposed to appoint an overseas representative for Africa, to be located in Kinshasa, the CBFZ General Assembly first (in 1981) gave provisional approval to the idea, then rescinded its decision the following year. It is clear that both the CBFZ and ECZ leadership feared an attempt to recreate the powers of the old Field Secretary. Following the rejection of the proposal, Angus MacNeill suggested to the 1982 Assembly that consideration be given to the appointment of a missionary counsellor to work within CBFZ structures. However, even this more limited proposal was rejected by the Assembly in 1983.[50]

Over the next few years concern grew within the Society about the number of its Zaire missionaries who were leaving the field after short and sometimes unhappy periods of service. Within the CBFZ there was parallel disquiet about the operation of the 1973 convention, and the apparent failure of some missionaries to observe its provisions. As a result of this unease on both sides of the partnership, the BMS proposed to the CBFZ Assembly in 1987 that a consultation be held to review the nature and operation of the 1973 convention. The Assembly welcomed the idea, and plans were made to hold the consultation in 1989. However, the CBFZ requested a delay of one year, and the consultation did not take place until 28 May-2 June 1990. Twelve CBFZ and four BMS representatives met at

---

50. Didcot; CR 548, Report of Rev. H. F. Drake's Visit to Zaire from 4 May to 6 June 1981; H. F. Drake file, MacNeill to Drake, 25 June 1982; Overseas Sub-Committee Minutes, 14 June 1983, p. 257; interview with Rev. A. T. MacNeill, 8.6.90.

Kisantu in Bas-Zaire to discuss a ten-point agenda covering issues of general theological principle as well as specific questions of policy. Most time was given to the future role of BMS missionaries within the CBFZ, and to how the CBFZ could make progress towards the ultimate goal of financial self-sufficiency.

Although the consultation was at times a painful experience for both parties, the potential was created for a new era in the partnership of church and mission. The CBFZ representatives suggested that a CBFZ pastor who was also a BMS missionary should be appointed to assist the CBFZ President in the discharge of his pastoral responsibilities for missionaries. That such a proposal - essentially identical to that rejected in 1983 - should now be made held promise for the future. The consultation established clearly that the CBFZ saw a continuing role for BMS missionaries in Zaire, and that the Society was keen to continue its partnership with the CBFZ.[51]

In April 1990 President Mobutu announced his intention to move Zaire towards a 'third republic', characterized by the re-emergence of multi-party politics (in fact three-party politics under his professedly impartial supervision). Hopes were raised that Mobutu's professed intentions signalled a new confidence in the cohesion and political maturity of the Zairean nation. During 1991 these hopes evaporated as the economic and political condition of the impoverished country deteriorated into chaos. On the night of 22 September one of Mobutu's paratroop brigades went on the rampage, destroying Ndjili international airport in Kinshasa. Law and order rapidly broke down, both in Kinshasa and in other Zairean cities. Most BMS personnel were evacuated, along with other expatriates, in early October.[52] By the end of 1991 only one BMS missionary was left in the country - Gwen Hunter at IME hospital, Kimpese. Although it is very probable that BMS missionaries will return to Zaire once the Mobutu regime comes to an end, there is no doubt that they will return to a Protestant church that has been deeply affected and changed by this latest crisis in the nation's turbulent history. 1991 marked the end of an era in BMS history in Zaire.

IV: Independence, Civil War and Reconstruction: Angola, 1975-1992

On 25 April 1974 an army coup toppled the Caetano regime in Portugal, and brought to an end fifty years of Salazarist rule. The new government was committed to bringing Portugal's African colonies to

---

51. Didcot, A. T. MacNeill, Report on the CBFZ/BMS Consultation, 28 May-2 June 1990.

52. *MH* (Nov. 1991), 3-8.

independence. These events in Lisbon soon brought about a ceasefire in Angola between the colonial government and the three liberation movements of FNLA, MPLA and UNITA. In January 1975 representatives of the three movements held talks with the government, at which it was agreed that Angola should become independent on 11 November 1975. A provisional government, comprising a coalition of the three movements plus the Portuguese, took control. From this point on, the Angolan refugees began to return from Zaire.

On 22 February F. J. Grenfell, H. F. Drake, and five Angolan church leaders commenced a three-week tour of northern Angola to make contact with the Christians and investigate the condition of the churches. The São Salvador church building had been returned to the Christians five months previously, but was in a sorry state, having been used as a dance hall and bar. The Portuguese army finally withdrew its garrison on 3 March. The mission stations at Bembe and Kibokolo had been completely destroyed, and most of the Bembe area had been almost entirely depopulated. Of the over 200 Baptist church buildings which had existed in 1961, only two were still standing. Medical care was fragmentary. There were some government dispensaries, and state hospitals at São Salvador and Carmona, but few doctors. Primary schools existed in the populated villages, but secondary education was virtually non-existent. It was a daunting prospect, both for the returning refugees as a whole, and for the churches in particular. Nevertheless, by September many of the villages had been re-built, and gardens planted with crops. In November Grenfell returned to São Salvador on a more permanent basis. For two months he worked with returning church leaders in helping to re-establish Baptist churches and organize relief supplies throughout the former BMS area. By the end of the year, pastoral oversight had been restored to almost the whole of the region.[53]

The prospects of a speedy return to normality in northern Angola were cruelly dashed by the rapid disintegration of the fragile unity between the three liberation movements. On Independence Day, 11 November 1975, the Portuguese formally acknowledged Angolan independence, but no one nationalist movement possessed the universal recognition within the country that was necessary to receive a legal transfer of power from Portugal. Two rival Angolan governments were set up, one by the MPLA in Luanda, and the other in Huambo by a coalition of the FNLA and UNITA. MPLA forces, with substantial Cuban and Soviet backing, now began a rapid advance on the FNLA in the north and UNITA in the south. On 6 January

53. Didcot, CR 479, Report of BMS Delegation's Visit to Angola Feb./Mar. 1975; *BMS Annual Report*, 1975-6, p. 15.

1976 the MPLA captured Uige, the FNLA capital. 15,000 refugees took shelter in Mbanza Kongo, where Baptist pastors participated in the distribution of food. By the second week of February, Mbanza Kongo itself was under threat, and many of the refugees were evacuated to the frontier. F. J. Grenfell and an Angolan pastor, João Matwawana, made repeated journeys across the frontier with relief supplies. On 15 February, with Mbanza Kongo about to fall to the MPLA troops, the frontier was opened, and the refugees crossed into Zaire. The frontier was soon closed again, separating those in Zaire from the larger proportion of the population who had remained in Angola.

Some unofficial border crossings by church leaders continued, supplying those in Zaire with reports of the gradual re-establishment of Baptist church life, under the supervision of a body of forty-two pastors and evangelists, and over 150 catechists. In many areas the church was growing rapidly, in spite of all the obstacles. The new church district of Nova Caipemba - formed only the previous year - had 5,800 members by June 1976.[54] Following Drake and Grenfell's visit in February/March 1975, a co-ordinating committee, representing the four church regions of Mbanza Kongo, Kibokolo, Bembe and Caipemba, had been set up to prepare the ground for the creation of a unified, autonomous church. Despite the civil war, the committee managed to meet four times. At its last meeting in Luanda in May 1977, the committee drafted a constitution for the new church. At the first General Assembly, held at Uige from 21 to 26 July 1977, the constitution was adopted, and the Evangelical Baptist Church of Angola (IEBA) came into being. Pedro Manuel Timoteo, previously pastor at Bembe, was appointed General Secretary.[55]

Meanwhile, in the Kimpese-Songolo district of Bas-Zaire, Grenfell, Matwawana, Alvaro Rodrigues, and others organized the distribution of relief supplies provided by a variety of humanitarian and Christian organizations, including BMS. At first the numbers of refugees were small in comparison with those who had fled in the 1960s - about 13,000 by June 1976. However, during 1977-8 the MPLA intensified its drive against FNLA guerrillas in the forests of northern Angola, and by August 1978 about 80,000 more Angolans (most of whom were refugees for the second time) had fled across the frontier. After nine months of furlough in Britain, Grenfell returned in July 1978 to the work of organizing refugee aid

54. Didcot, CR 502, Report from F. J. Grenfell on Angola.

55. Didcot, CR 509, Report of Rev. H. F. Drake's Visit to Angola from 9 July to 1 Aug. 1977.

projects, and assisting Angolan pastors and evangelists in the provision of Christian ministry in the refugee villages. From mid-1978 relations between the Angola and Zaire governments (which had been almost nonexistent since 1975) began to improve, and from early 1979 some groups of refugees, mainly from the Bazombo people, began to return to Angola. At the same time the accent of the work amongst the refugees in Zaire began to shift from the giving of direct aid to the promotion of development projects.[56] F. J. Grenfell left later that year to join the staff of St Andrew's Hall in Birmingham.

From its inception the IEBA was short of trained leaders. Many of its early pastors had received some training in Zaire between 1961 and 1975 at the Bible schools at Kimpese or Kinkonzi. Some of these were among a group of seventeen ordained to the pastoral ministry during the inaugural Assembly in 1977. Alvaro Rodrigues, the Yaoundé graduate, had pastored the Mbanza Kongo church from January 1975 to February 1976, but was not formally ordained until May 1979, during his second period of exile at Kimpese. Rodrigues replaced Pedro Timoteo as General Secretary in August 1981. João Makondekwa, the first President of IEBA, had also gained his preparation for ministry during the anti-colonial war: Makondekwa studied at Spurgeon's College and the School of Oriental and African Studies in London, before being appointed Director of the Bible School at Kimpese. After independence he returned to Angola, and was appointed Director of the Commission for Evangelism of the Angolan Council of Evangelical Churches (CAIE). Later he became General Secretary of the Bible Society in Angola. Few Angolan Baptists had enjoyed the educational opportunities of Makondekwa or Rodrigues. The IEBA's first Bible School, originally planned for Uige, in fact opened at Kibokolo in February 1983, but was compelled by the protracted instability of the area to move to Luanda in May 1988. For four years before the move to Luanda, the troubles had dictated that not a single student had completed his course.[57] Even in 1992, many of the leaders of local IEBA congregations had received little or no formal training.

The Angolan civil war continued into the 1980s, with the MPLA government, backed by Cuban forces, being challenged by UNITA, supported in the south by South African troops based in Namibia. The MPLA government maintained a Marxist and atheistic stance. All Christians were debarred from party membership, and until 1986 no religious

56. F. J. Grenfell papers, 'Refugee and Angola Notes', 1978-9.

57. Didcot, D. A. Rumbol, Report of a Visit to Angola, Feb. 1988.

organization was granted official recognition or the right to hold property. In practice, however, relations between the IEBA and the government were generally quite amicable. The only significant limitation on religious freedom was a ban on open-air evangelism.

In 1982 the first two BMS missionaries returned to Angola: on his retirement as BMS Overseas Secretary, H. F. Drake served in the IEBA secretariat in Luanda, and his wife Marjorie in women's work, until 1984. Although the IEBA was keen to receive several BMS missionaries, the Society found it hard to attract candidates for Angola, and it was August 1987 before another missionary, Colin Pavitt, was sent to Luanda to work as a builder, assisting the IEBA in the task of constructing office and other premises in the capital. The stationing of missionaries in Luanda was in part a consequence of the continuing hostilities in the north, but also a reflection of the fact that the IEBA was becoming less of a purely northern Angolan community. The civil war had forced numbers of Bakongo to move south to the capital, leading the IEBA to plant churches there. Although primarily catering for the Kikongo-speaking community, these churches have begun to attract those of other tribes.

In December 1988 a peace accord was signed between the governments of Angola, South Africa and Cuba. The agreement led to the independence of Namibia, and to the withdrawal of Cuban and South African forces from Angola. Although these objectives were partially achieved during 1989, UNITA itself had not been a party to the agreement. UNITA forces continued military action against the government until a peace agreement was signed at the end of May 1991. By then, the Angolan economy was in a parlous state after thirty years of war. During those thirty years the Baptist churches had suffered the martyrdom of some of their leaders, the almost total destruction of their premises, and the prolonged disruption of their community life by two long periods of exile. In spite of all this, these churches had attained their autonomy, and continued to grow (from 10,856 members in 1959 to 20,129 in 1987).[58] As so often in the history of the people of God, the experience of exile had brought about the rejuvenation rather than the extinction of spiritual life. The BMS can look back with satisfaction on what has been achieved in one of the most eventful chapters in its history. It can also look forward in faith to future co-operation with the IEBA in reaping a still more substantial harvest in the years of peace for which Angola has waited so long.

---

58. Ibid.; *BMS Annual Report*, 1959-60, p. 12.

XV

Brazil, 1953-1992

I: The Brazil Experiment, 1953-1956

The enforced exodus of missionaries from China after 1949 released resources of personnel and finance which many within the BMS wished to see used to strengthen hard-pressed existing fields, notably the Congo. Others, however, saw in the course of events a providential opportunity to open a new sphere of work. Most influential among them was Victor Hayward, the former China missionary who succeeded H. R. Williamson as General Foreign Secretary in 1951. Hayward's eyes were turning towards Latin America, for so long the forgotten continent in Protestant missionary thinking. Latin America now offered the prospect, not merely of a new and potentially productive BMS field, but more fundamentally of a new and radical approach to mission.

Half a century previously the BMS had in fact considered opening a Latin American mission under the auspices of the Arthington Fund. Two exploratory expeditions were dispatched: the former Congo missionaries, Robert Glennie and R. D. Darby, visited the Amazon basin in 1908;[1] a year later Glennie returned, this time with G. S. Blake, a Baptist layman, to investigate the possibilities of work among tribal peoples in Mato Grosso and Bolivia. Glennie and Blake's report concluded that the openings among the Indian tribes were few and relatively insignificant, and hinted at the unrealistic nature of their brief, to consider only those Indians 'untouched by Roman Catholics'. It was not surprising that the Society declined to commence even the very limited work in Mato Grosso which Glennie and Blake recommended.[2] Even Baptists were influenced to some extent by the

1. *MH* (Apr.) 1907, 99-102; (Mar. 1908), 70.
2. Misc/1, Report of the Possibility of Work among South American Indians; General Committee Minutes, 20 July 1910, p. 173.

reluctance of many Anglicans to regard the Catholic population of Latin America as appropriate objects of Protestant missionary activity - a sentiment which led to the exclusion of Latin America from the terms of reference of the World Missionary Conference at Edinburgh in 1910.

The question of the legitimacy of addressing Protestant missionary effort to the conversion of Roman Catholics was still a live issue among Baptists in the 1950s. The first BMS minutes to refer to a possible South American mission - those of the Officers' meeting of 5 June 1952 - record that 'the question would need to be considered whether the Society would adopt a policy of seeking to convert Roman Catholics'. It was suggested that a distinction might have to be drawn between practising and nominal Catholics. Hayward shared with the Officers his vision of a small mission with a strong evangelistic and church-planting emphasis, reflecting the ideas of Roland Allen's book, *The Spontaneous Expansion of the Church*.[3] No particular South American country was mentioned, though reference was made to the fact that Arthur Elder, recently returned with his wife Kathleen from the BMS Shaanxi mission, had been born in Argentina, and was now considering service in South America. Hayward had written to Arthur Elder in Hongkong in 1951, informing him that the Officers were considering work in Latin America, and asking whether he might be interested. The Officers' meeting in June 1952 agreed that further enquiries about the missionary prospects of the continent should be made, initially at the July meeting of the International Missionary Council in Willingen, and also through a forthcoming visit to South America by the President of the Baptist World Alliance, Dr F. Townley Lord of Bloomsbury.[4]

Attendance at the Willingen conference as one of the British delegates confirmed Victor Hayward in his view that Latin America was a continent of great need and opportunity. The conference report spoke of Latin America competing with Africa as the 'continent of tomorrow'. Even the Catholic Church was now appealing for missionaries for Latin America, which suggested that the field should now be deemed open for Protestant

3.   R. Allen, *The Spontaneous Expansion of the Church and the Causes which Hinder it* (London, 1927). Hayward was not the only ex-China missionary to have been drawn by the China experience to a re-discovery of Allen's writings; see G. Hood, *Neither Bang nor Whimper: The End of a Missionary Era in China* (Singapore, 1991), 204-12.

4.   Officers' Meeting Minute Book 4, pp. 137-8; interview with Rev. A. C. and Mrs K. Elder, 9 July 1990. J. B. Middlebrook's claim in his MS autobiography that it fell to Hayward merely to 'implement the Brazil project behind which H. R. W. and I had already thrown our weight' understates Hayward's role. (Didcot, J. B. Middlebrook papers).

missions also. Indeed, American evangelical missions, in Brazil particularly, were already witnessing rapid church growth. The report concluded that South American Protestants needed wider external contacts, both for their own sake, and for the enrichment of the world Church; this was an echo of the 'Macedonian' call for new sources of missionary help, voiced by the Latin American representatives at Willingen.[5]

Thus encouraged, Hayward reported to the BMS Officers in September that he was pursuing two possible avenues of development: one was for BMS missionaries to be seconded to work under the auspices of the Southern Baptist Convention; the other was collaboration with the Canadian Baptists in Bolivia.[6] By December, Hayward was able to report a specific suggestion, arising from Dr Townley Lord's visit, that the Elders should serve in Brazil in collaboration with the Southern Baptist Convention. The idea had the support of the executive secretary of the Convention's Foreign Mission Board, but the Officers agreed to keep the Bolivian alternative open for the time being. When nothing came of the Bolivian possibility, a written proposal was sent to the Southern Baptists.[7] By March 1953 a favourable response had been received, and the Officers felt on sufficiently firm ground to report the matter to the General Purposes sub-committee, in relation to the other two 'special projects' in Hongkong and Malaya, being developed as a result of the exodus from China. The Elders' secondment to Brazil was to be described as 'new work' rather than as 'a new field'; it was a small-scale project involving the Elders, and possibly, towards the end of their first term of service, one other couple.[8]

The recommendations of the General Purposes sub-committee regarding the three 'special projects' were brought to the General Committee on 24 April 1953. Those relating to Hongkong and Malaya were approved without qualification, but the modest proposal that approval be given for the secondment of the Elders to Brazil provoked 'a full and prolonged discussion'. It was eventually passed with the addition of the proviso that the Elders should be permitted to branch out into work independent of the Southern Baptists only if the initial period of collaboration with the Convention produced a satisfactory report; three members still voted

5. N. Goodall (ed.), *Missions under the Cross* (London, 1953), 174-6. For a reference to the 'Macedonian call', see Didcot, CR 101.

6. Officers' Meeting Minute Book 4, pp. 157-8, minutes for 11 Sept. 1952.

7. Ibid., pp. 198, 204, minutes for 4 Dec. 1952, 8 Jan. 1953.

8. Officers' Meeting Minute Book 5, p. 4, minutes for 5 Mar. 1953.

Map 11: Brazil

against the motion. Some within the Society may have feared - despite explicit assurances from the Officers to the contrary - that the Elders' venture would grow to a size that might divert resources from other fields. Others may have been suspicious of the anti-ecumenical stance of the Southern Baptists, although on this point also Hayward had obtained a pledge that the ecumenical policy of the BMS would be respected.[9]

Arthur and Kathleen Elder sailed for South America early in May 1953. They spent a year of language study at a language school in Campinas, run at that stage by the Presbyterians. The Elders' first major contact with Brazilian Baptists was made through attending the Baptist Youth Conference at Rio de Janeiro in July. There they received an invitation from Walter Kaschel, pastor of the Baptist church at Curitiba, capital of Paraná, Brazil's fastest growing state, to visit the town. The Elders did so, and were impressed by the opportunities open to Baptists there. A second visit to Paraná followed, at the invitation of the Southern Baptist missionary who was director of the small Bible institute in Curitiba. As a result of a tour of the south-western part of the state, Arthur Elder was invited to assume pastoral charge of a newly-planted congregation in Ponta Grossa, a town of some 70,000 inhabitants.[10]

9.   General Committee Minutes, 24 Apr. 1953, pp. 39-40.

10. Interview with Rev. A. C. and Mrs K. Elder, 9 July 1990.

The first Southern Baptist missionaries had entered Brazil in 1881. Baptist work in Paraná dates from the early years of the twentieth century. By 1953 there were forty-three Baptist churches in the state, twenty-six of them in the interior, an area of Brazil which was only just being opened up to large-scale settlement by the development of coffee cultivation. Total Baptist membership in Paraná in 1953 was well under 5,000.[11] After their year at Campinas, the Elders duly began work in Ponta Grossa. Soon after their arrival, the Paraná Baptist Convention - a body still at an embryonic stage of organization - invited Arthur Elder to be its part-time executive secretary; subsequently Kathleen was asked to become secretary for the incipient work among women. The Elders promptly accepted these invitations, and thus gained a strategic opportunity to assess the prospects for church-planting work by travelling widely in Paraná.[12] In 1956 the Southern Baptists had only three missionary couples in the state - one in Curitiba, one in Londrina, and one in Maringá. Apart from a few missionaries from other evangelical agencies, Paraná could be reckoned virgin territory for possible BMS work. In particular, the whole of the interior of the state to the west and south of the Ivaí river, struck the Elders as being 'practically unevangelized', with virtually no Baptist work, and very little by any other Protestant denomination.[13]

In September 1956 the BMS received a lengthy report from Arthur Elder, reviewing the three years of the Brazil 'experiment'. Elder's report, entitled 'Brazil, Land of the Future', cited an article by a Roman Catholic writer describing Brazil as 'the Protestant country of the future' and predicting that, if the present rate of Protestant growth continued, within forty-nine years there would be more Protestants than Catholics in Brazil. Conscious of the questions that would be raised by some Baptists in Britain, Elder was at pains to stress that the assumption that Roman Catholicism was the religion of the majority of Brazilians was highly questionable. Indigenous candidates for the priesthood were so scarce that there were actually more Brazilian Protestant pastors than Catholic priests. At the last census only 47 per cent of the population had registered as Roman Catholics, most of whom were 'purely (or impurely) nominal'. The bulk of the people subscribed to a mixture of African fetishism, spiritism and

---

11. *MH* (Sept. 1972), 135. Paraná Baptist membership in 1955 was 6,300, according to W. R. Read and F. A. Ineson, *Brazil 1980: The Protestant Handbook* (Monrovia, 1973), 95. Figures cited by Elder in 1956 suggest a considerably lower figure.

12. A. C. Elder papers, Elder to Hayward, 13 Apr. 1955.

13. Didcot, CR 120, Elder to Hayward, 29 Oct. 1956.

veneration of the saints that could not merit the label 'Christian'. In this land of the Protestant future, Paraná presented unique opportunities. As the state at the forefront of Brazil's expanding coffee economy, Paraná was multiplying its population at the rate of nearly 100,000 a year. In the north of the state, where the new city of Londrina had risen out of the forest, Baptist church growth had been 'phenomenal'. Elder urged the BMS to reap a similar harvest in as yet unevangelized areas, particularly in the west.[14]

Arthur Elder's report, together with a paper by Victor Hayward reviewing the origins and history of the Brazil project, was considered by the General Purposes sub-committee, and then brought to the General Committee on 7 November 1956 with a recommendation that the Society's involvement in Brazil should now be put on a more permanent footing. As in 1953, the recommendation emphasized that the Brazilian venture would not be allowed to divert missionary resources from other fields: there was a tacit understanding that the Brazil project would remain of limited size for the foreseeable future. Despite this re-assurance, there was again protracted debate in the General Committee. Influential persons in the Society urged caution, and reminded the Committee of the claims of the Congo and Angola missions. Nevertheless, no-one actually spoke against the proposition, and the eventual vote was unanimous. The Society committed itself to continue its work in Brazil, resolved to appoint two accepted candidates, Derek and Beryl Winter, to join the Elders, and agreed to re-name its West Indies sub-committee as the 'West Indies and Brazil sub-committee'.[15] Derek Winter, pastor at Waterbeach in Cambridgeshire, had been in touch with Victor Hayward about possible service in Brazil since his student days at Spurgeon's College, but had been given strict instructions by Hayward in 1954 not to publicize his probable destination until the Society had committed itself to continue the Brazil experiment.[16] Now, in November 1956, that commitment had been made: the BMS had entered its first new field since the beginning of the Congo mission in 1879.

II: Baptist Church Growth in a Frontier State: Paraná, 1956-1965

The Paraná Baptist Convention reported almost 700 baptisms during 1956, bringing total membership to nearly 6,000, a rate of Baptist growth

14. Didcot, CR 96, 'Brazil, Land of the Future'.

15. General Committee Minutes, 7 Nov. 1956, pp. 133-5; A. C. Elder papers, Hayward to Elder, 8 Nov. 1956.

16. Interview with Rev. D. G. Winter, 9 Aug. 1990; D. G. Winter papers, Hayward to Winter, 26 Mar. 1954.

which Arthur Elder believed to be without parallel in Brazil.[17] The Baptist experience in Paraná in the 1950s and early 1960s constitutes a classic example of David Martin's generalization that Protestantism in Brazil has flourished 'either where there was movement, as on the frontier, or where there was modest independence'.[18] In western Paraná, both conditions applied. The flood of migrants into the state was constantly pushing forward the frontier of cultivation and urban development, creating new towns such as Cianorte, Cascavel, and Pato Branco. The ready availability of land meant that most migrants settling in Paraná in this period soon acquired economic independence as small proprietors or businessmen, even though few, if any, were originally wealthy. Some of the migrants had been Baptist members in other states, and these tended to form the nuclei of new Baptist congregations in Paraná. Thus in the vicinity of the company town of Cianorte (developed by the North Paraná Land Development Company, and still barely four years old) there were by October 1956 about 140 Baptist members newly arrived from other states. Apart from one small house congregation, supervised from a distance by the pastor at Maringá, these scattered Baptists were totally without organization or leadership. With new migrants crossing the river Ivaí to set up home in Cianorte at a rate of about thirty families a day, the town appeared to be ideally placed for an experiment in the spontaneous expansion of the Church.[19]

By the time news reached him of the decisions of the November 1956 General Committee, Arthur Elder had already reached the conclusion that western Paraná (the area west and south of the Ivaí river) should be the sphere of BMS operations. He listed three possible locations for consideration by the Society - Cianorte in the north of the region, Cascavel in the centre, and Pato Branco in the south. His clear preference was for Cianorte. In January 1957 the West Indies and Brazil sub-committee accepted his suggestion, and resolved to recommend to the Paraná Baptist Convention that the Elders be appointed to Cianorte.[20] In late April the Elders accordingly moved there from Ponta Grossa. Shortly afterwards Derek and Beryl Winter visited Cianorte in a break from their language study in Campinas, and were greatly impressed with the suitability of the town as a

17. Didcot, CR 136, Report of Activities of A. C. and K. Elder for 1956.

18. D. Martin, *Tongues of Fire: The Explosion of Protestantism in Latin America* (Oxford, 1990), 64.

19. Didcot, CR 120, Elder to Hayward, 29 Oct. 1956; information from Mrs K. Elder.

20. Didcot, CR 121, Memorandum on Western Paraná; W. Indies Sub-Committee Minute Book 3, p. 54, minutes for 8 Jan. 1957.

missionary bridgehead. On 23 June 1957 the Baptist church at Cianorte was formally constituted with 139 members, and Elder then set about organizing its constituent congregations. In September special evangelistic meetings were held, which elicited a warm response. Sixteen candidates were baptized during October, and others were being prepared. The next month work began on building a house for the Winters. By the end of the year the Cianorte church had two hundred baptized members, worshipping in six organized congregations. Reflecting on the interest aroused by the September campaign, Arthur Elder observed, 'One senses a spiritual vacuum which organised Roman Catholicism does not fill, and also a dangerous political disillusionment which augurs ill for the future'. Even in relatively affluent Paraná there were signs of dissatisfaction with the failure of the rapidly expanding Brazilian economy, fuelled as it was primarily by foreign capital and technology, to bring substantial benefits to ordinary people.[21]

Derek and Beryl Winter joined Arthur and Kathleen Elder in Cianorte early in 1958, and took over their responsibilities when the Elders left for furlough in June. On home deputation in 1958-9, the Elders found intense interest in the Brazil mission. The stirring image of pioneer evangelism on Brazil's advancing frontier appealed to the home constituency, and amply justified Victor Hayward's feeling in the early 1950s that a new BMS field would serve to rejuvenate enthusiasm for the Society in the churches, particularly those with a strong evangelical emphasis.[22] But the novelty of the Brazil mission was a matter of substance, and not merely of image. From the outset, there was a studied and self-conscious attempt to fulfil Hayward's vision of a mission which embodied the principles of Roland Allen. There were to be no 'mission stations' and no costly institutions financed by overseas funds. Mobility and the three-self principles of self-government, self-support and self-propagation were the watchwords. The lessons of the China experience, so clear in Victor Hayward's mind, were to be put into practice in Brazil.

The goal of self-government was to be attained by a strategy of leadership training directed towards the education of the many rather than the setting apart of the few. 'It would be unwise,' wrote Arthur Elder, 'to try and

---

21. *BMS Annual Report*, 1957-8, pp. xxx-xxxii; W. Indies Sub-Committee Minute Book 3, p. 71, minutes for 19 June 1957; A. C. Elder papers, Report by A. C. Elder on Work in Brazil during 1957.

22. W. Indies Sub-Committee Minute Book 3, p. 145, minutes for 2 June 1959; interviews with Rev. A. C. and Mrs K. Elder, and Rev. D. G. Winter, 9 Aug. 1990.

reproduce overseas the exact set-up of church and ministry which has not been altogether successful' in Britain. 'There is need for trained leadership, but not necessarily of a professional leadership which might become a financial burden to the young church'. The Southern Baptist method of using the Sunday School as the central agency of Christian education for adults was enthusiastically espoused, while those with leadership potential were to be encouraged to become lay pastors, assisted by a rudimentary training. Furthermore, there was no question of setting up a distinct 'BMS church'. Full co-operation with the Southern Baptists and the Brazilian Baptist Convention was the premise on which all BMS work would be based.[23]

Self-support was seen, not as a distant goal to be aimed at, but as a constant principle determining priorities and practice. No BMS funds would be made available for building projects. Church buildings must be financed from local resources, even though the end result, as in the case of the Jussara church building near Cianorte, might be 'architecturally non-descript'. Stewardship was to be taught as an integral part of Christian discipleship. The tithing of members' income - again a Southern Baptist practice - was enjoined by Arthur Elder on the Cianorte church, and accepted initially by about 30 per cent of the membership. Tithing has continued to be the policy and general practice of the Convention churches.[24]

The aim of establishing a self-propagating church, an ideal which the BMS had subscribed to from its earliest days, attained new spontaneity and meaning in the Brazilian context. No longer was it simply a question of the mission working towards the goal of establishing a mature church in a locality, and then moving on to evangelize a fresh area; rather, every Baptist church from its infancy was the primary instrument of mission in its locality. Although this emphasis was wholly in conformity with Victor Hayward's theoretical vision for the Brazil field, it was less an objective imposed from Britain than a recognition of existing reality in Brazil. Evangelism in the Brazilian churches was a largely spontaneous, home-based, lay movement. Under the slogan of 'every Baptist home a preaching station', Brazilian Baptists used their homes to spread the Christian message to their friends and neighbours.[25] Clusters of converts won in this way formed the nuclei of new congregations. The role of BMS missionaries in western Paraná in this period was to channel and manage this autonomous

23. A. C. Elder papers, undated paper by A. C. Elder on 'The BMS in Brazil' [late 1950s].

24. Ibid.

25. Ibid.

process, organizing home groups into congregations, and congregations into churches, and providing a focus of pastoral leadership for the Baptist community in each town or locality.

Nevertheless, the continuing role of the ordained pastor was given a more precise definition amongst Brazilian Baptists than amongst the various Pentecostal bodies which witnessed such phenomenal growth in Brazil from the 1930s. In conformity with Southern Baptist custom, the Brazilian Baptist Convention has confined the right to baptize and celebrate communion to ordained pastors, and it is arguable that this limitation of the scope of lay leadership is a primary explanation of the marked differential in rates of growth between Baptists and Pentecostals in Brazil.[26] Thus, whilst Baptist membership in Paraná grew from between 5,000 and 6,000 in 1955 to 10,800 in 1965, membership of the Assemblies of God in the state rocketed from 9,200 in 1955 to 38,450 in 1965.[27] The Baptist option to retain fairly tight control in the hands of the ordained pastorate has undoubtedly secured a higher standard of orthodoxy and theological understanding amongst the membership, but such concern for 'the grammar of doctrine', argues David Martin, has weakened the appeal of Baptist churches to the poor and marginalized in Brazilian society. The secret of Pentecostal success in Brazil, on the other hand, lies in the offer of active leadership participation to ordinary, uneducated people: 'Pentecostals recognize that their life-blood depends on breaking the cordons of clerical caste, Protestant or Catholic'.[28] Brazilian Baptists, though affirming the priesthood of all believers in theory, and indeed practising it in their evangelism, have been less radical in applying this principle to their church life, less radical than many BMS missionaries would have wished.

In 1958 the Paraná Baptist Convention asked the BMS to respond to the growing opportunities in Paraná by sending two additional missionary couples to the field, and permitting Arthur Elder to become full-time executive secretary of the Convention. The Society declined the second request, believing it would divert Elder from his pioneering role, but agreed to increase its missionary force in Brazil by the recruitment of one additional couple. Accordingly in December 1959 Andrew Brunton and Sheila Scott arrived in Brazil, and commenced their language training. In September

---

26. Interview with Rev. A. Ferreira, 23 Mar. 1987.

27. Read and Ineson, *Brazil 1980,* 95, 97; see above, p. 475, n. 11.

28. Martin, *Tongues of Fire,* 63, 65, 66. A more fundamental reason for the slower growth of the Baptists has been their resistance to charismatic Christianity; see below, p. 498.

1960, the three BMS missionary couples (the Elders, the Winters and the Scotts) made a formal request to BMS that at least one new couple each year should be sent out, in order to keep pace with the growing responsibilities in West Paraná.[29] Arthur Elder had already opened up a second centre of BMS work at Umuarama, where a church of 165 members was organized in October 1960. In January 1961 Brunton Scott assumed the pastorate at Umuarama, and with it acquired responsibility for a vast area extending northwards and westwards to the river Paraná.[30] The Society now faced a fundamental decision about the future scale of the Brazil mission, which had so far remained within the very limited parameters envisaged by the General Committee in 1956.

Of crucial importance in determining the Society's response was the fact that both Ernest Madge and J. B. Middlebrook had just visited Brazil to attend the Baptist World Alliance Congress in Rio de Janeiro at the end of June. Following the Congress meetings, Madge and Middlebrook led a team of BWA representatives from BMS-related churches - comprising Samuel Koli of Congo, Benjamin Pradhan of India, W. G. Wickramasinghe of Ceylon, and Sushil Adhikari of East Pakistan – to West Paraná, to see at first hand the immense evangelistic opportunities confronting the Society. The team were greatly impressed. 'How thrilling it was', exclaimed the BMS annual report enthusiastically, 'to see the Elders and Winters working out in Brazil the missionary pattern that Paul and Barnabas employed in Asia Minor, as recorded in the Acts of Apostles'.[31] Ernest Madge, reporting to the West Indies and Brazil sub-committee on 1 November 1960, 'strongly recommended that the Society should plan gradually to increase the number of missionaries working in Brazil'. Certain doubts were expressed by some members of the committee. Gordon Hastings, the influential minister of Queen's Road, Coventry, who had also attended the Rio Congress, drew attention to the strong nationalistic spirit in the country, which was likely to affect the church, and anticipated difficulties in co-operating with the Southern Baptists. Hastings was also one of those who still had reservations about the BMS appearing to 'proselytize' Roman Catholics. The eventual decision of the committee was cautious: to recommend that at least one further couple be sent to Brazil 'when financial considerations permit'. The finance sub-committee warmly endorsed the

---

29. W. Indies Sub-Committee Minute Book 3, p. 178, minutes for 1 Nov. 1960.

30. *BMS Annual Reports,* 1960-1, p. xxxviii; 1961-2, p. xl.

31. *BMS Annual Report,* 1960-1, pp. xxxvii, xlii-xliii.

recommendation, confident that the 'very strong interest shown by the constituency in South America' would ensure that an increase in the Brazil mission would actually increase the Society's support.[32]

The decision to exceed the previously agreed limit of three missionary couples in Brazil proved a significant mile-stone in the history of the mission, which now entered a phase of expansion that soon transcended the cautious commitment made in November 1960. In 1961 the executive committee of the Paraná State Convention urged the BMS to send 'as great a number of workers as possible'. The Society, discerning a 'Divine imperative' behind this appeal, resolved to send an additional couple to Brazil each year for the next three years, commencing in 1962-3. The Society's Officers were now explicitly committed to a policy of advance in Brazil, although they were anxious to dispel any suggestion that this was a pragmatic response to closing doors elsewhere, particularly in Angola.[33] As a result, by 1965 the BMS missionary force in Brazil had grown to eight couples. Six of the eight male missionaries had been trained at Spurgeon's College. Although this preponderance of Spurgeon's men in the early years of the Brazil mission was a largely fortuitous development, it established a pattern which continued in more recent years, and helped to reinforce the distinctive appeal of the Brazil mission to those parts of the Baptist denomination loyal to the evangelical tradition of C. H. Spurgeon.

The first new recruits to arrive were Roy and Margaret Deller, who had been appointed in 1961 in response to the November 1960 decision. After a period of orientation in Cianorte, the Dellers were sent to Cascavel early in 1963, and set out to plant a Baptist church, beginning with just three members. The new frontier town of Cascavel was strategically placed at the junction of two distinct population movements into Paraná: the first from the southern states of Rio Grande do Sul and Santa Catarina, where the mechanization of agriculture was displacing much of the farming population; and the second, a much larger flow of poorer migrants from the north and north-east, attracted by the expanding coffee economy of Paraná. The first group were mainly of European stock, and proved comparatively resistant to evangelical Protestantism. The second, comprising people of African and mixed racial origin, were far more responsive. The church in Cascavel was formally constituted in August 1964, with a membership of

---

32. W. Indies Sub-Committee Minute Book 3, pp. 177-80, 183, 231, minutes for 1 Nov. 1960, 11 Jan. 1961, 11 Apr. 1962. See Clyde Binfield, *Pastors and People: The Biography of a Baptist Church Queen's Road, Coventry* (Coventry, 1984), 298-300.

33. W. Indies Sub-Committee Minute Book 3, pp. 209-13, minutes for 27 Sept. 1961.

about eighty. The growth of the Baptist community in the town paralleled the growth of Cascavel into one of the principal cities of Paraná: by 1990 there were several Baptist churches in the city, with a membership of over 1,000.[34]

The Dellers were closely followed in 1962 by Tony and Gill Boorne, Kibokolo missionaries who had been compelled to leave Angola in 1961 by the fighting there. The Boornes began work in Porto Guaira, an important town on the river Paraná, bordering Paraguay and the state of Mato Grosso (then a single state stretching from the borders of Amazonas in the north to the river Paraná in the south). A Baptist church had been formed here in June 1962, largely due to the initiative of a Christian naval officer stationed in the town.[35] Meanwhile the Elders had moved in October 1961 to the state capital of Curitiba. In response to the repeated pleas of the Paraná churches, Ernest Madge had eventually persuaded the West Indies and Brazil sub-committee that the pioneering character of the Brazil mission would not be infringed by releasing Arthur Elder to move to Curitiba, as requested, to establish and run a central office for the Paraná Baptist Convention.[36] Derek and Beryl Winter, returning from furlough in 1963, also assumed a new role, initiating a new church-planting ministry at Goio Erê. Three additional missionary couples arrived between 1963 and 1965: Jim and Eileen Clarke, and David and Doris Doonan in 1963, and Avelino and Ana Ferreira in mid-1964. After a period of language learning at Campinas and orientation at Umuarama, the Clarkes settled in the extreme north-west of the state at Loanda. The Doonans took up the work at Umuarama in 1964, when Andrew Brunton Scott accepted a post in Curitiba as organizer for Paraná of a nationwide evangelistic crusade planned for 1965. The Ferreiras, Portuguese missionaries of the Society whose service in Angola had been brought to an end in 1963 by the repression of the 1961 revolt, had been invited to consider service in Paraná by Arthur Elder. Their first posting in Brazil from 1965 was at Jacarézinho in the north-east, where Avelino, a natural extrovert, rapidly won the affection of the local people. He assumed responsibility for a scattered and generally moribund group of churches, some of which were twenty years old.[37]

34. Interview with Rev R. and Mrs M. Deller, 18 Sept. 1990.

35. *BMS Annual Report*, 1961-2, pp. xl-xli.

36. W. Indies Sub-Committee Minute Book 3, pp. 220, 255, minutes for 26 Sept. 1962; D. G. Winter papers, Madge to Winter, 29 Mar. 1962.

37. Interview with Rev. A. Ferreira, 23 Mar. 1987; A. C. Elder papers, Elder to Madge, n.d. [mid-1965].

III: Debates over Strategic Priorities, 1964-1965

With the exception of the Elders in Curitiba, all BMS personnel in 1965 were engaged in church-planting or evangelistic ministries. Most were based in rapidly growing towns organizing town-centre churches, whilst devoting much of their energy to the planting and nursing towards autonomous life of new satellite congregations. Nonetheless, even before 1965 it was clear that the end of the pioneering era in Paraná was not that far distant. The flow of migration into the state was drying up, while new economic pressures were carrying the population westwards and north-wards into the states of Mato Grosso, Pará, and Amazonas. In church life also, there were indications that something more than pioneering would soon be needed in Paraná. With these trends in mind, Arthur Elder in early 1964 drafted a 'Memorandum on future policy and plans for the Brazil mission'. It was a major policy document, which Elder (then on furlough) presented in person to the West Indies and Brazil sub-committee on 23 April 1964.[38]

Elder's memorandum raised two strategic questions. The first was the possibility, indeed the necessity, of broadening the range of BMS work in Paraná. Involvement in theological education would have to be a higher priority if the newly-planted churches were to be given adequate leadership. BMS missionaries were already involved in the training of lay leaders in the congregations which they had helped to plant, but there was an evident need for higher-level pastoral training. Graduates of existing Baptist seminaries, notably the South Brazil Baptist Seminary in Rio de Janeiro, were not finding their way to pastorates in Paraná, preferring more attractive opportunities in other states. Paraná itself had only a low-level Bible institute in Curitiba, founded in the 1940s to prepare students with little secular education for entry to the Rio seminary. The Elders were already teaching part-time in the Curitiba institute, and there were hopes that the academic standard might in future be raised to seminary level. BMS participation in the up-graded institution seemed to Elder an appropriate goal. Equally important would be the setting aside of one missionary couple to run training courses for lay leaders in various centres. There was also a need for quality Christian literature, particularly of a type that would make Christianity intelligible to the intellectual, and challenge the flood of Communist publications now deluging Brazil. Elder also pointed out the educational and medical needs of Brazil. In Paraná the great majority of the

---

38. Didcot, CR 333. A draft of the memorandum, retrospectively dated 1963, is preserved in the A. C. Elder papers.

population had little prospect of secondary education, whilst government medical provision was inadequate, especially outside the large urban centres. Although he did not suggest a major investment by the BMS in educational or medical work (to have done so would have been to reverse the whole emphasis of the Brazil mission), Elder did raise the possibility of the Society sending out a nurse to do mobile clinic and public health work.

The second question raised by Elder's memorandum was the appropriateness of the BMS extending its activities beyond Paraná to other states and even other Latin American countries. The most obvious next step would be to follow the migration flow westwards into Mato Grosso. To do so would probably necessitate the Society establishing some official relationship with the national Baptist body, the Brazilian Baptist Convention, as well as relating to the various state conventions. More radically, Elder did not hesitate to lay before the Society the challenge of the 'unconquered territories and unreached millions' of the continent as a whole. Although he was now speaking the language of consolidation in Paraná, the frontier spirit in Arthur Elder was still very much alive.[39]

Discussion of Elder's memorandum took place initially at the committee meeting on 23 April 1964, subsequently in the context of the Society's Officers' meeting, and then more fully at a further meeting of the West Indies and Brazil sub-committee meeting on 20 October, when Elder was again present. On the last occasion a 'full and lengthy discussion' took place. Several speakers urged the BMS to accept the challenge of further advance, at least into Mato Grosso. Others, notably J. B. Middlebrook, then vice-chairman of the Society, Alberic Clement, Middlebrook's successor as Home Secretary, and Dr G. Henton Davies, Principal of Regent's Park College, warned against over-extension, and argued for the priority of devoting resources to theological education in Paraná. It was finally resolved to recommend to the General Committee that BMS activity in Paraná be expanded by the sending out of at least one missionary couple per year, if possible, although the work in Paraná was now said, rather ambiguously, 'to include the following of migrants across the river into Mato Grosso'. It was also agreed to ask Elder and his colleagues to prepare plans for further participation in theological education, and to explore the possibility of sending single missionaries to Brazil, a further point Elder had raised for consideration.[40]

39. Didcot, CR 333.

40. W. Indies and Brazil Sub-Committee Minute Book 4, pp. 30-9, 47, 56-9, minutes for 23 Apr., 30 June and 20 Oct. 1964.

The Officers had already formed the view that no final decision on future policy in Brazil should be made until after Ernest Madge and Alberic Clement had visited the country after attending the BWA Congress in Miami in June 1965. Madge and Clement made a four-week tour of Brazil from mid-July to mid-August, which included a visit to Campo Grande in Mato Grosso. On 25 July they attended a meeting of all the BMS Brazil missionaries in Londrina. There was an extended discussion of potential openings in theological training, including a request for BMS help from the theological faculty of the São Paulo Baptist College, and the possibility of sending Brazilian pastors for further training in Britain. Jim Clarke gave a report of a recent visit to Mato Grosso to consult with Baptist leaders there about possible BMS involvement; mention was also made of invitations to enter Rio Grande do Sul and Santa Catarina. Missionary opinion was strongly in favour of making some positive response to these requests, but the secretaries could see little prospect of the necessary resources of personnel or money being available within the next few years: theological education, rather than geographical expansion, was the most logical next step in BMS Brazil policy. The meeting agreed reluctantly that it would not be possible for the time being to accept invitations to engage in church and evangelistic work outside Paraná.[41]

The secretaries thus brought to the West Indies and Brazil sub-committee in October 1965 a recommendation that BMS work in Brazil be confined to the state of Paraná for the immediate future. Some members of the committee still argued strongly that the Society should not flinch from presenting the challenge of new openings in other states to the churches. Nevertheless, the committee concluded that it was not possible at present for the BMS to accept invitations from other state conventions, save in cases of special secondment. This recommendation was adopted by the General Committee on 3 November.[42] In fact nearly ten years were to elapse before the Society felt able to respond to invitations to become involved in church work in other states. There remained a feeling among some of the missionaries who had been present at the Londrina meeting on 25 July that the BMS had failed in 1965 to seize the opportunity created by the onward movement of population beyond Paraná into

41. Didcot, CR 373-374, Report on Visit of Foreign and Home Secretaries to Brazil, and Minutes of Meeting of Brazil Missionaries, 25 July 1965; interview with Rev. D. W. Doonan, 5 Sept. 1990.

42. W. Indies and Brazil Sub-Committee Minute Book 4, pp. 79-80, minutes for 19 Oct. 1965; General Committee Minutes, 3 Nov. 1965, pp. 72-4.

Mato Grosso.[43] Be that as it may, the report written by Ernest Madge on the 1965 visit charted a course of future development for the Society in Brazil which was to be closely followed over the next decade.[44]

IV: New Forms of Ministry in Paraná, 1966-1973

The transition from pioneering to consolidation in Paraná after 1965 was a gradual process. The majority of BMS personnel continued to be involved in church-planting and evangelistic work throughout the 1960s, and even into the early 1970s. However, the diversification of ministry anticipated by Arthur Elder's memorandum was progressively realized. In theological education, the first significant development was the sponsorship by the Society of a young Paraná pastor, Waldemiro Tymchak, to undertake further theological study at Spurgeon's College. Tymchak, who commenced his course at Spurgeon's in the autumn of 1966, was the first of a series of Brazilians whose studies at British Baptist colleges, mainly Spurgeon's, were financed by the BMS over the next twenty-five years. This sponsorship programme enabled the Society to provide advanced theological education for some of the most promising of the Brazilian pastors, especially for those who were involved, or likely to become involved, in theological teaching in Curitiba or elsewhere. The programme had the disadvantages inherent in removing a student from his native land, but there were compensating advantages in introducing future Brazilian Baptist leaders to a more profound and penetrating theological perspective than was generally available in the Brazilian seminaries.

For some years the theological faculty of the São Paulo Baptist College had expressed a desire that a BMS missionary should be seconded to their staff. In 1965 the College made a request for the services of Derek Winter, one of the most gifted academically of the BMS missionaries, who was then about to leave Goio Erê for furlough. Ernest Madge and Alberic Clement supported the request in the report of their Brazilian visit, and approval was given by the General Committee in November 1965.[45] In the event, family circumstances prevented the Winters from returning to Brazil until 1968, when Derek joined the staff of the Curitiba Bible Institute. Soon after their return, Beryl Winter was killed in a road accident, leaving her husband with the care of five young children. Despite this tragedy, Winter decided to

---

43. Interviews with Rev. D. W. Doonan, 5 Sept. 1990, and Rev. R. and Mrs M. Deller, 18 Sept. 1990.

44. Didcot, CR 373.

45. General Committee Minutes, 3 Nov. 1965, p. 72.

remain in Brazil. The São Paulo faculty still desired his services, and for a semester in 1969 Winter commuted on a weekly basis the four hundred kilometers from Curitiba to São Paulo, where he taught New Testament Greek. This was an unsatisfactory arrangement, and in March 1969 the Society ruled that its 1965 agreement for Winter to be seconded to São Paulo no longer held good.[46] One reason for the change of view was a desire in the home Committee to retain strict limits on the proportion of missionaries engaged in institutional rather than pioneering roles. In the previous year, the Society had agreed to second Tony Boorne to the Recife Baptist Seminary in the north-east, where some students from Paraná were being trained. The Elders also were now more fully involved in teaching at the Curitiba institute, during the absence of its director on furlough in the USA. More fundamentally, the plans to up-grade the Curitiba institute to seminary level were now maturing, and both the home staff and senior missionaries in Brazil felt that the BMS should accordingly concentrate its investment in theological teaching in Curitiba. Despite a formal request from São Paulo for his full-time services, Derek Winter thus remained on the staff at Curitiba until 1970, when the needs of his children compelled him to return to England to take up a teaching post.[47]

After 1970 the Curitiba Bible Institute increasingly became the focus of the Society's strategy for theological education in Paraná. In addition to the institute's main courses of evening study (most Brazilian theological students have to support themselves by paid employment during the day), growing emphasis was placed on a programme of extension study aimed at lay leaders, which was developed by David Doonan and Avelino Ferreira, initially from Cianorte, and then integrated in the work of the institute after the Doonans joined the staff at Curitiba in 1970. In the early 1970s the institute remained heavily dependent on missionary staff: the only full-time Brazilian lecturer in 1971 was Waldemiro Tymchak, who had joined the staff on completion of his studies in Britain. The institute was up-graded to seminary status in 1974.

The increasing involvement of the BMS in theological education brought into sharper focus the differences in cultural and theological

---

46. W. Indies and Brazil Sub-Committee Minute Book 4, p. 169, minutes for 13 Mar. 1969.

47. W. Indies and Brazil Sub-Committee Minute Book 4, p. 176, minutes for 3 June 1969. Didcot, CR 403, minutes of meeting of Brazil missionaries, 9 Apr. 1969; CR 404, minutes of meeting of Brazil missionaries, 24-26 June 1969. Interview with Rev. D. G. Winter, 9 Aug. 1990.

emphasis between British Baptist missionaries and the American Southern Baptists who remain a significant influence on contemporary Brazilian Baptist life. These differences had been fully recognized by the BMS from the beginning, but they had not been sufficiently serious to prevent BMS missionaries from co-operating harmoniously with American missionaries in the pioneer work of church-planting in Paraná. In theological education, however, the potential for conflict was that much greater between BMS missionaries, whose theology was evangelical, but with varying degrees of conservatism, and Southern Baptists and their Brazilian protegés, whose theological orientation was often more fundamentalist in character. The fact that this potential for conflict was not realized within Paraná was due largely to the respect which BMS missionaries had already earned by their zeal for evangelism and pioneer work. Beyond Paraná it is possible that Southern Baptist perceptions of the theological stance of British Baptists tended to debar BMS missionaries from entry into teaching posts in the more traditional seminaries, such as that in Rio de Janeiro.[48] Nonetheless, BMS missionaries earned widespread respect throughout the Brazilian Baptist Convention for their role in theological education. In recent years several have held the post of Principal in various Baptist seminaries: David Grainger in Curitiba, David Doonan and Eric Westwood in Cuiabá, and John Clark in Campo Grande.

In comparison with theological education, BMS medical work in Brazil was slow to develop. Arthur Elder's 1964 suggestion that a BMS nurse might profitably be appointed to engage in mobile clinic work in Paraná did not become a reality for some years, despite the fact that health care in the frontier regions of West Paraná in the mid-1960s was very sporadic. Those missionary wives who were nurses or midwives by training, such as Margaret Deller at Cascavel, found that their professional services were in great demand, albeit on an unofficial basis. Mainly because British nursing qualifications were not officially recognized in Brazil, it was April 1968 before the BMS made a firm decision to recruit nurses for Brazil.[49] The first nurse to be recruited, Angela Parish, arrived in Brazil in 1969, but had to return home a year later owing to ill health. The second nurse, Helen Watson, went out in 1970, and then had to spend time in language study and gaining the requisite Brazilian nursing qualifications. It was thus October 1971 before the Society was able to approve a proposal for a pilot

---

48. Interview with Rev. D. W. Doonan, 5 Sept. 1990.

49. W. Indies and Brazil Sub-Committee Minute Book 4, pp. 153-6, minutes for 4 Apr. 1968, with inserted report by H. F. Drake on Visit to Brazil, Jan.-Feb. 1968.

medical project, to be staffed by Helen Watson, and a Brazilian worker supported by the Paraná Baptist Convention, with an emphasis on mobile dispensary work.[50] The mobile dispensary, which was funded by British Baptist young people, performed a useful function from 1973 to 1975 in the Pato Branco area, staffed by Helen Watson and a Brazilian teacher, Lydia Klava. Another BMS nurse, Mary Rasmussen, served in Curitiba from 1973 to 1975. The irony was that by the mid-1970s, state medical provision in West Paraná had become much more substantial, and the need for Christian medical work correspondingly less great. Through no fault of its own, the Society had been unable to move fast enough to respond to the needs of the moment in Brazil's rapidly changing society.[51] Not until the mid-1980s did the Society again send nurses to Brazil - Margaret Swires in 1985, and Mary Parsons in 1986.[52]

The one area of Paraná where there was an obvious and continuing need throughout the 1970s for medical work was the Litoral, the low-lying and wet coastal strip. Here the standard of living was extremely low, and communications poor. Three pastors and a teacher served a small Baptist community. The Baptist Convention had a dispensary at Tagaçaba, run by a single nurse. Following an approach to the Society from the Paraná Baptist Convention, H. F. Drake made a point of visiting the Litoral during a tour of Brazil in early 1968, and reported that a group of forty to fifty villages to the north and west of Tagaçaba were largely without schools, medical facilities, or churches. On Drake's recommendation, the BMS resolved to ask the Convention for a formal invitation to enter the Litoral, and set aside John and Norma Clark, new missionaries currently undertaking language study in Campinas, to work with the pastor at Antonina, on the western side of the Litoral.[53] After a year's orientation at Antonina, the Clarks moved in 1969 to the port of Paranaguá, the chief town of the Litoral. Again, however, it was some years before the Society was in a position to place a suitably qualified missionary nurse at Tagaçaba.

As the least developed part of Paraná, the Litoral needed not merely primary health care, but also programmes of agricultural development to

---

50. W. Indies and Brazil Sub-Committee Minute Book 4, p. 220, minutes for 14 Oct. 1971.

51. Overseas Sub-Committee Minute Book 1, p. 25, minutes for 10 Oct. 1974; interview with Rev. D. W. Doonan, 5 Sept. 1990.

52. Margaret Swires was accepted for development rather than nursing work. Mary Parsons (née Rasmussen) is Clifford Parsons' second wife and widow.

53. W. Indies and Brazil Sub-Committee Minute Book 4, pp. 153-6, minutes for 4 Apr. 1968, with inserted report by H. F. Drake on Visit to Brazil, Jan.-Feb. 1968.

raise the subsistence levels of the population. In late 1970 Avelino Ferreira and John Clark led a stewardship conference for the leaders of the Litoral Baptist Association. In addressing the meeting, Ferreira happened to mention the range of work undertaken by the BMS in Angola, including agricultural work. He was asked to say more on the subject, and the eventual outcome was a request by the Paraná Convention to the Society to supply an agriculturalist to initiate an agricultural project on behalf of the Convention. The BMS responded favourably, but was unable to find a qualified agriculturalist, offering instead the services of Walter and Jane Fulbrook, veterans of the Angola mission. Walter Fulbrook, although from a farming background, was a pastor rather than an agriculturalist, and the Convention accepted the Society's offer with some reluctance. The Fulbrooks pioneered the project, located at Potinga, between 1974 and 1976, but the Brazilians still pressed the BMS for a professional agriculturalist. The Society was able to supply Frank Gouthwaite, who had a keen interest in rural development, but was not an agriculturalist as such. Not until 1985 did the Potinga project (known from 1979 as CEBADER - *Centro Batista de Desenvolvimento Rural*) gain the professional agricultural expertise which it needed in order to make a substantial impact on the local farmers. The Bangladesh missionary, David Stockley, had been brought over as a consultant to advise the Society on the operation of the project, and made such an impression that the Brazilians requested, successfully, that David and Joyce Stockley should be re-located permanently in Brazil to direct the CEBADER work. Under the Stockleys' leadership, the CEBADER project made a significant contribution to agricultural improvement in this part of the Litoral.[54]

The growing size of the BMS operation in Paraná necessitated some clarification of the status and organization of the mission. Arthur Elder served as Field Secretary until he assumed increased teaching responsibilities at the Curitiba Bible Institute in 1968. In 1970 the Elders left Brazil, when Arthur was appointed to the staff of St. Andrew's Hall in the Selly Oak Colleges. During the Elder years, the Society had no legal existence in Brazil independently of the Paraná Baptist Convention, and virtually no administrative structure. All BMS missionaries met periodically for discussion, but this meeting had no official status within the Society, and no executive authority. In July 1966 this meeting resolved to establish a small administrative committee, comprising Elder, Ferreira, and Brunton Scott, to assist Elder in his duties; the committee was increased to four members in

---

54. Interview with Rev. D. W. Doonan, 5 Sept. 1990; information from Rev. F. W. J. Clark, 2 Jan. 1991.

1968.[55] Under Elder's successor, Roy Deller, Field Secretary from 1968 to 1972, the BMS was recognized as a separate legal entity, and gained an official committee. A formal working agreement with the Paraná Baptist Convention was concluded in 1972.[56] In addition, the Society entered into official discussions with the national Baptist body, the Brazilian Baptist Convention, which led in 1972 to an agreed basis of co-operation between the Convention and all its overseas missionary partners.[57]

Following the conclusion of the working agreement with the Paraná Convention, the Society decided in March 1973 to discontinue the office of Brazil Field Secretary, and appoint instead a Secretary for Missionary Affairs, with a more limited brief.[58] The change was in conformity with trends in the Society's African and Asian fields, but was not fully welcomed by the Paraná Baptist leaders. There was never much danger of BMS missionaries dominating the life of the Convention, and Brazilian church leaders would have preferred to relate to a person with clear executive responsibility. The sense of a leadership vacuum was reinforced by the departure from Brazil of the first generation of BMS personnel: the Elders, Derek Winter, the Scotts, and in 1973 the Dellers also, had left. It was in part to fill this vacuum that Clifford Parsons was sent from BMS headquarters to serve in Curitiba as an interim Secretary for Missionary Affairs. Although Parsons filled this post only for a few months before moving to São Paulo, his presence on the field was crucial in enabling the Society's committees to appreciate that the dynamics of church-mission relationships in Brazil were very different from those in Zaire, and that a rigid limitation of missionaries' freedom of action was not desired by the churches. David Doonan replaced Parsons as Secretary for Missionary Affairs in late 1973. The Society's later policy decision to appoint regional representatives for its various fields gave the Brazilian churches the officially responsible person they desired: Andrew Brunton Scott returned to Brazil in 1977 and became the first regional representative for the West Indies and Brazil.[59]

---

55. W. Indies and Brazil Sub-Committee Minute Book 4, p. 122, minutes for 1 Nov. 1966; Dicot, CR 401, Minutes of Meeting of Brazil Field Missionaries, 16 Oct. 1968.

56. W. Indies and Brazil Sub-Committee Minute Book 4, pp. 250-1, minutes for 23 Mar. 1973.

57. Didcot, CR 469.

58. W.Indies and Brazil Sub-Committee Minute Book 4, p. 251, minutes for 23 Mar. 1973.

59. Interview with Rev. D. W. Doonan, 5 Sept. 1990.

By 1973 the Paraná Baptist Convention had a membership of 13,000, distributed among 100 churches and a further 300 congregations and preaching points. The churches were still growing, but now at a much slower rate than in the days of the massive population influx into Paraná. There were now few opportunities for BMS missionaries to be engaged in frontier evangelism: 'the tasks now', reported Ernest Madge after a tour of Brazil in August, 'are consolidation and leadership training'.[60] It was time for the vision of moving beyond Paraná to be fulfilled.

V: Keeping Pace With a Moving Frontier: Expansion Beyond Paraná, 1974-1992

1968 to 1974 were the years of Brazil's 'economic miracle', during which foreign capital and technological expertise fuelled an annual increase in the Gross Domestic Product of ten per cent - more than double the rate achieved by the world's advanced industrial economies at this time.[61] This economic revolution, whilst it did little or nothing to benefit the poorest sectors of the population, accelerated the rate of urbanization and stimulated the second wave of rural migration, away from the populous states of the south-east towards the undeveloped territories of the north and west. The population of Rondônia grew from only 37,000 in 1950 to 100,000 in 1970, reaching about 450,000 by 1976.[62] These new patterns of social and economic life gave fresh urgency to the question of whether the BMS should accept invitations to begin work in states other than Paraná.

The first state convention other than Paraná to issue a formal invitation to the BMS was the Baptist Convention of Amazonas, Acre and Adjacent Territories in February 1968. The Society gave the request considerable prominence through a leaflet, 'Blueprint for Brazil', produced for the Baptist Union Assembly in 1968. A possible advance into Amazonas was a major challenge. It was a vast territory, previously undeveloped, but now rapidly being opened up by government investment and road-building. In 1968 there were only twenty-two Baptist churches, served by eighteen pastors.[63] H. F. Drake made a brief visit to Manaus, the state capital, in

60. Didcot, CR 466, Report on General Overseas Secretary's Visit to Jamaica, Trinidad and Brazil.

61. *Brazil: State and Struggle* (Latin American Bureau, London, 1982), 47.

62. T. Beeson and J. Pearce, *A Vision of Hope: The Churches and Change in Latin America* (London, 1984), 83.

63. Didcot, 'Blueprint for Brazil' (1968).

1971, but was unable to make contact with any representative of the State Convention. However, the following year Roy Deller attended the Amazonas State Convention meetings. The Convention (now comprising thirty churches) covered the territories of Rondônia and Acre as well as Amazonas, and Deller was able to visit Porto Velho, capital of Rondônia, and Rio Branco, capital of Acre. Deller was impressed by the opportunities created by the two great roads which were being constructed to encourage population movement into the Amazon region: the trans-Amazonian highway, to stretch from the cities of the north-east to Peru in the west; and a second highway running northwards from Cuiabá, capital of Mato Grosso, to Santarem in Para. Deller wrote an enthusiastic report on his trip for the *Missionary Herald*, suggesting that the Amazon basin had a 'tremendous future in terms of population movement, perhaps greater than anything we have yet seen in Brazil and the challenge to the Church of Jesus Christ is obvious'.[64]

Ernest Madge, sent out to Brazil the following year to advise the Society on the strategic development of the mission, endorsed Deller's view of the opportunities in the north, but saw the continuing call to enter Mato Grosso as an even higher priority. As a result, the Society resolved in October 1973 to appoint missionaries to Amazônia by 1975, to work with both the Mato Grosso and the Amazonas State Conventions. In Mato Grosso, the focus was now clearly on the fast developing northern half of the state, rather than, as in the mid-1960s, on the south. In Amazonas, Porto Velho was identified as the most promising initial location. Both initiatives were seen as part of an overall strategy of following the mainstream of human migration northwards from Paraná, through Mato Grosso to the Amazon basin.[65] In January 1974 H. F. Drake met leaders of both the Mato Grosso and Amazonas Conventions at the National Convention meetings in Brasília, and was able to report continuing enthusiasm for co-operation with the BMS.[66]

The first BMS missionaries to settle in Mato Grosso, John and Yvonne Pullin, arrived in Cáceres, a town of some 140,000 people west of Cuiabá, in October 1974. There was already a Baptist church with a membership of 347, but the majority of these were located in eight daughter congregations scattered at distances of up to 235 kilometers from Cáceres itself. John

64. *MH* (Sept. 1972), 140-2.

65. Didcot, CR 466; W. Indies and Brazil Sub-Committee Minute Book 5, p. 11, minutes for 11 Oct. 1973.

66. Didcot, CR 470, Report on Associate Overseas Secretary's Visit to Brazil 6 Jan.-1 Feb. 1974.

Pullin was given responsibility for these eight congregations, and their associated preaching points.[67] The Pullins experienced a number of difficulties in their work, and returned to the United Kingdom on completion of their third term of service in 1978. Despite these initial problems, the Society increased its commitment of personnel to Mato Grosso. Peter and Susan Cousins began work at Cuiabá in 1978. In 1979 Stuart and Georgie Christine were sent to Jaciara, to nurture the development of the five mission centres of the Baptist church, in a town which grew from 14,000 to 20,000 during the three years of their residence there. Similar work was undertaken by David and Irene McClenaghan in Alta Floresta and by the Cousins in Sinop, both new towns on the route of the Cuiabá/Santarém highway. A Bible institute was opened at Cuiabá in February 1980 under the principalship of David Doonan. The old state of Mato Grosso had been divided in January 1979 into two - Mato Grosso to the north and Mato Grosso do Sul to the south. The early BMS work was in the north, under the auspices of the Center of America Baptist Convention, formed after the division of the state.[68] The more established churches of Mato Grosso do Sul did not require foreign missionaries for church planting work, but in 1980 they asked the BMS for help in staffing the Baptist Theological Faculty at Campo Grande, opened in March, and in initiating a programme of lay training by extension. John and Norma Clark moved to Campo Grande in October 1982; John taught in the Faculty and pastored a local church.

The Society's declared objective of sending missionaries to Rondônia was not fulfilled so rapidly. It was 1979 before the first BMS couple, John and Maria Dyer, settled in Porto Velho for a six-month period of orientation, after which they moved to Vilhena, where John assumed the pastorate of a small congregation. It was a lonely assignment, which left the Dyers many miles from British or Brazilian Baptist colleagues. The Amazonas Convention had been divided in 1976, to form the Amazonas/Roraima and Rondônia/Acre Conventions. The partnership into which the BMS entered in 1979 was thus with the Rondônia/Acre Convention, a group of sixteen churches, thirteen of which were less than ten years old. The Amazonas/Roraima Convention, however, tended to feel that the Society had yet to redeem its promise made in the days of the undivided Convention in 1973 to send missionaries to Amazonas. The BMS remained sympathetic

67. Didcot, CR 493, Report on Rev. H. F. Drake's Visit to Brazil, 29 July-25 Aug. 1975.

68. Didcot, CR 523, Report of Rev. H. F. Drake's Visit to Brazil, Trinidad, and Jamaica, 8 Jan.-1 Mar. 1979.

to the prospect of entering the state, but resolved in 1983 to inform the Convention of the 'unlikelihood of help from us over the next five years'.[69] Whilst the BMS presence in Rondônia was well established by 1992, the possibility of entering Amazonas itself remained unrealized.

1974 - the year in which the BMS moved into Mato Grosso - also saw the beginnings of a BMS presence in the vast metropolis of São Paulo. The Society had lost a number of missionaries from the Brazil field because of difficulties in finding suitable education for their children. São Paulo had an English-medium school, St Paul's, which provided a good education to 'O' Level standard. The Society accordingly decided to open a hostel for missionaries' children in São Paulo, and a property in the Vila Sônia district of the city was purchased in 1974. Clifford and Lottie Parsons were the first house-parents. Those who served in this capacity were inevitably confronted with the desperate social and spiritual needs of the *favelas*, the shanty towns which mushroomed in and around São Paulo in response to the city's burgeoning industrial development. In 1979 the growing numbers of missionary children compelled the Society to buy another house in São Paulo. The house-parents, Frank and Dorothy Vaughan, had time and opportunity to devote themselves to work in the *favelas*. By 1981 the growing involvement of both the Vaughans and John and Norma Clark (in charge of the main hostel) in work in the *favelas* had led the Society, at the invitation of the executive secretary of the State Convention, to consider appointing missionaries specifically to this urban ministry.[70] Accordingly in 1982 the Vaughans were set aside for a new evangelistic role in one of the São Paulo *favelas*. Over the next decade, BMS personnel were allocated to work among the urban poor, not merely in São Paulo, but also in Curitiba (which had grown to a city of over one million inhabitants by 1981) and Campo Grande. Increasingly these ministries had a social as well as an evangelistic dimension. In Campo Grande Frank and Peggy Gouthwaite and Margaret Swires helped the State Convention to set up a community programme, known as the 'Baptist House of Friendship', dedicated to meeting the needs of the slum areas of the city.

In the course of the 1980s, the geographical spread of BMS work in Brazil expanded enormously from the original concentration in Paraná. In 1985 Roy and Margaret Deller returned to Brazil to the southern state of Rio Grande do Sul, to teach in the seminary at Porto Alegre. The Baptist community in Rio Grande do Sul was relatively weak and small (about

---

69. Didcot, CR 572, Policy Guidelines for Brazil (1983).

70. Overseas Sub-Committee Minute Book 1, p. 193, minutes for 19 Feb. 1981.

4,000 in 1990), a weakness which reflected the high proportion of the population whose origins were German or Italian, with a traditional but largely nominal commitment to the Lutheran or Roman Catholic Church. Most communities in Rio Grande do Sul were also settled and long-established, and hence less responsive to the evangelical Protestant message.[71]

By 1986, of the forty-eight BMS personnel in Brazil, only twelve were in Paraná - the remainder being located in São Paulo, Mato Grosso, Mato Grosso do Sul, Rondônia, Rio de Janeiro, and Rio Grande do Sul.[72] Recent geographical expansion by the Society has been into the poorest part of Brazil, the north-east, where two couples in 1991 were serving in Rio Grande do Norte and Ceará. Some BMS missionaries continued to work in Paraná - mainly in theological education or in the less developed areas, such as the Litoral. Others have exercised urban ministries which have combined church work with community involvement, such as Gerry and Johan Myhill, who have served continously at Nova Londrina since 1975. However, the coming years are likely to see a further shift in the concentration of BMS personnel away from Paraná to the more northerly states, and also to the extreme south: in November 1990 the BMS accepted an invitation to work with the Santa Catarina Baptist Convention. The Society has also played an increasing role in partnership with the World Missions Board of the Brazilian Baptist Convention: two BMS missionaries, Eric Westwood and David Brown, have served in the Board's headquarters in Rio de Janeiro, and in 1991 the Society began to provide financial support for Brazilian Baptist missionary work in Guyana.

By 1991 the strictly limited experiment initiated in 1953 had grown to the second largest BMS field, with fifty-nine serving missionaries. Victor Hayward's vision of a mission which should exemplify 'the spontaneous expansion of the church' had been amply fulfilled. British Baptist missionaries had played an increasing part in the life of the Brazilian Baptist Convention, whose membership had grown from 152,649 in 1955 to approximately 700,000 in 1991.[73]

VI: Baptists in the Brazilian Context: Church Growth and Social Justice

The growth of the Brazilian Baptist community needs to be seen against the backcloth of the rapid expansion of Protestantism as a whole, not merely

71. Interview with Rev. R. and Mrs M. Deller, 18 Sept. 1990.

72. Didcot CR 601, Report on Brazil and the Caribbean, 1986.

73. Read and Ineson, *Brazil 1980*, 68.

in Brazil, but also in many other parts of Latin America. David Martin estimates that in the late 1980s twenty per cent of the Brazilian population of 150 million was Protestant.[74] Baptist churches have flourished most readily among the middle ranks of Brazilian society, and especially among the frontier settler towns of the newly developed parts of the country. Independent-minded people who have embraced the challenges and op-portunities of migration have proved peculiarly open to the Protestant message. As the rate of population movement into Paraná tailed off in the 1960s, Baptist growth slowed also, while simultaneously accelerating in the newly expanding states further to the north. On a national scale, however, the indications are that the rate of Baptist church growth has been declining since the mid-1960s. One recent evangelical critic of Brazilian Baptist life predicted a stagnating future for the denomination unless Brazilian Baptists shifted their primary focus from the shrinking lower-middle class to the urban poor.[75]

The fact that Baptists have been markedly less successful than the Pentecostals in penetrating the poorest areas of Brazil's mushrooming cities is attributable partly to the greater reliance of the Pentecostal churches on lay leadership. Probably even more significant has been the general resist-ance of the Brazilian Baptist Convention to charismatic manifestations of Christianity. In a society still profoundly influenced by the spiritism inherited from the African past of the slave population, those varieties of Christianity which have appeared to offer guaranteed spiritual power and uninhibited emotional release from the realities of sickness and poverty have exerted the greatest appeal. Tensions within the Brazilian Baptist Convention on charismatic issues led to the exclusion in 1965 of some 165 churches, which then formed the National Baptist Convention. As British Baptist life in the 1970s and 1980s was increasingly influenced by the charismatic renewal, some BMS missionaries, although having no desire to duplicate the Pentecostal formula for church life, found the tendency to formalism within the Brazilian Baptist Convention a source of frustration. More recently, there have been signs of a more open attitude in the Convention to alternative styles of Christian worship.[76]

74. Martin, *Tongues of Fire*, 50.

75. G. Cook, *The Expectation of the Poor: Latin American Basic Ecclesial Communities in a Protestant Perspective* (Maryknoll, 1985), 219-20.

76. Interviews with Rev. A. Ferreira, 23 Mar. 1987, and Rev. R. and Mrs M. Deller, 18 Sept. 1990.

Fear of anything which appeared to depart from the classic hallmarks of Protestant worship (as understood within the Southern Baptist tradition) was one example of that limitation of theological and ecumenical perspective among Brazilian Baptists which, from the beginning, the BMS had recognized and sought to ameliorate: in 1956 Arthur Elder had expressed the hope that BMS missionaries in Brazil would act as a 'catalytic agent to break through the spirit of isolationism' evident among Brazilian Baptists.[77] In a context where almost all Baptist converts have come from a background at least nominally Catholic, the tendency to regard 'Christian' and 'Catholic' as mutually exclusive categories has proved an enduring one. Baptists in Brazil have been slow to perceive the magnitude of the changes which have transformed the face of the Catholic Church since the mid-1960s. Baptist understanding of the Catholic faith has been shaped by the folk Catholicism of the masses, permeated as it still is by spiritism and a superstitious devotion to the saints, rather than by the reforming orthodoxy of the ecclesiastical hierarchy. In particular, the radical social Catholicism pioneered by Dom Helder Camara in the 1950s, and now exemplified by the 100,000 or more *comunidades eclesiais de base* (basic Christian communities), is a development with which Brazilian Baptists have yet to come to terms.[78]

Baptists, like most other Brazilian Protestants, have been generally a-political in their thinking. At times of political or social upheaval, their leaders have tended to support the *status quo*, which has most frequently meant the political right. After the military coup of 1964, when the urban middle classes, fearful of a national slide towards 'Communism', lent their support to the overthrow of President João Goulart, the President of the Brazilian Baptist Convention presented the new military ruler, General Castelo Branco, with a New Testament. It was a gesture which inevitably acquired political significance, even if none were intended. In 1965 the Brazilian Baptist Convention (at the same assembly which expelled the charismatic churches) voted to close down its committee on social action.[79] The increasingly repressive character of the Brazilian military regime in the late 1960s and 1970s attracted little comment or criticism from Brazilian Baptist leaders. Some British Baptists deplored their silence, and called for the BMS also to make a more explicit commitment to solidarity with the

77. Didcot, CR 96, 'Brazil, Land of the Future'.

78. For an analysis of the various layers of Brazilian Catholicism, see T. C. Bruneau, *The Church in Brazil: the Politics of Religion* (Austin, Texas, 1982).

79. Interview with Rev. D. G. Winter, 9 Aug. 1990; see Beeson and Pearce, *A Vision of Hope*, 84.

Brazilian poor. In 1978 Derek Winter submitted a paper to the General Committee on 'Theology of Liberation and the Baptist Missionary Society', calling for the Society to put 'greater emphasis on the Word in action'. One of Winter's suggestions was for the BMS to consider further expansion out of prosperous Paraná, and face the new frontier of the huge urban sprawls - a proposal that was largely acted on during the 1980s.[80] Since his return from Brazil, Winter has become well-known as a sympathetic writer and commentator on Latin American political theology. A BMS promotional film on church growth in Mato Grosso - 'The Spreading Flame' - was criticized in the correspondence columns of the *Missionary Herald* in 1983 for its lack of concern for economic, political, or ecological issues. Subsequent letters from Brazil missionaries and the Society's officers defended the film as an accurate portrayal of Baptist work in Mato Grosso, and explained that the BMS could no longer expect to dominate the thinking of its partner churches, in this or in any other respect.[81]

In the course of the 1980s Brazilian Baptist leaders placed growing emphasis on the importance of social concern within the witness of the Church. The gradual process of *abertura* (opening-up to democracy) in Brazil's political life - culminating in 1989 in the first democratic presidential election for three decades - encouraged a cautious but significant opening up of Brazilian Baptists to the social dimensions of the Christian message, even though Baptist attitudes to liberation theology remained overwhelmingly negative. In January 1990 the Brazilian Baptist Convention established a junta for social action, whose stated aims included the interpretation to society and political authorities of 'the principles of Christian justice, solidarity and love, with the purpose of establishing a social order that guarantees the well-being and fulfilment of the human race'.[82] Although radical observers of the Brazilian Christian scene continue to complain of the political indifference of Brazilian Protestants, the gap in perception of the social implications of the gospel between Brazilian church leaders and their British missionary partners is now considerably less broad than once it was. In Paraná certainly, and possibly in other states also, British Baptist influence, mediated through the BMS and the British Baptist colleges where gifted Brazilian pastors have studied, has made a contribution to the degree of social awakening that has taken place in the

80. Didcot, CR 513.

81. *MH* (Dec. 1983), 237; (Mar. 1984), 56-7; (June 1984), 116-17.

82. Information from Rev. F. W. J. Clark, 2 Jan. 1991.

Brazilian Baptist Convention.[83] As the level of theological education available to the Brazilian pastors continues to rise, it may be expected that the social responsibility of the Church will occupy an increasingly high place on the Brazilian Baptist agenda.

83. Interview with Rev. D. W. Doonan, 5 Sept. 1990.

XVI

The Domestic Life and General Policy of the Society, 1962-1992

I: A New Context for Global Mission

The thirty years of the Society's life between 1962 and 1992 witnessed a fundamental transformation in the global context within which Christian mission was conducted. Throughout the previous history of the BMS, it had been possible to conceive of the missionary enterprise as an essentially one-way flow of personnel, funds and ideas from a broadly Christian Western world to a broadly non-Christian non-Western world. Both the theology and the practice of the Christian attempt to bridge this gulf between two worlds were ultimately fashioned by Westerners (although indigenous Christians had always done most of the spade-work of evangelism in the mission fields). In Protestant circles, the contours of thinking about mission were set by the boards of the historic denominational missionary societies, which found their collective voice in the International Missionary Council. All this missionary activity took place within a political context in which the supremacy of the European or North American - exercised either through formal colonial rule or through the more subtle mechanisms of cultural hegemony - was only rarely challenged and never wholly overturned.

By the mid-1960s these previously stable features of the missionary landscape had all but disintegrated under the impact of new political, cultural and religious forces. The end of the Western colonial era had been heralded by the nationalist and Communist revolutions of the 1940s and 1950s in Asia - but in Africa in the mid-1950s it still seemed to most missionaries no more than a distant possibility. Yet by 1965 the process of decolonisation was virtually complete across the African continent. Missionaries in Africa, no less than their colleagues in Asia, now found themselves, as chapter fourteen has indicated, exposed to the chill winds of nationalist sentiment and political upheaval.

It was not, however, the political context alone that had changed. The 1960s were a decade of cultural crisis in Europe and North America. Student revolution, repudiation of traditional authority, and an enthusiastic adoption of secular norms of thinking and behaviour were among the distinguishing marks of the age. This cultural radicalism found its theological counterpart in the construction of 'secular' and 'Death of God' theologies, which proclaimed the demise of the old supernaturalism. Ultimately more significant within world Christianity was the decisive shift from Western to non-Western dominance, in terms of the sheer numbers of Christians, the vitality of church life, and also global ecumenical politics. The integration of the International Missionary Council (IMC) within the World Council of Churches at the New Delhi assembly of the WCC in 1961 contributed to the shift in the balance of power. No longer could Western missionary statesmen construct their own independent strategies for the Church in the non-Western world. Rather, within the WCC, Third-World church leaders became increasingly vociferous in demanding an end to dependence on Western resources and Western theology. The tendency to brand Western missionary activity as an accomplice of the now discredited Western colonialism combined with the current questioning of all theological certainties to produce a widespread lack of confidence in the missionary imperative as traditionally understood. The new radicalism most clearly broke surface at the fourth assembly of the WCC at Uppsala in 1968, where even experienced ecumenical leaders such as Bishop Lesslie Newbigin were saddened by the anger and confusion which surrounded discussion of the Church's mission.[1] The transition from a traditional understanding of mission primarily in terms of missionary-led proselytism towards a new emphasis on mission as the task of the whole Church, with humanization as its central objective, was symbolized by the statement of the Bangkok conference of the WCC's Commission on World Mission and Evangelism in January 1973 that 'we have seen the end of one missionary era; we are beginning a new one in which the idea of world mission will be fundamental'.[2]

---

1 . L. Newbigin, *Unfinished Agenda: An Autobiography* (London, 1985), 231-2.

2 . E. Castro, 'Bangkok, the New Opportunity', *International Review of Mission* LXII, 246 (April 1973), 140.

II: Continuing Mission in a Transformed World

The effect of these profound changes in the context and interpretation of Christian mission was less immediately apparent in the BMS than in other strands of the Protestant missionary movement. The conservative theological alignment of most British Baptists ensured that a commitment to seeking conversion to Christ as the central goal of missionary activity remained undiminished in the churches, and hence also in BMS committees. A document on 'Future Policy' presented to the General Purposes sub-committee in May 1973 by Ernest Madge (who succeeded Victor Hayward as General Foreign Secretary in 1959) began with a trenchant statement that 'Our Lord's command "Go ye into all the world and preach the Gospel" comes to us down through the years as clear and as compelling as on the day He first issued it'.[3] Nevertheless, the Society could not remain indifferent to the changing context and emphases of Christian world mission. Whilst BMS policy documents in the 1960s and 1970s emphasized the continuing applicability of the evangelistic imperative deriving from the command of Christ, they also took great pains to help those whose theological perspective remained essentially conservative to perceive the radical changes which had taken place in the nature of the missionary task. In the spheres of ecumenical relationships, partnership with overseas churches, and the scope and theology of mission, the Society faced new and demanding challenges in this period.

Through its participation in the Conference of British Missionary Societies (CBMS) and the IMC, the BMS had been consistently exposed to the ecumenical mainstream of thinking on mission. The incorporation of the IMC within the WCC (a step which the BMS had, after considerable debate, supported)[4] inevitably raised questions about whether the CBMS should continue as a separate body from the British Council of Churches (BCC). The response of the BMS Officers to this proposed extension of the principle of integration was, however, very cautious. They expressed the fear in 1965 that integration might place the BMS in an invidious position by driving a sharper wedge between 'ecumenical' and 'evangelical' mission organizations and that the Society could suffer from too direct an association with the WCC, in view of the perceived 'growing concern' that missionary affairs in the World Council were receiving 'less and less attention'. Anxiety was also expressed that integration of the CBMS within the BCC might lead to the Society's representatives in a new BCC mission

---

3 . Didcot, CR 460A, Future Policy.

4 . *BMS Annual Report*, 1961-2, p. li.

department being nominated by the Baptist Union of Great Britain and Ireland.[5] In fact, progress towards integration proved slow. It was 1973 before the CBMS committed itself to the explicit goal of integration, and 1978 before the goal was achieved. The CBMS became a division of the BCC as the Conference on World Mission, of which the BMS remains a member.

Under Victor Hayward's leadership in the 1950s, the BMS had already been alerted to the implications for mission of Communism, nationalism, and decolonisation. The rapid transfer of control from mission to church in the Congo in 1960, followed in India after 1965 by the sharp reduction in the size of the BMS missionary presence and the withdrawal of missionaries from major administrative roles, transformed the nature of BMS work in its two largest fields. From now on, the Society defined its role increasingly as one of partnership with the overseas churches in their own missionary responsibility. Two themes in particular recurred with some regularity in committee discussions: the role of the BMS in supporting church institutions overseas and the problem of providing pastoral care for missionaries.

Particularly in India, the partner churches of the BMS inherited from the missionary era high-quality medical and educational institutions which they valued highly but were incapable of supporting from local resources. Naturally the churches looked to the BMS for substantial block grants to enable these institutions to survive. The Society responded sympathetically and generously, but with growing unease about the wisdom of perpetuating forms of Christian witness which re-inforced financial dependency. Thus Ernest Madge (whose period as India Field Secretary from 1954 to 1959 had given him first-hand experience of the problem) concluded a discussion of this topic in his 1973 paper on future policy with the statement: 'The day of large institutions linked with churches is coming to an end and we should help the overseas churches to find other ways of expressing Christian compassion, which they can support from their own resources'.[6] In practice, this goal proved hard to achieve. In July 1982 the Society found it necessary to clarify its policy on the support of overseas institutions: they were to be seen as servants of the churches, not as their masters; they should exist to serve the wider community, not merely the interests of church members; and they should be integrated as far as possible with government pro-

5 . Didcot, CR 358, Memo on CBMS/BCC Relationship in the Light of IMC/WCC Integration.

6 . Didcot, CR 460A, Future Policy.

Alberic Clement, Editorial Secretary of the BMS, 1952-62; Home Secretary, 1962-82.

Ernest G.T. Madge, Missionary in China, 1935-51 and India, 1951-9; General Foreign Secretary of the BMS, 1959-76.

R.G.S. Harvey, General Secretary of the BMS, 1982-

Angus T. MacNeill, Missionary in Zaire, 1960-73; Overseas Secretary of the BMS, 1982-

grammes, rather than competing with them. It followed that the Society's limited resources would be applied selectively to a limited number of institutions in accordance with these principles.[7]

Until the 1960s, BMS missionaries looked to senior colleagues on their stations and ultimately to the Field Secretary for their pastoral care. The transfer of power to autonomous national churches removed from missionaries any automatic voice in the making of policy on the field and placed them, at least in theory, in the same relationship to their local national pastor as that experienced by indigenous church members. As was observed in chapter fourteen in relation to Zaire, some missionaries found the new arrangements for pastoral care inadequate.[8] Western and non-Western conceptions of the role of the pastor were frequently found to be at variance. Missionaries whose problems consisted precisely in the nature of their relationship to the indigenous church had no-one at hand who could provide experienced and independent counsel. Partly as a result of the changing profile of the foreign missionary, which made missionary roles more specialised and temporary in nature, and partly in response to the cultural shift within Western society from long-term to short-term vocational and personal commitment, the average length of field service in the BMS (as in other missions) declined markedly. In consequence, there were now far fewer experienced missionaries on the field to smooth the path of younger colleagues, particularly in a field like Zaire, where distances were vast and transport poor.

These problems first became a major concern of the Society during the period of office of H. F. Drake as Overseas Secretary (1975-82).[9] It is probable that the deficiencies were felt most acutely by the growing proportion of the Society's missionaries from the 1970s onwards who had been influenced by the charismatic movement in Britain, with its emphasis on close, supportive and intimate fellowship. The fact that pastoral care - especially in Zaire or Bangladesh - did not always correspond to this model caused disappointment. A study commissioned by the Society in September 1989 reported that the breakdown of relationships with the national church was the third most common cause of resignation from the Society's service (behind family and health reasons) during the thirty years from 1959 to

---

7 . Didcot, CR 559, Continuing Support for Church Institutions.

8 . See above, ch. XIV, p. 465.

9 . Didcot, CR 489 and 534, two papers on Pastoral Care of Missionaries (1975 and 1980).

1989.[10] The transformation in the status and professional role of the foreign missionary during the last thirty years has been profound. The BMS, in common with all mission organizations, has had a number of emotional and psychological casualties as a result.

Awareness of the deficiencies of current provision for the pastoral care of missionaries was a primary factor behind the Society's decision in 1980-1, as part of the re-structuring of the secretariat then in process, to appoint three regional representatives for Brazil and the Caribbean, Africa, and Asia, to be resident within their region.[11] Although objections from the CBFZ made it impossible to proceed with the intention to appoint a regional representative for Africa,[12] the other two representatives have exercised a crucial role in pastoral guidance as well as in other ways.

One of the more significant missiological trends apparent from the early 1960s onwards was an explosion of Christian interest in issues of world development, agriculture and alternative technologies. Programmes to raise the standard of living of rural populations by agrarian or simple technological innovation won an assured place in mission strategy among a wide theological spectrum of mission agencies. Specifically agricultural mission work within the BMS was pioneered by David Stockley in what is now Bangladesh from 1952.[13] By 1961 the Society had four missionaries engaged primarily in agricultural work. In that year the Baptist Men's Movement launched the 'Operation Agri' project, whose initial object was to provide tools, seeds and livestock for the use of BMS agricultural missionaries.[14] Whilst supported particularly by men's organizations in Baptist churches, Operation Agri has exerted a wider influence in making British Baptists more aware of the place of agricultural development within contemporary Christian mission, notably by means of the annual harvest thanksgiving appeals, whose proceeds have been divided between Operation Agri and the direct support of the Society's agricultural missionaries. In 1982 the scope of Operation Agri was broadened to include all aspects of rural development.

10 . Didcot, CR 699, Report of the Working Group on Missionary Resignations.

11. The pattern for such regional representatives resident on the field had already been set by the appointment in 1977 of A. Brunton Scott as representative for Brazil and the Caribbean. Didcot, CR 540 and 550, Reports of the General Purposes Sub-Committee on the Secretariat (Nov. 1980 and July 1981.

12. See above, ch. XIV, p. 465.

13 . See above, ch. XIII, p. 406.

14 . *BMS Annual Report*, 1961-2, p. xlviii; K. W. Bennett, *Men in the Service of God: Seventy Years of the Baptist Men's Movement* (London, 1987), 38-9; M. Putnam, *The Story of Operation Agri 1961-1990* (n.d, n.p.).

Operation Agri was one example of the greater willingness of British Baptists from the 1960s onwards to adopt a more holistic approach to mission. To some extent this trend reflected the prominence of socio-political issues in ecumenical thinking about mission, but from the 1970s it was a trend shared increasingly by all parts of the denomination, as evangelicalism as a whole broadened its understanding of the place of social responsibility in Christian mission. The Evangelical Alliance Relief Fund (TEAR Fund), founded in 1968, attracted widespread support from the more conservative churches within the denomination. Although BMS work benefited from TEAR Fund grants, the popularity and novelty of TEAR Fund, and of other Christian relief agencies, to some extent diverted funds and enthusiasm from Operation Agri and the BMS.

A further sign of the current ferment in thinking about mission was the fact that in 1989 the BMS General Committee issued a lengthy theological statement on mission which could serve, not as a basis of faith, but as an indication to the Society's partner churches and other mission agencies of its essential understanding of the missionary task.[15] Even in the most conservative of the Free Church denominations in Britain, a ready consensus on the meaning and scope of Christian mission could no longer be assumed.

III: The Leadership of the Society

The complexity and rapidity of change in the landscape of world mission in this period placed an exceptional premium on the quality of leadership provided by its senior secretaries. Those who served as Home Secretary had in some ways an even harder task than their colleagues who held the overseas portfolio, for to them fell the challenge of interpreting the missiological revolution to British Baptists in ways that did not cut the nerve of the popular missionary enthusiasm on which the financial survival of the Society depended.

J.B. Middlebrook was succeeded on his retirement in 1962 by A.S. Clement, who had served the BMS since 1952 as its editor. Alberic Clement was by background a pastor with strong interests in education. While minister of Hearsall Baptist Church in Coventry between 1944 and 1952, he had served on the city's Education Committee. Appointed on Middlebrook's initiative as the Society's editor in succession to H.L. Hemmens, Clement retained the full confidence of his superior. As

15 . Didcot, CR 653, Statement on Mission.

Middlebrook's successor after 1962, he maintained many of his policies, particularly with regard to relations with the Baptist Union of Great Britain and Ireland. Initially Clement shared responsibility for the home life of the Society with a promising young accountant, Bruce Glenny, who was appointed as a third senior secretary and designated 'Finance Secretary'. Glenny demonstrated great potential for re-shaping the administrative structure of the Society. However, he was suddenly taken ill and died in 1963. The short-lived experiment of a triumvirate of senior secretaries was abandoned.[16] The disruption caused by Glenny's illness and death was compounded by the tragic discovery in 1964 that the Society's recently retired and long-serving accountant had been guilty over the years of a systematic fraud which had cost the BMS approximately £18,000.[17] Alberic Clement proved himself capable of surmounting these formidable obstacles. He was an able administrator who demonstrated a sharp mind, sound judgment and caustic wit in committee discussions. He was also widely respected in Baptist World Alliance circles. Although his detailed inside knowledge of the Society was a great asset, he had less flair than his predecessor in the pulpit or on the platform. Alberic Clement's contribution to the BMS was not primarily in the public sphere: one of his more significant achievements from the historian's standpoint was to ensure that the Society's archives were more adequately housed and cared for.[18]

Ever since 1912, the BMS had been led by a team of two senior secretaries of equal status, one responsible for the overseas work and one for home affairs.[19] The advisability of this arrangement, which had not been without its difficulties, was debated in 1974-5, when Ernest Madge was approaching retirement. It was, however, decided to perpetuate the system of two joint-secretaries during the term of office of Madge's successor as Overseas Secretary, H. F. Drake.[20] By 1980, with the prospect of both senior secretaries approaching retirement in 1982, it was possible and appropriate

16 . W. M. S. West, *To Be a Pilgrim: A Memoir of Ernest Payne* (Guildford, 1983), 121; *BMS Annual Reports*, 1961 -2, p. 8; 1963-4, pp. 7-8; Didcot, J. B. Middlebrook papers.

17 . The accountant had been in the Society's service since 1924. *BMS Annual Reports*, 1963-4, p. 44; 1964-5, p. 49; Didcot, J. B. Middlebrook papers.

18 . Didcot, J. B. Middlebrook papers.

19 . This statement requires two qualifications. Between 1925 and 1946 the Medical Secretary and Women's Secretary possessed in theory (but not in practice) equal status to the Home and Foreign Secretaries. In 1962-3 Bruce Glenny as Finance Secretary was given equal status to Madge and Clement.

20 . Didcot, CR 478A, Report of the General Purposes Sub-Committee on the Retirement of the General Overseas Secretary and its Consequences.

for the question to be reviewed in a more fundamental way. The General Purposes sub-committee, influenced by clear advice from the world of business management that to have one person in overall control was preferable, recommended a new administrative structure for the Society, in which leadership would be exercised by a General Secretary, assisted by a Deputy General Secretary. It was envisaged that one of the two senior secretaries would be a person primarily of home experience, and the other more experienced in foreign affairs, but there was no stipulation as to which of the two should be General Secretary. A further dimension to the proposals was the intention to appoint three regional (or overseas) representatives with responsibility not only for the pastoral care of missionaries but also for the cultivation of closer links with the partner churches.[21]

These proposals were endorsed by the General Committee, and at the BMS annual meeting in 1981 it was agreed to appoint two senior secretaries in accordance with this new management structure. The then chairman of the Society, R. G. S. Harvey, was appointed as General Secretary from April 1982. Reg Harvey, pastor of Rugby Baptist Church since 1972, had wide experience of BMS committees, having served in particular as chairman of the Candidates' Board. The Society appointed as Overseas Secretary (and Deputy General Secretary), Angus MacNeill, formerly Field Secretary in Zaire, and currently pastor of Kilmarnock Baptist Church. These two new senior appointments were to be assisted by a team of eight assistant secretaries, with responsibilities for personnel, finance, administration and promotion, and by the proposed overseas representatives.[22]

The leadership team appointed in 1982 proved stable and harmonious, and remained in place as the Society reached its bicentenary. The new administrative structure gave the BMS the benefit of a more coherent, forceful and innovative lead from the top, although perhaps at the price of over-loading the two senior secretaries with administrative tasks.

IV: The Society and its Domestic Constituency

During the nineteenth century, and arguably also for the first two decades of the twentieth, the BMS was the principal force unifying British Baptists. The symbolic role of the Society as the body which brought together the relatively diverse elements of English, Welsh and Scottish Baptists (plus a small number from Ireland) in a common enterprise was at

21 . Didcot, CR 540, Report of the General Purposes Sub-Committee on the Secretariat; General Committee Minutes, 4 Nov. 1980, p. 24.

22 . Didcot, CR 557, Report on the Secretariat (Mar. 1982).

its strongest between the fusion of the BMS and the General Baptist Missionary Society in 1891 and the early 1920s. These were years, as was seen in chapter twelve, in which missionary enthusiasm was at its peak, denominational identity was strong, and the claims of the BMS for the support of Baptist church members were warmly received. However, the theological tensions within evangelicalism which surfaced in the early 1920s had long-term implications for the Society. Although the unity of the BMS was preserved in 1922, from that date onwards the tendency strengthened for the conservative evangelical wing of the denomination to support interdenominational evangelical missions alongside, or even instead of, the BMS.

The global ecumenical developments of the 1950s and 1960s, and the profound changes in missiology which we have noted, had the effect of widening the divergence within British Protestantism between 'conservative evangelicals' and those of broader theological inclination. A further factor, which acquired enormous significance for all aspects of Baptist life in the 1970s and 1980s, was the marked weakening of traditional denominational loyalties among the younger generation in Baptist churches, leading to what the Society's annual report in 1988 termed 'a crisis of Baptist Denominational identity'.[23] The resurgence of conservative evangelicalism in the student world, and among the churches generally, together with the impact of the charismatic renewal movement, diluted traditional Baptist allegiance and increased the appeal of interdenominational missions with a strong evangelistic emphasis.[24] It was also the case that in the post-colonial period, the spiritual horizons of much of British Christianity narrowed, so that all missionary advocates now faced a much harder task than before. Thus the BMS found itself in an increasingly competitive market-place when seeking to raise missionary support in the churches, and it was in this respect that the absence from the Society's staff in the 1960s and 1970s of an outstanding communicator of the mission cause began to tell. The Society was not helped by the fact that, with the notable exception of Brazil, its fields were of a long-established kind, and hence less obviously marked by an emphasis on pioneer evangelism than were the fields of service of some of the newer conservative evangelical missions.

The cumulative effect of these trends on the BMS was two-fold. Firstly, opinion within the General Committee strengthened in favour of an increase in the relatively small proportion of the Society's resources previ-

---

23 . *MH* (May 1988), 30.

24 . The background of British evangelicalism in this period is most ably treated by D. W. Bebbington, *Evangelicalism in Modern Britain* (London, 1989), chs. 7-8.

ously devoted to promotion. The traditional reliance of the BMS on the good-will of ministers and the voluntary service of secretaries of missionary auxiliaries was, in the judgment of some members of General Committee, no longer adequate to meet the changed demands of the age.

The BMS had employed one full-time representative in Wales since 1916 (and subsequently appointed a second Welsh representative) and one such agent in Scotland since 1937. The possibility of appointing full-time paid area representatives for England (as other missions had done) was considered by the Home Organization sub-committee in 1976, but rejected by the majority.[25] Nevertheless, in the following year the Society appointed Vivian Lewis to the new post of Assistant Secretary for Promotion, with responsibility for 'devising co-ordinated and integrated schemes of approach to the churches'.[26] In 1979 the General Committee agreed to make a serious exploration of the possibilities of appointing area representatives on either a full-time or a part-time basis.[27] The next year saw the appointment of the first full-time area representative in England, when Roy Turvey was appointed to the North-West region, on a five-year experimental basis. The review of this experimental appointment in 1985 concluded that the Society ought to invest more heavily in paid promotional agency; five more area representatives were accordingly appointed, to cover the rest of England.[28] The work of the six area representatives was reviewed in 1989, and a decision taken to continue their employment for a further five years.[29]

A second consequence of the trends outlined above was that the BMS in the 1960s and 1970s came to be perceived by some churches in the more conservative wing of the denomination as too liberal in its theology and yet too traditional in its methods and structures. Specific questions from conservative evangelicals about the theological stance of the Society were raised comparatively rarely, although there was a continuing undercurrent of disquiet, notably in the 1970s, about the nature of the ecumenical theological training given to the Society's candidates at Selly Oak in Birmingham, where the separate institutions of Carey Hall for women and St Andrew's College for men had been amalgamated in 1966 to form St Andrew's Hall.[30]

25 . General Committee Minutes, 6-7 July 1976, p. 31.

26 . General Committee Minutes, 29 Mar. 1977, p. 2.

27 . General Committee Minutes, 28 Mar. 1979, p. 7.

28 . Didcot, CR 594, Report of Working Group on Area Representatives and Promotion.

29 . Didcot, CR 669, Working Group: Review of Area Representatives.

30 . See, for example, General Committee Minutes, 28 Mar. 1973, p. 16; 6 Nov. 1973, pp. 52-5; 27 Mar. 1974, pp. 10-13; 2 July 1974, p. 23. The questions over St Andrew's

More characteristic were complaints that the BMS had lost its cutting edge of evangelistic vision, and had become cumbersome in its committee structures. A paper submitted in 1978 by Lesley Partridge, one of the Society's young people's secretaries, attempted to explain why the BMS had, on the whole, 'such a bad image with young people', and identified in response the self-defeating nature of appeals to the younger generation to support their denominational society, the tendency of committee procedures to stifle initiative and spontaneity, and the unexciting nature of BMS promotional literature.[31] A similar note was struck by a memorandum submitted to the General Committee in 1984 by a group of ten Scottish ministers, which compared the BMS unfavourably with interdenominational mission agencies in terms of their ability to communicate to church members a vision of the continuing need for pioneer evangelism.[32]

Comments of this kind were made, not so much by those who were fundamentally unsympathetic to the Society, but more often by those who wished to see the BMS more widely and enthusiastically supported but had been frustrated in their efforts. Those who held a conservative evangelical position continued to support the BMS in large numbers, and, as their influence in the churches grew, supplied an increasing proportion of the missionary force. The level of candidate applications considered by the Candidates' Board remained fairly consistent throughout this period, and indeed rose from a mean of 24.5 per annum in the 1960s to 26.3 in the 1970s, before falling again to 22.5 in the 1980s.[33] The sustained ability of BMS voluntary income over these thirty years to keep pace with constantly escalating overseas expenditure was a further indication of the continuing strength of commitment to the Society in the churches; in comparison with other denominational mission organizations, the BMS, although certainly not free from deficits, maintained a relatively stable financial position.

The 1980s in fact saw determined efforts by the BMS to modernize its image and procedures. The standard of promotional literature was improved enormously, increased resources were devoted to the production of

Hall were partly financial in nature, in view of the fact that at any one time there might be only 2 or 3 BMS candidates training in an institution which received substantial BMS funding.

31 . Didcot, CR 516A, 'The Way Forward'.

32 . Didcot, CR 589.

33 . Figures compiled from Candidates' Board minutes by Miss K. Tubbs. It should be noted that candidates were often persuaded to withdraw an application before appearing at the Candidates' Board. Thus these figures may not reflect accurately trends in initial applications.

films, videos and other forms of audio-visual communication, and effective use was made in promotion of those who exerted wide influence among Baptist young people, such as the evangelist, Steve Chalke. Two major attempts were made to overhaul the long-standing system of deputation agency, which in some respects still adhered to a nineteenth-century pattern. Increasingly this model had been felt to be unsatisfactory, as churches competed for the services of a limited number of missionaries on furlough. In January 1988 the method of the deputation system was changed: instead of churches taking the initiative in requesting deputation speakers for their own independently arranged meetings, the Society now offered teams of speakers to different areas of the country in a co-ordinated fashion. A more radical departure was introduced in 1991, with the replacement of the deputation system altogether by a new concept known as 'World Mission Link', which emphasized the cultivation of a long-term two-way relationship between a missionary or missionary couple and a group of local churches.[34] The change symbolized a recognition that the classic nineteenth-century model of the returned missionary touring the country to drum up support in public meetings and gatherings was no longer applicable in the more privatized cultural environment of the late twentieth century.

In 1988 the committee structure of the Society was radically simplified in an attempt to minimize the amount of time devoted to routine business and promote more meaningful involvement in policy-making by the members of the General Committee: the number of permanent committees was reduced to four, with *ad hoc* working groups being set up to accomplish specific tasks as occasion demanded.[35] Perhaps inevitably, the BMS still finds it difficult to attract enough young lay church members to the General Committee (which comprises some 140 elected members) to make it genuinely representative of current Baptist church life. There is a sense in which the BMS finds itself torn between its characteristicallly Baptist conviction that the government of the Society should to the maximum possible extent be accountable to the representatives of the churches, and the more pragmatic reflection that large and diverse committees are notoriously inefficient as agents of policy-making.

There is little doubt that over the decade before its bicentenary the BMS made considerable progress in up-dating its image. If an image problem still

34 . Didcot, CR 686, Draft Proposals on New Deputation Patterns.

35 . Didcot, CR 634, Report and Recomendations of the Working Group on Committee Structures. The four surviving committees were the General Committee, General Purposes and Finance Committee, Candidates' Board, and Officers' Committee.

remained to some extent, it was in large measure the consequence of being a long-established denominational organization in an increasingly undenominational and unhistorical Christian generation. The Society also shared the difficulty faced by all contemporary mission organizations which now had to communicate the message that the days were over when Western missionary societies could partition the continents between them into spheres of ecclesiastical influence. In the nature of the case, the partnership approach to global mission does not arouse the same intensity of popular enthusiasm as the heroic mood of the nineteenth-century pioneers, on whose efforts the eternal destiny of the heathen was believed to depend. The challenge which confronts the Society today is how to convince British Baptists that the global mission of the Church, although it can no longer be presented as the prerogative of Western Christians alone, remains an inescapable spiritual imperative no less urgent than it was in the days of William Carey.

V: New Fields of Service

Between 1986 and 1992, the BMS entered six new fields of service, either through the direct input of missionary personnel or through other forms of co-operation - France, Thailand, El Salvador, Nicaragua, Belgium and Italy. These new openings should be interpreted, not as marking a return to a Victorian pattern of unilateral missionary expansion, but as the outcome of a widespread feeling within the Society in the mid-1980s that a partnership approach to world mission should not exclude an openness to fresh geographical initiatives. Although these initiatives were not greeted with universal enthusiasm in the Baptist constituency (for example, some questioned whether Europe was a proper object of the Society's endeavour), the sense that the BMS was seizing fresh mission opportunities played its part in raising morale within the Society as it approached its bicentenary.

The Society's return to its former field in France had its origins in a fraternal visit made in May 1985 to the Federation of Evangelical Baptist Churches of France by the BMS chairman and General Secretary, together with three representatives of the Baptist Union of Great Britain and Ireland. The trip was a return visit for one made to Britain in 1982 by representatives of the Federation, and was an expression of the wider sense of fellowship experienced within the European Baptist Federation.[36] The 1985 visit made it clear that the French Federation - an expanding group then comprising some seventy-five Baptist churches - was open to the possibility of co-

---

36 . The European Baptist Federation was founded in 1950.

operation with the BMS.[37] A subsequent visit to Paris by Angus MacNeill in March 1986 led to a firm invitation from the Federation to the BMS to give assistance, particularly through the provision of pastors with a vision for church-planting.[38] A formal convention between the Federation and the Society was signed in December 1986. The first BMS missionary couple, John and Sue Wilson, left for language training in France in September 1988. By 1992 the Society had three couples working with the Federation, and a fourth in prospect.

Just as the Society's return to France arose out of the confessional fellowship of the European Baptist Federation, the entry of the BMS into Thailand had its origins within the global confessional family of the Baptist World Alliance (BWA).[39] In this case, however, the opening arose in response to an active quest by the Society's Officers for an appropriate new field of service, and reflected in particular the contacts made by the General Secretary as a member of the BWA Council and its Conference of International Mission Secretaries. Conversations with American, Australian and Swedish Baptist mission leaders at the Baptist World Alliance Congress at Los Angeles in 1985 indicated that there was scope for the BMS to join these existing Baptist mission agencies in working with various church groups in Thailand.[40] A visit to Thailand in May-June 1986 by Angus MacNeill and the BMS Asia representative, Neil McVicar, identified a number of possible spheres in which BMS personnel might usefully operate under the auspices of the Thailand Baptist Missionary Fellowship (TBMF), a body formed in 1974 to co-ordinate the work of American and Australian Baptist missionaries under the auspices of the ecumenical Church of Christ in Thailand (CCT). The TBMF had subsequently broadened the scope of its work to include co-operation with various Baptist groups not in membership with the CCT; missionaries from the Baptist Union of Sweden had also joined the Fellowship in 1976. In November 1986 the General Committee gave approval to the principle of BMS involvement in Thailand, thus opening the way for specific church groups associated with the TBMF to issue definite invitations to the Society.[41] As a result, the first BMS missionary, Jacqui Wells, who had

37 . Didcot, CR 599, Report on Visit to France, May 16th/19th, 1985.

38 . Didcot, CR 607, Translation of Letter Sent by Pasteur André Thobois.

39 . The Baptist World Alliance was formed in 1905.

40 . The American Baptist mission concerned was the Board of International Ministries of the American Baptist Churches.

41 . *MH* (Jan. 1987), 3; General Committee Minutes, 5 Nov. 1986, p. 20.

served the Society for a number of years in Bangladesh, arrived in Thailand in November 1988 to work with the Karen Baptist Convention, which linked together fifty-four churches among the tribal Karen people in the north of the country. A missionary couple, Geoffrey and Christine Bland, followed early in 1989, to assist the CCT church in the Udon Thani district.

In contrast to France or Thailand, the origins of BMS work in El Salvador lie, not directly in confessional contacts within the global Baptist family, but in the personal convictions of a young Baptist minister, David Mee. Mee's interest in the war-torn country of El Salvador was first aroused by the assassination of Archbishop Oscar Romero of San Salvador in March 1980, and was fanned into more active commitment by the visit to Britain in 1982 of a Salvadorean Baptist church worker, Marta Benavides.[42] Two years later, Mee visited El Salvador and formed a resolve to work there in the future. Mee's personal interest led by degrees to full corporate involvement by the BMS in 1987. Following a visit to El Salvador in April-May 1987 by Angus MacNeill, the General Committee agreed in August to accept the invitation of the El Salvador Baptist Association to work in the country. Mee returned to El Salvador as a BMS missionary in 1988 to serve in Sensuntepeque, the capital of Cabañas province.

Amidst the bitter civil war between the American-backed government and military of President Alfredo Cristiani and the *Farabundo Martí de Liberacion Nacional* (FMLN) guerrillas, Salvadorean Baptists were adopting a wide variety of political stances, ranging from firm support for the government to clear sympathies with the guerrillas' objectives. Increasingly, however, Christian appreciation of the justice of the FMLN cause was drawing upon the churches and humanitarian organizations savage and undiscriminating repression by the army. On 5 April 1989 a Baptist teacher in San Salvador, María Cristina Gomez, was taken from her school by gunmen and shot dead, presumably because she had, amongst other political concerns, agitated on behalf of persons who had 'disappeared' at the hands of the authorities. The news of the shooting gave added force to a prepared resolution passed two weeks later at the BMS annual members' meeting as part of the Baptist assembly at Leicester. The resolution called on the government of El Salvador to respect human rights and pursue peace and reconciliation at all levels of society.[43]

In November 1989 there was a sudden and unprecedented escalation in the civil war. An offensive by the FMLN against San Salvador was met by

42 . *MH* (Sept. 1987), 176.

43 . *MH* (June 1989), 130-1.

heightened military oppression, culminating on the night of 16 November in the murder of six Jesuit priests sympathetic to the guerrilla cause, their housekeeper and her daughter. The deteriorating situation led to an urgent request to Brian Tucker, the chairman of the Society, and David Martin, its Assistant Overseas Secretary with responsibility for Central America, to visit El Salvador. Tucker and Martin's report on their brief visit painted a sombre picture of 'systematic persecution of many church and humanitarian groups' and of widespread oppression of the poorest sections of the community by the government forces. They returned to Britain in December bearing a promise to do all they could to alert Christian opinion in Britain to the reality of events in El Salvador.[44] The January 1990 *Missionary Herald* devoted several pages to 'El Salvador - the Struggle for Justice' in what was possibly the most politically outspoken edition of the magazine since the Angolan crisis of 1961.[45] The high profile given by the Society to what was a very small field in terms of numbers of BMS personnel helped ensure that parts of the British Baptist constituency developed a greater awareness of human rights issues in Central America, although Baptist concern never attained the dimensions which it did over Angola in 1961.[46] It must also be said that there were other BMS fields - notably Sri Lanka - where widespread contemporary violations of human rights failed to arouse the same degree of concern amongst Baptists in Britain.

More recently still, the door opened for the Society into a second Central American state. Exploratory visits to Nicaragua in 1989 by John Clark from Brazil and in February-March 1990 by David Martin (who had taken over the Central America portfolio from Clark) led to the BMS signing a partnership agreement with the Nicaragua Baptist Convention.[47] The Society received invitations to supply the Convention with medical doctors and a co-ordinator for the Managua Baptist Theological Seminary. Whilst it is too early to predict the precise nature of the role which the Society will play in Nicaragua, there can be no doubt that the partnership agreement was concluded at a critical point in the nation's history, following the years

44 . Didcot, CR 666, Report on the Visit of Rev. Brian Tucker and Rev. David Martin to El Salvador, 27 Nov. to 3 Dec. 1989.

45 . *MH* (Jan. 1990), 2-8. The magazine went to press before David Martin's report was available.

46 . In 1991 the BMS had two couples in El Salvador: David and Rachel Quinney Mee, and James and Sue Grote.

47 . General Committee Minutes, 28 Mar. 1990, p. 7; Didcot, CR 670 and 712, Reports on Visits to Central America by David Martin, 19 Feb.-7 Mar. and 20 Nov.-5 Dec. 1990; *MH* (May 1991), 28-9.

of civil war between the Sandinista government and the Contra rebels, and the electoral overthrow of the Sandinista government in February 1990 by Violeta Chamarro's multi-party coalition.

The partnership agreement between the BMS and the Union of Baptists in Belgium, concluded in 1990, and the multilateral understanding reached in 1991 between the Society, the Baptist Unions of Great Britain, Wales and Scotland and the Union of Evangelical Christian Baptists in Italy provided further evidence of the readiness of the Society to explore new avenues of missionary opportunity.[48] More fundamentally, the variety of constitutional arrangements established in this period between British Baptists and their partners in continental Europe also indicates something of the difficulty which now confronted the BMS and the three British Baptist Unions in defining the nature of their mutual relationship. The resumption by the BMS of activity in Europe was one of the stimuli forcing the issues of the constitutional basis of the Society and its relationship to other Baptist denominational structures to the head of its agenda for the 1990s.[49]

VI: The BMS, the Baptist Unions and Future Patterns of Christian Mission

At the BMS annual members' meeting in 1961 J.B. Middlebrook moved and Ernest Payne seconded a resolution giving the General Committee authority, jointly with the Baptist Union of Great Britain and Ireland, to build or acquire premises which would be suitable for the joint headquarters of the two bodies. A similar resolution was passed at the Baptist Union Council, moved by Payne and seconded by Middlebrook.[50] The objective which had come so close to being realized in 1938 was thus still very much on the agenda of both Baptist organizations. Early in 1965 negotiations took place with a view to a possible re-development of the site of Beechen Grove Baptist Church in Watford for the purposes of a joint headquarters building, together with new church premises. However, a joint meeting of the General Purposes committees of the BMS and BU resolved not to proceed with the Watford project. The site was not large enough, there was a strong inclination to remain, if possible, in London, and the fundamental

---

48 . On Belgium see *MH* (Aug. 1990), 16 and (July 1991), 14; also General Committee Minutes, 26-27 June 1990, p. 17. On Italy see above, ch. VII, p. 222.

49 . Didcot, CR 672, A Response to Europe, by A. T. MacNeill (Mar. 1990).

50 . *BMS Annual Report*, 1960-1, p. 8; West, *To Be a Pilgrim*, 120.

will to proceed was insufficiently widely held.[51] Further discussions between the BMS and the BU took place in 1966-7, but proved inconclusive. In the provinces, there was a considerable body of feeling in favour, not just of the idea of joint headquarters, but also of progress towards actual integration. The Northamptonshire Baptist Association sought an assurance in January 1967 that the BMS General Committee and the Baptist Union Council were 'working towards an organic integration of the two bodies', and encouraged its churches to raise funds jointly for the BU and BMS.[52]

The climate of opinion in the denomination in favour of a closer relationship between the BMS and the three Baptist Unions, together with pressure from the Scottish Baptist Union for parity of status with the Baptist Union of Great Britain and Ireland, led to a joint meeting of the officers of the four bodies in October 1967. The officers agreed that regular meetings of their number would be valuable as a means of fostering mutual understanding and trust.[53] The resulting series of meetings between the officers of the four bodies led in February 1971 to the establishment of a joint consultative committee, made up of the officers and two representatives of each body.[54] This committee has had an unbroken history since 1971. There has been some limited participation also by the Irish Baptist Union. The joint consultative committee became increasingly important as a forum in which matters of common denominational concern and issues of relationship between the four bodies could be discussed. Three dimensions of these relationships warrant particular discussion in terms of their implications for the BMS over the two decades prior to 1992.

The first was the resumption in the 1980s, and prosecution to a successful outcome in 1989, of the search for joint headquarters between the BMS and the Baptist Union of Great Britain and Ireland.[55] The fact that what had previously proved a fruitless quest now proved possible was evidence that the ghost of the 1938 débacle had finally been laid to rest and that the delicacy which had characterised the relationship between the BMS

---

51 . West, *To Be a Pilgrim*, 141-2; General Committee Minutes, 29 April 1965, p. 25; Didcot, CR 382, Joint Headquarters Report.

52 . General Committee Minutes, 18 Jan. 1967, p. 12; 5 July 1967, p. 40.

53 . Didcot, CR 391, paper for General Committee (Jan. 1968).

54 . Didcot, Joint Consultative Committee Draft Minutes, 2 Feb. 1971. In 1990 the membership of the committee was reduced to three representatives of each body.

55 . In 1988 the title was changed to the Baptist Union of Great Britain.

and the BU in the 1950s was largely a thing of the past.[56] The warmer relationships between the two bodies in the 1980s were founded on the close personal friendship and mutual trust which existed between Reg Harvey as General Secretary of the BMS and Bernard Green as Secretary of the Union from 1982 to 1991. The search for suitable premises was no more straightforward than on previous occasions - indeed, as late as May 1988 it seemed that a site in the King's Cross area of north London was destined to be the new Baptist headquarters.[57] However, later that year purpose-built new office premises in Didcot, Oxfordshire, became available. On 18 October 1988 a joint meeting of the BMS General Committee and the Baptist Union Council (the first such meeting ever held) voted by large majorities of both bodies to purchase the freehold of the Didcot premises.[58] In August 1989 the Society and the Union moved to occupy their new joint headquarters in Didcot. No longer could the relationship between the BMS and its younger partner be complicated by the potential for misunderstanding or poor communication which even a few miles of geographical distance can create.

The second aspect of British Baptist affairs in the twenty years up to 1992 which possessed special relevance for the BMS was the growing concern within the denomination about the challenge to Christian mission within Britain posed by the extremely large communities of people of non-Western ethnic origin. Some members of General Committee, especially those who resided in areas with substantial non-Western populations, began to question the clause in the BMS constitution limiting the Society to work beyond the British Isles.[59] The question was first fully debated in the General Purposes sub-committee and General Committee in June 1978, but arguments were put against the removal of the limiting clause, notably by Alberic Clement, who saw the clause as a necessary safeguard of the Society's independence, clearly demarcating the respective spheres of the BMS and the Baptist Unions.[60] However, during the 1980s advocates of the removal, or at least modification, of the clause became more numerous. In 1990 the Society set up a working group to consider whether any change in the stated object of the Society was desirable, with particular reference to

---

56 . See above, ch. XII, pp. 386-8.

57 . *MH* (May 1988), 31.

58 . General Committee Minutes, 18 Oct. 1988, pp. 24-5; *MH* (May 1989), 18-19.

59 . For the origins of this clause see above, ch. VII, pp. 215-17.

60 . General Committee Minutes, 28 June 1978, p. 16; Didcot, CR 516, Work among People in the British Isles.

the words 'beyond the British Isles'.[61] As a result of recommendations made by the working group, the General Committee in October 1991 agreed that the time had come for an entirely new definition of the object of the Society to be drafted. Various attempts were made at a revised wording which would express the idea that the task of making known the gospel of Jesus Christ was one to which British Baptist churches were called in common with all God's people. Although no final agreement was reached in October 1991 on a form of words to be submitted to the 1992 annual meeting for approval, it was agreed that the future object should include the phrase 'principally beyond the British Isles'.[62]

At its annual meeting in April 1992, the Society obtained agreement on a new statement of its object which contained the phrase 'principally beyond the British Isles'. In its bicentennial year, the BMS thus decided to revert to the original geographical emphasis which governed its work in the days of Andrew Fuller. As was the case before 1815, the BMS has again become an institution which maintains a primary commitment to the spread of the gospel overseas whilst also being ready to respond appropriately to mission opportunities within Britain.

A third relevant dimension of the British Baptist scene in the 1970s and 1980s was the forging of increasingly strong relationships between the Baptist Unions (especially the Baptist Union of Great Britain and Ireland) and Baptist unions and conventions overseas. The heightened activity of the Baptist World Alliance and its affiliated federations established global confessional ties which led the Baptist Unions, as well as the BMS, to speak the language of partnership in Christian mission across international frontiers. As has been seen, the forging of relationships between national Baptist bodies within Europe posed the issue particularly sharply: what was the rationale behind the renewed involvement of the Society as an autonomous body in France, when elsewhere in Europe bilateral relationships of partnership were being developed between the Baptist Union and its continental counterparts? Discussions of this question within the joint consultative committee led to the conclusion in January 1990 that the involvement in Europe of the BMS and the UK Baptist Unions should be seen as complementary rather than mutually exclusive.[63] This assumption of complementarity of relationships was reflected in the subsequent agreements concluded with the Belgian and Italian Baptist Unions.

61 . Minutes of the Working Group on the Object of the Society, 17 Dec. 1990.

62 . General Committee Minutes, 29-30 Oct. 1991.

63 . Didcot, CR 672, A Response to Europe; Joint Consultative Committee Minutes, 17 Jan. 1990.

At the joint consultative committee meeting in January 1990 the BMS and the three Baptist Unions acknowledged the need to

> affirm a structure that will enable them to cooperate together with some federal understanding of how to relate to the needs of Baptist churches in other countries and of how to benefit in turn from the insights and gifts of these Churches.[64]

Discussion within the committee in 1990-1 hence focused on the possibility of moving towards some form of federal linkage between the three Baptist Unions in the United Kingdom and the BMS. It may be anticipated that under such an arrangement, recognition would be given to the Society's status as the primary channel through which the Baptist churches represented by the Unions engage in overseas missionary partnerships. Differences between the three Unions in size, national identity and theological outlook mean that a federal outcome cannot be assumed. What is undeniable, however, is that the BMS, as an autonomous voluntary society born in the days when national Baptist denominational structures were virtually non-existent, now desires to express its relationship to the three unions of Baptist churches in a new and more ecclesiologically coherent fashion.

As the Society approached its bicentenary, it faced major issues of objective and orientation arising both from the domestic and from the global context. Of even greater significance than the discussions about the relations of the BMS with the Baptist Unions within the United Kingdom was the question of to what extent, and in what way, the voice of the Society's partner churches should be heard at the point of policy-making in Britain. This was one of the questions discussed in August 1990, when fourteen leaders of the BMS partner churches in Bangladesh, Brazil, El Salvador, India, Jamaica, Sri Lanka, Thailand and Zaire met with Reg Harvey and Angus MacNeill in Seoul, Korea, prior to the sixteenth Baptist World Alliance Congress. The consultation ranged widely in its exploration of ways in which the concept of a multilateral partnership of giving and receiving of resources within a common missionary endeavour might become a reality amongst this global family of Baptist churches. Specifically, the consultation recommended that a small international group be formed, representing all the partner churches and the BMS itself, with

---

64 . Joint Consultative Committee Minutes, 17 Jan. 1990.

powers to allocate financial and human resources made available to the group by its constituent churches and bodies.[65]

To a limited extent, the vision expressed at Seoul of mutuality in mission was already a reality by 1992. Gifted pastors from the partner churches had for some years been awarded BMS scholarships for further study in Britain. In addition to the benefit they and their churches have received from their studies, they have been able to share with British Baptists something of the cultural insights and vibrant experience of non-Western Christianity. BMS funds were also beginning to be used to assist the partner churches in their own cross-cultural evangelistic activity. The Society began to give financial help to a missionary from the Zoram Baptist Mission (the missionary agency of the Baptist Church of Mizoram) working in Thailand. Following a request from the Zoram Baptist Mission in October 1990, it is likely that this pattern will be reproduced more widely through BMS support of the Mission's work outside India. Similarly, in 1991 the BMS undertook a major share of the financial support of a Brazilian couple, serving with the World Mission Board of the Brazilian Baptist Convention in Guyana.[66]

Thus, within the final decade of its bicentenary, the pace of change in both the geographical scope and the character of the work of the BMS quickened considerably. It seems likely that the bicentenary of Britain's oldest evangelical missionary society will prove to be more than a purely symbolic landmark. The Society was born in an era of turbulent political change, in which the political geography of much of the Western world was re-constituting itself into radically new patterns. Today the Baptist Missionary Society is called to proclaim the gospel of Jesus Christ in a world whose political and ideological contours are changing no less markedly. William Carey would have interpreted such turbulence as a sign that God was about to do 'great things' in and through the historical process, and hence as a call to the Church to attempt 'great things' for God. In an age which, like Carey's, views the very idea of Christian mission with puzzlement or derision, his successors face no less a challenge in seeking to follow the path of missionary obedience.

---

65. Didcot, CR 698, Report on Special Consultation at Seoul, Korea; *MH* (Oct. 1990), 3-4; *MH* (May 1991), 29.

66. Didcot, CR 709, Co-operation in Mission; *MH* (Nov. 1991), 18-19.

Select Bibliography

1. **Manuscript and archival sources**
Note: The sources given below list the records which have been used directly in the writing of the history. They do not represent an exhaustive list of all relevant archival material. In particular, researchers of the early years of the Society should note the list of MS sources contained in E. Daniel Potts, *British Baptist Missionaries in India 1793-1837,* Cambridge, 1967.

1.1 **Oxford, Regent's Park College, Angus Library**

(i) **Baptist Missionary Society archives** (a large collection which will not be listed in detail here. The footnotes indicate which sections of the archives have been most useful in the writing of the history. All unpublished material referred to in the footnotes is to be found in the archives unless otherwise indicated). The archives now contain the following sets of family papers:
Bushill Papers:
Circular letters from, and diary of P. N. Bushill.
F. G. Harrison papers:
Photocopies of diaries, notebooks and logbook of   F. G. Harrison.

(ii) Letters of William Carey to Jabez Carey, 1814-32.

(iii) Typed transcripts of letters from Andrew Fuller to various correspondents (Ref. 4/5/1).

1.2 **Didcot, Baptist House**

(i) Current records of the Baptist Missionary Society (these are not normally available to researchers; a 30-year bar is in operation; material older than 30 years is mostly to be found in the archives in the Angus Library).

(ii) J. B. Middlebrook papers (in possession of the General Secretary of the BMS).

(iii) Joint Consultative Committee minutes, 1971-92.

1.3 **Birmingham, Selly Oak Colleges Library**
MS letters of Robert Hall to John Ryland, 1791-1824.

1.4 **University of York, Borthwick Institute of Historical Research**
W. D. Grenfell papers, box GR3 and microfilm 66.

1.5 **Bottoms MS (in possession of Professor A. E. Bottoms, Cambridge).**
J. W. Bottoms, "'I'd no idea": A Study of Medical Missionary Work',
unpublished MS.

1.6 **A. C. Elder papers** (in possession of Rev. D. G. Winter, Bredwardine,
Herefordshire; to be deposited in BMS archives)
Correspondence of A. C. Elder with V. E. W. Hayward and E. G. T.
Madge, and miscellaneous Brazil papers.

1.7 **F. J. Grenfell papers** (in possession of Rev. F. J. Grenfell, Nottingham)
Personal and BMS papers on Angola.

1.8 **P. J. Manicom, 'Light and Shadows in Congo'**
(unpublished MS in possession of Mrs J. Manicom, Nottingham).

1.9 **H. W. Spillett papers** (in possession of Mr A. H. Spillett, New Addington,
Croydon, Surrey)
MS autobiography of H. W. Spillett.

1.10 **F. Stainthorpe papers** (in possession of Rev. F. Stainthorpe, Willenhall,
West Midlands)
Personal diary of Rev. F. Stainthorpe for July 1960.

1.11 **West Croydon Baptist Church archives, West Croydon, Surrey**
Deacons' minutes and *West Croydon Baptist Magazine* for 1921.

1.12 **C. E. Wilson family letters** (in possession of Mrs E. M. Vicary, Princes
Risborough, Buckinghamshire)

1.13 **D. G. Winter papers** (in possession of Rev. D. G. Winter, Bredwardine,
Herefordshire)
Correspondence of D. G. Winter with V. E. W. Hayward and E. G. T.
Madge.

1.14 **India, West Bengal, Calcutta, Lower Circular Road Baptist Church
archives**
Minutes of Church Meetings, 1819-present day (5 vols.).

1.15 India, West Bengal, Serampore College archives
Serampore College Council minutes, 1931-48.

1.16 India, Orissa, Cuttack diocesan archives
Minutes of the Utkal Baptist Central Church Council, 1938-53.
Minutes of the Utkal Christian Central Church Council, 1953-70.
Annual reports of diocese of Cuttack, 1970-.

1.17 India, Orissa, Berhampur Christian Hospital archives
Berhampur station committee minutes, 1938-47.
Hospital managing committee minutes, 1943-61.
Christian Hospital Berhampur: Souvenir Programme, November 4th, 1967.

1.18 Bangladesh, Dhaka, Bangladesh Baptist Sangha archives
Minutes of the Bengal Baptist Union, 1932-46.

1.19 Zaire, Kinshasa, Omedis-Nlemvo Centre de Santé
Wathen (Ngombe Lutete) church roll, 1889-1904.
Wathen (Ngombe Lutete) church meeting minutes, 1895 -1907 (3 vols., in Kikongo).

1.20 Zaire, Ngombe Lutete, CBFZ pastor's office
Wathen (Ngombe Lutete) station minutes, 1900-25. (pp. 307-21 contain J. S. Bowskill's MS, 'Notes on the "Prophet" movement').
Wathen (Ngombe Lutete) church meeting minutes, 1908-.
Miscellaneous correspondence.

1.21 Zaire, Mbanzu Ngungu, CBFZ pastor's office
Kibentele church minute book, 1918-59 (in Kikongo).
Thysville (Mbanza Ngungu) church minute book, c. 1919-54 (in Kikongo).
Wathen (Ngombe Lutete) station minutes, 1925-53.

1.22 Zaire, Yakusu, CBFZ pastor's office
Yakusu log book, 1923-38.
'Recent correspondence on Congo affairs between the BMS and the Belgian Colonial Minister', 1911.

1.23 Zaire, Upoto, CBFZ pastor's office
Upoto station minutes, 1936 to present day.
Log book of Upoto-Pimu station, 1955-82.
Typescript log for 1-23 Aug. 1964.
Baptist Church of the Upper River at Upoto and Binga: Annual Report, 1964.

1.24 Zaire, Pimu Hospital archives
Letter from S. G. Browne to S. Henderson-Smith, 1 July 1954.
Annual Reports on Pimu Hospital.

2. Newspapers and periodicals

The Baptist Annual Register (ed. J. Rippon)
Baptist Magazine
Baptist Missionary Society: Annual Reports
Baptist Missionary Society: Directory and Financial Reports
Baptist Quarterly
Baptist Revival Fellowship Bulletin
Baptist Times
Baptist Union Directory
Baptist Zenana Mission: Annual Reports
Church Union News and Views
Evangelical Magazine
The Freeman
The Friend of India
General Baptist Missionary Society: Annual Reports
General Baptist Repository and Missionary Observer (continued as *General Baptist
        Magazine, Repository and Missionary Observer,* later as *General Baptist Magazine*)
The Guardian
Indian Reports of the Orissa Baptist Mission (continued as *Baptist Missionary Society
        Orissa Reports*)
Juvenile Missionary Herald
Ladies' Association...in connexion with the Baptist Missionary Society: Annual Reports
Missionary Herald (for most of the nineteenth century this was bound as a
        supplement to the *Baptist Magazine,* and is cited accordingly)
Parliamentary Debates (Hansard)
Periodical Accounts relative to the Baptist Missionary Society
Yakusu Notes

3. Previous General Histories of the Society

Amey, Basil, *The Unfinished Story: A Study-Guide History of the Baptist Missionary
        Society,* Baptist Union of Great Britain, 1991.
Cox, F. A., *History of the Baptist Missionary Society, from 1792 to 1842,* 2 vols.,
        London, 1842.
Lord, F. Townley, *Achievement: A Short History of the Baptist Missionary Society
        1792-1942,* London, n.d. [1942].
Myers, J. B., ed., *The Centenary Volume of the Baptist Missionary Society 1792-1892,*
        London, 1892.

4.   Books, articles and unpublished theses

4.1   The Origins and Early Domestic History of the Society to 1815

> **Note:** biographical studies of Carey and other early India missionaries appear under section 4.2 on the Indian sub-continent.

Amey, Basil, 'Baptist Missionary Society radicals', *BQ* 26 (1975-6), 363-76.

Anderson, Hugh, *The Life and Letters of Christopher Anderson,* Edinburgh, 1854.

Bebbington, D. W., ed., *The Baptists in Scotland: A History,* Glasgow, 1988.

Brown, Raymond, *The English Baptists of the Eighteenth Century,* London, 1986.

Carey, S. P., *Samuel Pearce, MA: the Baptist Brainerd,* London, n.d.

Carey, William, *An Enquiry into the Obligations of Christians, to Use Means for the Conversion of the Heathens,* facsimile edn., London, 1961.

Clipsham, E. F., 'Andrew Fuller and Fullerism: a study in Evangelical Calvinism', *BQ* 20 (1963-4), 99-114, 146-54, 214-25, 268-76.

Elwyn, T. S. H., *The Northamptonshire Baptist Association,* London, 1964.

Evans, Caleb, *The Kingdom of God,* Bristol, 1775.

[J. Fawcett, junior], *An Account of the Life, Ministry, and Writings of the late Rev. John Fawcett, DD,* London, 1818.

Finnemore, W., *The Story of a Hundred Years 1823-1923: Being the Centenary Booklet of the Birmingham Auxiliary of the Baptist Missionary Society,* Oxford, n.d. [1923].

Fuller, A. G., *The Complete Works of the Revd Andrew Fuller, with a Memoir of his Life,* London, 1841.

Gregory, Olinthus, ed., *The Works of Robert Hall, AM,* 6 vols., London, 1832.

Hayden, R., 'Kettering 1792 and Philadelphia 1814', *BQ* 21 (1965-6), 3-20, 64-72.

Hickman, E., ed., *The Works of Jonathan Edwards, A M,* 2 vols., London, 1834.

Horne, Melvill, *Letters on Missions: Addressed to the Protestant Ministers of the British Churches,* Bristol, 1794.

Ivimey, Joseph, *A History of the English Baptists,* 4 vols., London, 1811-30.

Laws, Gilbert, *Andrew Fuller: Pastor, Theologian, Ropeholder,* London, 1942.

Lovegrove, D. W., 'English Evangelical Dissent and the European conflict', in W. J. Sheils, ed., *The Church and War* (Studies in Church History 20), Oxford, 1983, 263-76.

Lovegrove, D. W., *Established Church, Sectarian People: Itinerancy and the Transformation of English Dissent, 1780-1830,* Cambridge, 1988.

Martin, R. H., *Evangelicals United: Ecumenical Stirrings in Pre-Victorian Britain, 1795-1830,* Metuchen, N.J., and London, 1983.

Morris, J. W., *Memoirs of the Life and Writings of the Revd Andrew Fuller,* London, 1816.

Nuttall, G. F., 'Northamptonshire and the modern question: A turning-point in eighteenth-century Dissent', *Journal of Theological Studies* 16 (1965), 101-23.

Nuttall, G. F., 'Continental pietism and the Evangelical movement in Britain', in J. van den Berg and J. P. van Dooren, eds., *Pietismus und Réveil*, Leiden, 1978, 207-36.

Payne, E. A., *The First Generation: Early Leaders of the Baptist Missionary Society in England and India*, London, n.d. [1936].

Payne, E. A., *The Prayer Call of 1784*, London, 1941.

Payne, E. A., 'Doddridge and the missionary enterprise', in G. F. Nuttall, ed., *Philip Doddridge 1702-51*, London, 1951, 79-101.

Payne, E. A., *The Baptist Union: A Short History*, London, 1959.

Payne, E. A., 'John Dyer's memoir of Carey', *BQ* 22 (1967-8), 326-7.

Ryland, John, *The Work of Faith, the Labour of Love, and the Patience of Hope Illustrated; in the Life and Death of the Reverend Andrew Fuller ...*, London, 1816.

Smith, A. Christopher, 'The spirit and the letter of Carey's catalytic watchword', *BQ* 33 (1989-90), 226-37.

Smith, A. Christopher, 'The Edinburgh connection: between the Serampore mission and Western missiology', *Missiology* 18 (1990), 185-209.

Smith, A. Christopher, 'William Ward, radical reform, and missions in the 1790s', *American Baptist Quarterly* 10 (1991), 218-44.

Steane, Edward, *Memoir of the Life of Joseph Gutteridge, Esq.*, London, 1850.

[Sutcliff, John], *Jealousy for the Lord of Hosts: and, the Pernicious Influence of Delay in Religious Concerns: Two Discourses Delivered at a Meeting of Ministers at Clipstone ... The Former by John Sutcliff of Olney ...*, London, 1791.

Underwood, A. C., *A History of the English Baptists*, London, 1947.

Vickers, John, *Thomas Coke: Apostle of Methodism*, London, 1969.

Ward, W. R., 'The Baptists and the transformation of the church, 1780-1830', *BQ* 25 (1973-4), 167-84.

Wilkin, M. H., *Joseph Kinghorn of Norwich*, Norwich, 1855.

[Wilson, J.], *Memoir of ... Thomas Wilson, Esq.*, 2nd edn., London, 1849.

4:2 The Indian Sub-Continent

Baptist Missionary Society, *Reports and Documents on the Indian Mission, Prepared for the Use of the Committee of the Baptist Missionary Society*, London, 1872.

Belcher, Joseph, *William Carey: A Biography*, Philadelphia, 1853.

Bennett, Clinton, 'A Theological Appreciation of the Reverend Lewis Bevan Jones (1880-1960): Baptist Pioneer in Christian-Muslim Relations', *BQ* 32 (1987-8), 237-52.

Boal, Barbara, *The Konds: Human Sacrifice and Religious Change*, Warminster, 1982.

Bridges, Harold, *The Kingdom of Christ in East Bengal*, Dhaka, 1984.

Brock, William, *A Biographical Sketch of Sir Henry Havelock, K.C.B.*, 4th edn., London, 1858.

Carey, [Esther], *Eustace Carey: A Missionary in India*, London, 1857.

Carey, Eustace, *Memoir of William Carey, D.D.*, London, 1836.

Carey, S. P., *William Carey, D.D., Fellow of Linnaean Society,* 7th edn., London, 1926.

Carey, S. P., *Dawn on the Kond Hills,* London, 1936.

Carey, William, *Thoughts upon the Discussions which Have Arisen from the Separation between the Baptist Missionary Society and the Serampore Missionaries,* Liverpool, 1830.

Carson, P. S. E., 'Soldiers of Christ: Evangelicals and India, 1784-1833', Ph.D. thesis, London, 1988.

Chapman, E., and Clark, M., *Mizo Miracle,* ed. M. Sykes, Madras, 1968.

Charter, H. J., *Ceylon Advancing,* London, 1955.

Chatterjee, S. K., *Hannah Marshman: The First Woman Missionary in India,* Hooghly, 1987.

Chaturvedi, B., and Sykes, M., *Charles Freer Andrews,* London, 1949.

Drewery, Mary, *William Carey: Shoemaker and Missionary,* London, 1978.

Evans, E. W. Price, *Dr George Howells: Missionary Statesman and Scholar,* Baptist Union of Wales, n.p., 1966.

Forrester, Duncan B., *Caste and Christianity: Attitudes and Policies on Caste of Anglo-Saxon Protestant Missions in India,* London, 1980.

French, W. E., *The Gospel in India,* London, 1946.

Gulati, C. J., *Bangladesh: Liberation to Fundamentalism,* New Delhi, 1988.

Hanwella, D. W. M., 'The educational activities of the Baptist Missionary Society in Ceylon 1812-1912', M.A. thesis, Univ. of Ceylon, 1965 (copy in BMS archives).

Hayward, Victor E. W., ed., *The Church as Christian Community: Three Studies of North Indian Churches,* London, 1966.

-         *Historical Sketch of the Baptist Mission in Ceylon; from its Commencement to the Present Time,* Kandy, 1850.

Hminga, H. L., *The Life and Witness of the Churches in Mizoram,* Serkawn, Mizoram, 1987.

Hoby, James, *Memoir of William Yates, D.D., of Calcutta,* London, 1847.

Hodne, Olaf, *L. O. Skrefsrud, Missionary and Social Reformer among the Santals of Santal Parganas,* Oslo, 1966.

Howells, George, *The Soul of India: An Introduction to the Study of Hinduism,* London, 1913.

Howells, George, and Underwood, A. C., *The Story of Serampore and its College,* Serampore, 1918.

Howells, George, et. al, *The Story of Serampore and its College,* Serampore, 1927.

Ingham, Kenneth, *Reformers in India 1793-1833,* Cambridge, 1956.

Ivimey, Joseph, *Letters on the Serampore Controversy, Addressed to the Rev. Christopher Anderson,* London, 1831.

Jones, Lewis Bevan, *The People of the Mosque: An Introduction to the Study of Islam, with Special Reference to India,* London, 1932.

Jones, Lewis Bevan, *Christianity Explained to Muslims: A Manual for Christian Workers,* Calcutta, 1938.

Jones, Violet Rhoda, and Jones, Lewis Bevan, *Woman in Islam: A Manual with Special Reference to Conditions in India,* Lucknow, 1941.

Laird, M. A., *Missionaries and Education in Bengal 1793-1837*, Oxford, 1972.

Lewis, C. B., *The Life of John Thomas*, London, 1873.

Lindell, Jonathan, *Nepal and the Gospel of God*, Kathmandu, 1979.

Malalgoda, K., *Buddhism in Sinhalese Society 1750-1900*, Berkeley, 1976.

Marshall, P. J., *Bengal: The British Bridgehead. Eastern India 1740-1828* (The New Cambridge History of India, II.2), Cambridge, 1987.

Marshall, W. J., *A United Church: Faith and Order in the North India/Pakistan Unity Plan*, Delhi, 1987.

Marshman, John Clark, *The Life and Times of Carey, Marshman, and Ward*, 2 vols., London, 1859.

Marshman, John Clark, *Memoirs of Major-General Sir Henry Havelock, K.C.B.*, 3rd edn., London, 1867.

Marshman, Joshua, *Letters from the Rev. Dr Carey...*, 3rd edn., London, 1828.

Mathew, A., *Christian Missions, Education and Nationalism: From Dominance to Compromise 1870-1930*, New Delhi, 1988.

Mathew, K. V., *Walking Humbly With God: A Biography of the Rev. C. E. Abraham*, Kottayam, 1986.

Mitra, S. K., 'The Vellore mutiny of 1806 and the question of Christian mission to India', *Indian Church History Review* 8 (1974), 75-82.

O'Connor, Daniel, *Gospel, Raj and Swaraj: The Missionary Years of C. F. Andrews 1904-14*, Frankfurt-am-Main, 1990.

O'Donnell, C. P., *Bangladesh: Biography of a Muslim Nation*, Boulder and London, 1984.

Oddie, G. A., *Social Protest in India: British Protestant Missionaries and Social Reforms 1850-1900*, New Delhi, 1979.

Oussoren, A. H., *William Carey, Especially his Missionary Principles*, Leiden, 1945.

Payne, E. A., *South-East from Serampore*, London, 1945.

Peggs, James, *India's Cries to British Humanity*, 2nd edn., London, 1830.

Peggs, James, *A History of the General Baptist Mission*, London, 1846.

Pickett, J. W., *Christian Mass Movements in India*, New York, 1933.

Piggin, Stuart, *Making Evangelical Missionaries 1789-1858: The Social Background, Motives and Training of British Protestant Missionaries to India*, Sutton Courtenay Press, 1984.

Plan of Church Union in North India and Pakistan, 3rd revised edn., Madras, 1957.

Potts, E. Daniel, 'A note on the Serampore Trio', *BQ* 20 (1963-4), 115-17.

Potts, E. Daniel, *British Baptist Missionaries in India 1793-1837: The History of Serampore and its Missions*, Cambridge, 1967.

Report of the Commission on Christian Higher Education in India: An Enquiry into the Place of the Christian College in Modern India, London, 1931.

Reynolds, C., *Punjab Pioneer*, Bombay, 1968.

- *Scheme of Church Union in Ceylon*, 3rd revised edn., Madras, 1955.

Sharpe, Eric J., *Not to Destroy but to Fulfil: The Contribution of J. N. Farquhar to Protestant Missionary Thought in India before 1914*, Uppsala, 1965.

Sharpe, Eric J., *Faith Meets Faith: Some Christian Attitudes to Hinduism in the Nineteenth and Twentieth Centuries*, London, 1977.

Silva, K. M. de, *Social Policy and Missionary Organizations in Ceylon 1840-1855*, London, 1965.

Silva, K. M. de, *A History of Sri Lanka*, London, 1981.

Smith, George, *The Life of Alexander Duff, D.D., LL.D.*, 2 vols., London, 1879.

Smith, George, *The Life of William Carey, D.D. Shoemaker and Missionary*, London, 1885.

Soddy, Gordon, *Baptists in Bangladesh*, Dhaka, 1984.

[Sri Lanka Baptist Sangamaya], *1812-1987: Baptists in Sri Lanka, Heirs of a Noble Heritage*, Sri Lanka Baptist Sangamaya, n.d. [1987].

Stanley, Brian, 'Christian responses to the Indian Mutiny of 1857', in W. J. Sheils, ed., *The Church and War* (Studies in Church History 20), Oxford, 1983, 277-89.

Stennett, Samuel, *Memoirs of the Life of the Rev. William Ward*, London, 1825.

Stewart, W. S., ed., *The Story of Serampore and its College*, Serampore, 1961.

Studdert-Kennedy, Gerald, *British Christians, Indian Nationalists and the Raj*, New Delhi, 1991.

Underhill, E. B., *The Case of the Baropakhya Christians*, London, 1856.

Underhill, E. B., *The Life of John Wenger of Calcutta*, London, 1886.

Underhill, E. B., *Principles and Methods of Missionary Labour*, London, 1896.

United Mission to Nepal: Constitution and Bye-Laws, n.p., 1983.

Weber, H-R, *Asia and the Ecumenical Movement, 1895-1961*, London, 1966.

Wells, D. S., comp., *Ye Are My Witnesses 1792-1942: One Hundred and Fiftieth Anniversary of the Baptist Missionary Society in India*, Calcutta, 1942.

Wenger, E. S., *The Story of the Lall Bazar Baptist Church Calcutta*, Calcutta, 1908.

Wilkins, E. G., *By Hands, Bullocks and Prayers: Building the Moorshead Memorial Hospital Kond Hills, Orissa, India*, n.p., 1987.

Wilson, D. K., *The Christian Church in Sri Lanka: Her Problems and Influence*, Colombo, 1975.

Yates, William, *Memoirs of Mr John Chamberlain*, London, 1826.

4.3 The Caribbean

Barrett, W. G., *Baptist Mission in Jamaica: An Exposition of the System Pursued by the Baptist Missionaries in Jamaica*, London, 1842.

Bolt, C., and Drescher, S., eds., *Anti-Slavery, Religion and Reform*, Folkestone, 1980.

Brewer, Peter D., 'The Baptist churches of South Trinidad and their missionaries 1815-1892', M.Th. thesis, Glasgow, 1988.

Brewer, Peter D., 'British Baptist missionaries and Baptist work in the Bahamas', *BQ* 32 (1987-8), 295-301.

Burchell, W. F., *Memoir of Thomas Burchell*, London, 1849.

Catherall, G. A., 'Thomas Burchell, gentle rebel', *BQ* 21 (1965-6), 349-63.

Catherall, G. A., 'George William Gordon: saint or sinner', *BQ* 27 (1977-8), 163-72.

Catherall, G. A.,'Baptist War and Peace: A Study of British Baptist Involvement in Jamaica 1783-1865', unpublished MS, n.d. [1988], copy in BMS archives.

Cooper, R. E., 'The diary of William Newman - II', *BQ* 18 (1959-60), 275-82.

Curtin, P. D., *Two Jamaicas: The Role of Ideas in a Tropical Colony 1830-1865,* Cambridge, Mass., 1955.

Gamble, W. H., *Trinidad: Historical and Descriptive,* London, 1866.

Gardner, W. J., *A History of Jamaica,* new edn., London, 1909.

Gayle, Clement, *George Liele: Pioneer Missionary to Jamaica,* Kingston, n.d. [1982].

Henriques, F., *Family and Colour in Jamaica,* 2nd edn., London, 1968.

Hinton, J. H., *Memoir of William Knibb,* London, 1847.

Holmes, E. A., 'George Liele: Negro slavery's prophet of deliverance', *BQ* 20 (1963-4), 340-51, 361.

Jakobsson, Stiv, *Am I not a Man and a Brother? British Missions and the Abolition of the Slave Trade and Slavery in West Africa and the West Indies 1786-1838,* Uppsala, 1972.

Lorimer, Douglas A., *Colour, Class and the Victorians,* Leicester, 1978.

Payne, E. A., *Freedom in Jamaica,* London, n.d. [1933].

Payne, E. A., 'Baptist work in Jamaica before the arrival of the missionaries', *BQ* 7 (1934-5), 20-6.

Reckord, Mary, 'The Jamaican slave rebellion of 1831', *Past and Present* 39 (1968), 108-25.

Rooke, P. T., 'Evangelical missionary rivalry in the British West Indies', *BQ* 29 (1981-2), 341-55.

Russell, H. O.,'A question of indigenous mission: the Jamaican Baptist Missionary Society', *BQ* 25 (1973-4), 86-93.

Russell, H. O., 'An overview of the Church in Jamaica during the past twenty-five years', *The Fraternal* 223 (July 1988), 14-21.

Semmel, Bernard, *The Governor Eyre Controversy,* London, 1962.

Short, K. R. M., 'Jamaican Christian missions and the great slave rebellion of 1831-2', *Journal of Ecclesiastical History* 27 (1976), 57-72.

Sturge, J., and Harvey, T., *The West Indies in 1837,* London, 1838.

Symonette, M. C., and Canzoneri, A., *Baptists in the Bahamas: An Historical Review,* El Paso, 1977.

Turner, Mary, *Slaves and Missionaries: The Disintegration of Jamaican Slave Society, 1787-1834,* Urbana, 1982.

Tyrrell, A., 'The "Moral Radical Party" and the Anglo-Jamaican campaign for the abolition of the Negro apprenticeship system', *English Historical Review* 392 (1984), 481-502.

Underhill, E. B., *The West Indies: Their Social and Religious Condition,* London, 1862.

Underhill, E. B., *A Letter Addressed to the Rt. Honourable E. Cardwell...,* London, n.d. [1865].

Underhill, E. B., *Life of James Mursell Phillippo: Missionary in Jamaica,* London, 1881.

Wilmot, S., 'The peacemakers: Baptist missionaries and ex-slaves in Western Jamaica, 1838/40', *The Jamaican Historical Review* 13 (1982), 42-8.

Wright, P., *Knibb 'the Notorious': Slaves' Missionary 1803-1845,* London, 1973.

4:4 The Cameroons, Congo, Zaire, and Angola

Adam, T. B., *Africa Revisited: A Medical Deputation to the Baptist Missionary Society's Congo Field,* BMS, London, n.d. [1931].

Addicott, L. E., *Cry Angola!,* London, 1962.

Bentley, H. M., *W. Holman Bentley, D.D....The Life and Labours of a Congo Pioneer,* London, 1907.

Bentley, H. M., '"Kiambote" Nlemvo: true knight of the Cross', unpublished MS, 1938.

Bentley, W. Holman, *Pioneering on the Congo,* 2 vols., London, 1900.

Braekman, E. M., *Histoire du Protestantisme au Congo,* Brussels, 1961.

Brock, William, *From Mill Hill to the Congo,* London, n.d. [1908].

Carter, Hazel, 'Malcolm Guthrie 1903-72', *Proceedings of the British Academy* 59 (1973), 473-98.

Congo-Angola Border Enquiry: Report on the Visit of Mr George Thomas, M.P., and the Rev. Eric L. Blakebrough to the Congo-Angola Border, August, 1961, Southend-on-Sea, n.d.

Curtin, P. D., *The Image of Africa: British Ideas and Action, 1780-1850,* Madison, 1964.

Fullerton, W. Y., *The Christ of the Congo River,* London, n.d. [1928].

Graham, R. H. Carson, *Under Seven Congo Kings,* London, n.d.

Grenfell, W. D., *The Dawn Breaks: The Story of Missionary Work at São Salvador, Portuguese Congo,* London, 1948.

Guinness, F. E., *The First Christian Mission on the Congo,* 4th edn., London, n.d. [1882].

Hastings, Adrian, *A History of African Christianity 1950 -1975,* Cambridge, 1979.

Hawker, George, *The Life of George Grenfell,* London, 1909.

Hughes, J. W., *D. Christy Davies: A Brief Memoir,* London, 1962.

Iliffe, John, *The African Poor: A History,* Cambridge, 1987.

Innes, Alexander, *Cruelties Committed on the West Coast of Africa by an Agent of the Baptist Mission...,* London, 1862.

Innes, Alexander, *More Light...The Only True Biography of Alfred Saker and his Cruelties,* Birkenhead, 1895.

Irvine, Cecilia, 'Birth of the Kimbanguist movement in the Bas-Zaire, 1921', *Journal of Religion in Africa* 6 (1974), 24-76.

Johnston, H. H., *George Grenfell and the Congo,* 2 vols., London, 1908.

Kwast, L. E., *The Discipling of West Cameroon,* Grand Rapids, 1971.

Lagergren, David, *Mission and State in the Congo: A Study of the Relations between Protestant Missions and the Congo Independent State Authorities with Special Reference to the Equator District,* Uppsala, 1970.

Lewis, Thomas, *These Seventy Years,* 2nd edn., London, 1930.

MacBeath, A., 'The Revival in Bolobo, Belgian Congo', *International Review of Missions* 27 (1938), 415-23.

Mackay, D. J., 'Simon Kimbangu and the BMS tradition', *Journal of Religion in Africa* 17 (1987), 113-71.

Makulo Akambu, *La Vie de Disasi Makulo,* Kinshasa, 1983.

Marcum, John, *The Angolan Revolution: Volume I: The Anatomy of an Explosion (1950-1962); Volume II: Exile, Politics and Guerrilla Warfare (1962-1976);* Cambridge, Mass., and London, 1969, 1978.

Mason, P., ed., *Angola: A Symposium,* London, 1962.

Munayi Muntu-Monji, *Les Vingt-Cinq Ans de la Faculté de Théologie Protestante au Zaire 1959-1984,* Kinshasa, 1984.

Myers, J. B., *Thomas J. Comber: Missionary Pioneer to the Congo,* 3rd edn., London, n.d. [1888].

Myers, J. B., *The Congo for Christ,* London, n.d. [1895].

Nzongola-Ntalaza, ed., *The Crisis in Zaire: Myths and Realities,* Trenton, N. J.,1986.

Parsons, Clifford J., 'The Baptist Missionary Society in Africa', four unpublished Whitley lectures (copies in BMS archives).

Pélissier, R., *Les Guerres Grises: Résistance et Révoltes en Angola (1845-1941),* Orgaval, 1977.
Report of Second Education Conference Kimpese, Congo Belge 25 July-2 August, 1933, Kimpese, 1934.

Sabben-Clare, E. E., et. al., eds., *Health in Tropical Africa During the Colonial Period,* Oxford, 1980.
San Salvador: Mr Bowskill's Letters on the Native War of 1913-4, and Other Documents, BMS, London, n.d. [1914].

Samarin, W. J., 'Protestant missions and the history of Lingala', *Journal of Religion in Africa* 16 (1986), 138-63.

Slade, Ruth M., *English-Speaking Missions in the Congo Independent State (1878-1908),* Brussels, 1959.

Slageren, J. van, *Les Origines de L'Eglise Evangélique du Cameroun,* Leiden, 1972.

Stanley, Brian, 'The East African Revival: African initiative within a European tradition', *Churchman* 92 (1978), 6-22.

Sutton Smith, H., *Yakusu: The Very Heart of Africa,* London, n.d. [1912].

Thompson, Phyllis, *Mister Leprosy,* London, 1980.

Tuttle, G. W., 'IME: Institut Médical Evangélique: The First Twenty-Five Years', unpublished MS, 1983 (copy in BMS archives).

Underhill, E. B., *Alfred Saker Missionary to Africa,* London, 1884.

Wilson, C., *The History of Unilever,* 2 vols., London, 1954.

Wilson, C. E., et.al., *After Forty Years,* BMS, London, n.d. [1919].

4.5 China

Anderson, G. W., 'Harold Henry Rowley 1890-1969', *Proceedings of the British Academy* 56 (1970), 309-19.

Balme, Harold, *China and Modern Medicine,* London, 1921.

Bohr, Paul R., *Famine in China and the Missionary: Timothy Richard as Relief Administrator and Advocate of National Reform, 1876-1884,* Cambridge, Mass., 1972.

Borst-Smith, E. F., *Caught in the Chinese Revolution,* 2nd edn., London, 1913.

Broomhall, A. J., *Hudson Taylor and China's Open Century,* 7 vols., London, 1981-9.

Cohen, P. A., 'Missionary approaches: Hudson Taylor and Timothy Richard', *Papers on China,* vol. 11, Harvard University, 1957, 29-62.

Cohen, P. A., *China and Christianity: The Missionary Movement and the Growth of Chinese Antiforeignism 1860 - 1870,* Cambridge., Mass., 1963.

Evans, E. W. Price, *Timothy Richard: A Narrative of Christian Enterprise and Statesmanship in China,* London, n.d.[1945].

Fairbank, John K. ed., *The Missionary Enterprise in China and America,* Cambridge, Mass., 1974.

Fairbank, John K., *The Great Chinese Revolution: 1800-1985,* London, 1987.

Fullerton, W. Y., and Wilson, C. E., *New China: A Story of Modern Travel,* 2 vols., London, 1910.

Garnier, Albert J., *A Maker of Modern China,* London, n.d.[1945].

Glover, Richard, *Herbert Stanley Jenkins,* London, 1914.

Gregory, J. S., *Great Britain and the Taipings,* London, 1969.

Hayward, Victor E. W., *Christians and China,* Belfast, 1974.

Hood, G. A., *Mission Accomplished? The English Presbyterian Mission in Lingtung, South China,* Frankfurt, 1986.

Hood, G. A., *Neither Bang nor Whimper: The End of a Missionary Era in China,* Singapore, 1991.

James, John Angell, 'God's Voice from China to the British and Irish Churches, Both Established and Unestablished', in *The Works of John Angell James, edited by his son,* 17 vols., London, 1862, vol. 16, 477-554.

Keyte, J. C., *Andrew Young of Shensi,* London, 1924.

Keyte, J. C., *The Passing of the Dragon,* London, 1913.

Lambert, Tony, *The Resurrection of the Chinese Church,* London, 1991.

Latourette, K. S., *A History of Christian Missions in China,* London, 1929.

Meyer, F. B., *Memorials of Cecil Robertson F.R.C.S. of Sianfu,* London, 1913.

Middlebrook, J. B., *Memoir of H. R. Williamson: In Journeyings Oft,* London, 1969.

Nevius, H. S. C., *The Life of John Livingston Nevius,* New York, 1895.

Nevius, J. L., *Methods of Mission Work,* new edn., London, 1898.

Paton, David M., *Christian Missions and the Judgment of God,* London, 1953.

Payne, E. A., *Harry Wyatt of Shansi 1895-1938,* London, 1939.

Richard, Timothy, *Conversion by the Million in China: Being Biographies and Articles,* 2 vols., Shanghai, 1907.

Richard, Timothy, *Forty-Five Years in China,* London, 1916.
Soothill, W. E., *Timothy Richard of China,* London, 1924.
Thompson, R. W., *Griffith John,* revised edn., London, 1908.
  Through Toil and Tribulation: Missionary Experiences in China during the War of 1937-1945, London, 1947.
Whyte, Bob, *Unfinished Encounter: China and Christianity,* London, 1988.
Wickeri, Philip L., *Seeking the Common Ground: Protestant Christianity, the Three-Self Movement and China's United Front,* Maryknoll, 1988.
Williamson, H. R., *China among the Nations,* London, 1943.
Williamson, H. R., *British Baptists in China 1845-1952,* London, 1957.
Young, G. A., *The Living Christ in Modern China,* London, 1947.

4.6 Brazil

Beeson, Trevor, and Pearce, Jenny, *A Vision of Hope: The Churches and Change in Latin America,* London, 1982.
  Brazil: State and Struggle, Latin American Bureau, London, 1982.
Bruneau, T. C., *The Church in Brazil: The Politics of Religion,* Austin, Texas, 1982.
Cook, Guillermo, *The Expectation of the Poor: Latin American Basic Ecclesial Communities in a Protestant Perspective,* Maryknoll, 1985.
Martin, David, *Tongues of Fire: The Explosion of Protestantism in Latin America,* Oxford, 1990.
Read, W. R. and Ineson, F. A., *Brazil 1980: The Protestant Handbook,* Monrovia, 1973.

4.7 The Domestic Life and General Policy of the Society since 1815, and Relevant Works on the British Churches

Acres, Ian, 'Partners in Healing', unpublished BMS MS, 1983.
  Address of the Committee of the General Baptist Missionary Society, Derby, 1816.
Anderson, Olive, 'The growth of Christian militarism in mid-Victorian Britain', *English Historical Review* 86 (1971), 46-72.
Angus, D., *The Favour of a Commission: The Life of Isabel M. Angus 1858-1939,* London, n.d., 1939.
  Baptist Missionary Society: Ter-Jubilee Celebrations: 1942-4, London, 1945.
Bassett, T. M., *The Baptists of Wales and the Baptist Missionary Society,* Swansea, 1991.
Bebbington, David W., 'Baptist M.P.'s in the nineteenth century', *BQ* 29 (1981-2), 3-24.
Bebbington, David W., *Evangelicalism in Modern Britain: A History from the 1730s to the 1980s,* London, 1989.
Bebbington, David W., 'Baptists and Fundamentalism', in K. Robbins, ed., *Protestant Evangelicalism* (Studies in Church History, Subsidia 7), Oxford, 1990, 297-326.

Bennett, K. W., *Men in the Service of God: Seventy Years of the Baptist Men's Movement,* London, 1987.

Binfield, Clyde, *Pastors and People: The Biography of a Baptist Church Queen's Road, Coventry,* Coventry, 1984.

Bollen, J. D., 'English-Australian Baptist relations 1830 -1860', *BQ* 25 (1973-4), 290-305.

Bowers, B. and F., 'Bloomsbury Chapel and mercantile morality', *BQ* 30 (1983-4), 210-20.

Briggs, John H. Y., 'Evangelical ecumenism: the amalgamation of General and Particular Baptists in 1891', *BQ* 34 (1991-2), 99-115, 160-79.

Causton, Mary I. M., *For the Healing of the Nations: The Story of British Baptist Medical Missions 1792-1951,* London, 1951.

Chesterman, C. C., *In the Service of Suffering,* London, 1940.

Chirgwin, A. M., *Arthington's Million: The Romance of the Arthington Trust,* London, n.d. [1936].

Dictionary of National Biography.

Fullerton, W. Y., *At the Sixtieth Milestone,* London, 1917.

Hay, R. Wright, *Untrue to the Bible: A Reply to a Pamphlet Issued by the Baptist Missionary Society,* London, n.d. [1923].

Hayden, R., 'Still at the Crossroads? Revd J. H. Shakespeare and Ecumenism', in K. W. Clements, ed., *Baptists in the Twentieth Century,* London, 1983.

Hemmens, H. L., *Such Has Been My Life,* London, 1953.

Jubilee 1867-1917: Fifty Years' Work among Women in the Far East, London, n.d.

Landels, T. D., *William Landels D.D.: A Memoir,* London, 1900.

Landels, William, *Memorials of a Consecrated Life: A Biographical Sketch of John Landels, Missionary in Genoa,* London, 1881.

Larcombe, H. V., *First, the Kingdom! The Story of Robert Fletcher Moorshead, Physician,* London, 1936.

Le Quesne, C. T., *Sir Alfred Pearce Gould K.C.V.O.,* London, 1946.

Middlebrook, J. B., *The High Places of the Field,* London, 1959.

Middlebrook, J. B., *Memoir of H. R. Williamson: In Journeyings Oft,* London, 1969.

Moorshead, R. F., *'Heal the Sick': The Story of the Medical Mission Auxiliary of the Baptist Missionary Society,* London, 1929.

Myers, J. B., ed., *The Centenary Celebration of the Baptist Missionary Society, 1892-3,* London, 1893.

Norman, E. R., *Church and Society in England 1770-1970,* Oxford, 1976.

Orr, J. Edwin, *The Second Evangelical Awakening in Britain,* London, 1949.

Payne, E. A., *The Baptist Union: A Short History,* London, 1959.

Payne, E. A., *The Great Succession: Leaders of the Baptist Missionary Society during the Nineteenth Century,* London, n.d.

Payne, E. A., *Henry Wheeler Robinson,* London, 1946.

Pike, J. B. and J. C., eds., *A Memoir and Remains of the Late Rev. John Gregory Pike,* London, 1855.

Prochaska, F. K., *Women and Philanthropy in Nineteenth-Century England,* Oxford, 1908.

Putnam, Michael, *The Story of Operation Agri 1961-1990,* n.d., n.p.

Stanley, Brian, 'Home support for overseas missions in early Victorian England, c. 1838-1873', Ph.D. thesis, Cambridge, 1979.

Stanley, Brian, 'C. H. Spurgeon and the Baptist Missionary Society, 1863-1866', *BQ* 29 (1981-2), 319-28.

Stanley, Brian, '"The miser of Headingley": Robert Arthington and the Baptist Missionary Society, 1877-1900', in W. J. Sheils and D. Wood., eds., *The Church and Wealth* (Studies in Church History 24), Oxford, 1987, 371-82.

Thorne, R. G., ed., *The House of Commons 1790-1820, vol. 5. Members, Q-Y* (The History of Parliament), London, 1986.

Trestrail, [E. R.], *The Short Story of a Long Life: Memorials of Frederick Trestrail D.D., F.R.G.S...edited by his widow,* London, 1892.

Underhill, E. B., *Christian Missions in the East and West,* London, 1873.

Underhill, E. B., *Principles and Methods of Missionary Labour,* London, 1896.

West, W. M. S., *To Be a Pilgrim: A Memoir of Ernest A. Payne,* Guildford, 1983.

West, W. M. S., 'The Reverend Secretary Aubrey: Part II', *BQ* 34 (1991-2), 263-81.

Wheeler, B. R., *Alfred Henry Baynes, J.P.,* London, n.d.

Williamson, H. R., *Fresh Ventures in Fellowship,* BMS, London, 1944.

Williamson, H. R., *The Christian Challenge of the Changing World,* BMS, London, 1946.

Wilmot, J., and Pizey, J. H., *God's Work in God's Way: A Memoir of the Life and Ministry of James Stephens,* London, 1934.

Wilson, C. E., 'The BMS and Bible translation', *BQ* 10 (1940-1), 97-105, 159-67.

Wilson, C. E., *Sir George Watson Macalpine, J. P., LL.D.,* London, n.d.

Wilson, C. E., ed., *Bible League Criticism and the Baptist Missionary Society: Reprints and Parallels with an Introductory Note by C. E. Wilson,* London, 1923.

4:8 Relevant Works on Other Missionary Societies and the Missionary Movement as a Whole

Allen, Roland, *Missionary Methods: St Paul's or Ours?,* London, 1912.

Allen, Roland, *The Spontaneous Expansion of the Church and the Causes which Hinder it,* London, 1927.

Browne, Stanley G., et. al., eds., *Heralds of Health: The Saga of Christian Medical Initiatives,* London, 1985.

Castro, Emilio, 'Bangkok, the new opportunity', *International Review of Mission,* LXII, 246 (April 1973), 136-43.

Christensen, Torben, and Hutchison, William R., *Missionary Ideologies in the Imperialist Era: 1880-1920,* Aarhus, 1982.

Conference on Missions Held in 1860 at Liverpool... Edited by the Secretaries to the Conference, London, 1860.

Findlay, G. G., and Holdsworth, W. W., *The History of the Wesleyan Methodist Missionary Society,* 5 vols., London, 1921-4.

Goodall, Norman, ed., *Missions under the Cross,* London, 1953.

Goodall, Norman, *A History of the London Missionary Society 1895-1945,* London, 1954.

Hewat, Elizabeth G. K., *Vision and Achievement 1796-1956: A History of The Foreign Missions of the Churches United in the Church of Scotland,* London, 1960.

Hewitt, Gordon, *The Problems of Success: A History of the Church Missionary Society 1910-1942,* 2 vols., London, 1971, 1977.

Hocking, W. E. ed., *Re-Thinking Missions: A Laymen's Inquiry After One Hundred Years,* New York and London, 1932.

Hooton, W. S., and Wright, J. S., *The First Twenty-Five Years of the Bible Churchmen's Missionary Society,* London, 1947.

Hopkins, C. H., *John R. Mott 1865-1955,* Grand Rapids, 1979.

Hutchison, William R., *Errand to the World: American Protestant Thought and Foreign Missions,* Chicago and London, 1987.

Jackson, Eleanor M., *Red Tape and the Gospel: A Study of the Significance of the Ecumenical Missionary Struggle of William Paton (1886-1943),* Birmingham, 1980.

Kraemer, Hendrik, *The Christian Message in a Non-Christian World,* London, 1938.

Lovett, Richard, *The History of the London Missionary Society 1795-1895,* 2 vols., London, 1895.

Murray, Jocelyn, *Proclaim the Good News: A Short History of the Church Missionary Society,* London, 1985.

Newbigin, Lesslie, *Unfinished Agenda: An Autobiography,* London, 1985.

Spangenberg, A.G., *An Account of the Manner in which the Protestant Church of the Unitas Fratrum ... Carry on their Missions among the Heathen,* Eng. transl., London, 1788.

Stanley, Brian, *The Bible and the Flag: Protestant Missions and British Imperialism in the Nineteenth and Twentieth Centuries,* Leicester, 1990.

Stock, Eugene, *The History of the Church Missionary Society: its Environment, its Men and its Work,* 4 vols., London, 1899-1916.

Tatlow, Tissington, *The Story of the Student Christian Movement of Great Britain and Ireland,* London, 1933.

Thompson, H. P., *Into All Lands: The History of the Society for the Propagation of the Gospel in Foreign Parts 1701-1950,* London, 1951.

Walls, Andrew F., '"The heavy artillery of the missionary army": the domestic importance of the nineteenth-century medical missionary', in W. J. Sheils, ed., *The Church and Healing* (Studies in Church History 19), Oxford, 1982, 287-97.

Warren, Max A. C., *To Apply the Gospel: Selections from the Writings of Henry Venn*, Grand Rapids, 1971.

Williams, C. Peter, 'Healing and evangelism: the place of medicine in later Victorian Protestant missionary thinking', in W. J. Sheils, ed., *The Church and Healing* (Studies in Church History 19), Oxford, 1982, 271-85.

Williams, C. Peter, *The Ideal of the Self-Governing Church: A Study in Victorian Missionary Strategy*, Leiden, 1990.

World Missionary Conference, Edinburgh 1910: Reports of Commissions, 9 vols., Edinburgh and London, 1910.

Index

Lewis & Clark College - Watzek Library

3 5209 00804 5094